The MOTHER of All Windows® 98 Books

*MOM once again plumbs the depths,
this time tackling Windows 98.
Introducing Woody and Barry's iconic alter egos
and, of course, Billy98.*

Woody Leonhard & Barry Simon

ADDISON-WESLEY

An imprint of Addison Wesley Longman, Inc.
Reading, Massachusetts • Harlow, England • Menlo Park, California
Berkeley, California • Don Mills, Ontario • Sydney
Bonn • Amsterdam • Tokyo • Mexico City

Many of the designations used by manufacturers and sellers to distinguish their products are claimed as trademarks. Where those designations appear in this book and Addison-Wesley was aware of the trademark claim, the designations have been printed in initial caps or all caps.

The author and publishers have taken care in preparation of this book, but make no expressed or implied warranty of any kind and assume no responsibility for errors or omissions. No liability is assumed for incidental or consequential damages in connection with or arising out of the uses of the information or programs contained herein.

The publisher offers discounts on this book when ordered in quantity of special sales. For more information, please contact:

Corporate, Government and Special Sales Group
Addison Wesley Longman, Inc.
One Jacob Way
Reading, Massachusetts 01867

Library of Congress Cataloging-in-Publication Data

Leonhard, Woody.
    The mother of all Windows 98 books / Woody Leonhard and Barry Simon.
      p.   cm.
    ISBN 0-201-43312-5
    1. Microsoft Windows (Computer file)   2. Operating systems
(Computers)   I. Simon, Barry.   II. Title.
QA76.76.063L47   1999
005.4'469—dc21

                 98-39309
                    CIP

ISBN 0-201-43312-5
Text printed on recycled and acid-free paper.
1 2 3 4 5 6 7 8 9 10-CRS-02010099
First Printing, October 1998

LET MOM VISIT TWICE A MONTH—FOR FREE!

Get the latest news on Windows from the guys who brought you *The Mother of All Windows (3.1) Books, The Mother of All Windows 95 Books,* and the all-new *The Mother of All Windows 98 Books.* They'll even cover NT Workstation.

Woody and Barry will send you the latest news, gossip, tips, and tricks FREE by email in *Woody's Windows Watch—WWW!*

You'll hear about:

- updates to Windows; what's good and what's bad
- the latest tips for getting the most out of Windows 3.1, 95, 98, and NT
- news on third-party freeware, shareware, and commercial utilities
- links to handy Web sites and resources

WWW tells it like it is—with bouquets and brickbats given without fear or favor.

Special Feature!

Get the inside track on Windows from YEOW—Your Expert on Windows— a.k.a. Barry Simon, appearing exclusively in *Woody's Windows Watch.*

JOIN TODAY!
Go to http://www.wopr.com/books/mom98.htm or send a message to www@wopr.com

While you're at it, subscribe to *WOW, Woody's Office Watch,* the **FREE** weekly newsletter covering Microsoft Office. You can subscribe at the same Web site as above or email to wow@wopr.com.

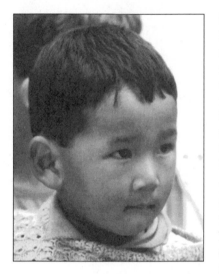

In 1959 the Communist Chinese invaded Tibet, driving its 24-year-old leader, the Dalai Lama, into exile. The Chinese unleashed a pogrom of ethnic and cultural genocide. Millions of Tibetans were imprisoned, tortured, murdered; their artistic, religious and cultural heritage reduced to rubble. Reliable estimates place the number of Tibetans slaughtered since the Chinese invasion at 3,000,000. According to Amnesty International and other leading human rights organizations, arbitrary arrest, torture, and Chinese government-sanctioned killings in Tibet continue to this day.

The Dalai Lama settled in northern India. Millions of Tibetans followed him into exile. Most moved into refugee camps scattered throughout Nepal and India. Life in the camps is hard. Few families have more than one room to call their own. Many eke out a hand-to-mouth existence as subsistence farmers, manual laborers, handicraft workers, traders—often with "shops" consisting of no more than a couple of pieces of bamboo and a plastic tarp.

The Tibetan Children's Fund was founded in 1993 to provide food, shelter and education for Tibetan refugee children living in northern India. TCF's center of operation is in Darjeeling—renowned to westerners as a source of tea, but better known to Tibetans and many other Asians as a respected center of education. For more than a hundred years, English-language boarding schools in and around Darjeeling have prepared leaders of government, education and commerce.

As of this writing, TCF sponsors almost 150 Tibetan children around Darjeeling, Gangtok, and parts of Nepal. The children are chosen for their scholastic ability and financial need. TCF volunteers (who pay for their own trips to India) interview the children and their parents, select the children, and monitor their progress in school each semester. Scholastic evaluation emphasizes proficiency in English, math, the sciences and humanities.

A little hard currency goes a long way in India. US$ 75 will sponsor a refugee child for a full year in one of the government-run schools. US$ 250 covers a full year—including tuition, room and board—in one of the top English-language schools.

TCF is an all-volunteer organization. Overhead expenses are paid by TCF's corporate sponsors. Every penny donated by individuals goes straight to the children. If you would like to help a deserving Tibetan refugee child, please contact:

Tibetan Children's Fund
Post Office Box 473, Pinecliffe, Colorado USA 80471
Voice: 303-642-0492, Fax: 303-642-0491

Part of the profits from the sale of this book are donated to the TCF.

Barry
To the gang: Martha, light of my life; Rivka and Sanford;
Zippy and Chaim; Binyomin and Penina;
Zvi, Ari and Chana.

Woody
To Linda, my loving wife of twenty years;
and Justin, the computer nerd in training.

The stress of putting together an enormously complex
book like this on a short deadline is hard to imagine . . . or
even describe. Writers' spouses, more than any others, feel
that stress take its toll every day. Words can't express how
much we appreciate the support you've given us.

Thanks to Jay Munro, for the most excellent
"Woody," "Barry," and "Billy98" icons.

Yes, we really *are* as handsome as our charicatures.
Well, OK, Bill isn't quite that cute.

■■ Contents

Do You Need MOM98?

The old order changeth, yielding place to new.

—ALFRED TENNYSON, *The Passing of Arthur*, 1869

 What makes *The Mother of All Windows 98 Books*—MOM98 for short —different from the other five hundred or so Windows 98 books on the market? Three reasons. First, it's the only book that shows you what's *really going on* inside Win98, from a user's point of view. Second, it's the only place you'll find hundreds of unique tips—and straightforward, down-to-earth explanations—for configuring Win98 to work *for* you, not against you. And third, it's the only Windows 98 book on the market that was written from the ground up based on the final, shrinkwrapped, shipped version of the software.

 It continues to amaze me how many books on store shelves are based on very, very early beta-test versions of Windows 98—and how many books amount to nothing more than minor rewrites of their Windows 95 versions. While it's true that Windows 98 looks a lot like Windows 95 from the outside—you know, pointing and clicking and all that—the simple fact is that Win95 has gone through major, even apocalyptic, changes on the inside. While you might not bump into those big changes the first time you use Win98, by the end of a week I guarantee you will.

And then there are all those books and magazine articles that say, "Windows is great but it won't do this and this and this." We spent months figuring out new ways to make Win98 do what the experts say it can't and making it cookbook-easy to put those tricks to use. Whether you're supporting a company full of Win98 users or simply sitting at home and trying to get the bloody thing to start, *MOM98* shows you hundreds of ways to make Win98 work better, faster, easier, and more reliably, the first time, every time, day after day after day. And we do it all in plain English.

For those of you who cut your teeth (if not your fingers) on Windows 95, we have a chapter designed specifically to bring you up to speed on Windows 98—with a curmudgeonly emphasis on what does and doesn't work. Not all of the "improvements" Microsoft talks about radiate sweetness and light. In fact, if you don't know where the problems lie, you might find yourself wasting days of effort and hundreds of bucks on Win98 features that just plain don't work.

On the other hand, Win98 has an enormous array of new features that *do* work—and you need to know about them, too. Some of the most important new features are buried so deep, you'd never find them without a guide map. And that's just what our first chapter provides: knowledgeable, detailed discussion of what to look for and where.

Windows for Dullards NOT!

If you're looking for a book to show you how to push the Windows 98 Start button, well, you're in the wrong place. The Win98 tutorial shows you all you need to know to get started, and the proliferation of built-in Windows Wizards can run you through the most common procedures. For nearly all the "click here, drag there" basic stuff, Windows online help shows you step by step what you need.

But Windows 98 is such a rich environment and the provided docs and online help so skimpy, you'll need *MOM98* just for its collections of tips and pointers, its plain-language explanation of what's really happening, and its authoritative exploration of Win98's seamier side. The shortcuts you find on just about any page of this book will save you lots of frustration every time you boot up.

Manual Labor

 At this point you're probably wondering, "Why doesn't Microsoft tell us about all these cool, albeit weird, things?" Or maybe "Why should I pay for a book when the documentation I already have undoubtedly covers all the important stuff—if I ever get around to reading it" Or "Why doesn't my favorite aftermarket Windows book give me at least some little hint that all this funky stuff is going on under the covers?" Let me clue you in on a little behind-the-scenes stuff, a few of the dirty secrets of the publishing biz.

First, all the official Win98 documentation and all the aftermarket Win98 books were written before the final code for Windows 98 was ready. That means that everything on the bookstore shelves and in the shrinkwrapped Win98 box—including the official docs, the Help files, and the Wizards—every bit of it is based on beta-test code and an idealized concept of how Win98 should work, once/if all the problems were resolved.

MOM98, in blazing contrast, was written by, for, and with the final, shipping Win98 product. That made us last on the bookstore shelves and probably hurt *MOM98*'s sales, but it was the only way we could be sure you'd get the straight story.

Second, the aftermarket books are based almost entirely on the official documentation. Where the Windows Resource Kit or online Help is wrong or ambiguous, virtually every book glosses over those points—or are wrong or ambiguous. MOM wouldn't let us get away with parroting Microsoft, even if we wanted to. She wields a mean rolling pin. We went back to original principles, as the saying goes, and reported only on what we could see: what's really there, as opposed to what somebody thought should be there.

 More than that, we had a chance to talk with many of the Windows designers and developers to pull together detailed descriptions of how the final, shipping product works, how each individual piece really functions, and how the pieces fit together in the overall scheme of Win98 things. We worked meticulously to make sure all the details are right, so when you have to figure out a solution to your own problems, you can rely on the most accurate information available anywhere—right here on these pages. You won't find these kinds of detailed, accurate, no-bull explanations anywhere else.

Third, the amount of documentation Microsoft produces—and it's the Microsoft documentation that drives the rest of the book-writing industry—has dwindled away. Consider the decline and fall of the windows manual.

Windows 2.0	568 pages	
Windows 3.0	640 pages	
Windows 3.1	754 pages	(with 104 in the *Getting Started* booklet)
Windows 3.11	477 pages	
Windows 95	95 pages	
Windows 98	129 pages	

Microsoft claims that they are backing away from longer manuals because readers don't want them, but that's a bunch of hooey. Their real goal is to drive down the COG—Cost of Goods. Paper manuals are the single most expensive part of the whole equation. Look at it this way: if shipping a 129-page manual instead of a 750-page manual saves $2.00 a package and 50 million copies ship . . . well, that's some nice pocket change, yes?

MOM's Point of View

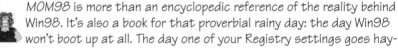 *MOM98* is more than an encyclopedic reference of the reality behind Win98. It's also a book for that proverbial rainy day: the day Win98 won't boot up at all. The day one of your Registry settings goes haywire. The day you delete or move a program and can't figure out how to get it working again. The day you need to do something Windows' designers didn't think of. The day you want to do something the designers thought you shouldn't be allowed to do.

If you want to get under Windows' skin—whether for the sheer pleasure of understanding what's happening in that box on your desk or to ward off the sheer terror of a machine that won't work right—this is the book you need.

MOM98 concentrates on the parts of Win98 that are hard to "get"—the tough concepts underlying Win98 font technology, for example, or what a

Shortcut really entails. You'll find never-before-seen tips on how to make Win98 work better, on how to customize it to support the way you work. You'll see how the Desktop connects to your applications and how folders control what you see on the screen. You'll learn how Win98 starts itself, and what's really happening in Safe mode. You'll see where vestiges of Windows 3.1 and even DOS creep into Win98, and how a rudimentary knowledge of those "archaic" operating systems can keep you out of a whole lot of hot water.

 And if you've ever tried to understand the Registry—the single repository of all Windows knowledge, where all the bodies are buried—by using the incredibly unenlightening official documentation in the Windows Resource Kit or online Help, you'll appreciate MOM98's unique, detailed report on what we found there . . . including all sorts of errors in the WRK, the Help files, and just about everywhere else we looked. A very large part of Chapter 3 and practically all of Chapters 8 and 9 work directly, down and dirty, with the Registry. That's more than 200 pages of Registry stuff, much of it previously unpublished. Now you know why we say that The Mother of All Windows 98 Books contains The Mother of All Registry Books.

 Most important of all is what you won't see: the Microsoft Party Line. MOM98 doesn't crib from the official, often erroneous, Windows manuals and books: it's a fresh, untainted look at what's really happening in the Win98 ooze. Mom, Woody, and I would sooner starve than serve up rehashed Redmond cant.

What you'll find here is the straight story, as best we can tell it, about the most pervasive, most important computer program ever created. In short, we think that every single Windows 98 user beyond the "What is the Start button?" stage needs *MOM98*. Sooner or later, it'll save your butt.

Enjoy!

Woody Leonhard
Coal Creek Canyon, Colorado

Barry Simon
Los Angeles, California

Conventions

*Metaphor is of the highest value in both prose and poetry,
but one must give special attention to the use of metaphor in prose—
for the resources of prose are less abundant than those of poetry.*

—ARISTOTLE, *Rhetoric*, ca. 322 B.C.

Most of MOM98 is in plain English. Sometimes, though, Mom has to lapse into computer-speak—as infrequently as possible, I promise!—and when computer terminology comes to the forefront, conventions can't be far behind.

I put filenames in a monospace font, just to warn you that a computer thing is coming. Like this: `system.dat.` Stuff on the keyboard receives similar treatment; I might say Hit `Esc`. Rarely do I talk about pushing keys (so *pedestrian!*), but if I want you to hold down two or more keys at once I use a `+` plus sign, e.g.: `Ctrl+Alt+Del`.

So much for the technical gobbledygook.

You might've noticed that these pages are populated—some would say littered—with three guys and one grizzled, uh, MOM, who chime in from time to time, spreading wit, wisdom, enlightenment, and more than a little fertilizer. If you've read any of the previous MOM books, you may be acquainted with the literary technique.

For this book, Mom decided to use Woody and Barry in the flesh—and Billy 98 *in absentia*. The icons appear here to break up this dry technical stuff with a bit of much-needed humor, bantering with opposing points of view when appropriate. Hmmmmm . . . come to think of it, maybe the techie stuff is here to break up the icons' bone-headed wit. Whatever.

Bowing to the obvious protocol—and an iron-tight contractual restriction—we start with MOM herself, the Mother of All . . . well, you get the idea . . . and let her do the introductions. MOM runs the show. What she says goes. *Capice*?

Windows 98 has been selling like hotcakes—faster than Windows 95 at its inception. Yes, it's true that Windows 95 was known, internally, as "version 4.0" and Win98 is just "version 4.1." Yes, Win95 looks a lot like Win98 from the outside. But the farther we wriggled down the Win98 rabbit hole, the more we discovered that Win98 has major differences deep down inside. So I figured I'd ditch all the old icons this time and bring in the, uh, heavyweights.

I resemble that.

 For those of you who don't know him, Woody has been writing books and magazine articles for so long he has callouses on his fingertips, and they're starting to migrate to his knuckles. Since the first *Mother* book in 1993 (at least two lifetimes in Net-dog years), Woody has gone on to achieve prominence in Hollywood as Mel Gibson's double in *Lethal Weapon 5*.

 Wait a minute, wait a minute! Are you sure we're talking about the same person, MOM? I mean, Woody is about twice Mel Gibson's size, he has these horrible scars on his forehead from more than a decade of banging his head against walls. He can write, sorta, but he can't act.

 Hey, hey, hey. Put a cork in it, Barry, or I'll tell them all about your office, and how you have to be a contortionist to . . .

 Boys, boys. Quit the bickering and shape up! You said you'd be on your best behavior for this book. Let's see. I guess that brings us to Barry, who's an internationally famous mathematician and physicist. Even though he blushes every time I say that.

 <blush>

 Barry is an authority on the Windows interface, utilities, and the things that make Windows tick. He, too, has been writing for me since the first *Mom* book in 1993. You've undoubtedly read his features and reviews in *PC Magazine*. Barry's been taking it easy lately, with a publication schedule that includes this book, numerous magazine articles, scientific articles and monographs, a lecture regimen that would give Madeline Albright jet lag, in addition to his day job teaching the best and brightest . . .

 Uh, MOM. You missed the point. By writing this book, Barry *is* teaching the best and brightest.

 Woody's also been goofing off. He writes up his storm in *PC Computing*. His articles there and his books have won him five Computer Press Association Awards. He's the publisher of the software product WOPR— Woody's Office POWER Pack™, "The #1 Enhancement to Microsoft Office." He and editor Peter Deegan put out WOW—*Woody's Office Watch*—the weekly free Internet newsletter on Office.

What about me?

 Oh yes. I almost forgot our fifty-billion-dollar Microsoft rep. (Or is it sixty?) The richest shill in the world. Billy98 appears on these pages to present the Microsoft® Point of View™ Version 4.1. He has many good points—sometimes Woody and Barry don't see all the sides of the equation—and you should listen to him. Anyway, I am proud to introduce to you our quasiofficial, on-site, in-book Microsoft rep, Billy98. You've probably seen him: he's done all the talk shows, and his Q rating recently surpassed his IQ. Just don't make fun of his name, OK?

 Oh, MOM, being here is so cool. I'm glad to have this opportunity to explain the position of America's most forward-looking and user-friendly corporation. People think we have a lot of power, but that's not true. Consumers have the power, when they buy their software, to choose whichever products they feel are best. We're always glad to serve the interests of the industry and our users.

 Tell it to Ralph Nader.

 Woody, lay off the poor little guy. I'm puzzled though. Three years ago, Billy95 was a spanking new baby and now he looks a lot older than 3. What's up?

 Those three years musta been Internet years—everyone knows Internet time runs a lot faster than ordinary time.

 But, like a dog year, an Internet year is about seven years. So Billy should be about 21 now rather than 8. What happened to the other years?

 Janet made me give 'em back.

 Billy98 is here to help us understand the reasoning behind Microsoft's choices and to shed light on where the folks in Redmond might be heading. He's a mouthpiece, all right? Besides, could anyone with Billy's love of Internet jokes be all bad?

I also like top ten lists and knock knock jokes. By the way, I just posted this list of top ten proposed Windows 2002 error messages:

1. Smash forehead on keyboard to continue.
2. Enter any 11-digit prime number to continue.
3. Press any key to continue or any other key to quit.
4. Press any key except . . . no, No, NO, NOT THAT ONE!
5. File not found. Should I fake it? (Y/N)
6. Bad or missing mouse. Spank the cat? (Y/N)
7. Bad command or filename! Go stand in the corner.
8. This will end your Windows session. Do you want to play another game?
9. Windows message: "Error saving file! Format drive now? (Y/Y)"
10. Message from Gates: "Rebooting the world. Please log off."

As you've probably guessed, the opinions expressed by any of the icons are not necessarily their own. Unless you happen to agree with them . . .

Billy98's Road Map

What is done hastily cannot be done prudently.

—Publilius Syrus, *Sententiae*, ca. 50 B.C.

 So you're still reading the introduction, eh? Kinda low bandwidth, aren't you? Anyway, MOM wanted me to say that MOM98 is designed to be read from beginning to end. Or at least beginning to middle.

Everybody should read Chapter 1, right off the bat. While it's specifically intended to bring Windows 95 cognoscenti up to speed on Windows 98, it also contains lots of important information for first-time Windows users.

Then, if you haven't yet installed Win98, go directly to Chapter 6. Do not pass go. Do not shell out another $200. When you're done with Chapter 6, hop back to Chapter 2, and learn what it was you really did.

Chapter 2 takes you through the panoply of Windows concepts, leaving no tern . . . uh, no stone unturned. These are the things you must understand before digging into the belly of Windows itself.

Chapters 3 and 4 shows you Windows' components from the inside out—how they work together, how they don't work at all, how they can be molded to get more work done, your way. The basic components are in Chapter 3 and the "little guys" are in Chapter 4.

Chapter 5 lets you know about Win98 add-ons, from Microsoft and others.

That's where you should stop reading sequentially. Chapters 6, 7, 8, and 9 are Reference Chapters, capital R, captial C, designed to help you diagnose and fix problems: this is the only place you'll find the whole story on installing Win98, on Win98 startup, those odd files that Windows 98 insists on scattering various places, plus the inside scoop on the Control Panel and most of all details on the Registry and other behind-the-scenes topics crucial to your continued sanity.

That's about it! Remember, you can read straight through to the end of Chapter 5, but beyond that point, sequential scanning is appropriate only for people who get a kick out of reading the encyclopedia from cover to cover.

 Like me.

Chapter 1

Fast Track

Did you cut your teeth on Windows 95? Have you spent hours, days, weeks sweating over the details of how Windows 95 works—and how it doesn't? Well, you're in the right place. Welcome to my Fast Track chapter, my home for wayward children of the Windows 95 night. This is where poor, abused Windows 95 veterans will find everything they need to know about Windows 98—new features, changing concepts, what's better and what's worse.

I'll even toss in a little gratuitous advice on renewing your vows with Win98. The upgrade is not for everybody, you know. Gettin' hitched to Windows 95 was a no-brainer—if the sweet siren song of all those fancy new features didn't pull ya, the sawed-off shotgun known as Windows 3.1 sat in the back, ready to go off if you looked at it sideways.

But Windows 98 is a different story altogether. She's hardly the blushing bride in lily white, pure and untouched, waiting for the perfect guy to come along. Nope, Win98 is more like a grizzled old battleaxe, prone to chewin' and spittin' in the wrong direction, who's been around the block a few times and knows where the bodies are buried. Kinda like, uh, somebody we all know, eh? And who better to tell you about it . . .

I've been writing books about Windows since the early days, back when you held a mouse in one hand and a club in the other, watching out for low-flying pterodactyls. I've seen everything Windows has to offer. I've heard the hype and seen the ads. I've watched people on the Windows team come and go. I've kicked and cried and pounded and sworn like a sailor on shore leave. But I tell ya, I have never in my sweet, short life seen anything like Windows 98. It's like the ultimate bug fix, with a few really amazing goodies thrown in for good measure.

I'll let Barry, Woody, and Billy98 show you what I mean.

But if you're totally new to Windows 9X, don't worry your sweet little head. Skim this chapter and then leap into Chapter 2. The rest of the book discusses all the elements of Windows 98, both the new . . . and the old.

■ The Facts

Every change of scene is a delight.

—SENECA, *Epistulae moralis ad Lucilium*, ca. 63 A.D.

On June 25, 1998, the long-awaited upgrade to Windows 95 hit store shelves. Unlike Windows 95, which arrived with a monologue from Jay Leno, media hype rarely (if ever) equaled in the annals of advertising history, and a very cool riff from the Rolling Stones, Windows 98's birthday went by relatively unheralded—but hardly unnoticed.

Even with the cards stacked against it—release at the beginning of the traditionally languid summer season, clouds of obfuscating fury from the Department of Justice, and lukewarm reviews from the computer press—Win98 took off, rapidly outselling even Windows 95.

There's a simple reason why Win98 sold and continues to sell so well. It's a hell of an operating system. Spend a few hours trying to get some real work done with it running in the background, and you'll come away convinced: Microsoft learned a lot in the three years between '95 and '98.

 Windows 98 (known as "Memphis" back then) first appeared in testers' hands in late December 1996. Beta testing took almost 18 months, an extraordinary length of time, even by Microsoft's standards. More than 150,000 people tested the software, making it far and away the most heavily tested piece of software in the history of computers.

 I guess that's true, Billy, if you exclude Windows 95, which some people insist was a "shipped beta" made available to millions of unsuspecting testers, who paid for the privilege.

 Win98 consists of more than 13,000,000 lines of program code. We made 3,000 specific, identified improvements to Windows 95. It runs more reliably and faster, and it makes applications run faster. Our new FAT32 disk format can add 20% to 30% of more usable space on many Win95 users' disks. And we've opened up new technologies for millions of people: the Universal Serial Bus, Digital VideoDiscs, and all sorts of TV-based capabilities.

 Well, yes, but at the same time you're pushing an "orphaned" operating system. Microsoft itself acknowledges that this is the end of the Windows 3.x-Windows 95 line and that the future belongs to Windows NT. You're telling people that they can upgrade from Windows 3.1 directly to Win98—a highly unlikely proposition, given Win98's substantial hardware requirements.

Think of Windows 98 as a brilliant .1 upgrade, sort of like the shift from Windows 3.0 to Windows 3.1. Even knowing that Windows 3.x was going to be replaced three years later by Windows 95, would you have recommended that users not upgrade from Windows 3.0 to Windows 3.1? Of course you would have recommended that upgrade, as you should this one.

Yeah, well, Win3.1 was a no-brainer because it was so much less buggy than Windows 3.0. Oh, I get your point! That is a compelling argument in favor of this .1 upgrade.

Ah, well. As you can see, Windows 98 represents a new pinnacle in operating system software. At the same time, it's stirred quite a bit of controversy.

That's about par for the course for a new version of Windows, wouldn't you say?

■ System Requirements

At a minimum, your system should include a 486 or higher processor with a math coprocessor and 16 MB of RAM.

—Windows 98 Reviewer's Guide

We've been criticized in the past for unrealistic system requirement specifications. Reviewers usually take what we say and double it. So this time around we decided to play it conservative and tell people what they really need to run Win98.

According to the Official Microsoft Party Line, as published in the *Getting Started* booklet for Windows 98, here's what you need to run Win98:

- 486DX/66 or higher processor
- 16 MB of memory
- 195 to 225 MB of additional hard disk space (although it's possible that you'll need as much as 355 MB, if you start with a blank hard drive, install the old-fashioned FAT16 file system, and choose to install every single option)

That seems to be a little closer to the mark—it certainly beats the *Reviewer's Guide* (implied) minimum of a 486DX/25. You could have a kid or two and watch them graduate from college before a DX/25 could boot Win98 twice.

Far as I'm concerned, you'd be crazy to run Windows 98 on anything less than this:

- Pentium processor
- 32 MB memory
- 100 MB of available hard disk space. If you're using a 1 GB or larger disk and can shuffle some of that data off the disk while installing Windows 98, converting to FAT32 will free up enough additional space to hold Win98.

 Well, we debated the memory requirements. We agree that it really needs 32 MB of RAM, but we knew if we said that, people would think we really meant 64 MB. So we decided to say 16 MB of RAM knowing that users would know that really means 32 MB.

 Yeah, Billy, a dishonest past can haunt you, can't it? You should have said 32 MB RAM on the box but added a footnote that read, "This time we really mean it."

 I've had excellent results running Windows 98 on a Pentium-90 with 64 MB of memory. The machine goes faster than it ever did with Windows 95—and with the price of memory so low these days, Win98 (using FAT32) and a couple of memory boards proved a wonderful, cheap, midlife kicker for this older PC.

■ What's New in 98?

Men love . . . newfangledness.

—GEOFFREY CHAUCER, *Canterbury Tales (Squire's Tale),* ca. 1386

The first time you start Windows 98, you're bound to be a bit disappointed. It looks an awful lot like Windows 95 (Figure 1-1). But don't let this somber scene put you off. Underneath the Desktop lurks the heart of a lion—and a whole bunch of improvements.

Figure 1-1. Bone-stock Windows 98 Desktop

All the Patches, All the Time

Today Microsoft shocked us all as they announced that their latest operating system—Windows 98—is to be renamed prior to launch as Diana, Princess of Windows. A spokesman for Microsoft said that this was in tribute to the late ex-royal and is a fitting name in that the product will look flashy, be mostly superficial, consume vast amounts of resources, and crash spectacularly.

—Posted on the Oracle website

 My number-one favorite new Win98 application, and the reason I think most people should upgrade to Win98 is the Windows Update Wizard. How many hours have you lost trying to find the latest drivers for all your hardware? When was the last time you *checked* for new drivers, for that matter? Not only *does* Win98 ship with 1200 or so new drivers, it has a built-in way to keep those drivers—and all the Windows files—up to date.

The **Windows Update Wizard** sits on top of the Start Menu, where it's only a click away (Figure 1-2).

When you click on Windows Update, Win98 launches your Web browser and attaches to the Windows Update page (Figure 1-3). The Wizard, with your permission, takes a look at the software you have installed on your PC and presents you with a "catalog" of available software, tailored to your specific situation. It then lets you download and update any Windows component you feel appropriate, with installation handled automatically. There's even a roll-back provision so that, at least in theory, you can "undo" any updates that cause more havoc than they alleviate. This is one impressive piece of software, which should set the standard for years to come.

We strongly recommend that you run the Windows Update Wizard at least once a month and preferably once a week.

**Figure 1-2.
Update Wizard**

**Figure 1-3.
Windows 98
Update Site**

Some folks (and I hope they don't tell Janet) would claim that this Update Wizard was inspired by Cybermedia's Oil Change and that the big bad Redmond Gorilla is aiming to put the Cybermedia folks outta business.

 Let me get this one straight. You're complaining that we've put something that is clearly an operating system function into the operating system and saved users from having to buy a third-party product?

 Actually, Billy, I was playing devil's advocate. I agree this sort of stuff belongs in the operating system and users only gain by it being there. But enough experts in antitrust and economics who don't know beans about computing mouth this stuff that I had to state their contention.

New Utilities

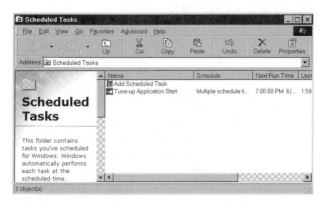

Figure 1-4. Improved Task Scheduler

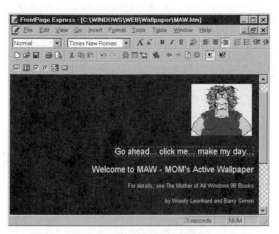

Figure 1-5. MAW in FrontPage Express

Windows 98 contains a couple of new applications that make it easier than ever to set up, customize, and run your PC.

Win98's new **Task Scheduler** (Figure 1-4) lets you schedule any program to run at any time. Although it resembles the old scheduler from the Windows 95 Plus! Pack, this one is built into Windows itself, and it works flawlessly.

Those of you who struggled with editing World Wide Web pages in "native HTML" (the code language used to create Web pages) can breathe a sigh of relief. Microsoft has included a "lite" version of its award-winning Web construction kit, FrontPage, as a freebie in Win98. Dubbed **FrontPage Express** (Figure 1-5), this amazingly versatile tool includes all the HTML editing features in FrontPage, plus a couple of bells and whistles. Microsoft is betting that a big dose of FrontPage Express will leave you wishing for the full package. Frankly, if you do much with Web pages, we bet you will, too.

Stability

It's been my experience that Windows 98 crashes and freezes about half as often as Windows 95 running Internet Explorer 4.01 SP1. I know that's a subjective statement, and I tend to run Windows very hard, but I think it's fair to say that Windows 98, right out of the box, is considerably more stable than Windows 95. Microsoft has done more than improve the stability: they've thrown in a handful of utilities that make it much easier to track down problems and possibly prevent problems before they occur.

I think the **ScanReg** utility, which scans the Registry for errors and prunes dead Registry keys once they are over 500K in waste space, is an important element of the increased stability. I talk about this more in the section "Integrity."

Microsoft's System Information Utility 4.1—better known as **SysInfo**—provides an enormous amount of information about your Win98 system (Figure 1-6). The folks in Redmond spent a lot of money coming up with the most thorough system reporting utility the PC has ever seen. They have an ulterior motive: a phone support tech can have you run SysInfo and gather an enormous amount of information about your system in no time flat. That saves Microsoft lots of bucks in the no-profit-here world of telephone support. But it's a win-win utility, because you can use it, too, to track down every little detail about your machine and what it's running.

Traditional reporting software also has some hardware diagnostic tests and this is missing from SysInfo—it's only a reporting tool.

Speaking of reliability improvements, the Win98 installer goes above and beyond the call of duty by searching for and *disabling* a Microsoft product called **Find Fast**. As many of you Office users know, Find Fast was the vehicle for

Figure 1-6. Extraordinarily detailed SysInfo report

Office's ill-fated attempt to index documents during the PC's idle moments. Find Fast was notorious for taking control of the machine while the user was typing on the keyboard. It also had a marvelous propensity for cascading General Protection Faults—leave it alone overnight and you could come back to a dozen or more neatly stacked GPF warning boxes in the middle of the screen, all attributable to Find Fast. In other books (for example, *Word 97 Annoyances* by Leonhard, Hudspeth, and Lee) we've urged Office users to turn off Find Fast. If you install

Win98, Microsoft's own installer does it for you. Now *that's* a stability improvement of the first degree!

Making a reappearance, the new, improved **Dr. Watson** sits in the background, waiting for Windows to hiccup. When a program dies, Dr. Watson— Windows 98's official coroner—takes over, gives you a reasonable explanation for the problem, then gathers information that could prove valuable to the program's designers to help prevent problems like that in the future.

 By default, Dr. Watson doesn't get loaded. I think that's fine unless you have a persistent software problem, in which case you'll want to load it to have a truly comprehensive bug report to send to the tech support department of the offending product. I'll tell you how to load it in Chapter 4.

It's hard to believe that Microsoft could improve on a humble utility like the **Disk Defragmenter**, but the Windows 98 flavor of this classic does much more than simply defrag a hard drive. ("Defragmenting" is the process of scanning a disk and relocating pieces of files so they sit next to each other, thus speeding up access to those files in the future.) This defragmenter maintains a log of the files you use most commonly, then rearranges file locations during the defrag process to make frequently used files and related files load even faster.

The old **ScanDisk** comes back with a new twist—Windows 98 watches to see if you shut down properly (using the Startup, Shutdown Menu). If for some reason you didn't shut down the right way, the next time Windows 98 starts, it runs ScanDisk. Since files are most likely to get scrambled when your system crashes, this forced ScanDisk run stands a very good chance of catching most file problems at the earliest possible moment.

Another new program, **Disk Cleanup**, offers to delete the usual crop of temporary files, empty the Recycle Bin, and otherwise delete unnecessary files from your hard drive. It goes one step farther, though, by offering to remove portions of Windows and other applications that you don't seem to be using (Figure 1-7).

The new **Maintenance Wizard** combines operation of the Disk Defragmenter, ScanDisk, and Disk Cleanup. Run the Wizard (Figure 1-8), and those

Figure 1-7. Disk Cleanup goes an extra mile in offering to delete files from your drives

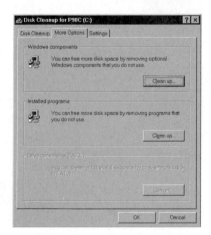

Figure 1-8. The Maintenance Wizard: Defrag, ScanDisk, and temporary file delete, all in one

three activities are scheduled to run in the middle of the night—using Task Scheduler, of course.

Finally, Windows 98 has a completely new version of the **Backup** program, written by Seagate, that many people find much easier to use than earlier incarnations. It includes support for SCSI-based media.

Integrity

Where Windows 95 pretty much assumed that its system files would be changed only if change was warranted—what kind of application would replace a Windows system file without issuing dire warnings?—Windows 98 isn't so trusting.

The **System File Checker** keeps on top of the primary Windows 98 files and warns you if some wayward program has replaced them or if they've somehow been deleted or renamed. Should that happen, you're asked what you want to do, and if you follow the recommended steps, backup copies of all the files are restored.

The **Registry Checker** keeps five (count 'em!) cycled backups of the Windows 98 Registry. Each time you restart Windows, a backup is automatically made unless a backup was already made earlier the same day. So you should have a Registry at least five days old around. If something goes terribly awry, you can restore the Registry to a stable state, at least in theory. Registry restoration is much, much simpler than ever before, particularly because the Registry Checker includes a DOS-mode program to perform the restore. Microsoft claims that Registry Checker also has some built-in smarts to resolve Registry problems. The jury's still out on whether that part does anything worthwhile, at least in the real world.

 I'll have a lot more to say about Registry backup in Chapter 9. In particular, you can keep more than five copies and you can add your own files to the list of what is backed up.

The **System Configuration Utility** puts most of your potential configuration problems in one place (Figure 1-9). Yes, you can edit **autoexec.bat**, **config.sys**, **system.ini**, and **win.ini** here (just as you could with **sysedit,** an archaic Windows 3.x tool that somehow survives in both Win95 and Win98). But you can also do much, much more: choose which of the startup files to run, and how; make backups; even disable some of Win98's more dicey features.

It's a very useful, very comprehensive feature. There's just one teeny-tiny problem with the System Configuration Utility. You can't find any information

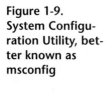
Figure 1-9.
System Configuration Utility, better known as msconfig

about it anywhere in the online Help (except buried deep in a couple of troubleshooting sequences), and it doesn't appear on any of the menus. To bring it to life, you have to know the secret incantation: click Start, Run, type **msconfig**, and hit Enter.

FATter Disks

FAT32 (short for "32-bit file allocation table") is the new, more efficient method of storing data on hard disk drives—and the *only* built-in way to store data on drive partitions larger than 2 GB under Windows 9X. (NT has had NTFS, the NT File System, which supports disks of up to 64 GB and various flavors of UNIX allow large disks.) Introduced in a later version of Windows 95 (the so-called OSR2, or OEM Service Release 2 version), FAT32 can reclaim 25% to 30% of your hard drive space if you're using the older FAT16 storage method (Figure 1-10).

Figure 1-10.
To see what kind of FAT method your drives use, go into Windows Explorer (right click on My Computer, pick Explore), then right click on the drive and pick Properties

Almost everyone with hard disks over 1 GB in size should convert their hard disks to FAT32 and take advantage of the 10% to 25% space savings. (We'll discuss the exceptions in Chapter 6.) Windows 98 offers a FAT32 converter that makes the conversion easy and—hard to believe—safe. Run **fat32win.exe** in the Resource Kit Sampler (described later in this chapter in "Windows Resource Kit Sampler") to find out how much space you'll gain by changing over. We think you'll be pleasantly surprised.

 But be warned that the FAT32 converter from Microsoft only works if your disk has no bad clusters.

Speed

Microsoft claims that Windows 98 runs substantially faster than Windows 95—and they have the test data to back that claim. In our experience, Win98 does shut down considerably faster than Win95. It boots marginally faster. And it loads and starts applications faster, but not enough faster to write home to MOM about it.

Win98 also has a fast boot capability that relies on new hardware (the so-called Fast Boot BIOS). We didn't have that hardware on hand in time to test before we went to press.

Microsoft claims that it has speeded up both startup and shutdown. In our testing, we didn't notice much of a speedup on startup on systems without the special new BIOS. The increased speed of shutdown, though, was dramatic. Of course, there is a cost for this increased speed. The system no longer properly logs out of networks, so when other systems on the network scan it, the scan seems to take longer if a Win98 machine has recently shut down.

Startup

In addition to the Registry backup and restore built into the Registry Checker (mentioned earlier), Win98 includes several important features that make booting your PC easier, more reliable, and at least a little less intimidating than it has been in the past.

Tops on the list: the **Emergency Startup Disk** with built-in CD support. Windows has been able to create an Emergency Startup Disk (ESD; MOM calls it a "panic disk") since the dawn of time. The ESD boots you into DOS so that you can perform emergency surgery on your system. But ESDs have always had one fatal flaw—they never supported CD drives. As a result, many Windows 95 users found themselves booting to a DOS prompt and then discovering they had hit a brick wall when the software they wanted to run (frequently the Windows installer) existed only on CD! Win98 overcomes that problem by endowing the ESD with CD drivers that work for most—but not all—CD drives.

The ESD goes one step farther. It stores a number of important DOS programs on one floppy diskette, in compressed form, and extracts those programs on the fly as it starts during an emergency boot. That's a great idea, with only a few drawbacks, which we'll cover in Chapter 6.

Another important improvement: Win98's **Automatic Skip Driver** feature, which you'll probably never see, intelligently bypasses loading drivers that have caused problems in earlier boot sequences. ASD does yeoman's work bypassing the all-too-common problem of not being able to boot Windows at all because of a bad piece of hardware or a driver that locks up the system.

Power Management

Windows 98 works with two power management standards called Advanced Configuration and Power Interface (ACPI) and Advanced Power Management (APM). If you've bought a notebook computer recently, you no doubt have built-in ACPI and/or APM support; in fact, many desktop systems now include APM. There's a whole slew of new power management settings, which we'll cover in Chapter 8.

Webby

Yes, indeed, the Web is everywhere in Windows 98, at times almost indistinguishable from the "rest" of Windows—if, indeed, there still is a "rest."

In addition to FrontPage Express, Win98 has a new Web look and feel to the My Computer icon and Windows Explorer application. It's very hard to tell where Windows Explorer ends and Internet Explorer begins—which is just as well, as more people stay connected to the Web all the time, and the Web becomes a simple (if painfully slow) extension of the Desktop.

Microsoft's Windows 98 **Personal Web Server** puts training wheels on the outstanding Windows NT Web Server. The result leaves much to be desired, but if you need to set up an intranet based on Windows 98 peer-to-peer networking, it's a serviceable choice. And the price is right—it comes bundled, free, with Win98.

The **Web Publishing Wizard** will help first-time Web publishers gather their files and send them to a Web server, but if you know how to use FTP, the Wizard offers little except a glitzy interface.

Networking

If you can get it to work, Win98's **Multilink Channel Aggregation** (gad, what a name!) combines two modems to double the amount of data you can shove over the phone lines. In theory. Here's the fine print.

- You have to have two modems and two phone lines, of course.
- The people on the other end of the phone call (typically, your Internet Service Provider or your company's network) has to support MCA.
- Even then, Microsoft advises that "using analog [as opposed to ISDN] modems can cause serial overrun errors that impair the performance of the multilink connection." Seems that MCA was built for ISDN, the super-fast phone lines, and not all the kinks have been worked out for normal phone lines.

With an overwhelming endorsement like that, how can you resist? We never did get MCA to amount to much. Kinda makes you want to go out and buy two expensive new modems, install two expensive phone lines, and give it a whirl, doesn't it?

Monitors

Unlike MCA, **multiple monitor support** in Windows 98 really does work. You use two video cards and attach two monitors to one machine. The Desktop then expands to fill both monitors. You resize your applications, usually, so that one appears on one monitor and the other appears on the second. You can then drag and drop between the monitors, just as you would on one huge desktop. Some people like it, some people hate it. Here's the fine print.

- Both video cards have to be PCI video cards. You can't use old-fashioned ISA bus cards. Nor can you use the newer, faster AGP cards or a video outlet that's on the motherboard (unless it's connected to the PCI bus). You can't mix and match, either. Two PCI cards, period, although they don't have to be the same brand.

- Your mouse doesn't "bang up against" the right side of the first monitor. Many lazy people (Woody included) rely on that "banging" all the time to hit the up-and-down scrollbar that usually appears on the right side of an application's full-screen window. Instead of banging on the right of the screen, the mouse pointer keeps on sailing onto the second monitor's screen, and it's nerve-wracking trying to bring it back.

 If you place the monitors one above the other, you will be able to bang against the side but not the top or bottom.

- You have to arrange both monitors so that you can see them. That may sound trivial, but for many people it isn't: either the left monitor is easy to see and the right monitor requires some twisting and straining or vice versa.

 Ah, but that misses the point! Wait till you look at a demo of Flight Simulator where you can see both a cockpit and tower view at the same time but on separate monitors. Then there are the two-person strategy games played on a single PC, action games, and so on. There's no doubt that serious game players will want multiple monitors. Given the cost of the second monitor and the desk space problems, I doubt home users other than the gamers will use this feature. But gamers are going to go ga-ga.

Before you spend $100 on a PCI video card (better make that $200 for two PCI video cards, if you currently have video on the motherboard or AGP video) and $150 to $200 for a second monitor, it would be very smart to try this feature for a couple of hours on some real work. When you're done, do the arithmetic, and check to make sure you have two free PCI slots. You may well end up springing for a single, larger monitor.

Windows 98 also includes video support for **font smoothing** (formerly available in the Windows 95 Plus! Pack and by download from the Microsoft Web site) and on-the-fly changes in color depth and **screen resolution** (from, say, 800 × 600 to 1024 × 768 pixels).

Figure 1-11.
Windows 98
Electronic
Program Guide

TV Connection

If you have a TV tuner card, Windows 98 brings you full TV viewing support in the form of something called **WebTV for Windows**. At this point, you get to watch TV on your screen (again, if you have the special kind of video card), and you'll have access to the **Windows 98 Electronic Program Guide**, which is shown in Figure 1-11 (there's a thumbnail in the blank window at the upper right of the show in progress if you are highlighting the current time period, but our screen capture software doesn't capture the TV picture).

 As WebTV for Windows evolves, you'll also be able to see Web-based information simulcast with the TV shows (click on an icon for *Baywatch* and see close-ups of each actor's biceps! Ooooh! Aaaaaah!) and retrieve data from the unused portion of the TV signal called the Vertical Blanking Interval. As we went to press, all this seemed possible, but very little of it was real.

Er, Woody, it isn't the *Baywatch* biceps that most guys look at.

The program guide can be updated overnight using the VBI (Vertical Blanking Interval) of PBS stations or can be downloaded over the Internet. For now you get only a two-day window, but it's free. It is likely that the third party currently providing it (for the rights to include ads like that shown in Figure 1-11) will eventually provide weekly or longer guides for a fee.

 The TV picture is drawn by the electron gun sweeping along the screen from the upper left to lower right, one horizontal line at a time. When the bottom corner is reached, the gun turns off and moves back to the start at the top of the screen. The time while the gun is off is called the VBI, and it means that a standard TV signal has about 15% dead time when it is sending nothing waiting for the electron gun to get back into place. Various people realized one could send useful information during that period. That's when the Program Guide can be downloaded, and it is also when **WaveTop**, another new Windows 98 component, does its magic.

 WaveTop downloads news and entertainment sources (see Figure 1-12). One warning, though. I have a TV tuner attached to an outside antenna. My local PBS station comes through loud and clear when I want to view it on Web TV and the ATI All-In-Wonder Pro (a video card with attached TV tuner), but WaveTop complains it can't locate any PBS channels, so I couldn't get it to work for me. Maybe you can.

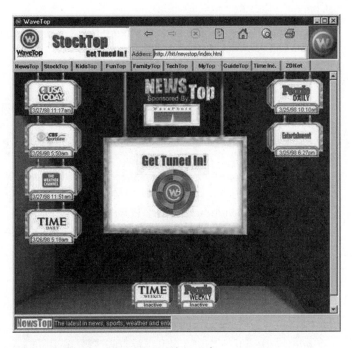

Figure 1-12. WaveTop News Channel

New Hardware

The single most important hardware development since the onslaught of Plug 'n' Play has to be the Universal Serial Bus, or USB. Win98 includes full, native **USB support**, so you can install a new USB device (such as a mouse or a scanner or a modem) and have it work immediately, with no driver headaches and no futzing with IRQs or DMA addresses. This is another area just beginning to develop as we went to press, and it holds a great deal of promise.

Win98 also includes built-in support for the Intel **MMX** processor (which runs fine with Win95 but needs Win98 for applications to take full advantage of the features), **AGP** video, **DVD** video discs, and some support for the **IEEE 1394** "Fire Wire" bus. For you notebook users, Win98 includes **PC Card32** support, for higher 32-bit communication bandwidth between the PC and the Card.

Finally, Win98 has built-in support for the Infrared Data Association (**IrDA**) standard to connect PCs to peripherals through infrared links. Win98 has drivers for printers, file transfer, and general network connection via infrared.

Windows Resource Kit Sampler

There's also a subset of the *Windows Resource Kit* called the Sampler. While the *WRK* itself weighs in at 1,500 pages and about $70—you can find it at most bookstores—almost everything that most Win98 users will need from the *WRK* proper can be found in the Sampler, right on the Win98 CD. A partial list (see Chapter 5 for further discussion):

- **checklinks.exe** to scan your hard drives and find "dead" links and shortcuts
- **cliptray.exe** to put five (or more) different, independently manageable "buckets" in the Win98 Clipboard
- **fat32win.exe** to check your hard drive(s) and tell you how much space you can save by using the FAT32 storage method
- **netmon**, the Network Monitor, to remotely monitor network performance on Win98 PCs
- **quiktray.exe** to add quick-launch icons to the Win98 system tray notification area
- **tweakui**, the ultimate Win98 PowerToy
- **usbview.exe** to watch what's happening with your USB peripherals
- **windiff.exe**, an excellent tool for comparing the differences between two text files
- **wshadmin.hlp**, a Help file that describes the Windows Scripting Host, a method for (finally!) building "Windows macro programs"

All these files, examples, and much more are installed when you put the Windows Resource Kit Sampler on your PC. Just run **setup.exe** in the **\tools\reskit** folder on the Win98 CD.

For Fun . . .

Win98 ships with **DirectX 5.0**, the gamer's delight, with full AGP, MMX, and force-feedback joystick support. It also has **Real Audio 4.0**—why it doesn't include RA 5.0 (the later version, widely available) is a mystery to me. There's also **ActiveMovie**, which uses data streaming to improve playback of MPEG, AVI, and QuickTime clips.

There's also the usual tomfoolery: Desktop themes (all of the themes in the Win95 Plus! Pack, plus four themes designed specifically for kids), screensavers, and the old Win95 games (Free Cell, Hearts, Minesweeper, and Solitaire).

 Aw, shoot. The one thing I looked forward to with a new version of Windows was a new little teaser game, but all you get here are the classics. Of course, given the time I've spent with Minesweeper and Free Cell, it's probably just as well.

Windows 3.1 Upgrade

 Microsoft says you can upgrade directly from Windows 3.1 to Windows 98, and that's undoubtedly true. We didn't spend a whole lot of time worrying about it. Fact is, you should have a Pentium-class machine to run Windows 98. And if you're still running Win3.1 on a Pentium, well, there isn't much hope for you, is there?

The IE 4 Changes

For those of you who bypassed the upgrade to Internet Explorer 4, there's a whole new world of features that come standard in Windows 98. We can't really call them Win98 features, because they came in through the IE 4 back door. But they may well be new to you.

The **Start Menu** is now fully configurable so that you can add, delete, and move items on the menu using the familiar drag and drop actions. Unfortunately, when you install new programs, they get added to the bottom of the Programs menu and—unlike Windows 95—they never get sorted into the main list. So, instead of seeing an alphabetized list of folders and shortcuts under the Programs menu, you'll get a mishmash of what was originally there plus the programs you've dragged onto the menu, followed by all the programs you've installed, in chronological order. You can reorder them yourself by dragging and dropping on the menu, though.

There's a **Favorites** list on the Start Menu. Fully configurable, you can add, change, or delete folders or files and make them readily available here.

 But alas, the use of a single Favorites folder shared by Explorer, Internet Explorer, and Office means that any Word documents you care enough to appear as Favorites in Word will also appear on the Favorites dropdown in IE. Too bad.

Figure 1-13. Placing Internet Explorer's Address Bar on the Win98 Taskbar

You can put the Internet Explorer **Address Bar** down on Windows' Taskbar (Figure 1-13). That makes it very easy to type in a Web address—a URL—and have IE 4 pop up and grab that Web page lickety-split. In fact, you can use the "?" option to have IE 4 search for whatever you like: type `Bill Clinton?` In the Address Bar, and IE 4 immediately launches into a full-scale search, using the Web search engine(s) you specify.

 Windows 98 also ships with **Outlook Express,** a stunted version of the enormously powerful Outlook 98 program bundled with Microsoft Office. Outlook Express, as a freebie, beats out almost all the other e-mail and newsgroup reader programs on the market.

 Actually, I don't think Outlook and Outlook Express share much more than a name—so OE is hardly a stunted version of Outlook 98. Rather, they are both e-mail programs. Outlook is more powerful and larger and better, but OE isn't half bad.

The new version of **NetMeeting** includes a wide range of tools for conferencing over the Net—cameras, voice, and file transfer are all supported.

Then there's the **Active Desktop**, which replaces Windows' standard Desktop with a Web page (that is, an HTML file) of your choice. We'll play with those quite a bit in Chapter 7.

And, lest we forget, the **Active Channel Bar** also appears in Win98. It allows you to subscribe to, oh, the Disney Web site or ESPN or PointCast and be notified of changes at those sites immediately or even have them downloaded immediately. Talk about a waste of real estate. And bandwidth.

■ Is Win98 for You?

See one promontory (said Socrates of old), one mountain, one sea, one river, and see all.

—ROBERT BURTON, *The Anatomy of Melancholy I,* 1621

So there you have it. That's as complete a list of Windows 98 improvements—the good, the bad, and the ever-so-ugly—as you'll find anywhere. Perhaps one or two new features caught your eye. Then again, maybe not.

The question you have to ask yourself: Is all of this worth $89 (or whatever the going price for the upgrade might be), plus the hassles of upgrading?

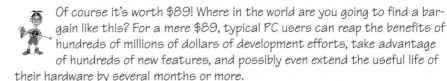 Of course it's worth $89! Where in the world are you going to find a bargain like this? For a mere $89, typical PC users can reap the benefits of hundreds of millions of dollars of development efforts, take advantage of hundreds of new features, and possibly even extend the useful life of their hardware by several months or more.

I tend to agree, if only for the new utilities, which can be mighty helpful in a pinch. But that only applies to individuals. In companies, where the cost of rolling out an operating system update is often many times the purchase price of the software, this isn't such a slam-dunk decision. In fact, unless there are very specific reasons to take on the agony of upgrading, I'm not sure I'd recommend Win98 to most companies. Get it when you buy new PCs, sure. But retrofitting may well be more hassle than it's worth.

I just wish Billy had pegged the price lower by about half. At $39 or even $49, upgrading's a no-brainer, at least for individuals. But at $89, it's hard to say. Guess it depends on how hard you use your PC, and how much you need the new features. If you have a hard disk with more than 1 GB, it isn't already running FAT32 (the Properties Tab for the Drive will tell you if it is running FAT32 or not) and you have 32 MB RAM, then the increased disk space makes Win98 close to a no-brainer. Otherwise, it's a tossup.

As you ponder your decision to buy and install Win98, consider a few disadvantages.

- The fax software isn't integrated into the e-mail program and is a bit tricky to find since it is not part of the standard installation.

 Lots of reviews missed the fact that right there on the CD is the old fax software that you can install. I'll talk about it in Chapter 3.

- You can't use DriveSpace, the hard disk compression software, on FAT32 drives. While converting to FAT32 may reclaim 25% of your hard disk space, DriveSpace compresses many files by about 50%.
- Any way you look at it, Windows 98 is an orphan. There won't be a Windows 2000—at least not as an extension of the Win3.1-Win95-Win98 lineage.
- In other words, sooner or later, you're almost undoubtedly going to end up with NT. Yes, NT takes a heftier machine than Win98, but many machines you buy nowadays can run NT with no problems. Yes, there are difficulties with NT drivers for all sorts of hardware, but those problems are decreasing (albeit gradually) in most areas. Yes, the interface in NT isn't quite as friendly as in Windows 98, especially when you get into more of the technical places, but NT 5.0 may address that. Maybe you should just take the plunge and move to NT now. . . .

My main machine is now a Windows NT workstation.

As MOM would tell ya, there are no easy answers.

■ Plus

Forget not on every occasion to ask thyself, Is this not one of the unnecessary things?
—Marcus Aurelius, *Meditations, IV,* ca. 170 A.D.

Unlike the quandary over Win98, there's a very simple answer to whether you should shell out real money for the Windows 98 Plus! Pack: just say no. Or at least, just say ho, ho, ho.

Here's what you'll find in the Plus! Pack.

- McAfee VirusScan, from Network Associates, including a six-month subscription to their online update service. McAfee certainly does make a decent antivirus package, but why not just buy it outright?

- An enhanced Maintenance Wizard and File Cleaner, from Cybermedia, which snags certain oddball files and offers to delete them for you, including screen savers, help files, icons that don't point anywhere, and several others. If you need to clean files this badly, you should buy a new hard drive.

- Compressed Folders, which treats Zip files as if they were folders. It works pretty well, but it won't let you create self-extracting Zip files, and it's nowhere near as usable as WinZip.

 If you like the Zips as folders, Zip Magic is much better.

- PictureIt! Express, a pared-down version of Microsoft Photo Editor, which ships with Office. Since you probably have Office (statistically speaking anyway), you probably have the real thing.

- Deluxe CD player, which can download details about CDs (track names, playing times, and so on) from the Web. Pardon me while I yawn.

- Themes, wallpaper, and a couple of semiinteresting games. This is the ho, ho, ho part. If you want to blow a few bucks on some sorta fun stuff, these might interest you. If you're really bored and you're easily amused, anyway.

All in all, we think you'll find the Plus! Pack to be a real yawner.

■ Janet and the Grasshoppers

Getting kicked to death by grasshoppers is a painful and ignominious way to go. Even if Microsoft escapes this legal round unscathed, the boys at the top may finally understand it's time to start acting like grown-ups, who are running one of the most important, most visible and most scrutinized companies in the world.

—CHARLES MORRIS, *Los Angeles Times,* May 17, 1998

We just couldn't let the Department of Justice antitrust action against Microsoft go without comment. Here's MOM's gang's take on the subject . . .

On Monopolies

 If you're talking about PC operating systems, Microsoft has a monopoly, period.

 If you're talking about PC operating systems, Microsoft has a monopoly, period.

 While it's true that Microsoft is the dominant player in the PC operating system market, there are many alternatives, from BeOS to Linux. I don't think the government should dictate to people what kind of software they should buy.

On the Effect of Monopolies

 Software is a funny commodity. The value to the consumer is so much higher than the cost to the producer that one has to rely on market competition to set the price at a reasonable level. Think about something like optical character recognition—during the past seven years, because of competition and a huge increase in the market, the price has dropped from $395 to $39, a factor of 10. But Windows pricing hasn't changed despite a huge increase in user base. That's because there is a monopoly and no competition.

 The 'Softies are fond of pointing out how much cheaper Windows is than the SunOS or other flavors of UNIX, but that's not the right analogy. Mac OS pricing wasn't usually this high. The bottom line is that $90 is unconscionable for what MS itself says is a ".1 upgrade" from Win95 to Win98. I've no problem with that price for upgraders from Win 3.1, but Win95 users should be paying more like $45 or $50 and would be if there were competition. And Microsoft would make a pretty penny at that price because even at that price, their profit after marketing cost would be $10 a copy (rather than the $25 or $30 a copy they make now).

Never in the history of mankind has there been an industry as competitive as the computer software industry. For a mere $90, PC users can take advantage of hundreds of millions of dollars' worth of development. Yes, it's a profitable venture—but if the profits weren't there, you wouldn't see the kind of innovation we've seen in software.

What Belongs in the Operating System

Microsoft (and all of its competitors!) has been absorbing new features into its software for years. Let's take just three examples: 386 memory management, disk compression, and fonts. In each case, the real innovators were outside Microsoft—Qualitas (386Max) and Quarterdeck (QEMM) with 386 Memory Management, STAC (Stacker) for disk compression, and Adobe and Bitstream with fonts. The first two features are so obviously OS functions that until they were absorbed into the OS, there were conflicts and problems galore. Fonts don't produce conflicts but are systemwide.

From the users' perspective, it is hard to claim that they have lost by the demise of QEMM, 386Max, Stacker, and the $50-per-font-family font packages. Indeed, they'd have to do without or put out a total of several hundred dollars for these pieces of software. And they wouldn't work so well because there really are advantages to integrating these functions into the OS and advantages to a single source that third-party applications can rely on. So integration of these features into the OS is a huge financial and functional gain for users.

So it comes down to what some economists and some Justice Department spokespeople have hyped as users being hurt by a lack of innovation. This too is a hard case to make. There is no dearth of entrepreneurs willing to carve a niche from what was left out of the current OS. If they are smart, they sock some of it away knowing that eventually the OS will steamroller them. The Quarterdeck founders have done very well, thank you. Of course, some were oblivious to the train roaring down the tracks and spent their gains on futile attempts to avoid the inevitable. So one can grab some sympathy for the entrepreneurs who were foolhardy, but it hasn't stopped new innovators from popping up nor has it hurt users. And Microsoft for all the bellyaching about bloatwear has been innovative. Excel, Access, Word, EnCarta have all been pioneering in their own way. Windows 95 was not a mere clone of the Mac as the anti-MS chorus would have it. It was genuinely innovative in many, many ways.

With regard to the core of the Justice Department case, it comes down to whether the browser belongs in the OS. That the two are indelibly entwined can be seen by the noise Netscape and Oracle made several years ago about turning the browser into an OS. The browser does belong in the OS. Not only that, if it weren't there, users would be paying Netscape $50 for their browser, maybe more, since Netscape would have exploited *its* monopoly!

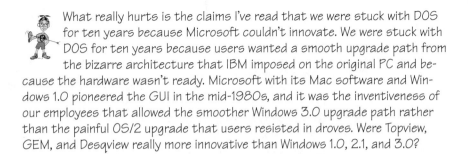

What really hurts is the claims I've read that we were stuck with DOS for ten years because Microsoft couldn't innovate. We were stuck with DOS for ten years because users wanted a smooth upgrade path from the bizarre architecture that IBM imposed on the original PC and because the hardware wasn't ready. Microsoft with its Mac software and Windows 1.0 pioneered the GUI in the mid-1980s, and it was the inventiveness of our employees that allowed the smoother Windows 3.0 upgrade path rather than the painful OS/2 upgrade that users resisted in droves. Were Topview, GEM, and Desqview really more innovative than Windows 1.0, 2.1, and 3.0?

I can hardly believe the U.S. Department of Justice has the temerity to sue Microsoft for rolling features into the operating system. We'd still be typing EDLIN at the DOS 3.2 command prompt if it weren't for expansion in the operating system. The whole thing's a red herring. It's only received attention recently because Microsoft's competitors have spent enough money and made enough friends inside the Beltway to turn it into a political fight. Once the D.C. sharks smelled blood, the various states' attorneys general started swarming, hoping to grab a piece of the publicity carcass. That stinks. Netscape and Oracle should be competing with better products, not with high-paid politicians and lawyers. The Senator from Novell embarrasses me. Do you think for one moment that any of these people know Type 1 from TrueType? Or a URL from a hole in the ground? They're all johnny-pol-come-latelies, with massive gaps in their knowledge and understanding of the PC software business.

We have an acronym around here for our enemies—NOISE—for Netscape, Oracle, IBM, and Sun.

What's the E stand for?

Everyone else <grin>!

You know, Billy, some of the problem is Microsoft's making. Of course, the attorneys general are on this because of the publicity and interest by the public. Most attorneys general are governor wannabes. But the public interest isn't fueled merely by jealous or frightened competitors. There is a significant fraction of the public that hates Microsoft, often vehemently, because of its arrogance, uncompetitive behavior I'll turn to in the next section, and a generally disdainful attitude towards consumers.

How can you say that we disdain our consumers? They are our bread and butter.

Too often, you substitute marketing for substance. You treat your consumers like jerks, throwing them stuff that will wow them, ignoring some of the serious bugs, and not providing them with proper documentation. The Microsoft attitude is really very patronizing toward users.

 One shouldn't forget Microsoft's secret weapon in the OS wars—the small developer. Sure, Microsoft steals their ideas and sometimes puts them out of business, but generally Microsoft woos the small developer in a way Apple and IBM didn't understand. And that served MS in great stead—Windows won in part because it had so many third-party applications.

 At one level, it is a puzzle that Oracle and Sun are involved in the anti-Microsoft jihad. What do an enterprisewide database company and a non-Intel hardware manufacturer have to do with Windows on the desktop? The answer has to do with a long-term view and a proper understanding of the biggest threat to their core businesses. The push of Windows NT up the food chain is a huge threat to Sun. Already Compaq has eaten into a piece of the midrange server business that used to be Sun's. And once the 64-bit Merced chip is out there, the Wintel-based hardware manufacturers will move farther up the food chain. And Oracle is afraid that once NT Server takes over, Microsoft's SQL database will threaten Oracle's bread and butter. So they are preemptively attacking now, realizing that a part of NT server's success is its links to Windows on the desktop.

On Using Monopolies Unfairly

 While asking Microsoft to unlink IE or forcing it to ship Netscape are crazy to me, there are big problems with how Microsoft has used and continues to use its monopoly power to improve its other businesses. Applications and Internet businesses that Microsoft has invested in get an undeserved boost all the time. Oracle is right to worry that Microsoft will use NT server to boost SQL unfairly if NT server takes over the *Enterprise*.

 In the original *The Mother of All Windows Books*, we documented a case of this—the Wave Mapper scandal, where Microsoft was clearly giving its consumer division a boost over its competitors by giving its products early access to some useful sound technology. And one reason the Microsoft Office won the suite wars was because it had an advantage in incorporating OLE technology—an advantage it got because of its links to the OS group at Microsoft.

 You guys have it all wrong. The Wave Mapper technology was developed by our consumer folks and OLE by the Office group, and big Bill then ordered this neat technology be incorporated into the OS, benefiting our customers.

You know as well as I do that these technologies used lots of undocumented features in the OS and that the OS was modified to accommodate them. That some of the code was written by another group within Microsoft is irrelevant. The point is that technology that is naturally a part of the OS needs to be made available to all application developers as soon as it is made available to Microsoft's application developers.

Cruder and even less acceptable is Microsoft's using its control of the desktop to push its other businesses. MSN had a preferred place on the Windows 95 Desktop, and looking at Figure 1-1 you see it still does on Win98. Why the heck should Hotmail, a product that Microsoft owns, get a place on the links bar? And why should Microsoft be able to trade with online service providers the right to an icon in the Online Services folder on every Windows 98 desktop in exchange for showing a preference for IE over Netscape? One can even question the demos for other Microsoft products that are included on the Windows CD.

That's not fair, Woody. Adobe includes demos of its other products on its installation CDs. Why should Microsoft be any different?

Monopolies have to play by different rules, Billy.

Hardware OEMs should get to pick the initial wallpaper and the content of the nonessential desktop icons and folders, and they should be able to ignore anything Microsoft provides for these. And somehow, Microsoft shouldn't be able to control these goodies on the upgrades.

First of all, MSN shows that the preferred positioning isn't that important. AOL ate our lunch in spite of that icon on the Windows 95 desktop. Secondly, it is important that users have the same Windows 95 experience on all machines. The commonness of the interface is a critical part of what makes Windows so successful. You learn to use it at your office and change jobs and it's the same Windows everywhere.

Gimme a break, Billy. That the icon hasn't let MSN dominate only shows that the benefit isn't always decisive. It is still real enough that we are puzzled that long ago the Justice Department didn't object to the icon. And it is a real stretch to claim that who is in the Online Services folder, what gets put on the initial Links toolbar, what the default Web home site is, or who is in the Channels toolbar has much to do with having the same experience with Windows on different machines. What it has to do with is Microsoft's other businesses and other interests. It's an abuse of your monopoly power pure and simple, and I hope Janet and the grasshoppers win on this one.

Rather than penalizing Microsoft for being so successful, the U.S. government should be helping new companies emulate our success. There's still room for enormous innovation in the software industry—we've hardly even begun—and the Microsofts of tomorrow are running out of garages and off kitchen tables today.

■ MOM98 for Upgraders

In my early years I read very hard. It is a sad reflection, but a true one, that I knew almost as much at eighteen as I do now.

—SAMUEL JOHNSON, *Boswell's Life,* July 20, 1763

If you know Win95 pretty well—in particular, if you scoured *The Mother of All Windows 95 Books* and remember most of it—and you're interested in learning all about Win98, we have a fast track for you, sprinkled throughout this book in the discussion of the features that have carried over from Windows 95. Here's what's new and where to look for it.

In Chapter 2, look for some of the subtle changes in the overall Windows framework, including the expansion of the folder tree-based menu from Start Menu to embrace the new Links and Favorites. The common dialogs have added a zip to the desktop button that you'll use a lot once you realize it is there. I'll discuss some theoretical background on what FAT32 is and why you might like it!

In Chapter 3, the new Desktop is discussed, including the new toolbars, especially the Quick Launch and Address bars. There is a new way to organize the Start Menu and a new Thumbnail view of the files in a folder. The new Control Panel applets are introduced, although the detailed discussion of most of them appears in Chapter 8. One exception that is discussed in this chapter is the new Users applet that improves the interface on Windows' multiple profiles feature. We have a collection of ten IE tips, ten Web sites, and ten mailing lists. There is extensive discussion of Outlook Express and where Windows' built-in fax software is hidden. There is discussion of Windows 98's new HTML Help format.

In Chapter 4, the home of built-in utilities discusses a raft of new ones (as well as the old ones), including Imagining for Windows, Task Scheduler, SysInfo, Dr. Watson, the new Defrag, the new ScanDisk, Disk Cleanup, the Maintenance Wizard, the New Backup, Active Channel Bar, Personal Web Server, NetMeeting, Microsoft Chat, NetShow Player, Web Publishing Wizard, and FrontPage Express. Whew!

In Chapter 5, I discuss some third-party products, most of them new since the release of Windows 95, in particular, the free WRK samples on the CD as well as two extra cost options from Microsoft: Plus! and the full *WRK* (*Windows Resource Kit*).

In Chapter 6, we go into the new Win98 installation procedures, give you a few pointers on wiping out all last vestiges of Windows 95 when you upgrade to Win98, and follow through Windows 98's new booting sequence, creating and using one of the new Emergency Startup Disks. We explain the effects of Automatic Skip Driver. There's a heavy dose of the System Configuration Utility here, too. I'll also discuss the Windows Update Wizard and FAT32 conversion.

In Chapter 7, VBScript comes front and center, with tips for creating your own scripts and tying them into Active Desktop HTML pages, using Front-Page Express. Look here for detailed step-by-step procedures for writing scripts you can use every day, as well as information on the Windows Scripting Host. I also discuss System File Checker, Version Conflict Manager, and System Configuration Utility.

In Chapter 8, we look at the new Control Panel applets provided in Win98. Of special note is TweakUI, Power Management, and some of the features in the new Display applet, including the Display Setting icon in the notification area.

In Chapter 9, the Registry chapter, look for information on all the new Registry keys, in addition to tips for running the Registry Checker, keeping on top of Registry backups and how to restore a backed-up Registry. We'll also explore Windiff as a competent tool for tracking Registry changes.

That's about it for the fast track. Don't forget to thumb back and refresh your memory on all those gory little details! MOM's threatening to have a test at the end . . .

Chapter 2

Windows Concepts

 The *Hitchhiker's Guide to the Galaxy* has, in what we laughingly call the past, had a great deal to say on the subject of parallel universes. Very little of this is, however, at all comprehensible to anyone below the level of advanced god. . . .

One encouraging thing the *Guide* does have to say on the subject of parallel universes is that you don't stand the remotest chance of understanding it. You can therefore say "What?" and "Eh?" and even go cross-eyed and start to blither if you like without any fear of making a fool of yourself.

The first thing to realize about parallel universes, the *Guide* says, is that they are not parallel.

It is also important to realize that they are not, strictly, speaking, universes either, but it is easiest if you don't try to realize that until a little later, after you've realized that everything you've realized up to that moment is not true.

The reason they are not universes is that any given universe is not actually a thing as such, but is just a way of looking at what is technically known as the WSOGMM, or Whole Sort of General Mish Mash. The Whole Sort of General Mish Mash doesn't actually exist either, but is just the sum total of all the different ways there would be of looking at it if it did. . . .

Please feel free to blither now.

—Douglas Adams, *Mostly Harmless*

 Those other books start up telling you how to click and clack and tip and tap. We won't forget that one of the reasons that you bought this book is for that sort of stuff. But our philosophy is that by first understanding some of the ideas that motivate the Windows interface, you'll be able to figure out the tips yourself and—more important—remember the ones I give you. So we start with an overview of the ideas behind not only windows, menus, and the common dialogs but also the Internet, fonts, MIDI, and video.

 Listen up, fans. You probably figure this is the chapter you can skip because it deals with abstract stuff, but it's exactly the opposite. If you read only one chapter in this book, read this one! It'll save you time each and every day and make your computing more pleasant to boot.

■ Of Mice and Menus

The goal of science is to build better mousetraps.
The goal of nature is to build better mice.

—Oscar Wilde

 No two ways about it; you have to learn the lingo. If you're on the phone to tech support and they tell you to choose the second radio button, you have to know they don't mean to switch from Rush to Howard using the presets you've configured on the portable radio next to your computer. So part of this first section just tells you the names of things. But it's more. I'll also give you the functionality tips that, once you learn them, can save you lotsa time, for example, the title bar double click.

 We had a cross-reference issue to settle because there's so much happening on your screen. We start with simple windows, but then when we discuss minimizing, the Taskbar needs to be mentioned. But we've not told you what the Taskbar is! In fact, the Taskbar is not discussed in detail until Chapter 3. We decided to make some undefined cross-references because you may come to this book with some terminology, and if not, the dynamite index should help you out.

 Microsoft provides a document to developers called *The Windows Interface Guidelines for Software Design.* It should be the bible for how objects act, for that way the user interface will be consistent across applications. I'll refer to it often as *The Interface Guidelines.*

Anatomy of a Window

Anatomy is destiny.

—Sigmund Freud, 1912

 Here's some rocket science for ya. They call it Windows® because it has a lotta windows running around on screen.

Figure 2-1 shows a minimal window with as little extra as possible. There is actually a lot more there than meets the glance. The most obvious feature of this window is the three buttons on the right side of strip at the top. That colored strip at the top is called the **title bar**, and I'll talk about it more in a moment. The extreme right-hand button, which looks like ✕, is called a **close button** and it closes the window—more rocket science, eh? Actually, all it really does is send a message to the window that says, "Hey,

Figure 2-1. Innocent little window

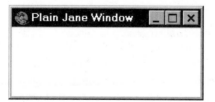

buddy, boss man says it's time to close shop." The window can then go gentle into that good night or it can rage, rage against the dying of the light . . . oops, I mean it can post a message back to the user to confirm the action, perhaps giving some additional information. For example, if the window were your word processor, it might first ask about saving some unsaved work. To the left of the close button are a pair—the **maximize button**, which looks like ▢, and the **minimize button**, which looks like ▬. The maximize button is called that because it makes the window as large as can be. Under Windows 3.1, that normally meant filling the whole screen. Under Windows 95 and 98, the window expands to the whole screen except for the Taskbar.

There are inevitable exceptions. Some users will configure their systems so that the toolbar doesn't usually appear (autohidden) and then maximize will take the whole screen. Others will like the Application Bar that ships with Microsoft Office and will place it as a second bar along the right side of the screen. Then maximizing will cover the part of the screen taken by all but *both* bars. Windowed DOS sessions treat maximize in a special way—the window expands to show the standard 80×25 character screen in whatever the current font size is.

 While on the subject of exceptions, some applications, like Windows Calculator, have the maximize button grayed out. (In Windows, an unavailable option appears as totally gray. Interestingly enough, under Windows 3.x, the calculator shows no maximize button at all, but the Windows 95 team decided that consistency was a good idea and showed a maximize button on all standard windows—sometimes grayed out. What was good for Windows 95 remained good for Windows 98.)

The minimize button is named so for historical reasons—under Windows 3.1, the window was iconized, that is, replaced with an icon at the bottom of the screen and so replaced by its minimum-size object. Under Windows 9X, the window disappears even though it is still running. Normally you can tell it is still running because it remains as a button at the bottom of the screen on the Taskbar like so: ⊙ Plain Jane Window. But that button is there even when the window is open. Again, there are exceptions—a program can choose to hide itself totally or can become an icon in the area of the Taskbar where the time appears.

When you maximize a window, the maximize button (▢) is replaced by a different button called the **restore button**, which looks like ▣. It returns the window to the state it was in before you maximized it.

 The look of the buttons is supposed to be descriptive. The maximize button is supposed to look like a full-screen window, the minimize like a blob on the Taskbar, and the restore button like several windows on screen rather than a maximized window taking the whole desktop.

 The **Quick Launch Toolbar** that you can add to the Taskbar includes a handy icon that looks like a kid's shovel in a sandbox (▨). It is called **Show Desktop** and if you click it, it minimizes all open windows and lets you access desktop icons. Despite the name, it's actually a toggle, so if you use it a second time, it will restore the windows it previously iconized.

Er, Barry, the icon isn't a shovel but a desk blotter with a pencil and eraser writing on a piece of paper.

Whatever. Pretty impressionistic. You can do the same thing by right clicking on a blank area on the Taskbar and choosing Minimize All. The second part of the toggle is then called Undo Minimize All on the right-click menu.

Moving right along, the title bar at the top of the window is usually blue (on some systems, a gradient from dark to light blue). The text in the title bar is called the **window caption**. The name is a holdover from the Windows 3.x days when it appeared underneath the icon as a caption. Now it appears as a title on Taskbar button.

*The title bar is a really useful device to control a window. Double clicking it is the same as clicking the maximize or restore button, that is, it will toggle between the normal and maximized window state. You can put your mouse pointer over the title bar, press the left button, and move the mouse (this is called **click and drag**), and the window moves! Normally, an outline of the window shows as you move it, but the Effects Tab of the Display Properties Dialog (right click on the Desktop and pick Properties to access this dialog) has a check box labeled "Show window contents while dragging" that lets you turn on a mode where the window is drawn as it moves. On all but the slowest of machines, you'll want to turn this on. I'll tell you about right click on the title bar in a moment.*

The icon at the extreme left of the window title bar is called the **system menu button**. If you click once on it (or hit **Alt+Space**), you get the menu shown in

Figure 2-2. System menu

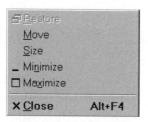

Figure 2-2. It's called the window's **system menu**. All the actions on the menu are available with the mouse in more direct ways, as we've seen, except for Size, which I'll discuss in a moment. Note two things about the last item on the list. First it is bold-face. That's an indication that if you double click the system menu button, the boldface action takes place. That is, double clicking the icon on the left is the same as single clicking the ❌ button on the right side of the title bar. Second, note that the keystroke **Alt+F4** is shown by that choice. It indicates this is a shortcut key to close the window if it is the active window.

If you right click on the title bar, the system menu for the window pops up.

The final element of the window in Figure 2-1 is the border. It is shown there in a different color, from the rest of the window but there are cases where it may not be. As you move your mouse pointer over the border, the pointer changes shape to ↕ over the top and bottom borders, to ↔ over the sides, and to ↖ or ↗ over the corners. At that point, if you press the left mouse button and drag, you resize your window in the obvious way.

 Some windows cannot be resized, and they don't have a cursor change over their borders. The Calculator is a good example. Also, a user can change the pointers, so the shapes I just described may not be the ones that actually appear on your system.

So much for the simple window. Figure 2-3 shows a window with lots of trimmings—an Explorer window with all its options turned on. Immediately below the title bar is the **menu bar** and below that a **toolbar**. I talk about their typical contents later in this chapter.

The last general feature in Figure 2-3 window is the bar at the bottom. It is called the **status bar** and is a place where well-designed applications show you information—it might be free disk space, as in this example, a page number in a word processor, or the date and time in some applications.

 The toolbar has also been called a lot of other names such as action bar and button bar. There are two common styles—the one you'll find in Office and the somewhat larger button type that you'll find in Internet Explorer and Windows Explorer that includes TextLabels.

 You can make Explorer toolbars look like Office toolbars if you want. You right click on the toolbar and uncheck TextLabels to remove them. Then you open Internet Explorer, go to the View/InternetOptions . . . menu item, pick the Advanced tab in that dialog, scroll down to the Toolbar options and check Small Icons. Violà an Office toolbar view.

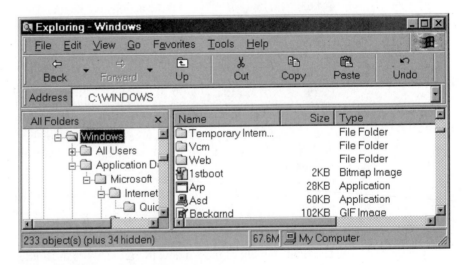

Figure 2-3. Fancy schmancy window

Talk about a confused interface! The way to change the size of the icons and whether or not they are labeled are in totally different places. Way to go Microsoft—NOT!

If you look at the right-hand side of the window in Figure 2-3, you see some objects that look like . These buttons are at either end of a **scroll bar** and it appears when a window or part of a window has more information than can be displayed in the view port on screen. You can have a vertical or a horizontal scroll bar, or, as in this case, both.

This scroll bar has four parts—the two **scroll arrows** at the left and right (or top and bottom), the **scroll shaft** (that's really what *The Interface Guidelines* calls it), which is the long strip between the arrows, and the thingy in the middle. Most folks call that thingy the **slider**; some call it the elevator ('cause it moves up and down the shaft on vertical scrollbars); *The Interface Guidelines* calls it the scroll box—no kidding. I'll call it the slider.

Let me describe how vertical scroll bars work. Clicking on the top or bottom arrows is supposed to move the contents of the window up or down by a single line or single other unit, if there is one. For a picture, there isn't a natural unit (other than a single line of dots, which is much too small), so the program is supposed to choose its own unit.

Clicking the top arrow scrolls into view a line above what was visible, so really it moves the view port up and the content actually moves down. It's the natural thing to do, although if you state it as "clicking the up arrow moves the contents down," you'll get a headache, which goes to prove that it sometimes doesn't pay to think something through.

Clicking an empty part of the shaft is supposed to move the content up by a screenful if you click above the slider and down a screenful if you click below. Actually, as *The Interface Guidelines* explains, not quite a full screen—a single line of overlap should be preserved (so it moves by a screen minus one line) to keep your bearings.

Finally, you can drag the slider. Dragging to the top of the shaft takes you to the top of the document and dragging to the bottom of the shaft takes you to the end of the document. For something like a spreadsheet that has empty rows at its bottom, dragging to the bottom of the shaft takes you to the end of the data, not the last empty row of the spreadsheet.

If you drag the slider 30% of the way down, the document scrolls to the 30% mark. If you scroll with the keyboard, for example by using **PgUp/PgDn**, the slider moves to give you a visual clue of where you are.

In Windows 98, the size of the slider indicates the fraction of the document currently on screen, so the slider in a two-screenful document takes up half the shaft. On a 10-page document, it would be a tenth of the shaft and on a 100-page document, it would be a thin line.

Microsoft Word shows the kind of innovation in design that I applaud—an extra that doesn't disconcert when it is absent in other applications—namely, when you press on the slider, a box pops up with the current page number. I hope this idea is widely copied.

Waiter—Menu, Please

While our Plain Jane Window doesn't have one, most application windows have a menu underneath the title bar. The menu usually has the names of submenus. Hitting the **Alt** key with nothing else will move you to the menu bar where you can use the arrow keys and **Enter**. If a menu item has an underlined letter, like <u>F</u>ile or <u>E</u>dit or Mi<u>d</u>dle, hitting **Alt+F** or **Alt+E** or **Alt+D** (no, you don't need to shift to capital F to get **Alt+F**) pulls down the menu, and it's often easier to do that when you have just been typing than to grab the mouse.

A combo such as **Alt+F** is called an **accelerator key**. You'll sometimes see someone write &File or Mi&ddle, because that's what Windows programmers do to tell Windows about accelerator keys. You need to know about this funny "&" convention because it carries over to quite a few programs that let you build your own menus or customize the ones the program already has. In Windows 98, when you customize the context menu for a file type, if you add a new action (call up **View/Options** in Explorer, go to the File Types tab, and hit **Edit** and then **New**), placing an & in front of a letter in the name makes that letter the accelerator key for the new command.

Select a submenu name with the mouse or accelerator key and down pops a **submenu**. There are many conventions about what symbols in a submenu mean.

- No special symbol means that an immediate action is taken. Since top menu choices normally invoke submenus in those rare programs that take immediate actions from the top menu bar, they carry an exclamation point to signal that this is going to happen. So if a menu item says **Forma<u>t</u>!** *rather than* **Forma<u>t</u>**, you'd better be sure you know what's about to be formatted with no questions asked!

- If the choice is going to just invoke a further submenu, then the symbol ▶ appears to the right of the menu choice. The subsubmenu is called a cascading submenu.

- If the menu choice is going to invoke a dialog box (I'll talk about them later), the choice is followed by an ellipsis (. . .).

- If a submenu choice isn't available, it will often still appear in light gray (said to be "grayed out").

- Some menu items act as a toggle, for example determining whether a toolbar is displayed or not. If the option is toggled on, it will appear with a ✓ to its left (not to the right, as for other symbols).

- If there is an accelerator key for a menu option, giving you a shortcut to invoke the item without traversing the menus, then the accelerator key is shown to the right of the menu choice; it is right justified. Not all programs are thoughtful enough to provide this great educational tool into their shortcuts—kudos to those that do. Special kudos to those programs that let you assign your own choices of accelerator keys to menu items and then display those choices for you on the menus.

The Interface Guidelines discusses five common submenus found on the menu bar of many applications. While the Windows 3.1 *Interface Guide* goes into these menu items in great detail, the Windows 9X *Interface Guidelines* are much more relaxed, probably because the standards for what **Open** and other common commands mean are so well understood. I'll mainly quote from the Windows 3.1 *Guide* since it still applies. (I've changed Print and added a discussion of Send . . .)

File menu

New or New . . .	Ctrl+N	Always the first item; creates a new document with a standard name like Untitled; the ellipsis is for programs that let you set document size, pick a template to base the new document on, or otherwise ask for information first.
Open . . .	Ctrl+O	Leads to the Windows common dialog, discussed later.
Close		Optional item for programs that allow multiple documents to be open. Closes the active document. Note that the Close command on the system menu closes the application, so it is like an Exit command on the File menu rather than like the Close command. A certain logic, but confusing nonetheless.
Save	Ctrl+S	If the document has never been saved, this entry invokes Save As. . . . Otherwise, it just saves the file.
Save As . . .		Also invokes the Windows common dialog. Allows renaming of the document before saving, as well as change of format.
Print or Print . . .	Ctrl+P	Normally occurs with the ellipsis and invokes the Windows Print common dialog.
Print Setup		You shouldn't find this command on programs written for Windows 98, since what used to be called Print Setup has been subsumed into the Properties button in the Print Common Dialog. But some upgrades from Windows 3.1 left this in.
Send . . . or Send To		Invokes a mail program to let you "print" to a fax or send the document via e-mail.
Exit		Last command on the File menu

 In *The Mother of All Windows Books*, Mom complained that the Windows 3.1 *Interface Guide* listed no accelerator keys for Save and the other File menu commands. I am pleased to say that Microsoft listens, and with Windows 95 and 98, we list **Ctrl+O**, **Ctrl+S**, and **Ctrl+P** for Open, Save, and Print. So **Ctrl+S** should save without reaching for the mouse.

The Edit menu largely refers to clipboard-related commands—I discuss the clipboard later in detail; for now, all you need to know is that it's a place where programs can exchange data both within an application and between distinct applications. I defer the discussion of commands like Paste Special, Link, and Object—OLE object commands—until our discussion of OLE.

Edit menu		
Undo	`Ctrl+Z`	Not appropriate for all programs, but it separates the user-friendly program from the pack. Those few programs with a multilevel undo are especially blessed. If the last action can't be undone, this command is grayed and optionally changed to Can't Undo.
Cut	`Ctrl+X` `(Shift+Del)`	Copies selected data to the clipboard and deletes them from the application. "Selected data" has a special meaning in Windows, which I'll explain in the section "For the Select Few" later. This command is grayed out if there are no currently selected data.
Copy	`Ctrl+C` `(Ctrl+Ins)`	Copies the selected data to the clipboard without deleting them from the application. Like Cut, is grayed out if nothing is selected.
Paste	`Ctrl+V` `(Shift+Ins)`	Copies data from the clipboard to the current insertion point (for text, where typing would enter text) in your document. If there are selected data, the clipboard contents should replace that data. This item is grayed out if the clipboard has no data or does not have data in a form appropriate for the current insertion point.
Delete		Like Cut, it removes the current selection from the document, but it doesn't change the clipboard.
Repeat		Repeats the last action.
Find and Replace		Can invoke Windows common dialogs, although some applications need to use specialized dialogs.

The accelerator key combinations in parentheses are the ones that were standard in Windows 2.x and 3.0. With Windows 3.1, Microsoft, in what I think was a terrible blunder in interface consistency, changed them to something close to the Mac keystrokes (the Macintosh doesn't have a `Ctrl` key, but it has a key called `Command`—Paste on a Mac is `Command+V`). I guess they figured they'd rather be like the Mac than like OS/2!

 The *Interface Guidelines* clearly states that while the new keystrokes should be implemented and appear on the Edit menu, the old-style keystrokes should also be implemented but undocumented. Alas, too many vendors don't pay attention, so we have a mishmash—some programs that use only the old keystrokes, some that use only the new, and some that allow both. As usual, we poor users take it on the chin. The moral is that if you are used to one accelerator key combination and it doesn't work in some application, try the other or go to the menus rather than assume something is broken. Cheer up—in about five years, it should be cleared up.

The <u>V</u>iew menu, the third menu, gives ways to change the view of the data and turn on/off special panels, like a toolbox in a paint program. The last two menus are the <u>W</u>indow menu, relevant for multiple document applications, and the <u>H</u>elp menu.

Good Dialogs Are the Key to a Healthy Relationship

It's like Britain, only with buttons.

—RINGO STARR, describing the
United States in a 1965 BBC interview

 More terminology. Menu items that end with an ellipsis, and a variety of buttons and other actions while you run Windows, produce dialog boxes—panels, sometimes without a border, that allow you to communicate with the program. The elements of the dialog are called controls. Programs can implement their own custom controls. I'll describe the most common controls partly to keep you in touch with the lingo.

**Figure 2-4.
Let's dialog
personal, like**

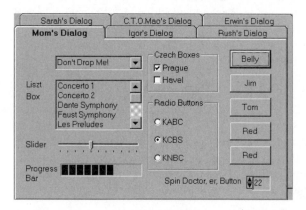

Figure 2-4 shows a **dialog** with lots of trimmings. At the right side are what are called **command buttons** or just **buttons**. Most often, you execute the command associated with a button by clicking the button. If you look closely, one of the buttons sometimes has a highlight around it. That's the one that will get executed if you hit the **Enter** key. If a nonbutton control is highlighted—say you are typing in a string, and there is a button labeled OK, then **Enter** is supposed to execute it. If there is a button marked Cancel, then the **Esc** key should close the dialog with no action taken.

 I get the Belly and the pair of Reds but what's with Jim and Tom?

 Jim Button was the author of PC File and one of the fathers of shareware. Tom Button is an obscure Microsoft executive in the Visual Basic Group—at least, he used to be obscure.

I'll pay a lot of attention to keyboard ways to drive a dialog box. If the dialog has some places you need to type in a word, moving your hand from the keyboard to mouse and back can be a pain and a half, so it pays to learn the keyboard methods.

Often a button has an underlined character, like menu titles have. As in a menu title the underscore is an indication of an accelerator key. A button called Tom with an underlined T can be executed from anywhere by hitting `Alt+T`. But there is one difference with a menu. If you have a *menu* called Format, you can pull it down with either `Alt+T` or first hitting `Alt` and then `T`. With a *button* called Format, you can use only `Alt+T`, not the two separate keystrokes.

Several controls in a dialog can be grouped together by surrounding them with a big box called a **frame**. It's especially common to group together several check boxes and/or radio buttons, so I'll talk about those next.

One control consists of some text to the right of a box ☐ that sometimes appears with an ✓ like so: ☑. It is called a check box and when the check is there the box is "checked." Check boxes are for options that are on or off—checked means on. Sometimes a dialog refers to several objects at once; for example, you might select some text in a word processor and call up a character-formatting dialog that includes a check box for italic. If all the selected text is italic, the box is checked and if none is, it is unchecked. But what if some of the text is italic and some not? In that case, the box is gray. Clicking once checks it and turns on the option for all selected items, and clicking again turns it off for all.

The keyboard way to toggle a check box is to use the space bar.

A dialog can have any number of check boxes, grouped or not, and each box can be checked/unchecked independently of the others, even if others are in the same group.

A **radio button** is a control with some text to the right of a circle ○. Sometimes the circle is filled in like so ⊙. The name comes from the fact that these are supposed to look like the on/off switches on old radio—talk about obscure! Normally several radio buttons are grouped together inside a single group.

 The Interface Guidelines calls them "option buttons," not "radio buttons," but the rest of the world uses "radio button."

Radio buttons are intended for mutually exclusive choices. That means that only a single radio button in each group can be clicked. A dialog can have several groups of radio buttons. If there is a set of related choices to be made that are not mutually exclusive, they'll appear as several check boxes in a single frame. Check boxes are used for true/false questions and radio buttons for multiple-choice questions. (Windows programmers hate grading essay questions, so you won't find many of those.)

Figure 2-4 illustrates a number of other elements of dialog boxes.

- As Windows programs became feature rich, dialogs became more and more complex or invoked additional dialogs with scores of buttons. Then someone has the idea of the **tabbed dialog**, as shown in the figure. The metaphor is like a box of cards in a file with divider tabs sticking up. Click on the tab you want to access the underlying dialog.

- Dialogs often require you to choose from canned lists. The most common controls for displaying such lists are the **list box** and the **drop-down list**, both shown in Figure 2-4.

- Increasing a number is often done with a **slider** or with a **spin button**. Both are shown in Figure 2-4.

- A **progress bar** is a control that a program can use to indicate, er, progress.

Some of these simple controls are combined with an edit box to provide "combo controls." The most common examples are combo dropdown list boxes and combo edit/spin controls.

For items in a list of alphabetized names, hitting a letter key is supposed to take you to the first item that starts with that letter, hitting the letter a second time will take you to the next item, etc. That means that the default Windows behavior for dropdown lists won't let you easily get to the first item starting with "St" if you have lots of "S" items. For combo boxes, where you'll start entering a full name, "St" should scroll to the first "St" item. This different behavior in the two cases is doubly unfortunate—it means that two controls with a similar look behave differently, and it prevents an attractive behavior for list boxes of multiletter searches.

Four keystrokes help you navigate dialogs when you don't want to take your hands off the keyboard.

Tab	Moves to the next control in the dialog
Shift+Tab	Moves to the previous control in the dialog
Ctrl+Tab	Moves to the next tab in tabbed dialogs
Ctrl+Shift+Tab	Moves to the previous tab in tabbed dialogs

 Each dialog has a **tab order** set by the programmer assigning a number to each button, dropdown list, and other control. As you hit **Tab**, you cycle through successively higher numbers (until you reach the highest number, in which case **Tab** moves to the control with the lowest tab order number). **Shift+Tab** cycles in the opposite direction.

The Wizard Behind the Curtain

Toto, we're not in Kansas anymore.

—L. FRANK BAUM, *The Wonderful Wizard of Oz,* 1900

Windows is peopled with **Wizards** to help with common tasks. Not only that, the Windows SDK (Software Development Kit) makes Wizard technology available to application vendors so you see Wizards a lot. The main point is that you know what the name means so that when I or someone else refers to a Wizard, you don't think "huh?" A typical Wizard screen is shown later in the chapter in Figure 2-22. Wizards take you through a sequence of dialogs that have you fill in the blanks in little steps. Usually there are three buttons at the bottom of each dialog box: `<Back`, `Next>`, and `Cancel`. In the first screen, `<Back` is grayed out, and in the final screen, `Next>` becomes `Finish`. Wizards often branch on what you choose in earlier screens. You get to step back if you realize that you made a mistake in any earlier screen.

There isn't much to say except to point out that using Wizards usually is a pleasure and that you'll find Wizards to help with the installation of Windows 98, with adding a printer or new hardware, and with doing many other actions.

 I'm not real fond of Microsoft but I have to admit they did a great job on this Wizard stuff. Not only is the basic scheme a good one, but whoever designed the actual Wizards in Windows 98 did a great job. Even formerly unpleasant tasks are kinda fun. Hmm. Maybe they could design a root canal Wizard?

Belly Up to the Button Bar

If you press exactly the right buttons and are also lucky, justice may show up.

—RAYMOND CHANDLER, *The Long Goodbye,* 1953

 User interfaces evolve—no doubt about it. They are not quite given from on high and set in stone. Vendors experiment with devices that go beyond the defined UI, and users, by their reactions, can cause de facto standards to arise. A great example of this is the toolbar, aka button bar, aka a lot of other names.

 Made up of often inscrutable little icons that puzzled users, button bars were nevertheless such an effective shortcut that they became wildly popular, inscrutability and all.

Obviously, the easiest way to avoid inscrutability is to have some standard buttons used by all applications; that way even the inscrutable can become scrutable. *The Interface Guidelines* defines the 24 standard icons shown in Figure 2-5. The first 13 are standard menu functions, the next is appropriate for situations where objects have property sheets, and the next 3 are font attributes. The 18th button is for context-sensitive help and the 19th for the contents page

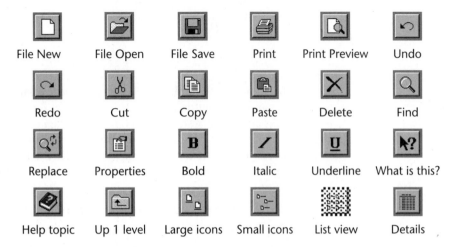

File New   File Open   File Save   Print   Print Preview   Undo

Redo   Cut   Copy   Paste   Delete   Find

Replace   Properties   Bold   Italic   Underline   What is this?

Help topic   Up 1 level   Large icons   Small icons   List view   Details

Figure 2-5. Button, button, who's got the button?

of the full application Help file. The last 4 have to do with the views available for the common list control that I'll discuss in the section "Common Controls."

The Guidelines defines three other less usual icons.

Let's see how the theory of *The Interface Guidelines* stands up against the actual button bars used by Windows 98 itself. Figure 2-6 shows the toolbars of three applications included with Win98.

WordPad is really very close. Of the 11 buttons in the top row, all are standard except the binoculars used for Find and the nonstandard Insert Date/Time button at the right. Internet Explorer (shown here as small buttons without text) does fairly well. The Browse Forward/Backward buttons with dropdowns are nonstandard, as is the View Dropdown at the right. Imagining's buttons are almost entirely nonstandard. They are not incompatible with the standard—just specialized. So Windows does fairly well meeting the standard—"Do not only what I say but what I do"!

 With one exception. The writer of the *Interface Guide* decided that Find is a magnifying glass, but the rest of the world, including WordPad and Word, thinks Find is binoculars, like so .

Figure 2-6.
A tale of three
toolbars

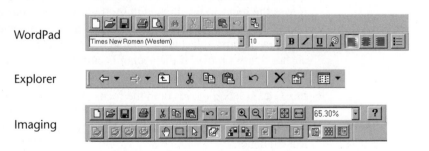

WordPad

Explorer

Imaging

Hey, 1 out of 24 is only about a 4% error. You guys sure are a tough crowd.

Besides standardized buttons, the other standard help for defeating inscrutable icons is the **ToolTip**, a little floating box of text that explains what a button does (rest the cursor over a button in WordPad to see what I mean). These do not display until the cursor has rested for a moment, so when trying to figure out what a funny-looking button does, be sure to rest the cursor on it for more than a fleeting instant. Also be aware that some applications let you turn tooltips on/off with a check box in an Options dialog. So look for that if an application doesn't seem to have tooltips.

One last point about toolbars is that the best of breed are customizable and let you determine what functions appear there and in what order. Many Winword users aren't aware that you can customize the toolbars (right click in the toolbar area and pick Customize…). Similarly, Outlook 98 has customizable toolbars. Of the three Windows toolbars, none lets you customize it.

For the Select Few

Many lists in windows dialogs are single-choice lists, lists that allow you to make only a single choice, just as if there were a radio button next to each item. But a few lists are multiple-choice lists—you can choose more than one item. There's a convention on using a mouse to select multiple that is specified in *The Interface Guidelines*. I'm going to start describing the Classic style selection method. I'll discuss Web style selection at the end of this section.

When there are chosen items, there is one called the **anchor**, which can be the same as the item with focus—the currently active item, usually with a dotted around it—but can be different. The anchor is usually but not always a selected item, as I'll explain shortly. If there are no selected items, the anchor can be regarded as being identical to the item with focus.

Here is a summary.

- **Clicking** an item deselects any items already selected, selects the clicked item, and moves both the anchor and focus to the clicked item

- **Shift+Clicking**, that is, clicking while holding down either Shift key, moves the focus to the clicked item. If the anchor is currently selected, all items between the anchor and the clicked item are selected; any other items, even those selected before the **Shift+Click** are not selected; the anchor doesn't move. If the anchor is currently not selected, all items are removed from the selection list.

- **Ctrl+Clicking** moves both the focus and the anchor to the clicked item. It toggles the selection state of the clicked item to the opposite of what it was. If you **Ctrl+Click** a selected item, the new item becomes an unselected anchor.

- **Shift+Ctrl+Clicking** (you only like this if you can wiggle your nose and twiddle your thumbs at the same time). If the anchor is currently selected, all items between the anchor and the clicked item are added to the selection list. Items outside that range remain selected if they were previously selected. The anchor is not moved. If the anchor is currently not selected, all items between the anchor and the clicked item are taken off the selected list and the anchor doesn't move.

As an example, suppose you have items 1, . . . ,10 in order and you do the following: **Click 2**, **Shift+Click 9**, **Ctrl+Click 4**, and finally **Shift+Ctrl+Click 6**. Here's the state after each mouse action:

After Action	Selected Items	Focus	Anchor
Click 2	2	2	2
Shift+Click 9	2,3,4,5,6,7,8,9	9	2
Ctrl+Click 4	2,3,5,6,7,8,9	4	4
Shift+Ctrl+Click 6	2,3,7,8,9	6	4

Click and drag will select contiguously; that is, act as if you clicked the item where you start the drag and then shift clicked the item where you stopped the drag.

In Windows 3.x, there was a keyboard method for multiple selection using the **Shift+F8** key combination. It is no longer mentioned in *The Interface Guidelines* and seems not to be supported. Indeed, I could find no way to use the keyboard to make multiple noncontiguous selections in Explorer (although **Ctrl+Click** works fine).

The undocumented **Ctrl+/** and **Ctrl+** that worked in Windows 3.x File Manager don't work in Explorer and presumably have gone the way of the dodo.

Most of these selection techniques work inside applications like your word processor and spreadsheet except that noncontiguous selection may not always be *sensible*. For example Winword doesn't allow noncontiguous selection of text and uses **Ctrl+Click** to select the current sentence.

What I've described so far is what Microsoft calls Classic style selection. If you call up Folder Options from the View menu in a folder view, you can shift to Web style (Figure 2-7). Folders then look like Figure 2-8 with filenames underlined. What has most changed, though, is the method of selection and choosing. In Classic style, you *select* with a single click and *choose* with a double click. With Web style, you select by hovering over the item (pausing the mouse cursor over the item for a moment) and select with single click. The shifts work the same way in either style, although **Ctrl-hovering** is a little strange, to put it mildly.

 Of all the crazy ideas, Web style selection wins a prize. Sure, it acts like a Web page, but it is awkward and alien to anyone who has used Windows for awhile. Microsoft is right to call the original style Classic—the Classic Coke/New Coke fiasco is a good analogy to this idiocy.

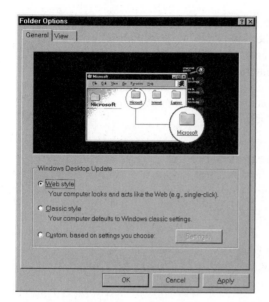

Figure 2-7. Weaving a tangled web

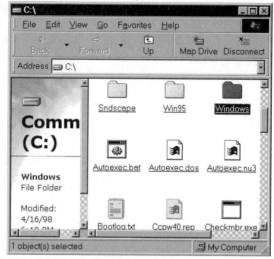

Figure 2-8. Web-like folder interactions

 Our focus groups with new and inexperienced users showed that they were confused by the fact that they single click on the Web and double click in *File* windows, so we introduced Web style with Internet Explorer 4.0 and made it the default.

 But beta testers howled so much, you pulled back and made Classic the default, and you even give a warning about single click before shifting if the user picks Web style. This Web style crap deserves the death it got.

 In many ways, it is now worse than before. The default has shifted back to Classic view, so even if new users *would* prefer Web view, they won't see it when they start out. And there is a chance that a novice fooling around will turn on Web style and not understand what the heck has happened to his/her system.

Keys to the Kingdom

Giving money and power to government is like
giving whiskey and car keys to teenage boys.

—P. J. O'ROURKE, *Why God Is a Republican*
and Santa Claus Is a Democrat, 1991.

It pays to remember the reserved keystrokes that Windows uses and that are common to most Windows applications to avoid inadvertently assigning them

Global Keystrokes

Note: These keystrokes work even in full-screen DOS sessions; however, if some DOS application uses one of them—say your favorite word processor, *foowrite,* uses **Ctrl+Esc** to access its menus—you can reserve its use for that DOS session on the Misc. tab of the application's property sheet.

Ctrl+Esc
Brings up the Start menu. Using keystrokes can often be a quick route—for example hitting **Ctrl+Esc**, **F**, **F** will bring up the Find Files dialog a lot quicker than mousing around.

Alt+Tab
One of the most underused neat things in Windows 3.x, and it's even neater in Win98! Hitting **Alt+Tab** cycles through your applications without actually cycling through them! Instead it displays a panel like that shown in Figure 2-9 with an icon for each running program and the window caption in text below it. The trick is to hold the **Alt** key down and hit the **Tab** key multiple times. It cycles through the applications. If you start **Alt+Tab** and change your mind, hitting **Esc** while **Alt** is still down will get you out. **Alt+Tab** visits only applications, not things like Property Sheets and Wizards.

Alt+Shift+Tab
Like **Alt+Tab**, but cycles in the opposite direction. It's unlikely you'd want to start moving with **Alt+Shift+Tab** (how could you remember which one of the currently open applications you used the longest time ago?), but if you start **Alt+Tab**bing and overshoot, **Alt+Shift+Tab** (remembering to keep the **Alt** down) will let you back up.

Alt+Esc
Like **Alt+Tab** except for two things. First, rather than showing you just the name of the application, it shifts to it, redrawing the screen. Second, unlike **Alt+Tab**, it does visit Property Sheets and the like. It may be the quickest way to locate a Property Sheet lost behind some maximized windows.

Alt+Shift+Esc
Like **Alt+Esc**, except cycles in the opposite direction.

PrintScreen
Another underused goodie. Did you know that Windows comes with its own screen capture utility—you know, the kind of thing you pay $39 to get all by itself? Hit **PrintScreen** (**Shift+PrtScr** on some keyboards) and Windows copies the current screen to the clipboard. When on the Windows Desktop, it is copied as a picture; in DOS text mode, it is copied as text. You do lose the convenience of DOS PrintScreen going straight to the printer, although by pasting from the clipboard into WordPad, shifting to Courier font, and printing, you can duplicate what DOS PrintScreen does—albeit awkwardly. This is half of the Screen Capture utility—I'll describe the other half following this table.

Alt+PrintScreen
In DOS mode, does what **PrintScreen** does, but on the Windows desktop, it copies the current window only to the clipboard (as a bitmap).

Alt+Spacebar
Invokes the system menu. There's a change from Windows 3.x in how this key combination works in full-screen DOS sessions. Under Windows 3.x, it shifted to a windowed DOS session, pulling down the system menu! Under Windows 98, you get shifted to the Windows Desktop with the toolbar button for the DOS session highlighted and the system menu for it popped up. But the DOS session is not put into a window.

Figure 2-9.
Where do you
want to go today?

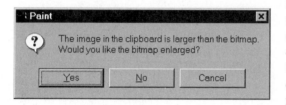

Figure 2-10.
Clean capture

to macros and as shortcut keys. Later on, in Chapter 3, as I come to specific core components like Desktop and Explorer, I'll discuss keystrokes specific to those components. Note that in the section "Good Dialogs Are the Key to a Healthy Relationship," I described the special use that **Tab** with various shifts (**Shift**, **Ctrl**, and **Ctrl+Shift**) has in dialogs.

Other common keystrokes that you need to know about, even though they are application dependent, are the **Cut/Copy/Paste** commands (discussed earlier in "Waiter—Menu, Please," The keystrokes are either **Ctrl+X/Ctrl+C/Ctrl+V** or **Shift+Del/Ctrl+Ins/Shift+Ins**, depending on the application), the DOS session **Alt+Enter** (which toggles between full screen and windowed DOS session and which I discuss in Chapter 3), and **Alt+F4** (which closes most applications).

The free **screen capture** is so useful, let me describe it in detail. Hit **PrintScreen** or **Alt+PrintScreen** to place the whole screen or the active window on the clipboard. Then start Paint. Go to the Image/Attributes . . . menu choice and make sure the height and width are smaller than what you captured (for example, you could pick 400×300 if you captured an 800×600 screen). Now choose Paste from the Edit menu and answer Yes to the dialog in Figure 2-10.

Other keystrokes that *The Interface Guidelines* encourage applications to use where appropriate are **Ctrl+S**, **Ctrl+O**, **Ctrl+P**, and **Ctrl+Z** for the File/Save, File/Open, File/Print and Edit/Undo menu choices. Also **F1** is the same as Help Topics, and **Shift+F1** is the same as the "What is this?" button (🔳). **Shift+F10** brings up an object's context menu just like right clicking on it.

 Hey, you! Pay attention. Look at me when I talk to you. Understand? I'm tired of your skimming the good stuff and missing it. You probably figure keystrokes are boring, and you are looking at this section hoping for some good jokes, not looking much at what it says. And there I tell you about **Shift+F10** in a single sentence you could easily miss. This is a *really neat* keyboard shortcut. It works in Windows itself and in well-behaved Windows 98 applications. For example, if you are typing in Winword and see a wavy underline indicating a spelling error, no need to reach for the mouse if you remember that **Shift+F10** will do the same thing as a right mouse click.

Super Natural Keyboard

Whatever the scientists may say, if we take the supernatural out of life, we leave only the unnatural.

—AMELIA BARR, *All the Days of My Life*

The Microsoft Natural Keyboard includes three keys special to Windows 9X. Many other keyboards come with them also. Two are identical and squeezed in between the two sets of **Ctrl** and **Alt** keys and are marked with the Windows logo. Their behavior is the same—they are called the **Windows key** and I'll call them **Win**. As with **Alt**, **Win** is a shift, that is, it can be used with other keys—you press down **Win** and holding it down, press the second key. The third special key is the **application key**, located to the right of the right-hand **Win**. The application key pops up the context menu for any active object in the shell—for example a selected drive or the Desktop as a whole. It thus acts the same as a right mouse click on the object. However, it is *not* a keyboard equivalent of the right mouse button or **Shift+F10** within all applications—the application can define it to have a special meaning, if it likes.

Here are the special things you can do with **Win** (the ones after **Shift+Win+M** work with the Microsoft Natural Keyboard and may not work with others).

Win	Pops up Start Menu (same as **Ctrl+Esc**)
Win+F	Pops up Find File dialog (same as **Ctrl+Esc, F, F**)
Win+Ctrl+F	Pops up Find Computer dialog (same as **Ctrl+Esc, F, C**)
Win+F1	Pops up Windows Help Topics (same as **Ctrl+Esc, H**)
Win+R	Pops up Run dialog (same as **Ctrl+Esc, R**)
Win+E	Explore My Computer (same as right click on My Computer, Explore)
Win+M	Minimize All Windows (same as right click on Taskbar, Minimize . . .)
Shift+Win+M	Undo Minimize All Windows (same as right click on Taskbar, Undo . . .)
Win+P	Open Printers folder
Win+C	Open Control Panel
Win+V	View clipboard
Win+K	Open Keyboard Properties
Win+I	Open Mouse Properties
Win+A	Open Accessibility Options
Win+Space	Pops up a list of **Win+** hot keys
Win+Break	Open System Properties

I didn't much like the Natural Keyboard when I tried it. The feel is mushy and I'm a lover of the IBM/Northgate/Lexmark firm keyboard. And the split and twist was something I couldn't get used to. But hey, the P in PC stands for something, and some folks probably like these aspects.

Mice Is Nice but MouseKeys Is Slicker

There isn't much to say about mouse actions because there aren't many actions: you can move the beast, you can click (quickly press and release) one or both buttons, you can double click either button, or you can drag and drop (drag means to press a button down and move the mouse while keeping the button depressed; drop means to then release the button). On three-button mice, you obviously have other options.

 There is my favorite obscure mouse trick that is habit forming once you get used to it. If you press down the Alt key while double clicking an object, the property sheet for that object should open. It certainly works for objects controlled by the Windows 98 shell, like the icons on the Desktop.

 The wheelie mouse from Microsoft really is habit forming. Between the buttons is a wheel that can be used for quick scrolling. Really wonderful when surfing or coping with long documents in Word or Excel.

Windows 98 includes a really neat option called **MouseKeys** that, except for one flaw, is an ultimate version of the kind of programs intended to give mouse functionality to laptop users without mice. It's part of the Accessibility package, so you might miss it because the other components of Accessibility are of interest to the otherwise enabled. While MouseKeys is clearly of interest to some users with disabilities, it is also of interest to users who like the keyboard and hate reaching for the mouse. To get it, you may need to install the Accessibility Options applet in Control Panel. If that applet isn't present, you'll want to run the Add/Remove Programs applet, go to the Windows SetUp tab and be sure the Accessibility Options box is checked (either by checking the Accessibility box or going to Details and picking just Accessibility Options). You then install Mouse-Keys by running that applet, going to the Mouse tab and checking the Use MouseKeys box. The settings can be found in Figure 2-11. You'll want to click Settings at least the first time to configure how it works.

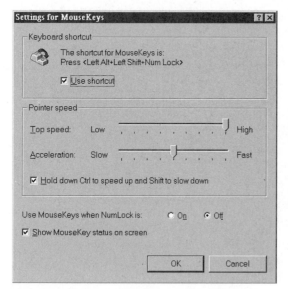

Figure 2-11. Nibble, nibble little MouseKeys

When MouseKeys is on and active, the arrow keys on the numeric keypad move the cursor in the direction of the arrows and **Home/End/PgUp/PgDn** move the cursor diagonally. By holding down **Ctrl** or **Shift** while moving the cursor, you can speed up or slow down the cursor motion.

Center (5 on the keypad) is the same as single click, and the number pad **Plus** is the same as double click. By default, these clicks are with the left mouse button. However, if you hit the **Minus** on the numberpad, you shift to the mode where **Center/Plus** have the effect of clicking the right button. Hitting the numberpad **Slash** returns to the mode where the left button is simulated.

The **Ins** key is the same as pressing the mouse button and holding it down, so after pressing **Ins**, moving the cursor keys will drag. After **Ins** is pressed, **Del** has the effect of dropping the object: it simulates releasing the mouse button. Normally, these keys simulate a left button drag, but if you've pressed the **Minus** key, they will simulate a right button drag.

When the MouseKeys option is turned on, **NumLock** toggles between whether MouseKeys is active or not. If you check the "Show MouseKey status on screen" box in the MouseKeys Settings dialog (Figure 2-11), a mouse icon is displayed in the notification area of the Taskbar with a "not" symbol superimposed on it when the option is on but MouseKeys is inactive. A radio button in that dialog determines whether the active state is with **NumLock** on or off.

 If you are used to using the cursor keys on the numeric keypad but don't use the number pad much, configure MouseKeys to be active when **NumLock** is on. If you tend to use the cursor tee for movement of the typewriter cursor, then configure MouseKeys to be active when **NumLock** is off. When you configure it that way, you get typewriter cursor motion from the cursor keys, mouse cursor motion from the number pad cursor mode, and number pad when you turn **NumLock** on.

If you check the Use Shortcut box you can toggle between MouseKeys being enabled by using the **Left Alt+Left Shift+NumLock** combination.

 MouseKeys is incredibly nice for users with full-size keyboards, but it sure does leave laptop users in the lurch. Lots of laptop users would love to have a hotkey that turned on a MouseKey-like feature applied to the cursor keys on the laptop. Since they simulate not the numeric keypad but instead the cursor T, MouseKeys as currently implemented doesn't help laptop users a bit. Sigh.

 You may think it strange that MouseKeys doesn't do squat on a laptop. But you have to realize that it was originally developed by the hardware group that makes the Natural Keyboard, so it was (naturally) made for that keyboard. The Windows group coopted the software for Accessibility purposes, but it was already written. Since several laptop vendors are pressuring Microsoft to make MouseKeys work with a laptop, it inevitably will before too long.

Er, Billy, you said the same thing three years ago, and there still isn't a laptop version, is there?

While we can knock Microsoft for not making a laptop version of MouseKeys, they deserve lots of kudos for the Accessibility support they've added to Windows. Those with sight or mobility problems have special options they can turn on to help make the human/computer interface easier to use.

New to Windows 98 is a program called Windows Magnifier for those with sight difficulties.

■ Objection, Your Honor

To make *oneself an object, to* make *oneself passive,*
is a very different thing from being *a passive object.*

—SIMONE DE BEAUVOIR, *The Second Sex,* 1953

Everything you see on the screen is an object. That goes for program windows, for dialogs, and for buttons in dialogs, and it goes for the Desktop, the Start button and the TaskBar. To say something is an **object** is to say that it is something on which you can perform actions. This idea of objects and actions will be central as we look at some common threads in the Windows 98 user interface.

Studies have shown that some users freak out at the mention of objects; they stare off in space and . . . Well, relax, it's just a fancy word for a piece of the user interface you can interact with!

Right On

Inanimate objects are classified scientifically into three major categories—those that don't work, those that break down, and those that get lost.

—RUSSELL BAKER, *New York Times,* June 18, 1968

If I have any piece of advice to someone who is exploring the interface of Windows 98 or a program written to run with Windows 98, it's "Don't forget the mouse's right button." Especially, don't forget to right click everywhere to see what pops up.

The Windows 98 interface is based on the notion that when you right-click on an object, it brings up a menu of actions and options for that object. There is even a right-click menu in the edit boxes that you find in dialogs where you are asked to type in text strings!

This menu is called a **Context Menu** or sometimes a **Right Click Menu**. That means, for example, that if you open My Computer (by double clicking on it) and right click on a diskette drive (or even better, drag the drive to your desktop for easy access), you'll get a menu that includes Copy Disk . . . and Format. . . . You might also like to find ScanDisk there but it won't be, at least not on the menu. You can pick Properties and get ScanDisk from there. But that's only the default menu. Most context menus can be configured. How depends on the object and will be a recurring theme as our discussion of the details of the interface picks up speed. In particular, I'll explain how to add ScanDisk to drive menus in Chapter 3. Some menu changes will require editing of the Registry and will be described in Chapters 3 and 9.

Not only can you change most of the built-in context menus but you can even make some changes to their cascading submenus. File objects (including drives, files on the desktop and in Explorer windows) have a menu item called Send To. I'll explain how to configure that later in this chapter in the section "The Tree-Based Menu." Blank pieces of Explorer windows and the Desktop have a branching submenu called New. I'll show you how to configure that in Chapter 9.

Basically, almost anything in Windows can be configured with only a few exceptions, the most notable being the right click menu that pops up over the Desktop (where I only know how to change the New submenu). If you figure you can configure something but don't know how, look it up in the index to this book!

Keep in mind that what you may think of as a single object may be many and may have many context menus depending on precisely where you right click. You may think of the Taskbar as a single thingy, but you get separate context menus for the Start button, for each toolbar, for a blank part of the Taskbar, for each task button, and for each different icon in the notification area! With the addition of the Windows 98/IE 4 toolbars, the Taskbar can also have subsections for Internet Addresses, Links, and Quick Launch buttons.

At the bottom of each context menu is typically a choice called Properties, which lets you change intrinsic aspects of an object. Some objects call up Property sheets you might not expect, but they provide thereby very quick shortcuts. The Properties choice on My Computer brings up the Control Panel System applet. The Desktop Properties is the same as the Display applet of Control Panel. The Taskbar Properties is the same as hitting Start, then Settings, then Taskbar. Properties of Network Neighborhood is, not too surprisingly, the same as the Network applet of Control Panel. Properties of the Internet Explorer icon is the same as the Options dialog for that program.

Drag 'til You Drop

A drawing is always dragged down to the level of its caption.

—JAMES THURBER, *The New Yorker,* August 2, 1930

 Oh, you think you're a hotshot, don't you? You heard my advice about right clicking everywhere, so now you think you know it all. Well, I haven't finished reading you your rights. It's also important to know about right drag and drop!

Windows 98 is highly drag and drop enabled. That means you should expect that, under most circumstances, the shell and well-written programs for Windows 98 will accept transfer of information via drag and dropping. This works in cases you might not expect. Open both a windowed DOS session and an Explorer window. Grab a filename in the Explorer window and drag it to the DOS window. When you drop the file, its full pathname will be entered at the DOS command line. This happens also in any DOS program, which can be very handy for dealing with an old DOS program that doesn't have a "browse for file" capability.

 Yeah, but what about programs that won't take full pathnames? There is no way to enter just the directory name or just the filename. It would be good if a right drag could bring up a menu of choices like "full name," "directory," and "filename" or if **Ctrl** or **Shift** would work. But they don't—you get the full pathname whether you want it or not.

 Yes, but at least we are smart enough not to paste long filenames. The assumption is that DOS programs don't understand long file names so if you drag **My long file name.doc** in **D:\my documents** to a DOS command line, what gets pasted in is something like[†] **D:\mydocu~1\mylong~1.doc**.

And, of course, the Windows shell is usually drag and drop enabled. If you open the Run dialog and drag a filename to it from Explorer, the full pathname is pasted in. Since you can run a program by double clicking it, you won't often use this for programs, but if a program needs another filename as a parameter, it is often simplest to use Start Menu's Find command to locate the file and then drag it from the Find results window to a Run window. Another time this comes in handy is when you locate a program you want to run in Explorer but you want to run it with parameters. Hit **Ctrl+Esc**, **R**, **Del** (the final **Del** blanks the Run box), drag the name to the Run box, and add the parameters.

 Ah, but the design team fell down in at least two places. You'd certainly expect that the target field in a shortcut's property sheet could get a file name by dragging the file from an Explorer window, but it can't. Similarly, the filename part of the File/Open common dialog isn't a drag and drop target. That's really a pain if your target has a long path that would be a nuisance to either type in (and risk typos) or find by navigating through a Browse dialog.

---

† I'll discuss how short 8+3 filenames are associated with long filenames a few sections from now.

Under such circumstances, I've found it useful to hit **Ctrl+Esc**, **R**, **Del**, drag the file to the Run box, hit **Shift+Del**, **Esc** to cut that file name to the clipboard, close the Run dialog, and finally paste the name into the shortcut property sheet. It may not be any less effort, but you feel more in control!

 An even better solution is to pick up the SendTo Extensions Power Toys (I'll discuss Power Toys in Chapter 5). It includes the possibility of clicking on a file in Explorer and sending just the filename to the clipboard.

When drag and dropping a file from one Explorer window to another or to the Desktop, there are generally three actions that can occur. The file can be moved or copied, or a shortcut to the file can be created. As seen in Figure 2-12, Windows gives subtle feedback to tell you what is going to happen. You see pieces of actual screen shots of dragging a file in suitable ways. If the result of the drag will be to move the file, the cursor "picks up" the filename as seen on the left. If the result is going to be a copy then a plus is added as in the middle panel. Finally, the standard shortcut symbol is added if a shortcut is going to be made.

**Figure 2-12.
A tale of three
dragons**

Move File

Copy File

Make Shortcut

 The visual clues are important because Explorer isn't consistent about what drag and drop does. Its action depends on the file type and on whether the source and destination drives are the same or different. The basic rules are that, by default, dragging a program creates a shortcut to the program, dragging a nonprogram file within the same drive moves it, and dragging it between drives copies it. Such behavior is downright confusing.

 Actually, Barry, it is disconcerting to users who always pay attention and feel they have to learn these rules. But if you think about it, you'll agree that the default does what the naive user wants 90% of the time, probably more. And if someone doesn't want the default they can always use right drag and drop or the Shift keys.

I'd better expand on Billy's ways out. The first is the way Barry mentioned at the start of this section. Targets for a drag and drop operation can provide you with several different options when you drag and drop, although one must be the default option. If you drag and drop with the left button, then when you drop, the default action happens. If you right drag and drop, then when you drop, a menu of options pops up with the default option in bold. You then get to pick among the options. For example, if you right drag and drop a program to the Desktop, you'll get the menu shown in Figure 2-13.

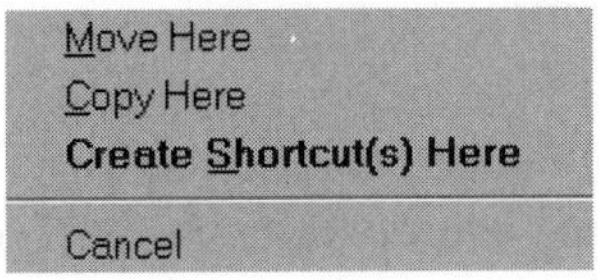

**Figure 2-13.
Right is better**

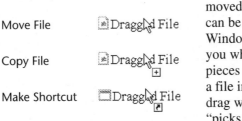

The second set of methods for controlling what happens on the drop concerns the special meaning of shifts when you left drag and drop on a target that is part of the Windows 98 shell, such as the Desktop or an Explorer window. If you hold down **Shift**, the object is always moved. If you hold down **Ctrl**, the object is always copied. If you hold down **Ctrl+Shift**, you get the same menu you would if you right dragged.

 It is especially important to note that you don't need to be holding down the shifts at the time you start to drag, but you do at the point you drop. This has two important consequences. First, if you forget whether **Ctrl** or **Shift** means copy and which means move, but you remember that copy gives the plus sign in the icon, you can just try each shift and see what happens to the drag icon. Second, if you realize in mid-drag that you really wanted to right drag and drop because you know the default action is wrong, you can always hold down **Ctrl+Shift** and get the same effect as if you did right drag and drop.

If you press **Ctrl+Shift**, the shortcut symbol is added to the icon, but that only indicates that "Create Shortcut(s) Here," will be the default—you always get the right drag menu with those keys down.

 But remember that these keystrokes are sure to work only if the target is a Windows 98 shell object. They may not work in other places, whereas the right drag always produces a menu.

 Yeah, Barry, maybe that's the theory, but Winword 7.0 sure didn't understand that. Right drag a ***.txt** file to that first Windows 95 version of Winword and you should get a menu with Cancel as one of the options—but that ain't what it does. Merely inserts it as an object, it does. If Microsoft can't even get it right in their flagship application . . .

 But Woody. We fixed that in Word 97. Microsoft heard MOM's complaint in *The Mother of All Windows 95 Books*, and our newest version does give you a proper right drag and drop menu.

It will sometimes happen that you start a drag and realize that you don't want to drag after all. Hitting **Esc** will cancel the drag. You can also look for a target that isn't legal—the mouse cursor turns into the universal "no" sign of a circle with a slash—and drop it there, which is the same as aborting the drag.

One final drag and drop trick to mention. Suppose you want to drag something to a running application on the toolbar—it might be minimized or it might be behind some other window. For example, suppose you have a ***.doc** file in Explorer that you want to open in a copy of Word that is already running. If the Word window were visible, you could drop the file to the Word title bar and it would open that document. Instead, drag it to the Word button on the Taskbar and hold it there—do not drop it on the button. After you hold it over the button for a moment, Word will open and you can drop it where you want. This will work for any program, not just Word.

Bah, humbug. Why not just let me drop the filename on the button? Why make me hold it over the button until the application opens?

 Because the program may act differently depending on where the filename is dropped. Word will open the file if you drop the name on the toolbar but will imbed it if you drop it in an open document.

Common Dialogs

The greatest benefit of a GUI has nothing to do with the "graphical" part—it's really something called a CUI. CUI, the Common User Interface, refers to the fact that well-written Windows programs look and behave very similarly.

—*The Mother of All Windows Books,* 1993

In the Wild West that was DOS, every time you got a new program, you had to learn its idiosyncratic way of opening files, printing them, saving them, and so on. When Sheriff Windows rode into town, this changed. A new paradigm arose: standard actions in programs should go through a standard series of steps so that, once you've learned to open a file in one program, you can open it in all programs. This not only means common menu locations (such as File/Open) and accelerator keys (such as **Ctrl+O**) but that the same dialog should be used. To this end, Windows, starting with Windows 3.1, provides a set of common dialogs that programs are strongly encouraged to use for a variety of functions:

- **File functions**, most notably for **Open** and **Save As** but also for actions like **Inset Picture**
- **Print** and **Print Setup** (this last only in Windows 3.1 applications but not Windows 98 applications); **Page Setup** (in Windows 98)
- **Find** and **Find and Replace**
- **Font** picking and **Color** picking

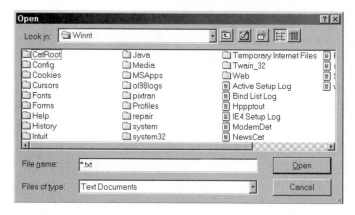

Figure 2-14. Open common dialog

Most of these dialogs are fairly straightforward, so there is nothing much to say about them. The main exception is the File functions dialog—there are some tips you need to know about. I'll also mention the Print dialog. I show the color picker in Figure 2-40 and discuss custom colors near that figure.

Figure 2-14 shows the Windows 98 Open common dialog. A similar dialog is used for Save As. Much of the dialog is obvious—there's a drive dropdown list at the top but it shows more than drives. As you choose directories in the large area, the directory is listed and the dropdown will show the directory and its parents. You can also use the first button ( ) to go up the tree one step—**Backspace** will do the same.

 If you keep going up, at the top you reach Desktop, which is a little strange, since Desktop is also **C:\windows\desktop**. New with Windows 98, there is an icon ( ) that takes you directly to the Desktop folder.

There is logic to placing Desktop at the top, where it is the most accessible. Users with simple needs are always losing their files. We encourage them to save files on the Desktop where they are "in sight." It is also convenient to have Desktop at the top because it gives you direct access to Network Neighborhood and files on any hard drive shared over the network.

To expand on what Billy says, if you open the drive dropdown, you'll find Network Neighborhood on it—choose it and you'll be able to access files as you can from a normal Network Neighborhood Window. You can also type UNCs directly into the box that says "File name." I'll say more about Network Neighborhood and UNC names at the end of this chapter and in Chapter 3.

The other buttons on the top of the Open dialog are also worth noting. will make a new subdirectory. ▦ shifts from the view in Figure 2-14 where there are several columns of directory/filenames to a "details view" where there is only one file or folder per row but that row has columns for name, size, file type, and modification date. ▦ shifts back to the view with lots of rows of files. By the way, in details view, clicking on the column headers sorts on that column and clicking twice sorts in reverse order.

But just looking at these buttons and the dropdown list misses the power of this dialog. The Open dialog file list area is essentially a small Explorer window with all the power that it entails.

What Woody is saying is that the Open dialog has right click context menus and that it can be a drag and drop source or a target. You don't need the New Subdirectory button—if you right click on a blank space in the file list, you'll get a right click menu with a New submenu from which you can pick Folder. If you single click on a file or folder name to select it and then right click, you get the same kind of context menu you get in Explorer (and which I'll describe in some detail in Chapter 3)—for example, you can Quick View files that have quick viewers and the entire SendTo menu is accessible to you.

You can also delete files from the Open or Save dialog either with **Del** or by dragging them to the Recycle Bin.

As for drag and drop and the Open dialog, you can move and copy (and so on) from an Open dialog to the Desktop or an Explorer window or in the other direction. You could even drag a file in an Open dialog to a folder icon in the same dialog and thereby move the file from the current folder to the subfolder you dragged it to!

Windows 3.1 programs that are run under Windows 98 will not use the new Open dialogs. In essence they use the old common dialogs (Figure 2-15), albeit with a new look (Figure 2-16). The Windows 3.1 dialogs not only lack the power of the Windows 98 dialogs but they don't support long filenames.

 Bah, humbug. Microsoft should have included long filename support in the dialogs that Win 3.1 programs use when running under Windows 95. But they don't even do it for Windows 98! Initially they said they expected to, but then they claimed they were unable to do it. But guess what? Norton has done it in Norton Navigator as have several other utilities makers. So much for being unable to do it.

 The problem is that Win16 applications are linked with a fixed stack size. Many Win16 applications that use the common dialogs were tested under Windows 3.1 and may be close to running out of stack space when using these dialogs. If we were to change the in-memory size of these dialogs to support long filenames, we might cause existing Win16 applications to run out of stack space. At the very least, long filename support would add 260 bytes just for the possible file buffer, plus whatever code was necessary to parse/convert the long filenames into 8+3 filenames. Norton Navigator can get away with adding this support because it is an ancillary product that the user doesn't have to run. If their common dialogs blow up, so what? They don't have to test their shell with 2,500 existing applications. If we add this support to Windows, however, then there's nowhere to turn if the application blows up. It would have added a huge extra testing effort on our part and on the part of the beta user community. Besides, Windows 3.1 applications are surely passé now.

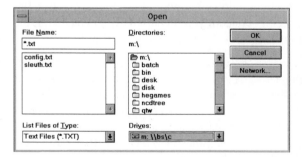

Figure 2-15. Windows 3.1 common dialog

Figure 2-16. Windows 98 common dialog for 16-bit applications

As usual, the Microsoft Office team marches to its own drummer—the File dialogs in Office 97 look a lot like common dialogs but they aren't! In particular, they do not behave like little Explorer windows, so they have less power in some ways. They do, however, add one dynamite feature—the Favorites folder. I talk about Favorites when I discuss shortcuts in a few sections. Let me just say that this is such a lovely idea, that I almost—notice that I said almost!—forgive them for deciding they are above the standard. In any event, I'm sorry Windows 98 doesn't use the Favorites folder for its standard Open dialog.

**Figure 2-17.
Print common
dialog**

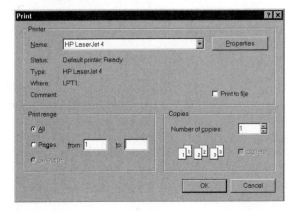

The Print common dialog is shown in Figure 2-17. Again, pretty straightforward except that you can change the printer in the dropdown list (that will just change it temporarily in the current program—I discuss permanent changes when I talk about the Printer folder in Chapter 3). And by clicking on Properties, you can access the Printer settings—for example whether a color printer prints in black or in color.

Common Controls

Common-looking people are the best in the world:
that is the reason the Lord makes so many of them.

—Abraham Lincoln

Windows 95 introduced a library of common controls beyond the simple stuff like buttons that were provided by Windows 3.x, and these controls are used in Windows 98. Most of them needn't concern you much—what do you care if the spin buttons come from common controls or are from third parties?[†]

 You'd care if you were visually impaired. Our common controls now all support standard internal text labels for all functions that blind-access technology screen readers can extract to enunciate to the end user. Many roll-your-own third-party controls do not support this functionality. Hence the blind user cannot tell that this collection of bitmaps is in reality a toolbar. This is a very big deal in light of the Americans with Civil Disabilities Act that requires equal access in buildings, offices, software, and so on.

[†] You care because controls licensed from the same vendor look the same and you needn't wonder, "Whazzat?"

There are a few controls that you should know about because some of their neat features may not be so obvious. There are three.

- **Header controls** display lists in columns with column names in gray at the tops.
- **Tree View controls** display objects in a hierarchy.
- **List View controls** display icon/text combinations in alternate views.

 Well, header controls are displayed in gray only by default; you can change the color scheme in Windows 98 to your heart's content, and Desktop Themes will definitely change them for you. Technically, it's the color called 3D Objects in the Display applet that is used for the column names in header controls.

An Explorer window such as the one in Figure 2-3 illustrates all three controls. The right pane in the window shows a header control, the left pane a tree control. The file side (right pane) shows a List View control in Details View.

The point about a header control is what you can do with the headers. If you hold the mouse cursor over the gap between two headers, it changes shape to **+** which indicates that one can change the position of the column separator by pressing and dragging the mouse. Even more important is knowing that pressing a column header will sort that column in ascending order. If the column is already sorted in ascending order, pressing on the header will sort it in descending order.

The only thing to remember about Tree View controls is that each branch can be open or closed, and there are different symbols for open/closed in different applications. In Explorer, they are a minus signs and a plus sign, but the tree controls used in Help Contents are an open and a closed book. New to Windows 98, if you drag an object and hover over a closed list view entry (with a plus sign next to it), then the entry will open up to display the subfolders or other subobjects.

List View controls can be displayed in four modes that can usually be chosen from a View menu or from a button bar that looks like ▣▤▥▦. Taking it from the left, the four views are Large Icons, Small Icons, List View, and Details View. Small Icons and List View show the same icons but sort differently and have windows that scroll differently. Rather than trying to put it into words, view a large directory in an Explorer window and you'll see how the views differ.

 In addition to these four views, Explorer windows can be viewed as thumbnails and as a Web page—something that is vastly overrated by the Microsoft PR machine. I'll have more to say about thumbnail and Web views later.

Clip Bored

Philosophy will clip an angel's wings

—JOHN KEATS, *Lamia*

The two sections "ClipBoard" and "DDE" have nothing to do with objects, but they are preliminary to the discussion of OLE, which is object city—think of the clipboard as the delivery van for OLE and DDE (Dynamic Date Exchange) as its bill of lading.

The clipboard is an area of memory that Windows sets aside for storing data to facilitate data transfer between applications and even within an application. In its simplest form, you select data in an application, Copy or Cut it to the clipboard, and Paste it into an application, which can be the same one or a different one.

We'll give both the "preferred" hotkeys for these operations under Windows 3.0 (and before) and under Windows 3.1 (and later including Windows 9x)—they changed from one version to the other. Ideally, both will work, and they do work in applications that follow *The Interface Guidelines*. The *Guidelines* suggests that programs accept the older keys but not document them! Alas, you need to know both sets of keys because there are applications in which only one of the two sets works; if all else fails, you can use the Edit menu.

Copy (hotkey is **Ctrl+Ins** or **Ctrl+C**) leaves the source document alone but places the data on the clipboard. Cut (hotkey is **Shift+Del** or **Ctrl+X**) copies to the clipboard and deletes the material from the source. Paste (hotkey is **Shift+Ins** or **Ctrl+V**) copies the data from the clipboard to the target application. In some text controls, right clicking will bring up a menu with Copy, Cut, and Paste options.

That's the simple idea, but the question is, In what format does the clipboard transfer data? Does it include font information if you copy from one word processor to another? How about a spreadsheet formula if you copy between spreadsheets? The answer is, That depends on the source and the target.

The clipboard itself is very flexible. If you have Excel 97, open it, load a spreadsheet, mark some data, and copy them to the clipboard. Then run Windows Clipbook viewer (which I discuss in Chapter 4). One of the menu items in that viewer is View. Pull it down and it gives you a list of 30 formats—9 are black and 21 are gray (Figure 2-18 shows the menu split to fit on the page!). What does that mean? The 9 black formats are actually placed on the clipboard by Excel. For the other 21, Excel places only a promise on the clipboard. Essentially, it tells target applications, "If you have a need for the data in a promised format, let the clipboard know and it will get that format from me to give to you." By only promising data, not as much memory is used and the copy operation is faster.

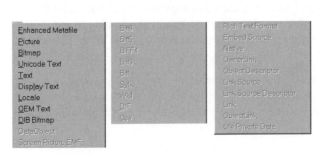

Figure 2-18. Sure is a lot loaded on that clipboard!

The downside of promised rather than actual data is that you have to keep the source application open to fulfill the promise. If you close an application before pasting, the clipboard notices and removes the promised formats from the list it offers to transfer. So if you are trying to transfer anything more complex than straight text, be sure to keep the source application open until after you paste.

The clipboard uses terms that may differ from those that applications use. It will say Picture for what many applications call Windows Metafile or WMF and it will say Bitmap for what applications may call BMP. If you never look at the viewer, this terminology is irrelevant because the applications and clipboard can talk about these standard formats, but it may confuse you if you do look and aren't aware of the terms.

When you paste into an application, that application will pick the format to use if there are several. The Edit menu sometimes has a Paste Special choice—you then get to pick the format used from the ones that are both on the clipboard and understood by the target application.

How well does the clipboard do on the transfer of formatted data? Remarkably well. When MOM tested it in 1993 for *The Mother of All Windows Books,* she was unable to transfer boldface attributes on text between any pair of the word processors Microsoft Word, Write, and Word Perfect. Similarly, attempting to paste a column of numbers with a SUM formula at the bottom pasted only the numbers, not the formula, when going in either direction between Excel and Quattro Pro. For *The Mother of All Windows 95 Books*, MOM tested Office 95 products and the Perfect Office products released in early 1995 and the results were heartening. Pasting formatted text including font and size and bold/italic information worked between all pairs of Word, WordPad, and Word Perfect. Formulae pasted OK from Excel to Quattro but not the other way. And this communication remains true in Windows 98.

 Wow. The industry really can get its act together. I'm impressed.

 The key to pasting formatted text is the adaptation by all word processing vendors of a format called RTF (Rich Text Format). It may become the standard for formatted e-mail also.

For some users, the biggest disappointment in the clipboard is that there is no Append command. Copy or Cut anything to the clipboard and whatever was there is gone, vaporized, moved to the great electron graveyard. What was there is replaced by the new cut. It's unfortunate that Windows doesn't have an append command built in for the special case where the clipboard has text and what you try to append is also text.

 For those who want an enhanced clipboard, there are various third-party shareware products available; among the best are ClipMate (**http://www.thornsoft.com/**) and SmartBoard (**http://www.smartcode.com/isshtml/smtbrd.htm**).

DDE

DDE stands for **Dynamic Data Exchange**. It's a built-in part of the Windows architecture that is of special importance for programmers. Indeed, it was added to the Windows spec in 1989–1990 at the request of Aldus and Microsoft's Power Point groups. It affects end users mainly through a command called **Paste Link**. If you write really fancy macros, you may need to know about DDE at the level beyond Paste Link, and we recommend that you find a copy of Woody's *Windows 95 Programming for Mere Mortals*. But as long as you are communicating between applications that use Microsoft's Visual Basic as a macro language, you are likely to have better choices than DDE for programming purposes. If you aren't going to do programming (including macro programming), don't worry your pretty head about anything but Paste Link.

 In many ways, DDE as a programming device is passé—replaced by OLE automation. But that isn't totally true. When you press Start Menu and chose Find/File or Find/Folder, the Start Menu actually sends a DDE command to Explorer to tell it to display the Find dialog!

Paste Link extends the idea of promised data to the idea of future promises. Not only does the source provide data now but it promises to provide data again in the future. Why would you want to do that? Suppose you are preparing a daily report for your boss in WinWord and part of it is a table of data that need to be computed in Excel. If you link the data rather than just paste them, the data can be updated automatically so the today's data is used without you having to do an explicit Copy and Paste again.

So, for example, if you have an Excel sheet called **daily.xls** and position **R6:C2** is a formula that you want to link into a Word document called **report.doc**, you select the cell in Excel, pick Copy from the Edit menu, go to Word and pick Paste Special from its Edit menu. The dialog that pops up has a pair of radio buttons marked Paste and Paste Link. Pick the latter and Paste as unformatted text, and it picks its formatting from Word, not from Excel. Word not only stores and displays the current value of the number in that cell but stores the application it is linked to (Excel), the filename (**daily.xls**), and the topic—the identifying tag it needs to send Excel to get that number back in future (**R6:C2** in this case).

Links come in two main varieties: automatic and manual. A **manual link** is updated only when you explicitly ask for it to be updated; you'd need to use a command in the target file to do the update. **Automatic links** are updated whenever you open the file with the target link (the Word **doc** file in the example). With automatic links, the target application also asks the source application to inform it whenever the source of the link is changed. It's impressive to make a link like the Excel/Word link we describe and type in changes in Excel while you have the Word window visible on the screen. You see the numbers updated in real time as you change the values in the spreadsheet that are involved in the formula!

If the link is automatic and the source of the DDE link isn't open when the target application loads the file with the target link (for example, if Excel isn't open when Word loads `report.doc`), then the target will offer to open the source and update the links. Either way, Word begins a DDE conversation with Excel that begins "Hey, Excel, ol' buddy, how ya been?" Quite literally, the first step in a DDE exchange is initialization. It continues with asking for and getting the linked data. The line is kept open for Excel to inform Word of further changes in real time. Often, users don't get to determine which kind of link it is—that's set by the target application—but it is important that you understand which kind of link it is so you know whether and when to ask for an explicit update. Civilized applications give you control over the links through a Links . . . command in the Edit menu.

 While you needn't worry about understanding DDE beyond Paste Link if you aren't going to program, you should care a great deal whether your applications support DDE and/or OLE automation and/or VBA because of the potential third-party add-ins possible when they are available.

OLÉ, José

Every country gets the circus it deserves. Spain gets bullfights.
Italy gets the Catholic Church. America gets Hollywood.

—ERICA JONG, *How To Save Your Own Life*, 1977

Objects truly come into their own with the notion of compound documents. If you had an Ami word processing file that had in it a piece of an Excel spreadsheet, a photo touched up with Picture Publisher, and a Corel Draw graphic, Windows 3.0 thought of that as a file made with Ami that happened to have pieces pasted in from other applications. Most likely, the files from Picture Publisher and Corel were saved to disk and just copied into the Ami document, although the Excel spreadsheet fragment might have been DDE Paste Linked.

The object/compound document paradigm would view such a document as one that had a single piece whose parts you would edit and act on with four separate tools—the four programs that made up the pieces. New Wave, an environment from Hewlett Packard that ran over Windows, pioneered this idea.

New Wave could never reach the critical momentum for its glue to catch on, but it and related ideas in the academic literature and other platforms captured Microsoft's and the industry's imagination. According to Microsoft's version of the history, OLE came out of a proposal of Lotus, and the OLE 1.0 spec was formulated by a committee of programmers from Lotus, Word Perfect, Aldus, and Microsoft's application programming group with input from Micrografx, Samna, Borland, Metaphor, and Iris. About six months before Windows 3.1 shipped, Microsoft released OLE program libraries that third parties could distribute, and these OLE 1.0 spec libraries were included with Windows 3.1. In the middle of 1993, Microsoft released libraries implementing the OLE 2.0 spec based on input from many software vendors.

 While there is no doubt that Microsoft has listened to other vendors, it is clearly first among equals. It is a remarkable coincidence that Microsoft's applications and languages seem to be the first ones to implement the various versions of OLE.

 Not surprising at all. OLE 2.0 was actually developed by the application division, which was then ordered by big Bill to turn it over to the Windows group for inclusion in the operating system.

 Still, there is no question that the synergy between the applications and OS groups over OLE was a factor in the victory of the Office Suite in the office products war of the early 1990s. We went from Word Perfect as the best-selling word processor and 1-2-3 as the best-selling spreadsheet to Microsoft Office's dominant position. One can't use the word "monopoly" because Windows was not the dominant OS it is now. Indeed, one could argue that Office contributed as much to Windows' success as vice-versa. Still, many think that the collusion between the Office and Windows groups wasn't a way of playing fair.

OLE is not automatically built into all applications—they have to have code to support it. Any recent application and, in particular, any application with the Windows 9X logo, has OLE 2.0 support, but older applications have OLE 1.0 or no OLE support.

OLE stands for **object linking and embedding,** although "object linking *or* embedding" might be clearer. Before OLE, the bitmap you edited with Picture Publisher would be embedded in your Ami[†] document as a picture. If you didn't like the way it looked, you'd launch Picture Publisher from Program Manager or your favorite launcher, load the on-disk file, edit it, save it to disk, and tell Ami to update it. Not hard, but certainly tedious.

The OLE 1.0 spec presented a better way. If the photo is an on-disk file placed inside the Ami document, when you place it there, it is linked as a PCX file to Picture Publisher. A database is kept by Windows specifying that OLE PCX objects are to be edited by Picture Publisher (if that happens to be your photo editor). Double click on the picture in the Ami document and Picture Publisher is loaded with the picture already opened. Edit it and close Picture Publisher and you are asked if you want to update the linked object. The tedium is somewhat reduced, and you have much more of the feel of working on a single document.

It isn't even necessary to have an on-disk file. You can instead "embed" the object in the target document, that is, save the data that Picture Publisher needs to describe a bitmap as part of the Ami document. You do this by creating the

---

† The Lotus word processor is now called Word Pro, but in the historical context I'm discussing, its old name of Ami is appropriate.

object while in Ami by telling Ami you want to embed a PCX object and have it load Picture Publisher for you.

At a technical level, the difference between linking and embedding is that linking only stores display data in the document and to edit it a file needs to be loaded from disk; embedding also stores the native data an editor needs. At the user level, linking is the way to go if you have a file, for example a company logo, that you want to share among several documents; editing it once affects all documents using it. Embedding is the best thing to use if you want to send the document to someone else without worrying about also sending extra files or about problems with the directory structure's being different on the receiving machine.

While the OLE 1.0 spec started us down the docucentric road, where users are supposed to think more in terms of documents and less of individual applications, there is still a feel of separate programs, because you double click when you want to edit and editing takes place in a separate window that feels like (and is!) a separate program. OLE 2.0 introduced the idea of in-place editing. Click on a photo inside a word processor **doc**, and, if the word processor and photo editor support OLE 2.0 in-place editing, the menus change to those of your photo editor. You have much more the feel of a single application acting on a single document with menus changing as appropriate to the part of the document you are editing.

OLE really does pass responsibility for the embedded or linked object to the program that created it. When a document is printed and gets to an embedded object, it passes commands to the program that understands the object asking for the object be rendered in a way that can be passed on to the printing subsystem.

A second important element of the OLE 2.0 spec was OLE automation, a protocol for programs to drive each other. It went way beyond the DDE spec and allows the potential of universal macro languages. Examples of application programs that supported OLE automation are Excel and Visio.

As for automation, the next step was the decision of Microsoft to license its Visual Basic for Applications (VBA) to third parties. That means that Excel and Visio and dozens of other applications share a common macro language.

You may hear bandied about some acronyms related to OLE. **OLE DB** (database) and **distributed OLE** are extensions of the current spec to allow sharing of objects across networks. The grand architecture on which these and other OLE extensions are based is called **COM** for **common object model**. The extension of COM to support distributed OLE is called **DCOM** for **distributed common object model**.

The program doing the driving—either sending the automation commands or asking for the embedded object—is usually called a **client**, and the program whose strings are being pulled or which is providing the embedded object is usually called a **server**. Microsoft says that with the release of OLE 2.0, the terms have been changed from client and server to container and object.

I think I'll scream if anything else is called an object. I assume some purist at Microsoft thinking of an object hierarchy thought themselves really clever to use the word "object" to refer to the controlled program in an OLE 2 conversation. But that's a big mistake. Oy. I think I'll shoot the next thing that is called an object!

There are two OLE file types that are implemented in Windows 98. The first is known as **Scrap** (it has the extension `.shs`). It allows you to take a fragment of an OLE document and save it to a file—you'd most often save it on your Desktop. For example, you could take some text in a Winword document, select it, and drag it to the Desktop. You can later drag a copy of it into WinWord or to any OLE 2.0 client that supports being a drag and drop client. Even in WinWord, the scrap is treated as a separate object, but since you can edit it, it almost behaves as an intrinsic part of the document. The second new file type is called **A Shortcut into a Document** (and has a filename with the extension `.shb`). I'll discuss it when I get into the subject of shortcuts in a few sections. If you right drag and drop some text from WinWord to the Desktop, you get a menu that lets you choose whether to make the text into scrap, make it into a document shortcut, or cancel. As usual, if you start left dragging, you can hit `Ctrl+Shift` and have the drop pop up a context menu.

Scrap seems to be of limited value, but document shortcuts are a wonderful but underused feature.

WordPad implements scrap with left drag and drop of selected text. It has no document shortcuts—you can't right drag and drop selected text at all.

■ A First Look Under the Hood

Being willing to look under the hood is what distinguishes users who want to squeeze performance from their system from those who don't. Four whole chapters at the end of this book look in the engine room and show you a lot of what is happening. In this group of sections, I give a first look at some parts of the engine room, in part to expose you to notions that help in understanding how to optimally use Explorer and the other core components discussed in Chapter 3.

Of course there are those who say that being willing to look under the hood is a sure sign of someone who spends all their time fooling with their computers rather than getting work done. But, what the hey—sure beats TV for entertainment.

Directories and Folders, Folders and Directories

I have been a soreheaded occupant of a file drawer labeled "Science
Fiction" . . . and I would like out, particularly since so many
serious critics regularly mistake the drawer for a urinal.

—KURT VONNEGUT, JR., *Wampeters,*
Foma and Granfallons, 1974

With Windows 95, Microsoft started using the term "folder" instead of "directory." That's the truth but not the whole truth. In some ways it is more accurate to say that "folder" is a term that encompasses what used to be called a directory. Every directory is a folder, but not every folder is a directory.

A folder is basically a collection of objects that the operating system understands. Just as a compound document can be thought of as a container for objects like pictures and text, so a folder is a container for files and, er, other things. In fact, it is useful to continue to use the term directory to refer to a folder whose contents are just disk files. I do that in this section.

 Ha! You can look in the Registry to learn what the designers of Windows 9X really think about the names of these things. Classes of objects have both a techie name that you'd never see if you didn't look in the Registry and a public name, which is what is used in the FileTypes tab of Explorer's View/Options dialog. For example, what is publicly called Microsoft Word Document has the techie name **Word.Document.8** (presumably because the file format is that of Word 8.0). The object with the public name "File Folder" has the techie name **Directory**.

To give you an idea of a folder that is not a directory, consider the one folder that is on everyone's Desktop—**My Computer**. It is hardwired in. You can change its name, and, if you go to the Effects tab of the Display applet, you can change its icon, but it is hardwired into the Desktop. Open it up and you won't find a file in sight. You'll find an icon for each drive. These drives should also be thought of as folders—indeed they correspond to the root directory of the drives. If you doubt it, pop up Run from the Start menu and type in **c:** and hit OK. The folder that opens is identical to the one that opens if you click the C drive icon in My Computer.

You could argue that since My Computer has folders corresponding to the directories such as **A:**, it is essentially a folder like a directory. But wait a minute. You'll notice that My Computer has some icons that do not correspond to drives—at least three will be there: **Control Panel**, **Printers**, and **Scheduled Tasks**. If you installed **Dial-Up Networking** when you ran setup for Win98, there will be a Dial-Up Networking folder also. Control Panel, Printers, and Dial-Up Networking do not correspond to directories—they are folders of a totally different type from file folders. They have objects that don't correspond to files. Of course, this means that My Computer is a kind of hybrid with some objects that are files and some that are not.

Scheduled Tasks is a different kind of hybrid. There is a directory called `C:\Windows\Tasks` and the objects in the Scheduled Tasks folder correspond to the `*.job` files in this directory. But the property sheet of the objects in the Scheduled Tasks folder is only a subset of the property sheet of the `C:\windows\tasks\*.job` files.

There are some other hybrid folders, each with its own weird twist on the paradigm. One is the **Fonts** folder, which can contain objects that are totally virtual. I'll talk about it later at the end of the group of sections on fonts.

Another hybrid folder is **Network Neighborhood**, which is hardwired[†] into the Desktop if you've installed network drivers. By default all it shows are workgroups and workstations on the network. But you can put files in it—presumably Microsoft assumes that you'll put shortcuts to places on the network there. To put any files there, you must physically place the files in a directory called `C:\windows\nethood`. So Network Neighborhood displays the top-level network nodes and all the files in `C:\windows\nethood`.

 And then there is The Mother of All Folders. The Desktop. If you don't believe me, run Explorer and keep hitting **Backspace**. Each hit takes you one up in the folder hierarchy. You'll probably start in `C:\`. **Backspace** will take you to My Computer, the parent of `C:\`. A second **Backspace** will take you to it's parent, which is Desktop. Further hitting of **Backspace** does nothing—Desktop is the top of the folder hierarchy.

In reality, as we'll explore in Chapter 3, the visible Desktop, which shows the contents of the Desktop folder, is another hybrid. It shows one icon for each file or folder in the disk directory `C:\windows\desktop`. There is a second folder whose objects are displayed on the Desktop—it is called `C:\windows\All Users\desktop.` The Desktop also shows the two hardwired folders My Computer and Network Neighborhood. Finally, it displays icons that are installed in a special way in the Registry, which is how Windows adds the icons for Recycle Bin, My Documents, and Internet Explorer. It appears that these are hardwired in and that you can't delete them. But see Chapter 9.

 If you've turned on multiple user login, the Desktop folder is not `C:\windows\desktop`, so you shouldn't be surprised if that folder isn't the one that corresponds to what is on your Desktop. I discuss this further in Chapter 3.

 This putting the Desktop at the top is just crazy. How can `desktop\my computer\windows\desktop` be contemplated without out a bad case of vertigo caused by circular reasoning? And it serves no purpose.

---

† Actually, in Chapter 9, I'll explain several ways to remove Network Neighborhood from your Desktop.

You're wrong, old spot. Putting the Desktop at the top is a brilliant coup for two reasons. First, naive users like the hierarchical idea of Desktop containing the icons it obviously contains. They'll happily drag to and from it never knowing there is a directory—a hidden directory by the way— that holds the files they drag there. Second, the Desktop is a terribly convenient place to put temporary files. Maybe you want to make a Zip, send it to someone via e-mail, and delete it. Put it on the Desktop when you make it and you can drag it into the e-mail message and then later drag it to the Recycle Bin. Because the Desktop is the top of the, er, heap, in any File/SaveAs dialog you can just keep hitting **Backspace** or keep hitting the 🔲 button or just hit 🗐 once and get to the Desktop—awfully handy if you want to leave stuff there.

 I've got to hand you one thing, though. Sensible users will place short-cuts to folders they use all the time and to their drives on the Desktop. If I choose such a shortcut on the Desktop in a File/Open dialog, the di-alog should move to the folder that the shortcut points toward. That's true under Windows 98, but it works incorrectly in Windows 95 where it offers to open the actual shortcut file. That was dumb! MOM complained about it. Thanks for fixing it, Billy boy.

Windows 98 introduces still additional special folders connected with Internet Explorer Toolbars—Links, Favorites, and Quick Launch. I'll say more about them in Chapter 3.

Hidden Pleasures

The knowingness of little girls
Is hidden underneath their curls.

—Phyllis McGinley, *What Every Woman Knows,* 1960

Figure 2-19. Letting it all hang out

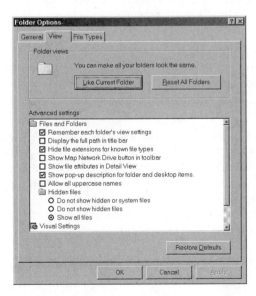

Billy98 just referred to the fact that `C:\windows\desktop` is a hidden directory. The modifier "hidden" makes it sound like some deep dark secret—hidden directories sound rather under-handed. In fact, "hidden" isn't very hidden. If you go to the View tab of Explorer's FolderOptions/View dialog (Fig-ure 2-19), you'll find three radio buttons under Files and Folders\Hidden files. The default is to pick "Do not show hidden or system files." I strongly urge you to pick "Show all files." When the default radio button is picked,

`C:\windows\desktop` won't appear on the directory list under `C:\windows` when you open Explorer. If "Show all files" is picked, it will appear. Similarly, if you do a `dir` at the DOS command prompt, you won't see hidden files, but if you do `dir/a:h`, you will see (only) hidden files. Using DOS's `attrib` command or the property sheet of a file in Explorer, you can hide or unhide a file or folder.

So "hidden" means hidden only from naive users, so don't hold much store by it for real security issues! In fact, it should be thought of as "kept out of the way of naive users" rather than "hidden." Serious users will probably want to pick the radio button to show hidden files.

 DOS has long had a hidden attribute, and eight of the nine directories that come into view when you pick "Show all files" have the hidden attribute turned on. But what is truly bizarre is that whether the Desktop folder appears is determined by the "Show all files" radio button, but this folder does not have a hidden attribute.

 To add to the bizarre, the subfolders of the Windows folder that are displayed are the same whether you pick "Do not show hidden or system files" or not, despite the fact that there are six folders with the System attribute turned on. I wonder what Windows means by "system files."

 While you're at it, you should consider unchecking "Hide file extensions for known file types" and checking "Display full path in title bar" and "Show file attributes in Detail View." If you are on a network, you may want to check "Show Map Network Drive button in toolbar."

Windows places eight hidden subdirectories in its own directory† (`nethood` is not always there):

- **`applog`** contains the application logs that Windows stores to track loading of programs for efficient defragmentation of your disk. I discuss this further in Chapter 4.

- **`inf`** contains files used to set up additional components of Windows. Most of these files have the extension `.inf`. Some are intended to be run via the Add/Remove programs applet in Control Panel, but they can also be run by right clicking them and choosing Install. Others are for hardware installation.

- **`nethood`** is discussed in detail earlier. Its behavior has changed from Windows 95 where the folder appeared only if you dragged a shortcut into the Network Neighborhood folder. The actual shortcuts were stored there. Now the folder is always present if you installed networking, and you cannot drag shortcuts into the Network Neighborhood folder. However, you can drag shortcuts into `C:\windows\nethood`, and they will appear when you open the Network Neighborhood folder.

---

† If you have multiple user support installed, some of these folders appear in the Profiles folder rather than Windows folder.

- **printhood** sure sounds like it should act like **nethood** for the printers folder. But it doesn't. Darned if I can figure out what it does.

- **recent** stores the shortcuts that appear in the Start Menu's Document command.

- **shellnew** is the default location for templates used in documents made from the New submenu of the Desktop context menu.

- **spool** is where files waiting to be printed are stored.

- **sysbckup** stores copies of the most basic Windows system files—if some rude installation program overwrites them, Windows tries to restore them from here.

The Windows directory also normally includes six hidden files—the two files that make up the Registry (**user.dat** and **system.dat**), a font cache (**ttfcache**), a cache for icons (**shelliconcache**), a file that stores information on hardware obtained during setup (**hwinfo.dat**), and an html template file for controlling default html views of folders (**folder.htt**). If you've turned on Thumbnail View for the Widows folder, you'll find a seventh hidden file (**desktop.ini**).

 It's not unreasonable that these files and directories are hidden. All but the most serious users won't need to access them, and they could confuse naive users.

 Actually, I explain in Chapter 9 why some users will want to delete **shelliconcache** and force Windows to reconstruct it, but I admit only rather sophisticated users will want to do that.

 Expect an explosion of hidden directories. Microsoft's setup recommendation to application developers is to place all the funny binary files in a hidden subdirectory of the main application directory called **system**.
No doubt some paranoids will rant and rave about all this hidden stuff, but you and I know better: hidden is just a name, and a user who wants access to these directories can easily get at them.

 desktop.ini sure is a weird one. Windows 95 was supposed to move us away from text **ini** files and put everything into the binary Registry. For backward compatibility some **ini** files were kept, but the word was clearly not to introduce new ones. So where the heck did this new **ini** file come from? It wasn't in Windows 95!

 It was introduced with IE 4.0, not Windows 98. Among other things, every time you turn on Thumbnail View in a folder, Windows makes a hidden file in that folder called **desktop.ini** with that information. So your disk is probably littered with hidden **desktop.ini** files in different folders!

Special Windows Folders

Besides the Desktop and the eight hidden folders I just discussed, the Windows folder contains lots of other special folders. As with other special items, if multiple users is turned on, some of these folders appear in the Profiles folder instead of the Windows folder.

Windows places six folders inside the Windows folder that have the system attribute set:

- **Cookies** stores data used by World Wide Web sites. I'll talk more about cookies in the section "Me Love Cookies."
- **Downloaded Program Files** stores ActiveX controls that your Browser gets off the Web.
- **Favorites** stores the shortcuts that appear on the Favorites menu of Internet Explorer and the Start Menu. I say more about it in Chapter 3.
- **Fonts** stores information about your fonts. I say more about it in the section "Installing and Removing Fonts in Windows 98."
- **History** stores shortcuts to the last 20 days' worth of World Wide Web sites you've visited. When you hit the **History** button in Internet Explorer, the information comes from **History**. You can change the number of days saved in the Internet Options dialog (see the discussion in Chapter 8).
- **Temporary Internet Files** is the browser cache. It's because of what is stored there that the browser doesn't have to reload a page from the Web when you use the Back button.

Besides these folders, which are set explicitly as system folders, there are a number of other "ordinary" folders that have special meaning as far as Windows is concerned.

- **All Users** is a folder that can contain additional desktop items in **All Users\Desktop**. Also, additional automatically started shortcuts can be placed in **C:\windows\All Users\Start Menu\Programs\Startup**.

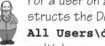 For a user on a single-user system, the bizarre way Windows constructs the Desktop from **C:\windows\desktop** and **C:\windows\All Users\desktop** is strange. This method is in place because of multiple-user support, discussed in the section "User Profiles" in Chapter 3. With multiple users, especially in a situation with a system administrator, it is useful to have common elements of the desktop and startup group in a one location.

- **Application Data** is a folder that applications are encouraged to store their data files in. For example, Outlook Express stores its message folders in **C:\Windows\Application Data\Microsoft\Outlook Express\Mail**.
- **Command** is a folder that contains DOS programs for the Startup Disk and for you to use if you ever have to boot to a DOS prompt. The EBD subfolder

of this folder contains a set of tools that are stored in compressed form on the Startup Disk. The EBD is discussed in Chapter 7.

- The **Config** folder stores MIDI configurations. MIDI is discussed in the section "'Mid the MIDI."

- **Cursors** are where Windows stores, er, whatchamacallits. You choose which cursors to use in the Mouse applet of Control Panel.

- **Drwatson** is where Windows stores crash logs. If you have crash problems and contact tech support, they may want files from this folder. Unless you explicitly load **drwatson.exe**, these complete logs will not be kept.

- **Help** is where Windows stores help files for its applications. Help files are further discussed at the end of Chapter 3. Applications often store their help files in their program directory.

- **Java** is used by Internet Explorer to store the code needed to interpret Java applets from the Web.

- **Media** is where Windows places the MIDI and **wav** sound files it installs.

- **pif** involves PIF (short for program information file) files that discuss in detail in the sections on DOS in Chapter 3. PIFs serve many purposes, but in particular, if you try to run a DOS program directly, Windows 98 will make a PIF for it. If the DOS program is on a local hard drive, the PIF file is placed in the same directory as the program. If the DOS program is on a CD-ROM or a network drive, the PIF files are placed in **C:\windows\pif**.

- **SendTo** is a special folder discussed in Chapter 3.

- **Start Menu** is a special folder discussed in Chapter 3.

- **Subscriptions** stores information on the various channels you've subscribed to. Channels are discussed in Chapter 4.

- **System** and **System32** is where Windows and third-party applications store dynamic link libraries (dlls), which are shared code libraries for programs to use.

- **Tasks** are where scheduled items are saved. The Scheduler is discussed in Chapter 4.

- **Temp** is used for temporary files. Disk Cleanup, discussed in Chapter 4, will get rid of files left in this directory by mistake.

- The **Web** directory is where Windows stores gifs and icons for various Microsoft business partners.

 Bah, humbug. It is disturbing that Microsoft gets to throw stuff from its friends on your hard disk. That's the way it stays powerful—by leveraging its ability to favor its friends.

 The Web directory has files from popular channels like CNET and CNN. The user only gains by not having to download these files from the Web.

Don't Be a FAThead

What if nothing exists and we're all in somebody's dream? Or what's worse, what if only that fat guy in the third row exists?

—WOODY ALLEN, *Without Feathers*

 The FAT, the File Allocation Table, is so low level that I normally wouldn't discuss it in a book like this, but, because the FAT32 converter is a key feature of Windows 98, I'll give you some background. This section is more for your curiosity. The actual conversion tools are covered in Chapter 6.

 You should come away from this section with two important understandings: what slack is and why FAT32 decreases it and where the 2-GB barrier in FAT16 comes from.

All PC disks are divided at a very low level into 512-byte units called sectors.

The FAT file system is based on dividing your disk into units called clusters that have to be an integral number of sectors. This number is normally a power of 2, so allowed cluster sizes are 512, 1,024, 2,048, 4,096, 8,192, 16,384, or 32,768.

 The next size up is 64 KB, or 65,536 bytes. Microsoft made a decision to never allow clusters greater than 32 KB and not allow 64-KB clusters because too many third-party programs would break. These program allocated 2 bytes, which are 16 bits, to store the cluster size. In binary, 64 K is 1 followed by 16 zeros, or 17 bits, too big to fit into the 16-bit storage.

Files are allocated space in whole clusters. The FAT itself is a database that keeps track of which clusters are in use and the order in which files are using.

 The details are interesting, but I won't take the time to explain them here. You can read about them, for example, in my article in *PC Magazine* on the Web at `http://www.zdnet.com/pcmag/issues/1607/pcmg0170.htm` (or search on "Barry Simon FAT" on the *PC Magazine* Web site).

 I'll restrain myself and skip the fat jokes.

The actual entries in the FAT are cluster numbers so the data size becomes critical. FAT16 uses 2 bytes = 16-bit entries, while FAT32 uses 4 bytes = 32 bits. That means that FAT16 disks can have up to 2^{16} = 64 K = 65,536 clusters, while FAT32 can have 2^{32} = 4 G = 4,294,967,296 clusters.

 If you like to do arithmetic in your head, it is useful to remember that 2^{10} is 1,024, a K. That means in reading powers of 2, each 10 is another K, so 2^{20} is a mega and 2^{30} is a giga. So 2^{32} is $2^{30} \times 2^2$ is 4 giga.

C'mon, Barry, your readers aren't going to care about or understand such numerical stuff.

Look, Billy, your standard assumption is that your customers are dumb and interested in fluff, but mine is that my readers are smart and interested in substance.

You can now understand where FAT16's limit of 2-GB partitions comes from. Clusters are limited to no more than 32 KB and there is a limit of 64 K of clusters and $32 \text{ K} \times 64 \text{ K} = 2^{15} \times 2^{16} = 2^{31} = 2$ G.

As I explained, the limit of 32-KB clusters is somewhat artificial, put in place to avoid breaking third-party programs. These programs may break with FAT32, so why didn't we allow larger cluster size than 32 KB? In fact, we could have gone to 64 KB but not up to 128 KB because of a different limit in FAT16 that allows clusters to have no more than 128 sectors. So we could have pushed FAT16 up to 4-GB partitions, but then FAT32 would have been necessary. Rather than a temporary fix that would last only a while and break stuff without the benefit of the small cluster size that the boys discuss shortly, we bit the bullet and went for the full change to FAT32.

The 4 gigabytes of clusters that FAT32 allows is huge. Even if FAT32 stuck to 512-byte clusters, that would allow disks up to 2 terabytes. In fact, at 2 terabytes, a different limitation is reached, and that's where FAT32 will break, so, strictly speaking, cluster sizes over 512 bytes aren't ever required for FAT32 to be able to count the clusters.

Typical capacities of hard disks double every 18 months (what is known as Moore's law). If that continues to be the case, we'll hit the 2-terabyte boundary in about 15 years and we'll need to move to FAT64 or some other file system.

Figure 2-20. FAT32 cluster sizes

Disk Size	FAT32 Cluster Size
Up to 512 MB	Not supported
512 MB–8 GB	4 KB
8+ GB–16 GB	8 KB
16+ GB–32 GB	16 KB
>32 GB	32 KB

Nevertheless, Microsoft uses larger cluster sizes than the minimum, as shown in Figure 2-20. While the smaller cluster size would save slack space, as I'll explain in a moment, there are benefits from the larger cluster size: the FAT size is smaller and files are less fragmented.

For 4-KB clusters, the FAT size is 14 MB smaller per GB of disk space. We estimate the slack is greater by about 28 MB per GB of disk space. So the FAT size, while important, is not the sole reason for the use of 4-KB clusters—it's the improved performance that led to the decision to use that size.

Besides the breaking of the 2-GB barrier, FAT32 can save considerable disk space. This has to do with what is known as slack. Recall that files are allocated an integral number of clusters. If you make a text file with "Hello, World!" in it, Explorer will say that the file is 15 bytes in size. But it takes a full cluster, that's 32 KB on a 2-GB FAT16 disk partition. The difference between the total cluster size and the file size is called slack. It is wasted space. For very small files, the slack is about one whole cluster, but for files much larger than the cluster size, the slack will average about half a cluster.

Thus on average if you move from 32-KB clusters to 4-KB clusters, you'll gain about 14 KB per file (the difference of 16 KB of slack to 2 KB). To figure out the total savings, you need to know how many files there are on disk. We've done the calculation assuming that an average file is 64 KB in size and the disk is entirely filled. The results are in Figure 2-21.

With a 512-KB disk, this is hardly worth spitting at, but with 2-GB partitions, we're talking real space.

You may have seen figures of 30% savings. How can that be while we only get 22%? One reason is that we computed the fraction of the total disk that you'd save, and it is 22% with our assumptions. Microsoft and those that follow their lead do the calculation as follows. With FAT16, you can fit in only about 1.5 GB of files (total file size rather than total allocated size), so Microsoft computes the 444-MB improvement as a percentage of 1.5 GB, not 2 GB, and that's 29%. And our 64-KB average file size is a bit high; 50 KB might be more accurate, which would also up the numbers.

Any way you want to look at it, with 2-GB partitions the savings are so large that the Windows 98 upgrade will almost pay for itself with disk savings alone.

There are two situations where the Windows 98 upgrade will *not* save you disk space.

- If you already have FAT32 on the disk, which may be the case for a machine bought in the last 18 months, right click on the drive in Explorer and choose Properties. Under File System, it will tell you FAT32 or FAT16.

Partition Size	F16 CSize	F16 Slack	F32 CSize	F32 Slack	Change in Slack	Change in FAT	Gain with FAT32	% Gain
512 MB	8 KB	32 MB	4 KB	16 MB	16 MB	− .75 MB	15.25 MB	3.0
1 GB	16 KB	128 M	4 KB	32 MB	96 MB	−1.75 MB	94.25 MB	9.2
2 GB	32 KB	512 M	4 KB	64 MB	448 MB	−3.75 MB	444.25 M	22

Figure 2-21. FAT32 space savings

- If you are using DriveSpace (Windows disk compression), there is very little slack because of how files are stored, and FAT32 won't gain you any space. Indeed, since you also lose the benefits of compression, you'll actually lose, not gain, free space, but not that much. Note that there is no disk compression available with FAT32. There still may be a reason to switch to FAT32: there is a performance hit with DriveSpace that there isn't with FAT32. The transition from FAT16 with DriveSpace to FAT32 is hairy—I tell you what to do in Chapter 6.

If you have a hard disk with more than 2 GB and so multiple partitions, there is no way to merge partitions using only Windows tools (check out Partition Magic if you really feel you have to do this). You don't even have the option with the standard Windows 98 upgrade of rerunning fdisk, repartitioning, reformatting, and starting all over because the upgrade won't install on a freshly formatted drive—it explicitly looks for Windows 95!

Shortcuts

What Romantic terminology called genius or talent or inspiration is nothing other than finding the right road empirically, following one's nose, taking shortcuts.

—ITALO CALVINO, *Cybernetics and Ghosts,* lecture, November 1969

I know what a shortcut is. It's one file that points to a program or document so when you double click on the shortcut, the program runs or the document is launched in its associated program. Shortcuts have the extension .**lnk**.

That's a pretty good summary and one that many people would agree with, but it's not the whole truth by a long shot. First of all, even shortcuts with the extension .**lnk** can point toward objects in the folder hierarchy that are executable but not programs in the usual sense. And I'm aware of at least four other extensions used for specialized shortcuts by Windows 98! And applications can define their own shortcut types.

A shortcut, as defined by the *Programmer's Guide to Windows,* is "a data object that contains information used to access another object in the system, such as a file, folder, disk drive, or printer." Double clicking on the shortcut is supposed to access the object that the shortcut points toward.

To understand why the notion was needed, it helps to consider Window 3.x's Program Manager, if you are familiar with it. The main Program Manager window had subwindows called groups. The groups contained items (represented by icons), and when you double clicked one of them, it launched the object that the item was supposed to point toward. In a sense, the Program Manager items were already shortcuts, but they were of a very different makeup from the objects to which they pointed. The target objects were always files in the file system. The Program Manager items were bits of binary fluff inside the files that were associated with groups.

Given the folder emphasis in Windows 98, it was natural that Program Manager groups would evolve into folders of some sort—it turns out that they are folders exactly corresponding to disk directories (namely subdirectories of `C:\windows\start menu\programs`). But then what happens to the launch items? They couldn't always be the actual executable files since often programs insist on being in a directory with lots of other files. So the shortcut was born—the icons in a Program Manager folder would evolve into shortcuts to executable programs—files that could launch other files. But the designers then pushed the concept to new heights.

That shortcuts are the evolution of Program Manager items is clear in several ways. Just as items had working directories, hotkeys, and icons, so do shortcuts. I'll discuss these in detail in Chapter 3. More telling, Windows 95 had a conversion program to turn `.grp` files, the binary files representing groups, into subfolders of `C:\windows\start menu\programs`. Items get translated into `.lnk` files in the folders. When you install a Windows 3.1 program in Windows 98, the items become shortcuts in the Start Menu directory if the install is properly designed.

So far, the picture is exactly like that presented by Woody. But links can point to things other than programs and documents. They can point to folders, for example, the command in a shortcut could be `C:\windows`. The shortcut would then open the folder in Explorer running in Folder View. As I explain in Chapter 3, drives (folders like `C:\`) are treated specially.

You can add a link shortcut by dragging an object to the Desktop or from one folder to another in a suitable way. For **exe** files, making shortcuts is the default action after a drag and drop. For other files you need to right drag. To get drive shortcuts by dragging, you can drag from the My Computer folder.

You can also right click Desktop or on a blank part of an Explorer window, choose New and then Shortcut from the menu, and invoke a Create Shortcut Wizard (see Figure 2-22). This lets you pick the command line by browsing and assign a name to the shortcut.

The folder-based object system has other objects besides files. For example, Control Panel, the Printers folder, Dial-Up Networking, and Network Neighborhood have their own type of objects (applets, printers, dial-up connec-

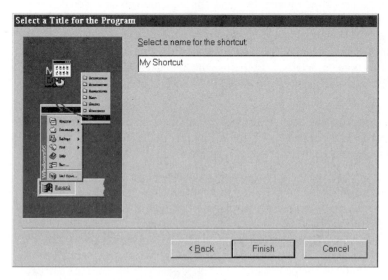

Figure 2-22. Create Shortcut Wizard

tions, and computers). The Windows 98 shell is consistent and lets you drag these objects to the Desktop and create shortcuts that launch them.

A second kind of shortcut is the DOS PIF file that could be used as a launch shortcut under Windows 3.x. I discuss it in detail in Chapter 3. It's a clever piece of design that `.lnk` shortcuts and DOS PIF files are presented to the user as conceptually the same thing. That they are different in some ways is shown by the fact that their property sheets are very different. PIF files have the extension `.pif`.

A third kind of shortcut—my favorite—is the shortcut into a document. Programs that fully support the OLE spec (for servers) let you select a piece of a document and drag it to the Desktop (or an Explorer folder) and make that piece into a shortcut (which happens to have the extension `.shb`). For example, right drag a piece of a WinWord document to the Desktop and choose to make a shortcut. When you later double click that shortcut, WinWord will be launched if it is not already running, the document will be loaded if it isn't already loaded, and Winword will scroll to the location of the original text and reselect it.

 This is ideal for saving a bookmark to where you are currently working on a project like, oh, writing an 800+ page book on Windows 98!

If you drag a Dial-Up Networking connection to the Desktop, it produces a fourth kind of shortcut with extension `.dun`.

There is a fifth kind of file-based shortcut—one to an Internet Web site with the extension `.url`. Double clicking will dial up your Internet connection, launch Internet Explorer, and connect to the Web site that you were visiting when you created the shortcut.

URL shortcuts can be e-mailed to other Windows users, who should be able to access them directly, and they are the basis of the Favorites menus. The simplest way to make Internet shortcuts is using the Add to Favorites command on the Favorites menu in IE. You can also take a link on the page currently displayed in IE and drag it to the Desktop (or other folder), where a shortcut to that link will be made.

 There is a further kind of phantom shortcut—that to a font. I discuss why I call it a phantom when I get to fonts a bit later in this chapter.

 Well, I think I was basically right at the start. Sure, there are other extensions than `.lnk`, but who cares? That's techie stuff! And sure, the shortcut can point to objects other than programs, but conceptually they are all the same.

There is one aspect of shortcuts that has caused some complaints from the learned magazine writers, namely how well shortcuts locate the program they point to if the program is moved. If that happens, you get the dialog shown at the left of Figure 2-23. In the initial release of Windows 95, it did an excellent

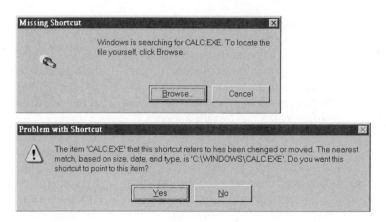

Figure 2-23. It's 10 o'clock. Do you know where your program is?

job of locating the file as long as it had been moved in the same drive. It searches based on more than name—look at the dialog from Windows 95 at the right of Figure 2-23, which located the Windows 3.1 `calc.exe` when Windows 95 `calc.exe` was moved to another drive. It didn't just match the names. If a file has been moved to a different drive, you can always use the Browse button.

 But somewhere on the way to Windows 98, this admittedly flawed but not bad recovery method got replaced by something much worse. Some bozo apparently decided that the dialogs in Figure 2-23 are too confusing. So the process is much faster, so fast that when the dialog on top flashes on the screen you can barely see it, and you are spared the second dialog entirely. The result is that moving `calc.exe` from `C:\windows` to `C:\` (the same drive!) and running Calculator from the Start Menu causes Windows to run CleanUp Manager and change the shortcut to CleanUp Manager without even asking. This is progress?

 The sad thing is that it wouldn't be that hard for Windows to keep track of which executables are connected to shortcuts so it could adjust shortcuts as files are moved. But the 'softies seem to have opted for a slick fix that often doesn't work!

Files can be registered with the operating system to never display extensions.[†] Since shortcuts are so registered, you won't see extensions for any of the shortcut types on the Desktop or in Explorer even if you uncheck the Explorer option "Hide MS-DOS extensions for file types that are registered." You will see them if you do a `dir` at a DOS prompt and in some third-party file managers. And when you look at the General tab of the Properties sheet for a shortcut, you'll also see the extension.

---

† This is distinct from the option in the Explorer View/Options dialog; I talk about it further in Chapter 3.

The Tree-based Menu

Tree at my window, window tree,
My sash is lowered when night comes on;
But let there never be curtain drawn
Between you and me.

—Robert Frost, *Tree at My Window*

There is one paradigm that is reused several times by Windows 98 and its applications and it is important to understand: a menu that is built based on a subtree of the folder system. There is a top level of the menu associated with a specific folder, which I'll call the **root folder for the menu**. Items on the menu are associated with files in the root folder. Submenus are associated with subfolders. Items on the submenu associated with a given subfolder are associated with files in that subfolder and subsubmenus to subsubfolders of the subfolder. This process keeps going on as long as the folders last. The names of the menu items and submenus are precisely the names of the files and subfolders. When a menu item is chosen, the corresponding file is run. It is useful to make the file items shortcuts—they run properly and their names display without their extensions.

 Sometimes—for example, with Internet Explorer-related toolbars, only the top-level correspondence works—that is, a menu corresponds to shortcuts but there are no submenus and subfolders are opened when clicked in the menu.

The Mother of All Tree-based Menus is the Start Menu. Its root folder[†] is `C:\windows\Start Menu`. It has items in its top level that are more than what's in the root folder, but the `Programs` submenu is precisely built from the `C:\windows\Start Menu\Programs` folder. You can add additional items to the main Start Menu by adding shortcuts to the `C:\windows\Start Menu` folder and you can make additional submenus by putting subfolders in that same folder.

The point of understanding the paradigm is that it tells you how to modify your Start Menu. You want to use Explorer to view this part of the folder tree and move/add/delete shortcuts and subfolders. This is much, much more efficient than calling up Start/Settings/ Taskbar . . . from the Start Menu, choosing the Start Menu Programs tab and using the Add . . . and Remove . . . buttons. One way to access Explorer in these folders is the Advanced . . . button in that same dialog, but it is hardly the most efficient. You can right click the Start button and choose Explore and get to the folders that way. In Chapter 3, I'll encourage you make an Edit Start Menu item on your Start Menu, which is better still.

 New to Windows 98, you can move Start Menu Items from the Start Menu itself, but you cannot rename them. I discuss this further in Chapter 3.

---

† As usual, things aren't quite like this if you have Multiple User profiles turned on.

A second place that this paradigm is used is for the Send To submenu on the context menu that you get if you right click on file and folder objects in Explorer. This is a tree-based menu with root folder `C:\windows\sendto`. Yeah, that's right, there is a space between "send" and "to" in the submenu name but not in the folder name. You can add or remove items from the Send To menu by manipulating the files in the folder. If you want, you can add submenus to Send To by adding subfolders to the SendTo folder.

 A third place where one would expect Windows to use a tree-based menu is on the Documents submenu of the Start Menu. The items on this submenu are related to shortcuts in the folder `C:\windows\recent`, but it is not a simple tree-based menu—it's kinda techie, one might even say irrelevant. I tell you about it when the Start Menu is discussed in Chapter 3.

The Favorites menu is a tree-based menu based on `C:\windows\favorites`. It is accessible as a top-level submenu in Explorer and Internet Explorer as well as on the Favorites submenu of the Start Menu. There is also a Favorites button on the Internet Explorer toolbar that opens a Favorites view on a left-hand pane, as seen in Figure 2-24.

If you had any doubts that this was a tree-based menu, the Organize Favorites … item on the Favorites menu opens up a window that looks and acts much like the mini-explorer window that is part of the common Open dialog.

Figure 2-24. Girls in white dresses with blue satin sashes,/Snowflakes that fall on my nose and eyelashes

The designers of Internet Explorer made a huge mistake in using the same **C:\Windows\Favorites** folder that Microsoft Office uses for its favorites. Office uses favorites to speed up exploration when in a File/Open or File/Save As dialog. You probably don't want your favorite Web pages in a Word Open dialog or your favorite Word documents in the drop-down list in Internet Explorer.

Long Filenames

. . . one needs long arms; it is better to have them too long than too short.

—SARAH BERNHARDT, *Memories of My Life,* 1907

Hey, what's there to say about long filenames? You can have 'em— that's great—but what more is there to be said? Shortest section in the book, eh?

Other than the obvious need to explain how long they can be and what characters are allowed, for the curious and to warn readers how fragile the system behind long filenames is, I'll explain how long filenames are stored. But there are two more important issues to discuss. In a world that suddenly allows spaces and periods in filenames, how do you deal with ex-tensions and multiple parameters in a command line? And how do programs written for 8+3 filenames cope in a world with long filenames?

Filenames under versions of DOS or Windows prior to Windows 95 had ex-tensions of up to 3 characters and prenames up to 8. The full pathname for a file, including **c:**, the backslashes, and the period between the prename and the extension, was limited to 80 characters. Under Windows 95 and 98, file-names can be up to 255 characters and pathnames up to 260. Extensions can be more than 3 characters—and since multiple periods are allowed, the exten-sion is the part after the last period.

Forbidden in filenames and directory are any control character (one with codes below ASCII 32, for example, ^A=ASCII 001) and the following special characters:

```
\ / : * ? " < > |
```

In particular, both spaces and periods are allowed, as well as the following characters that are forbidden in older versions of DOS:

```
+ , ; = [ ]
```

I understand why those characters are forbidden: **:** and **** are for drive and directory names, **/** is for parameters, ***** and **?** are wildcards, **"** is for quoted names, and **>**, **<**, and **|** are for DOS redirection.

Right, but there is a scheme that would allow any character. One could use **$** as an "escape." You could have ***** in a filename and still use ***** for a wildcard. You'd use **$*** when referring to that character as part of a filename. **$$** would mean a single **$**.

 Oh, how UNIX-like. One could use an escape character to allow anything in filenames, but what would that gain except to tickle the fancy of the computer science crowd? Real users would be as confused as all get-out. Nope. We made the right decision to just forbid these characters, although some users will no doubt try to use **?** or **<** or **>** in a name and be puzzled at the error message.

 I did find a buglet in the way that DOS rename handles illegal characters. If you type **ren config.sys ^G.sys** at the DOS command line (where **^G** is entered as **Ctrl+G**), DOS will reply: **File not found – config.sys**. Oh, how I love a nice bug in the mornin'.

 Well, at least they make it impossible to put control characters in when renaming in Explorer. You get a beep if you try to. That's been fixed since Windows 95.

Microsoft says that long filenames are stored in Unicode,[†] which says something about the future.

For compatibility with programs that don't understand long filenames, Windows 98, like Windows 95 before it, assigns each file an 8+3 filename without any of the characters that are illegal in earlier versions of DOS. The short filename is determined by the following rules:

1. If the long filename is legal under earlier versions (no more than 8 + 3 characters, no more than one period, and none of the newly allowed characters), then the short filename is the same as the long filename.

2. If the long filename is illegal under earlier versions of DOS, keep up to 3 characters after the last period. From the characters before the last period, drop all periods and all spaces. Then keep the first 6 of the remaining characters or all of them if there are fewer than 6. This gives a preliminary 6+3 name.

3. In the preliminary 6+3 name, replace all the newly allowed characters, such as **+** and **<space>** by **_** .

4. Tack **~1** onto the end of the 6-character part to get an 8+3 filename. Use this name as the short filename if there isn't already another file in the directory with that name.

5. If the first try already exists, try **~2**, **~3**, and so on instead of **~1**.

---

† Unicode is a scheme for handling multiple alphabets; I discuss it in the collection of sections on fonts.

So assuming that a **~1** file doesn't already exist, here are some examples:

LONG NAME	Short Name	LONG NAME	Short Name
winutil.doc	winutil.doc	win util.doc	winuti~1.doc
winutil.do;	winuti~1.do_	A very long.name	Avery1~1.nam
winutil.docs	winuti~1.doc	a;;;;;.abc	a_____~1.abc

If you look at these names, you see that the convention is rather silly. Why shouldn't **winutil.docs** and **win util.doc** just become **winutil.doc**? You could imagine a saner system where the **~1** is used only if absolutely necessary.

 What happens if you use up **~1**, . . . , **~9** and add another?

 Windows uses the first 5 characters and appends **~10**.

 How about if you go over 999,999 files?

 You are in big trouble!

If you want to refer to a long filename with spaces or other characters that might be confusing (like **+** or **;**), you can use quotes. Thus, to distinguish renaming **this file** to **that file** from **this file that** to **file** at the DOS command line, you could use

```
ren "this file" "that file"
```

 An unusual case where you need to use quotes is the following. Suppose you want to save a file in Notepad to the name **foo.bar**. If you just type that name in the Save dialog, Notepad happily tacks on a **txt** extension and saves it as **foo.bar.txt** (!). To save it as **foo.bar**, you need type **"foo.bar"** in the Save dialog. Notepad is smart enough not to try to tack **.txt** onto **.bat** and **.ini** files. Word and WordPad behave similarly in insisting on tagging on their extensions.

I had a tricky situation with using quotes properly that I needed explained to me. I figure it could be a pointer to you. I wanted to add Norton's antivirus scanner to the scheduler. If you just run the program, it sits there in interactive mode, but I wanted to run it while I sleep. If you pass the program **C:** as a parameter it scans drive C and exits if no problems are found. No problemo, I figured. Norton was installed in the **C:\program files\norton antivirus** folder, so it ran the Add Tasks Wizard and browsed to the program **C:\program files\ norton antivirus\navw32.exe**. The wizard placed

"C:\program files\norton antivirus\navw32.exe"

into the Run box of the resulting scheduled Task. Since I wanted to add the parameter **C:**, I changed this to

"C:\program files\norton antivirus\navw32.exe C:"

but then the scheduler complained.

 Woody needed to use

"C:\program files\norton antivirus\navw32.exe" C:

Alas, Windows 3.x applications don't understand long filenames. You might hope that if the application used calls to the Windows 3.1–type common File dialogs, then that dialog could display the long filenames for the user but pass the short filename on to the application. Windows 98 doesn't work that way for reasons Billy elucidated earlier.

 To see how Windows 9X stores long filenames, I made a file called **This is a very long file name with a period in the middle. Isn't it.txt.** (Hey, I bet you don't spell so good late at night, either.) The resulting directory is shown in Figure 2-25. Notice that the DOS **dir** command shows the associated short name on the left and the long name on the right.

**Figure 2-25.
Directory listing**

```
C:\Test>dir

 Volume in drive C has no label
 Volume Serial Number is 2E11-11E8
 Directory of C:\Test

.              <DIR>         07-31-95  10:51p .
..             <DIR>         07-31-95  10:51p ..
THISIS~1 TXT            0    07-31-95  10:51p This is a very long file name with a
peirod in the middle. Isn't it.txt
        1 file(s)                  0 bytes
        2 dir(s)      511,623,168 bytes free
```

Figure 2-26.
LFN directory file

```
Name      .Ext  ID          Size      Date       Time     Cluster  76 A R S H D V
Cluster 2,533, Sector 81,527
.                Dir          0    7-31-95    10:51 pm   2,533   - - - - D -
..               Dir          0    7-31-95    10:51 pm       0   - - - - D -
ment.txt         Del LFN                                      0   - R S H - V
New Text Docu    Del LFN                                      0   - R S H - V
σEWTEX~1 TXT     Erased       0    7-31-95    10:51 pm       0   A - - - - -
it.txt           LFN                                         0   - R S H - V
iddle. Isn't     LFN                                         0   - R S H - V
irod in the m    LFN                                         0   - R S H - V
ame with a pe    LFN                                         0   - R S H - V
y long file n    LFN                                         0   - R S H - V
This is a ver    LFN                                         0   - R S H - V
THISIS~1 TXT     File         0    7-31-95    10:51 pm       0   A - - - - -
                  Unused directory entry
                   Unused directory entry
                    Unused directory entry
                     Unused directory entry
Cluster 2,533, Sector 81,528
                     Unused directory entry
                      Unused directory entry
```

I then fired up Diskedit from Norton Utilities for Windows 95, which has to be run in DOS-exclusive mode. The data actually stored in the on-disk directory are displayed† in Figure 2-26. The actual file is shown as the last item before the **Unused** directory entries. You see it with its assigned short filename. Old DOS and Windows programs will normally find only such entries. But immediately above it appear six entries that manage to squeeze 13 characters to a line and put them in order of the long filename if you read upward from the true file entry.

Note the cluster assigned to these entries—it's **0**, which is normally used for erased file entries. And if you look to the extreme right, where the file attributes are stored, you'll see that each of these babies is a read-only, hidden system file, which happens to be a volume label. This scheme depends on the fact that most programs totally ignore volume labels. Weird—but slick, isn't it?

This scheme is fairly fragile in that the association of long filenames depends on the exact location of the long filename entries. They have to be in the directory immediately prior to the associated short filename. This means that if you do something like run a pre-Win95 directory-sorting utility (like Norton's DS), you'll lose all your long filenames. In fact, you should assume that any pre-Win95 utility that directly manipulates file directories will foul up long filenames if you run it. *Totally* foul them up.

If you really need to run some kind of pre-Win95 utility and want to save a long filename, look at **lfnbk**, the long filename backup utility. You'll find it on the Windows CD in the directory **\tools\reskit\file\lfnback**. You'll find documentation for it in **\tools\reskit\help\win98rk.hlp**. Using it is like having a root canal, only less fun.

'Softies sometimes use "LFN" for long filename and "SFN" for the old-fashioned 8+3 name.

---

† The discussion in the rest of this section is a little technical and assumes you know about file attributes, clusters, and how directory entries are stored on disk. Feel free to skip to the next section.

Drivers

KERMIT: Where did you learn to drive?
FOZZIE: I took a correspondence course.

—*The Muppet Movie*

To understand Windows, it sometimes pays to look at the real world, but a somewhat skewed real world. The plumbing industry has settled on standard pipe sizes and connectors, but suppose it didn't and you want a new sink connected to the city lines. The poor plumber would have to ask you exactly what brand and model sink you have and what kind of incoming pipe you have and make sure that he has the right connection to join them. If there were 40 kinds of sinks and 30 kinds of pipes, the plumber would need 1,200 (40 times 30, see) connectors to cover all the possibilities.

Pretty heavy toolbox to carry around. If the plumber were really clever, she might figure out the following. Develop a special standard intermediate piping. Then all she'd need is 40 connectors to connect the sink to the special intermediate piping and 30 connectors for the other side. Only 70 (the sum) rather than 1,200. Big improvement.

If the plumber really had clout in the industry, she'd convince the sink makers that *they* should supply the 40 connectors for the sinks to the standard. True, with the extra connectors, there would be more chance of leaks, but if handled right, this would simplify everything.

The same idea is central to much in the world of computing. Rather than have everything connect directly to each other, we use a protocol (like the standard pipe) and need only the sum of the possibilities, not the product. This is important to the understanding the Windows API (application programing interface) and the role of drivers.

 Take printing. Please. The confused world of 1,200 connectors is the DOS world. Each printer had its own quirks and command set. Each application had to provide its own connector—called a printer driver—for each printer out there. Lots of duplicated effort, lots of application programmer time wasted writing drivers, and the people who knew the quirks of individual printers best—the printer manufacturers—were not those who wrote the drivers.

Windows is like the smart plumber. It provides a standard intermediate connector, the Windows API, for printing. The applications talk to the API. The printers connect to the API by providing drivers that are loaded as part of Windows. Not only is this paradigm used for printers, it's used for monitor adapters (screen drivers), sound cards, and more.

An advantage of this scheme is that the hardware manufacturers who presumably know their products best are responsible for the drivers. Another advantage is that a manufacturer can provide a fancy new piece of hardware and have its features work with most Windows software just by writing the driver. For example, Hewlett Packard could up the printer resolution from 300 dpi to 600 dpi and then to 1,200 dpi without waiting for application software to catch up if they supplied a new printer driver to which the software would automatically catch up!

If you got the impression that drivers are pretty important parts of your system, you're right. Probably no third-party component of Windows is used more than your screen driver. These drivers tended to be unruly stepchildren under Windows 3.1. The hardware vendors didn't always expend the resources they needed to and Microsoft didn't always provide the help to driver writers when the companies did take them seriously. As a result, the drivers were responsible for a lot of crashes.

We realized this and attempted to address the problem in two ways under Windows 95. First, we worked closely with vendors of mainstream hardware to make their drivers stable. And some learned their lessons well. For example, after working with us to write Windows 95 drivers, ATI went back to their Windows 3.1 drivers and improved them. Second, we shifted the screen driver over to the Unidriver model that worked well with Windows 3.1 for printers. Basically, Unidriver, written by Microsoft, provided the core of functionality that drivers need, and third parties wrote minidrivers, which are essentially add-ons for the Unidriver module. For Windows 95, we also created an analog of Unidriver but for video—it is called the DIB engine.

You'll see mention of a special driver called a **VxD**. These are virtual device drivers that are loaded as extensions of the Windows core and live at the lowest level of the system software. They have the advantage that they can provide services to DOS sessions while taking no conventional memory footprint. They are the key to the increased memory that Windows 98 can provide for such DOS sessions. They also provide improved performance in Windows programs. The 32-bit file system, the CD file system, the protect mode Network clients, the comm port driver, support for file sharing, and the print spooler are all implemented in VxDs.

Windows knows which VxDs to load by looking in at subkeys of the Registry key **HKLM\system\currentcontrolset\services\VxD**. If you ever need to prevent a VxD from loading, you can remove the associated key from the Registry. But bear in mind that you are dealing with a loaded gun pointed at you, so don't even think about such surgery if you aren't 1,000% sure that the VxD you are preventing from loading is from a third party and isn't needed for some aspect of the system you haven't thought of. Because if you prevent a VxD that is essential from loading, Windows itself may no longer load, and you may be forced to reinstall Windows and maybe even all your applications.

I'm glad to say that Windows 98 includes a new **Win32 Driver Model (WDM)**. This allows vendors to write a single driver that works for both Windows 98 and Windows NT. This was accomplished by adding some of the features of the Windows NT kernel to Windows 98. Many third-party drivers will continue to use the older driver model, but Windows 98 includes WDM drivers for keyboard, mouse, modems, scanners, DVD, and USB.

One of the big advantages of WDM has to do with Windows NT, not Windows 98. Hardware support for Windows NT is often less than ideal—with the WDM, we will likely see more peripherals that work with NT without hassles.

One more comment on drivers involves the extension of the notion of printer drivers to a heck of a lot of "virtual" printer drivers. "Printing" is just a way of outputting a document from an application, usually as a set of dots. If you want to send the document over the phone lines to someone's fax machine, it's just like printing, so one way to implement faxing from Windows is via a printer driver that doesn't print! Instead, the driver pops up a box asking who you want to send the fax to, and then it sends the bit pattern out the serial port to your fax modem instead of out a parallel port to your printer! Actually, if Windows fax software finds either another Windows fax program on the receiving end or a stand-alone fax machine that understands Windows fax, then it does something more efficient that just blast a bitmap across the phone line.

Windows 98 prefers to implement fax as part of MAPI[†], and you'll use a Send or Mail command in mail-enabled applications to send faxes. But while Windows 98 prefers to think of MAPI for programs that are not mail enabled, when you install Microsoft fax, it also installs a Microsoft fax print driver. If a program doesn't support MAPI, you can just print to this driver to send a fax to it.

Similarly, the portable document idea I'll discuss in the section "Portable Documents" later in this chapter depends on "printing" a document to a file. The moral is to keep in mind that "printer drivers" are really "output drivers" and may not actually print.

The Registry

*History . . . is, indeed, little more than the register of the crimes,
follies, and misfortunes of mankind.*

> —EDWARD GIBBON, *The Decline and Fall of the Roman Empire*, 1776

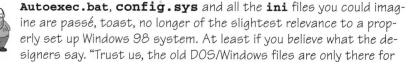 **`Autoexec.bat`, `config.sys`** *and all the* **`ini`** *files you could imagine are passé, toast, no longer of the slightest relevance to a properly set up Windows 98 system. At least if you believe what the designers say. "Trust us, the old DOS/Windows files are only there for compatibility." Our testing systematically shows that this isn't entirely true; there is some information in the* **`ini`** *files that still gets used. But that's an anomaly. It really is true that the oodles of information stored about system details and your preferences is almost entirely in a single* logical *object called the Registry.*

I emphasized the word "logical" after "single" because the **Registry** in most systems is built from two files—**user.dat** and **system.dat** in the **C:\windows** directory. There is even a good reason for this, as I explain when the rubber

---

† MAPI is discussed at the end of this chapter.

meets the road on the Registry in Chapter 9. Most of the discussion is there, but I want to note a few general facts here.

- The amount of stuff stored in the Registry is overwhelming. It includes OLE registration information, the most intimate details of the life of your hardware, and configuration information, such as what goes on the New submenu of the Desktop context menu and what icon is used for My Computer. The Windows **ini** files were typically 40,000 to 100,000 bytes. Figure 25 times that for the Windows 98 Registry.

- The **ini** files are ASCII. The Registry files are binary to allow a more elaborate structure and quicker reading by the system. This means that a special program is needed to view the Registry. Windows 98 comes with such a program, called Regedit. It is installed in the Windows 98 directory but is not added to the Accessories (or any other group) in the Start Menu. You can add it yourself or just type **regedit** into the Run box. So long as you don't use the Add or Modify commands, you can't do anything wrong, so you might want to take a quick look—or better, jump to Chapter 9 and look at it in some detail.

- Windows 98 includes a **ScanReg** program that checks the Registry each time you reboot Windows and makes a backup at that time (if it hasn't made a backup earlier the same day). This program keeps five generations of the Registry in compressed format and includes a DOS component that lets you restore a backup if your Registry becomes totally hosed.

- The structure is more involved than the old **ini** files. The **ini** files had sections (like **[386Enh]**) and value pairs like **com1autoassign=2** in them. Sections are now called **keys** and are hierarchically designed like the folder structure, so believe it or not, if you choose to have your Start Menu directory renamed to "Barry's Menu," the information is stored in the key

**\HKEY_CURRENT_USER\Software\Microsoft\Windows
   \CurrentVersion\Explorer\Shell Folders**

(that's all one long path!) with the value pair

StartMenu=C:\windows\Barry's Menu.

 It takes some getting used to, but once you pick it up it's not as bad as those huge key names look. Besides, the first time you reel off something like the just-mentioned key name, the jaws of the people you are talking to will drop and they'll think, "My, wotta guru."

 Explorer is smart about renaming the core folders. If you rename Start Menu in Explorer, the Registry is automatically adjusted. This may not be true in third-party tools and is not true if you do the renaming at a DOS prompt.

Plug 'n' Whatever

 Now the truth can be told about where Plug 'n' Play came from. One day big Bill was driving along in one of his souped-up sports cars, happy as a clam. But when he looked in the mirror—whoops, there was a smoky. Yet another ticket to be shoved in the glove compartment for Bill Neukom[†] to take care of. Being the world's richest human being means not having to worry what a ticket will do to your insurance rates, but still big Bill was steamed, so he turned on the radio to relax. Then he heard it—an Apple ad called "Readings from the Microsoft® Windows™ Manual" poking fun at the complications of dealing with comm ports under Windows. Bill stormed onto the corporate campus and let the Windows team have it. Why couldn't a PC be as easy to configure as a Mac? The result was Plug 'n' Play.

In 1981, when IBM released the first PCs, configuration of add-ons wasn't hard. First, there weren't many boards you could add to the computer, and those you could came from IBM, who could arrange for them to have no conflicts. The computers weren't very smart—they were several hundred times slower than current PCs—and IBM could assume that most users understood technical stuff about IRQs and DMAs or else would like nothing better than to learn.

But as time went on, add-on hell sprang up. An explosion of wonderful add-on boards occurred and conflicts arose. Yet users were forced to use 1981 technology because the industry couldn't get its act together. You'd set some dip switches on the board, turn on your computer, and hope things worked—it was Plug 'n' Pray.

 Intel and Microsoft decided to put their considerable combined weight behind a specification that has been embraced by the industry and which finally reached fruition with Windows 95. This spec is called **Plug 'n' Play**.

The idea is simplicity itself. Plug 'n' Play hardware can be configured by the operating system. When you put a new board in the system, it doesn't grab any system resources, but during bootup, when Windows 98 asks if anyone new is here, the board says, "Me, oh, me. Could you set me up to work with the rest of the stuff?" Windows 98 then figures out what settings to use for the board, if need be adjusting the settings of other Plug 'n' Play peripherals to prevent conflicts. It finds out what kind of peripheral it is, and, if it has drivers for that peripheral, it automatically installs them.

---

† Bill Neukom is Microsoft's general counsel. He started with the company when, as a junior partner in a prestigious Seattle law firm, his boss told him that his son had just moved his company from Albuquerque to Seattle, and could Neukom keep an eye on their legal affairs? Neukom may not handle Bill's tickets, but Bill does have a reputation for getting them. Mr. Neukom has been rather busy of late with Bill's, er, other speeding tickets.

That's the theory. I've no doubt that within the next few years that's the way virtually everything will work. For now, it often does but not always because of two issues. First, users still have what is called **legacy hardware**, that is, boards and peripherals that are not Plug 'n' Play. Windows 95 provides some help for installing such hardware, as I'll describe in Chapter 8, but it's not transparent. Second, Plug 'n' Play needs a bit of a shakedown cruise, especially for somewhat unconventional hardware.

I like to think of Plug 'n' Play as the little girl with the little curl in the middle of her forehead of the Windows world. When it works, it works flawlessly, but when it doesn't, it is horrid; if Windows fouls up, you often can't override what it insists on doing.

One confusion often occurs. Users assume that if their computer doesn't have a Plug 'n' Play BIOS, then Plug 'n' Play boards won't work. That's not true for most kinds of plugins and certainly not for CDs and sound, the two biggest headaches for most users.

Crash 'em, Bash 'em

A car crash harnesses elements of eroticism, aggression, desire, speed, drama, kinesthetic factors, the stylizing of motion, consumer goods, status—all these in one event. I myself see the car crash as a tremendous sexual event, really: a liberation of human and machine libido (if there is such a thing).

—J. G. BALLARD, interview in *Penthouse*

I wonder what Ballard would think about a crash of Windows?

Anyone who tells you that the program they've just shipped has no bugs in it is either a liar or a fool. Anyone who tells you that the program they've just shipped has no *known* bugs in it is either a liar or an incompetent. Any modern program is so complex that it is bound to have some kind of glitches, hopefully small. Indeed, vendors of complex programs keep lists of bugs found during the beta test, and invariably some wind up on the list of bugs that won't get fixed before this version is shipped. Since fixing one set of bugs can introduce a new set, if a vendor waited until the product was known to be bug-free, the product would never ship.

Some fraction of program bugs will result in the program doing something that causes the operating system to close the program down, lock, stock, and barrel. Up pops a message that says "This program has performed an illegal operation and will be shut down." If you hit the Details>> button, you get the view seen in Figure 2-27.

The most common problem is that a program will try to access memory owned by another program. Essentially, Mother Windows then says: "Naughty,

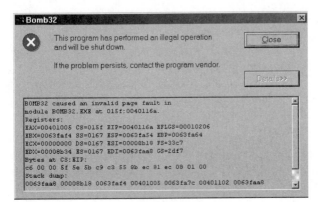

Figure 2-27. It's not my fault

naughty. That's Johnny's. Put it down and go to your room." The error is not so much that the program is making a power play for someone else's memory but that it passes Windows an address to send data to and the address is wrong. These kinds of errors are called **protection violation errors**. If the address points to nowhere, the error is called an **invalid page fault**.

In Windows 3.x, if some program crashed, the best plan of attack was to save your work and reboot. In Windows 98, unless it is Explorer that has crashed, you can probably safely continue working without rebooting. If you get a Windows error message with a Details tab and you plan on contacting the vendor, be sure to click the Details>> button and save the information shown. You can select it with a mouse and hit **Ctrl+C** to copy it to the clipboard, open Notepad and paste it in, and save it to a file. Saving the information could help the vendor out a lot.

 If some program crashes more than once, you'll want to be sure the Dr. Watson utility is loaded because it saves much more information for you to forward to tech support. I discuss Dr. Watson in Chapter 4.

 I always reboot whenever I get an IllOp...,er, Illegal Operation. I'm still superstitious, and rebooting is such a small price to pay. Besides, I've seen applications crash with an IllOp, then, when restarted, crash with a similar IllOp, and so on—as if something got stuck and won't shake loose until I reboot. And while we're on the subject of IllOps, why in blue blazes didn't Microsoft include a Copy or Print button along with Details? I always need to copy or print the information, just so I can yell at the manufacturer.

 You are overly cautious, Woody. My practice is to save all files in other applications that are running and reload the problem program—if it has a problem reloading, then I do the reboot. Otherwise I continue, happy as a clam.

The other common crash is when the hourglass pops up and won't go away or the program just beeps if you click something. After being sure you haven't missed some message from the program telling you what to do, you can hit **Ctrl+Alt+Del** and wrap the sucker in concrete galoshes and drop it in the deep blue sea.

 Various third-party programs can sometimes help you recover from a crash without closing the offending program so you can save your work. The best-known ones are included with Cybermedia's First Aid, Helix's Nuts & Bolts and Symantec's Norton Utilities.

■ And Dots Not All

I could never make out what those damned dots meant.

—WINSTON CHURCHILL (speaking of decimal points)

Well, Blast My Raster

Beware of Geeks bearing gifs.

—Heard on the Net

Run your finger over a piece of glass. GET YOUR FINGER AWAY FROM THAT MONITOR!!! It's a little-known fact that computer monitor screens are treated with special chemicals that draw the grease out of your fingertips. Some advanced models have the ability to draw it out from across the room. So run your finger over a window. NO, NOT THAT KIND OF WINDOW!

Is the piece of glass a smooth surface or is it a bunch of tiny beadlike atoms spread out in two dimensions? It's "really" a set of atoms, but it's useful to think of it both ways. If you want to understand the sound made when you hit a glass with a spoon, the smooth surface model may be better, but to understand how the kind of sand used to make the glass affects its strength, the atomic model may be better.

In the same way, what you see on a screen or what is printed out on a piece of paper is really a bunch of dots. And the computer or printer thinks of it that way. Before the display on your screen reaches the monitor it is put into the language of **pixels**; the color of each and every dot on your screen needs to be specified. (*Pixel* is short for "picture element.") In $1,024 \times 768$ mode, there are 786,432 pixels on the screen. With that kind of job to do, it's no wonder Windows can be slow! Similarly, when printing graphics on a 300-dpi laser printer on 11-by-8.5-inch paper, the computer needs to send 8,415,000 dots per page to the printer!

With those kinds of numbers involved, it is often better to think on an abstract level in terms of lines and suitable curves. Windows accelerated display cards work on that principle; in detail,

This is the line that Windows wants to draw.

This is the driver that was passed the line that Windows wants to draw.

This is the accelerator chip that understands lines that got one from the driver that was passed the line that Windows wants to draw.

This is the adapter RAM where bits were placed by the accelerator chip that understands lines that got one from the driver that was passed the line that Windows wants to draw.

This is the monitor that turns on the pixels sent to it by the adapter RAM where bits were placed by the accelerator chip that understands lines that got one from the driver that was passed the line that Windows wants to draw.

All without your CPU worrying its pretty head.

Similarly, if a file can describe a graphic in terms of lines and other objects—say solid rectangles, text, and so on—it can be a lot smaller than if it has to describe every color. Twenty-four bit color is called that because it takes 3 bytes (24 bits) to describe the color of each pixel. So a 24-bit color, 1,024 × 768 file-describing bits, would require 2,359,296 bytes (1024 × 768 × 3)—that's over 2 megabytes on disk!

Alas, lines and shapes do have their limits. If you have a solid blue large rectangular shape, you can hope to use a description in terms of lines, but if you have a photo of the sky, the subtle variations in the shade of blue can't be captured in terms of higher-order graphics but only via "This here dot is royal blue, that one over there is kinda cyan. . . ."

So both descriptions via dots and descriptions with graphics objects have their place. If you ever want to manipulate either, you'd better know which is which, so you have to learn some names and file types.

 Files that describe graphics in terms of dots (or pixels) are called bit–mapped files, bitmapped files or just plain **bitmaps**. They are also called **raster based**. Windows has a native bitmapped file format distinguished by the file extension **bmp**. Wallpaper has to be a ***.bmp** file, and Windows ships with a whole bunch of them that it probably installed on your disk. Other bitmapped formats are PC Paintbrush (***.pcx**), TIFF (Tagged Image File Format—***.tif**), CompuServe's Graphics Image Format (***.gif**), and the Joint Photographic Expert Group compressed file format (JPEG— ***.jpg**).

 *.gif and ***.jpg** are the Web standards, so much so that Internet Explorer is a viewer for both kinds of files. Windows assigns these file types to IE, so clicking on one of them will open the file in IE itself.

Programs that manipulate bitmaps are sometimes called **paint** programs, although the higher-class name is **image editor**. Occasionally, the paint name is for programs that focus on creating bitmaps (Fractal Painter is the best example) and the image editor for programs that focus more on editing a photo you've gotten (by purchase or scanning). MOM's favorite bitmap editor is Picture Publisher, and the standard for the photographic professional is Adobe Photoshop. Windows itself comes with Paint and Imaging, which are both bitmap manipulation programs. Each of the high-end paint programs has its own internal file format, adding to the oversupply of formats in this area.

 The popularity of digital cameras has produced a plethora of under-$100 popular photo editors, of which the best known is Adobe Photo Deluxe.

Files that describe graphics in terms of higher-order objects are called **vector graphics** or **object graphics**. Different formats support different kinds of objects, but almost all support lines, some kinds of curves, and text. Many allow a special kind of complicated curve called a Bezier. Alas, there isn't really anything like a common standard in vector graphics. The closest things are the Windows built-in format called Windows Metafile (***.wmf**) and Encapsulated PostScript (***.eps**).

The WMF format that was used in Windows 3.1 had limitations, such as no support for Bezier curves and limited ability to embed bitmaps. Windows 9X has an Enhanced Metafile Format (***.emf**) that removes these limitations and is likely, over time, to become the standard for vector graphics.

 Ha! Dream on. Vendors like to think they are adding something with their own formats—like trapped customers. There will never be an overwhelming standard in graphics files. If there were, Windows BMP files would have replaced TIFF and PCX and they haven't.

EPS is intended for use with PostScript printers only, and displaying an EPS in native format requires a full-scale PostScript interpreter built into the program. However, most EPS files include a TIFF bitmap implementation, and programs can read and display those on screen. They can then send the real PostScript code on to a PostScript printer even if the program itself doesn't understand PostScript. There is a subset of EPS used by Adobe Illustrator (AI), and some programs that can't deal with arbitrary EPS can deal with AI files.

A third common format is a holdover from DOS called Computer Graphics Metafile (***.cgm**), and because Word Perfect had so many users, its Word Perfect Graphics (***.wpg**) files is a fourth common format.

Programs that manipulate vector graphics are called **draw programs**, **drawing programs**, or **illustration programs**. The leading products are Adobe Illustrator, Corel Draw, and Micrografx Designer. A draw program with less power but a unique, especially easy to use interface is Visio. Its idea is to provide you a large library of building blocks out of which to make your drawings.

In addition to solid colors, many vector formats allow **gradient fills**—a smooth interpolation of colors in a region of the drawing.

For special effects, most vector formats allow a bitmap to be an object as part of their graphic. And several recently released bitmap edit programs (Adobe Photoshop and Picture Publisher, for example) allow an object layer in their files, so that, for instance, they can leave text as separate letters rather than embedding it as a bunch of pixels.

Many of the high-end bitmap and vector graphics editors have their own file formats, making the area confusing. Even worse, many programs that use **.tif** or **.cgm** files support only some of the files that have that designation.

Generally, photographs that you get from third parties and items that you scan are bitmaps. Most high-end clip art is vector. You should want your clip art to be vector because it scales to different sizes (as I'll discuss in the next section) and prints on different printers with no loss of quality. If you upgrade from a 300-dpi (dpi = dots per inch) printer to a 600-dpi printer, your vector clip art will automatically use the higher resolution while bitmaps will effectively print out no better.

So if you get an offer for a wonderful CD with oodles of clip art, find out if it is vector or raster and don't bother to get it if it is raster.

Besides the two basic graphics file families, multimedia has introduced its own graphics types. Most notable are the two main video types: Microsoft audio-visual interleave (`*.avi`) and Apple's Quicktime Movie (`*.mov`). There are also animation files (where the standard is Autodesk Animator—`*.flc`), sound (which I discuss later), and 3D graphics.

The Web has multiplied this further with Real Audio (`*.ra`) and Real Video file formats.

The Scales of Just Us

Vector graphics have a special advantage because they are scaleable. Consider a cap A. In a font like Arial, it consists of three straight lines—two forming a tent and one a crossbar. TrueType stores it as a vector graphic. Of course, when you type an A, it has to be shown on the screen as bits, so the TrueType engine makes the translation. The process of changing from vector to raster is called **rasterization**. Figure 2-28 (a) shows a blowup of a boldface 10-point Arial capital A on a pixel-sized grid to see the rasterization. Suppose we blindly blow it up to double size. Thus every black pixel becomes a 2 × 2 grid of pixels, and you get the blown-up A in Figure 2-28 (b). In (c), you see a blowup of the True-Type rasterized Arial 20-point bold cap A. Notice that the straight blowup is blocky and ugly compared to the A made directly from the vector rasterized at the higher size. The blockiness is even evident in (d), where the letters are shown (in the same orientation) without the blowup.

Actually, this example involves more than just rasterization of lines—in the 20-point A, the rather delicate (and effective) single-pixel black rows at the bottom and single white row just above the cross bar are a consequence of hinting. We'll see what that means in the section "Could You Gimme a Hint?"

The moral of this is that vector graphics are scaleable. Bitmaps are not. If you scan in line art and want to blow it up, try to convert it to a vector graphic, blow that up, and convert back (I'll talk about conversion in a bit).

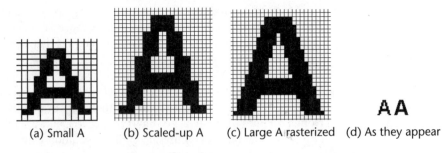

| (a) Small A | (b) Scaled-up A | (c) Large A rasterized | (d) As they appear |

Figure 2-28. A, A, who's got the A?

That's a Cockroach of a Different Color

Another wrinkle in rasterization concerns the use of colors, a process known as **antialiasing**. Allow me to explain.

If you were computing in the ancient days when VGAs were first introduced, you may recall that they had two "spectacular" new graphics modes. (The modern equivalent of telling your kid about trudging through the snow to school may be recalling the CGA—"Gee, I remember when graphics modes had only four colors." "Was that before or after the end of the Civil War, Dad?" But I digress.) There was 640×400 in 16 colors and 320×200 in 256 colors. The remarkable thing was that the lower-resolution but higher-color mode looked more lifelike and actually seemed to be higher resolution than the 16-color mode.

This is an example of the phenomenon that, as far as perception is concerned, you can often trade color depth for resolution. This can place a monitor that is low resolution ($1,024 \times 768$ on a 15-inch monitor works out to about 85 dpi) but has lots of colors on a closer footing with the latest popular laser printers that are high resolution (1,200 dpi) but have only two colors (black and white!).

In one direction, consider how a laser printer handles gray-scale printing. The printer has no gray ink. It mimics gray by putting down black dots in differing densities. A light gray will print as a few dots on the white background while darker shades have more dots for the same area. If the resolution is high enough, you don't see the dots but perceive shades of gray. What is effectively a "gray dot" is a mix of several black dots and white space so there is less resolution when printing grays. The printer has traded resolution for extra colors.

 Current HP printers use variable-size dots as well to help mimic gray scales, a procedure they called RET— resolution enhancement technology—but the idea is the same.

The precise way grays are translated depends on an algorithm that has to be carefully chosen to avoid banding and other artifacts. Usually your applications and the printer handle this for you, but if you read or hear about halftone frequency and angle, or error diffusion, someone is talking about this gray-to-dot-pattern translation.

On screen, when translating from a vector object like a line at some angle to dots, the problem is that rasterization occurs in block-size units—the ideal rasterization might be to take only a third of some block, but pixels don't come in thirds. Or do they? When the object suggests that one take only a third of pixel, why not use a shade of light gray, roughly one third of the way from white to black? That's what antialiasing does.

To illustrate this, we looked at a 20-point Arial cap A as entered in the paint program PhotoMagic with and without antialiasing, an option it supports. On the extreme right of Figure 2-29, you see the two As normal size with the antialiased

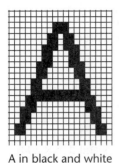
A in black and white

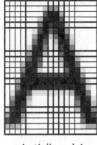
Antialiased A

A A

Figure 2-29. What was the name of that masked A?

version on the right. If you look closely, you'll see that the normal A has a more noticeable staircase effect. The anti-aliased letter is smoother, although a little fuzzy. The other two parts of the figure show blowups of the two letters. There are several different gray-scale levels used to produce the effect.

So what does antialiasing mean for you? One option is that you can turn on antialiased screen fonts as long as you are running with at least 256 colors. To check whether it has been turned on and turn it on if it hasn't been, go to the Display Properties sheet (right click on the Desktop and pick Properties or run the Display applet in Control Panel), go to the Effects tab, and check the box labeled "Smooth edges of screen fonts."

 Call me an aesthetic yahoo if you want—I know antialiased screen fonts are supposed to be the bees' knees, but they make the letters look so fuzzy to me I keep thinking I've got to get my eyeglass prescription changed. So I experimented but then turned the checkbox off. But you should at least try it.

In addition, some bitmap editing programs give you antialiased fonts and curves as an option. If you plan to print out a bitmap, if there is any way to keep the font as a vector object (for example, in programs with a vector layer), that is preferable. Rather than turn on gray scale and then have the printer turn those gray areas to thinned-out black areas, it is better to have the rasterization done at the higher resolution by the printer. If you are sending a presentation out to a service bureau to make slides, the same considerations are true—try to keep anything that can be a vector object as one. But if your goal is to display fonts in an on-screen presentation, it will pay to use antialiasing if it is an option when you prepare the final screens.

Ain't Just Missionaries That Do Conversions

Domini, domini, domini
You're all converted now

—Firesign Theater

Graphics files are a Tower of Babel. Not only are there bitmaps and vector graphics, but there are oodles of formats for each. You really need a method to transfer between one format and another, a translation utility.

You have to realize that there are four kinds of translations and each faces a different set of problems:

- **Raster to raster**   This is the most straightforward. The different formats have different headers (the start of bitmapped files contains information like the dimensions and color depth; it is called a header because it comes at the start of the file) and use different compression schemes (some formats use data compression schemes that allow you to take less space without losing any information), but basically they list each and every pixel color, one after the other. So translation is relatively straightforward. If you have a decent bitmap editor, you can usually convert between formats by loading in one and saving in another without the need for a special utility. Most of the time you'll want to keep your files in **pcx** or **tif** format, which are accepted by virtually any program that supports bitmaps at all.

- **Vector to raster**   This is the second-easiest conversion—it is what we called rasterization and has all the issues of antialiasing. Still, you can expect a decent conversion program (like Quarterdesk's Hijaak) to handle this conversion without surprises.

- **Vector to vector**   This is tricky and fraught with peril. The biggest problem is that different formats support different objects. If a program tries to translate from a format that understands Bezier curves to one that doesn't, the best it can do is use a polyline—something that looks like a curve but is really a bunch of short lines strung together. So the file swells in size and complexity. Avoid such conversions if you possibly can.

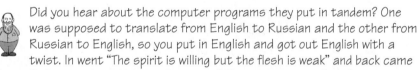

Did you hear about the computer programs they put in tandem? One was supposed to translate from English to Russian and the other from Russian to English, so you put in English and got out English with a twist. In went "The spirit is willing but the flesh is weak" and back came "The vodka's great but the meat is rotten." If you try to translate from **cgm** to **wmf** and back, you should expect similar results—at best.

- **Raster to vector**   This is really an art rather than a conversion! It used to be available only in special programs called autotrace programs. Now such capability is available with drawing packages and with Hijaak. If you have a complicated bitmap with subtle colors, successful autotracing is close to impossible. If you want to scan in line art or a logo in a fancy font and blow it up, you can hope to use autotrace successfully, but be prepared to do some correcting of the trace by hand in a drawing program—most likely, the trace will put too many nodes on a polyline and you'll want to smooth it out.

To be clear about blowing up a line art logo you have on paper, you

- Scan in the line art. This will produce a TIFF file in bitmapped format. If you can set the scanner for line art or two colors rather than gray scale, do so.

- Run the bitmap through an autotrace program. This will change the file to some vector format, for example, **ai** (a variant of **eps**) in Adobe Illustrator.

- Look at the vector file in a draw program that uses that file as its native format—presumably you'd use Illustrator, Designer, or Corel Draw. See if you need to clean it up.

- Ideally, you'll use the logo in a program that understands your vector format so that blowing up is as simple as setting dimensions in a dialog or dragging on some handles. If you really need a bitmap, blow up the vector image in a draw program and use a conversion program for vector to bitmap. Your draw program may allow you to save as a bitmap, or you may need to use a program like Hijaak.

■ Putting Up a Good Font

As soon as he learned that I was writing a Windows book, Billy, who has been taking font lessons, started bugging me to be sure that when I talked about fonts, he could get a chance to tell you about 'em. So, here's Billy.

 To explain fonts to folks, you print out samples of the good fonts and the bad fonts. Then you hold the page of good fonts up to the light and twirl it. You give a knowing look and remark, "1984 was an exquisite year for Caslons." Then you bring the page of good fonts carefully up to your nose and say, "Quelle arôme, quel bouquet."

Whoops; it appears that Billy mixed up the wine lessons he's been getting with the font lessons. That's the point. You've probably learned to ignore the wine snobs. That doesn't mean you have to drink rotgut. You can enjoy a good wine and learn some basics, like when to serve a white wine without becoming a wine snob yourself and without paying any real attention to the wine snobs.

But the same folks who don't let the wine snobs and the hi-fi snobs faze 'em turn to Jell-O in the face of font snobs. Funny thing is that while we know a few sensible font experts, most font snobs are pompous fools. If you don't believe me, just ask the other font snobs. So *illigitimus non carborundum.*[†]

Both to cope with the font snobs and to understand the simple dos and don'ts, you need to learn some of the basic language, so, forthwith, I present the basics, a kind of first course in fonts, and then an intermediate course the section after. If you want to know more, say, enough to know what it means when you tell a font snob to go kern himself, you'll want the advanced course in the section after that. Then I give you some practical advice on using fonts, and I talk about font technology in Windows 98. Even if you skip the rest because you decide you don't want to know about the theory of fonts, be sure to read the sections "Font Tools in Windows 98" and "Installing and Removing Fonts in Windows 98."

In understanding the language of fonts, you need to remember that you are dealing with an art that goes back over 500 years, so the terms reflect the technology of 100 years ago more than the changes of the past 15, revolutionary though they may be. Most of all, they deal with movable metal type.

[†] Don't let the bast—er, illegitimate ones get you down.

The terminology enters in places you may not realize. A printer set type by grabbing the letters from two boxes, each with compartments for the individual letters. The boxes were typically laid out one over the other. The capital letters were in the box on top because they were used less often and the other letters on the bottom. These boxes were called cases, the upper case and the lower case. I kid you not.

Fonts 101

Here are the basic terms. The first thing you have to realize is that what you think is a font, you know, something like Arial or Times or Courier, isn't a font (nor is it a parallel universe). It's a type family. A **font** is a set of letterforms (fancy name for shapes of letters) at a given size, weight, style, and type family. The **type family** is the family of similar-looking fonts. **Size** is a measure of the vertical height of the font (normally the width scales as the height does, so an 11-point font is not only 10% taller than a 10-point font but also 10% wider). **Weight** refers to a measure of how heavy the strokes in the font are—the most common weights are **normal** and **bold**, but some families have an **extra bold** or a **light** at the heavier and lighter ends of the spectrum. **Style** is an expression of orientation—the most common styles are **roman** and **italic**.

Fonts are also called **typefaces** and, as the irreducible typographical unit, go back to those cases of type that contained letters from a single font. A set of fonts where all that is varied is the size should have a convenient simple name, given current practice in computer typesetting, but there doesn't seem to be one. I'll call it a **scaleable typeface**.

 While font purists use font in this way, common usage these days is to talk about the Arial "font" when you really mean the Arial "type family."

You can also have fonts with the same type family name and weight that are distinguished by how wide the letters are. If the font is made less wide for a given height, it is called **condensed** or **narrow**. If it is made wider, it is called **expanded**; expanded faces are rare. Condensed fonts are useful in situations where you want to squeeze a lot of text into a headline.

Here are typical examples in the Arial family:

Normal:	ABCDEFGHIJKLMnopqrstuvwxyz
Bold:	**ABCDEFGHIJKLMnopqrstuvwxyz**
Extra bold:	**ABCDEFGHIJKLMnopqrstuvwxyz**
Black (extra, extra bold!):	**ABCDEFGHIJKLMnopqrstuvwxyz**
Extra Bold Condensed:	**ABCDEFGHIJKLMnopqrstuvwxyz**
Narrow:	ABCDEFGHIJKLMnopqrstuvwxyz
Italic:	*ABCDEFGHIJKLMnopqrstuvwxyz*
Bold italic:	***ABCDEFGHIJKLMnopqrstuvwxyz***

Bear in mind that a well-made italic is not merely the font with a slant added nor is a condensed font made by blindly scaling the widths—there are subtle design changes that a skillful type designer makes when italicizing or condensing. Of course, if the font is a schlock font made by scanning and autotracing, it is likely that the italic is made by simple slanting the outlines. In this case the font should be called oblique rather than italic.

Interestingly enough, while a good font design is a work of art, fonts cannot be copyrighted in the United States or directly protected. Some bozo in the copyright office decided years ago that after all, the alphabet is the alphabet so what's to copyright. That doesn't mean that you can buy a font pack and give all the files on it to all your friends. Those files are computer programs and as such *are* protected. What it does mean is that if you are a font producer, you can try to make a perfect copy of a fancy new font you see; you can even print out that font, scan it in, autotrace it, and sell it as your own. However, font names can be trademarked, so you have the phenomenon that the same basic design can be produced under many names. Helvetica, for example, is called Aristocrat, Claro, Corvus, Europa Grotesk, Geneva, Hamilton, Helios, Holsatia, Megaron, Newton, Spectra, Swiss, Vega, and Video Spectra among other names.

 Heehee, Europa Grotesk! I like that. I'll have to remember that name when I next have a run-in with the Swiss gendarmes.

Monotype's Arial is not a copy of Helvetica, as some might think, but a separate font, although it has some similar characteristics and was designed to have identical widths to the Adobe Helvetica font. But enough of culture! Let's return to our list of font terminology.

How are sizes measured? Fonts define a number of horizontal lines, all shown in Figure 2-30. The letters cap E and lower-case x are especially regular. The line at their bottoms that also lies at the bottom of most letters is called the **baseline**. An imaginary line at the top of the cap E is called the **cap height**. Most caps go up to the same line but some, like cap S, often extend slightly above. The height of the letter x, called the **x-height**—another one of those obscure technical terms—is the typical height of many lower-case letters but won't really concern us. Any lower-case letter that extends above the x-height is said to have an **ascender**. Typical examples are the letters t, h, and f (note that the t does not extend above the cap height but is still considered to have an ascender). Lower-case letters that fall below the baseline are said to have a **descender**. Typical letters are g, j, and y.

Figure 2-30. Definition of point size for a font

The point size of metal type was easy to define; it was the height of the slug of metal that the letter was cast on. The type designer would include an extra space below the lowest descender to avoid a too cramped look. If even more space was desired between lines, a strip of lead was inserted, and the practice was called leading.

So **point size** is the distance between baselines of two successive lines of text. It is the distance from the top of the highest ascender and the bottom of the longest descender plus the default spacing that the designer wants.

The space taken by a line of type on a page is not determined only by the point size because the blank space between the bottom of the descenders of one row and the top of the ascenders of the next can be adjusted. This is called **leading**, after the lead that printers once used to change that space. The term is pronounced to rhyme with "bedding," not with "seeding." With computer type, unlike the metal version, one can even have negative leading! A 10-point font with an extra 1 point of leading between lines is called a 10-point font with an 11-point spacing or just "10 on 11."

As the name point size suggests, the height is usually measured in a unit called **points**. A point was once about $\frac{1}{72}$ inch, but since the United States is the hand that rocks the computer cradle, it is now considered to be exactly $\frac{1}{72}$ inch. The rest of the world may be metric, but we continue to impose our weird measurements on them. So an 8-point font is $\frac{1}{9}$ of an inch and an 11-point font with 12-point spacing fits 6 lines to the inch.

 Having told you that a font isn't a font but is a scaleable typeface, I'll misuse the terms and talk about fonts unless there is an especial need for clarity. What do vendors do? Why, of course, they use the terms in a way that will let them blazon the largest number of "fonts" in their packages. When fonts were sold in bitmapped form so that size mattered, a vendor could sell you two type families in the standard 4 weights/styles (normal, bold, italic, and bold italic) and in 7 point sizes (say 6, 8, 10, 11, 12, 14, 18) and yell about selling you 56 fonts ($2 \times 4 \times 7$).

Now that most fonts are outlines, vendors don't get to multiply by the number of font sizes, but you can bet they still count different weights/styles as separate fonts. So, for example, the Monotype Value Pack says it provides 57 typefaces. In fact the pack contains 7 type families in the standard 4 weights/styles, 21 display/symbol/script-type families in 25 combinations, four Arial fonts, and one Times New Roman at weights that supplement the ones in Windows. I'm not sure how they count 57, since by their rules I count 58, but it's only a 2% error and no doubt it makes Heinz happy, so why complain? However, by what a naive user would think fonts means, this package has 30.

Monotype isn't to be singled out. Every vendor counts the way they do and every naive user misunderstands! In the naive terms, it is not atypical for a package that claims N fonts to have N/2 or N/2.5 type families. Indeed the celebrated 35 PostScript fonts are actually 8 families of the standard four weights/styles and three specialized fonts for a total of only 11 type families.

Type families are often grouped together in various ways. The simplest is fixed pitch vs. proportional spacing. **Fixed-pitch**, aka **monospace**, fonts have a common width for all letters; M takes the same space as i. **Proportional fonts** have variable letter widths within the single font. Here is a comparison of Courier, a fixed-pitch font, vs. Arial, a proportional one:

Courier:	MMMMMMMMMM	Arial:	MMMMMMMMMM
	iiiiiiiiii		iiiiiiiiii
	1234567890		1234567890
	1111144444		1111144444

To have numbers vertically line up in columns, all numbers have a common width in either fixed-pitch or proportional fonts.

Fonts 201

A more complex but useful style breakdown is into **serif, sans serif, script, display,** and **symbol**. The first two sets are the workhorses of typography—the ones you'd normally use for body text. A serif is the funny hook that some fonts have

Figure 2-31.
Serif vs. sans serif

at their edges. Look at the four letters shown in Figure 2-31. The letters on the left are in a sans serif font (Arial) and the ones on the right are in a serif font (Times New Roman). Serif fonts are more common and include Century Schoolbook, Garamond, Palatino, and Times. Sans serif fonts include Avant Garde, Futura, and Helvetica.

Script fonts are ones you might use for invitations, like *Shelley Allegro*, *Shelley Andante*, and *Shelley Volante*. Display fonts are usually used for specific purposes, mainly in headlines or letterheads. Among the more famous ones are **Cooper Black** and **Bodoni**. Symbol fonts include foreign alphabets—notably Greek ($\alpha\beta\gamma\delta\epsilon\kappa\lambda\mu\nu\pi$)—math symbols ($\int, \otimes, \Sigma, \notin$), and dingbats, those little pieces of fluff that make bulleted lists less dull (☎, ▱, ➔, ✎, ☺).

It turns out that making dingbat fonts is fraught with peril! If you take the letters NYC, highlight them and change the font to Wingdings, you get

☠   ✡   ☝

A New York-based consultant discovered this shortly after Windows 3.1 shipped and the *New York Post* blazoned on its front page

Software Company Vows Death to New York Jews

I kid you not—it really happened. Ain't technology grand?

 If you're really into Microsoft conspiracy theories, there's a better one. The story about the Wingdings was short-lived because the Los Angeles riots broke out the next day and moved the story off the front page even in the *Post*.

It's an interesting sidelight to the story that six high-ranking Microsoft executives met the next day to decide how to react to the story. Of the six, four were Jewish, including the managers of the font and Windows units.

 Personally, I think what the message really means is "If you take poison, see a Jewish doctor and you'll feel better." It's also interesting that they didn't complain about Mr. Zapf. In *his* dingbats, $A4 becomes ✂ ✡ ✔. Surely, the *Post* could have made something of that.

Fonts 378

Herewith, a primer of some of the more esoteric font terminology.

- **Tracking**   Letter spacing in a font as a whole or in a chunk of text as a whole. Useful only for special situations. Here's an example that should make it clear.

How big did you say that fish was? It was a real WOPR, sir.	How big did you say that fish was? It was a real WOPR, sir.	How big did you say that fish was? It was a real WOPR, sir.
Default tracking	Tracked (too) tight	Tracked (too) loose

- **Kerning**   Spacing between pairs of letters. Without kerning each letter has a fixed width—different width for different letters but, in the absence of kerning, all occurrences of one letter have the same width as all other occurrences; the space next to a **T** is the same for **Th** as for **To**. But there is room to slightly tuck the o under the T, an attractive possibility at larger point sizes. Look at the three examples below: the one where the o is nudged under the T is more attractive. High-class fonts come with kerning information—tables to tell programs how to kern if the user wants the program to kern automatically. For headlines at large point sizes, you may want to kern manually.

To	To	T o
No kerning	Kerned condensed	Kerned expanded

- **Hanging indent**   Name given to a paragraph where the first line starts to the left of the rest of the paragraph, like the example below:

  This text has a hanging indent. You'll notice that the second and subsequent lines start indented. Hanging indents are most naturally used when discussing a list of items. The indentation makes it easy for the eye to see when a new item has begun. Often with such a list, the first line has a number or bullet or dingbat and the text on the lower lines are actually aligned at the left with line one. Typographers still regard this as a hanging indent, since they include the bullet in line one! The items in this bulleted list have a hanging indent.

- **Dropped caps** and **Raised caps**

This is a dropped cap, determined by making the initial letter large and dropping it down into the text. A few programs allow you to pick dropped caps from a menu, but usually you need to fool around with frames. Dropped caps should be arranged so that they base align on the baseline of a lower line of type. In Microsoft Word, you can get a drop cap by picking the Drop Cap... item from the Format menu.

This is a raised cap. It is made by picking a large point size for the initial letter. It isn't as effective as a drop cap.

- **Rules**   Typographical name for lines.

> The most famous rules are ones that are used for **pull quotes**, quotes from your text that you pull out and then make stand out by placing lines, I mean rules, above and below.

- **En** and **em**   Font-dependent measures of horizontal space. At one time, the em was the width of the letter M and the en was half an em. Now, an em is a horizontal space exactly equal to the point size and an en is half an em. Most important for referring to dashes of that width, specifically – and —.

- **Small caps**   If you want SMALL CAPS, you can try to use capital letters of a smaller point size, but the proportions aren't quite what a typographic purist would want. Some type families have special small caps fonts. These are available in a few PostScript fonts but not in TrueType.

- **Lower case or old-style numerals**   The numerals included with modern fonts are called **lining numerals** because they are fixed width and will line up under one another. For a spreadsheet, you want to use lining numerals, but they look funny if you are typing the time where 1:11 should have very different letter widths than 6:00. Quite a few TrueType fonts with old style numerals are available.

- **Justification**   Your word processor probably supports four varieties as shown below

Text that lines up at the left side of the page but not at the right side is often called **ragged right**, sometimes **left justified**.

Text that lines up at both sides is called **justified**. Your word processor adds extra spaces between words to arrange for the text to line up.

Text that lines up at the right side only is called **right justified**. It is useful only in special circumstances like entering the date in a letter.

Centered text also is useful only in special circumstances. Use it sparingly.

- **Widows** and **orphans**   Yeah, I know, you gave at the office. To adequately tell you about these terms, I need to talk about my poor friend Sylvia from Boston, who married John from London. One day, Sylvia's parents and John were in a terrible car accident and they were all killed. So Sylvia is a widow in England but an orphan in the United States. In the same way, at one point the short last line of a paragraph all on its own at the top of a page was called a widow in England and an orphan in the United States. Since then, an array of books on desktop publishing has so muddied the waters that it is not clear what exactly is a widow and what an orphan. The thing to avoid is either a single first line of a paragraph at the bottom of a page or a single last line of a paragraph at the top of a page. When you see either, flip a coin and then knowingly say, "Oh, my, an orphan" or "Oh, my, a widow" depending on whether the coin is heads or tails. Half the know-it-alls will think you right and the other half will think you wrong. "Widow" also refers to a single word or part of a word on the last line of a paragraph. Desktop publishers need to worry about this. You can safely ignore it for one-page correspondence or standard memos.

- **Ligatures**   Certain combinations of letters, namely, fi, fl, ffi, and ffl, should be spaced so close together that they really should be treated as a single character (and the i's dot is wrong if you just kern the letters). In some specialized fonts they are. These characters are called ligatures.

- **Panose numbers** are numbers assigned to fonts based on various characteristics; fonts with nearby Panose numbers are similar to each other. When you list fonts in Win98 by similarity, the ranking is derived from Panose numbers.

  Panose is so named because if you take the measurements of the upper-case P, A, N, O, S, and E from any roman font, you can derive a very high-fidelity measurement of the overall font's style. In other words, the P tells you the basic shape of the B and R since they (generally) share the same upper bowl. The N tells you the shape of the M, X, W, Y, Z, and V since they will have the same diagonal strokes in the center. E tells you what the F will look like, while O tells you the basic shape of the Q, C, G, D, and lower portion of the U. The system is designed to be mathematically repeatable, meaning that if you teach 100 monkeys how to measure a font using the PANOSE method and lock them in a room, they will all arrive at the same answer for the same font, unlike other font measurement methods that depend on the subjective "feel" from a group of "experts." It's sort of like wine tasting vs. using a mass spectrometer to determine differences between types of wine.

- The **standard 35 PostScript** fonts are the eleven font families that were included on the earliest printers that licensed PostScript from Adobe, most notably, Apple's LaserWriter. They are eight families of body fonts in the standard four weights and three symbol (or decorative) fonts. The accompanying table shows the PostScript names and the Monotype equivalents. These equivalents are not the same fonts or even fonts with the precise same shapes. For example, Arial and Helvetica are *not* the same font with different names. But the Monotype equivalents do use the same width tables, so you could replace them on a one-to-one basis.

PostScript Name	Number	Monotype Name
Courier	4	Courier New
Helvetica	4	Arial
Symbol	1	Symbol
Times Roman	4	Times New Roman
Avant Garde	4	Century Gothic
Bookman	4	Bookman Old Style
Helvetica Condensed	4	Arial Narrow
New Century Schoolbook	4	Century Schoolbook
Palatino	4	Book Antiqua
Zapf Chancery	1	Monotype Corsiva
Zapf Dingbats	1	Monotype Sorts

The thirteen fonts above the line are included with Windows. The twenty-two afterward are among those available in the Monotype Value Pack and in the Microsoft Font Pack.

 These extra fonts are also on the Office 97 CD. Some are in `D:\os\fonts` and others are in `D:\valupack\msfonts`.

Windows TrueType Fonts

Windows comes with 27 scaleable TrueType fonts:

- Arial in five weights/styles (the four standards and black)—a proportionally spaced sans serif font.
- `Courier New in four weights/styles`—a monospaced serif font.
- Times New Roman in four weights/styles—a proportionally spaced serif font.
- Symbol, including Greek—ΑΒΧΔΕΦΓΗΙϑΚαβχδεφγηιφκ—and math—≅∃⊥≡ℑ↑∞
- Wingdings, including ✌✍✊✏✐☞☺☹☻☂🗁🗎🗏🗐🗑📠🖐🔹🗆✒✂✈✌🖑🔔 ✉☎①
- Webdings, including 🏭🏨🏪🏦🏫🏬🏢📸✔♿☐♥🏠🏠🏠🏃
- **Comic Sans in two weights and Impact in one**

- `Lucida Console` for use in DOS Windows—a monospace sans serif font.
- Tahoma in two weights and Verdana in four—produced for Internet Explorer
- Marlett, of which I'll say more.

 Marlett was new with Windows 95. In Windows 95, it was hidden and didn't appear in the fonts folder, but Windows 98 has removed that mystery.

Marlett is a monospace font, and here are some of the characters (with the corresponding characters in Courier New below them):

_	⊟	□	×	?	▲	⁄⁄	⌐	˅
0	2	1	r	s	t	p	c	a

If you look at the buttons at the upper right of a Windows 98 window, you'll recognize the Marlett characters 02r or 01r on those buttons. The other characters are also used for system drawing. For example, look at the symbol associated with the letter p and at the lower right corner of an Explorer window.

While it seems to be documented nowhere, Marlett is clearly a system-level font.

 But Microsoft does supply you with a TrueType file with this font, so, for example, Woody and Barry could pass said font file on to their publisher for use on the Macs (gack!) on which the book is typeset. The file is marlett.ttf and it's in the fonts folder.

Good Writing Needs Character Development

Simplicity of character is no hindrance to subtlety of intellect.

—JOHN MORELY, *Life of Gladstone,* 1903

In addition to the physical characteristics of size, weight, and style, a font has a character set, the actual mapping of computer codes to symbols, not only letters like A or x but special symbols like ™ or ½. The initial starting point for PC character sets is the **ASCII code** (ASCII is short for American Standard Codes for Information Interchange), a 7-bit assignment of a specific symbol to each number from 0 to 127. It starts with 32 control characters (holdovers from the days of Teletypes) with codes 0 to 31. It is followed by 32 symbols starting with space at code 32, punctuation like !, ., and ,, and the ten numerals. At code 64 is the character @ followed by the 26 capital letters in alphabetical order and then five more symbols to round out the third set of 32. The final 32 starts with ` and then has the 26 lower-case letters, each exactly 32 codes beyond the corresponding caps. The basic ASCII set is rounded out by 5 final symbols (see Figure 2-32—the codes from 32 to 127).

**Figure 2-32.
ASCII codes in
decimal**

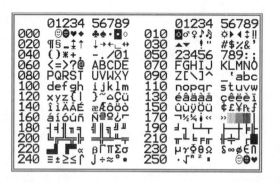

**Figure 2-32.
ASCII codes in
decimal**

**Figure 2-33.
ASCII codes in
hexadecimal**

When IBM introduced the PC, the architecture of the system CPU made it natural to use 8-bit characters, so IBM extended the ASCII set in two ways. It gave symbols to the codes below 32, strange ones like the playing card suits and the closest things to dingbats the original PC had. In the area above 128, it placed accented letters like ê or á, line-drawing characters to allow the placement of frames, and a pitifully small selection of Greek letters and mathematical symbols. In Figures 2-32 and 2-33 are two views of the IBM character set (also called extended ASCII).

In Figure 2-32 is a decimal-labeled table; cap A is in the 060 row and the 5 column, so its ASCII code is 65 decimal. In Figure 2-33 is a hexadecimal (base-16-labeled) table. Here A is in row 40 and column 1, so its code is 41H (= 65 decimal, of course).

These character sets are mainly of historical interest, although Windows 98 does supply (in the United States) several fonts that use the Extended IBM sets:

- For displaying data pasted from DOS sessions in the clipboard viewer, a bitmapped font with **oem** in its name,[†] for example, **8514oem.fon** at high screen resolutions.

- Bitmapped fonts for displaying DOS sessions in a window. For weird historical reasons, these are stored in five files: **dosapp.fon, ega40woa.fon, ega80woa.fon, cga40woa.fon, cga80woa.fon**. **woa** stands for "Windows old apps," in other words, DOS.

- A bitmapped font called Terminal for display of terminal mode in communication programs.

- Lucida Console fixed-pitch TrueType, used for DOS sessions.

For other Windows fonts, a different character set is normally used—it is called the Windows ANSI character set. ANSI is short for American National Standards Institute, and you'll see their name pop up all the time as you learn about

---

[†] OEM means "original equipment manufacturer," but it is really Microsoft-speak for IBM.

computers. Microsoft has modified the set and continues to make refinements as time goes on. In particular, some of the ASCII codes in the 140–160 range were not in Windows 3.0 but were added in Windows 3.1. A few of these “new” codes only codified what you could call black market codes—for example, codes for typographically proper “curly” quotation marks that the main desktop publishers had set up. The Windows ANSI set appears in Figure 2-34.

<table>
<tr><td> </td><td>!</td><td>"</td><td>#</td><td>$</td><td>%</td><td>&</td><td>'</td><td>(</td><td>)</td><td>*</td><td>+</td><td>,</td><td>-</td><td>.</td><td>/</td><td>0</td><td>1</td><td>2</td><td>3</td><td>4</td><td>5</td><td>6</td><td>7</td><td>8</td><td>9</td><td>:</td><td>;</td><td><</td><td>=</td><td>></td><td>?</td></tr>
<tr><td>@</td><td>A</td><td>B</td><td>C</td><td>D</td><td>E</td><td>F</td><td>G</td><td>H</td><td>I</td><td>J</td><td>K</td><td>L</td><td>M</td><td>N</td><td>O</td><td>P</td><td>Q</td><td>R</td><td>S</td><td>T</td><td>U</td><td>V</td><td>W</td><td>X</td><td>Y</td><td>Z</td><td>[</td><td>\</td><td>]</td><td>^</td><td>_</td></tr>
<tr><td>`</td><td>a</td><td>b</td><td>c</td><td>d</td><td>e</td><td>f</td><td>g</td><td>h</td><td>i</td><td>j</td><td>k</td><td>l</td><td>m</td><td>n</td><td>o</td><td>p</td><td>q</td><td>r</td><td>s</td><td>t</td><td>u</td><td>v</td><td>w</td><td>x</td><td>y</td><td>z</td><td>{</td><td>|</td><td>}</td><td>~</td><td>□</td></tr>
<tr><td>□</td><td>□</td><td>‚</td><td>ƒ</td><td>„</td><td>…</td><td>†</td><td>‡</td><td>ˆ</td><td>‰</td><td>Š</td><td>‹</td><td>Œ</td><td>□</td><td>□</td><td>□</td><td>□</td><td>‘</td><td>’</td><td>“</td><td>”</td><td>•</td><td>–</td><td>—</td><td>˜</td><td>™</td><td>š</td><td>›</td><td>œ</td><td>□</td><td>□</td><td>Ÿ</td></tr>
<tr><td> </td><td>¡</td><td>¢</td><td>£</td><td>¤</td><td>¥</td><td>¦</td><td>§</td><td>¨</td><td>©</td><td>ª</td><td>«</td><td>¬</td><td>-</td><td>®</td><td>¯</td><td>°</td><td>±</td><td>²</td><td>³</td><td>´</td><td>µ</td><td>¶</td><td>·</td><td>¸</td><td>¹</td><td>º</td><td>»</td><td>¼</td><td>½</td><td>¾</td><td>¿</td></tr>
<tr><td>À</td><td>Á</td><td>Â</td><td>Ã</td><td>Ä</td><td>Å</td><td>Æ</td><td>Ç</td><td>È</td><td>É</td><td>Ê</td><td>Ë</td><td>Ì</td><td>Í</td><td>Î</td><td>Ï</td><td>Ð</td><td>Ñ</td><td>Ò</td><td>Ó</td><td>Ô</td><td>Õ</td><td>Ö</td><td>×</td><td>Ø</td><td>Ù</td><td>Ú</td><td>Û</td><td>Ü</td><td>Ý</td><td>Þ</td><td>ß</td></tr>
<tr><td>à</td><td>á</td><td>â</td><td>ã</td><td>ä</td><td>å</td><td>æ</td><td>ç</td><td>è</td><td>é</td><td>ê</td><td>ë</td><td>ì</td><td>í</td><td>î</td><td>ï</td><td>ð</td><td>ñ</td><td>ò</td><td>ó</td><td>ô</td><td>õ</td><td>ö</td><td>÷</td><td>ø</td><td>ù</td><td>ú</td><td>û</td><td>ü</td><td>ý</td><td>þ</td><td>ÿ</td></tr>
</table>

Figure 2-34. Getting ANSI

It’s displayed with 32 characters in each row and starts with character 32, the space. Unassigned codes are shown with a box. The first three rows are the standard ASCII characters from code 32 to 126. The 0 in row one is at position 16, which is a useful marking point, so, for example, the box below the 0 in row 4 is at position 128+16 = 144 and the quotes are at 145–148.

You’ll occasionally need to know these character numbers so we selectively list the following ones.

Types of Characters	*Examples*	*Codes*
Typographical quotes	‘ ’ “ ”	145–148
En and em dash	– —	150, 151
Trademark, etc.	™ ® ©	153, 169, 174
Fractions	¼ ½ ¾	188–190
Currency	¢ £ ¥	162, 163, 165
Dots and daggers	• † ‡	134, 135, 149
Typographic symbols	§ ¶	167, 182
Accented letters	ä Ø ç ñ	192–256

How do you enter these funny ANSI characters? There are three ways.

- You can use the Windows applet Character Map, which I discuss in Chapter 4.
- You can enter a character with code 192 by making sure **`NumLock`** is on and then holding down the **`Alt`** key and hitting

  `0 1 9 2`

  on the numerical keypad.

- Word processors may have automated ways to enter them. For example, Winword automagically replaces " by " at the start of a word and by " at the end. And by default, (c) becomes © with similar replacements for ®. I'd recommend you consider going into Winword's autocorrect dialog and replace -- by —, an em dash. To make such specialized replacements in Winword, you'll need to know the codes at the time you set up (or use Character Map).

If Word replaces (c) by © and you want (c), just hit Ctrl-Z right away to undo the automatic replacement.

IBM (woops, OEM) and Windows ANSI aren't the whole story for the forward-looking Windows maven. Extended ASCII and Windows ANSI are one-byte character codes, which means only 256 codes. This is stretched already, but if one thinks of the ideographs of Japan and China, it is clearly too restricted. Unicode is a proposed two-byte scheme that allows 65,536 possible characters. It would be quite a bit of homework for you to learn them all, wouldn't it? The codes are described in two 600+-page volumes, the second devoted solely to East Asian ideographs. Volume One starts with ASCII and then includes the Greek, Cyrillic, Armenian, Hebrew, Arabic, Devanagari, Bengali, Gurmukhi, Gujarti, Oriya, Tamil, Telugu, Kannada, Malayalam, Thai, Lao, Tibetan, and Georgian alphabets, as well as assorted dingbats, math symbols, arrows, and currency symbols.

Microsoft has announced its intention to move to Unicode in a future version of Windows. Think of all the symbols you'll have and think of all the programs that could break! Progress is rarely cheap.

Actually, grasshopper, Windows already supports Unicode to some extent. Every TrueType font that Microsoft has shipped has been internally coded as Unicode. At one point, full Unicode support was promised for Windows 95, but that promise was not fulfilled even for Windows 98. Use of some non-Latin alphabets (for example, Hebrew) in English versions of Windows remains a disaster with no standard and each program that uses such fonts marching to its own drummer. Sigh.

American Windows does have support, though, for standard roman characters that involve accents, for example, French or Spanish characters. You can explore this by calling up the keyboard applet in Control Panel and clicking on the Language tab.

Microsoft has hinted that Office 2000 will have support for all languages in one common program.

Most of the TrueType fonts in Windows 98 have the option of including multiple character sets inside a single font. Indeed, the Courier New font that comes with Windows includes both the Windows ANSI and the OEM sets. By default, programs accessing those fonts will get the ANSI set, but a program can request OEM characters, and that is exactly what DOS boxes do.

The Windows CD comes with two sets of font files for twelve of the basic core fonts (four weights each of Arial, Courier, and Times). The "small" versions of the fonts take almost exactly 1 MB but there are "large" versions that take almost 2 MB. ("Small" and "large" do not refer to font size—these are scaleable fonts after all—but to the number of extra characters squeezed in.) The large fonts include up to 652 characters in Cyrillic, Greek, Turkish, the Baltic languages and the languages of Eastern Europe—and even the Mac character set.

Except we couldn't get permission to include the character in the Mac character set that is the Apple logo. Too bad.

On my test system, the large variants were installed. I'm not sure when the small version gets installed.

The Font of All Wisdom

Barry got the part of Polonius in a production of *Hamlet*. In preparation, he decided to give some pompous advice on the use of fonts. So, heeere's Barreee!

Avoid ransom note typography. It is the biggest type sin in a world with hundreds of fonts.

Ransom note typography is the name given to material that uses too many fonts—sort of like the infamous ransom notes that are cut out of magazine ads with each letter in a different font. You'll see rules of thumb, but they may be too generous to the fontoholic. The advice is somewhat different for **heading text**, the words used as section titles, and **body text**, the bulk of what you are saying.

Certainly do not use multiple fonts for body text on a single page. Indeed, consider using a single body text font in each document. Some of the font etiquette books suggest using a serif font for body text and a sans serif font for headings. That's OK, but it is often more elegant to use the same font for headings and body with the heading bold and larger. Normally, you'd want to use the same typeface for headings and for page headers/footers but there are special reasons to violate that rule.

Consider 11-point text for correspondence.

Ten-point text is more usual but it looks small. Some users jump to 12 point. Before scaleable fonts, many font collections had only 10- and 12-point, skipping 11, but if you are using scaleable fonts, 11 is easy. And it's a good compromise.

 Pitch out your fixed-pitch fonts.

Well, don't exactly throw them out. Fixed-pitch fonts are a holdover from obsolete technology. Typewriters couldn't handle proportional spacing so fixed-pitch fonts were introduced, even though they were unknown before then. The two fonts used in IBM typewriters—Courier and Elite—became so standard for business correspondence that even now law offices and some other businesses tend to use them. But they are ugly. Avoid their use except for special purposes like our use of a fixed-pitch font for keyboard keys and pathnames.

Don't think that to get numbers to line up in a column you need a fixed-pitch font. All fonts used a fixed pitch for their numerals. And a proper use of tabs, especially of right as well as left tabs, is a more effective way to align columns with text.

 Neither a borrower nor a lender be.

 Woody, you cut that one out from the wrong part of the book! Besides, isn't that Tobias, not Barry?

 Well, from someone guilty of Polonius assault.

 As a general rule, set body text in a serif font.

The general wisdom is that for large chunks of text a serif font is easier to read because the serifs sweep the eyes along. But there is an exception to this rule.

 Use sans serif fonts for smaller point sizes.

Eight-point and smaller type is more legible without the clutter of serifs. So if you are typing up a legal contract, use Arial for the fine print. This rule is an artifact of computer-generated fonts. Hot-metal fonts compensated for smaller sizes by thickening strokes and increasing x-heights, so serif fonts were more legible at smaller sizes also, but this is not true for computer-generated fonts.

Think about your audience when using fonts.

This may be obvious but users caught up in the excitement of fontitis forget it. Fonts are important because, in unseen ways, they can set the tone of a document. You should use the template/style sheet feature of your word processor to pick the fonts for different kinds of documents and stick with them. You can make exceptions for the announcement of the company picnic.

 So he's saying, To thine own self be true!

 Oy, Woody. The Bard is too much with thee.

 Avoid using dingbats and other doohickeys too much. Similarly avoid using too many rules.

Remember that the point of using fonts is to make your point—to get a message across. You risk having the messenger get in the way if you overload the text with stuff that distracts rather than complements. Again, you can make exceptions for the announcement of the company picnic.

 Yo, Billy. Did ya see what he said about avoiding too many rules? Kids would sure like that!

 He meant typographical rules—the lines that make up boxes or break text.

 For long documents, use ragged right text. For short business correspondence and memos of less than a page, you can consider using justified text.

This advice is somewhat controversial. Justified text is definitely harder to read (which is why you want to avoid it in long documents), less elegant to my taste (it can make for unevenly spaced lines) and enough to make the font snobs wince. But it looks more businesslike.

Use typographical quotes " . . . " and ' . . . ' and the real apostrophe ' rather than the lower ASCII characters " and '. Also use the en dash – and em dash — where they are appropriate rather than a hyphen -.

It is a pain to enter these characters from the keyboard so you'll need some method to help. See the discussion in the last section about ways to enter special characters.

 Be consistent—a good rule in dealing with children, employees, and type. Use the same font, including weight and point size, for parallel headings throughout a document.

 Avoid too much dense text. If you want people to read and understand what you write, make the paragraphs short. Be sure to place some white space between single-spaced paragraphs. Remember that the concentration span of the MTV generation for written text is about three words.

 *AVOID USING ALL CAPS. They are actually harder to read because the eye prefers variation, and they don't even produce the desired emphasis. Besides, needing to use all caps for emphasis is the sign of a limited typographic environment, such as you find with a typewriter or in online messages. Use italic for emphasis, **bold** for special terms or phrases.*

 Use real bold and italic. If you use a font that doesn't have a bold or an italic, Windows will try to fake it, and the results are not as good as a font that has the extra weights/styles. Alas, the only way to know if the bold and italic are real is to remember from the ad for the font (!) or by checking out the Fonts Folder.

 Don't be cowed by this advice or the advice of others. Do experiment and do consider breaking rules (the rules that are pontificated, not the rules that are really straight lines!). If you've understood the reason for a rule and have reason to break it, you're almost sure to do the right thing.

Could You Gimme a Hint?

. . . that faculty of beholding at a hint the face of his desire and the shape of his dream, without which the earth would know no lover and no adventurer.

—Joseph Conrad, *Lord Jim*, 1900

When you hear about how good Microsoft's hinting is, most likely the speaker is not referring to how well their press agency seeds rumors but to the care put into their TrueType fonts.

If you print a 72-point character on a 2,200-dpi Linotronic, the letter will be at least a thousand dots high and a few dots won't matter. But consider a 15-inch monitor running at 800×600. A 15-inch diagonal at a 4×3 aspect ratio means a 9-inch height or fewer than 72 dots per inch, so on screen an 8-point letter could have only 5 or 6 dots in it.

Hey, how come he didn't say 2,200 dots for the Linotronic and 8 dots for the 8 point?

Remember that point size is measured from the top of the tallest letter to the bottom of the letter that drops down the most plus a default line spacing. So no letter has a height equal to its point size!

The best fonts in Windows are scaleable fonts that are stored as outlines that are rasterized before being displayed on your screen or printer. In case you skipped it, I discussed rasterization in the first part of the section "And Dots Not All."

The two main outline formats in terms of usage are TrueType and PostScript Type 1. TrueType is included in Windows 98. To rasterize PostScript fonts on screen, you need a copy of Adobe Type Manager, called ATM. You can purchase ATM separately or find it bundled with a variety of programs from Adobe.

The dumb algorithm for rasterizing an outline font is to pretend to draw the objects at a much higher resolution on top of a grid representing the available resolution. If a box is more than 50% covered, fill in the corresponding dot as black. Otherwise leave it blank. This algorithm could do violence to a letterform. In many fonts, W is left–right symmetric. But if the grid is aligned to the exact character width, using the dumb algorithm could destroy that symmetry. So an intelligent font rasterization scheme allows for information about symmetry. **Hints** is the name given to all information beyond the pure outlines that is included with a font.

Hints include information to be sure serifs aren't dropped, that essential type elements like a crossbar on the t aren't dropped and are uniform from left to right when they need to be. Both TrueType and PostScript Type 1 have hinting engines built into them so that font vendors can supply this extra information.

Hinting has three levels of sophistication. Some fonts in these formats have no hinting because the vendor didn't bother. Some are autohinted—an automated program was used to make the hints. A few have hand-tuned hints—hints added by a professional type designer usually after autohinting is done.

Both ATM and TrueType include font caches. They save in memory the raster patterns for recently rasterized letters and don't have to do it again and again. On slower machines you may note a pause the first time you use a font in a session compared to later usage—that's the effect of the font not being in the cache the first time around.

The biggest font vendors have their own programs for internal use. And they also hand-tune afterward. Microsoft did all the right things when it added TrueType to Windows. First they started with a good specification. Indeed, TrueType hinting is a superset of what is in PostScript. Second, they introduced new printing technology that substantially sped up printing on HP laser (and related) printers compared to ATM 1.0. That version of ATM rasterized a page of text as dots and sent it to the printer as a graphic. Suppose that page had the letter A 200 times on the page, in the precisely identical font. Because of the font cache, ATM would rasterize it only once and get it the other times from the cache. But because the dot pattern is sent as a graphic, the dot pattern for that A would get sent to the printer 200 times on that page. Since the parallel port is one of the slowest links on a computer, that's a lengthy process.

Windows TrueType engine instead used the ability of laser printers to understand downloadable fonts. It would send the characters needed for that page to the printer as a soft font, sending each dot pattern only once. Then those 200 A's could be sent as characters requiring only one byte each. ATM added that feature in version 2.0, but the speed boost was a welcome addition for which Microsoft deserves the bulk of the credit.

Third, Microsoft provided with Windows 14 TrueType fonts—not merely OK fonts but great ones. There were four weights each of three basic typefaces, Times New Roman, Arial, and Courier New. All were licensed from Monotype and all had hand-tuned hints. Times New Roman is certainly my favorite variant of Times and one of the best fonts, period. The 12 character fonts were supplemented by a symbol font and the Wingdings font.

Finally, Microsoft broke the back of high font prices with its first TrueType font pack—but more of that in the section after the next.

Love Me True (Type)

The advantage of love at first sight is that it delays a second sight.

—Natalie Clifford Barney

The $64,000 question for fonts is "Do I need PostScript and ATM if I already have TrueType under Windows?" There's a simple answer and a complicated answer.

The simple answer is: TrueType is a superb engine, it offers lots of inexpensive, well-done fonts, and it's built into Windows, so you save no memory by not using TrueType. And you can be sure that any application supports it. ATM's font cache, on the other hand, takes a significant chunk of memory and is supported by most but not all applications. So no, you don't need ATM.

The complex answer is: TrueType is a superb engine, it offers lots of inexpensive, well-done fonts, and it's built into Windows, so you save no memory by not using TrueType. And you can be sure that any application supports it. ATM's font cache, on the other hand, takes a significant chunk of memory and is supported by most but not all applications. So no, you don't need ATM unless you are doing heavy-duty desktop publishing or need some of the special font families that come from Adobe.

 Hmm, I'll bet John Warnock (the founder and CEO of Adobe) never talks to me again, but I gotta tell you the truth, don't I?

I agree this point of view regarding PostScript fonts—most users don't need 'em—but I'm less sure about ATM, which is a superb tool for organizing fonts. So if you have a lot of fonts and want to organize them, get ATM, but don't use the PostScript fonts if you are going to share your documents with others who might not have ATM.

 What about the memory taken by the ATM font cache?

 When ATM first came out, the 500-KB to 1-MB cache took up significant space on machines with 4 or 8 MB of RAM. Now that 16 MB is a minimal machine and 32 MB is common, it is a less significant factor.

How Much Is That Font Pack for Windows, the One with the Shiny Ohs?

The heaping together of paintings by Old Masters in museums is a catastrophe; likewise, a collection of a hundred Great Brains makes one big fathead.

—CARL JUNG, *Civilization in Transition,* 1934

There are a few fonts suitable for body text that you'll use most of the time—bread-and-butter fonts. The fonts that come with Windows are so good that you could happily use only those, but they are so common that if you want to show some individuality, you may decide to buy some more fonts. You won't be alone. But be careful, because the font business really is a classic case of Gresham's law: the schlock fonts have come close to driving the class foundries out of business.

Fonts used to be a boutique kind of business but in the early 1990s they soared. I estimate that in 1992, fonts were over $100-million-a-year business.

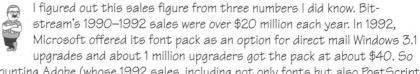 I figured out this sales figure from three numbers I did know. Bitstream's 1990–1992 sales were over $20 million each year. In 1992, Microsoft offered its font pack as an option for direct mail Windows 3.1 upgrades and about 1 million upgraders got the pack at about $40. So counting Adobe (whose 1992 sales, including not only fonts but also PostScript licenses and their software programs, was over $250 million), I figure it must be over $100 million.

Fonts are the potato chips of the Windows world. You can't eat only one. Not so long ago, a better analogy might have been nicotine or harder drugs. The font companies had their few samples to hook you—their Joe Camels. All sorts of programs were bundled with Bitstream Dutch and Swiss, which vendors got for very little. But if they hooked you, boy, did you have to raid the cookie jar. A single typeface (in four outlines for the standard weights/styles) beyond the basics went for $200–$300. That's $50 or more per font.

But then Microsoft went and spoiled the party! Their first font pack gave you 44 fonts for a street price of under $50. Fonts were suddenly only a buck each. At that price, you could afford to nibble quite a few potato chips. The major font foundries gritted their teeth and, gasp, competed. They kept some of their fonts at the old rate to catch the pathetic guys huddled in the corner shooting up every new font that shows up but they also produced font packs at the buck-a-font street price. And, surprise, they did quite well, because the volumes were enormous compared to those of the $50-per-font market.

The schlock font vendors competed, too, with deals like "250 fonts for $49.99." Those fonts tended to run 20–25 cents each. The high-class fonts should have won, but alas, the difference between schlock and class is subtle and not so easy for the novice to see. So the junk sold and the good stuff didn't. Monotype and Adobe pulled back from the mass market and sold expensive fonts to the cognoscenti. Bitstream competed and put out a superb library of 500 fonts for $50. That's 10 cents apiece. If I needed to go out and buy fonts, my top pick would be the Bitstream CD, if I could find it.

If you get Corel Draw or certain other packages, you'll find hundreds of fonts are included. Microsoft Office includes oodles of fonts. So maybe you don't need to buy more fonts after all! But if you do, avoid the schlock. If you install more than about 100 fonts, your font list will be enormous and you'll want a font organizer like ATM.

You know, Janet Reno should read the story you guys just told very carefully. Fonts used to be a specialized niche with pricing out of reach for most consumers. Many settled for investing a coupla hundred bucks to get a handful of fonts. Then Microsoft put fonts firmly into the operating system and paid Monotype big bucks for hand-tuned fonts to include free with Windows. We even broke the back of the $50 font packs by throwing in fonts with Office. This was bad news for the font vendors but absolutely wonderful news for consumers. You have to ask if preventing the operating system from expanding its technological reach would be good news for consumers or only for competitors who couldn't otherwise survive in the marketplace.

Portable Documents

Barbarism is the absence of standards.

—José Ortega y Gasset,
The Revolt of the Masses, 1930

The only universal format for exchange of textual information is ASCII, a format that has been in place for many years. Clearly, we need a format that supports font information, pictures, and all that so we can transmit "portable documents." Adobe Acrobat seems to be the sure winner.

Well, you could say that HTML is also a format of exchange of textual information and it supports **.gif** and **.jpg** pictures. With the extensions supported by Internet Explorer and Netscape Navigator, it supports font information.

 It may well happen that HTML, especially with the XML extensions, eventually displaces Acrobat, but for now, HTML doesn't smoothly handle multiple-page documents or have the option of embedding fonts so that the user can see documents without the font being present in the receiving PC.

Acrobat Reader, which will display PDF files, is free for the download from **http://www.adobe.com/prodindex/acrobat/readstep.html**. It includes a plugin for the two main browsers as well as a stand-alone program. The PDF includes general information on the fonts used in the document, and the reader has the technology to produce an approximation of the font on your screen and printer even if you don't own the actual font. The output won't make a font lover do cartwheels, but it will look a lot like the true original.

Acrobat 3.0 for Windows (which is a commercial product with a street price of $179) includes a "printer driver" that lets you "print" a document to a PDF file. The included Distiller program allows you to take PostScript output (as you'd get if you used a PostScript printer driver and printed to a file). Distiller plus Reader is one of the best PostScript interpreters currently available. Acrobat 3.0 also has a PDF editor that lets you add hyperlinks, annotations, and more to a PDF file.

 By using compression technology and settling for approximations of the actual document, PDF files can be much smaller than the original document. In one sample that Adobe talks about, an 80-MB Page-Maker document (with lots of big bitmaps) produces a PDF of under 2 MB. Impressive technology.

With Adobe's name and technology behind it, Acrobat's format should have an even larger following, but initially, Adobe used a stupid marketing model where you had to buy the Reader. That meant it couldn't spread on BBS or be used as a universal format. This delayed the acceptance of the format.

But Adobe shifted to the right moves before any competitor could get established. First, in 1994, they convinced the IRS to put all their forms in PDF format, and Adobe posted them on CompuServe with a free reader to download. The next year they were posted in many places. You could download the forms and Acrobat Reader and print them out looking as good as the originals without trekking to the library or calling the IRS.

 It's still true that you can download a tax form in Acrobat format from the IRS Web site and print out a better-looking version than you can pick up at the public library.

Font Tools in Windows 98

There is a great satisfaction in building good tools for other people to use.

—FREEMAN DYSON, *Disturbing the Universe*, 1979

The tools for organizing fonts provided in Windows 98, while virtually identical to those in Windows 95, are vastly superior to those in Windows 3.1.

 That ain't saying much—Windows 3.1 provided almost nothing to organize fonts.

 There are some technical differences in how Windows 98 handles the fonts folder that are an improvement. Windows 95 hid the `*.ttf` files associated with TrueType fonts in a way that MOM complained about. It's been fixed in Windows 98, so that now you can do a search on `C:\*.tff` files in the Find dialog and see the ones in the Fonts folder.

Many of the tools are associated with the Fonts folder, an object found in My Computer with a shortcut to it in Control Panel. This folder is an entirely different beast from any other folder in Windows 98, and it can be a little confusing. Most folders correspond to a directory of on-disk files. Open the `C:\windows` folder and you see the same files you'd get by opening a DOS window and typing `dir C:\windows` at the DOS command line. There are other folders like the Printers folder that are entirely virtual. The objects shown do not correspond to files anywhere.

The Fonts folder is different because there is an on-disk directory by default, `C:\windows\fonts`, which is associated with it but there is not a simple one-to-one correspondence between the files that `dir C:\windows\fonts` will turn up and the icons shown when you open the Fonts folder. In the first place, when you open the Fonts folder, you will never see any icons but those associated with TrueType fonts (with the extension `.ttf`) and those associated with Windows bitmapped fonts (with extension `.fon`). If you copy a file called `readme.txt` to `C:\windows\fonts`, the DOS `dir` command will show it there but you'll never see it in a folder view of the directory or with Explorer, since those show you the sort of virtual directory that is the Font folder and not the actual contents of `C:\windows\fonts`.

 There is another folder that is neither entirely virtual nor a disk directory and that's Network Neighborhood. It shows icons for machines and other resources on the network that don't correspond to local files, but it also shows files in the directory `C:\windows\nethood`. The purpose of those files is to place shortcuts to network resources, but if you make a text file in the `C:\windows\nethood` directory, it'll happily show up in Network Neighborhood. Moreover, if you view `C:\windows\nethood` in Folder or Explorer view, you see the actual files in that directory without the virtual objects included in Network Neighborhood. So Network Neighborhood, while neither totally disk based nor totally virtual, is very different from the Fonts folder.

The story gets even stranger, though. If you or a program installs a font into a directory other than `C:\windows\fonts`, it shows up in the Fonts folder as a shortcut. I'll explain in the next section how you can install fonts in other directories. But here's the weird part. The font shortcut does not correspond to any disk file. Make a shortcut to an executable and a `*.lnk` file is made; make a shortcut to a DOS program and a `*.pif` file is made. Make a font shortcut and no additional file is made. In some sense the shortcut corresponds to an entry in the Registry.

 The lack of a file corresponding to font shortcuts is partly a curiosity, but since it is a player in a dangerous removal problem I explain in the next section, it is more than a mere curiosity.

The icons in the Fonts folder show either a TT for `*.ttf` TrueType files or an A for bitmapped `*.fon` files. Double click on either and you pop up a box like that shown in Figure 2-35 with the name of the font, some general samples, the alphabet and samples in 12, 18, 24, 36, 48, 60, and 72 points. You can view the sample on screen or print it by using the handy button provided on the sample.

Here's the neatest thing about this viewer: it works on fonts you haven't yet installed! If you have a CD filled with fonts and want to figure out which to install, you can double click on the `*.ttf` on that CD and look at samples.

 There is no real magic here. There is a program called **fontview.exe** in the Windows directory. Running it is assigned as the default action when you double click on a `*.ttf` or `*.fon` file. If you want to print out the sample of the font, you can right click on the font and choose print. That just runs **fontview.exe** with the `/p` switch to get it to print the font and exit.

Figure 2-35. Windows font viewer

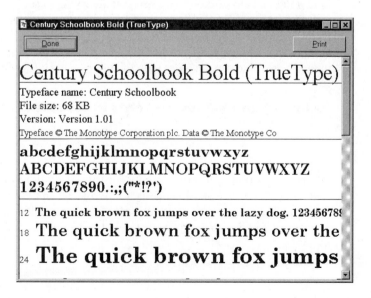

I guess the spec sheets you print/display are so much better than what you used to get that I shouldn't complain, but it is a pretty limited applet. How about at least letting us see the full ANSI character set in the font? That would sure be useful for Dingbats and other symbol fonts, for Hebrew fonts and the like. And rather than make us look at a bunch of fonts one at a time, how about a way to print out single lines in all the fonts in some directory?

Figure 2-36. The font folder View menu

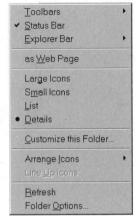

Figure 2-37. A normal folder View menu

The only other font tools to mention are options in the View menu. Figure 2-36 shows the View menu in a Fonts folder while Figure 2-37 shows the View menu in a normal folder. The items missing from the Fonts folder (small icons, web view, icon line-up commands) aren't important. What is are the two items special to Font Folders: Hide Variations, which is an on/off check box and List Fonts By Similarity, which is one of four list options. Hide Variations shows a single font from a family rather than the usual four—normal, italic, bold, and bold italic. It's a useful option when you are trying to see what fonts are installed. List Fonts By Similarity uses Panose numbers to take any font you choose and list the other fonts in four categories: very similar, fairly similar, not similar, and "No PANOSE information available." The button bar when you are in the Fonts folder has an extra icon to allow quick shift to Similarity view.

Installing and Removing Fonts in Windows 98

Do not use a hatchet to remove a fly from your friend's forehead.

—Chinese proverb

The way for a user to install a font in Windows is easy. Just open the Fonts folder, locate the `*.ttf` file you want in Explorer, and drag and drop the `ttf` file to the Fonts folder. The default action (no matter what the source drive) is to copy the `tff` file to the `C:\windows\fonts` directory and install the font into Windows.

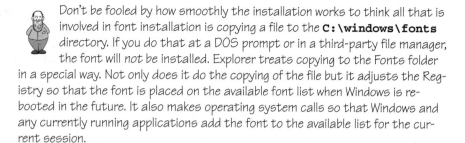

Don't be fooled by how smoothly the installation works to think all that is involved in font installation is copying a file to the **C:\windows\fonts** directory. If you do that at a DOS prompt or in a third-party file manager, the font will *not* be installed. Explorer treats copying to the Fonts folder in a special way. Not only does it do the copying of the file but it adjusts the Registry so that the font is placed on the available font list when Windows is rebooted in the future. It also makes operating system calls so that Windows and any currently running applications add the font to the available list for the current session.

I'll talk about the Registry in Chapter 9. Font information is stored in the key **HKEY_Local_Machine\Software\Microsoft\Windows\CurrentVersion\Fonts**. Fonts whose **ttf** file is in **C:\windows\fonts** just have the name of the **ttf** file listed (without the full pathname). Fonts located elsewhere are listed with their full pathnames.

This method of simply storing directory information in Registry is much smoother than the procedure used in Windows 3.x. That model used an extra binary file called an **fot** file. The **win.ini** entries pointed toward the **fot** file and the pathname of the **ttf** file was embedded inside the **fot** file.

This change was made only after considerable thought because it broke a number of font utilities. Most fonts under Windows 3.x were placed in the system directory. So if you had 400 fonts installed, you had 800 extra files in your system directory—400 **ttf** files and 400 **fot**s. Every time any program wanted a **dll**, it needed to read the system directory, and those extra 800 files had a noticeable impact on performance. So we removed the **fot** and moved the fonts to their own directory.

But doesn't this break the installation model for Windows 3.x programs installing under Windows 98? Won't they just put their fonts and **fot** files in the system directory and adjust **win.ini**?

We realized that could be a problem, so when Windows 98 boots, it looks for entries in the **[fonts]** section of **win.ini**. If it finds them, it looks for the **fot** file and uses that to figure out where the corresponding **ttf** file is. It then properly installs the font in the Registry, moving the **ttf** file to **C:\windows\fonts** if it was in **C:\windows\system**. The entry in **win.ini** and the **fot** file are then deleted.

If you want to install a font in Windows without moving it to **C:\windows\fonts**, you right drag it to the Fonts folder. On the context menu that pops up, one of the choices is "Create Shortcut(s) Here." If you choose that, Windows will not copy the `ttf` file but will instead install the font using the full path-name in the Registry. In the Explorer view of the Fonts folder, the font name will appear but with a shortcut symbol indicated. As I mentioned in the last section, there is no file placed in `C:\windows\fonts` corresponding to the shortcut.

 I have lots of fonts installed—more than 900 at last count—and I've encountered lots of problems installing new fonts. With one font, I can double click on a `ttf` file and get the full font information, print it, and whatnot. I can install the file by dragging it to the `C:\windows\fonts` directory. But if I use the File/Install New Fonts option, I get a message that the font file is damaged. With a different font, double clicking works fine, but dragging into `C:\windows\fonts` gives the same bogus damaged file message. Oh, how I love a nice bug in the middle of 900 fonts!

 Hey, anyone who tries to install 900 fonts gets what they deserve.

Removal of fonts is as easy. If you select a font icon (which is not a shortcut) in the Fonts folder and delete it, the corresponding `ttf` file is deleted from `C:\windows\fonts`. And the font will no longer appear on the list of available fonts. If you select an icon corresponding to a shortcut and hit **Del**, you get exactly the behavior you'd expect: the original `ttf` file pointed to by the shortcut is unaffected, but the font is no longer installed in Windows.

But if you drag a font shortcut from the Fonts folder to the Recycle Bin, then Windows not only removes the font from the list of installed fonts but deletes the original `ttf` that the shortcut pointed to.

 Ooo! A bug, a big fat juicy squishy one. Gotta be. You drag any other kind of shortcut to the Recycle Bin and only the shortcut is deleted, not the file it points to. And in every other place in Explorer, hitting **Del** and dragging to the Recycle Bin are the same thing. Bug! Bug! Bug! In fact, this one is so blatant, it should have been fixed in going to Windows 98 but it wasn't.

 Perhaps not; it may be a design flaw. It seems unlikely that the differing behavior for **Del** and Recycle Bin drag is accidental. The reasoning may have gone like this. When you hit **Del** on the shortcut, it uninstalls the font, but since there is no actual file corresponding to the shortcut, there is no file placed in the Recycle Bin. If it started empty, it'll stay empty. If the user dragged the shortcut to an empty Recycle Bin and the icon didn't change to indicate a bin with something there, the user might get very confused. So the shell designers made the choice to blow away the `ttf` file that could have been a family heirloom to avoid a little confusion. Dumb design—but sorta understandable.

Well, users hardly care if it's a bug or a bonehead design decision. The bottom line is that if a user uses the capability to install fonts via shortcuts, she'd better be sure not to delete them by dragging to the Recycle Bin!

As for not fixing it, the number of users who use shortcuts to fonts is very small, so we couldn't justify the resources for the fix.

■ Winning on the First Palette

The next few sections are gonna be colorful, that's for sure. Well, at least color full.

Which One Is Burnt Umber?

But soft! what light through yonder window breaks?

—WILLIAM SHAKESPEARE, *Romeo and Juliet,*
Act II, Scene ii

Remember when Mom got you your first 64-crayon Crayola set? Your friend said, "Gimme that brown," but you couldn't figure out which crayon she meant since the one you were using was called burnt umber. Well, you're gonna have to pick colors a lot in Windows applications if you get at all graphical, so you'd better learn the way colors are named.

Alas, it ain't as simple as remembering which one is burnt umber. Colors are labeled by numbers and there are at least four different color-numbering standards that are in common use: RGB, CYMK, HSB, and HLS.

RGB stands for red, green, blue. Each can have a level from 0 to 255. It is a model of light, where RGB are the primary colors. As the numbers get higher, the color gets brighter: (R = 0, G = 0, B = 0) is black and (R = 255, G = 255, B = 255) is white. The color space is a cube. This is the most common color model used in Windows.

You may have heard that light has a continuous parameter called frequency, representing variation in space and time. Light of wavelength midway between red and green is yellow but then how can that also be a mixture of 50% red light and 50% green light? Physically, the two wave trains are very different. The answer is in our eyes. Color is perceived by three types of cones in the retina. Roughly speaking, the cones are sensitive to light frequencies near pure red, near pure green, and near pure blue. True yellow light, that is, light whose frequency is midway between red light and green light, stimulates both the red- and green-sensitive cones in roughly the same way that a combination of red and green light do, so they are perceived similarly, even though the physical light waves are different.

CMY (we'll get to K soon) stand for cyan, magenta, and yellow, the complementary colors to red (cyan is green/blue), blue, and green. It is a model of ink; indeed color printers normally use ink in those exact colors to make the rainbow of colors. In an ink model, higher numbers are darker, so (C = 0, M = 0, Y = 0) is white and theoretically (C = 255, M = 255, Y = 255) is black. In fact, if you mix together those inks in high concentration, you don't get black but instead a kind of muddy dark ooze.

Muddy dark ooze. Sorta sounds like Mom's coffee. Have to remember that—CMY crouches in wait.

Because mixing colored inks makes a lousy black, high-class color printers use a fourth ink, namely blacK. K is used to avoid confusion with Blue. Programs that prepare pictures for actual color printing often use CMYK, but most users will hardly see that.

**Figure 2-38.
HSB color model**

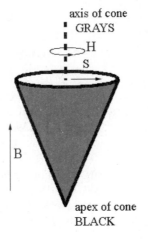

HSB stands for hue, saturation, and brightness. It uses a color cone model (Figure 2-38). Think of the cone as upright on end, like an ice cream cone, with the apex at the bottom and an axis running through the middle. The colors along that axis are grays. Black is at the apex and white at the center of the circle that lies at the top of the cone. The B parameter measures the distance along the axis from the apex (brightness 0) toward the brighter colors.

Hue is a discriminator of the pure color. It is connected to the color wheel. Imagine a wheel with pure red (R = 255) at 3 o'clock, yellow (R = G = 255) at 5 o'clock, green (G = 255) at 7 o'clock, cyan (R = G = 255) at 9 o'clock, and blue (B = 255) and magenta (R = G = 255) at 11 and 1 o'clock. As you move around, the red value is 255 from 1 to 5 o'clock and 0 from 7 to 11 o'clock and changes linearly in the transition areas. Many programs meas-ure H in degrees from 0 to 360. Windows measures from 0 to 240 so that red is H = 0, yellow is H = 40, green is H = 80, and so on.

In the HSB model, the color wheel is put on the circle at the top of the cone and H is a measure of the angle around the axis. The color wheel is more naturally a hexagon with the colors at the vertices, so the cone should be a hexagonal pyramid (Figure 2-39).

**Figure 2-39.
Color hexagon**

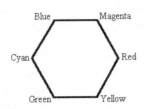

Saturation measures the distance from the axis toward the edge. S = 0 is gray. As saturation increases, the color gets purer.

HLS stands for hue, saturation, and luminosity. It's model is a double cone, two cones shaped like the HSB cone with one turned over and put on top of the other so that the points are at the top and the bottom. L = 0 is black while L = 240 (in Windows units) is white at the points of the double cone. The pure color wheel is in the middle at L = 120. If you fix S = 0, you still go through the grays. If you fix S = 240 and H = 0 (red) and move from L = 1 down to 0, you move from white through pink, red, and dark red to black.

Many color theorists regard the HSB/HLS models as more intuitive. In RGB, pink, which is a mixture of white and red, has RGB values (255, 128, 128), which says pink is made up of red and half green and half blue, which certainly isn't what one thinks of as pink. In the HSL model, pink is a pure red hue of luminosity ¾ of the way from black to white. Moreover, the color wheel is in line with the actual physical wavelength of colored light.

Windows standard color dialog uses the HLS model. You'll find it if you run the Display applet in Control Panel (or right click the Desktop and choose Properties, which is the same thing), click the Appearance tab, hit the Color button and choose Other. It is also used in any program using the common dialog, such as Windows Paint. But it doesn't use cones or circles, it uses squares (see Figure 2-40). The slider on the right changes the L values. Slide it all the way to the top or bottom and you get white or black, no matter what color you pick in the middle area. In that middle area, the top is the pure color wheel if L is 120 (midway). The bottom is a shade of gray no matter how you shift from left to right. That's because the top of the square is really a circle and the bottom is really a single point representing the center of the circle. Leave it to Microsoft to square the circle!

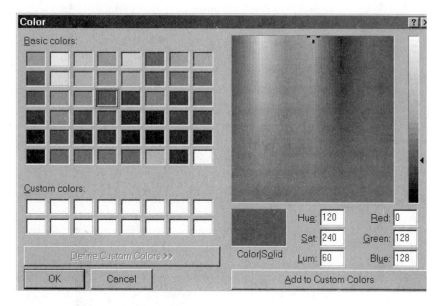

Figure 2-40. Color common dialog

Some of My Friends Are Pals and Some Are Palettes

If you are going to fool around with color schemes (and you may as well confess that you already have!), you should understand how Windows controls what colors you can access. I'll discuss 256 color drivers because that's what some of you will be using. If you have only 16 colors, those are normally hardcoded, although a very few programs will manipulate them (if you use any program much that does, you really do want to shift to 256 colors, even if it requires a new video card). In 24- and 16-bit color (called True Color and High Color, respectively, they have roughly 16 million and 64,000 colors), the palette and dither (sic) stuff I discuss aren't used. Everything is represented as a pure color, so much of what I'll say is irrelevant if you are running at that number of colors.

 Microsoft is to be commended for using the Windows 95 Plus! Pack to nudge the user community toward High Color. Many of its Desktop themes require this number of colors. That and the decreasing cost and improved performance of video led to many more of you using High Color now than when Windows 95 shipped. There is a performance penalty associated with the higher color depth, but on an accelerated video card it is not large, and I urge you to seriously consider moving to High Color if you haven't already. Unless you are an artiste, there isn't much reason to go to 24-bit color. For those who won't or can't shift to High Color, I'll discuss 256 colors here.

Drivers that display 256 colors are capable of picking those 256 colors from among either 262,144 colors (2 to the power 18) or 16,777,216 colors (2 to the power 24). VGA cards and older SuperVGA cards have the smaller number while higher-end adapters and cards that have a 24-bit mode have the larger number.

 "Oh, boy," you must be thinking, "I get to pick what color my title bar is from hundreds of thousands of colors." Alas, no; read on.

 What I'm about to say about the 20-color limitation for title bars and related issues is true only for 256 color mode. For High Color and True Color (16- and 24-bit color), you can choose any colors you like. These considerations will hopefully go the way of the dodo.

Windows keeps track of which 256 colors of those 262,144 or 16,777,216 are to be displayed, and such an assignment is called a **palette**. If a program asks for a color not in the current palette, Windows fakes it—it uses a **dithered** color that combines nearby dots of two different colors, which sorta gives the desired color. Pure colors look great; dithered colors often look awful. For example (assuming you are running at 16 or 256 colors), call up the Common Color dialog that I described in the last section. I'm sure several of the 48 colors shown don't look like colors but like polka dots. Assuming that your screen driver uses the standard colors for 256 color drivers (while a driver can define different color sets, I'm not aware of any that don't use those supplied in the Windows Super-

VGA scheme), it has the worst polka dots in row 2, columns 6 and 7, and row 1, column 7.

Programs can also attempt to manipulate the palette and tell Windows to change what colors are used. If colors can be manipulated by programs, how does Windows deal with the fact that you want your title bar color to be consistent across applications? It makes a compromise. Twenty colors of the 256 are **reserved** for all 256 color drivers. The other 236 colors can be freely changed by applications that need to. (Actually, programs that really need to are allowed to change 254 of the colors, leaving only black and white alone, but that is very rare—indeed, I know of no program that takes advantage of this.)

As you switch from one program to another, Windows changes the palette to the one that the active program has set. Since most programs don't change the default palette, you most often do not see any changes, but image editors and some other graphics programs change the palette, and then you often see funny flashes as you switch and perhaps fouled-up colors on your wallpaper when you are in certain programs.

Some image editors, when displaying several images, adjust the palette to be ideal for the one you are working on; others adjust it so that all the images display in a not too bad way but still save most of the 236 colors for the foreground image.

Because Windows is worried about what other programs may do to their 236 colors, it will only let you use the 20 reserved colors for title bars, menu bars, and the like. Moreover, you cannot change those 20 colors, in part because applications assume that they haven't changed. It would have been nice if Windows had reserved an additional 4 or so slots for user-mixed custom pure colors, but it didn't.

In the following discussion RGB values are always given 123/235/68, which means values R = 123, G = 235, B = 68. You can ignore them, but they will tell you something about the colors if you think in the right way.

The 20 colors include the 16 that have been standard on the PC since the CGA's text mode. Those 16 colors are the 6 primary color wheel colors in dark and light (for example, red is 255/0/0 and dark red is 128/0/0; magenta is 255/0/255 and dark magenta is 128/0/128) plus white (255/255/255), black (0/0/0), dark gray (128/128/128), and light gray (192/192/192).

How come dark red is R = 128, a smaller value than true red at R = 255?

Remember that RGB is a model of *light*, so R = 255 means more intense red light, which appears brighter!

Our Name	Red	Green	Blue
Medium gray	160	160	164
Eggshell white	255	251	240
Army olive	192	220	192
Powder blue	166	202	240

Figure 2-41. Extra four solid system colors

Besides the 16 standard colors, there are an extra 4 colors that must have been picked by Bill Gates's interior decorator; they are shown in Figure 2-41.

I've a theory that the medium gray should really be 160/160/160, a true gray. First of all, why pick something so close to a gray and not take a real gray? My most compelling reason, though, has to do with Windows 3.1. There, the default colors in the common dialog had 19 of the 20 reserved colors. The missing one was medium gray. On the other hand, one of the most polka-dotted colors had RGB values 160/160/160. So the Color dialog designer thought it should be 160/160/160 but whoever actually set the colors typed a number in wrong! I'd have thought that with the adjustments made to powder blue, they would have also fixed medium gray during the move to Windows 95, but they didn't.

The slight change in the RGB values of powder blue in the passage from Windows 3.x to Windows 95—from 164/200/240 to 166/202/240— is mysterious. Why did they do it? Maybe big Bill's interior decorator came in and said, "A smidgen more red and green would make it just *parfait*."

If you go back to the Appearance tab in Display Properties and click on the Color button, you get a dropdown of exactly 20 colors above the word Other. Guess what? Those are precisely the 20 solid colors. Choose them for your Windows colors and you won't get anything dithered. On the other hand, some of the dithered colors don't look too bad; indeed, the default tool tip color is dithered. So you may want to look at the Other colors. For those objects like title bars that Windows insists be solid, the dithered colors are grayed out. For all others, you get the 8 × 6 array that follows.

The boxes marked BUG are there because those colors are the same. It's remarkable how many of the dithered colors look pretty good and that they bothered to include the awful ones I marked with a –.

Common Dialog Colors

–	+	+	+	+	–	–	–
red	yellow	+	+	cyan	–	–	magenta
+	–	green	dark cyan	+	–	+	+
dark red	–	dark green	+	blue	+	dark magenta	+
+	+	+	+	dark blue	+	BUG	+
black	brown	+	dark gray	+	light gray	BUG	white

But there sure are a bunch of mysteries in this little corner of Windows land. Most of the solid colors are in the same locations they were in Windows 3.1. So why did they move yellow? And why not fix the duplicate color rather than have some users decide they have gone color blind? And why oh why didn't they include the extra four solid colors in the 48 that are displayed so they'd be easily accessible in other programs like Paint that use the common Color dialog?

 I have a theory about the boxes marked BUG. At a product review, Mr. Gates complimented the designers on putting two subtly different shades next to each other, the product managers were afraid to tell him they were the same color, and no one's dared to change it since.

 By the way, powder blue is a particularly good choice for the color of the thing called 3D Objects in the Item dropdown list on the Appearance tab.

■ Putting Windows on a Sound Basis

The power of sound has always been greater than the power of sense.

—JOSEPH CONRAD, *A Personal Record,* 1912

Wav and MIDI

IBM included a kludgy speaker in the original PC and, in the interest of compatibility, until recently, that's what virtually all PCs used for sound, if you can call it that. Early on, Macs had real sound allowing both voice and music, as did Amigas, Ataris, Suns, NeXT, and others. PC sound solutions going beyond the speaker were largely driven by the needs of games with successive standards set by Ad Lib and then Sound Blaster cards. But sound has even entered the business mainstream with sound annotation, multimedia presentations (whatever that means), and most especially Windows support for sound in version 3.1 and then Windows 95 and 98. And future developments in voice synthesis and recognition will only make sound capabilities more important.

There are two types of sounds you can record and play under Windows. It's rasters and vectors all over again but at the sound level. One kind of sound is **digital**, the analog of a bitmap—the actual sampling or playing of sound levels. Just as the standard Windows bitmap file is the **bmp**, the Windows digital sound file standard is called a **wave file** with the extension **wav**. A **wav** file literally gives directions to a speaker to oscillate in a certain way.

The sound analog of vector graphics is the **synthesized** sound file, under Windows, a MIDI file, with extension **mid**. Instead of telling the sound card to oscillate in a given way, a MIDI file has commands like "Play a middle C for X amount of time and do it as if you were playing it on a piano."

Microsoft has developed a general header for various kinds of multimedia files. The header contains binary information that can be useful to programs using the files. The header format is called RIFF for resource interchange file format, and **wav** files have RIFF headers as part of the spec. MIDI files, which predate the RIFF spec, do not have RIFF headers. A hybrid file format that has a RIFF header followed by a MIDI file for content is now the format recommended by Microsoft. These RIFF–MIDI files are called RMID files by Microsoft and have the extension **.rmi**. Windows 98 installs seven superb RMID files in the **C:\windows\media** directory. I'll say more about them later.

To see the dramatic size difference between MIDI and digital files, consider this. The RMID of the first movement of Beethoven's Fifth symphony takes about 90 KB of disk space for over 6 minutes of music. The Utopia Sound Scheme Windows Start sound file is about 150 KB of disk space for less than 4 seconds of sound. That's about a factor of 150. To add to the drama, the wave file in question isn't even of top quality (it is mono, not stereo, and FM radio quality rather than CD audio), and it uses digital audio compression.

 Of course, since the Utopia Start sound isn't instrumental music, it couldn't be duplicated in MIDI. The point is that each format has its uses but that while orchestral music can be put in digital files, MIDI is much more efficient for such sounds. It boggles the mind to think that an hour of music can be stored in 1 MB of disk space!

Just as it pays to keep in mind whether a graphic is raster or vector, you'll want to bear in mind the difference between digitized and synthesized sounds. Here are more details on the two types.

Riding the Perfect Wav

. . . here shall thy proud waves be stayed.

—Job 38:11.

Bitmaps files are characterized by the number of colors and sometimes by their intended resolution. In the same way, **wav** files have some basic parameters that describe the native format of the data. Of course, just as Windows can display a 16-million-color file on a 256-color screen by doing its best, it can play a stereo **wav** file on a mono sound card by merging the two channels. The point of a stereo file is that it can play stereo on appropriate hardware.

Wav files have three basic parameters.

1. Look at whether the sound is **mono** or **stereo**. You know the difference. Most presentations don't need stereo. Some games do. Stereo sound files run twice the size of mono for rather obvious reasons.

2. They come with something called **sample size**, a measure of how much information about a single sound sample is kept around. For low-fidelity

voice recordings, 4-bit sampling suffices; 8-bit sampling does a good job of reproducing speech; but 16-bit—the sample size used in CD audio—is necessary for high-quality sound. Basically, sample size measures the number of different sound levels that are distinguished—4-bit has 16 levels (2 to the power 4), 8-bit has 256 levels (2 to the power 8), and 16-bit has 65,536 levels (2 to the power 16).

3. They include **sample rate**, a measure of how often the computer looks at the incoming sound and translates it into numbers. Sample rate has to do with how high a frequency can be distinguished and how much one can hear differing amounts of harmonic overtones. 11-kHz sampling (sampled 11,000 times per second, natch) sounds like AM radio. 22-kHz sampling sounds like FM radio. And 44-kHz sampling sounds like CD audio—because it *is* CD audio.

Most soundboards nowadays can record 8-bit mono sound at 22 kHz. Few can record at CD audio rates (16-bit stereo at 44 kHz). Even if they could, you probably wouldn't want them to: one minute of 8-bit mono 22 kHz sound generates 1.3 MB of data, hefty by any standard; one minute of 16-bit stereo 44 kHz sound would produce a 10.6 MB file. Fidelity hath its price!

 You get 1.3 MB by multiplying 22,000 by 60 seconds (since 8 bits is a byte) and 10.6 MB by multiplying 44,000 by 60 seconds, then by 2 (16 bits is 2 bytes), and then by 2 again for the stereo.

There are other digital sound file types, but they are less common than alternate bitmap types because sound has less of a pre-Windows history. The ones you may see are **voc** (the Sound Blaster standard—PC-digitized sound at games-player prices started on the Sound Blaster), **au** (used on NeXT and Sun), **snd** (used on the Mac and Amiga and the most common pre-**wav** type), and **vox** (dialogic phone-answering system voice files). Just as bitmap-to-bitmap conversion is straightforward, so is conversion from one digitized sound format to another. One program that will do such conversions for you as well as edit is Sonic Foundry's Sound Forge XP (**http://www.sonicfoundry.com/**).

 There is another source of digitized sound on some systems with both a sound card and CD-ROM—so called Red Book audio. No, not Chairman Mao's Red Book, but the standard document used to define audio CDs. Red Book audio is essentially audio CD tracks embedded in the middle of a CD-ROM. Multimedia CDs sometimes have sound in that format. One way you can hear such sounds is by connecting the output jack on your CD (assuming it has one!) to a pair of speakers. If you use that route, you'll need a mixer to use the same speakers on your sound card output. A better solution is to connect the CD output to one of your sound card inputs and have the sound card send out to the speakers.

Ideally, you should use internal connections on CD and sound card, assuming that the CD is internal. But be warned that the internal connectors are anything but standard. After a year of trying I gave up on finding an internal connector to send the Red Book audio from my Toshiba CD-ROM to my Sound Blaster Pro. Fortunately, the external connectors are standard, so a modular audio cable I picked up at Radio Shack did the trick. But it sure is silly to have a cable snaking out from the front of my CD around to the external audio input on the back of the Sound Blaster.

'Mid the MIDI

MIDI is short for musical instrument digital interface. It's a standard invented to drive high-end musical devices such as might be used in a recording studio, and it was already fairly common in non-IBM compatible computer systems (for example, the Mac) before it was adapted to Windows in version 3.1. Microsoft is to be complemented for using an external standard rather than rolling its own, although there are Windows-specific modifications in the implementation.

There is considerable confusion surrounding MIDI under Windows. To start with, there are really three separate MIDI devices relevant to a sound setup—the device used to play **mid** and **rmi** files, a midi in port and a midi out port.

As a preliminary, you should know that there are basically two routes to synthesis on sound cards. One is called **FM synthesis**, usually based on a Yamaha chip. The chip understands the general features that make something sound like a piano or an organ or a flute, and given a command to play a middle C as a piano would, the chip makes up, er, synthesizes the sound on the spot.

The second is **wave table lookup**. The sound card has actual recorded samples of a piano and other instruments playing various notes and "looks them up" to do the synthesis. Typically, the wave table information is stored in ROM with 2 or even 4 MB of wave tables possible. Some cards are available with wave tables stored on your hard disk and a buffer on card.

The difference between these two sources are dramatic. FM synthesis sounds tinny and wave table lookup sounds rich. It's the same kind of dramatic difference as that between a dot matrix and a laser printer. Whatever you do, if your budget can't afford a wave table card, don't listen to one or else you'll have an unrequited yearning. The good news is that wave table sound has come down in price. There was essentially a single card with a street price over $800 in mid-1992, but now wave table is available in all but the very lowest-end sound solutions. Still, not including wave table is a way that some computer vendors cut corners on unsuspecting consumers, so be sure it is on your checklist when you buy a system.

 While wave table is desirable, don't totally despair if you discover your sound card uses FM synthesis. Most of the sound you play on your computer will be digital or Red Book audio so it is only a mild calamity if your MIDI isn't up to snuff.

Figure 2-42. Where do you want your MIDI output to go today?

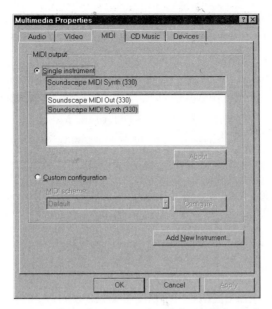

Any sound card that includes a synthesizer will allow you to play **mid** files directly from the card. If you have a MIDI out port, there is usually a choice between the internal card and the external out port as the place that **mid** files are played. You choose where **mid** files are by calling up the Multimedia Properties applet in Control Panel, shifting to the MIDI tab, and choosing there. Figure 2-42 shows the dialog for an Ensoniq Soundscape with a choice of external MIDI and internal wave table synthesis.

 If you have a card with both FM synthesis and wave table lookup, be sure to call up this dialog and check that the wave table option is picked (the FM synthesis will use the name FM Synthesis while the term "wave table" may not be mentioned explicitly; try the choices that are not labeled FM Synthesis!).

While MIDI in and out ports are part of the MPC spec, for many users they are not so important and they tend to be an extra cost item that you can happily skip (for example, Sound Blaster cards have a box that attaches to their joy stick ports with MIDI In, MIDI Out, and Pass Through Joy Stick Ports on the box).

MIDI is used to attached a MIDI keyboard or other MIDI instrument. If you want to make your own music, you'll want a MIDI in port. MIDI out ports are for attaching high-end MIDI synthesizers like the Roland Sound Canvas. They present one way of adding a wave table output device to a sound card that has just an FM synthesizer—although a pricey one.

Other synthesized sound file types include **rol** (the Ad Lib standard, quite popular on BBS at one time), **cmf** (the Sound Blaster attempt to replace **rol**; because **rol** worked on Sound Blaster, **cmf**, a subset of **mid**, never really took off), and **mod** (an Amiga spec that includes the instrument data as part of the file).

Windows 98 includes seven **rmi** samples that are so well done they are to kill for! They are an optional component (Multimedia/Sample Sounds in the Add/Remove Programs applet) and take about 350 KB:

BACH'S~1 RMI	Bach's Brandenburg Concerto No. 3.rmi
BEETHO~1 RMI	Beethoven's 5th Symphony.rmi
BEETHO~2 RMI	Beethoven's Fur Elise.rmi
DANCEO~1 RMI	Dance of the Sugar-Plum Fairy.rmi
DEBUSS~1 RMI	Debussy's Claire de Lune.rmi
INTHEH~1 RMI	In the Hall of the Mountain King.rmi
MOZART~1 RMI	Mozart's Symphony No. 40.rmi

So far, to most Windows users, MIDI has played a minor role compared to **wav** files. One reason is that only **wav** files can be assigned to system events, and that's what has most captured the public's attention. Second, until wave table sound becomes common, **mid** files just don't sound as rich as the sound you can get with Red Book audio or with **wav** files. Finally, the cost of a decent midi editor is two to three times what a wav file editor costs and requires a lot more knowledge to use.

Wasn't General MIDI in the Battle of the Choral C?

 This section gets into the guts of MIDI and may be more than you want to know. So you can skip it. It's here to show the scope of MIDI. In Windows 3.1, you needed this information to cope with the MIDI mapper— fortunately a thing of the past!

MIDI used to be a Tower of Babel. MIDI instructions refer to instruments by number and exactly which number referred to which instrument was determined by the MIDI device manufacturer and/or software company. In 1991, a consortium of the leading MIDI suppliers—the MIDI Manufacturer's Association—produced a standard called General MIDI Level 1 (sometimes called GM and sometimes just MIDI level 1). Interestingly, the original call for a spec came from a publisher of multimedia titles (Warner New Media), and the key to adopting it was a hardware manufacturer (Roland, whose Sound Canvas was the first GM device).

To overwhelm you with how rich the MIDI spec is, let me list the 128 instruments: Acoustic Grand Piano, Bright Acoustic Piano, Electric Grand Piano, Honky-Tonk Piano, Elect. Piano 1 (Rhodes), Elect. Piano 2 (Chorused), Harpsichord, Clav, Celesta, Glockenspiel, Music Box, Vibraphone, Marimba, Xylophone, Tubular Bells, Dulcimer, Hammond Organ, Percussive Organ, Rock Organ, Church Organ, Reed Organ, Accordion, Harmonica, Tango Accordion, Acoustic Guitar (nylon), Acoustic Guitar (steel), Electric Guitar (jazz) , Electric Guitar (clean), Electric Guitar (muted), Overdriven Guitar, Distortion Guitar, Guitar Harmonics, Acoustic Bass, Electric Bass (fingered), Electric Bass (picked), Fretless Bass, Slap Bass 1, Slap Bass 2, Synth Bass 1, Synth Bass 2, Violin, Viola, Cello, Contrabass, Tremolo Strings, Pizzicato Strings, Orchestral

Harp, Timpani, String Ensemble 1, String Ensemble 2, SynthStrings 1, Synth-Strings 2, Choir Aahs, Voice Oohs, Synth Voice, Orchestra Hit, Trumpet, Trombone, Tuba, Muted Trumpet, French Horn, Brass Section, SynthBrass 1, Synth-Brass 2, Soprano Sax, Alto Sax, Tenor Sax, Baritone Sax, Oboe, English Horn, Bassoon, Clarinet, Piccolo, Flute, Recorder, Pan Flute, Blown Bottle, Skakuhachi, Whistle, Ocarina, Lead 1 (square), Lead 2 (sawtooth), Lead 3 (calliope), Lead 4 (chiff), Lead 5 (charang), Lead 6 (voice), Lead 7 (fifths), Lead 8 (bass+lead), SynthPad 1 (new age), SynthPad 2 (warm), SynthPad 3 (polysynth), SynthPad 4 (choir), SynthPad 5 (bowed), SynthPad 6 (metallic), SynthPad 7 (halo), SynthPad 8 (sweep), FX 1 (rain), FX 2 (soundtrack), FX 3 (crystal), FX 4 (atmosphere), FX 5 (brightness), FX 6 (goblins), FX 7 (echoes), FX 8 (sci-fi), Sitar, Banjo, Shamisen, Koto, Kalimba, Bagpipe, Fiddle, Shanai, Tinkle Bell, Agogo, Steel Drums, Woodblock, Taiko Drum, Melodic Tom, Synth Drum, Reverse Cymbal, Guitar Fret Noise, Breath Noise, Seashore, Bird Tweet, Telephone Ring, Helicopter, Applause, Gunshot.

 Wow! One doesn't think of Helicopter or Gunshot as an instrument. Is Tinkle Bell Peter Pan's friend in the ladies' room?

And there are 47 percussion sounds: Acoustic Bass Drum, Bass Drum 1, Side Stick, Acoustic Snare, Hand Clap, Electric Snare, Low Floor Tom, Closed Hi-Hat, High Floor Tom, Pedal Hi-Hat, Low Tom, Open Hi-Hat, Low-Mid Tom, Hi-Mid Tom, Crash Cymbal 1, High Tom, Ride Cymbal 1, Chinese Cymbal, Ride Bell, Tambourine, Splash Cymbal, Cowbell, Crash Cymbal 2, Vibraslap, Ride Cymbal 2, Hi Bongo, Low Bongo, Mute Hi Conga, Open Hi Conga, Low Conga, High Timbale, Low Timbale, High Agogo, Low Agogo, Cabasa, Maracas, Short Whistle, Long Whistle, Short Guiro, Long Guiro, Claves, Hi Wood Block, Low Wood Block, Mute Cuica, Open Cuica, Mute Triangle, Open Triangle.

MIDI supports polyphony, which is multiple notes. These notes can be played on multiple instruments that are assigned to distinct channels. General MIDI devices are supposed to allow 32-note polyphony and to respond to 16 channels with the first 9 sets for instruments and the tenth for percussion. A GM file can do whatever it wants with channels 11–16, although usually they aren't used.

Trip the Light Fantastic: Video

Maxim for the computer age:
C:/ is the root of all directories.

—HEARD ON THE WEB

In just a few short years, video has gone from an exotic computer add-on to something users expect. The Windows CD even comes with 34 video clips. A video clip is a sequence of pictures interleaved with a sound track. From the point of view of playback, there is no difference between animation and movies, although obviously very different tools are needed for their creation. For this reason, there are special animation formats, most notably `*.flc` for files made with Autodesk Animator. But most videos you'll see are in one of three formats: Microsoft Audio-Visual Interleaved (`*.avi`), a RIFF-based type, MPEG compressed (`*.mpg`), and Quick Time (`*.mov`), an Apple format developed for the Mac.

 The Windows 95 CD had some interesting clips including an MTV video and a movie trailer. The videos on the Windows 98 CD are all ads for Microsoft products as Microsoft uses its Windows monopoly to tout its CD offerings. Lack of class, Billy boy, lack of class.

Besides the obvious picture parameters (size and number of colors), videos have one other parameter of importance—their frame rate. Motion pictures have a rate of 30 frames per second, but many computer videos have a rate of only 15 frames per second, which makes them rather jerky.

 There are two reasons the frame rate was set low. First, videos take a lot of disk space and halving the frame rate cuts the disk space used by a factor of two for rather obvious reasons. In addition, drawing 30 frames per second on the screen would bring the best PC of several years ago to its knees begging for mercy. As disk storage prices continue to plummet and hardware improves, the 15 frames per second video will go the way of the dodo or the CGA.

Compression

A definition is a sack of flour compressed into a thimble.

—RÉMY DE GOURMONT

 A picture is worth a thousand words only if it is black and white and less than a tenth of a super VGA screen in size.

Why does Barry say that? Well, a typical word is about 5 bytes counting the space, so 1,000 words are 5,000 bytes or 40,000 bits. That's enough disk space for a 200×200 black-and-white bitmap.

 A $1,024 \times 768$ True Color picture requires a whopping 2.25 MB of space, so, with my, sniff, high standards, I like to say that a picture is worth 450,000 words.

And if pictures take a lot of space, videos take even more. What often saves the day is compression. Files often have a lot of inefficiently presented data in them. For example, if a black-and-white bitmap is presented a series of bits indicating black and white dots as 0's and 1's, that's not going to be too efficient for "typical" pictures. Because pictures are usually made of blobs, if a given dot is black, it is likely that the next dot will be black. It is clearly more efficient to code most pictures by describing them as "first so many black dots, then so many white dots, then . . ."

 That's a simple compression technique known as run length encoding (RLE). Another set of algorithms, of which the best known is Huffman compression, depends on the fact that something like a text file will use the letter e a lot more often than the letter q, not to mention the ASCII code for ©! Huffman schemes use fewer than 8 bits for e's and more for characters like © and gain space in the bargain.

 By far the most common compression algorithms, though, depend on the fact that bit patterns tend to be repeated over and over and over. It may be more efficient to use shorthand meaning "the three letters that occurred 27 letters ago" than to reuse the word "the." The Mother of All Repeating-Pattern Algorithms is Lempel-Ziv and a variant on it called Lempel-Ziv-Welch (LZ and LZW). These algorithms are behind **zip** and **gif** files and Drive Space.

 Abraham Lempel and Jacob Ziv are two Israeli academic computer scientists who pioneered the technology in the late 1970s. Terry Welch worked for one of the companies that merged to become Unisys, which claims a patent on LZW. There have been huge arguments over how much of the technology was already in LZ and so in the public domain. Periodically, Unisys tries to assert its claims, most recently demanding royalties on all the **gif** files on the World Wide Web. Sigh.

All these schemes are lossless compression schemes, which means that one can recover the original file byte for byte from the compressed file. This is obviously a requirement if you are going to compress programs or highly structured data like that in a spreadsheet. But if the colors of a few pixels in a picture are changed, the eye won't notice; if the high-frequency part of a recorded sound is dropped, your dog's ear might notice but yours won't. So multimedia files can use lossless compression schemes where the original file can't be reconstructed byte for byte. JPEG and MPEG (for pictures and videos, respectively) are the two best known lossless compression schemes.

 I had to restrain Barry from bending your ears with all the technical details behind these schemes since he finds the mathematical ideas so lovely. But I told him that readers could go and look at the two pieces on compression that he wrote for *PC Magazine* in 1993 if they want more details.

**Figure 2-43.
Multimedia
Properties tab**

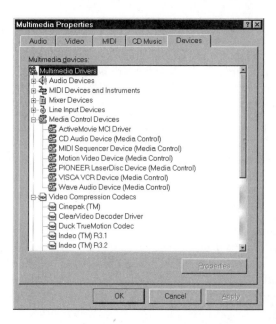

Programs that play compressed videos or audios have to know how to decompress them or have to have the decompression done for them automatically by the operating system. Windows is built around the second idea and provides many built-in decompression schemes. When you record something and save it to disk, you may want to compress it automatically. The drivers that compress and decompress are called Codecs—get it? COmpress/DECompress.

The Advanced tab of the Multimedia applet in Control Panel (Figure 2-43) displays the installed Video and Audio Codecs. Windows should have installed them during setup, but if they aren't there and you plan to run any videos or play **wav** files, you can install them by running Add/Remove Programs, going to Windows Setup, highlighting Multimedia, hitting the Details button and making sure both Audio Compression and Video Compression are checked.

If you read the original Mother of All Windows Books, *for Windows 3.1, you may wonder whatever happened to the Wave Mapper. It's become the Audio Compression Manager. Go to the part of the Devices tab of the Multimedia dialog labeled Audio Compression Codecs, open it, highlight Microsoft PCM Converter, click Properties and About. You'll see the bits per sample converter that was at the heart of "le scandale du Wave Mapper."*

I hope Janet doesn't read that book!

Media Control Interface—Do You Mean Mike McCurry?

Windows' support for multimedia is extensible; drivers written to what Microsoft calls **MCI**, for Media Control Interface, can be plugged into any program that uses the MCI API. If you get a new multimedia device, say a video disc player, the Media Player applet can play files from it, if the vendor supplies a driver that supports MCI.

MCI defines the following standard device types:

animation	animation device, such as an Autodesk **flc** player
cdaudio	Red Book audio from a CD
dat	digital audio tape player
digitalvideo	digital video in a window
other	undefined **MCI** type
overlay	analog video in a window
scanner	image scanner
sequencer	MIDI sequencer to play **mid** and **rmi** files
vcr	video recorder or player
videodisc	videodisc player
waveaudio	audio device that plays digitized **wav** files

An MCI driver has to respond to two types of commands—a **command message interface** and a **command string interface**. The command message interface uses the Windows API called **mcisendcommand**. It is intended for C programmers and is much like any other part of the Windows API. The command string interface uses what appears to be English language. Here's a little program written in the command string interface (with comments on each line in {...}):

open tada.wav type waveaudio	{gets control of the **wav** player; gives it a file to open}
play waveaudio	{tells the driver to play the sound}
close waveaudio	{returns control of the **wav** player to Windows}

The presence of a command string interface is an indication that Microsoft expects sophisticated users to try to use MCI in macro languages. As a first step, Visual Basic has an MCI custom control that uses a variant of the command string interface. Moreover, when Media Player pauses, you can hit **Ctrl+F5** and open a special window that lets you send **MCI** commands to the current device. For a video, try typing in **status frames skipped** or choose CD audio in the Device menu and type in **set door open** to eject the CD.

The full documentation for the command string interface is available as part of the Windows 98 SDK. To give you an idea of the power of the command string interface, note that the commands include Open, Close, Play, Record, Pause, Resume, Seek, Stop, Status, Freeze (for video), and Set Tempo (for MIDI).

Windows stores the list of installed MCI types in the Registry (where it stores nearly everything else) in the key (see Chapter 9):

```
HKEY_LOCAL_MACHINE\system\currentcontrolset\control
   \mediaresources\mci
```

You have access to the list in the Devices tab of the Control Panel Multimedia Properties applet. Figure 2-43 shows the list with the seven MCI drivers built into Windows.

 Media Player uses a rather involved scheme to get the items it shows on its Device menu and to pick up the File extensions it uses in the File dialog that then pops up. First it looks in the **[mci]** section of **system.ini** to find the names of all the MCI drivers. Then it makes calls to the drivers themselves to find out the user-friendly names to use. When it pops up the File/Open dialog, it looks in the **[mci extensions]** section of **win.ini** to figure out what extensions are associated to the various devices.

 C'mon, Barry, ol' buddy. That's quite a whopper you've made up there! Microsoft says **ini** files were no longer used by Windows 95 and its components; surely any residual that was there in Windows 95 must have been scoured out for Windows 98. Your scheme doesn't even mention the Registry, where we know all this sort of information goes. Have you any evidence to back up this preposterous theory?

 My esteemed Mr. Woody, of course I wouldn't posit such a theory without an experiment to back it up. I did the following. First I copied the driver **midseq.drv** to **midseq1.drv**. I loaded that copy into a binary file editor I have and located the string **MIDI Sequencer** near the end of the driver. That was the name that appeared on Media Player's Device menu but was nowhere to be found in the entire Registry, so I figured this might be significant and I changed it to **MOMS Sequencer**. Then I loaded up **System Configuration Utility** and changed the line in **system.ini's** **[mci]** section that said **sequencer=mciseq.drv** to instead say **sequencer=mciseq1.drv**. And I added the line **barry=Sequencer** to the **[mci extensions]** section of **win.ini**. I saved those files and started up Media Player. On the Device menu, what had been MIDI Sequencer now said MOMS Sequencer, and the Open dialog I saw is in Figure 2-44. Look at what it says under "File of Type" at the bottom of that dialog.

Figure 2-44. Barry's experiment

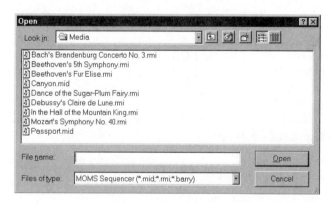

Bravo! But why, oh, why did Microsoft do that?

 Hey, guys, we had code that worked perfectly well in Windows 3.1. Why change it merely to keep some "We don't want no stinking inifiles" purists happy?

CD Mania

Bill Gates is a CD visionary. In 1986, he organized the first international conference on CD-ROM technology, calling it "The New Papyrus." One of the first products on the PC to show what could be done was Microsoft's Multimedia Beethoven (which wasn't made by Microsoft, but was successfully marketed by the Redmondians). Microsoft has been a major player in several types of CD-ROMs, so, for example, EnCarta, its encyclopedia, outsells the best-selling print encyclopedia by more than a factor of 10.

Yet when it came to the operating system, CDs were treated as an afterthought. Support for CDs was not built into the core of DOS but was provided by a program called MSCDEX (for MicroSoft CD EXtensions) that took over 40K of valuable below-1-M RAM. Until DOS 6.0, this program wasn't even included with DOS but was provided by CD-ROM manufacturers, which meant that users had the hassle of getting a new version from their hardware supplier whenever they got a new version of DOS.

With Windows 9X, CD technology is finally being taken seriously. Of course, this is no surprise; except for some low-end portables, every PC now sold has a CD drive with it. Here's what Windows 98 provides for CDs.

- **Built-in CD file system** that is handled via a VxD
- **Autoplay for audio CDs**   Put an audio CD into the drive and Windows 98 CD Player will pop up and start playing the CD. If you hold down a Shift key while popping the CD into the drive, it won't autoplay. In Chapter 4, I'll explain how to disable autoplay so that the CD will not automatically start playing. You'll still be able to start playing by right clicking the CD icon and choosing Play.
- **Audio CD track support**   You can drag a specific track of a specific CD to the Desktop or Start menu, pick it, and have Windows tell you which CD to put in and then play that track. I'll discuss this further in Chapter 4.
- **CD Plus support**   This is an enhanced audio CD specification from SONY and Phillips that allows audio CDs to come with data; the idea is that pictures of the stars, video clips, and more on the music CD would enhance the experience. The CD could be played on a standard audio CD player, but if you load it under Windows 98, you get the extra goodies. The spec depends critically on multisession technology, so you'll need a CD drive with multisession support. Most single-speed and some very early double-speed CDs don't have this, but any recently manufactured CD drive will.

This format was introduced in Windows 95 to great fanfare but its been pretty much an unused failure.

- **Autoplay for CD-ROMs**   A CD maker can arrange that when a CD is placed in the drive the CD will just start running. This will be ideal for younger kids and also for users who don't want to worry about what drive letter their CD drive is. As with audio CDs, if you hold down a Shift key while popping the CD into the drive, it won't autoplay. Unlike audio CD, there is no way to prevent automatic autoplay while keeping autoplay capability on a context menu.

- **Informative CD icons**   If you look at a CD drive in My Computer or drag a shortcut to a drive onto the Desktop, a CD-ROM maker can arrange for a special icon to replace the default and so let you know what CD is in the drive. Place an audio CD in the drive and see 🖴 replaced by 💿. Or pop the Windows CD in and see the icon become 💿.

- New with Windows 98, the **Emergency Boot Diskettes** include generic IDE and SCSI drivers for CDs.

- New with Windows 98, **support for DVD**, the probable successor to the CD spec.

■ No PC Is an Island

Networking Light

Only connect! That was the whole of her sermon. Only connect the prose and the passion, and both will be exalted, and human love will be seen at its height. Live in fragments no longer.

—E. M. FORSTER, *Howards End,* 1910

If you want to know about using Windows 98 with a "real" network, which these days most often means with a Windows NT server, you are looking in the wrong place. Dealing with the issues raised by large-scale networks requires a book of its own at least the size of this book.

But Windows 98 has built in peer-to-peer networking, which is ideal for a small business or home office with a few machines to connect to each other and useful for what we expect to become a common scenario in the home, a den with more than one computer that the modern family will need as the kids want to do homework or play games at the same time Mom wants to check her e-mail. So we want to say something about setting up a simple peer-to-peer network.

Even more significantly, even if the idea of ethernet and peer-to-peer networking gives you the willies and you wouldn't think of using anything but a stand-alone PC, you're going to get brushed pretty hard by networking if you want to connect to the Internet because the Internet is a network and Windows 98 treats it as such. Dial-Up Networking is the name that Windows 98 gives to network connections over a phone line, be it to an Internet provider or to your corporate network or from your portable computer to a stand-alone machine at home!

I'll give you some of the basic terminology here and discuss Dial-Up Networking and Internet access in Chapter 4.

There are four components to a network as far as Windows 98 is concerned.

1. **Adapters**   Most typically an ethernet hardware board that needs to be installed through the Network applet of Control Panel. But it can also be the virtual adapter called Dial-Up Adapter that you install to do "networking" over the phone line.

 If you have a Plug 'n' Play Ethernet card, the automatic install should set up all the drivers you need.

2. **Protocols**   Methods networks use to talk to one another. If you are connecting to a large-scale network, you'll probably want to use the protocols the network's maker provides, but for the kind of networks I'm discussing, you'll want the Microsoft protocols IPX/SP, NetBUI, and TCP/IP. When you install the adapter, the associated protocols should be installed.

3. **Client**   Software that allows your computer to use the protocols and adapters to actually do stuff over the network. For the kind of connections I'm discussing, you'll want the Client for Microsoft Networks. Again, this should be installed when you install the adapter.

4. **Services**   Provides extras. If you want other machines to be able to access files on your machine, you'll need to add "File and printer sharing for Microsoft Networks." Rather than add this explicitly, you press the File and Printer Sharing button in the Network applet, and when you hit the check boxes, the necessary service is turned on. Be sure to check what I say in Chapter 8 about the need to separate turn-on sharing for individual drives even after turning on general File and Printer Sharing.

TCP/IP is the standard protocol of the Internet. When you have an Internet provider that gives you direct access to the net, they'll normally establish a PPP account for you, and you'll need TCP/IP support (a **TCP/IP stack**) on your machine.

 TCP/IP = Transmission Control Protocol/Internet Protocol; PPP = point–to–point protocol. Thoroughly useless information but I thought you'd be curious.

A Windows dll that provides TCP/IP is called a **Winsock**, and before Windows 95 there were lots of third-party Winsocks floating around.

 When Microsoft introduced its own Winsock in Windows 95, certain people howled about it putting the third-party Winsock makers out of business. But there is no question that this functionality belongs in the operating system, and users gained: a single Winsock avoided capability problems and precluded the need to locate and perhaps purchase another product.

Before you worry about installing TCP/IP, you'll want to read about the Internet Connection Wizard I talk about in Chapter 4.

A final general networking issue concerns **UNC**† **filenames** that are fully supported in Windows 98. Every workstation on a network has a name. Newt's machine might be called Aye. If you want to refer to a file in `C:\windows` on that machine, you could type in `\\aye\c\windows` any place Windows 98 accepts a filename. Of course, Windows 3.1 applications and DOS applications aren't likely to understand this terminology. But Windows 98 understands it so well that if you type the line in the Run box, it will open that folder in Folder/View!

With this understanding of UNC names, drive mapping becomes a thing of the past. You no longer need to refer to drives with associated letters—which you can run out if you link a number of machines together.

The Mother of All Networks

A century or so from now, observers looking back on the 1990s will consider the advent of the Internet and the World-Wide Web one of the great watersheds of history—comparable technologically to the invention of movable type, artistically to the Renaissance, and socially to the Declaration of Independence. You may think this assessment grandiose, but look around you: The great on-line body of individually authored and hyperlinked information that Ted Nelson envisioned decades ago as the Xanadu project is day by day crystallizing before our eyes. Tens of thousands of creative network citizens across the world are setting up their own information servers and joining the Web. In the process, those net citizens are completely bypassing the Establishment with its bureaucracies, class hierarchies, and power structures, not to mention the entire monolithic apparatus of the traditional publishing industry!

—RAY DUNCAN, *PC Magazine,* May 16, 1995

Duncan is right. There is no question that history books a hundred years from now will remember the 1990s for the Web, not Monica or OJ. There is no source of communications or information that isn't being profoundly affected

---

† Universal Naming Convention, if you must know!

by the advent of the Internet: newspapers and scholarly journals, books, travel reservations, the phone system. It boggles the mind to think about what is happening. We certainly live in interesting times!

"May you live in interesting times" is a Chinese curse. For many businesses, this is indeed true. Think of it: local phone companies could get wiped out in the next 30 years if some other Internet connection takes off. Stockbrokers are losing a lot of customers to the under-$25 online brokers. Scientific journal publishers could disappear. The list goes on and on.

The Internet began as Arpanet—the Army advanced project network—connecting together mainly a bunch of academics. But e-mail and discussion were so incredibly convenient and powerful that word spread and academics outside ARPA wanted in. Eventually, the NSF took over responsibility for what came to be called NSFNet and then the Internet. With the advent of the Web and browsers, things really took off.

Basically the Internet is a collection of computers all wired together using a basic binary protocol called TCP/IP. There is an alphabet soup of higher-level data exchange protocols like HTTP, HTML, FTP, and POP that I'll discuss in the next section.

It is estimated that over 150 million users have access to the Internet. Growth isn't the 100%+ it was for a few years, but it certainly is still well into double digits. And the World Wide Web's growth has been phenomenal. It too has slowed somewhat, but at the height of its growth in mid-1995, it was estimated that the number of "pages" on the Web was doubling every 23 days. Clearly, the Internet and its components are an important part of computing.

One has to take some of the Internet numbers with a huge grain of salt. Many of those 150 million users have e-mail accounts only. And when a Web site brags of 3 million hits a day, that doesn't mean 3 million people visiting; the counts typically include every page visited and however many times the user's browser downloads it when they return to it. Still 500,000 visitors a day and 50 million people browsing the Web are mind-numbing numbers.

The large numbers of users and sites and the variety of different information providers give the Internet something of an unruly nature. It will be a frequent occurrence that you'll click on a link on a Web page or request a file through the Archie search engine and get a message that the resource you are looking for isn't available. This can have two different causes. First, the site you are searching for may have literally disappeared—the owner of the site may have stopped paying the bills of the service provider, or the machine the site was on may be down, temporarily or permanently. When a piece of the Net disappears, the pointers to it elsewhere on the Net will long remain.

The second cause for unavailability is that there may be more users accessing the resource than the resource is able to handle. Sometimes you'll get an explicit message from the resource telling you this, but sometimes you'll just be unable to make the connection and not know why. Sometimes if there are too many users, performance just slows to a crawl. Speaking of performance, Web browsing is graphically intensive, and that means large files. You won't find browsing at 28,800 bps that pleasant. If you do a lot of browsing, look into a 55K modem or ISDN—or true nirvana: a cable modem or xDSL connection.

Many phone companies shot themselves in the foot on ISDN. For example, Pacific Bell came close to offering home users unlimited access accounts a few times but then pulled back to per-minute charges after an initial 200 channel hours per month (and high speed is two channels so those 200 hours are really 100). They are talking the same way about xSDL. If they don't wake up, the cable companies will eat their lunch.

Internet for Smartypants

*I've discovered the killer application that will establish
Internet. No, it's not the World Wide Web. It's e-mail.*

—MOM

So what can you do on the Internet? Here's a list of the main functions, listed roughly in the ranking of importance (according to Mom):

- **e-mail**   Short for electronic mail, not that anyone uses that term any more. There truly is a way to send messages to millions of other people, have them get them at their convenience, and transfer them as cheaply to someone around the world as around the corner. Windows 98 supports e-mail through Outlook Express (discussed in detail in Chapter 3).

- **World Wide Web**, aka **the Web**   A collection of information resources that are hyperlinked together. Providers produce one or more "home pages" of information with links to other pages that let you jump by pointing and clicking. There are literally millions of pages out there with useful information varying from daily postings by *Time* magazine to access to parts of the Library of Congress. A high school student cannot only locate information on hundreds of colleges but often requests an application while on the Web. Because of the links, you can wander from Web site to Web site searching and even sometimes enjoying. This is called "surfing the Web" or "surfing the Net." Programs that let you surf the Net are called Web browsers. Of course, the Web browser built into Windows is Internet Explorer. Its most prominent competitor is Netscape (Navigator and Communicator).

The Web truly is wonderful. If you have an idea of what you want to find, you can often get useful information quickly. But it is also the most overhyped service on the Internet. Random fooling can spend enormous gobs of time without much to show for it. That surfing the Web beats TV for entertainment is a negative statement about TV rather than a positive one about the Web.

 Learning to use search engines is essential. I prefer Yahoo and Alta Vista but know others who swear by Excite or Infoseek or Hotbot.

- **FTP**   Short for File Transfer Protocol, the standard, or, protocol for transferring files over the Internet. Actually, the name is used not so much for the protocol as for transferring files from special Internet nodes called **anonymous FTP sites**. That name comes from the fact that you can log onto the nodes as a user called "anonymous" with a password equal to your e-mail address. You'll find software libraries, drivers from many vendors, and more at various FTP sites. You can do FTP transfer from Internet Explorer. Windows 98 comes with a DOS (!) program called FTP (see Chapter 4). In Chapter 5, I'll discuss a third-party program called FTP Voyager for those who use FTP a lot.

- **Mailing lists**   An interesting hybrid of the discussion forums you'll find on the online services and plain mail. Different mailing lists have different focuses. They may be as specific as support groups for parents of children with cancer or as general as U.S. politics. Once you find out the source of a mailing list you want, you subscribe to it (typically by sending e-mail to an address that starts with `listserv@...` with text that says SUSCRIBE), and it appears once a day in your mailbox with all the messages for that day. Or you can often ask the list server to send you messages individually as they come in. There is usually some process you have to go through to be authorized to add messages of your own to the list. When you subscribe, you'll get back a message telling you how to unsubscribe and usually providing other options. The `listserv` address is totally automated, so it is important that you follow syntax directions precisely.

Some lists are moderated (someone authorizes which messages are placed on the list) and some are not. There are also private lists that are used to send messages out with no way for outsiders to submit their own messages—an example is the Exploring Windows newsletter on Windows 98 put out by Microsoft. To subscribe to it, you go to the Web page `http://register.microsoft.com /regwiz/forms/pic.asp`. In Chapter 3, I talk about MOM's top ten mailing lists.

You don't need any special software to access mailing lists other than e-mail software. Some lists will send you the mail in HTML format, so you need a mail program (like Outlook Express) that understands that format of e-mail.

In between mailing lists and e-mail are personalized information sources that will send you regular information by mail. My favorite is Infobeat (`http://www.infobeat.com/`), which includes news clips, stock quotes, sports, comics, and more. For most of their services the "cost" is in the banner ads in the mail.

- **Newsgroups**, aka **uunet** or **usenet**   Publicly posted groups of messages in forums that run the gamut from `rec.humor.funny` and `biz.jobs.offered` to `alt.tv.dinosaur.barney.die.die.die` and `alt.sex.fetish.tickling`. Outlook Express includes newsgroup capabilities.

`alt.sex.fetish.tickling` is for real and brings up the point that there are parts of the Internet that are pretty raunchy. A kid looking not too hard can find pictures of naked ladies—and I do mean naked—in about 5 minutes. He can also find pictures at a local magazine stand, but he's more noticeable there. If your kids surf the Net, they'll need some supervision.

- **Telnet**   A protocol for remote login from one machine to another in dumb text mode. This is probably only relevant to you if you have an account on a UNIX-based network, if you get into MUDs (see the discussion of MUDs later in this list) or if you want to access a BBS system via Telnet. Windows 98 includes a GUI Telnet program that I discuss in Chapter 4.

- **Archie**   Search tools for files on FTP sites. Various Archie sites are accessible via the Web and so via Internet Explorer, as I explain later.

- **Gopher**   An older method than the World Wide Web for dispersing information on the Internet. It involves text databases with fill-in-the-blanks forms for searching. There is still some amount of information out there in gophers. You can access gopher via Internet Explorer or via Telnet.

- **Veronica**   Search tools for "gopherspace" that try to locate a gopher with some particular information. Various Veronica sites are accessible via the Web and also via Internet Explorer.

- **Chat**, aka **IRC**   Short for Internet Relay Chat. It's what it sounds like—a CB simulator but text based. Windows 98 doesn't come with any software for IRC. You'll need third-party software for it. You can find shareware IRC programs on the Internet.

If you want to send messages to and from others, I like the free program ICQ (`http://www.icq.com/`) from Mirabilis. As long as the people you want to talk with are connected to the Internet and have ICQ, you can easily send text messages back and forth. ICQ uses not IRC but the Mirabilis servers to do the transfer. Similarly, NetMeeting (discussed in Chapter 4) can be used for discussions over the Net.

ICQ = I Seek U; cute, I guess.

- **MUD**   Short for MultiUser Dungeons, MUDs are Internet text-based games with elaborate rules. You log onto most MUDs via Telnet. Windows 98 includes a Telnet program. There are beginning to be Web-based GUI MUDs.

 Just so you know what HTTP, HTML, and XML mean when you see them, allow me a techie aside. The Web works by using protocols that browsers understand and that Web page editors know about. HTTP, short for HyperText Transfer Protocol, is the command language the browser uses to send out commands to the Web to access certain pages. That's why addresses are prefaced by "http:\\." What is sent back is text written in HTML = HyperText Markup Language. If you want to have a feel for what that looks like, go to a Web page in IE and pick Source from the View menu. HTML provides extra information in tags. For example, you turn on boldface by including the text **** and turn it off with ****. XML, short for eXtended Markup Language, is the new kid on the block. It allows systematic extensions to HTML such as MathML.

 Similarly, ASP stands for Active Server Pages, a feature of the full-blown Microsoft Web Server. If you see a Web address that ends in **.asp**, you know that's what it is.

Me Love Cookies

C is for cookie, it's good enough for me;
Oh cookie cookie cookie starts with C.

—COOKIE MONSTER

Often when you visit a site, it needs information about you, the same information you gave it the last time that you logged on. Rather than force you to reenter the information each time you visit, the site can store the information. Some sites store the information on their server, which can be convenient if you log in from somewhere else. Others store the information in what are called **cookies**—text files that are kept on your local machine in **C:\windows\cookies**.

 There is a totally unwarranted level of hysteria in some quarters over cookies. The exact concern makes no sense, since the server could store the information on its own disk, making you log in each time. You'd have less control over it than you do when it is on your local machine.

Part of the concern is that it is totally transparent. It can store the information without telling you and reuse the information when you next visit, again without telling you. At least with a login mechanism, you can log in as someone else each time. Still, the concern is overblown.

There are real privacy concerns on the Internet, but focusing them on cookie technology is the wrong way to express them. I'd like to see an industrywide (not government) privacy standard that sites adopt and proudly advertise that they are using, with a set of strong privacy requirements like a page where you could go to find out and correct all the information the site has on you. Sites should also agree not to disclose any of your personal information unless you explicitly permit it.

MAPI and TAPI

One of Microsoft's ways of controlling the software market is to place high barriers for the entry of small, innovative companies. Their favorite device for making it hard for the small developer is the API of the month.

—A DISGRUNTLED PROGRAMMER

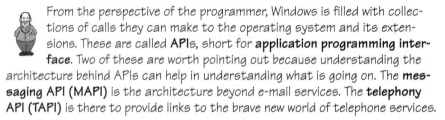

From the perspective of the programmer, Windows is filled with collections of calls they can make to the operating system and its extensions. These are called **APIs**, short for **application programming interface**. Two of these are worth pointing out because understanding the architecture behind APIs can help in understanding what is going on. The **messaging API (MAPI)** is the architecture beyond e-mail services. The **telephony API (TAPI)** is there to provide links to the brave new world of telephone services.

MAPI is intended to provide a universal inbox, a single place where all your e-mail is collected and stored. At the same time, it provides a uniform place to store name, address, and telephone number information. The MAPI architecture has five components.

1. **Message store provider**   Message stores are files with a specified format that store messages and other personal information. These files have an extension `.pst` and are sometimes referred to as a **personal information store**. If you installed Exchange under Windows 95, it will make such a file for you. Outlook does also. Outlook Express does not use MAPI.

2. **Address book provider**   MAPI specifies a format for address books and allows other service providers to extend the information stored in an address book record so that, for example, CompuServe can define the formats it requires for e-mail messages sent via CompuServe. **Personal address books** have the extension `.pab`. Again, Outlook can set up such a file for you, although the preferred mode in Outlook 98 is to store contact information in your `.pst` file.

3. **Transport service providers**   Provide the back-end links to various places that mail can be sent to. These providers respond to requests from clients and message-aware applications to send or collect mail. Under Windows 95, Exchange automatically offered to install two transport providers when you installed it—Microsoft FAX and the Microsoft Network. The Windows CD had a transport provider supplied by CompuServe. Internet Explorer offered to install a fourth provider for Internet Mail. MCI Mail introduced a MAPI service provider.

4. **MAPI client**   Basic user interface to the whole shebang. The client accesses the address book and information store to allow the user to read and compose mail and then calls the transport providers to actually send and collect the mail. Exchange was the MAPI client provided with Windows 95. Windows 98 comes with the plumbing for MAPI but does not come with a built-in MAPI client. Outlook and TalkWorks Pro are two MAPI clients that you can use with Windows 98.

5. **Message-aware applications**   When they sense that a MAPI client is installed in the system, programs can add a Send . . . command to their File menus that will send the current document to the message store and then invoke the client to handle addressing and the actual sending of the messages.

The wonderful thing about this architecture is that it sets standards. Third parties can produce their own MAPI clients with more features than Exchange or with the ability to more easily manipulate the message store or the address book. Since the file specifications are standard, files manipulated with one client should be readable in another. And the transport providers should work with any client.

 To me, one of the most exciting parts of the whole specification is the common address book. I don't want to count the number of times I've had to reenter hundreds of addresses and phone numbers because I changed PIMs (PIM = personal information manager) or because my envelope addresser didn't understand my PIM's format. At this point I'm only interested in PIMs that use the MAPI address book to get addresses, phone numbers, and so on.

TAPI provides a common set of calls that allow programs access to the telephone without having to reinvent the wheel. A program after installation can offer to register their product by phone without knowing anything about modems. Once the program determines that a TAPI provider is present in the system, it just sends commands to dial. A PIM could track incoming phone calls by using caller ID with calls to the TAPI provider. This use of caller ID needs specialized hardware in your computer.

You may hear references to subsets of these basic APIs that are useful to programmers because they are easier to use. For TAPI, this subset is called **assisted telephony**. For MAPI, it is called **common message calls (CMC)**.

I have a favorite acronym in these specs, **POTS**, that is sprinkled through the TAPI documentation. What does POTS stand for? Plain Old Telephone Service. I kid you not.

 My favorite is TSAPI, the TAPI competitor offered by Novell. What's so cool about the acronym? Well, unless you live in Ogden (Novell's home turf), it's pronounced "sappy." Proof positive that engineers have a tin ear for marketing!

Chapter 3

Core Components

A fierce unrest seethes at the core,
Of all existing things,
It was the eager wish to soar,
That gave the gods their wings.

—Don Marquis, *Unrest*

They call it the Windows 98 shell. It's the console you use to drive spaceship Windows. The most important functions are task management, file manipulation, program launching, and Web browsing. And that's what I start with. Pay particular attention to the discussion in the section "Configuring Context Menus and Associations" because that's a wondrous power feature of Windows 98 that seems to have gotten lost in most magazines' meandering on the product. Be sure to check out "Sarah's Smart Setup Step by Step," the power user's preferred way to have folders and drives open. Then I talk about some of the other core components, including a first brush at Control Panel (continued in Chapter 8), Network Neighborhood, Help, and how Windows handles DOS sessions. Finally, there's Outlook Express. Many would argue it's an applet, not a core component, but I think e-mail is the most important part of computing for many and a core component for all.

Yeah, but you're well advised to use Outlook, not Outlook Express, as both you and I do, Barry.

Me, too.

Taken to Taskbar

. . . the task itself arises only when the material conditions necessary for its solution already exist . . .

—KARL MARX, *A Contribution to the Critique of Political Economy*

 There's no feature of Windows 98 more obvious to a new user sitting down to a new machine than the Taskbar (see Figure 3-1). So what better place to start than the Taskbar? Besides, the Start button is there (although this is not the group of sections where my team will discuss the Start Menu itself; that'll come after the Taskbar and Explorer discussions).

When someone starts up Windows 98 and there are no programs in the StartUp group, they get a "Click here to begin" and an arrow bouncing up against the

Figure 3-1. This must be the start of something grand

Start button, as shown in Figure 3-1. Kinda tacky, but it wows them newbies.

 The irony of the fancy start is that if the Welcome application runs—the one that pops a message about Windows onto the screen (Figure 3-2)—at startup, then the moving "Click here . . ." message is not displayed.

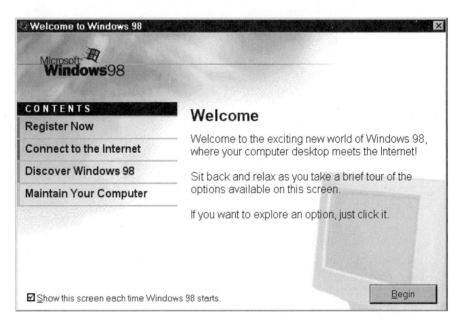

Figure 3-2. "Come into my parlor," said the spider to the fly

The Welcome screen in Windows 98 is a sad comedown from that of Windows 95. In 95, the tips got old fast, but at least there were useful tips to read. Now you have glitz, and the buttons lead to Microsoft patting itself on the back if you pick an option like Discover Windows 98. My advice is to Register and then uncheck the box that requests the program to load every time Windows starts. Get rid of this as soon as you can! If you have unchecked the box and ever need the Welcome screen again, just type Welcome into the Run applet.

Of all the idiocy, the music that accompanies the Welcome screen takes the cake. It might be cool for home users, but I'll bet you'd be embarrassed if your boss walked into your office the first time you started up Windows 98 to that music.

Hey, we have to do something to convince business users to move to NT, don't we?

Taskbar Basics

The hardest task of a girl's life, nowadays, is to prove to a man that his intentions are serious.

—HELEN ROWLAND, *A Guide to Men,* 1922

The Taskbar has five parts.

Five? I only see four: the Start button, the task buttons, the bunch of cute little icons that start with the Internet Explorer "e" and that area on the extreme right with the time and tiny icons.

The bunch of icons is the Quick Launch Toolbar, and the area with tiny icons is called the Notification Area. And the fifth part is the blank, unoccupied part of the task button area in the middle. The blank area is important because it lets you do quite a few things. First, you can right click and get the menu shown in Figure 3-3. The first item gives you a submenu that lets you control which toolbars appear on the Taskbar. By default only the Quick Launch Toolbar does, but you can change that, as I explain shortly. The next three menu items rearrange all open Windows—cascading places them overlapping along a diagonal. Tile cancels the overlapping function. Minimize All Windows gives you access to the Desktop with all the Windows gone.

Figure 3-3. Taskbar context menu

It is important to note the fact that if you pick any of the middle four items, the menu picks up an Undo option. With the first three choices, Undo is an extra option; if you pick

Minimize All Windows, then the next time you invoke the menu that option is grayed out, and in essence, the Undo Minimize All is a replacement. This has two important consequences. First, you can experiment with Tile and Cascade, the results of which won't always be to your liking.

 Second, you can pick Minimize All Windows to get at the Desktop, launch an icon on the Desktop, and then Undo Minimize All, since that command stays on the Taskbar context menu for several actions afterwards.

I talk about the Taskbar Properties menu, which you can access from the context menu, in a bit. I first want to note that the unoccupied part of the Taskbar is also what you use to move the Taskbar. Click and hold the mouse cursor over a blank part of the Taskbar and experiment with what happens if you drag it. You can repeat the process to drag the Taskbar back. You'll notice that you can place the Taskbar in any of the four edges of the screen. It's as if the blank part of the Taskbar were playing the role played by the title bar of a normal window.

 It's clear that most users will leave it at the bottom of the screen, if only because they don't know you can move it, but it is clear that sophisticated users are already split into warring camps—much like Swift's bottom enders and top enders, there are the bottom taskers and right side taskers and. . . . And, as we'll see, there are also arguments about Autohide. I don't cotton much to theological arguments so I'll let you figure out which you prefer.

 Even if you like the Taskbar at the bottom of the screen very much, thank you, there are two reasons you need to know about moving the Taskbar. First, you can move it by mistake. You reach to click a button, your hand slips and suddenly your lovely Taskbar has moved from the bottom to the side and you haven't the foggiest idea how to move it back. Well, you do if you read what I just told you.

 Second, there is a neato stupid Desktop trick. I like a nice neat column of drive icons along the right edge of my screen. How do I line them up? Simple: I sort of line them up along the right side. Then I drag the Taskbar to the right side and maybe stretch it to be a little wider. It lines the icons up nice and neat to the left side of the Taskbar. Then I just drag the Taskbar back, lasso the column of icons and move them in bulk.

You can also resize the Taskbar, that is, make it higher when it is horizontal and wider when it is vertical. Just let your cursor hover over the edge of the Taskbar opposite from the screen edge until it changes into a double header arrow; then press and drag.

 Certainly at 1,024 × 768 resolution and maybe at 800 × 600, I recommend that the horizontal Taskbar have two rows. In fact, with the new toolbars, I like to use a three-row Taskbar at 1,024 × 768 with the bottom row taken by three toolbars (Figure 3-4).

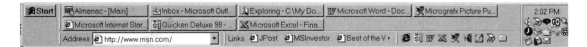

Figure 3-4. A tiskit, a Taskit, a three-row basket

A final remark on getting at the blank part of the Taskbar. If you have a two-row or deeper Taskbar, there is always a blank area beneath the Start button. Even if you only have a one-row Taskbar, there is usually a thin line between the recessed notification area and the rightmost task button and an even thinner line to the right of the recessed notification area. You can right click on those areas to get at the Taskbar context menu.

 In Windows 95, Microsoft made the mistake of keeping the notification area a single row high and wasting the space below it on multiple-row taskbars. Windows 98 not only uses the whole area but presses the icons to fit more rows than there are in the rest of the taskbar. In Figure 3-4 you see four rows in the notification area and three elsewhere. Way to go, Microsoft. Thanks for fixing this one.

There isn't much to say about the buttons on the Taskbar. Each brings its application to the top when pressed whether the program is minimized or just behind another program. If you right click on a button, the system menu for that program will pop up. If the full caption for a program won't fit on the button, an ellipsis appears, and then if you place the mouse cursor over the button and let it rest for a moment, a ToolTip appears with the full caption. This is especially useful for Explorer buttons since they often have long directory names, and the Windows designers made the mistake of placing the program name before the directory name.

 You might expect that dragging an icon to a button on the Taskbar and dropping it would open the window and tell the program to open the dropped file. But you'd be wrong. If you do that, Windows punishes you with the dumb dialog in Figure 3-5. What it's telling you to do is to let the icon hover over the button until the window opens and then drop the icon into the open window. In other words, it makes it quite clear that it understands what you want even though it doesn't do it.

 We had to do this since a window can have multiple drag and drop targets. For example if you drop a Word file into a Word file, it OLE embeds it, while if you drop it on the Word toolbar, it opens it in a new window.

Figure 3-5. That'll teach you to expect things to work reasonably!

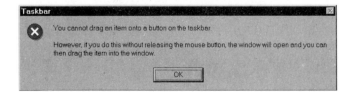

C'mon, Billy, do some intelligent default thing. At a minimum, change the specs so a program can be given a drop-on toolbar message to react to.

Figure 3-6. Taskbar property sheet

If you choose Properties from the Taskbar context menu (or Settings/Taskbar & Start Menu . . . from the Start Menu), you get the property sheet shown in Figure 3-6. I'll talk about the Start Menu tab and about the third check box when I discuss the Start Menu. The Show Clock check box obviously determines whether the time is shown at the extreme right of the Taskbar. I can't imagine why anyone would want to, but you can turn off the display of the time.

"Always on top" controls whether other windows can cover the Taskbar. If the box is checked (the default) when a program asks Windows to maximize a window, it fills only the part of the screen other than the Taskbar. I can't imagine why anyone would want this option independently of Auto hide.

The Auto hide choice is an interesting one that causes the Taskbar to normally appear as a single thin line. Move the mouse cursor to the thin line and the Taskbar pops up to its normal size; move the cursor away and the Taskbar disappears again.

 If you are running at 640 × 480, screen real estate is so valuable that Auto hide will be extremely tempting for any user. As resolutions go up, the case is less compelling, so much so that I wouldn't turn Auto hide on at 1,024 × 768.

 Well, I wouldn't think about running without Auto hide on no matter what the resolution, and I'd urge all our readers to at least give it a try.

 We agree it's something everyone should try. To my taste, it only makes sense at the bottom of the screen because every other edge is used by many programs' windows. For example, if you have a maximized window with a scroll bar on the right side and an autohidden Taskbar on the right, when you reach for the scroll bar, the Taskbar pops out and you can't reach the scroll bar! While the right edge is used the most, the top and left side of main windows are edges you often need to reach. In most programs, the bottom of the window is a status area and you don't need to move your mouse there. But there are programs—Claris's File Maker Pro comes to mind—that place popup menus at the bottom of their windows. If Auto hide is on and the File Maker Pro window is maximized, you can't reach the File Maker Pro popups without the Taskbar getting in the way.

Notification Area

All publicity is good, except an obituary notice.

—BRENDAN BEHAN, *Sunday Express,* January 5, 1964

One of the most innovative ideas in the basic design of the Desktop is the area on the extreme right of the Taskbar called the **Notification Area** (Figure 3-7). As its name implies, one of its main purposes is for programs to notify you of some situation, for example, for the e-mail program to inform you that new mail has arrived. But it is also a very tempting location for background programs to use to give you access to them without their having to take a full button in the middle area of the Taskbar.

Icons in the Notification Area can communicate with you in five different ways:

**Figure 3-7.
Notify me when
that part comes in**

- **Through their icons**   The presence of the icon—for example, the one that shows that New Mail has arrived—can convey information, but the icon itself can also change. For example, in Figure 3-7, the last icon is Windows' own Resource Meter, and the level changes to indicate the amount of free system resources. The Power Toys audio CD player uses a "not" band through it to mean that there isn't an audio CD in the drive. (I'll discuss Power Toys in Chapter 5).

Free resources remains a problem so I recommend you add Resource Meter to your StartUp group. You can copy the icon from Programs/ Accessories/System Tools/Resource Meter on the Start Menu or else use the program name **C:\windows\rsrcmtr.exe**. Nice to see such an intelligent use of long filenames in rsrcmtr.

- **Through a ToolTip**   If you rest your mouse cursor over the time on the notification area, you'll see the day of the week and the date in a ToolTip. Some ToolTips are just the name of the program, but others convey useful information.

- **Through a single click**   A single click on a Notification Area icon normally pops up a small interactive control. A typical example is the volume control, which pops up a single master volume slider and mute check box (Figure 3-8). But some programs react only to a double click, not a single one (for example, the Task Scheduler). And a program can take whatever action it deems appropriate on a single click. For example, the Power Toys audio CD player uses a single click to start or pause CD playing.

- **Through a double click**   A double click normally pops up a more extensive interactive control. For example, double clicking the volume icon brings up a full-fledged mixer (Figure 3-9).

- **Through a context menu**   Right clicking an icon can invoke a menu. For example, the Power Toys CD player lets you get to an audio track list that way.

**Figure 3-8.
Simple volume
control**

Volume

Mute

**Figure 3-9.
Full-fledged
volume control**

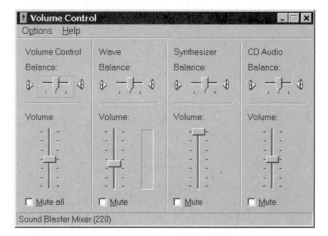

Not every icon in the Notification Area uses all five ways—indeed, very few use them all—but you need to know of them all. When a new icon appears in the area, you should experiment with it to see which of the methods it uses.

The only Notification Area icon built into Windows on all systems is the time. On systems with a sound driver, there is a volume icon (which can be turned off via a check box in the Audio tab of the Multimedia applet of the Control Panel). Most systems also have the Task Scheduler and Display Changer icons. Portables will have a battery icon and usually an icon for PCMIA cards.

When there are jobs waiting to be printed in the spooler of your printer, an icon will appear that gives you quick access to the Spooler control. Many third-party utilities use the Notification Area.

Several third-party products let you move any programs you want from the Taskbar to the Notification Area. My favorite is Icon Corral. Its author seems to have disappeared, but you can download it from **www.hotfiles.com** (search on Icon Corral). It even lets you open multiple Outlook Windows and move only some of them to the Notification Area.

Launch and Web Toolbars

New with Internet Explorer 4.0 and included with Windows 98 is a group of toolbars you can add to the Taskbar.

You may not have seen these if you upgraded to IE 4.0 over Windows 95 or NT 4.0 because they were part of the optional "new Desktop," but this new Desktop is built into Windows 98 and you can't turn it off (although you can turn off the Web page view of the Desktop, which many users find annoying; see the section "*The Active Desktop*").

Figure 3-10.
Step right up to the toolbar

There are five new toolbars, as seen in the menu choices in Figure 3-10. You turn them on and off by right clicking on the Taskbar, selecting Toolbars, and checking or unchecking the items on the submenu (except for "New Toolbar . . ." which I'll discuss below).

- **Address**   Allows you to directly type in a Web address and launch IE to that address. It has a dropdown that contains the names of items you recently typed into the box. But it will autocomplete addresses you type in if it can find them in the IE history list, even if you entered them into an open copy of IE. So if you type in **www.**, the program will fill in the rest from the last such address you entered. As you enter more of the address, it adjusts the autocompletion appropriately.

A neat feature of the Address box that is often overlooked is that you can type in folder names or even a filename and the intelligent thing will be done. Type in a folder name, even a UNC name for a network folder (like **\\eye\newt\c**) and hit Enter, and the folder will open in Explorer. Type in the full pathname of a file (for example, **C:\windows\win.ini**) and, if the file extension is associated with the program, the file will open in the appropriate program. File completion works even here—try typing in **C:\windows\w** and watch what happens!

- **Links**   Displays buttons for each shortcut in the directory **C:\windows\ favorites\links**. There are seven default links, but you can add or remove links freely. This can be done by changing the shortcuts in the folder, using Explorer, or by dragging shortcuts (or even links on a page in your browser) to the links bar. You can right click a link on the bar and delete it.

Strangely enough, the only way to rename a link seems to be to do it in the **C:\windows\favorites\links** directory.

It's quite reasonable that Windows Update is built into the default set of Links that Windows installs. It is *not* reasonable that Free Hotmail is. Is it appropriate that Microsoft should be able to use its Windows monopoly to give its Web e-mail site a boost over similar sites?

- **Quick Launch**   This is the only toolbar turned on by default. Its default includes icons to launch Internet Explorer, Outlook Express, View Channels and a Show Desktop Icon. If you have a TV tuner card, WebTV for Windows is added. But this is only the default. The icons shown are exactly the shortcuts in the directory **c:\windows\application data\ microsoft\internet explorer\quick launch**. As with the Links bar, you can make changes in this toolbar either by using Explorer on the actual folder or by dragging to the Quick Launch bar, and right clicking and choosing Delete. Renaming the ToolTip that appears over the icon can be done only by renaming the shortcut in Explorer, and you can change the order of the icons only by drag and drop on the Quick Launch bar itself.

 That there are shortcuts involved here is shown by the fact that if you right click on an icon and pick Delete, it asks you about sending an item to the Recycle Bin—it's of course the shortcut from `C:\windows\application data\microsoft\internet explorer\quick launch` that goes to the Recycle Bin.

- **Desktop**   You can make something much like the Quick Launch Toolbar but with an icon for each shortcut on the Desktop. Alas, if you have the number of icons on the Desktop that Woody and Barry have, this isn't very practical.

- **New Toolbar . . .**   You can point to a folder and get a toolbar made out of all the shortcuts in that new folder. In many ways it acts like the Quick Launch Toolbar. The one difference is what happens when you turn it off. Once you add new toolbars, they appear as checked on the Toolbars menu. If you uncheck them, they are removed not only from the Taskbar but also from the Toolbar menu, so you can't easily turn them back on.

 These toolbars are really great additions to the user interface, but I wish I could add some toolbars to the menu that persist after I uncheck them.

 On a 1,024 × 768 screen, I'm quite happy with the Taskbar shown in Figure 3-4 where the bottom row is taken up roughly one third each with an Address bar, a Links bar and a Quick Launch bar.

You can move the toolbars around by placing the mouse just to the right of the raised ridge at the left of the bar and pressing down. You get a four-headed arrow indicating that you can drag the bar around. If you press over a ridge, you get a two-headed arrow that lets you move that edge left or right to grow or shrink the bar.

 You can grab a toolbar and drag it off the Taskbar area. You just grab it and move it off the area and it becomes free floating. You can keep it free floating or dock it at a side of the screen or at the top.

 The ability to float toolbars is neat but not to my taste. I like everything at the bottom of the screen.

 Docking the Desktop toolbar at the right of the screen with either small icons with text (using ToolTips) and/or using Auto hide is a neat way to have access to the Desktop launch icons at all times.

**Figure 3-11.
Seeing a toolbar
in context**

By default, the Quick Launch Toolbar is icons only, while Links, Desktop, and New show both icon and text. But you can change this. If you right click to the right of the toolbar ridge, you get the context menu shown in Figure 3-11. Whether just icons appear or icons and text is controlled by whether the Show Text item is checked or not. Similarly, the Show Title item determines whether or not text appears to the right of the toolbar ridge.

 The names Address and Links serve no useful purpose (although the bars themselves are great), so I suggest you remove them if you are using Links or Address bars on the Taskbar. What's weird is that while you can remove this useless text when these menus appear on the Taskbar, you can't when they appear in Internet Explorer.

 The only disadvantage of removing the names is that the area you need to press with the left button to move or with right button to get the context menu is very small if there is no toolbar name and it requires some care. With the name, you can press on the name to move or get the context menu.

Taskman Lives!

Windows installs a program called **taskman.exe**, aka. the Task Manager, into your Windows directory. It has much of the functionality of the Windows 3.1 Task Manager, functionality now built into Windows. You can start it by typing **Taskman** in the Run dialog, or, if you really like, you could assign it a hotkey.

 What a cockamamie thing. With the Taskbar here, who needs this piece of fluff?

 Well, I guess Microsoft put it there so the Windows 3.1 lovers wouldn't complain. It is also true that some perverse folks might like to have Taskman floating on top with the Taskbar autohidden.

Under Windows 95, there were times when Windows would get confused and unload Explorer without exiting. At that point, if you double clicked the Desktop, Taskman popped up. This is no longer true under Windows 98, so Taskman stays around mainly to remind us of old times, I guess.

■ Explorering the Great Unknown

I seem to have been only like a boy playing on the seashore, and diverting myself in now and then finding a smoother pebble or a prettier shell than ordinary, whilst the great ocean of truth lay all undiscovered before me.

—Isaac Newton

 You are likely to spend a lot of time with Explorer and folders, so you may as well learn how to interact with the beast efficiently. While the bulk of Explorer tips and tricks are in this section, the program affects so much else that there are important sidelights in a number of other places. I discuss Find File under Start Menu because most users will access it from the Start Menu, but the Find File window is just a special Explorer window. The Desktop is also just a special Explorer window, and some of the tips in the section "Desktop Dancing" are as much Explorer tips as they are about the Desktop. Finally, there is the mother lode of Explorer customization in the section "Configuring Context Menus and Associations" later in this chapter; check out especially the subsection "Sarah's Smart Setup Step by Step."

Fix Explorer Options

The first thing you want to be sure to do is to fix the default options that Explorer uses. These are in the View tab on the Folder Options dialog (Figure 3-12). The easiest way to reach this dialog and be sure that the changes are global is to choose Settings\Folder Options . . . from the Start menu. The defaults aren't unreasonable for naive users, but they are not the best for experienced ones. MOM's preferred choices are seen in Figure 3-13.

In many ways the most important change is the "Hidden files" radio buttons. This control determines whether Explorer displays certain files—those whose attributes indicate that they are hidden (I discussed what "hidden" means in Chapter 2 in the section "Hidden Pleasures") and files with five special extensions. You want to be able to see the files and folders hidden by the first two radio buttons because some of them are important (for example, `C:\windows\desktop`), so change the selected button to "Show all files."

Next be sure to uncheck the box that says, "Hide file extensions for known file types." The other changes are matters of taste, but I strongly prefer to have them as checked in Figure 3-13.

 You're wrong about the "Hide file extensions" check box. Why confuse users with inscrutable three-letter extensions that are passé? Registered files normally have their own icons and the Type column in Details view gives a more scrutable version of the type then the silly little extension.

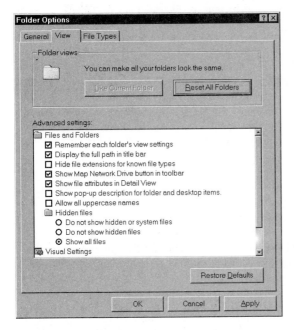

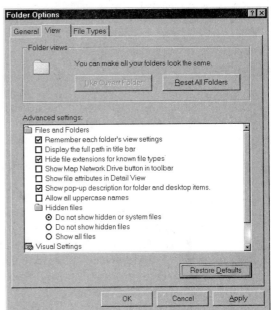

Figure 3-12. Default Explorer options

Figure 3-13. MOM's preferred options

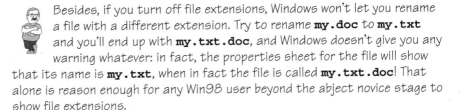

Yup, Billy. We've had real progress. Sometimes inscrutable extensions have been replaced by really inscrutable icons. Yup, real progress. The Type column is nice, but the eye has to move to it while extensions are right there and extensions show up in List view and the Icon views. Moreover, I want to see the difference between **.bmp** and **.tif** files even though on my machine both are registered as the type Micrografx Picture Publisher Image.

Besides, if you turn off file extensions, Windows won't let you rename a file with a different extension. Try to rename **my.doc** to **my.txt** and you'll end up with **my.txt.doc**, and Windows doesn't give you any warning whatever: in fact, the properties sheet for the file will show that its name is **my.txt**, when in fact the file is called **my.txt.doc**! That alone is reason enough for any Win98 user beyond the abject novice stage to show file extensions.

There are a number of strange elements in the Figure 3-12 dialog. First the radio buttons also determine whether **C:\windows\desktop** is visible in Explorer or not. But this directory is neither hidden nor does it have any of the special extensions. So the dialog doesn't tell the whole truth. Moreover, it seems that the list is hardcoded to the five specific extensions: **.dll**, **.sys**, **.vxd**, **.386**, and **.drv**. Users may need to find a missing **.dll**, but they can't if it's hidden, so this option is crazy. Moreover, by what logic does one hide the **.dll** files in the **windows\system** folder but not **.cpl** or **.ocx**. Bizarre.

All four types (to get real techie!) appear in the Registry with **EditFlags** set equal to **01 00 00 00** and with a value entry named **AlwaysShowExt**. And they are the only types with either of these value entry pairs. But adding a new type with such entries doesn't add the corresponding extension to the list of extensions that get hidden.

The check box that says, "Hide file extensions for known file types" doesn't quite mean what it says, either. Some types like Shortcut (with extension **.lnk**) have a Registry value pair named **NeverShowExt** and they, er, never show their extension no matter how the check box is checked. Similarly, those with a value pair named **AlwaysShowExt**, er, always show their extension.

Views, Filtering, and Sorting

There are a number of issues I want to discuss involving the view in an Explorer window. The first is Folder view vs. Explorer view, the next the four possible looks for the right-hand panel in Explorer, the third the Web view, then sorting and filtering.

The program Explorer can open a folder in two views. Folder view (Figure 3-14) just shows the contents of the folder and Explorer view (Figure 3-15) has two panes—a tree on the left and contents on the right. The designers of Win-

Figure 3-14. Explorer dumbed down

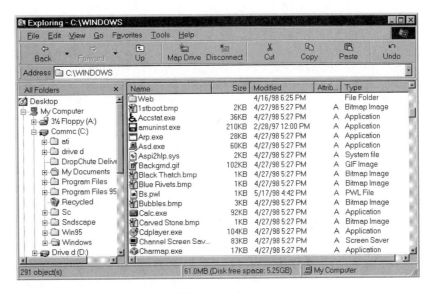

Figure 3-15. Explorer on steroids

dows assumed you'd normally want Folder view, which for experienced users is the wrong attitude. I think it's wrong even for naive users (who have to be aware of the folder tree to cope with it), but that's debatable.

In any event, the defaults in Windows are set up to strongly favor opening Folder views and lots of them. When you double click any drive or folder icon on the Desktop, by default it opens in Folder view. If you do this in Explorer (in the contents pane), it always uses the same window, although if you do it in Folder view it may or may not open a new window, depending on an option you set in the Folder Options . . . /General tab (under Custom Settings).

 The fact that you don't open a new window when you click on a folder in the right pane in Explorer is an improvement over Windows 95, which did by default. Microsoft is to be complemented for fixing this.

 But they made up for this positive change by hiding the option to not open multiple Folder view windows in a special dialog below the basic tabs.

In the sections "Stupid File Types Tricks" and "Sarah's Smart Setup Step by Step" later in this chapter, I explain how to change the defaults so that double clicking a drive or directory on the desktop or in a folder window opens Explorer. And I'll tell you how to do it while still having My Computer and Control Panel open in Folder view. Even after you set up your system this way, the Folder view choice is available on the right click context menu for drives and folders.

Another place that Windows prefers Folder view is with the Explorer command! Indeed, if you type **explorer C:** in the Run box, it opens in

Folder view! To get Explorer view, you either need to type in **explorer** with no parameters or **explorer /e,C:** (note the comma after the e). I discuss the Explorer command line later. There is no simple way around making **explorer C:** bring up Explorer view, but you could make a batch file **explore.bat** (or even **ex.bat** to keep it short) with the single line **@C:\windows\explorer.exe /e,%1** and with properties set to **Close on Exit** and **Run Minimized**. Typing in **Explore C:** (note **Explore**, without the **r**; not **Explorer**) would bring up Explorer view.

 If you insist on having **explorer C:** bring up Explorer view, it can be done, but this is just a thought experiment—because third-party programs will assume **explorer.exe** is in **C:\windows**, I urge you not to try this at home! You need to move **explorer.exe** from **C:\windows** to **C:\windows\command**. You can't do that in Windows since you'll get a complaint that **explorer.exe** is in use! But you can do it if you boot up in Command Prompt mode (hit F8 during startup and choose the Command Prompt option). Windows will still locate **explorer.exe** because **C:\windows\command** is in your path. You'll next need to search through your Registry and make sure all references (and there will be a lot!) to **C:\windows\explorer.exe** are changed to **C:\windows\command\explorer.exe**. Now make a batch file like the one mentioned in the previous paragraph, but put it in the Windows directory, call it **explorer.bat**, and have the line read **@C:\windows\command\ explorer.exe ,e/%1**. This is a stupid Desktop trick and only worth mentioning to expand your thinking.

The third place Windows has a preference for Folder view is when you type in the name of a folder in the Run box: Windows opens that folder in Folder view. This too can be changed.

 By far the best way to change it is to make all the changes I recommend in the section "Sarah's Smart Setup Step by Step," later in the chapter. But if you want a quick and dirty way (that will also change the default action when you click on My Computer and Control Panel, something you may not want), you can open up Regedit, go to the key **HKEY_CLASSES_ROOT\Folders\Shell**, and rename the subkey **Open** to **FolderView** and then **Explore** to **Open**. If you do that, typing in a folder name will open it in Explorer mode.

If you are in Folder view, you can easily bring up an Explorer view, if you want to. The little icon in the upper left corner of any Folder view is "live," and right clicking on it brings up the context menu (Figure 3-16). It has an entry for Explore (under the default menu scheme). With the simplest version of Sarah's Smart Setup, Explore is absent but you won't see many Folder views if you use Sarah's Setup, and it can be added by hand.

The other parts of view involve the Status bar and Toolbar—which are on the View menu—and which of the four views you pick for the content panel: Large Icons, Small Icons, List, or Details (I talk about a fifth view in the next

**Figure 3-16.
Folder window
context menu**

section!). You can make the choice in the View menu, or, if you have the Toolbar turned on (and your Explorer window is maximized, since the Views button is not displayed in most configurations in less than a maximized window), there is a Views button with a dropdown or the option of cycling through the four view types when you just press the button. Large Icons is the Mac-like view that feels right for Folder view but will rarely make sense in Explorer view. An exception would be when looking at a folder with lots of icons (`.ico`) that show as thumbnails. **Details** shows the filename, size, file type, and date/time modified. This is the most useful view for times when you are managing your files.

 In Details view, you can rearrange the columns by just drag and dropping the column headers. You can resize them by floating the mouse over a line between column headers until the cursor becomes a bar with a two-headed cursor. Then just press and drag to resize.

The entries in Small Icon and List view are the same—filename and small icon. List view lists in multiple columns sorted column by column with scroll bars to bring more columns into view if needed. The columns adjust if you resize the window. Small Icon view sorts rowwise and normally scrolls to bring additional rows into view, but it doesn't adjust for window resizing. I've found Small Icon view generally useless, although List view is often useful, especially in Open and Save dialogs (which are specialized Explorer windows).

Another place where you have a choice in picking a view is whether or not to view as a Web page. This is a check box on the View menu in both Explorer and Folder windows.

 The Web view for ordinary folders is worse than useless since it takes up space without providing anything useful—it fits the wag's description of breasts on a man: "neither useful nor ornamental." On drives and special folders like Control Panel, the descriptions provided may be useful, but even there the benefit is minimal. Web view is mainly important because of what it allows in the way of customizing your desktop.

 I found one specialized situation where Web view is exceedingly useful. While the info area for most files is kinda useless, for **.jpg** or **.gif**, the two graphics formats build into IE, the info area is a thumbnail of the file. The thumbnail view that I'll discuss in the next section shows thumbnails of all the files in the folder; the Web view shows a medium sized thumbnail of only the currently selected file. One place this is great is when I transfer the.**jpg** files from my digital camera to my computer. The files come in with names like **dsc0003.jpg**. I turn on Web view and rename the files using the thumbnail to figure out the name to give the file.

The Arrange Icons submenu of View will sort the items in the contents window, although in anything but Details view, it seems confusing to sort on anything but name since that's the only sort variable visible. The efficient way to sort in Details view is to click on a column header. That sorts Ascending unless the column is already sorted that way in which case it sorts Descending. So double clicking an unsorted column brings it to a Descending sort. Sorts on name always place subfolders at the top.

Explorer doesn't have a command to filter the view, say to only show `*.ico` files, but the Find File command is a most effective substitute because its results are displayed in a window with most Explorer capabilities. `F3` from Explorer will bring up a Find File dialog with the current directory name filled in.

Fifth View: Thumbnails

Uncle Ed's Rule of Thumb: Never use your thumb for a rule. You'll either hit it with a hammer or get a splinter in it.

Besides the four views already standard in Windows 95 (Large Icons, Small Icons, List, and Details), Internet Explorer 4.0 and Windows 98 have a fifth view you can enable on a folder-by-folder basis. For any folder, if you call up the Properties dialog, you can check a box near the bottom of the panel labeled "Enable thumbnail view" (Figure 3-17). Once enabled, you can pick Thumbnail view from the View menu or from the context menu of the panel displaying the files in the folder (Figure 3-18). For a large variety of graphics files (`.pcx`, `.bmp`, `.tif`, `.wmf`, even `.wmf`) you see thumbnails of the graphics! You also see thumbnails of HTML files and of Web pages for URL shortcuts.

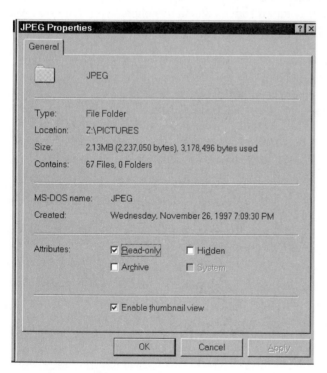

Figure 3-17. Turning on Thumbnail view

Figure 3-18.
Thumbnail view
of a folder of
JPEGs

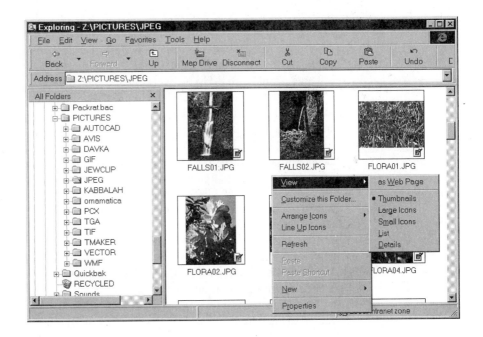

 One spectacular use of this concerns my Nikon Coolpix 900 camera that uses Compact Flash memory. I pull the memory card from the camera, pop it into a PCMIA adapter, and put it into my portable, where it appears as a disk drive with the JPEGs that the camera took in a folder. I turn on Thumbnail view in that folder and get thumbnails within Explorer! Thumbnails are also useful once I store the images on disk.

 While this is wondrous, it's unfortunate that it doesn't include Word, Excel, and PowerPoint files—it would be wonderful to be able to visually scan for that missing file.

 Be warned that for URL shortcuts, the page has to be in the IE cache to display. Otherwise, if you have a live connection to the Internet, you can right click on an Internet shortcut and ask for the thumbnail to be updated.

 One annoying gotcha. There doesn't seem to be a way to enable thumbnails globally. You have to do it on a folder-by-folder basis.

That's because Windows places a **desktop.ini** file in each and every folder for which you enable Thumbnail view. Once you actually view the thumbnails, it stores them in a file called **Thumbs.db**.

Directory Tree

The left pane in an Explorer view shows a folder tree (Figure 3-15) starting at Desktop with My Computer and its drives and then its idealized folders—Control Panel, Printer, Dial-Up Networking and Scheduled Tasks. At the same level as My Computer you'll have, where appropriate, Network Neighborhood, Recycle Bin, My Documents, Internet Explorer, and any folders that you've placed on the Desktop.

The tree is displayed in outline format with folders that have subfolders indicated with either a + or a − to the left. Those with a − have their subfolders displayed (they are open) and those with a + have their subfolders hidden from view (they are closed). Clicking on a folder selects it and changes the display in the contents window to that folder. Double clicking does what clicking does and toggles the folder between open and closed.

Clicking + or − will toggle between open or closed state without selecting the folder or changing the view in the contents pane. This is very important for file operations—see the section "Two Directories Conundrum." Hitting * will open the entire current branch of the tree completely.

The Backspace key or changes the folder displayed in the contents window to the parent. That means that hitting the Backspace key or the Up button repeatedly will take you to the Desktop. The Backspace key and the Up button work whichever pane is active, but * is effective only if the tree pane is active. There is also a dropdown address bar on the toolbar for quick change of the current folder.

 Here's a useful tip. Do you want to reach `c:\windows\profiles\` `barry\application data\microsoft\outlook`? Do you shudder at the thought of opening six levels of directory tree? The Address bar at the top of an Explorer window has autocompletion on folder/file names also. So just start typing. As you type, the name will complete with the first match. Once the folder name you want appears, hit the right arrow and slash and start typing in the next level. Works slickly.

Ha! Third-party DOS command line tools did this in 1985. It's about time Windows did it!

Property Sheets

Drives, file folders, and files each have their own property sheets (Figure 3-19). Each object you can select in Explorer has a property sheet that is accessible by hitting **Alt+Enter** or choosing Properties from the context menu or from the File menu. Figure 3-19 shows property sheets for the three main objects in the File system. The property sheet of a drive lets you relabel the drive and displays total and available space both graphically and as numbers (too bad percentages aren't given).

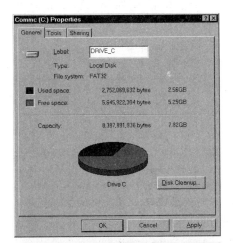

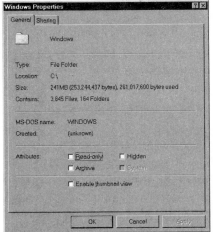

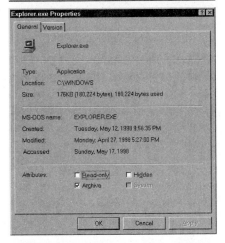

Figure 3-19: Property sheets for drive, directory (er, folder), and file

You'll note that the drive sheet shown is an 8-GB partition; you couldn't get that until FAT32 was introduced. Hooray for FAT32.

The property sheet of a directory includes the total size of the files that the directory and its subfolders have with a count of the number of files and folders. You get similar counts if you select multiple files and/or multiple folders and ask for Properties.

Notice the Sharing tabs on the drive and directory property sheets. On some machines a Sharing tab won't appear, even on a network with file sharing enabled. That's because a system administrator could have disabled file-sharing capabilities for that particular machine or that particular user via the system policies editor.

Notice that three dates are listed on the property sheet for the file—the date and time it was created, the date and time it was last modified, and the date it was last accessed. In this case—Windows' **explorer.exe**—the modified time is the time the file was made in Redmond, the created time is when it was loaded on Barry's disk, and the accessed date is the time it was last run. As contrary as it seems, the modified time is before the creation time, which goes to show that the names are less than ideal. Before Windows 95, the only time kept on a file was the modified time. The other two times were new to Windows 95.

The accessed time is especially neat because it lets there be utilities that will inform you which files on disk have not been used at all in the past six months and are therefore ripe for removal.

The four attributes listed at the bottom of the directory and file sheets will not be discussed here. **System** is grayed out because you can't change that attribute here. You can change the others by checking or unchecking a box.

Ha! Windows puts up a brave front to indicate that the System attribute is the system's and not the user's to change. But guess what? Using the DOS **attrib** command, included in the Windows package, you can change the system attribute. It's all a show of bravado by good ol' Windows.

Hey, Barry, I'm puzzled. When I select drive C and look at its property sheet, it tells me that the used space is 2,752,802,816 bytes. When I select all the directories and files in C and hit **Alt+Enter**, it tells me that the size is 2,630,211,270 bytes in 48,666 files and directories. What gives? Those numbers can't both be right. Have I a bug to report to Billy?

 Nope. Believe it or not, both numbers are correct! The second number is the total of the sizes of all the files and directories. File sizes are the size of the data in the file. But the DOS FAT system must allocate an integral number of clusters of disk space, so the space used by a file is more than its size. The difference, called the slack, is always less than a cluster per file. If all the files were very large and random in size, the average slack would be about half a cluster. Since small files have almost a whole cluster of slack and there are lots of small files around in Windows (shortcuts, for example), the average slack is generally more than half a cluster. On the disk you are asking about, the cluster size is 4 KB, and if you divide the difference of the two numbers you gave me by 48,666 you get about 2.52 KB—indeed between a half and a whole cluster. This slack was a serious space drain under FAT16—on larger disks as much as 20% of the total file size. In this case, with FAT32, it's 4.5%. On a 4-GB disk, the difference between 5% and 20% works out to 600 MB. That ain't chump change.

 If you run Scandisk, it will tell you the cluster size, although it calls them "allocation units." The basic rule under FAT32 is to use 4-KB clusters for hard disks between 0.5 and 8 GB, 8-KB clusters between 8 and 16 GB, 16-KB clusters between 16 and 32 GB, and 32-KB clusters above 32 GB.

 You may be amused to hear me talk about drives above 32 GB, but wait a few years—they'll be common!

If you look at the file property sheet in Figure 3-19, you'll notice a second tab called Version. That's special to **.exe**, **.vxd**, and **.dll** files. Windows (as in this case) or third parties can add extra tabs to property sheets.

I'll discuss the tools in the Tools tab for drives in Chapter 4.

 The most important thing to remember about property sheets for Explorer objects is that they are there and often have useful information.

File Operations

The most common operations you'll do in Explorer are the basic file management operations of deleting, copying, moving, and renaming. If you select one or more files and or folders and hit **Del** or drag them to the Recycle Bin, they'll get moved to the Recycle Bin. Until you explicitly empty the bin or selectively delete some files from it (opening Recycle Bin, selecting files, and hitting **Del** deletes them for real), the Recycle Bin fills up. When it gets too large, Windows complains and tells you, "Take out the trash, darn it." The advantage of this method is that recover of "deleted" files is 100% until you remove them from the Recycle Bin. The disadvantage is that Windows forces you to explicitly manage the Recycle Bin. It would be better if it let you specify a time period (I'd pick a week or two) and had the trash automatically deleted after that time—that is, Windows would automatically remove from the Recycle Bin files deleted for real if they'd been "deleted" by the user more than the specified time period ago.

 A second disadvantage is that the Recycle Bin captures only files that you delete from a local hard drive using Explorer. If you use a third-party file manager, if some program deletes them, if you delete them at a DOS prompt, or if you delete them from a floppy, they do not go to the Recycle Bin, and Windows provides no recovery tools other than the Recycle Bin.

 The Norton Utilities for Windows addresses all these lacks.

If you have a bunch of files that you are 100% sure you want to delete and you don't want them to go to the Recycle Bin, selecting them in Explorer and hitting **Shift+Del** (or holding down **Shift** when choosing Delete from their context menu) will delete them for real. If you hold down **Shift** and drag something to the Recycle Bin, it also gets deleted for real. Also be aware that if you delete (with plain old **Del** or by dragging to your Recycle Bin) files from a network or floppy drive, they are deleted for real.

 If you drag a file on a local hard drive to the Recycle Bin, it eats it silently, storing it away. If you do that from a diskette or network drive where it is going to delete the file without storing it in a Recycle Bin, it warns you. That's good. Under Windows 95, if you shift drag to the Recycle Bin, it deletes the file without storing without warning. MOM complained about the bug and Microsoft has fixed it! Under Windows 98, if you shift drag to the Recycle Bin, you get the warning you would if you shift deleted it.

You can copy or move files or folders between two Explorer windows or from one Explorer window to a directory in an Explorer tree. So one way to copy or move is to go to the source directory, pick the files you want, use the scroll bars on the tree to locate the destination, and drag the files from the contents pane to the destination on the tree. So long as you are careful to hit only the + signs, you can even open directories on the tree side.

Whether a drag produces a copy or a move depends on the type of files, whether you use the left or right mouse button, and whether you hold down various combination of **Ctrl** and **Shift**. I discussed the rules in Chapter 2 in the section "Drag 'til you Drop."

One neat new feature of Windows 98 is that you can drag some files to the name of a folder in the directory tree and hover there and the folder will open up. That's useful to remember if you forget to open up the folder before you start the drag.

You can rename a file or folder by selecting it and hitting **F2**, selecting it and picking Rename from a context menu, or from the File menu. Or you can select it and then click on the name. In all cases, the name in the Explorer window turns into an edit box where you can just retype the name. The name is initially selected so that if you start typing the name is replaced totally. If you just want to edit the name, click gently a second time or use **Home** or **End** and the arrow keys. If you hit **Esc**, you abort the rename. Hitting **Enter** or clicking outside the edit box accepts the edit.

After a Rename, you can use Edit/Undo to undo the Rename.

This clicking stuff is a pain and half. If you try to use it to select and rename, you have to noticeably pause in between or else Windows will interpret it as a double click. And often when you just mean to select, somehow you wind up in rename mode. This click to rename looks neat but on balance I wish it weren't there.

You can rename files and folders this way but not a drive. The drive name, called a label, can be changed from the property sheet for that drive (see the leftmost sheet in Figure 3-19). You create a new folder by selecting New and then Folder from the File menu or by right clicking on a blank area of the contents pane of the folder in which you want to create the new subfolder. This is awkward—there should be a single keystroke option to make a new folder (**Ins** was used in some third-party file managers for Windows 3.1). When you make a new folder it comes in with the name New Folder but is ready to rename immediately.

The New submenu of the blank area context menu or of the File menu also lets you create new documents. The application adding its documents to the New menu can arrange for a wizard to pop up to make the document or can arrange for the document to start out as some template. Information in the New menu is contained in the Registry. I have a lot to say about it in Chapter 9 where I explain how you can remove items you feel you'll never want and even how you can add some new New entries of your own.

Built into the New menu when you install Windows are seven entries: Folder, Shortcut, Text Document, WordPad Document, Bitmap Image, Wave Sound, and Briefcase. You may want to remove Bitmap Image and/or Wave Sound, using Tweak UI (see Chapter 8) or the methods I'll discuss in Chapter 9.

Using the Clipboard

Explorer supports an interesting use of the clipboard for file copying and moving. On the Edit menu in Explorer you'll see items Cut, Copy and Paste. The usual hotkeys work for them and the toolbar has the standard icons for the operations

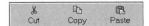

although larger than in other programs, such as WordPad.

You can select one or more files and/or folders in the contents pane, or a folder in the tree pane, and hit/pick Cut or Copy. Then move the focus of Explorer to the destination directory or use a second Explorer window, click on a blank area in the contents pane, and hit/pick Paste. If the original action was Copy, the files are copied to the destination, and if the original action was Cut, they are moved there. You can do multiple Pastes in different Explorer destinations.

When you choose Cut, the file(s) isn't actually deleted. That only happens after you do the Paste. Before then, the icon(s) of the Cut file(s) is grayed out.

You can Copy and Paste to the same location. If you do, the words "Copy of" are prepended to the file names. You can then rename the copies if you want. This is a rather efficient way to make backup copies of `config.sys` and similar files before you edit them.

When there are files that have been placed on the clipboard with Copy (but not with Cut), the Edit menu has an item that says Paste Shortcut. For those who don't much like dragging, this can be an efficient way to make shortcuts on the Desktop or in a Start Menu submenu. Remember that these clipboard options are available when you have several Explorer windows on a crowded screen and you have trouble getting the windows placed to do a simple drag and drop.

Alas, you cannot use this method to paste the names of files into DOS sessions, Open dialogs, or text editors. You can use it to paste OLE packages into applications that are OLE 2.0 clients.

Diskettes

 Diskettes are a media of the past. I can't wait for the era when kids say, "Diskette? What's that? A female hard disk?" With Windows built-in networking, CDs, and the advent of decent online speeds, you'll need diskettes less often than you used to. But you will still use them. Here are some tools for use with diskettes besides the general Scandisk, Backup, Defragger that I discuss in Chapter 4.

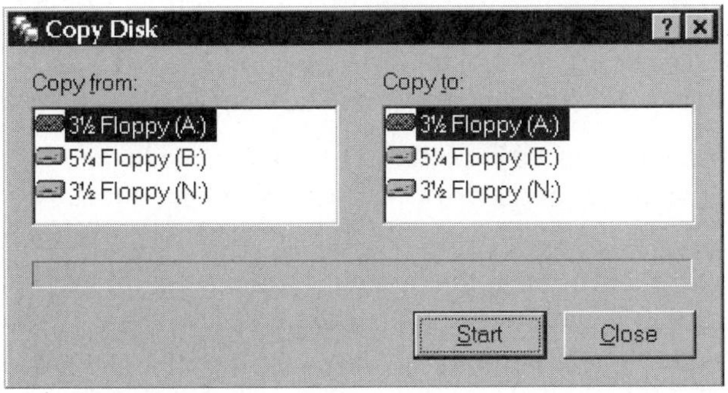

There is a simple Copy Disk program (Figure 3-20) accessible by right clicking on a diskette icon on the Desktop or in My Computer. It's just the Windows version of Disk Copy. It requires you to track which diskette formats are compatible. There is a Format utility (Figure 3-21), also available on a diskette's context menu. You get to pick the diskette

Figure 3-20. Diskcopy redux

Figure 3-21.
Format utility

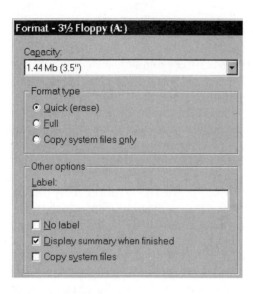

capacity and whether to make the diskette bootable. You also choose between Format/Quick (logical formatting only) or Format/Full (physical formatting also). "Copy system files" means copying only four system files (**io.sys**, **ms-dos.sys**, **command.com**, and **drvspace.bin**, taking a total of 378 KB). Such a diskette boots into a command prompt without support for long filenames.

Finally, don't forget to consider using diskettes with Drive Space file compression (I discuss Drive Space in Chapter 4). Figure that you'll normally be able to squeeze about 2 MB on a 1.4-MB diskette, maybe as much as 2.5 MB. Since Drive Space is now built into Windows, any Windows 9X user who gets a compressed diskette from you will be able to read it even if they aren't using any disk compression at all.

Explorer Command Line

The Explorer command can take some parameters. The syntax is

```
explorer [/n] [/e] [,root,object] [,subobject]
```

Here, I've left out a specialized and not very interesting parameter called **/select** (which opens Explorer with some files selected), and don't discuss the **/idlist** undocumented parameter (which appears in some Registry entries; I've no idea what it does). The [...] in the syntax summary means that the parameter is optional. *Object* and *subobject* are directory names—you can use UNC path names (of the form **\\network_computer_name\netpath**, for example, **\\aye\c\windows**) but not nondirectory filenames. If you try using **explorer "My Computer"** you'll get an error message. Here's what it all means when run from the Run box or a shortcut (there are special rules for actions run from context menus inside Explorer itself, as I explain later):

- **explorer** with no parameter opens Explorer in Explorer mode in the folder **c:** (or in the root folder of the drive with your Windows directory if it is not drive C).

- **explorer** *foldername* opens the folder in Folder view, not Explorer mode. The comma that the syntax suggests is needed is optional. If the precise folder is already open, then a second copy is not opened—instead the open one becomes the active window.

- **explorer /e,** *foldername* opens an Explorer window with the contents pane showing the folder. It is rooted on Desktop in that repeating **Backspace** will take you up to Desktop eventually.

- **explorer /n,** *foldername* opens the folder in Folder view. A new copy is opened even if the folder is already open. You can use **explorer /n, /e,** *foldername*, but the **/n,** has no effect whatever—a new Explorer window is opened whether the **/n,** is there or not. If you use **/n** without a comma, you get an error message.

Gack! When Windows 98 is installed an item is placed on the Programs submenu called Windows Explorer. The shortcut this points to has the following command line: **explorer /n, /e, C:**. The **/n,** does nothing, or rather it does nothing but confuse users who look at it. Even the Redmondians can't keep the syntax straight.

- **explorer /e, /root,** *foldername* opens Explorer view rooted at the folder and with the folder as the one displayed in the contents pane. Rooted in a certain folder means that you can't go to the parent of the folder with **Backspace** and the tree pane only shows the rooted folder and its subfolders.

- **explorer /e, /root,** *foldername,subfoldername* opens in Explorer view rooted at the folder with the subfolder displayed in the contents pane. The subfoldername must be a relative, not absolute, path to the foldername; use **explorer /e, /root,C:\,windows\system**, not **explorer /e, /root, C:\,C:\windows\system**, which would produce an error message.

- The last two commands work without the **/e,** for rooted folders.

There is one special situation where the syntax is slightly different and this is for Actions associated with folders, File folders, or drives and issued from a context menu of an object inside an Explorer window. I discuss such Actions and how you add them in the sections on file types later on, but I'll note the syntax rule here:

- If an object has an Action with the underlying command **explorer /e,** without **/n,** and if the action is invoked from the context menu inside an Explorer window, then a new Explorer window is *not* opened. If there is an **explorer /e,/n,** then a new window is always opened.

I use this Explorer command line syntax when I discuss various shortcuts to make in dealing with the Start Menu in the next group of sections and in the "Stupid File Type Tricks" section.

More Explorer Tips

- Undo is multiple steps and works even if you have exited Explorer but not if you reboot.

- You cannot undo a file deletion unless the file was deleted to the Recycle Bin; in particular, you can't undo a **Shift+Del** deletion.

- If you have a number of Folder windows open, **Shift** clicking on the close button on one folder will close it, its parent, and so on, as so long as the parent chain is unbroken.

- Don't forget the new Go menu in Explorer windows. It lets you go quickly back and forth through folder changes (you can also use the back/forward arrows and drop down) and go to My Computer and various Web places like Mail and News.

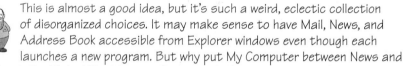 This is almost a good idea, but it's such a weird, eclectic collection of disorganized choices. It may make sense to have Mail, News, and Address Book accessible from Explorer windows even though each launches a new program. But why put My Computer between News and Address Book? And Net Meeting (Internet Call) is a specialized application that doesn't belong there. And anyway, why not let the user customize it?

- You can add Folders to the Favorites dropdown menu for easy access. The easiest way to do it is to display the desired directory in the contents pane and then choose Add to Favorites . . . from the Favorites menu.

 Oy. Talk about overusing the poor Favorites menu! Just as it is crazy to mix Office Favorites with Internet Favorites, it is crazy to further mix in Folder Favorites.

 But the Internet is just an extension of your machine. It's conceptually all the same—folders and URLs.

 Yeah, right. Tell that to Janet. There is a huge difference between ZDNET or Yahoo and **C:\windows** or **C:\my documents\books\MOM98**.

- If you place the mouse over the break between two column headers in Details view (so the cursor changes to a bar crossed by a double-headed arrow) and double click, the column to the left will auto-size so that the width precisely fits the text in it. This will happen with any other Windows list control—for example, the one in Regedit.

- If you hit **CTRL+Numpad Plus**, all columns will auto-size.

Hotkeys

Explorer Shortcut Keys

F1	Help	F2	Rename
F3	Find file	F4	Dropdown folder list
F5	Refresh current window	F6	Cycle among tree pane, dropdown list, and contents pane
Ctrl+Z	Undo	Shift+F10	Context menu
Alt+Enter	Properties	Backspace	Parent

 The original Windows 95 Explorer had **Ctrl+G** to pop up a GoTo box. It's gone. Too bad.

While on the subject of keystrokes, it is worth mentioning two keyboard modifications of the double-click action on a folder.

- **Shift+double click** opens the folder in Explorer view.
- **Ctrl+double click** toggles the browse folder option action. This is the radio button under "Browse folders as follows" in the Custom Setting subdialog of the Folder Options/General tab. That is, if you have picked the "Open each folder in its own window" radio button, then **Ctrl+double click** will shift to the new folder without opening a new window, whereas if you have picked the radio button marked "Open each folder in the same window," then **Ctrl+double click** will open a new window.

These two modifications are with the default setup where Windows opens in Folder view when you double click, but this last **Ctrl** as toggle also matters if you use Sarah's Smart Setup. If you right click and pick **Folder View** on a directory in Sarah's Setup, then the action depends on the radio button choice in the Custom Settings dialog and whether you hold down **Ctrl** when you click on Folder view in the context menu. Holding down **Ctrl** produces the same effect as switching the radio button in the dialog.

 Oy, these weird clicks with shift key tricks. I'd better tell our readers about the special **Ctrl+Shift Click** command built into Windows. You have to be pressing **F10**, **Backspace**, and **Del** while you do it, but if you do and it is the first Sunday in April between 2:30 A.M. and 2:45 A.M., then Windows 98 turns into Linux. Don't believe me? Try it out!

Two Directories Conundrum

Poor fellow, he suffers from files.

—Aneurin Bevan, referring to a bureaucrat

 If there's one bellyache I've heard in the press most about Windows 95 Explorer, it is that you have to open two copies of Explorer to copy files from one directory to another. They compare this with Windows 3.x File Manager, where it was claimed that you could get away with a single copy of File Manager. Of course, you did need two windows within File Manager, but it seemed like less. And in File Manager, you had drive icons just below the menu bar and could drag to diskette icons without a second window. Although I think the complaint has been overblown, at its core there is a real issue—it is more awkward than it has to be to copy or move files from one folder to another. So Barry and I are going to discuss some of the more efficient ways to do it.

 First, for copying to diskette, there are two special methods you can use without opening a second Explorer window.

- If you choose some files and right click, there is the Send To submenu, and on that you'll find an entry like 3½ Floppy (A). If you choose that, the files are copied there.

- If you drag a diskette drive from My Computer to the Desktop or if you make a shortcut whose command line is **A:** (not **Explorer /e,A:**), the diskette drive icon that appears on the Desktop is a drag and drop target. If you select some files in an Explorer window and drag them to the diskette icon, they'll get copied to the diskette. This is my preferred method because I can right drag and drop and get a Move option and because it is quicker than Send To.

 Actually neither of these methods is really diskette specific. If there is a folder on a hard disk you often need to copy files to, you can place a shortcut to it in the **C:\windows\sendto** folder or on the Desktop and have the same capabilities just mentioned. The only difference is that files on the same drive as the folder will be moved, not copied, if you do a Send To or a left-button drag and drop.

Here are some other ways to copy or move files easily:

- Use the clipboard. Remember that you go to the source directory in an Explorer window, select the files you want, pick Copy or Cut (for file copy or move, respectively) from the button bar or Edit menu, change to the destination directory (in the same or different Explorer window), and pick Paste from the button bar or Edit menu.

- Use the fact that you can scroll the tree pane in an Explorer window without changing which folder is displayed in the contents pane. Therefore, you can place the source folder in the contents pane, scroll the tree so that it shows the destination folder, select files in the contents pane, and drag them to the destination folder in the tree pane. While scrolling in the tree pane, you can even expand or contract parts of the tree without changing the folder displayed in the contents pane so long as you use the + or – and don't ever click on a folder name. And while dragging, you can open a closed subtree by hovering over it.
- Use the free Power Toys Send to Any Folder . . . Other Folder menu item. I discuss Power Toys in detail in Chapter 5, but these are utilities written by the Windows 9X team. As shown in Figure 3-22, after you select a bunch of files and choose this item from the **Send To** menu, you get a dialog with the names of the files, a pair of radio buttons for Copy or Move, and a place to enter the destination. You can enter the destination in this To: field by typing it in, choosing it from a dropdown lists of recent destinations, or using the Browse . . . button.

 Normally I wouldn't show a picture of a third-party product, but here it is so natural and the third party is more like a second-and-a-half party. Third-party products like PowerDesk include similar applets.

 You left out what I've always wanted as the solution—an easy way to load two nonoverlapping Explorer windows side by side, taking up the whole left and right sides of the Desktop.

 I left that out on purpose because I've seen it in Winbatch. It lets you easily launch such a setup, but there are two difficulties with it. The windows are a little too narrow, and even after you close both windows, the next one you launch has the same dimensions, which isn't good for browsing. Still, if this appeals to you, check out Winbatch. Or look at **www.wopr.com** for a free utility called Twofer.

Figure 3-22. Power Toys Any Folder

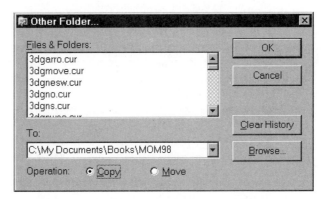

If you want to be able to quickly open a second Explorer window in cascade position, check out the section "Adding an Open New in Explorer" later in this chapter.

QuickView

It cannot be said that nude sunbathing on a beach is a form of expression likely to be understood by the viewer as an attempt to convey a particular point of view.

—VITO J. TITONE, Judge, New York State Court of Appeals,
October 21, 1986

One of the options on the context menu of certain files is QuickView. This brings up a set of bare-bones file viewers for a limited number of file types. Here is a list of the supported file types and extensions.

Text and word processors: .txt, **.asc**, **.ini**, **.inf** (ASCII text), **.wri** (Windows 3.x WRITE), **.rtf** (Rich Text Format), **.sam** (Ami, Ami Pro), **.doc** (Winword versions 1, 2, 95, 97), **.wps** (Works Word Processing)

Spreadsheets: .xls (Excel 4 and 5, 97), **.wk1**, **.wks**, **.wk3**, **.wk4** (Lotus 1-2-3 versions 1, 2, 3, 4), **.wq1**, **.wq2**, **.wb1** (Quattro Pro versions 4, 5 for DOS, version 1 for Windows), **.mod** (Multiplan)

Database formats: .wdb (Works Database)

Graphics formats: .bmp, **.dib**, **.rle** (Windows Bitmaps), **.xlc** (Excel 4 Chart), **.cdr** (Corel Draw, versions 4 and 5), **.drw** (Micrografx Draw), **.wmf** (Windows MetaFile), **.ppt** (Powerpoint version 4), **.pre** (Freelance)

Executable files: .exe, **.dll**

Except that Office 97 support has been added to the Word, Excel, and PowerPoint viewers, this is the identical product to what shipped with Windows 95. QuickView Plus is at version 4.5 with lots of extra features, but the built-in QuickView is basically three years old.

To say that QuickView has lacks is a huge understatement. No support for Word Perfect, for **.pcx**, **.tif**, or **.gif**, for **.wpg**, **.emf**, or **.cgm** or for any common database format. The list is heavy on obscure Microsoft formats (Multiplan?) and viewers for obsolete versions of products (no Quattro Pro Win 2.0). QuickView has no search or cut/paste or print capability, and the word processing doesn't show embedded graphics or much formatting.

It's a huge come-on. QuickView is based on technology from Inso. Inso is selling a product called QuickView Plus that's pretty good. I discuss it in Chapter 5. Given what Microsoft has done in the past, I'll bet dollars to donuts that Microsoft magnanimously allowed Inso to supply QuickView at no cost to Microsoft for the privilege of being a part of the Windows 95 product, and the license let them use it in later products.

Bellyaching again, Woody? Where's the beef? Our users come out ahead because they have viewers that even with faults aren't exactly chopped liver. Inso comes out ahead because they have an in with tens of millions of potential customers. Third-party vendors come out ahead because we've published the specs for them to add their own QuickView viewers. And Microsoft comes out ahead. So where's the beef?

The supported extensions and file types are stored in the Registry in the keys under **HKEY_CLASSES_ROOT\QuickView**. The viewers themselves are stored in directory **C:\windows\system\viewers** and use **quickview.exe** in that directory and the dynamic library **insoview.dll** in that same folder.

Internet Explorer is a viewer for two graphics file types common on the World Wide Web and not supported by QuickView—**.gif** and **.jpg**. Assuming that no program has changed the default file assignment, double clicking on a **.gif** or **.jpg** will open that file in IE. If some other program opens it (say a photo editor you've installed) and you want to view such files in IE, click on the Internet Explorer icon on your desktop and cancel out of the dialog that wants to dial up your Internet provider. Then you can either take a **.gif** or **.jpg** in Windows Explorer and drag it to the Internet Explorer window or pick File/Open in Internet Explorer and pick the Open File . . . in the resulting dialog.

Explorer Lacks

Here are some of the limitations and problems with Explorer—and a wish list.

- It's crazy that there is no way to switch a Folder view window to an Explorer view and vice versa. Outlook lets you do this for its analogs; why can't Explorer?

- The most infuriating aspect of Explorer is that it saves settings for windows only kinda sorta and doesn't give you any access to where it is storing the defaults. I have machines that seem to love to load Control Panel and My Computer in List mode even though I prefer them in Large Icons. I switch Control Panel to Large Icons and close the window, and for a while it opens in the right mode, but then I don't use it for a few days and bam—List mode. This affects the Desktop, which is after all just a special Explorer window in Folder view. It can happen that suddenly Windows loads and it puts your desktop icons alphabetically in columns, forgetting the arrangements you carefully laid out.

There is a third-party shareware product called EZDesk (it's available on **www.hotfiles.com** and on **www.download.com**) that will save and restore various desktop configurations. Why the heck doesn't Windows provide this service, especially given its ability to trash your carefully laid out arrangements?

And we know that Microsoft could add the capability of saving Desktop settings so that you could later restore them; the Windows NT Resource Kit comes with such a tool for NT 4.0.

- Disney may think the lion is king, but Microsoft thinks it's the mouse that is king. Little thought seems to have been given to an intelligent keyboard interface to Explorer and the other parts of Windows. No, I'm not arguing with the fact that the mouse is a requirement for Windows 98—I'd call Microsoft stupid if it wasn't. But that doesn't mean that those who use mice reluctantly or those who prefer to use the keyboard for quick stuff shouldn't have a decent set of keyboard methods for doing things.

- Explorer should have a configurable button bar. I'd prefer the kinds of configuration interface that Word has but even the one in Windows Messaging (that shipped with Windows 95) would be OK.

- In particular, there should be a single keystroke and button bar icon to make a new folder.

- The Power Toys Copy/Move to Any Folder should be built into Explorer but with hotkey access and directly on the context menu instead of buried a menu deep in Send To.

- The Sort design should be revised. If you are sorted on Name and the cursor is on, say, **aardvark.txt** and you hit the column label to sort Type, the view port will stay at the top of the list (where **aardvark.txt** was when sorted on Name) even though the selected file is now near the bottom of the list. Clearly when you resort, the view port should move to show the currently selected file.

- And what happened to sort by extension? The Type designations don't bear much relationship to what I want to find—say, all the .bat files, or all the .docs in a folder.

- There should be a dropdown, remembered from one session to the next, of recently accessed folders to go to. Here "recently accessed" means ones where Copy, Move, QuickView, or Delete was initiated.

We missed this in Windows 95 but we did add it to IE 4 (and Windows 98). The little arrow next to the Back button gives you exactly such a dropdown.

Not quite, Billy—that back arrow is a nice addition, but every time you exit Explorer, it forgets what's on the list, so you can't easily return to the folders you looked at yesterday.

- There should be a button for a Favorite Directories list that lets me quickly move Explorer to a directory I use often. In the section "Desktop Dancing," I describe a way to get some of this functionality, but it isn't as smooth as it could be if it were built into Explorer.

We missed this, too, in Windows 95, but it's there in IE 4 (and Windows 98). You can add directory shortcuts to the Favorites menu.

Well, sorta, Billy boy. Same ol' problem: Who wants a single menu with Web favorites, favorite folders, and favorite Office documents?

- The Recycle Bin should have a setting to automatically truly delete files older than a user-set time.

- There should be better viewers than currently provided in QuickView. Certainly the text viewer needs to include decent search capability.

- What was one of the biggest complaints about Program Manager? "They won't let me choose separate icons for my Program Manager groups!" Well, groups have become folders and guess what—they won't let you choose separate icons for your folders! In Chapter 9, I discuss the hooks that are there so that a third party could write a program to do this—but it really should be part of Windows itself.

- Two compressed formats—`.zip` and `.cab`—are so important that Windows Explorer should provide direct support for them. I'll discuss third-party tools for them in Chapter 5.

Ha. We missed that in Windows 95 but early on provided a PowerToy to view cabs, and it is built into Windows 98.

Yeah, the support for cabs (which only Microsoft uses) is nice but Zip is more common. Zip support should be in the OS.

But would Janet let me? We put it in the Plus! Pack where no one can complain we are jumping on Niko Mak and Mijenix.

If Janet is preventing this, she isn't doing users any favors, although she is protecting the makers of third-party Zip products.

Besides, Billy, you know that the real reason you keep some goodies for the Plus! Pack is to sell more of it. The Zip component is probably the most interesting thing in the whole package.

- Internet's FTP protocol is just a file copy utility. It should be possible to have FTP sites in your directory tree, from which you copy files (using FTP in the background) by drag and drop.

- There should be a GUI file compare rather than just the DOS `fc.exe` that comes with Windows.

■ You Gave Me Such a Start

When you start with a portrait and search for a pure form, a clear volume, through successive eliminations, you arrive inevitably at the egg. Likewise, starting with the egg and following the same process in reverse, one finishes with the portrait.

—PABLO PICASSO, 1932

**Figure 3-23.
Guess what?**

If the Start button is the most famous symbol in Windows 98, then the menu you get when you press it (the default form is shown in Figure 3-23) is the most notable source of user control. Rather than go through the ten choices in spatial order (starting from the bottom, of course!), I discuss them in what I regard as their order of significance. That means beginning with the Programs submenu and how to configure the submenu for more launch options. I'd be remiss while discussing launching if I didn't discuss hotkey launching, one of Windows 3.x's most underused goodies made more powerful in Windows 9X.

Then I jump down to the Find command, one of Windows 9X's most wonderful features. Next I talk about Documents and Run, which are two sides of the same coin. Only then will I turn to Shutdown and LogOff, where I'll bet you're in for some surprises. I end with some advanced topics on the subject of Start.

**Figure 3-24.
Set 'em up!**

You may note three players as missing in action. Favorites gives you a cascading menu of the items in your Favorites folder,—just like the one you get from the Favorites menu of Explorer or Internet Explorer. There isn't much to say about it. Help brings up the central Windows help file, which is discussed with the help engine in general at the end of this chapter.

**Figure 3-25.
Demure Start
Menu**

Settings brings up the submenu in Figure 3-24. There isn't much to say about it. The first two launch the Control Panel and Printers folders (I give you a better way to do that when I discuss configuring the Start Menu). Of course, there is a lot to say about the actual Printers and Control Panel folders—indeed, they are the major themes of the central part of this chapter and of Chapter 8. The Taskbar & Start Menu . . . submenu item has two tabs; one I discussed when I talked about the Taskbar, and the other will be mentioned in the very next section.

The Folder Options item on the Settings menu brings up the dialog I discussed in configuring Explorer. I'll discuss the Active Desktop subsubmenu in the subsection "Active Desktop" in the "Desktop Dancing" section. I discussed Windows Update in Chapter 1.

By checking the box labeled "Show Small Icon in Start Menu" in the Taskbar Properties menu (Figure 3-6), you can shift the look of the Start Menu from that shown in Figure 3-23 to the more demure look of Figure 3-25. And the ad for Windows 98 is gone too! I strongly recommend this setting at 640 × 480 resolution.

 If you have a portable with properly implemented Advanced Power Management support, the Start Menu will also include a Suspend item that puts the machine in a very low power-consumption state that saves the system—a Resume button on the keyboard reawakens the system. Depending on the laptop, expect the suspended state to persist for several hours to several days but never much longer than a week (assuming you don't plug the system into the wall).

Configuring the Start Menu

A journey of a thousand miles
Starts from beneath one's feet.

—Lao-Tzu, *Tao-te-ching*

If you want to manipulate the Start Menu, go to Chapter 2 and reread the section "The Tree-Based Menu." The Programs submenu of Start and the items above it that you can add are a reflection of the files and subfolders of the folder `C:\windows\Start Menu`.

 A suitable picture really is worth a thousand words. At the left of Figure 3-26, you see the top of Barry's Start Menu from Programs up. Notice that he has added three submenus (you know they are submenus by the ▶ to the right) and one item that runs a shortcut when you choose it. Now look at the right side of the figure at the Explorer view of Barry's `C:\windows\Start Menu` folder. You'll notice that the folder has four subfolders whose names are precisely the names of the four submenus at the left. In addition, the file panel at the extreme right has two files besides the four subfolders—shortcuts whose names are identical to the Start Menu items.

Figure 3-26.
Extra Start Menu items reflect a directory structure

 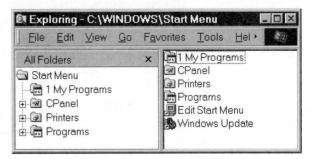

You may notice three unusual aspects of the extra folders I put in. First, there are folders named Cpanel and Printers with the Control Panel and Printer folder symbols next to them. Since their setup is a little bit techie, I'll tell you about them in the section "Advanced Start Menu Tips." Second, my other folder is called 1 My Programs. Why did I use that 1? Simple—it's a holdover from Windows 95 where you didn't get to choose the ordering of the submenus above Programs. They were alphabetical, and 1 happens to come before any letter in the alphabet (in the ASCII code list, which is what counts), so it's unobtrusive and always puts that menu at the very top. Some folks label subfolders starting with 1, 2, . . . to control their ordering. But as I explain in the very next section, you can control the order of the menu items directly under Windows 98.

 Don't let Barry's use of the words "techie" and "advanced" frighten you. The trick for putting a dynamic Control Panel on the Start Menu is simple if you are careful. Check it out.

This paradigm extends to submenus and subsubmenus. Figure 3-27 shows a fourth-level submenu branching off the Start Menu while Figure 3-28 shows the Explorer view of the corresponding folders and subfolders. This should make it clear that the way to arrange and reorganize your Start Menu and the way to add and remove submenus and items is exactly the same way you organize your files and folders. Since I strongly urged you to use Explorer mode to manipulate files, you won't be surprised that I encourage you to use Explorer to manage your Start Menu. You'll find Add . . . and Remove . . . buttons in the Start Menu Programs tab of Taskbar Properties. They may be useful for those who

Figure 3-27. Fourth-level submenu

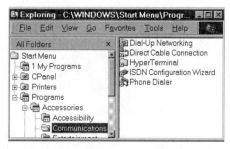

Figure 3-28. Corresponding third-level subfolder

don't understand the menu/folder paradigm—but since you do, you won't be interested in them!

There are two built-in ways to access Explorer to manage your Start Menu program items—but I recommend a third! First, if you right click on the Start button and pick Explore, Explorer will open up with `C:\windows\start menu` as the current folder. Second, if you pick Advanced . . . from the Start Menu/Programs tab of Taskbar Properties, you get a rooted Explorer starting at `C:\windows\start menu`. (Rooted Explorers and the Explorer command line are discussed earlier in this chapter). The rooted Explorer you get from the Advanced . . . button is more natural for this manipulation than the unrooted Explorer you get from right clicking on the Start button, but it is a pain to have to choose Start, then Settings, then Taskbar & Start Menu. . . , then click a second tab and a button to reach Advanced. . . . So I strongly recommend that you set up a shortcut to do essentially what the Advanced . . . button does. Right click on a blank part of the Desktop, pick New and then Shortcut. This will invoke the New Shortcut Wizard. For the command line, enter

```
C:\WINDOWS\EXPLORER.EXE /e, /root, C:\windows\start menu
```

and hit Next. You can use anything for the name of the shortcut. I doubt you'll like the one Windows suggests, which is `explorer.exe`. You might want to use Edit Start Menu the way Barry does, but you're the boss. You might want to double click on it to make sure it works. If you get an error message, check that you haven't forgotten the two commas; they're important. You might also want to change the icons—right click on the shortcut, choose Properties, go to the Shortcut tab, and pick Change Icon. . . .

Once the icon is on your desktop, you can assign a hotkey to it if you want and/or place it on the main Start Menu the way Barry does by dragging the shortcut and dropping it on the Start button. Once you have quick access to Edit Start Menu, you can easily manage the Start Menu. Removing an item is as simple as finding it in the folder tree and hitting **Del**. Adding a new item is as easy as setting the menu to display the folder corresponding to the submenu you want the item on, opening another Explorer window, locating the executable, and dragging it to the Edit Start Menu window. (Dragging an **.exe** creates a shortcut; if you are dragging a document or an existing shortcut, you may want to right drag and drop and pick Create Shortcut Here.) Adding a new submenu is just creating a New Folder and rearranging items; whole submenus are just drag and drop file or folder moving.

A few final remarks on organizing the program menus in Start Menu:

- In Windows 98, there is a graphical way to rearrange the menu items that I discuss in the next section. It has its uses, but so does the Explorer view.

- There is a special subfolder in the Programs subfolder of Start Menu called StartUp. Items in this folder (in `C:\windows\start menu\programs\startup`) are run when Windows starts up (unless you hold down **Shift**). As I discuss in Chapter 9, there are at least eight other places that program names can be placed and run when Windows starts up. So if some package is installed and the result is a new program that runs automatically, don't suppose that the entry for it is necessarily in the StartUp group.

- You can add an item to the top level of the Start Menu by dragging it to the Start button. Even if you don't want the item at the top level, this can be a quick way to get an item on the Desktop into the Start Menu where you can move Edit Start Menu to move it to a submenu below the top. In the next section I describe how to drag and drop to a submenu.

- If a Windows 3.1 package is installed but makes the proper DDE calls to Program Manager to add a new group, then Windows 98 intercepts them and instead makes a new subfolder in the Programs subfolder of Start. But some installs may not work quite right. If that happens, you may be able to add the subfolder by hand.

- If you install Windows 98 to a new directory, it won't translate your old Windows 3.1 or Program Groups to Start Menu subfolders (as it does if you install Windows 98 over Windows 3.1). But you can accomplish that on a group-by-group basis by double clicking the **.grp** files.

- You can rename or move the Start Menu folder. As long as you do so in Explorer, Explorer is smart enough to adjust the Registry entries necessary to make sure that Start Menu (and the StartUp group) still work. But I recommend against this—some dumb program may just blithely assume your Start Menu is in the Start Menu subfolder of the Windows folder.

Reordering and Reorganizing the Start Menu

Under the original release of Windows 95, the items on the Start Menu itself were inert—you could pick them to launch something but right clicking or dragging and dropping them had no effect. When OSR2 was released, a right click menu that let you delete menu items from the menu was added, but you still couldn't drag and drop. With Windows 98, the menu items have become full-fledged draggable objects.

 While it wasn't called that, there was a sort of Windows 96 released in August of 1996. It was called OSR2—short for OEM Service Release 2. OEM, which means original equipment manufacturer, refers to the computer "makers" like Dell, Compaq, and IBM. As the name implies, this version was available only to computer makers to ship with new PCs although some people figured out how to get copies to upgrade their existing machines. OSR2 had FAT32 and several UI upgrades, including better Dial-Up Networking and context menus on Start Menu items.

One thing you can now do is drag a shortcut from the Desktop or Explorer and do more than just plop it into the top of the Start Menu. Take the shortcut and hold it over the Start Menu for a moment and the whole menu will open. Now hold it over a submenu name, say Programs, and that submenu will open. You can do this down several levels until the menu where you want to place the shortcut opens and you can drop it there.

 This is kinda whizzy and it does have its uses—it's the best way to drag a single icon from the Desktop to the Start Menu—but it requires finer hand–eye coordination to do this drop with opening panels than a simple drag and drop between Explorer windows. So there is no question that the Explorer mode I describe in the previous section is the way to go for extensive rearrangements of the Start Menu.

 One place that drag and drop on the menu itself is essential is when you want to rearrange the order of menu items. You can do this only by opening the menu and dragging away.

 The menu order is stored in the Registry in a binary format. The key is **HKCU\Software\Microsoft\Windows\CurrentVersion\ Explorer\MenuOrder\StartMenu\Menu\Order**. I'll discuss more about Registry keys in Chapter 9, but this one isn't editable in any reasonable way so the only way to change is via drag and drop.

 Wow, Billy, you guys sure know how to make complicated-looking keys. It's a great touch to have both MenuOrder and Menu\Order in the same key. I'll bet there was an argument about which to use and upper management settled it by using both.

I'm Hot for Hotkeys

A woman is like a teabag—only in hot water do you realize how strong she is.

—Nancy Reagan

 If I had to pick the single most underused neato feature in Windows 95, it would have to be quick-launch hotkeys.

Barry's right. In the property sheet of a shortcut, there is a field, shown in Figure 3-29, for entering hotkeys. It's in the Shortcut tab of a Windows shortcut

Figure 3-29. Hotkeys, er, shortcut keys

Shortcut key: Shift + F11

(**.lnk** file), in the Program tab of a DOS shortcut (**.pif** file), and in the Internet Shortcut tab for Internet shortcuts (**.url** files).

 Internet shortcuts couldn't have hotkeys in the original Windows 95; they were added with IE 4.

Hotkeys either shift to a running program or start a program that isn't running. They work under two circumstances:

- If a program was launched from a shortcut with an assigned hotkey either directly (you double clicked on the shortcut) or indirectly (you launched it from Start Menu or via a hotkey), then hitting the hotkey will restore the program window (if minimized) and switch to the program in question. Hotkeys work no matter where the shortcut is located.

- If the shortcut is in the Desktop directory or one of its subfolders or in the Start Menu directory or one of its folders, then the program associated with the shortcut will be launched.

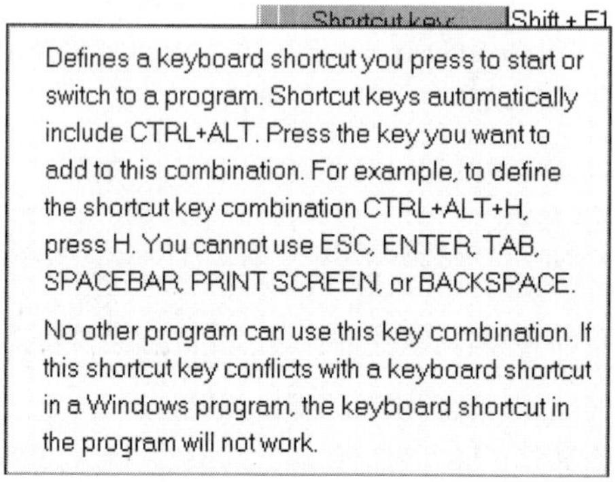

Figure 3-30. Hokey, er, hotkey help

Shortcut key: Shift + F1

Defines a keyboard shortcut you press to start or switch to a program. Shortcut keys automatically include CTRL+ALT. Press the key you want to add to this combination. For example, to define the shortcut key combination CTRL+ALT+H, press H. You cannot use ESC, ENTER, TAB, SPACEBAR, PRINT SCREEN, or BACKSPACE.

No other program can use this key combination. If this shortcut key conflicts with a keyboard shortcut in a Windows program, the keyboard shortcut in the program will not work.

The second item means that the program is launched no matter where you are, even inside a full-screen DOS window. It does sometimes take a little while for the hotkey to do the launch, which is unfortunate.

The official documentation for hotkeys (what you get if you hit the ? in the dialog and press the words Shortcut Key) is seen in Figure 3-30.

But it lies and lies badly. First of all **Ctrl+Shift** and **Alt+Shift** also work with any alphabetic key (and if you like violin practice, **Ctrl+Shift+Alt+[letter]** is also OK). And a single shift with a function key works too.

You assign a hotkey by placing the cursor in the Shortcut Key field and hitting the hotkey. To blank an assigned hotkey, hit **Backspace** in the same field. You won't normally be able to assign the same hotkey to two shortcuts because attempting to hit the hotkey to define the second one won't work. Instead, it will invoke the first program assigned the hotkey. If a hotkey is assigned to an action, figuring out exactly where the shortcut is that is producing the action may not be so easy. Alas, I know of no place where Windows stores this information.

Using FileFind

What affects men sharply about a foreign nation is not so much finding or not finding familiar things; it is rather not finding them in the familiar place.

—G. K. Chesterton, *Generally Speaking*

Windows FileFind is one of its shining moments. Not only does it have intelligent wildcard and multiple filespec support and the ability to search within files, but it's very speedy. Third-party unindexed file search utilities are a thing of the past.

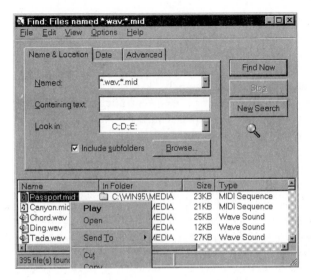

Figure 3-31. Finders, keepers

It's deceptively simple looking (Figure 3-31) but exceedingly powerful. You have to understand the capabilities of the entry fields in the main Name & Location tab and those of the additional options, and you have to know what you can do with the results of a search.

While the main place you'll probably invoke FileFind is off the Start Menu Find/File menu item (hit **Ctrl+Esc**, **F**, **F** real fast!), it can also be invoked by hitting **F3** in any Explorer window (including the Desktop). I explain how to assign it a hotkey later. There is no executable that invokes the dialog—rather, it is so much a part of Explorer that it is called via DDE commands to Explorer.

The three fill-in fields on the main tab are called "Named:", "Containing text:" and "Look in:". Here is the power of entry you have.

- The "Named :" field is for filenames. You can use the standard DOS filenames ***** and **?** but more flexibly than in DOS. ***a?b*.*** would look for files with an a and b in the middle separated by a single letter.

- If you enter a string with no wildcards and no **.**, then it looks for names with that string anywhere in the middle; for example, **win** is the same as ***win***, and FileFind would find both **win.ini** and **topwin.exe**.

- You can enter multiple filenames in the "Named:" field separated by spaces, commas, or semicolons, and the search will be for all of the types (the union of the lists for each of the types). I suggest remembering semicolons for reasons that will become clear in a second. Note that one cannot search for explicit filespecs with a space in them—names in quotes don't work. You can use **?** in place of the space (for example, **start?menu**) to find the file but you may find others, too.

- "Containing text:" allows you to search for text in ASCII files as well as Word **doc** files. Leave it blank if you don't want to limit the search to text.

 I applaud the wisdom of moving the containing text box from the Advanced tab to the main tab—it seems to have been done with IE4. It comes up enough that it shouldn't be buried.

- "Look in:" specifies a target directory. By default, an "Include subfolders" box is checked that can turn a search of **c:** into a search of an entire drive.

- There are two obvious ways to enter choices in the "Look in:" box. There is a dropdown list with any recent single directories you've searched in.

Also, Browse . . . lets you search for a particular directory whose name can be entered. One of the dropdown choices is My Computer. Pick that and all the local drives and any mapped network drives will be searched (at least if "Include subfolders" is checked).

- You can type a full pathname into the "Named:" box. If you type `C:\windows\*.exe`, when you hit **Enter**, `C:\windows` will magically get transferred to "Look in:" and `*.exe` will remain in "Named:". This does not work properly with multiple specs (separated by `,`, `;`, or space).

- The true power is that "Look in:" is a combo box—that is, you can type drives or directories into it. You can type multiple drive or directory names into it separated by semicolons but not by spaces or commas. This works as you expect if you also use multiple filespecs in the "Named:" field. For example, if you type `*.exe;*.com` in the "Named:" field and `C:\windows;D:\msoffice`, you'll get a list of all `.exe` and `.com` files in either directory (or their subdirectories). You'll often just do a multiple drive search, for example, `C:;D:`.

- The directories you type into "Look in:" can be UNC pathnames as well as local drives.

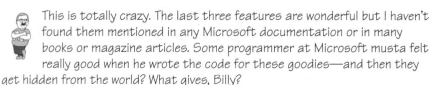 This is totally crazy. The last three features are wonderful but I haven't found them mentioned in any Microsoft documentation or in many books or magazine articles. Some programmer at Microsoft musta felt really good when he wrote the code for these goodies—and then they get hidden from the world? What gives, Billy?

Ah, you've discovered the MGS—the Microsoft Goody Specification. One key idea behind the committee that formulated this specification is that there can be no documentation errors if there is no documentation. If we'd documented this neat FileFind stuff, the writer might have made a small error—maybe he'd have said that a comma worked in "Look in:". If he had, you guys in the press would have made a bigger deal about the error than about the feature and you'd have forgotten about it being so great in a few weeks. But under the MGS, the goodies dribble out slowly. Instead of a few lines in the Resource Kit, maybe we'll get a whole column by Brian Livingston on the power of the Find dialog. And it'll last for months after the rollout. Yes, sir-ree—the MGS is one of our marketing team's most brilliant ploys. And I've got even better news for you—the same team that wrote the MGS is working on the MGAPI.

The **Date** tab (Figure 3-32) is pretty straightforward. The only thing to note is that the designer fouled up here. You'll often want to search files made today, but the "During the previous *N* day(s)" means today and the *N* days before that, so a 1 there means "yesterday" and "today." Alas, you can't make that 1 into a 0. But you can fool the designer and use the "between" option. It defaults to to-day's date in the final date—type today's date in the beginning date and you

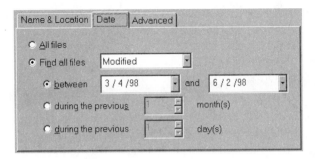

Figure 3-32. Finding by date

can search just for today's files. The Advanced tab is also straightforward. "Of type" refers to the File Types that I discuss extensively later in this chapter.

Once you've done the search, bear in mind that the results list is essentially a full-fledged Explorer window with a very few lacks. As shown in Figure 3-31, you can select a filename and right click to get the full context menu. You can launch the default action by double clicking. You can delete files (not just from the list but from the disk), rename them, and move or copy them to an Explorer window or the Desktop. If you have lots of folders in a Games folder, you could search for `C:\games\*.exe` and then drag the files to a Start Menu subfolder window to get shortcuts to all your games at once. If you want, you can use the View menu to change to large icons, and you can resize the window to see more rows of columns. The File menu includes the full context menu for selected file(s) together with a command to open the folder containing the selected file.

The final Find tip you need to know is that you can save a find with the File/Save Search menu item. Depending on whether you've checked the Save Results item on the Options menu, either the search criterion or the criterion and results get saved. If you pick this item, you get no feedback, no choice of file in which the data is saved, and no indication that the menu item did a darned thing. Ah, well, you think, something else broken. In fact, the search is saved in a file on the Desktop with extension `.fnd` and a name based on the title in the Find window, for example, `all files.fnd` or `@.exe.fnd`. Since `*` and `?` aren't permitted in a filename, they are replaced with `@` and `!`, respectively.

 Note that you must run the Find once (at least to the point of clicking Stop) before the search parameters "take." It isn't enough to type, say, `c:;d:` in the "Look in:" box and then click File, then Save Search. If you want the `c:;d:` to be included in the `.fnd` saved search, you must press Find Now first.

 As I explain soon, I'm all for using the Desktop as a convenient repository but this silent use of the Desktop violates several cardinal rules of good UI design—give the user feedback when something has been accomplished, let the user pick a meaningful filename, and warn the user before you overwrite a file—instead, File/Save Search just overwrites any prior search with the name it feels it should use. The moral is to be sure to move and/or rename any saved finds you want to keep.

One useful thing to do with saved searches is to place shortcuts to them on the Desktop or Start Menu and then assign a hotkey to the shortcut. Because calling up a **.fnd** file makes a DDE call to Explorer and DDE can be slow or even flaky, the response to the hotkey is sometimes slow and occasionally doesn't do anything at all, but by and large it's great.

 Find does have two limitations in its full text search. The searches are unindexed; they start from scratch each time rather than using the previous creation of indices to some or all of your files. While the search will locate text within proprietary file types if the text is stored in pure ASCII format, as soon as any formatting codes or other binary junk intervenes, the search may fail. For the Office file types, Fast Find (built into the Office Open dialog) doesn't have either of these limitations.

 Yeah, but Fast Find is so flaky that Windows 98's installer disables it, and I strongly recommend that you leave it disabled. Reenable it at your own risk!

The Run Box and the Documents Menu

Of all the thirty-six alternatives, running away is best.

—Chinese Proverb

The Run . . . command and the Documents submenu have in common access to a history of your recent actions. The Documents menu normally lists the last 15 documents you used. A document is any file with an extension that has an associated Open command. Such files are displayed in Explorer with an icon next to them, although not every file with an icon next to it is considered a document for the purposes of the document menu.

 To get supertechie, in the language of ProgIDs that I describe in the sections on File Types later, the extensions that are considered to be documents are precisely those that have an associated ProgID listed in the Registry with a **shell\open** subkey. There, aren't you sorry you asked?

Files can get listed in the Documents menu in several ways.

- If you double click on a document in Explorer, it becomes listed in this list.
- If you have a shortcut to a document and you double click on that, the document is placed in the list.
- If you use a Windows 98 application and either open or save a document (using the Win98 common dialogs), the document appears on the list.
- If some program wants to, it can add a document to the list. For example, the Office 97 applications don't use the Windows 98 common dialogs but they still list their documents files in this list—presumably by using custom code.

Surprisingly, if you type the full pathname of a document (or the name of a document in the DOS path, for example, **win.ini**) into the Run box, it does not appear in the Documents list. This may have been done on purpose because the entry will appear in the Run history, but it sounds like a bug to me. And one not fixed from Windows 95!

 The files in the Documents menu are associated to shortcuts in the directory **C:\windows\recent**. You can delete an individual document from the list by deleting the shortcut from that directory, but you cannot add a document to the menu by adding a shortcut to that directory. That's because the Documents menu also involves the Registry entries in the Registry key

HKEY_CURRENT_USER\Software\Microsoft\CurrentVersion\Explorer\RecentDocs.

This key tracks the order in which the documents were used so that Windows knows which of the 15 to remove when a new one needs to be added. There, aren't you sorry you asked?

You can also clear the Documents list completely from the Start Menu Programs tab of the Taskbar Properties sheet.

The Run . . . box has a dropdown list of the last 26 commands you issued from the Run box. (Well, it turns out to be a dropup list most of the time!) You can type in the full path to a command or Browse . . . for it. The command can be an executable or the name of a document (extension with an Open command, as I explained earlier). You can drag a file from Explorer to the Run box and have the full pathname entered there. As I explain in Chapter 2, this can be an efficient way to get a complicated pathname onto the clipboard.

The number 26 isn't random—it's the number of letters in the alphabet. The list is stored in the Registry (in a key similar to the one for documents but it ends with **\RunMRU** instead of **\RecentDocs**). There are 27 items in this Registry key, of which 26 have the names a, b, . . . , z with values equal to the command; the last is called MRUlist and has the 26 letters in the order the commands were run. The indirection of this list makes for efficiency in the code to change it. If the order was fixed to be commands a, b, c, . . . , then every time a new command was run, Windows would have to change 26 Registry entries, moving y to z, w to y, . . . , a to b, and putting the new command in slot a. With this indirect method, Windows looks at the last letter in the MRUlist string, places the new command in the key for that letter, and moves the last letter in the MRUlist string to the first place. Only two Registry entries are changed. And if a command is rerun to move it to the top of the list, all that needs be done is reorder the letters in the MRUlist string.

I'm Gonna Shut You Down

COSTELLO: *Hey, Abbot!*

ABBOT: *Yes, Lou?*

COSTELLO: *I heard that you are a real computer expert. I am having no problem turning it on, but I heard you should be very careful how you turn it off.*

ABBOT: *That's true.*

COSTELLO: *So, here I am working on my new computer and I want to turn it off. What do I do?*

ABBOT: *Well, first you press the Start button, and then—*

COSTELLO: *No, I told you, I want to turn it off.*

ABBOT: *I know. You press the Start button—*

COSTELLO: *Wait a second. I want to turn it OFF. I* know *how to start it. So tell me what to do. Look, if I want to turn off the computer, I am willing to press the Stop button, the End button, the Cease and Desist button, but no one in their right mind presses the Start to Stop.*

ABBOT: *But that's what you do.*

—Heard on the Web (abbreviated version)

 What's to say about the Shutdown option? It stops Windows and that's that. So what's to talk about?

Figure 3-33. Adios, baby

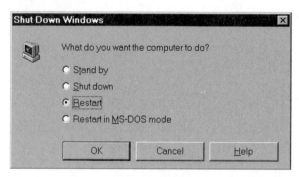

Well, Woody, there are actually four options in the Shutdown dialog box shown in Figure 3-33. And as I'll explain, there are secretly five options there! And there is a sixth option just above Shutdown on the Start Menu. The point is that the Shutdown option isn't just to shut down. It's also for restart, and there are many kinds of restarts.

 Standby may be there on your Desktop, Barry, but it sure ain't on mine. Readers may or may not have it on theirs.

I have to emphasize to the readers how important it is to shut down the system and not just turn it off, that is to pick the default "Shut down." There is sometimes important information to be stored in the Registry when Windows exits, and it won't be if you just turn off the machine. For example, programs can restore themselves after a reboot if you give them a chance to save their state by going through "Shut down," which informs each program that the system is about to shut down. For the same reason, don't just hit the Reset button to restart Windows—go through one of the levels of restart that I discuss in a moment.

 That said, don't freak out if your kid trips over the wire and pulls the plug from the wall so you don't have a proper shutdown. Well, don't freak out because you are concerned about the lack of a proper shutdown. If you have six hours of unsaved work, you do have my permission to say gently: "I wish you wouldn't do that!" Anyhow, the consequence of not shutting down properly is most likely going to be the loss of some option you changed that wasn't properly saved, not the end of civilization as we know it.

There are in essence five ways to restart Windows 98 itself. As a preliminary, I note there are normally three user-made files of commands that are run during a complete bootup of Windows: **C:\config.sys**, **C:\autoexec.bat**, and **C:\windows\winstart.bat**. These files and all aspects of the startup of Windows 98 are discussed extensively in Chapter 6. The five levels of restart (in order of how thoroughly they start over) follow.

1. **Cold reboot**   The system goes through POST (power on self-test), of which the most noticeable symptom is the memory count. Memory starts out zeroed out and all three user configuration files are processed. The only absolutely sure way to accomplish this is to choose "Shut down," wait for the "It's now safe . . ." message, and then hit a reset button or turn the machine on and off. (In reality, one could argue that this is two options; reset is subtly different from power off/on especially if you wait a minute or two between turning the machine off and on. Under Windows 3.x, I once saw the SCSI controller get so confused that hitting reset didn't help although power off/on did.)

2. **Warm reboot**   This is what happened in prior DOS versions if you hit **Ctrl+Alt+Del**. There is no POST and memory isn't zeroed out (but the operating system assumes all memory can be used by any program); otherwise it is just like a cold reboot. There may or may not be a way to cause a cold reboot. On all the systems I've seen, choosing Restart and choosing "Shut down," waiting for "It's now safe . . . ," and then hitting **Ctrl+Alt+Del** did the same thing. But what that same thing was seems to be system dependent. On some systems, these actions cause a cold reboot. On others they cause a warm reboot—in which case I'm not aware of any simple way to force a cold reboot short of hitting the Reset button.

3. **Restarting Windows . . .** This is the undocumented fifth option in the Shutdown dialog. If you choose the radio button that says Restart, hold down the Shift key and choose Yes, and keep the Shift key down until you see the message **"Windows is now restarting . . . ,"** then what occurs is essentially the Windows 3.1 equivalent of exiting Windows and typing **win** at the DOS command line. Windows itself and the programs loaded in it are closed, but the programs you loaded in **config.sys** and **autoexec.bat** remain in memory. **Winstart.bat** is run again (but what was previously in it is unloaded). Please note that if the Shift key is held down through the loading of Windows itself, then your StartUp group is skipped. So you have to be careful to remove your finger from the Shift key when you see the message (assuming you do want the program in StartUp loaded).

4. **Relogging Windows** The option on the Start Menu that reads "Log off <username> . . ." is primarily intended for situations where you've set up multiple user profiles or have logged into a network, an option I discuss later in this chapter, and in that case, it does what the question suggests. But you can use this option even if you are a single user to quickly unload all the running Windows applications without unloading Windows itself or rerunning **winstart.bat**. If you are a single user with no login password, you get the dialog that is shown in Figure 3-34. Just hit OK, and you'll preserve your no-login status.

The last option is not present on all systems. For it to be there, you either have to have turned on multiple user profiles (a procedure discussed later in this chapter) or you need to have some kind of networking turned on. I find the restart option associated with it—relogging—so useful that I think users might want to install Dial-Up Networking just to get this menu option! You can install Dial-Up Networking on any computer—you don't need a modem or a network card.

5. Some machines will show an option labeled "Stand by." This suspends the system in a very low-power state and you can later restore the system by moving a mouse or hitting the keyboard.

Figure 3-34. Will the next guest sign in?

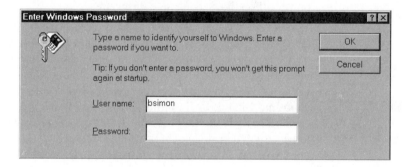

Well, that's what it's supposed to do, and it will on systems made to support the Advanced Power Management spec, but the menu option can appear on older systems where you are likely to get an error message instead of going into standby mode. That's what happens to me.

 Microsoft is pioneering low-power usage. Soon, you'll have systems that can go into a very low-power mode and instantly awaken when a fax comes in to your fax software or other external events happen that require action.

If you have some program that is eating resources or some other reason to "start afresh," option 4 is probably enough and is by far the quickest restart. You may learn that under some circumstances it isn't enough, in which case you should try option 3. Given the amount of time that it takes to boot up from scratch, options 3 and 4 are definitely worth trying first.

 On the machine my kids use, which has multiple user profiles, I find that after they've been playing certain games, resources are eaten up, and logging in to my profile doesn't restore them. So relogging may not be enough.

That leaves the option that says, "Restart in MS-DOS mode." This normally involves what is called MS-DOS Exclusive mode, an option I talk about more extensively in the section *"DOS Penalty Box"* later in this chapter. Exactly what happens when you choose this option depends on whether there is a file called **exit to DOS.pif** in the **C:\windows** directory. If there is no such file, Windows 98 makes one and runs it. This default **exit to DOS.pif** is set to run DOS Exclusive mode with the choice of "Use current MS-DOS configuration." If Windows is just going to run this standard **.pif**, why does it bother to make it? Because it gives you control over what this menu choice does. If you want it to restart in a configuration that has your real mode CD-ROM drivers present, change **exit to DOS.pif** to use a custom MS-DOS configuration that loads them. If you want to disable this Shutdown entry, you can make **exit to DOS.pif** run a batch file that displays a message saying "DOS Exclusive mode not allowed on this machine." A sophisticated user wouldn't be fooled but a less experienced user might. Heck, if you were a system administrator concerned that some user was booting this mode too often to play some DOS game, you could have **exit to DOS.pif** run a batch file that first sent a notification to your computer and then ran another **.pif** file that really did exit to DOS Exclusive mode.

An interesting fact to note. If you call up the Shutdown dialog and answer No, then Windows saves the Desktop icon position information in the Registry. You might want to do this right after a lot of Desktop rearranging as insurance against a crash before you've had a chance to properly shut down.

Advanced Start Menu Tips

My interest in desperation lies only in that sometimes I find myself having become desperate. Very seldom do I start out that way. I can see of course that, in the abstract, thinking and all activity is rather desperate.

—WILLEM DE KOONING

Here are one important tip and one stupid Desktop trick.

 You can easily add a shortcut to Control Panel to the Start Menu by just dragging the Control Panel entry from My Computer to the Start button. Such a menu item opens a Control Panel window and forces you to click on a second icon and close Control Panel afterward. You could make a subfolder of the Start Menu called CPanel and laboriously make shortcuts to each and every applet. That's not only time-consuming but if you add a new applet, you have to explicitly update the Start Menu. There's a better way.

Figure 3-35. Making a dynamic Control Panel

To get a dynamic Control Panel on the Start Menu at the top level, you need to open an Explorer window on the `C:\windows\start menu` directory, make a new folder, and then name that folder with the following strange name (see Figure 3-35):

CPanel.{21EC2020-3AEA-1069-A2DD-08002B30309D}

You can put anything you want before the `.` in place of **CPanel**, say **Control Panel** or **Applets**. But the funny string of 32 characters with the braces and dashes must be exactly as it appears here. When you hit **Enter** to complete the rename, the extension will no longer appear in Explorer (but it will be there, for example, in a DOS directory). If you choose that menu item from the Start Menu, you get a submenu with the names of all the Control Panel applets (part of the flyout menu is shown in Figure 3-36).

Figure 3-36. Dynamic Control Panel

You can get similar flyout lists of the Printers and Dial-Up Networking folders using the following magic strings.

Magic CLSIDs	
Control Panel	{21EC2020-3AEA-1069-A2DD-08002B30309D}
Printers	{2227A280-3AEA-1069-A2DE-08002B30309D}
Dial-Up Networking	{992CFFA0-F557-101A-88EC-00DD010CCC48}

The 32-character strings are hex digits (hex means base 16 and has the "digits" 0–9 and A–F, with A = 10, B = 11, . . . , F = 15) and they are called CLSIDs. I say a lot more about them in Chapter 9. Basically, they are just identifying numbers for shell objects, and the specific number says as much about the object as your Social Security number says about you. The Registry tells Windows what code library to use to deal with objects with a particular CLSID.

I dunno what all the hoopla is. I don't set things up with a dynamic Control Panel at the top of my Start Menu. There are two problems with this. First, if my mouse passes over that choice on my way to some other choice, there can be a noticeable pause while Windows reads the names of the applets from disk. Second, the menu is long and includes applets like Mouse and Date/Time that I use once in a blue moon. Instead, I have a subfolder of Start Menu called CP Applets. Inside, I've put shortcuts to the few applets I use all the time (Add/Remove Programs, Display, Fonts, System) and a shortcut to Control Panel, which I call Other Applets. I considered putting a dynamic Control Panel in that folder but didn't in the end.

So much for the important tip. Here's a weird trick, mainly a curiosity. Call up the Shutdown dialog from the Start Menu. Hold down **Ctrl**, **Alt**, and **Shift** at the same time and click Cancel. Explorer will unload itself totally. No Taskbar and no Desktop icon and no Explorer windows but all other programs will be running. About the only option at that point is to hit **Ctrl+Alt+Del** and choose "Shut down."

This weird state is there for programmers who need to debug a program without Explorer loaded.

Ye Olde Shell Game

There's no accounting for tastes. Some people actually liked Windows 3.1 Program Manager and miss it when faced with the rather dry and nongraphical Start Menu Programs submenu. If you liked the Program Manager shtick, use the following psuedo Program Manager.

Here's how you make a Folder view that will look and act a lot like Program Manager. Right click on the Desktop, pick New and Shortcut to invoke the new Shortcut Wizard. Type in the command line

```
C:\windows\explorer.exe/root,C:\windows\start menu\programs
```

and then name it whatever strikes your fancy, say, **progMan strikes back**. Next double click on the icon, go to the View menu and make sure that Large Icons are checked and that Toolbar and Status Bar are not. Go to Options . . .

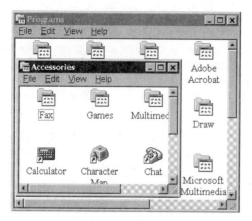

Figure 3-37. ProgMan impersonator

and make sure "Display the Full . . ." is not checked. Close the program. When you reopen that icon, it will remember these settings, at least most of the time. What you get sure looks a lot like Program Manager (Figure 3-37).

■ Desktop Dancing

Custom has made dancing sometimes necessary for a young man; therefore mind it while you learn it, that you may learn to do it well, and not be ridiculous, though in a ridiculous act.

—Lord Chesterfield, *The Letters of the Earl of Chesterfield to His Son*

 I used to consider calling the computer screen a desktop as slightly weird. First, the monitor is usually on your desktop, so there's a wheels-within-wheels phenomenon. More significantly, at least to Windows 3.1 users, it sure didn't resemble how I use my desktop—as the repository of all sorts of things that I want to keep handy. Windows 9X has changed that.

If this section has one lesson you should take away from it, it is that the Windows Desktop is the ideal place to put stuff while you are working with it, especially files you need for a while but which you want to toss out when some project is done or some e-mail is sent or—and so on. Tossing it out is easy—just drag it to the Recycle Bin. Accessing it is easy if the file is a document associated with a program—just double click on it.

So if you are saving a new file, ask yourself if you are going to need to access it again in the next day. If so, put it on your Desktop.

Windows actually makes it easy to save stuff on the Desktop and to access the Desktop in Explorer, because the Desktop is the Mother of All Folders. Literally. Figure 3-38 shows the right panel of Explorer when My Computer is

**Figure 3-38.
The mother of all
folders**

A

C

D

Control
Panel

Ye Olde
Recycle Bin

**Figure 3-39.
Gee, it sure
looks like a
Mac**

closed. Your disk drives appear on the Explorer tree because they are children of My Computer and My Computer is a child of Desktop, which is at the top. Since Desktop is the ultimate parent, it's easy to get there in Explorer—just hit **Backspace** or repeatedly and you are guaranteed to wind up there. The same is true in the Windows 98 Open and Save As dialogs, and there it is even easier since you have the button, which takes you directly to the Desktop.

Alas, Windows 3.x Open and Save As dialogs don't work that way, and those dialogs don't understand the folder structure above individual drives. So to save a file on the Desktop in a Windows 3.1 program, you need to know that it's "the same" as the file folder **C:\windows\desktop**.

Free the My Computer Four

*My desk, most loyal friend
thank you. You've been with me on
every road I've taken
My scar and my protection.*

—Marina Tsvetaeva, *Desk*

It's the hallmark of the Mac, but what the heck, it's a good idea. You want to place icons for each of your disk drives on your Desktop. But you have to choose which of two ways to do it.

There are two ways to add icons representing disk drives to your Desktop.

1. You can drag the drives from My Computer to the Desktop and make short-cuts—you'll get a dialog saying you can't move or copy the icon, but it offers to make a shortcut. Alternatively, you can right click on the Desktop and pick New Shortcut. If you type in **C:** for the command line, you get a shortcut equivalent to dragging the C drive from My Computer. You can type in **C:** instead and Windows will change it to **C:**. Do this for each of your drives, which for many people means three icons—floppy, hard drive, and CD. While you're at it, free a fourth icon from the confines of My Computer. Drag Control Panel to the Desktop. It's true that I gave you a method for putting a dynamic Control Panel on the Start Menu, but I like also having quicker access around.

2. Go through the New Shortcut Wizard specifying the command line as **C:\windows\explorer.exe /e, A:**. You'll get the Explorer icon , so you'll need to right click, choose Properties, go to the Shortcut tab, and choose Change Icon. . . . It will display icons from **C:\windows\system\shell32.dll**. If you scroll, you'll get a bunch of appropriate ones for disks:

Pick the right one for your floppy, hard drive, CD, and so on

You'll also find appropriate icons in **C:\windows\system\cool.dll**.

Once set up, I suggest putting the icons at the extreme right of your Desktop with the drive icons at the top and the Recycle Bin on the lower right. But, hey, you hardly need me as your interior decorator—put 'em where you want!

I strongly recommend using the first method. It has several advantages that outweigh one huge downside. One advantage is that you can copy by dragging files to icons set up by the first method but not the second. Another plus is that the drive icons automatically adjust to the type of drive. Finally, the icons shown for a CD drive can be adjusted by Windows or by the CD itself. Figure 3-40 shows the default CD icon, the one used for audio CDs, and the one taken from the Windows 98 CD when it is in the drive. The disadvantage is that with the default Windows setup, if you double click on a drive icon set up by the first method, it opens in Folder view; those set up by the second method open in Explorer view.

Plain   Audio   Windows 98

Figure 3-40. CD icons

The solution to the downside is easy. If you shift over to Sarah's Smart Setup, which I explain later in this chapter, then icons set up by the first method open in Explorer mode. So I say you should use Sarah's Setup and the direct icon method.

The Active Desktop

Whatever you are, be a good one.

—ABRAHAM LINCOLN

When Windows 98 installs, it includes a feature called the Active Desktop. Unless you turn on "View as a Web Page," the Desktop isn't very special.

In the beta version of Internet Explorer 4.0, Web view was turned on by default. Many users complained and we listened, so Web view is not the default when you install Windows 98 (unless you've previously installed IE 4.0 and turned on Web view).

You can adjust whether Web view is turned on from the Active Desktop menu (which is found off the Desktop context menu or off the Settings submenu of the Start Menu). Or you can pick from these menus **"Customize my Desktop . . ."** and get the dialog in Figure 3-41, which has a check mark that controls whether Web view is used.

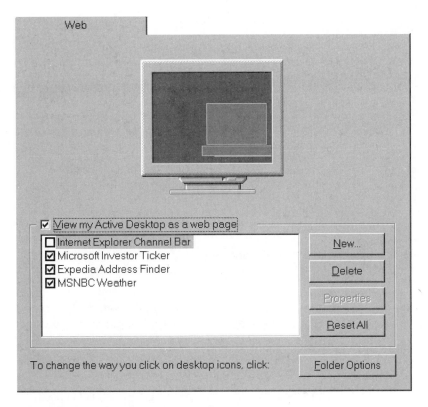

Figure 3-41. Adding ActiveX controls

Turning on the Web page view allows three possibilities you might want to play with. The first is HTML wallpaper.

 Customizing HTML wallpaper, especially if you use VBScript, is techie so I'm saving it for Chapter 7.

The second is the ability to add ActiveX controls, as you can in the dialog shown in Figure 3-41. You'll see three really neat controls chosen there that Barry added to his Desktop. Microsoft Investor Ticker shows a live stock ticker; in Expedia Address Finder, you can type in any address in the United States and go to a Web site that locates that address on a map; MSNBC shows a live weather map (Figure 3-42).

 If you click the New button in Figure 3-41, you get taken to a Web site (**http://www.microsoft.com/ie/ie40/gallery/**) with lots of Desktop ActiveX controls to pick from.

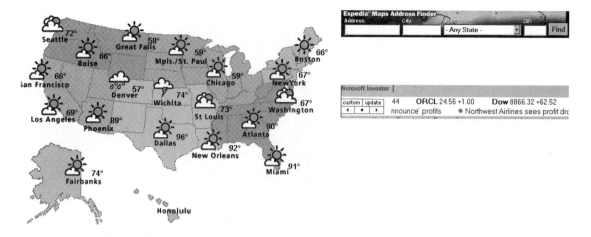

Figure 3-42. Some Desktop ActiveX controls

 The ActiveX controls are updated over the Internet. If you have a hard-wired connection to the Internet, these controls are fun additions to your Desktop. If not, you'll probably want to avoid them unless you like your system dialing the Internet at strange times when some control gets the urge to be updated.

Third, you can place any jpeg or gif as a movable background object allowing, for example, several pictures of your kids on your Desktop.

Desktop Tips and Tricks

When one wanted one's interests looking after whatever the cost, it was not so well for a lawyer to be over honest, else he might not be up to other people's tricks.

—GEORGE ELIOT, *Felix Holt, The Radical,* Introduction

Here are a bunch of suggestions for using your Desktop.

- You can hold down the mouse button and drag to lasso several icons, which you can then move together. You can also select multiple icons with **Ctrl+Click**. But, be careful—it is easy to drag several icons and wind up with some of them off the screen by accident! If you do, picking Line Up Icons from the Desktop's context menu will bring the icons in from the cold—but it could do some other icon rearranging you aren't so happy about.

- I'll repeat the tip on how to align icons in a column (remember the Taskbar?). Sort of line them up at one side or the other. Then drag the Taskbar to that side and make the now columnar Taskbar so wide, it covers up the column of icons. The icons will jump to the inside of the Taskbar and line up in a neat column. Now drag the Taskbar back to the bottom of the screen. Lasso the now neat column of icons and move it where you want. You can also use Line Up Icons but you'll probably want to adjust the icon spacing options in the Appearance tab of the Desktop property sheet; Icon Spacing (Horizontal) and Icon Spacing (Vertical) are on the Appearance dropdown.

- There is no easy way to save the location of all your Desktop icons so that you can restore them easily if Windows or you should foul up (a single Arrange Icons from the Desktop menu can ruin your whole day: it cannot be undone with Undo). But there is a complicated way that I tell you about in Chapter 9.

- Consider placing a shortcut to a folder that is under Start Menu on the Desktop. For example, you might make a subfolder called Current Projects in the C:\Windows\Start Menu folder. Then, using Explorer, right drag that folder to the Desktop and pick Create Shortcut (or use the Create Shortcut Wizard or Cut and Paste shortcut from Explorer). By double clicking on the shortcut, open a Folder view of the folder. Keep the view open and quite small. You can drag shortcuts to documents you are working on to this open folder window. They'll then be available on the Current Projects submenu of Start.

- Barry's office has two PCs in it, which he uses for different projects. They are networked. He has placed shortcuts to each machine's Desktop on the other machine's Desktop. The two machines are called **barry1** and **barry2**. On the Desktop of **barry1** he used the Create Shortcut Wizard to make a shortcut with command line **\\barry2\c\windows\desktop**. He can send files to the other machine by just dragging them to this shortcut. A boss and her secretary could use similar shortcuts to each other's Desktop.

- This idea works as well with Dial-Up Networking as with direct networking. You can connect to a machine with the Remote Access Server. The first time you make a Dial-Up connection, drag a shortcut of the Desktop on the remote machine to the local machine. Now, if you drag a file to this icon, Windows offers to use Dial-Up Networking, and when you answer Yes, it makes the connection and copies the file.

- Consider making a folder on your Desktop called Favorite Dirs. In it, place shortcuts to the directories you use a lot. While you are in Explorer, hitting **Backspace** or ▣ repeatedly will take you to Desktop, and you can click on Favorite Dirs and then a shortcut to move Explorer's focus to the directory in question.

The Mother of All Easter Eggs

The cocks may crow, but it's the hen that lays the egg.

—Margaret Thatcher

Fabergé made elaborate jeweled Easter eggs for the last czars of Russia. So credit screens for programs that were reached by elaborate steps came to be

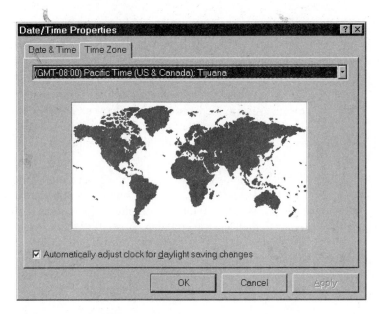

Figure 3-43. Calling up the egg

called Easter eggs also. Frankly, I call them Rube Goldberg eggs. In *The Mother of All Windows Books*, MOM gave Easter eggs the disdain they deserve as in-crowd tricks. But I know you don't care what MOM thinks about Easter eggs—you just want to know how to find the one that's in Windows 98.

Here's what you do to invoke "da egg."

1. Call up the Date/Time applet either from Control Panel or by double clicking on the time in the Notification Area.
2. Click on the Time Zone tab (Figure 3-43).
3. Depress the Ctrl, Alt, and Shift keys together and keep them depressed.
4. Hold the mouse button down on the location of Cairo, Egypt, drag it to the position of Memphis, Tennessee, and release the mouse button.
5. Release the three shifts.
6. Depress the three shifts again and hold them down.
7. Hold the mouse button down on the location of Memphis, Tennessee, drag it to the position of Redmond, Washington, and release the mouse button.
8. Release the shifts.

Voilá, the egg as seen in Figure 3-44.

 Cairo is the code name for Windows NT 5.0 and Memphis the code name for Windows 98. Redmond is of course the home campus of Microsoft. If you don't know where the cities are on the map, get an atlas!

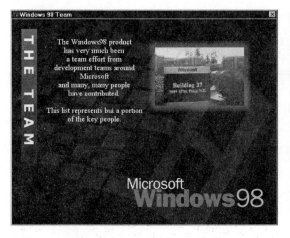

Figure 3-44. Egg all over your face

■ Configuring Context Menus and Associations

Menu, n.: A list of dishes which the restaurant has just run out of.

—AMBROSE BIERCE, *The Devil's Dictionary*

A columnist in one of the big magazines, and we won't mention *PC Computing* by name, complained that you couldn't change the right click menu for drives and, in particular, you couldn't arrange to have Scan-Disk a direct option on this menu (rather than having to click through the Properties menu). This section will let you in on the secret of changing the context menu for most objects in the Windows 98 shell (but, alas, not the context menu for a blank part of the Desktop). In particular, using some fancy footwork, we'll show you how to place a ScanDisk option on your Drive menu, which is a little tricky.

It's remarkable how poorly Microsoft has documented this power user stuff that lets you do things like change the context menu. They didn't even let the press in on it, so the magazines don't often discuss this sort of thing. And it's too bad that for some stuff you need to use Regedit, which can be a bit daunting.

Piece o' cake, guys, piece o' cake. And if you didn't sometimes need Regedit, we wouldn't have supplied it, now would we? As for the lack of documentation for the power user stuff, we wanted to give the magazine and book writers something to discover and talk about. Think of it as the *Barry and Woody Full Employment Act of 1998*.

Send To, which does have some limited uses, was too often presented in the press as a cure-all, when it is often a poor substitute for what is better and more flexibly done with File Types.

 The thorough treatment of File Types that follows can get a little hairy at times so you'll want to look ahead to the section "Stupid File Types Tricks" to see lots of examples of the theory in practice.

File Types Dialog: An Overview

1. Nothing in the known universe travels faster than a bad check.

2. A quarter-ounce of chocolate = four pounds of fat.

3. There are two types of dirt: the dark kind, which is attracted to light objects, and the light kind, which is attracted to dark objects.

—Slick's Three Laws of the Universe

Before I explain how you change actions associated with file extensions and shell objects, I need to give you a few terms that will come up again and again. You may think that **.txt** files are directly associated with Notepad—that was true under Windows 3.0. But in Windows 9X (and already in some cases under Windows 3.1), there are several layers between **.txt** and Notepad. Inside the Registry, extensions are assigned to hidden things called **application identifier keys.** I use the techie name **ProgID**s, taken from the OLE technical docs, to save ink. These keys cannot contain spaces. I call them hidden because you won't ever see them unless you look in the Registry. Several extensions can be assigned to a single ProgID. Associated with ProgIDs are three things of relevance for our discussion here—an **application description** (I call it a **public name**), an icon, and one or more actions that can be applied to the files whose extensions are assigned to that

Figure 3-45. The .txt context menu

ProgID. The actions themselves come in two parts—a name and the command that performs the action. One of the actions is normally the default action—it is run if you left double click on the object and is the boldface item on the right click menu. The icons are used to represent the associated files in Explorer or Folder windows, either as large icons or the tiny icons that appear in the margin in the other three views.

For example, **.txt** has an associated ProgID of **txtfile**. The public name for **txtfile** is Text Document, the default icon is not that for Notepad but an icon taken from the collection in **shell32.dll**. There are two actions assigned to **txtfile**, namely Open (the default) with action **C:\windows\notepad.exe %1** and Print with command **C:\windows\notepad.exe /p %1**.

The result is the context menu shown in Figure 3-45. The two actions assigned to the ProgID text file appear at the top. All the other choices are built into the Windows shell. Third-party products can add their own items to this menu using a Context Menu Handler, something I'll discuss in Chapter 9.

There are also shell identifier keys (I'll also use ProgID for them!). These are objects with special meaning to the Windows shell, such as AudioCD, Drive, and Directory, which do not have an associated file extension but otherwise have all the properties of a ProgID including a public name, an icon, and actions.

 MOM made me promise not to say much about Regedit before Chapter 9, but you get such a good idea of what I'm talking about by looking there that I will say something. Run Regedit (for example, by typing **regedit** in a Run box). Click on the plus sign in front of **HKEY_CLASSES_ROOT**. Scroll down and you'll see a bunch of **.abc**-type entries at the start. If you highlight one you'll see the word (Default) and the associated ProgID at the right. That's where extensions are associated to a ProgID. Now scroll down to a ProgID and highlight it. The associated public names with the familiar (Default) will be at the right. Look at **.txt** and follow it to **txtfile**. Highlight that and hit the asterisk key on your keyboard and you'll open up keys that show you how the icon and actions are stored.

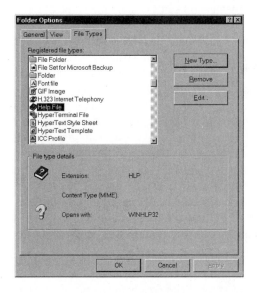

Figure 3-46. File Types dialog

You could change and add actions in Regedit. But Windows provides a more humane way to do this, the File Types dialog you see in Figure 3-46. You get to this by opening an Explorer or Folder window, dropping down the View menu, and picking Options. . . . The General tab is displayed; the last tab is File Types!

The most obvious thing in the File Types dialog is a scrolling list of items. What shows are the public names of the various ProgIDs. This is something of a pain, as you might not guess that the name associated with a batch file is "MS-DOS Batch File" or that a directory has become the politically correct "file folder," so you have to scroll through a long list. If you can't locate something that must be there, run Regedit and trace from the extension(!).

If you highlight an item on the list, you get several pieces of information displayed in the "File type details" panel, including the associated extension(s), the icon for the ProgID, and the name and icon of the program that "opens" the object. Normally, this is the program in the command for the default action for objects with a default. If there is no default, one of the actions is picked, but darned if I can figure out the algorithm.

From the main File Types dialog, you can take three actions that involve new and current file types. Remove blows away the highlighted item from the list. It removes at least two sets of keys from the Registry—the one defining the ProgID and the one or more defining the associated extension(s). Exercise extreme care: look at the discussion in Chapter 9 about making backups of your Registry before fooling with *any* of the options in the File Types dialog.

New Type . . . gives you a dialog almost identical to the Edit . . . option I discuss next. The main difference is that you can and must supply a "Description of type" and you have the option to fill in extensions. When you make a new file type, Windows chooses the ProgID—it takes the first listed extension, say, **foo**, and turns it into the ProgID **foofile**. Brilliant, no? This is not the place to change the program associated with a given extension—the dialog complains and won't let you assign your new type to an already taken extension. I talk about how to do that in the section "Open With Dialog."

If you hit the Edit . . . button, you get the dialog shown in Figure 3-47. At the top, you get to change the icon that is used when files with the extensions associated with this new type appear in the shell. If you pick the Change Icon button, you get the standard Change Icon dialog (Figure 3-78) that I discuss in the section "Take a Deep PIF" later in this chapter. The Description of type allows you to change the public name. It appears grayed out for system file types like Drive, which means you can't change the name of Drive. I talk more about this later. Normally, as in the text file case shown, you can change the public name, and it can be a name with spaces.

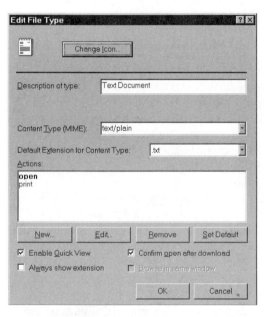

Figure 3-47. Edit File Type dialog

The Actions box lists the various actions assigned to the file type with the default action in bold. If you highlight an action and hit Set Default, it changes the default to the highlighted action if another action was the default or there was no default, but it acts as a toggle if the highlighted action was already the default—that is, it shifts to a mode where there is no default action so that double clicking has no effect. For an example of where you might like to have no default, look at the discussion of Audio CD in the section "Stupid File Types Tricks."

 All this stuff with Set Default affects only the context menu. It doesn't affect what happens if you just type the document name in the Start Menu Run box. When you type in a document name, Windows looks for a command called Open and runs it whether or not Open is the default. And if there is no command called Open, then Windows complains, "No application is associated with the specified file. Create an association by using the Explorer." Type **C:\windows\win.ini** in the Run box and Notepad opens the file even if you've made Print the default action that takes place when you double click the file. Double click a **.cpl** file and it opens the first Control Panel applet in that file. Type the name of that file into the Run box and you get an error message. Why? Because the action isn't called Open but Open with Control Panel? Not quite. Open with Control Panel is the public name, and what counts is the name buried in the Registry, which isn't **Open** but **cplopen**.

Of all the crazy conventions. It makes no sense that double clicking and "running" the file can do different things. Anyhow, you can at least fix the behavior of **.cpl** files. Open the Registry, go to the key

HKEY_CLASSES_ROOT\cplfile\shell\cplopen

right click on it, pick Rename, and change the name to Open. When you run **.cpl** files, what you'd expect to happen does.

The Edit . . . button calls up the dialog shown in Figure 3-48. The Action name is grayed out—the only ways of changing that are to do it in the Registry or else to

Figure 3-48. Edit Action dialog

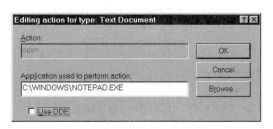

delete the action and reset it using New. . . . The second Edit field lets you change the command issued by the action. When you change actions this way, Windows automatically tacks a **%1** onto the command before storing it in the Registry. That means that the filename you clicked on to reach the context menu with this action gets passed to the command as an action. If done this way, the name is always tacked on after any other parameters. This is usually what you want, but if you don't want a **%1** or you need to place it before some parameters, you can arrange that but only by directly editing the Registry (see Chapter 9).

The New . . . button in the Figure 3-47 brings up an identical dialog to Edit . . . except that the action field isn't grayed out and you can enter a name for the new Action.

If you check the Use DDE field in the New . . . /Edit . . . dialog or if you edit an action that has it checked, the dialog expands to include what is shown in Figure 3-49. The fields shown in that figure come from the Find command that pops up the Find dialog that, as I explained earlier, was launched via DDE commands to Explorer. DDE is stuff for gurus. I doubt you'll ever want to look at this dialog for your own use.

Figure 3-49. DDE fields

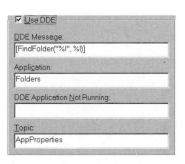

The Enable QuickView check box adds to the context menu a QuickView item that will try to pass the files of the given file type to Quick-View; for most files that means opening it in an ASCII text viewer. The check box marked "Always show extension" does what you'd expect: even if you've checked the box marked "Hide MS-DOS file extensions for file types that are registered," the extensions are shown if you check the Always . . . box for that type. Of course, since you followed my advice earlier in the chapter to uncheck "Hide . . . registered," this is irrelevant to you. The box

Confirm Open After Download has to do with downloads via Internet Explorer and whether files are automatically run or you are queried first. For example, Windows 98 installs with RealMedia files set up to run automatically when clicked in Explorer. That means this box is not checked for them.

 You may find that as you use the File Types and Edit Action dialogs that some buttons are mysteriously grayed out. You can't change the batch file default from Open to Edit even if you want to. Bah, humbug.

 We've placed keys called EditFlags in the Registry to stop you from doing stuff that might harm you. Think of it as a chastity belt to prevent you screwing around with important entries.

 Microsoft may not trust you but of course I do, so I'll give you the keys to the chastity belt. In Chapter 9, I describe these flags in loving detail. But for now, I'll give you the simple method. For any file type that has grayed-out items you don't like being grayed out, note the public name for the type in the File Type dialog. Then call up Regedit and search for the name; for example, for batch files you'd search on "MS-DOS Batch File." When you locate the name, you should find at the right side of the display the word **EditFlags** and to its right eight hex digits, such as **d0 04 00 00**, for batch files. You want to double click on the word **EditFlags** and change the value. For types like **batfiles** that are associated with an extension, change the flags to **00 00 00 00**. For types like File Folder (aka **directory**) that don't have an associated extension, use **02 00 00 00**. It's important that you not use all zeros for entries like this because Windows displays file types in the dialog only if they have an associated file type or if the seventh bit in the edit flags is turned on.

 Two ProgIDs have special meaning: *, which applies to all files, and unknown, which applies to files with extensions that are not registered. You can add them to the file types and you can add actions to them by running Regedit, opening **HKEY_CLASSES_ROOT**, scrolling down to **unknown**, and highlighting it. Choose Edit\New\Binary Value from the Regedit menu. Type in the name **EditFlags**, then double click on that name and enter the data **02 00 00 00**. Do the same with *, which is first on the list under this key.

Open With Dialog

Technology is dominated by two types of people: those who understand what they do not manage and those who manage what they do not understand.

—Putt's Law

If you double click on a file with an extension that has no associated file type, you get the dialog shown in Figure 3-50. As long as you leave the check box that says "Always use this program to open this file" checked (and that's the default) you have a back door for the creation of a new file type. If the extension is **foo**, the ProgID for the new file type will be **foo_auto_file**. The public

Figure 3-50.
Open With dialog

name will be whatever you fill in. (If you don't fill one in, Open With will pick **FOO File**.) The programs you get to choose from are precisely those that are associated with the **Open** command for existing file types. The exact command line for the existing **Open** command is transferred to be the command line for an Open command associated with the new ProgID. If you uncheck the bottom check box, the program is used this one time but no permanent file association is made. Note the Other . . . button, which lets you browse for a program in case the one you want isn't in the list.

 This is a natural for opening ASCII text files, which often pop up with random extensions. But that's the point. For 99 out of 100 users, 99 out of 100 times the program they'll want to use is Notepad. So why the heck did the designers of Windows 98 make you scroll halfway through a huge list? They shoulda treated Notepad as special. Even better, they should have let you choose a default editor somewhere and given that special treatment in Open With.

 Of course, there's a way to make Notepad the first program on the **Open With** list. Go into Explorer, click once on **\windows\notepad.exe**, and click Edit. Click Copy, then click Edit and Paste. Scroll down to the bottom of the list and change the name **copy of notepad.exe** to **_notepad.exe**. Then click View/Options, bring up the File Types tab, and click New Type. . . . In Description of Type use **Mom's Magical Mystery** and in Associated Extension type, oh, **mom**. Click New. . . . In the box marked Action type **Open**, in the box marked Application used to perform action type **c:\windows_notepad.exe**, and click OK all the way back out. Heh heh heh. If you want you can delete the **.mom** subkey from the HKCR key of the Registry. The key needed for this trick is the other one that is created, which will be called **momfile**.

If a program has an Open command that is the default, you can add an Open With . . . item to the context menu if you hold down the Shift key when you right click.

 What is this with the Shift key producing weird but useful alternative actions all the time? The designers of the shell seem to be Shift fixated. And why the heck isn't Open With . . . available if Open is a nondefault action or if there is no Open command at all? Truly bizarre.

It gets worse, grasshopper. The default if you use Open With . . . when an Open command exists is to have the "Always use this program . . . " option unchecked. That's sensible. But if you check the box, what you get may be unexpected. You might think it would act the way the dialog works when there is no Open command and create a new file type. Instead it changes the command line for the file type already associated with files with the clicked extension. Assigning only one extension to the file type could be desirable, but it won't be if there are multiple extensions assigned to one file type.

 So, for example, if you have a general bitmap program that handles **.pcx**, **.tif**, and **.gif**, and you get some kind of great **.gif** handler, there is no way you can use File Types or Open With to just change the assignment for **.gif** and leave **.pcx** and **.tif** alone. You can do it with the Registry, but that'll be hair-raising for many users.

 The design of the Windows shell is so good that normally only so-so components stick out like a sore thumb. And Open With . . . is so-so at best.

 There actually is a program that ships with Windows 98 that will let you break out a single extension from a situation where several are assigned to a single ProgID. The program is called File Manager, and you run it by typing **winfile** in the Run box or by double clicking on the program in Explorer. It is a pretty brain-dead upgrade of the Windows 3.11 File Manager! It does not understand long filenames, and it is still 16 bits. But it does have a File/Associate that can be useful.

**Figure 3-51.
File Manager to
the rescue!**

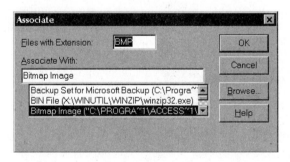

Figure 3-51 shows the dialog that results when you pick Associate from Fileman's File menu. It will normally fill in the extension of the highlighted file (**BMP** here), but you can type in another choice. You then scroll down to the file type you want—the public name and the program that is run are shown. File Manager acts exactly as you might expect it to (and expected Open With . . . to). It takes the extension you picked and only that extension and assigns it to the ProgID that you pointed to in the Associate dialog. It leaves any other extensions assigned to the same program as your extension used to be assigned to. You can even assign a new program to the extension and make a ProgID on the fly.

Because of some new features in Windows 9X, what File Manager does may not be precisely what you want. In the Registry, as subkeys of the entry for an extension, can be commands that set up an item on the New submenu for the context menus for the Desktop and any folders. When you change the ProgID using File Manager it leaves the old New items in place. If you find a spurious entry for the old file type on the New submenu, you need to go into the Registry and delete by hand the subkey of the extension called **shellnew**. The advantage of not deleting these subkeys is that if you make a mistake and reassign the wrong extension, you can easily recover.

 Or you may be able to use TweakUI to adjust the New submenu.

 You should note that all this File Type and association stuff is stored in the part of the Registry that is machine dependent, not the part that is user dependent. So if you are using multiple user profiles (which I'll discuss later in this chapter), changes one user makes in these things will affect all users. On such a machine, you should consult your fellow users before making changes.

If you assign an extension to an Open command using File Manager or Open With . . . , there is no default icon. In that case, as in any other where there is no document icon specified but there is an Open command whose associated program has an icon, Windows does a good job of faking it. It shrinks the program's icon and places it inside a document. Look at Figure 3-52. To the left, you see Notepad's icon and in the middle, the document icon made on the fly by Windows for a document assigned to Notepad. On the right, you see the generic icon Windows 98 uses if it can't figure out anything else to use. This ultimate default icon is used for extensions with no registration or if there is no default icon and no Open command.

**Figure 3-52.
A tale of three icons**

Stupid File Types Tricks

People who make puns are like wanton boys that put coppers on the railroad tracks. They amuse themselves and other children, but their little trick may upset a freight train of conversation for the sake of a battered witticism.

—OLIVER WENDELL HOLMES, SR., *The Autocrat of the Breakfast-Table*

 Here I am going to show you some explicit ways to use File Types to usefully configure your context menus. First, there will be the ScanDisk caper where I'll show how to add the item that the *PC/Computing* columnist complained about. Then there will be a bunch of tips about various individual changes. Finally, Sarah will tell you how she organizes her Folder and Drive menus. In doing so, she'll need to explain the File Types hierarchy that Microsoft has built for folders. In the section *Sarah's Smart Setup Step by Step*, she'll give you a step-by-step method for putting in place the tricks from this section involving context menus of various folder types.

ScanDisk Running ScanDisk for Windows on a drive isn't hard, but it sure is tedious. You can open My Computer, locate the drive, right click, find Properties, and then switch to the Tools tab, or you can click Start, move to Programs, then Accessories, then System Tools, then ScanDisk. Not only is this way tedious, you have to scroll to the right drive after startup. What a drag.

If you followed my advice earlier in this chapter, you have shortcuts to icons for each of your drives on the Desktop. Running ScanDisk with the default menus isn't helped by these icons; their property sheets are for the shortcut and don't have the Tools tab that true drives have.

 There is a convoluted way to go from the property sheet of a shortcut for a drive to ScanDisk. On the property sheet for the shortcut is a button labeled Find Target. It opens My Computer, and from there you can right click on the drive and choose Properties. Awkward, but at least it's there.

 And there is a Target Power Toy that gets you there a little faster, but it still isn't as quick as a direct context menu choice would be.

Clearly, you'd like to add a context menu item called Check the Disk that runs ScanDisk with the right drive letter. There is an obvious first try. Call up View/Folder Options in an Explorer window, click on the File Types tab, find Drive on the list, and hit Edit . . . and then New . . . for a new action. Call the action "Check the Disk," and browse to find ScanDisk for Windows—it is called **scandskw.exe** and is found in your Windows directory.

 Ah, my little chickadee, when you do that, ScanDisk gives you an error dialog entitled ScanDisk Cannot Start with the explanation "You typed parameters that are invalid for ScanDisk for Windows." The problem is that the folder name **C:** was passed to ScanDisk, which is happy with **C:** but doesn't like that ****. Yo, Barry, can we get around that?

 But of course, my friend. One way around it is to change the Registry. I discuss the Registry and Regedit in full glory in Chapter 9, but I can tell you now what to do. Call up the Run . . . dialog from the Start Menu and type in Regedit. Choose Find from the Edit menu and look for **scandskw**.

When it is found, you see on the right panel the data **C:\WINDOWS\ scandskw.exe %1**. It's that **%1** that is passing **C:** to ScanDisk. Double click on the word (Default) in the right panel, and remove the **%1** from the Value data box. Click OK and exit Regedit, and the Check item in the drive menu will invoke ScanDisk. Alas, it will start out highlighting the last drive you used on ScanDisk rather than the drive you right clicked; that's because by deleting the **%1**, you dropped any link to the particular drive letter.

But there is a better way. I'll assume that your hard drives are C: and D: and that you have two diskette drives. Using Notepad, make a batch file called **checkup.bat** that reads

```
@echo off
if %1==A:≠ scandskw A:
if %1==B:≠ scandskw B:
if %1==C:≠ scandskw C:
if %1==D:≠ scandskw D:
```

Let's suppose you place it in **C:\batfiles**. Now go back to the actions for Drives dialog (called from File Types), highlight Check the Disk, and choose Edit. . . . Make the command **C:\batfiles\ checkup.bat**. Instant ScanDisk!

Figure 3-53. Configuring batch file properties

If you've just gotten the impression that Windows has a built in macro language— namely the DOS batch language—you're right. I discuss this theme in some detail later. For now, though, I want to note that for the **checkup.bat** batch file and for the Quick Install example coming up, you want to be sure to set the Properties as shown in Figure 3-53. Explicitly, be sure to check "Close on exit" and to pick Minimized in the Run drop-down. If you don't check Close . . . the DOS window will stay open marked Finished until you explicitly close it. By running it mini-mized, you'll only see a flash on the Taskbar.

You can set properties by either running it once and setting the properties from the system menu in the Inactive DOS session or by copying the batch file to a shortcut in the same directory (by right drag and drop) and picking Properties from the shortcuts context menu.

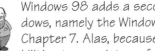 Windows 98 adds a second batch language that is intrinsic to Windows, namely the Windows Scripting Host (WSH). I discuss it in Chapter 7. Alas, because the model is to give the same scripting capabilities to a script run from a Web page to one you run locally, the scripting language has to be emasculated, so there is still a need for the DOS batch language.

You wish! The WSH lets you do pretty much what you want to your systems, which is good for a local scripting language. But it gives anyone writing a script on a Web page or sending you a script via e-mail the ability to do just about anything they want to your system.

But these external scripts aren't run unless you answer Yes to a security warning dialog, so there is no problem.

Naive users can answer Yes too readily. I return to this in Chapter 7.

There is of course another reason to use DOS batch languages rather than VBScript. There are many users who are willing to hack through a DOS batch file who go into shock when faced with the "real programming" model of VBScript.

That's true but as long as you remain calm, simple VBScripts aren't that bad as I'll explain in Chapter 7.

Disabling Autoplay of CDs   It's kinda neat to pop in an audio CD and have Windows automatically start the Windows 98 Audio CD player. But what if you have a favorite CD player program you want to use instead, or suppose you'd like to disable this Autoplay but still have playing capability a right click away? You'll notice that one of the built-in file types is Audio CD. If you look at its action, you'll see that it has exactly one, called Play, which is boldface and for which the command is **C:\windows\cdplayer.exe /play**. You can edit the action to replace the Windows CD player with your favorite or disable Autoplay by highlighting Play and hitting Set Default, which will toggle the default. If you do that, rather than delete the command, you have a setup where you don't have Autoplay but you can still play the CD by right clicking the CD drive (or the shortcut to it I told you to put on the Desktop!).

I think you'll definitely want to chuck the Windows CD player and use the Power Toys player (FlexiCD) instead (I talk about Power Toys in Chapter 5). The installation program for FlexiCD will change the Registry so that FlexiCD is run when you pop in an audio CD.

What's crazy is that while there is a way to toggle off Audio CD Autoplay, you can't do the same for CD-ROM Autorun.

You can avoid Autorun by holding down **Shift** while the CD loads, or you can totally disable Autorun by going to Device Manager, expanding CD-ROM, highlighting your drive letter, hitting Properties, going to the Settings tab, and unchecking "Auto insert notification."

 I know about that, Bill, but that's a very different thing from toggling off Autoplay. It's like the difference between tossing out the bath water and tossing out both the baby and the bath water. Because when you just untoggle Play as the default, Play is still available from the context menu. If you insert a CD-ROM and hold down **shift**, Autorun is still available from the context menu. But if you turn off Auto insert notification, the context menu has no idea whether there is a CD with Autorun capability or an Audio CD in the drive.

Editing Batch Files To me, it doesn't make sense that batch files are run by double clicking on them. If I want to run a batch file often I have a shortcut to it (a PIF file) that I can double click on. In fact if you've ever run the batch file and it is on a local hard drive, you'll have a shortcut there automatically. The only sensible default is Edit. Open (in other words, "run the file") is still on the right click menu in any event.

 Alas, Mother Windows doesn't let you change the default for MS-DOS batch files in the File Types dialog. It has the chastity belt on. So you'll need to first call up the Registry (using Regedit), search on **batfile**, and then double click on **EditFlags** and change the value to **00 00 00 00**.

Editing Generic Files More often than not a file with an unregistered extension, like **readme.1st** or **read.me**, will be an ASCII text file. Adding the unknown file type to the list of types you can edit, you can add an action called Notepad with command **C:\windows\notepad**.

Quick Install Here's a useful device for quickly getting to the setup for a new program. It is true that you can always call up the Add/Remove Programs applet in Control Panel and get to the installing operation that way, but it's a heck of lot quicker to just right click on the drive icon for the diskette drive or CD drive that you know has an install program on it. You make a batch file called **C:\batfiles\inst.bat** that reads

```
@echo off
if exist %1setup.exe goto setup
if exist %1install.exe goto install
start instmess.vbs
goto end
:setup
%1setup
goto end
:install
%1install
:end
```

This assumes that you have an ASCII file **instmess.vbs** in the same directory as the batch file with the line

```
foo=MsgBox "No Valid Install Available",0,"Hello"
```

 This mixes the DOS batch language and Windows scripting host. You could do everything in VBScript by writing your own subroutines to mimic what the DOS batch file's "If exist . . ." does, but that would be more involved than using the simple DOS batch file.

Converting a .doc File

So far, I've shown you how to use batch files to add neat context menu commands. Macros in programs can also be useful. Here's an example. Suppose you often want to convert a Winword **.doc** file into an ASCII **.txt** file. Open Winword, go to Tools/Macro, name the new macro **SaveAsText**, and click Create. Then type in the following macro:

```
Public Sub SaveAsText()
    Dim sFileName As String
    sFileName = Windows(1).Document.FullName
    sFileName = WordBasic.[filenameinfo$](sFileName, 5) &
    WordBasic.[filenameinfo$](sFileName, 4)
    ActiveDocument.SaveAs FileName:=sFileName & ".txt",
    FileFormat:=wdFormatDOSText
    ActiveWindow.Close Savechanges:=wdDoNotSaveChanges
    If Windows.Count = 0 Then Application.Quit
End Sub
```

Now go to File Types, highlight Microsoft Word Document, choose Edit. . . , then New. . . . Call the action **Convert to Text** and use the command line

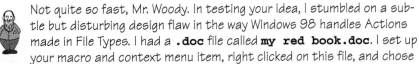

`C:\msoffice\winword\winword.exe /mSaveAsText`

Now you have an extra menu item on the right click menu for your **.doc** files. This sure is fun!

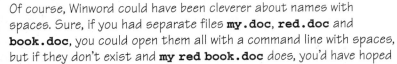 Not quite so fast, Mr. Woody. In testing your idea, I stumbled on a subtle but disturbing design flaw in the way Windows 98 handles Actions made in File Types. I had a **.doc** file called **my red book.doc**. I set up your macro and context menu item, right clicked on this file, and chose convert to text. Instead of converting it, Winword popped up an error message saying it couldn't locate **my.doc**. The problem is that when it stores the command in the Registry, windows appends a **%1** to it. But in order to accommodate long filenames with spaces, it should have appended a **"%1"**—with quotes. You can go into the Registry and fix this by hand, but it's a shame Windows doesn't do it automatically.

 Of course, Winword could have been cleverer about names with spaces. Sure, if you had separate files **my.doc**, **red.doc** and **book.doc**, you could open them all with a command line with spaces, but if they don't exist and **my red book.doc** does, you'd have hoped Winword would have done the right thing. So to me it looks like Redmond fouled up on the front end and on the back end. Oh, how I love a nice design flaw in the morning.

Adding a Local DOS Sometimes you can't beat DOS for some quick actions. Here is a way to add a menu item to the context menu for directories that will open a DOS box with that directory as the current one. Open up the File Types dialog, scroll down to File Folder, and add a new action called **Local-DOS**. For the action, type in **C:\command.com /k cd**.

 If you do this without the **/k cd**, the box will start fine but there will be a complaint from the system at the top of the DOS screen: **specified COMMAND search directory bad**. It's harmless but inelegant.

 The Power Toys collection includes one called Command Prompt Here that does nothing more than add this precise command to your Registry.

Printing a Directory Listing

Windows 9X can't do this. Windows 9X can't do that. It gets so tiresome to hear the critics who haven't bothered to understand the power of DOS as a batch language for Windows and the power of File Types. One learned book complained that Windows couldn't print a directory listing and while you could use DOS, by typing **dir > prn**, you'd have to eject the last page by hand. Mind you, Explorer should have some built-in directory printing smarts, but lacking them you can still do pretty well.

Make a batch file **C:\batfiles\dirlist.bat** that reads

```
dir %1 /-p /o:gn > "C:\temp\Directory Listing"
start /m /w notepad /p "C:\temp\Directory Listing"
del "C:\temp\Directory Listing"
```

Then do the same sets I told you about in discussing ScanDisk to run the batch file minimized and set to close after running. Next call up the File Types dialog, scroll down to File Folder, hit Edit . . . and then New. . . , and call the action **Print Directory Listing**; the command is **C:\batfiles\dirlist.bat**.

This file can be in any directory you want, assuming **C:\temp** exists. If you are distributing this tip to a bunch of users you could use **%temp%** in place of **C:\temp**.

This is an interesting batch file. The **/-p** switch on **dir** is just to overcome any default **/p** that the user might have to normally have output pause every screenful. The **/o:gn** sorts with directories first and by name. The need for the **start** command is especially interesting and comes from the fact that Windows is multitasking. Without it, Notepad loads, but before it can grab the file the directory output was saved in, the batch file has finished and erased that file. The **/w** after **start** says to wait for the program being started to finish before continuing the batch file. The **/m** runs Notepad minimized and is only for cosmetic reasons.

Looking at the Folders Hierarchy If you right click on a drive icon, you get the menu shown in Figure 3-54. As usual, the default action is boldface, so double clicking opens up the drive in Folder view. We already know how to change context menus for objects if the object is listed in the File Type tab of the dialog that pops up when you choose View/Folder Options from the Explorer menus.

Scroll down the list of file types and you'll find Drive as a type. Aha. We only need to click Edit . . . , get the expected list of actions—Open, Explore, Backup, and Find—highlight Explore, hit the Set Default button, and change the default. But that doesn't work! Despite the fact that the top of the context menu should come from the action list, the action list for drive has only two entries—Backup and Find.

Figure 3-54.
Default drive
menu

Hmm. Remember that a drive icon is just a special kind of folder. Folder is also a legitimate file type. Scroll down to it on the File Types list, pick Edit . . . and you get two actions—Explore and Open.

 It is indeed true that the Drive context menu is picking up the actions for both Folder objects and Drive objects. You can see this by adding an action to the Folder actions—you'll see it appear on the Drive context menu. There is a kind of hierarchy of objects, and Drive is treated as a type of folder. In the best spirit of object-oriented programs, it picks up the actions for both Drive and the parent of Drive, that is, Folder. File Folder, aka Directory, and Drive are the only children of Folder, and this is the only hierarchy within the set of shell objects. An abstract folder like My Computer or Control Panel picks up only the actions of Folder, drives pick up the actions of Folder and Drive, and directories pick up the actions of Folder and File Folder.

 It's too bad they didn't push the hierarchy farther to have diskette, CD, hard, and network drives as Subobjects of Drive. At some level Windows is already doing that. It uses different icons for the different kinds of drives, and of all drives, only diskette drives have a Copy Disk . . . option on their context menus. But this level is not accessible to the user fooling with file types.

Adding an Open New in Explorer I'd suggest adding an action to both Drive and File Folder called Open New with the command **c:\windows\ explorer.exe /e,/n,**. Note the commas after both **/e** and **/n**. What this does is open a new Explorer window starting from the current drive or directory. If you really want to, you could add a **/root,** (see the discussion of Explorer earlier in this chapter to see what that does).

This is a useful command for dealing with copying a lot of files from one place to another. Find the source or destination first in Explorer and use this command. That opens a second Explorer window. Then go to the other of the source or destination and you have the windows you need to drag and drop between.

Sarah's Context Menus

 Sarah is one of Mom's techies who played a prominent role in *The Mother of All Windows 95 Books*. Now that Mom has banished all the little icons to the back room, Sarah's not here, but her wonderful scheme from *WinMom 95* lives on. She's particular about how she wants the context menus for drives, directories, and other folders to work. After all, a lot of her interaction with the shell is through those objects. She likes the special folders like Control Panel and My Computer to open in Folder view with large icons. Control Panel in Explorer mode seems weird. On the other hand there is no question that she wants her drives and directories to open in Explorer mode with details, not large icons, showing.

She couldn't just call up the Edit File Type dialog for Folder and change the default from Open to Explore because that would open Control Panel and similar folders in Explorer mode. Being well versed in the theory of objects, she knew what to do. She just added an action to Drive and an action to File Folder called Explore and made that the default for those types.

But of all the dumb behaviors of Windows, when Sarah did that, she got a context menu with Explore shown twice! Of all the half-vast ways of implementing objects! It is well known that if the same action is defined for both an object and its parents, the parent definition is supposed to be ignored. Oh, well, maybe they'll get it right in Windows 2001.

So Sarah was caught between a rock and hard place. She decided that since she didn't care if she ever used Explorer on the special folders, she could change things so that double clicking on a special folder would open that folder in Folder view but double clicking on a drive or directory would open it in Explorer view. With the other tricks from this section, Sarah's drive context menu looks like Figure 3-55 as opposed to the default menu in Figure 3-54. And Open means to open in Explorer view, not Folder view, as it does in the Figure 3-55 menu. Setting this up is a little tricky, but the result is so worthwhile I've asked Sarah to explain what she did in the section "Sarah's Smart Setup Step by Step." Please check it out.

Figure 3-55. Sarah's drive menu

Send To Menu

Tell me what brand of whiskey Grant drinks. I would like to send a barrel of it to my other generals.

> —ABRAHAM LINCOLN, responding to tales that his most successful general was a drunk

Many context menus contain a cascading submenu marked Send To. The menus of all drives, directories, and file objects do. It appears that objects that are folders but neither directories nor drives (like Control Panel in My Computer) do not have a Send To submenu but shortcuts to such objects do. The hardcoded Desktop icons do not. But most objects do.

As described in Chapter 2, the Send To menu is built up with the same paradigm as the Start menu but rooted in the directory `C:\windows\SendTo`—yeah, it is Send To on the menu but `SendTo` in the directory. As we'll see, the designer of this part of the shell isn't big on consistency. As with Start Menu, subdirectories of the top directory (`C:\windows\SendTo` in this case) produce submenus of the Send To menu.

On most systems, before third-party software is installed there are normally six items preinstalled in the SendTo directory: shortcuts to your floppy drive(s) and to My Briefcase on the Desktop, a shortcut to an executable that invokes the Web Publishing Wizard, and items that are labeled Mail Recipient, My Documents, and Desktop as Shortcut.

These last three items are files with extensions, **.mapimail**, **.mydocs**, and **.desklink**, respectively. These extensions are in the list of extensions in the Registry, but rather than list ProgIDs they use the more techie CSLIDs, which point to particular **.dll** files that are run. So these files are small snippets that point to particular routines that their designers want run.

I wonder why they didn't just use an ordinary folder shortcut for My Documents.

Menu items mainly correspond to shortcuts but can include other files. Shortcuts to folders and drives are given special treatment.

- If one or more files on drive X are selected and a shortcut to a folder is picked from **Send To** and the folder is on a different drive Y, then the files are all copied there. This is true for any file including executable files. For folders, a copy of the folder is made in the target.

- If one or more files on drive X are selected and a shortcut to a folder is picked from **Send To** and the folder is on the same drive X, then all files and folders are moved to the new location except for executables, which pop up a message saying that they cannot be moved or copied and offering to make a shortcut.

Of all the crazy. . . . Why tell the user the file cannot be copied or moved when it clearly can be? And why treat it differently from dragging and dropping, which quietly makes a shortcut without popping up a message?

If the item on the Send To menu corresponds to anything but a shortcut to a folder, Windows runs the item, passing to it the selected filenames as parameters. If there are multiple files, they are passed as multiple parameters separated by spaces. The full pathnames are passed but with their shortname versions with the **~1**'s, not the long filenames.

Multiple selected files are treated very differently by general context menu commands and by Send To. For context menu items, the command is executed multiple times, once for each selected file, with the different selected files passed as parameters for each running of the command. Send To runs the command only once, with all the filenames passed in a long string. I wouldn't claim that either behavior is wrong, but it is unfortunate that the behaviors aren't consistent since, after all, the Send To command does cascade off the context menu. Why should users have to keep these different behaviors straight ?

When I tested what happens with parameters on the Shortcut command line, I found such inconsistent behavior that I'd have to regard it as a bug. Both DOS shortcuts (**.pif**) and Windows shortcuts (**.lnk**) have a place you enter the command to be executed, and both allow you to include parameters to the basic executable. If you double click on the shortcut or run it from the Run box, the command is executed with the included parameters passed to it. It is clear what the behavior should be if you run a shortcut that has internal parameters with extra parameters on the command line to the shortcut: both the internal parameters and the command line parameters should get passed to the executable. But that ain't the way it is. For Send To menu items, all internal parameters are dropped, which is a crimp on what you can do with Send To. It's even worse when you use the Run box from Start Menu. Internal parameters are passed for **.lnk** shortcuts but not for **.pif** shortcuts. Oh, how I love a nice bug in the morning!

It's remarkable that you see a lot more ink in the magazines and books on Send To than on the File Types dialog. Well, maybe not—it's easier to find Send To, and many writers prefer to complain that you can't modify the context menus instead of finding out what the story really is. But don't let those writers fool you into thinking that Send To is the cure for all that ails you. It's a pretty limited thing and broad-based in that it applies to all files rather than being extension-based. I think you'll want to add an Edit item to Send To—a shortcut to Notepad—but that's probably it.

There is one other item all users will want to add to their Send To menu and that's the AnyFolder . . . OtherFolder command in Power Toys, which I discuss in Chapter 5. Also Power Toys has Send To extensions that let you add things like **Send To Clipboard as Name**.

While I agree with the assessment that Send To is limited and that File Types is often more useful, you shouldn't lose sight of the incredible usefulness of the built-in items on the Send To menu. In particular, the Send To Diskette and Send To Briefcase commands are the quickest ways to copy files to those locations.

Sarah's Smart Setup Step by Step

Just remember: when you go to court, you are trusting your fate to twelve people who weren't smart enough to get out of jury duty!

—Heard on the Web

**Figure 3-56.
Dumb setup**

**Figure 3-57.
Smart drive setup**

**Figure 3-58.
Smart folder setup**

 I'm so pleased and proud. Sarah, my head of technical support, has broken into Windows' inner sanctum and figured out how to change the Registry so Windows' default behavior is to work in "smart" Explorer mode rather than "dumb" Folder view. And the good news is, if you follow the steps outlined here, you can do it yourself. The default user-configured parts of the context menus for Drive and Directory are shown in Figure 3-56 and Sarah's smart menus in Figures 3-57 and 3-58. See Figures 3-54 and 3-55 for the full menus.

- In dumb Windows, if you type the name of a folder or drive into the Start/Run box, or put a folder or drive in a shortcut, that drive or directory opens in dumb Folder view. Sarah's smart setup makes the drive or folder open in smart Explorer view.

- In dumb Windows, if you double click a drive or folder, it opens in dumb Folder view. With Sarah's setup, it opens up in smart Explorer view. (In dumb Windows, you can right click on a drive or folder to open it in Explorer view. In smart Windows, you can right click to open in dumb Folder view).

- In dumb Windows 95, if you double click on a drive or folder in the right pane of an Explorer window, you get a new window with that drive or folder—in dumb Folder view. With Sarah's smart Windows and in default Windows 98, double clicking just changes the active directory in Explorer, and you don't get that stupid extra window.

- In cases where you want that extra window, you can use the context menu, where Folder View will give you a new window in Folder view while Open New will give you a new Explorer window.

 Step 1. Make a binary backup of the registry. Call me ultracareful; I'm a belt-and-suspenders kinda gal. But since you're going to be fooling around in your Registry, I recommend that you first make binary backups of the Registry. In Explorer, make sure you are configured to display hidden files. Then go to the **C:\windows** directory, sort on Type, and look for **system.dat** and **user.dat**. Their type will be DAT File. Select them, copy to the clipboard, and paste from the clipboard. Scroll down to the bottom of the folder and you'll find files named **Copy of system.dat** and **Copy of user.dat**. Rename them to **system.bac** and **user.bac**. You'll get a couple of warnings about each rename. Just answer **Yes** to them.

While it can't hurt to make an extra binary copy, Windows 98 makes daily backups and keeps the last five. So you could go back to the last daily backup. In Chapter 9, I discuss ScanReg and how to restore a backup if you need to.

Step 2. Get used to working with the Registry. If you are already a Regedit maven, skip this step. Otherwise, you'll need to get used to working with it. Go to the Run box and type **regedit**. You should keep it running until the process is finished, but if you close it in error, just restart it from the Run box. You might want to read the beginning of Chapter 9, but here's a quick summary. You get a display that is much like Explorer with a tree at the left and a contents pane on the right. Be warned that there is no File Save here. Basically, as soon as you make any changes, Windows saves them to the Registry. And there is no built-in Undo!

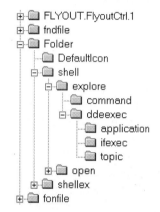

Figure 3-59. Register today

We'll need to worry about the top key (what the Registry calls the analog of folders) in the Regedit window. It is called **HKEY_CLASSES_ROOT**, and is abbreviated it **HKCR**. Double click on it (or click once on the **+** next to it) to open it. There will be a long list of subkeys starting with * and a bunch that begin with **..**. Scroll past them. We're interested in three subkeys that are near each other called **Directory**, **Drive**, and **Folder**. Scroll down to **Folder**, and open the keys **shell**, **explore** under it, and **ddeexec** under that. You should see something much like that in Figure 3-59.

Right Click on Folder and pick Rename. Then hit **Esc**. This was just for practice. Click on **Folder** and look at the right pane. You should see **EditFlags**. Double click on it and hit Cancel. Double click on (Default) and then Cancel. This is how you'll later edit some values, although, of course, you'll hit OK instead of Cancel!

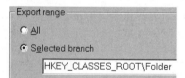 **Step 3. Make a .reg file to restore the initial setup.** Now Click on Folder again, go to the Registry menu, and choose Export Registry File. . . . In the resulting dialog (Figure 3-60) make sure the "Selected branch" radio button is selected and save the file on the Desktop as **folder.txt**. Similarly, scroll up and select Drive and export to **drive.txt** and select Directory and export to **dir.txt**.

Figure 3-60. Backing up the Registry

Now minimize Regedit and double click on each of the **.txt** files to open three Notepad windows. In the **drive.txt** window delete the first line (**REGEDIT4**) and the blank line below it, then choose Edit/Select All and Edit/Copy to put the rest of the file on the clipboard. Click on the **folder.txt** window, hit **Ctrl+End** to go to the bottom of the file, and then Edit/Paste. Repeat the operation with **dir.txt** (delete **REGEDIT4 . . .**).

You should now have in the **Folder.txt** window a file that is the combination of the three **.txt** files except that there is only one **REGEDIT4** line and it is at the top of the file. Now click File, then SaveAs and save on the Desktop as **dumbwin.reg**. You can delete the old **folder.txt**, **drive.txt**, and **dir.txt**.

Figure 3-61.
Editing the
Folder key
(Step 4)

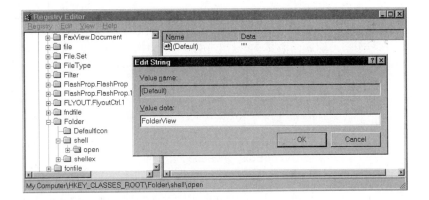

dumbwin.reg is your bailout file. If something goes wrong in the middle of the following steps, or if you find that smart Windows isn't to your liking after all, it's easy to bring back the old dumb version of Windows: all you need to do is go into Regedit, delete the Folder, Directory, and Drive keys by selecting each one in turn and hitting **Del**, then double click on **dumbwin.reg** to restore Windows 98 to its original dumb state.

As two last checks, first double click on **dumbwin.reg** to make sure the Regedit says it successfully updated the Registry. Then delete the Folder key in Regedit and double click on **dumbwin.reg** and confirm that the Folder key was indeed restored.

 Step 4. Adjustments in the HKCR\Folder\shell key. Now return to or restart Regedit, and open up and scroll down to the **HKCR\Folder\shell** and open it up so that you can see its two subkeys, **open** and **explore**. Do the following (to rename a key, you right click it and pick Rename from the context menu):

1. Rename the **open** key to **temp**.

2. Rename the **explore** key to **open**.

3. Select the new **open** key (that used to be called **explore**) and export it to a file you place on the Desktop named **sarah.txt**.

4. Delete the key that is now called **open**.

5. Rename the **temp** key to **open**. Select **open** and look at the right pane where you should see a single name **(Default)** with an empty value (which appears as **""**). Double click on the word **(Default)** and type in the value **FolderView**. Hit OK. See Figure 3-61.

 Step 5. Adjustments in Directory and Drive subkeys. Now you need to load **sarah.txt** into WordPad since you need to do a search and replace and Notepad won't do that. Type **WordPad** in the Run box and then open **sarah.txt**. Then:

1. Inside WordPad, click on Edit, then Replace and change occurrences of **\folder** to **\Drive**. WARNING!! It is very important to include the **"\"** in the search and replace strings because the file has two occurrences of the string **Folder** (without the ****) and they must not be changed.

2. Click File, then SaveAs, and save the file with the name **drive.reg**. It is important when you do SaveAs that you leave the format as Text Document. Don't exit WordPad yet.

3. Do a search and replace in the entire Word Pad document changing **Drive** to **Directory** and use SaveAs to save the new file on the Desktop as **dir.reg**. Close WordPad.

4. Double click on each of the files **drive.reg** and **dir.reg**. After each double click, Windows should claim that the Registry was successfully updated.

5. Delete the three files **sarah.txt**, **drive.reg**, and **dir.reg**.

 Step 6. Optional extra commands. There are five extra commands on my sample menus seen in Figures 3-57 and 3-58. Here's a table that shows where you can find them.

Menu Command	Drv	Dir	Batch File	Subsection of "Stupid File Types Tricks"
Check The Disk	✓		**checkup.bat** (page 229)	ScanDisk
Install	✓		**inst.bat** (page 232)	Quick Install
Local–DOS		✓		Adding a Local DOS
Open New	✓	✓		Adding an Open New in Explorer
Print Dir. Listing		✓	**dirlist.bat** (page 234)	Printing a Directory Listing

 Step 7. Fix EditFlags (optional). While you're fooling with these keys anyway, you may as well change the **EditFlags**. Select the key **HKCR\Directory** in Regedit. One of the value entries on the right side will have name **EditFlags** and value **d2 01 00 00**. Double click on **EditFlags** and replace it with the value **02 00 00 00**. Now do the same with the keys **HKCR\Drive** and **HKCR\Folder**. (**EditFlags** is discussed in Chapter 9.)

Step 8. Make a Windows "smart pill" .reg file. Repeat all the steps in Step 3, except name the combined file **smartwin.reg**.

Remember, if you ever need to dumb down Windows 98, go into Regedit and delete the three HKCR subkeys **Folder**, **Directory**, and **Drive**, then double click on **dumbwin.reg**. To make Windows 98 smart again, delete those three keys and double click on **smartwin.reg**.

 Barry, mind if I ask some questions? Why didn't Sarah just do it all with a **.reg** our readers could import?

 Two reasons. First, you can't delete/rename keys from a **.reg** file. Second, the path to Explorer isn't known since the Windows directory might be **C:\win98** or **D:\windows** or. . . .

 Why did Sarah name the key left under Folder **open** and have to fool with **(Default)**? Why not name the key **FolderView** instead of **open**?

 Because of a Windows weirdness. When you click on the Fonts or Printers shortcut in Control Panel, it doesn't run the default command but looks for an Open command. If you don't have an Open command, you get an error message!

 How does calling **(Default) FolderView** work?

 When it makes the context menu, Windows looks first to see if **(Default)** has a nonempty value. If it does, that name is used on the menu; otherwise the name of the key is used. This was put in to support foreign languages, but Sarah can use it also.

■ I've Got It Under Control Panel

The right half of the brain controls the left half of the body. This means that only left-handed people are in their right mind.

—F. M. HUBBARD

 As in Windows 3.x, an enormous number of user configuration options are encapsulated into Control Panel. Even more than in earlier versions, you have information-gathering utilities inside Control Panel—most notably, the Device Manager. Control Panel is so important it has its own chapter (Chapter 8), which deals with its more technical aspects and applets. Here, I give you an overview and discuss three of the more basic and less technical applets in detail.

A Fistful of Applets

It is now quite lawful for a Catholic woman to avoid pregnancy by a resort to mathematics, though she is still forbidden to resort to physics and chemistry.

—H. L. MENCKEN, speaking of birth control

You can access Control Panel in a variety of different ways. There is a Control Panel icon in My Computer. You can drag this icon to the Desktop or Start Menu and get another route. Or you can follow my advice in the section on the Start Menu and add a dynamic list of Control Panel applets to the Start Menu. You can also type **control** into a Run box or make a shortcut to the program **control.exe** in the **C:\windows** directory. In any event, Control Panel is merely a listing of individual programs (applets), each with its own icon.

In principle, Control Panel reads in its list of applets from three places:

1. Dynamic link libraries with the extension **.cpl** in the **C:\windows\system** folder

2. **.cpl** files in the directory from which **control.exe** is loaded, normally **C:\windows**

3. Programs entered in the Registry key **HKEY_CURRENT_USER\MMCPL**

 That's the theory, but all the applets that come with Windows 98 and every third-party applet I've seen uses the first method. This is a big change from Windows 3.1 where it was possible to add an applet by having a routine in a driver file. Another difference from Windows 3.1 is that third-party programs can add their own tabs to applet property sheets—for example, a mouse with three buttons could add an extra property sheet to the Mouse applet and the Microsoft Natural Keyboard adds some tabs to the Keyboard applet.

The applets installed with Windows 98 are normally among 22 standard ones in 16 **.cpl** files—4 applets are in **main.cpl** and 2 each in **inetcpl.cpl**, **mmsys.cpl**, and **sysdm.cpl**. Here are the standard 22 applets plus Tweak UI, which you should install from the Windows CD, described in the following chart.

 To install Tweak UI, the extra applet, put the CD in the drive, choose to browse the CD, go to the folder **D:\tools\reskit\powertoy**, right click on **tweakui.inf**, and pick Install. Or you can use the method I describe in the next section.

 Other Control Panel applets that Windows can install include Infrared, PC Card, and Scanners and Cameras. Third-party products can install additional applets such as Find Fast, which is installed by Microsoft Office.

 You may wonder why in the world the Users applet is part of inetcpl.cpl. Simple—it's a feature introduced with Internet Explorer 4.0. I guess Microsoft decided to cut down on the number of **.cpl** files.

	Accessibility Options	Loaded from `access.cpl`. This optional module is mainly for the otherwise enabled. I discussed MouseKeys in Chapter 2. I discuss the applet in Chapter 8.
	Add New Hardware	Loaded from `sysdm.cpl`. This is the Hardware Installation Wizard, which I discuss extensively in Chapter 8.
	Add/Remove Programs	Loaded from `appwiz.cpl`. Installation, Uninstall, StartUp Disk, and more. This is the subject of the section "Software Installation."
	Date/Time	Loaded from `timedate.cpl`. Also accessible by double clicking the time in the Notification Area. It sets the date, time, and time zone. See Chapter 8.
	Desktop Themes	Loaded from `themes.cpl`. This allows simultaneous changes in mouse, sounds, wallpaper, colors, etc. Windows ships with 18 themes and the Plus! Pack includes another 19 themes. See Chapter 8.
	Display	Loaded from `desk.cpl`. Also accessible if you right click on the Desktop and pick Properties. This controls display drivers, wallpaper, screen saver, and more. See Chapter 8.
	Fonts	Loaded from `main.cpl`. Also accessible in My Computer. This is a shortcut to the Fonts folder. See Chapter 2.
	Game Controllers	Loaded from `joy.cpl`. See Chapter 8.
	Internet	Loaded from `inetcpl.cpl`. This is identical to the dialog you get if you pick View/Internet Options in Internet Explorer and the Properties dialog for the Internet icon on the Desktop. See Chapter 8.
	Keyboard	Loaded from `main.cpl`. See Chapter 8.
	Modems	Loaded from `modem.cpl`. See Chapter 8.
	Mouse	Loaded from `main.cpl`. See Chapter 8.
	Multimedia	Loaded from `mmsys.cpl`. Has tabs for Audio, Video, MIDI, CD Music, and Devices. The Audio tab alone is accessible if you right click on the volume icon in the Notification Area and choose Adjust Audio Properties. See Chapter 8.
	Network	Loaded from `netcpl.cpl`. Also accessible if you right click on Network Neighborhood and pick Properties. See Chapter 8.
	Passwords	Loaded from `password.cpl`. This is where you get to change your password. It can be used to control multiple user profiles (and is briefly discussed in the section), but the Users applet is better for that. If you are on a single-user machine and are forced to log in when you don't want to, the way to turn it off is in the Network applet, not Passwords.
	Power Management	Loaded from `powercfg.cpl`. See Chapter 8.
	Printers	Loaded from `main.cpl`. Also accessible in My Computer or from the Setting submenu of the Start menu. This is a shortcut to the Printers folder. See the section "Printers."

	Regional Settings	Loaded from `intl.cpl`. Controls formatting of numbers, currency, date, and time. See Chapter 8.
	Sounds	Loaded from `mmsys.cpl`. This is where you can waste an inordinate amount of time trying to figure out what kind of whoosh you want to hear every time you minimize a window. See Chapter 8.
	System	Loaded from `sysdm.cpl`. Also accessible if you right click on My Computer and pick Properties. The Mother of All Applets, this includes Device Manager, and it's where you go to set up multiple hardware profiles. See Chapter 8.
	Telephony	Loaded from `Telephon.cpl`. Provides access to the dialing locations dialog and to configuration of TAPI service providers. See Chapter 8.
	Tweak UI	Loaded from `Tweakui.cpl`. Lets you set oodles of user interface options. See Chapter 8.
	Users	Loaded from `inetcpl.cpl`. Once you've enabled multiple users in the Passwords applet (or via the Wizard that this invokes), this applet lets you modify the list of users. Discussed in the section "User Profiles."

As I mentioned, but it is worth repeating, a number of applets are the property sheets of system objects and so accessible by choosing Properties from a context menu or by **Alt+Double click**. Explicitly, Display is Desktop Properties, System is My Computer Properties, Network is Network Neighborhood Properties, and Date/Time Properties are accessible by double clicking the time in the Notification Area.

You can also start a Control Panel applet from the Run box. The syntax for starting an applet is

```
control cpl-name applet-name,number
```

where **cpl-name** is the name (including the extension) of the `.cpl` file that contains the applet. I listed the `.cpl` for each applet in the Control Panel applet table. **Applet** is the name as it appears under the icon and in the applet table with spaces and all if the name is Regional Settings or one of the other applets with multiword names. *Number* is the number of the tab you want with labeling starting with zero. So, for example, if you want to start up Device Manager (which is the second tab and so numbered 1 with zero-based counting), you place the following as the command in a shortcut

```
control sysdm.cpl system,1
```

and the Appearance tab in Display Properties would be

```
control desk.cpl display,2
```

The number at the end is optional. If it is left out, a **0** is assumed—that is, the first tab is displayed.

Software Installation

An autobiography is an obituary in serial form with the last installment missing.

—Quentin Crisp, *The Naked Civil Servant*

The Add/Remove Programs applet (see Figure 3-64) serves many purposes.

- It has is a StartUp Disk tab that can be used to try to start your system in case of emergency. You probably made one when you installed Windows. I talk about what's on that disk in Chapter 7. One warning—you'll need the CD to make the StartUp disk. You'll be asked for it. You'd think there would at least be an option to store the files you need for the StartUp disk on your hard disk.

- There's an Install . . . button on the Install/Uninstall tab. All this does is look successively in the root directory of any diskette and CD drives you have for a program called **setup.exe** or **install.exe** and then offer to run it. This should successfully locate about 80% of programs but figure 20% will do something silly like put the setup in a subdirectory or name it something like **foostall.exe**.

If this install button doesn't appeal to you, you should instead look at the "Quick Install" subsection of "Stupid File Types Tricks" and add the context menu Install option, which is a lot quicker than calling up an applet.

- There's an Uninstall list on the Install/Uninstall tab. Highlight a program in it and choose Add/Remove. . . . At a minimum you should be offered a complete Uninstall. Some programs will take the Add part in the button seriously and also let you install extra components from this list. By the way, don't be fooled into thinking that the Uninstall list is limited to programs that you installed through the Install . . . button or that any program installed via that button will have an Uninstall. Uninstall routines and their registration with the system is a function of the SetUp program and will or will not work equally well if SetUp is run from the Install . . . button, by hand, or by an Autorun program when you pop the CD into the drive. The good news is that for a program to get the Windows logo, it is required to have an Uninstall routine that it registers with the system.

- The Windows SetUp tab can be used to add or remove programs that are part of the core of Windows itself. But it can also be used to install some of the extra goodies on the Windows CD and other programs that will tell you to install components that way.

The procedure for installing extras from the Windows CD is a little tricky, so let me explain how to install Tweak UI using that method.

1. Look through the CD for installable components. They will have the extension `.inf`, so Find File on `.inf` will be useful. In this case if your CD is D:, you'll find **tweakui.inf** in **D:\tools\reskit\powertoy**.

2. Call up the Add/Remove Programs applet, jump to the Windows Setup tab, and hit the Have Disk . . . button. Browse to the directory **D:\tools\reskit\powertoy**, double click on the **.inf** file, and pick OK (Figure 3-62). In the resulting dialog (Figure 3-63), you may be tempted to just click OK since the listed program is what you want, but you must first check the box next to the program you want!

3. You've completed the install, and since you installed the program from the Windows SetUp and it is from the Windows CD after all, you probably think that the Uninstall is also done through that tab. Nope! Tweak UI is added to the same list where third-party programs go on the Install/Uninstall tab (see Figure 3-64.)

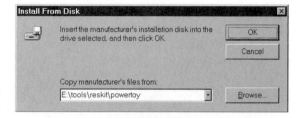

**Figure 3-62.
Picking the
directory**

Figure 3-63. Check the box!

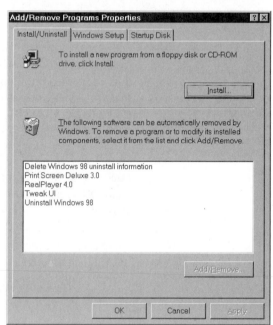

Figure 3-64. Uninstall list

It can't be emphasized too strongly how revolutionary the logo requirement for Uninstall routines is. The installing program is the right one to do the Uninstall. It will know a lot more than some special uninstall utility. Within a short period, these utilities have become a lot less essential than they once were. Bravo, Microsoft!

Printers

Line printer paper is strongest at the perforations.

—Wisdom from computer's dark ages

The Printers folder allows you to install printers and to access individual printer controls that let you adjust parameters and control the way documents spool. If

Figure 3-65. Printer Install: Step 1

you drag a printer icon to the Desktop and then drag a document to that icon or to the icon within the Printers folder, the document will print, assuming that the program that made the document registered a print routine.

I'm going to explain to you how to install a Printer. To illustrate some of the good stuff in Windows 98 and because local printer installation is similar, I'll install a Network Printer to a print server on a network.

1. Open the Printers folder and click on the Add Printers icon (Figure 3-65). This invokes the Add Printer Wizard. You OK through the first introductory panel.

2. In the next dialog (Figure 3-66) you need to pick whether the Printer is a local printer—that is, attached to your machine—or a network printer—that is, a separate network node or a printer attached to another machine on the network. If you pick "Local printer," Windows pauses to construct a database of printers and then displays a list of manufacturers/models to choose from.

3. If you pick "Network printer," you get a dialog that asks for the printer name and also asks, "Do you print from MS-DOS based programs?" You can browse the network to find the network printer, as shown in Figure 3-67. For a printer to show, the owner of the machine it is attached to has to have turned on Sharing for it.

4. If you answered Yes to the print-from-DOS query, you next get a panel requesting you to "capture" a printer port, in other words, assign a real port to it to fool DOS programs into sending output that Windows captures and shuffles off to the network. You hit a Capture Printer Port . . . button to actually pick the port, as shown in Figure 3-68. For a local printer, instead of capturing a port, you assign a port to the printer.

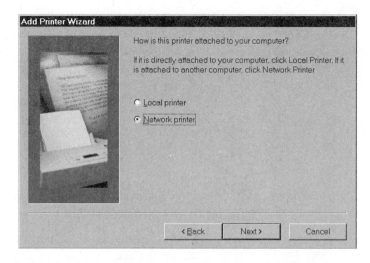

Figure 3-66. Printer Install: Step 2

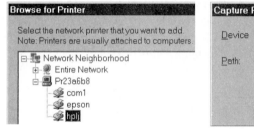

Figure 3-67. Printer Install: Step 3

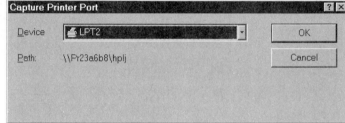

Figure 3-68. Printer Install: Step 4

5. In the next to last panel of the Add Printer Wizard, you name the printer (Figure 3-69). This is the name that appears in the Printers folder and that appears in the dropdown list in File/Print dialogs. By all means use a descriptive name like "4th Floor Broom Closet Printer." Be sure to choose the radio button on the next panel asking for a test printer page. If the network printer is also attached to a Windows 98 machine, the drivers are copied from the other machine. Otherwise, you'll need to pick manufacturer/model to get the right driver, often from the CD.

6. Success! Be sure to adjust the parameters in the Printer property sheet (which I'll get to in a moment). If you answer No to the question in this panel (Figure 3-70), you're thrown into the Print Troubleshooting part of Windows Help. If you have printer problems later, call up Windows Help, go to the Index tab, and find Printers/Troubleshooting.

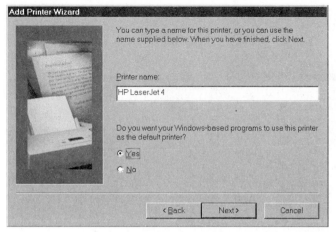

Figure 3-69. Printer Install: Step 5

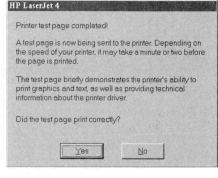

Figure 3-70. Printer Install: Step 6

You'll want to check your printer's property sheet as soon as you install it. You can invoke it by choosing Properties from the printer icon's context menu, from the File menu in the Printers folder, or from the File menu of the window that opens if you double click on a printer. These are also the places you find Set as Default, which lets you change which printer is the default. The actual dialog is shown in Figure 3-71 with one of the subdialogs superimposed. Looking at the tabs will give you an idea of the kinds of options there are. Device Options is where you go if you have a nonstandard amount of memory or other hardware enhancements. These days with TrueType fonts, font cartridges are about as common as the passenger pigeon, so you can probably ignore the Fonts tab. The Sharing tab is where you turn on the ability of other users on the network to use that printer. The General tab has one important choice for users of a shared printer—you can specify a special page to be used as a separator between print jobs. The one place you certainly want to look is the Spool Setting dialog in Figure 3-76, which you get by hitting the Spool Settings . . . button on the Details tab in Properties. If your goal is to get your machine back as soon as possible rather than to get output as soon as possible, make sure that the radio button marked "Start printing after last page is spooled" is chosen.

 The "Spool data format" dropdown involves an interesting enhancement in Windows 9X. Print data is now normally spooled in a metafile format (EMF = Enhanced MetaFile), which allows the driver to send as much data as possible in a high-level format that lets the printer do the translation to dots rather than sending everything over the parallel port as individual dots.

**Figure 3-71.
Printer Properties
and Spool Set-
tings dialogs**

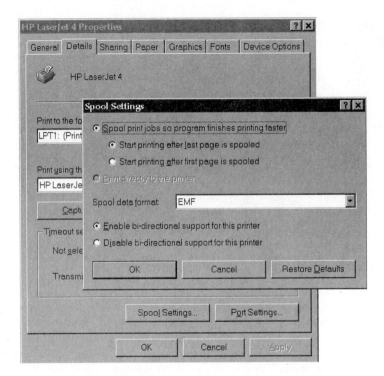

One final printer tip. Be sure to install the Generic/Text printer. The "manufacturer" is Generic and the "model" is Generic/Text Only. You'll want to be sure to assign it to the port **FILE:**. It allows you to print the ASCII text part of a document to a text file and is sometimes the only way to get such output. It doesn't always do exactly what you'd like, but it is a vast improvement over the similarly named driver in Windows 3.1. When you choose this printer to print to, you get a dialog asking you what file you want to print to.

But the dialog that you get to choose the file to print to is the Windows 3.1 File Save dialog with support for long filenames but with none of the other goodies in the Windows 98 dialog. Given that this is part of the operating system, I'd call the fact that this dialog isn't the Windows 98 dialog a shame! You also have to know to type in **FILE:** as a port; it isn't an option in the dropdown.

I realize that it can sometimes be foolish to demand consistency, but it seems a bit strange to me that if you go to install a modem, the first manufacturer is (Standard Modem Types), and if you install a video driver, the first choice is (Standard Display Types), but the Generic/Text printer driver is buried under that well-known manufacturer Generic.

User Profiles

Teenage boys . . . have only a brief season of exhilarating liberty between control by their mothers and control by their wives.

—CAMILLE PAGLIA, in *Esquire,* October 1991

Windows 98 has an optional feature called Multiple User Profiles. When it is set up appropriately, each user can have their own Desktop, their own Start Menu, their own list of recently used documents, and their own settings for things like wallpaper and Desktop colors. Moreover, third-party programs can save their options so that user-specific options can be different for different users. This is obviously useful in a business setting where a computer may be used by several people, but it is also useful for home users: each of your teenage children can have the exhilarating liberty of choosing their own wallpaper!

The first step for turning on User Profiles in Windows 95 still works (you invoke the Passwords applet in Control Panel and shift to the tab marked User Profiles), but it is highly recommended that instead you double click on the Users applet in Control Panel. This eventually leads to the dialog in Figure 3-72 where you get to decide which items are user specific. By doing this, the settings stored in the **HKEY_CURRENT_USER** key of the Registry, which includes Desktop wallpaper, colors, sound schemes, and so on, can be user dependent. The check boxes let you decide whether various sets of objects are user dependent including the Desktop icons and the Start Menu.

 You should give some thought to the issue of letting the Start Menu be user dependent, because some programs only install themselves in the current user's Start Menu, and someone may need to take responsibility for updating the Start Menus of other users by hand. I'll explain what is involved in a moment.

Figure 3-72. User Profiles Wizard

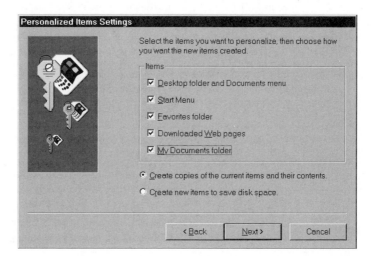

Eventually, installs will learn to use the All Users StartUp group, but it will take some time.

Figure 3-73. Windows login

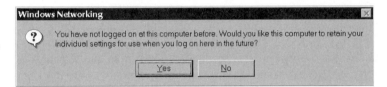

Figure 3-74. Psst! Answer Yes!

Once you've turned on this option and rebooted, you'll be greeted by the dialog in Figure 3-73. During the initial setup (if you went through the Wizard rather than the Passwords applet), you picked a user name and password, and you use those here.

There are two ways to add new users. The first is to type in a new user name in the login dialog. When that's done there is a critical question and it is important to answer it correctly. You are asked if you want to have individualized settings on the machine (Figure 3-74). You should answer Yes if you would like to turn on User Profiles for other users. If you answer No, you will wind up with common default settings so that changes any user makes affects all other users with these default options.

 If the user CTO Mao (Figure 3-73) answers Yes to this question the very first time he logs on, Windows 98 does the following. It makes a directory called **C:\windows\profiles\cto mao** using his login name as part of the directory name. In that directory, it places two hidden files and nine subdirectories. The hidden files are **user.dat** and its backup **user.da0**. These are the user half of the Registry. Initially they are just the default **user.dat** files with some obvious changes—for example, the entries that tell Windows where his Start Menu is will be adjusted to the new Start Menu location. Any changes he makes while he is logged in will get stored in the **user.dat** in his directory—which is why he can have his own wallpaper.

 The nine directories correspond to the Desktop, the collection of Recent Documents, the user shortcuts in Network Neighborhood, the programs in Start Menu, Favorites, My Documents, Application Data, and two IE-specific folders: History and Cookies. Windows no longer builds Mao's Start Menu from the directory **C:\windows\start menu**. Instead, it uses **C:\windows\profiles\cto mao\start menu**. It does some copying from the default but not all files. For example, it copies only the

**Figure 3-75.
The Users applet
after Multiple
Users is turned on**

shortcuts from the default
Desktop to his and not any
documents that might have
been there. Finally, a password
file **ctomao.pwl** is created in
the **C:\windows** directory.

Better than adding users on the
fly is invoking the Users applet
from an existing setup (Figure
3-75). Here you can modify
what is saved for a given user,
delete a user, or add new users.
If you add a new user, you get
to state the user name and
password in advance as well as
the options that the Wizard lets
you set initially.

 The Users applet lets you delete a user, a big advantage over Windows
95 where you had to delete users by hand. Of course, this means an
angry user could delete all his coworkers—but he could do that in Windows 95 if he knew what he was doing!

This is a great first step in giving multiple users on a PC control over their environment, but there are several gotchas you need to be aware of:

- There is no effective password protection for individual users' files. All
  users have access to all files on the machine. Thus a savvy user could modify another user's setup with ease.

 Unless, of course, you enable system policies and prevent your teenagers
from running an MS-DOS prompt or executing any Windows application
except the ones you specify ahead of time. You could also prevent them
from changing the Desktop, rooting around in My Computer, changing the
resolution, and so on.

 Gimme a break, Billy. If I tried that with my teenager, she'd get a boot
diskette and delete the darned **.pol** files. Windows 98 security may be
effective against confused corporate drones, but it is not serious
enough to defeat a determined teenager.

- You will probably need to install the same program multiple times, once
  for each user—you can use the same program directory so you won't have
  many duplicate files. Otherwise, you'll need to copy the Start Menu items
  from one user's Start Menu to another's by hand. For example, if **foowrite**
  installs Start Menu items in

```
C:\windows\profiles\dad\start menu\programs\foowrite
```

you may need to copy the shortcuts by hand to a new directory called

`C:\windows\profiles\ma\start menu\programs\foowrite`

if Ma also wants them on her menu.

- There are some other subtle gotchas. For example, while most directories are user specific, SendTo is not, and if one user renames the SendTo directory, the feature won't even work on other users' setups until their Registries are modified by hand.

 One thing really bugs me. The option whether Recycle Bin collects deleted files has to be the same for all users. I'm so competent (ahem!) that I prefer having it off, but Barry insists that for the sake of his kids, it needs to be on. There are lots of other settings that are systemwide that seem to me should be user specific.

 I often come to a machine with the password dialog up and want to turn the machine off. Do I have to login and then pick Shutdown from the Start Menu? Or can I just turn it off?

 If possible you should always run Shutdown, but there is no need to login. Hit **Ctrl+Alt+Del** and you get a dialog you can pick Shutdown from!

■ DOS v'danya

DOS is like the faithful worker who's agreed to delay retirement. He'd love it if the company would bring in some younger blood, but they can't seem to find anyone to replace him.

—SCOTT SPANBAUER

 The Mother of All Windows Books, our tome on Windows 3.1, had 22 pages on DOS. Now that DOS is integrated into Windows and Windows' DOS support has substantial improvements—the ability to start Windows applications from the DOS prompt, the windowed DOS button bar, scalable fonts, MS-DOS Exclusive mode, a comprehensive property sheet—you'd think that WinMom98 would have at least 40 pages. But The Mother of All Windows 95 Books had 25 pages (not counting the discussion of DOS commands), and WinMom 98 has about the same number. How come? Isn't DOS important? That's the right question. DOS isn't so important any more. I have a few DOS applications I've lived with for ten years or more, and I suspect you may have some too. But they tend to run fine with Windows 98. There are fewer than there were three years ago, and I'll bet there will be none in a year or two.

One reason that problems with DOS sessions are less an issue than they used to be is that there is more memory available. A lot of programs that used to take valuable DOS memory are run from Protect mode even in DOS sessions and take zero DOS memory: network, CD, and mouse drivers come to mind. On the three Windows 9x machines I currently have running in my office, two have 588 KB free (that's over 600,000 bytes) and one has 604 K free in a fresh DOS box. Under Windows 3.1, 600 KB would be regarded as spectacular. And all of those systems have network support at the DOS prompt, CDs, and sound cards.

I'm going to start by talking about the property sheet for DOS programs—the Windows 98 repository for what used to be in a PIF (Program Information File). Then we'll talk about DOS commands and the DOS batch language. The surprise is that with the Start command, DOS's batch language is a bare-bones but fairly useful batch language for all of Windows. Finally, I'll talk about DOS Exclusive mode.

Even if you have no DOS programs you use, you should care about DOS for three reasons. (1) For certain kinds of file operations, by far the fastest way to do what you want is to use the DOS command line. (2) DOS allows easier access to certain information that the Windows shell hides, for example, the real contents of the **C:\windows\fonts** directory. (3) DOS's batch language can be useful even for Windows applications.

Take a Deep PIF

Program Information Files, or PIFs, were first introduced with IBM's Topview, a clunky text-based task switcher that IBM tried to foist on the world in the mid-1980s. The sole lasting legacy of Topview is the PIF, which has gone through many changes since. Windows 9X expands the information that can be stored in PIFs and replaces the gangly Windows PIF editor with a property sheet metaphor (hooray).

The DOS session shown in Figure 3-76 shows DOS **Help,** useful if you want to use DOS commands, but not installed on your disk when you install Windows 98. Instead, you'll find it on the Windows CD in the **directory\tools\oldmsdos**. You'll need to copy **help.com, help.hlp**, and **qbasic.exe** to **C:\windows\command** if you want the Help available; I recommend copying the whole folder from the CD.

Whenever you run a DOS program or batch file directly, Windows first looks for a **.pif** file with the same name in the program's directory. If that fails, it looks in the **C:\windows\pif** directory, then **C:\windows**, then **C:\windows\system**, and finally the directories in the DOS path in order.

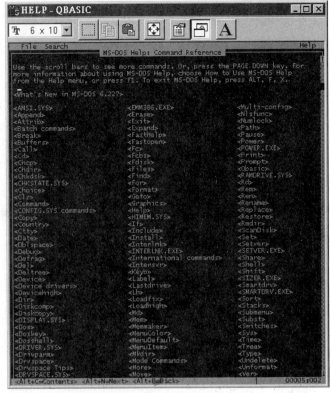

Figure 3-76. DOS session

If that fails to find an existing PIF, it makes a PIF for the program giving it the same name but the extension `.pif`. If Windows has to make a `.pif`, it looks for the name of the `.exe` in the ASCII text file `C:\windows\inf\apps.inf` in the `[PIF95]` section of that file and uses that information to make a `.pif` (I discuss the format of `apps.ini` later). If it doesn't find an entry there, it looks for a `_default.pif` file in the same sequence of directories it originally looked for a `.pif`. Failing that, it uses some defaults built into Windows itself. You'll have a `_default.pif` if you upgraded over Windows 3.x or if you made one in Windows 95—otherwise, you probably won't have one. If you care about the defaults, you can copy a convenient `.pif`—for example, `dosprmpt.pif`, which you'll find in `C:\windows` and which you can customize—to `_default.pif`.

That a `dosprmpt.pif` is still there is a weird sort of compatibility. Under Windows 3.1, the MS-DOS entry in the Main Program Manager group pointed to that `.pif` file (although even there it was otherwise not used). Under Windows 9X, there is still a `dosprmpt.pif`, but it is never used (unless you explicitly click on it, of course)—the MS-DOS Prompt entry on the Start Menu, of course corresponds to its own `.pif` file, namely `C:\windows\start menu\programs\MS-DOS prompt.pif`. By the way, if you just type in `command.com`, Windows uses an entry in `dosapps.inf` unless you've previously run Command and have a `command.pif` in the right place.

Once Windows makes a `.pif`, you can customize it to your heart's content. If you'd like to make a `.pif` directly, you can copy the DOS program or batch file in Explorer to the same directory and it will make a `.pif` (although you have to remove the extra Shortcut to MS-DOS that it prepends to the program name if you want this shortcut to be used when you double click on the program). If a `.pif` exists that would be used for the program if you double clicked on it, a copy of that `.pif` is used for the new shortcut.

And, of course, if you double click on a `.pif` itself, no matter where it is or what its name, it runs the program it is a shortcut to.

Here's the structure of the tabs in a `.pif`.

General Settings

Never let the other fellow set the agenda.

—James Baker

Figure 3-77. General settings

If you look at the Properties dialog of a running application, the first tab is the one shown in Figure 3-77. If you ask for the Properties of an actual PIF file, there is a General tab in first place with the standard ability to change attributes, see file date, and so on, and Program is the second tab. I number tabs using the count that puts Program first.

The top of the tab shows the icon used and the name used in the caption—the caption appears when the program is running in a windowed DOS session and on the Taskbar. Actually, Windows is so smart that if a program other than the initial one is running in the session, it adds the program name—see, for example, Figure 3-76, where Windows knows that DOS 6.22 Help loaded Qbasic to do its thing.

Four of the next five fields (**Cmdline**, **Working**, **Shortcut key**, and **Run**) are essentially identical to the fields in a Windows shortcut (**Target**, **Start in**, **Shortcut key**, and **Run**). When the `.pif` is run, either directly or by running a program that associates with the `.pif`, Windows switches to the directory in Working and tries to run the command in Cmdline. If you include a `?` in the command in Cmdline, when the `.pif` is run, Windows pops up a box inviting you to type in parameters for the command.

> But of all dumb things, this parameter box takes the cake. It doesn't have a Browse button to let you search for a file, and it's not be a drag and drop target so you can't drag and drop a filename from Explorer.
>
> Not only that but the dialog is system modal—that's just a fancy way of saying that you can't access any other program until you fill in the parameters Windows is asking for. Not only can't you drag and drop anything to the dialog, you can't even consult Explorer once the dialog is up! You'd have thought they'd have fixed this since Windows 95 shipped.

You know, not many users use DOS at all, and there are probably only a handful who use this funny **?** in the command.

But they are all readers of our books, Billy.

The kind of window the program runs in (normal, minimized, or maximized) is mainly determined by the Run dropdown in the Program tab, but it is also affected by choices in the Font and Screen tabs. The "Batch file" field lets you fill in a batch file to load before the program is run. You might want to load **doskey** that way. Actually, if all you want to load is **doskey**, just put `C:\windows\command\doskey` in this field; it may say "Batch file'" but it'll run any command.

Figure 3-78. Change Icon dialog

The check box "Close on exit" determines whether the window closes when the program is finished or stays open with the word Finished prepended to the window caption. For DOS programs that just display some information on the screen (like **.mem**) you'd want to leave the box unchecked, but you want to check it for most DOS programs.

If you want to change the icon used by the **.pif**, you hit the Change Icon . . . button and get the dialog shown in Figure 3-78. This elegant dialog is also used for shortcuts and in the Edit File Type Actions dialog. It displays all the icons in numeric order. If you ever need to place an icon number in a Registry entry, you can count them off in this dialog remembering that the first entry is 0. The Browse . . . button lets you look for another source of icons. The standard sources are **.ico**, **.dll**, and **.exe** files.

Faking 'em Out

Sincerity: if you can fake it, you've got it made.

—Daniel Schorr

The Advanced . . . button on the Program tab leads to an Advanced Programs Setting dialog (Figure 3-84), which is mainly concerned with DOS Exclusive mode, something I discuss in the section "Penalty Box." But here I want to note one check box on the dialog that you might miss: ☑ Prevent MS-DOS-based programs from detecting Windows. Its intention is to fool DOS programs, mainly games, that will run fine under Windows 98 but refuse to run because they have code that tests for Windows and posts a message that says, "I don't do no steenkin' Windows" if you try. The code is there because there are problems with Windows 3.x, sometimes only memory problems, and the vendor wants to preempt tech support calls. If you have a program that gives such a message, at least try this option before resorting to DOS Exclusive mode.

Fonts The Font tab (Figure 3-79) concerns the font used to display the text in the DOS session when it is running in a window. The sessions can use one of nine bitmap fonts or one of sixteen sizes of Lucida Console TrueType. All the fonts have the full IBM extended ASCII character set. The nine bitmapped fonts come in sizes 4×6, 5×12, 6×8, 7×12, 8×8, 8×12, 10×18, 10×20, and 12×16 (width × height). That means that a DOS screen with 80 columns and 25 lines with a 10×20 font will be 800×500 pixels—too big for a 640×480 screen and even too large for 800×600 if you remember the space needed for the title bar and toolbar. The bitmapped fonts are a Terminal typeface designed by Bitstream and used for DOS sessions over Windows for years. These fonts are all stored in a single file called **dosapp.fon**.

Figure 3-79. PIF Font tab

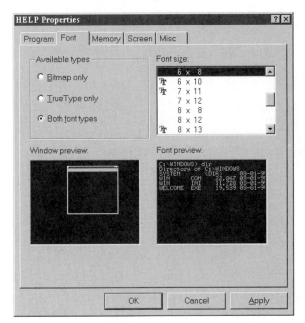

 This is a big improvement over the five files used for DOS's bitmapped fonts in Windows 3.1, as documented in *The Mother of All Windows Books*. Don't be surprised if you can't find this font file. It's in a hidden system file in the **C:\windows\fonts** directory, which is itself marked with the system attribute. Since the fonts are not installed in Windows as fonts accessible to Windows applications, they won't appear in the Fonts folder (Many of the other **.fon** files that are also hidden and system files are installed as fonts for Windows applications and appear in the Fonts folder.). To see dosapp.fon, you have to go to a DOS prompt and use the right switches on the **dir** command.

The DOS TrueType typeface has sizes 2×4, 3×5, 4×6, 4×7, 5×8, 5×9, 6×10, 7×11, 7×12, 8×13, 8×14, 9×15, 10×16, 11×18, 12×20, and 13×22. There was a 16×27 size in Windows 95 Plus! that was dropped.

 Gimme a break. Sizes 2×4, 3×5, and 4×6 are ludicrous—added for demos and marketing purposes, not for real users.

 The extremely small sizes are very handy sometimes. If you have a compile running in a DOS box, you can make the font really small and place it down in the corner of your screen. Seeing the little lines down there scrolling away lets you know that your compile is proceeding OK. If they stop, then you can quickly **Alt+Enter** to a full-screen mode to see what the problem may be.

from the Help menu,
Lucida Console

from the Help menu,
Terminal

Figure 3-80.
A tale of two typefaces

You'll notice that the Lucida options include many small pixel heights—8 sizes smaller than the 12-pixel height. Lucida and Terminal are sans serif (See the samples in Figure 3-80 taken from actual screen shots.), readable at small pixel counts.

 Courier, which is the DOS session TrueType font that shipped with Windows 95, is a remarkably ugly font created to work with typewriter-size type and typewriter technology. While Lucida is better, it just doesn't look as good as the hand-tuned bitmapped Terminal fonts. I tend to run my DOS sessions in the bitmapped 10×18 font. Works well on a $1,024 \times 768$ screen.

The Auto font choice adjusts the font size to fit the window as you adjust the screen size. This is a great idea in principle, but it doesn't work well in practice. First, as you resize, the screen jerks all over the place because the height-to-width ratio jumps all over the place (unless you have chosen TrueType only). Second, when Auto is turned on, I'm sometimes unable to resize the screen at all.

 You'd think if Microsoft was going to bother to do Autofont, they'd do it right, the way it is done on several other computer systems. You need a font that allows independent scaling in the two directions so that the font just resizes to fit the stretched screen.

Memory Settings   Figure 3-81 shows the last three tabs with a miscellany of settings.

 Finally, with Windows 9X, we see the beginning of the end of the DOS reliance on weird memory schemes with weird names to overcome the

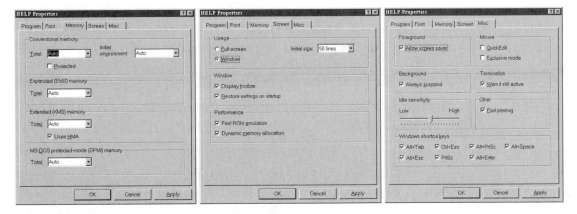

Figure 3-81. A tale of three tabs

640-K barrier built into the first PC. No more EMS. No more XMS. No more UMB. No more HMA. Hooray!

As long as you run DOS programs, you can't totally ignore these arcane memory issues, but Windows will usually handle them pretty well for you. The default settings (leftmost tab in Figure 3-81) for memory usage are set at **Auto**, which allows Windows to dole out memory resources as needed. A few rude programs will grab all the free EMS and XMS memory when they load, and such programs need to be given a fixed ration, but mainly you can ignore this tab.

Toolbar New with Windows 95, windowed DOS sessions came with a toolbar (Figure 3-82), which provides considerable functionality and which integrates well with the window (Figure 3-76). You can turn the display of the toolbar on or off with a check box in the Screen tab and by a choice on the title bar context menu. The functions are given in Figure 3-83.

Figure 3-82. DOS toolbar

Figure 3-83. DOS toolbar buttons

The Mark/Copy/Paste buttons work in concert. Mark brings up a cursor so that you can mark a block with the mouse, Copy copies the text to the clipboard, and Paste sends text from the clipboard to the DOS program through the keyboard. The Full Screen button jumps you to full-screen mode, as does **Alt+Enter**. The only easy way to get from full screen back to windowed mode is to use **Alt+Enter**, although from the Windows screen, you can call up the property sheet of a full-screen DOS session by right clicking on the Taskbar button for that session and shifting to windowed mode there. There are two ways to change the font from the toolbar—the dropdown and the button to the property sheet with the **Font** tab up. Pushing in the Background button lets the program run in the background; otherwise it will be suspended when you switch away from it.

Screen Setting

C:\DOS C:\DOS\RUN RUN\DOS\RUN

—Seen on a geek's T-shirt

The Screen tab (the middle tab in Figure 3-81) has three panels: Usage lets you choose whether the initial display is a full-screen or windowed DOS session and the number of screen lines. Window has a check box for whether you want the toolbar (I can't believe you don't!) and one called "Restore settings on startup" that I discuss in a moment.

I dunno, sure seems to me like the names of Window and Usage got switched.

Nope. The check boxes in Window matter only if you are in a windowed session.

The Performance panel means what it means so often in Windows—it's really a panel about troubleshooting. The two options here enhance performance and are turned on by default. If a DOS program is behaving flakily, try unchecking them and see if it helps.

I can imagine the meeting that must've gone on in the office of Brad Silverberg, the head of the Windows 95 project, when this tab was named. One of the engineers says, "You know, boss, we've got all these neat performance-boosting features that could cause problems under unusual circumstances. We should have Troubleshooting dialogs that let you check off options to turn them off." So the marketing guys say, "The public will think that Troubleshooting dialogs mean trouble. Let's call the dialogs Performance and have the options checked by default so the user unchecks them to turn them off. Whadya think, boss?" Brad starts to sing, "You have to accentuate the positive" and wonders if he could get Cole Porter to write an ad for Windows.

That leaves the "Restore settings on startup" option. You have to realize that it means exactly what it says—the settings in question (we'll see which ones in a moment) are stored in the **.pif** when the program exits. If the box is not checked, it also stores the settings in effect the last time you started up. If you don't check the box in the **.pif** before reloading the program, it reloads in the same place it was when last loaded, but if you do check it in the meantime, it loads with the settings in effect when the program exited.

Which settings? Well, let's see what happens when you press ? and point at that option. You are informed, "Restores window settings when you quit this program, including window size, position, and font."

 Oy. I guess what the Help writer meant was that it restores the settings to what they were when you last quit the program, but that isn't what it says.

 Worse, it's got the information wrong on what is saved. The window position is affected by this check box and, as long as you have the Run setting on the Program tab at Normal, so is the window size. But the window font together with settings like Background and Run are saved when you exit and restored when you restart whether this box is checked or not.

 Not quite. If the font is set to Auto, then the font size is adjusted according to the window size, so in that case, the font is restored. In others cases, well, er, er, the Help is wrong.

Other Settings The tab at the right in Figure 3-86 is called Misc—it is a hodgepodge of leftovers.

Foreground: Windows 98 screen savers kicks in even from a full-screen DOS session. If the box here is unchecked and the program in question has focus (is the active application), then the screen saver won't run; otherwise it will.

Background: If "Always suspend" is unchecked, then the program will continue to run in the background; if it is checked, the program will stop running when you switch away from it.

 Talk about poor design. There is a Background button on the toolbar whose meaning is the opposite of this check box. If the button is pushed in, the box is unchecked and if the box is unchecked the button is pushed out.

Idle Sensitivity: Lo, how the mighty are fallen. A fair number of Windows technical experts based their reputations on being able to compute the exact interplay of all the time-slice stuff built into Windows 3.1, and now they are reduced to a single slider. And guess what? It doesn't matter very often, so just leave it in the middle.

Mouse: Quick Edit is neat. When it is on, you can start marking by just pressing on the mouse. It would be neater if the right mouse button pasted but—hey, what's there is already nice to have. Basically, if a DOS program doesn't support the mouse, you want this box checked—

if it does, don't check the box. "Exclusive mode" turns off the mouse in all other programs including Windows. Avoid it if you possibly can.

Termination: Another neat setting. If "Warn if still active" is checked, then when you try to shut down Windows, you are sent to the DOS program to first close it. That's an improvement over Windows 3.x because this actually takes you to the relevant DOS sessions. But even neater is the option you should use with care to uncheck the box and have the DOS session automatically close when you shut down Windows. This setting also comes into play if you click the DOS Windows Close button. If the termination check box is unchecked, that will close the application with no questions asked; otherwise, it will issue a warning.

Other: Talk about ignominy. To be an Other setting on a Misc tab, you must be pretty random. In fact, "Fast pasting" is pretty simple and is one of those performance/troubleshooting things. Usually a program can accept keystrokes fast enough to keep up with the Fast Paste method. But sometimes it will beep or even go bananas when you try to paste in text from the clipboard. If that happens, try unchecking the box and see if it helps. The difference of speed of entry with the two methods is normally more than a factor of ten.

Windows shortcut keys: There are seven keys here that Windows normally wants for itself. Uncheck any key you want to go to the application instead.

The `apps.inf` File   As a final topic in `.pif` files I want to discuss the somewhat technical issue I alluded to at the start of the section: if a premade `.pif` can't be found for a program, Windows uses information in `C:\windows\inf\apps.inf`. This file has the structure of a Windows 3.x `.ini` file—there are sections with names inside square brackets and items in the sections of the form **name=value**. In the file are two generic sections called **[PIF95]** and **[Strings]** and other program-dependent sections. The syntax of the items in the **[PIF95]** section is

> **program=%*title*%,*icon*,*icon_number*,*X*,*section*,*Y*,*Z***

where X, Y, and Z are technical entries you can read about in the Windows Resource Kit. The entries can stop without specifying all options, and an option can be left blank by placing two commas next to each other. Here **%*title*%** is an indirect reference to an item in **[Strings]** that is used for the title bar caption for the program, **_icon,icon_number_** is the usual specification of an icon by giving a filename and the number of the icon in the file (starting with number 0), and **_section_** is a reference to a section of the **apps.inf** with additional information.

As an example, consider the references to Qbasic in the supplied **apps.inf** file:

```
[PIF95]
    QBASIC.EXE=%QBASIC.EXE%,moricons.dll,15,,QBASIC.EXE
[QBASIC.EXE]
    Params="?"
    LowMem=330
    EMSMem=None
    XMSMem=None
    Disable=win
[Strings]
    QBASIC.EXE="Microsoft QuickBASIC"
```

The first item says that the caption title will be found in the Strings section, so the caption **Microsoft QuickBASIC** will be used. Icon 16 in **moricons.dll** is used, and additional **.pif** information is retrieved from the section **[QBASIC.EXE]**.

There is nothing sacred about these entries. If you try to run the old shareware program PC-Write, whose name is **ed.exe**, and the PIF insists on setting itself up as WPOffice Editor, just go ahead and edit the PIF. Alternatively you can add your own entries to **apps.inf**. You wouldn't for a single machine, but you might if you were responsible for supporting a group of users.

Mom's Favorite DOS Commands

Windows '98 requires so much in the way of system resources, it should be called HOGGIN' DOS.

—Heard on the Net

 Here I get to talk about DOS commands. I can't help it—I'm a command line freak. Sometimes the quickest way to get something done is to start up a DOS prompt and just do it. First my top ten list. Then a few more useful commands. But I'm not going to attempt complete lists of available and now-missing DOS commands. Also DOS programs like **ftp**, which are really Internet utilities, are discussed in Chapter 4.

Help I'm not going to give you detailed syntax of all the commands. Help is available for any DOS command by typing its name followed by **/?**. There's also the full-screen DOS help engine from DOS 6.2. You'll find it on the Windows CD in the directory **\tools\oldmsdos**. Copy **help.com** and **help.hlp** to your **C:\windows\command** directory. You'll also need to copy **qbasic.exe** since the 1-KB executable **help.com** is only a wrapper to load **qbasic** in a special read-only mode.

Mem   You often need to know how much free memory you have in your DOS sessions, if only for bragging rights over your friends. **Mem** is a great tool for that. The **/c** and **/d** parameters give impressive amounts of detail. And **/p** tells it to pause after each screenful.

Start   This was new with Windows 95 and probably its most important new DOS element. The syntax is

```
start [options] prog_or_doc
```

where the options are **/m** for minimized, **/max** for maximized, and **/w** for wait. Normally when you run **start** it immediately returns to the DOS prompt or runs the next line in the batch file. With the **/w** switch it waits for the program it started to exit before continuing. See the listing of **dirlist.bat** and the discussion of that batch file on page 234 for an example of where the **/w** switch is needed. What appears after the options can be anything you could type into the Windows Run box—that means either program with parameters or a **doc** file.

You can start any Windows program from the DOS prompt by just typing its name. DOS **start** is more powerful in the following ways.

- It can start a new DOS session.
- You can specify a **/m** or **/max** switch.
- The command line gets passed to Windows without prior interpretation by DOS. That means you can have **doc** files, refer to the system directory (which is not normally in the DOS path), and use app paths and other Windows goodies.

The real use of **start** is in batch files, as I discuss in the section "Windows Batch Language."

Edit   DOS and Windows have a tradition of bare-bones editors starting with **edlin** and continuing through Notepad. Edit has been a kludgy shell for **qbasic** until now. With Windows 95, it suddenly blossomed into a blooming—well, maybe not an orchid but at least a daisy. I discuss it in detail in Chapter 4 when I discuss Notepad and WordPad. Check it out.

 You may wonder why Microsoft was wasting resources on DOS Edit. Undoubtedly, some employee wrote this on weekends as a lark, and Microsoft then used it.

 Edit isn't bad, but why did they name its help file **edit.hlp**? It is not a Windows Help file, and you'll get an error message if you double click on it.

Doskey It's hard to figure out why Microsoft didn't build **doskey** into DOS rather than require it as a program you have to know how to run. Basically, if you are going to use the DOS command line, you want **doskey** loaded: it gives you standard editing and recall of previous commands. You can load **doskey** in **autoexec.bat** and have it available in all DOS sessions. The command recall is independent in each window. If you use DOS a lot, check out **doskey**'s macro feature.

xcopy Long one of DOS's gems, **xcopy** has so many options they won't fit on a single 25-line screen. It will not only copy files but whole directories, preserving the subdirectory structure. It uses extended memory to enable it to copy more efficiently. Unlike DOS's copy command, it understands long filenames (you have to put them in quotes to settle ambiguities if there are spaces). It understands UNC names. It's great for complicated copy actions that would be awkward using GUI tools.

 Here's a weird one. If you look in **C:\windows\command**, you'll find two programs, **xcopy.exe** and **xcopy32.exe**. In Windows 95, the syntax and capabilities were identical (even though I've seen books that claimed **xcopy32** understands long filenames and **xcopy** doesn't— that's just false). **xcopy.exe** was just a shell that called **xcopy32.exe**. In Windows 98, the situation is even weirder! Now **xcopy.exe** and **xcopy32.exe** are byte-for-byte identical and call **xcopy32.mod**, a third DOS executable with a funny extension. Why have two identical programs? Weird, weird, weird.

dir Don't forget the lowly **dir**. It too has a fistful of options, and because of redirection, it can do some useful things like send the contents of a directory to a file. I'd suggest that you add

```
set dircmd=/o/p
```

to your **autoexec.bat**. Check out the DOS 6.22 Help under **dir**, and look at its Notes to see about **dircmd**. To have a directory of all files including hidden and system, use **/a** with no **:**.

deltree What the name advertises **deltree**—it puts concrete galoshes around a whole branch of a tree and drops it in the deep blue sea. No wimpy Recycle Bin to rescue you if you foul up (the Norton utilities can save you, by the way, usually even after the fact). Useful, if used with extreme care. But a single **deltree C:** can ruin your whole day.

move and copy Don't forget these two standbys. Because **copy** doesn't understand long filenames, **xcopy** is often more sensible. But **move** does understand long filenames.

One advantage of using DOS to copy or move is that you are spared the graphic of the paper floating from folder to folder. That graphic was really neat the first time, but it sure did get old fast, didn't it? Some vendor will make a mint selling randomized replacements for it—maybe darts zooming in on a poster of big Bill.

Other DOS Commands

Command, n.: Statement presented by a human and accepted by a computer in such a manner as to make the human feel as if he is in control.

—P. J. O'ROURKE

ansi.sys If you want to add color to full-screen DOS sessions, you want to place **ansi.sys** in your **config.sys**. There's a complete discussion of all the options and how to produce really fancy prompts in *The Mother of All PC Books*. For now, note that you can turn all DOS session text to yellow on blue by doing the following. First, in **config.sys** add

```
device=C:\windows\command\ansi.sys
```

or use **devicehigh**. In your **autoexec.bat** replace **prompt=pg** by

```
prompt=$e[1;33;44m$p$g
```

Windows NT handles color in DOS sessions in an intelligent way—by adding a **Color** tab to its equivalent of the PIF dialog.

Attrib.exe For several years, DOS has included a command to change file attributes (hidden, read only, archive, system) that complements the ability to change attributes in the property sheets of files. The DOS command line program has several uses. First, you can use it to change the system attribute, which you can't do with Explorer. Second, it is often easier to use its wildcards than to do the equivalent with Explorer—although you can use a wildcarded search in Find File, select all, pick Properties from the context menu, and change attributes there and have something even more powerful than the DOS program. The place you are most likely to need **attrib** (or the equivalent in Explorer) is after copying files from a CD to a hard disk. They will have the Read Only attribute set and you'll probably want to change that.

fc Windows 98 needs a decent File Compare utility. Failing that, there's **fc.exe**. As a comparison engine, **fc** is superb. It will compare ASCII files and show line differences and will then resynch the files to find more similarities and differences. The problem is that the display of results that spills out onto a DOS screen is almost unusable if the differences are extensive. Microsoft has done the hard work. How about putting a decent interface on it?

 Don't forget that Word has a File Compare that you can use to compare two ASCII files. You load one and then go to Tools/Track Changes/Compare Documents . . . to load the other.

 And the WRK sampler on the Windows CD includes WinDiff, discussed in Chapter 9.

 But there still isn't a good tool for comparing binary files.

Debug, Sort, Find   Debug, Sort, and Find are all clunky, venerable DOS utilities that have been around since DOS 2.x. You'll find plenty of books and articles with all sorts of neat tricks that use them. Some of the venerable tricks you can do with Debug may cause Windows to shut Debug down with a protect mode violation, but other than that, the tricks should work. And these programs are there in `C:\windows\command`.

Fdisk, Format   If you need to set up a new hard drive, you'll need to use `Fdisk` and `Format`. To do so, make a startup disk and copy these two programs to it. Then use them to partition and format the hard disk. If it is a replacement hard drive, you'll need to install Windows 98 on it.

 You'd think that Microsoft would improve the interface on **Fdisk**, but while it now understands FAT32, its interface is the same dumb DOS screen menu interface that was introduced in the early 1980s.

MSCDEX   When running under Windows 98, the protect mode CDFS should be in place and `mscdex` will be irrelevant. However, you'll need to know the syntax of `mscdex` if you plan to run a CD in the penalty box (our name for custom MS-DOS Exclusive mode). You use

```
C:\windows\command\mscdex /D:name /L:letter
```

where *letter* is the letter you want to assign to the drive (feel free to ignore this option if you don't mind the next available letter getting picked) and *name* is the name specified in the `config.sys` line loading the hardware driver for the CD.

Qbasic Microsoft Quick Basic, or Qbasic found in `\tools\oldmsdos` on the CD, is great to throw at a bright high school student. Visual Basic would be even better, but it isn't included free with Windows!

Windows Batch Language

Now, as always, the most automated appliance in a household is the mother.

—BEVERLY JONES, *The Florida Paper on Women's Liberation*

The DOS batch language is pretty primitive, but you can do a lot with it. There's a whole chapter in *The Mother of All PC Books* about it, and you'll find more tricks in books on DOS. With the ability to launch Windows applications from batch files and the **start** command (described above), you can use DOS batch files to do Windows tasks. Somewhat complicated examples appeared earlier in this chapter in the **checkup.bat**, **inst.bat**, and **dirlist.bat** listings on pages 229, 232, and 234. As a simpler example, if you have a project where you want to open Winword on a particular file, say **bookprop.doc** and Excel in **booksale.xls**, you'd just make a batch file that read

```
start bookprop.doc
start booksale.xls
```

and assign to it a shortcut set to run minimized and close when done. The important point is to remember that the batch language is there.

I found one disturbing compatibility problem with old batch files and the new DOS built into Windows 9X. There is a way under DOS to strip off the end of a string of fixed length, for example, pull the **C** out of **C:**. It uses the fact that DOS command lines are only 127 characters long: if a line in an old DOS batch file is more than 127 characters, then DOS uses only the first 127 characters. But they broke this part of the batch processor in Windows 95. First, while the DOS command line can still be only 127 characters long, DOS will happily process commands from within batch files that are up to 1,023 characters. In addition, they totally changed the order of processing of %1 parameter replacement so that DOS will process an even longer command line if it gets longer only after %1 replacement. The bottom line is that the batch trick doesn't work.

Ahem. We didn't break the batch language. We enhanced it. We figured with long filenames, batch files might actually need to deal with command lines longer than 127 characters. So we fixed them. If, in doing that, we broke some of the tricks that the DOS weenies so love, well, er, progress does have its price, doesn't it?

Don't forget that if you are willing to cope with a somewhat more complex language, there is Windows Scripting Host, discussed in Chapter 7.

Penalty Box

Come, children, let us shut up the box and the puppets, for our play is played out.

—WILLIAM MAKEPEACE THACKERAY, *Vanity Fair*

The enhanced support for DOS sessions of Windows 9X is supposed to be so good that just about any DOS program will run in Windows 9X. This is pretty much true. With the large memory typically available there, the ability to fool programs and make them think Windows isn't running (see the section "Faking 'em Out"), and more stable hardware drivers, Windows 9X can run a lot of DOS programs, especially games, that couldn't begin to run under Windows 3.x. But there are still some recalcitrant DOS programs, mainly games, that just won't run in a DOS session over Windows. For such programs, Windows 9X offers DOS Exclusive mode, where you can load a DOS environment without Windows.

Actually, there are two rather different DOS Exclusive modes, which could be called standard and custom. The custom mode is so ghastly to set up that I tend to think of it as a penalty box. You set up MS-DOS Exclusive mode by clicking the Advanced . . . button in the Program tab of a DOS property sheet. The key dialog is in Figure 3-84. You turn on the MS-DOS Exclusive mode capability by checking the box denoted **MS-DOS mode**. That turns on the check box and pair of radio buttons immediately below it. I urge you to always have the box marked "Warn before entering MS-DOS

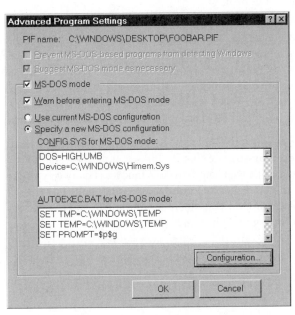

Figure 3-84. Advanced Program Settings

mode" checked since you don't want to click on such a `.pif` in error and wind up in MS-DOS mode.

The radio button determines whether you go into standard MS-DOS mode or into the penalty box. If you pick "Use current MS-DOS configuration" you go into standard mode when you run the `.pif`. "Specify a new MS-DOS configuration" puts you in custom mode.

Standard MS-DOS Exclusive Mode   If you run a `.pif` that starts up standard mode (including choosing "Restart in MS-DOS mode" from the Shutdown menu, assuming you haven't customized "Exit to **DOS.pif**"), here's what happens.

- All programs running under Windows are closed down.
- Windows exits, leaving only a small 4-KB stub in memory. Basically, the machine is returned to the state it was when **autoexec.bat** was run and before **winstart.bat** was run but with an additional 4-K piece of memory still controlled by Windows.
- The batch file **C:\windows\dosstart.bat** is run if it is present.
- The program specified in the `.pif` is run. If you specified **command.com** and did not check "Close on exit" (and in particular if you picked "Restart in MS-DOS mode" from the Shutdown menu), you wind up at the DOS prompt.
- When you exit the program you're running, Windows is restarted. If you've loaded no resident programs (either directly or through **dosstart.bat**), just Windows is loaded (similar to picking Restart with the Shift key held down) —otherwise, a reboot and reload of **autoexec.bat** and **config.sys** is performed (similar to picking Restart without the Shift key). You can tell which one Windows has picked because in the former case it says, "Restarting Windows 98" and in the latter it shows the splash screen.

When you install Windows 98, it makes a **dosstart.bat** file of commands in your **autoexec.bat** that it thinks you might want in DOS Exclusive mode but that it doesn't want run before Windows. The two typical examples are a real mode mouse driver and **mscdex**, the real mode CD file system. Of course, **mscdex** won't do you much good if you haven't kept a real mode hardware driver for your CD in **config.sys**.

 Don't be surprised if you don't have a **dosstart.bat** on your machine, especially if it was bought after Windows 95 shipped.

Custom MS-DOS Exclusive Mode, aka the Penalty Box—How It Works The problem is that the drivers you want in `config.sys` when you are running Windows are not likely to be the drivers you want for running DOS in Exclusive mode. For example, you may want a real mode hardware CD driver when running DOS, but you won't need it with Windows—while Windows won't use it, it also won't free up the memory it takes. A second problem is that, depending on the DOS program, you may have different needs for what you need loaded—say, a CD-ROM driver for one program and not for some other that needs every bit of RAM it can lay its hands on. For these reasons, there is the penalty box. It lets you specify a custom `config.sys` and `autoexec.bat`.

When you try to run a `.pif` with penalty box setup, Windows does the following.

- Renames your `config.sys` and `autoexec.bat` to `config.wos` and `autoexec.wos`. If you see such files on your disk during a custom exclusive session, do not under any circumstances erase or move them!

- Creates a new `config.sys` that starts with the line `dos=single` and then has all the lines in your custom `config.sys`; creates a new `autoexec.bat` consisting of the lines of your custom `autoexec.bat` followed by the three lines

  ```
  cd working-dir
  call program-name
  C:\windows\win.com /wx
  ```

  where *working-dir* and *program-name* are specified in the `.pif` as **Working** and **Cmd line** respectively.

- Sets a flag somewhere deep in the kernel that tells the system it is set for custom MS-DOS Exclusive mode.

- Reboots the system.

When the reboot takes place, the first thing that happens is that Windows displays the message "Windows 98 is now starting your MS-DOS based program." This message shows before the F8 Startup menu is looked for, before `drvspace` processing takes place, and before `config.sys` or `autoexec.bat` is loaded, and it is the result of the conjectured flag deep inside the kernel.

Windows 98 runs the custom `config.sys` and `autoexec.bat` and loads your program. When you are done with the program, the `autoexec.bat` file runs `win` with the `/wx` parameter, which resets the flag, does the `config/autoexec` renaming, and reboots.

This scheme as described has important consequences:

- Be sure to properly exit the program when you are done; don't just turn off the machine.
- With this fooling with **autoexec.bat** and **config.sys**, it is a good idea to make frequent backups of them if you run in the penalty box often.
- If disaster strikes and you get into some kind of loop in Exclusive mode, just hit F8 and go to confirm each step mode.

Setting Up the Penalty Box If you pick the radio button "Specify a new MS-DOS configuration," small edit boxes open up where you can type in your custom **config.sys** and **autoexec.bat** files. I call this mode the penalty box because the setup is so very awkward.

1. The edit boxes show only three lines at a time so you don't get a chance to see the entire files if they get very involved. There should be a way to at least specify files to be used that you could then edit with Notepad.

2. The width of the panels is not a fixed number of characters (since the font is proportional), but it is so narrow that complex paths or command lines don't fit without scrolling (and jerky scrolling at that) in the horizontal direction.

3. Under DOS 6, there was finally memmaker to help optimize upper memory usage for DOS configuration files, but here you are back at the need to hand optimize if you need just a little bit more memory for that DOS game. And the process between successive reboots/edits of the configuration files is lengthy since it requires Windows to load.

4. As I'll explain, there are some simple options Windows helps you set up, but they don't include some of the most important ones. Your CD and sound card commands aren't there, which I can forgive because they depend on your hardware so Windows could be clueless. But neither is a command to set up UMBs nor a command to move **drvspace** into UMB memory. Fear not—I can at least partly remedy this!

 Suddenly you need to become an expert on obscure DOS 6.22 commands. You didn't throw out the old DOS manuals and books, did you? None of this is discussed in the Windows 98 documentation.

When you first pick this mode, Windows normally sets up a simple starting **config.sys** consisting of the two lines

```
DOS=HIGH,UMB
Device=C:\windows\Himem.sys
```

and an **autoexec.bat** consisting entirely of **set** commands. Indeed, if you open a fresh windowed MS-DOS prompt and type **set** at the DOS command

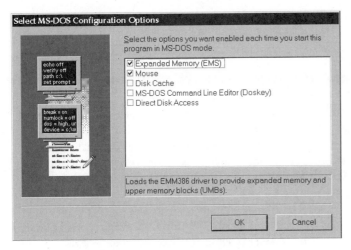

Figure 3-85. Advanced Configuration dialog

line, you'll get a list of environmental variables identical to the set commands in this initial **autoexec.bat,** including the order, except that two variables are dropped—**COMSPEC** and **windir**. You are free to edit these initial templates.

As an additional aid, in adding items to your custom configurations, there is a button marked Configuration . . . , which brings up the panel shown in Figure 3-85. Too bad such an elegant graphic is buried here! Two of the five items are checked, but you are free to pick and choose. The panel at the bottom provides a tip about the selected item.

 Actually, this is what happens normally. But it can be changed by entries in the Registry key **HKLM\Software\Microsoft\Windows\ CurrentVersion\MS-DOSOptions**. I discuss this in Chapter 9 where you'll see which items are checked and where the commands come both in the Advanced Configuration dialog and in the initial templates. In particular, a hardware vendor can add items to both the initial templates and the dialog in Figure 3-85.

The five options that are by default in the Figure 3-85 dialog set up EMS memory, Mouse, Smartdrv (the disk cache), Doskey and a special mode that allows programs like Norton Disk Editor to access the hard drive directly. As I said, some important options are missing.

 Many machines no longer have the Mouse entry.

 Microsoft's intentions are made clear in the Registry key I mentioned. In it are three subkeys, turned off and without specific commands: CD-ROM, Net, and VESA (the VESA spec is a video scheme for high-resolution DOS modes that some DOS game makers use; many video cards require special programs be run in **autoexec.bat** to turn on VESA support), as well as Mouse on those machines that don't have it enabled. Clearly the Redmondians hope that vendors selling new hardware for Windows 98 users will arrange that those keys have the right commands to turn on support for those three options and that the hardware vendors will then arrange to have choices in the Figure 3-85 dialog to turn on these options. So maybe you are lucky and you have a CD-ROM option in the list in Figure 3-85.

But most vendors seem to have ignored the hint and don't bother to give you much in the way of DOS support. Sigh. So, here is some information for dealing with the items that Microsoft left out.

Turning On UMBs The tip text for the item Expanded Memory(EMS) in the list in Figure 3-85 says, "Loads the EMM386 driver to provide expanded memory and upper memory blocks (UMBs)." But that's false for the command that is actually placed in `config.sys` if you select that item. The command is `devicehigh=C:\windows\emm386.exe`. (I'll ignore the fact that it should be `device` not `devicehigh` because the high is ignored). This form of the command loads EMS support but not UMB support. Here's the correct syntax:

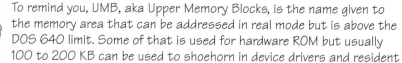

UMB and EMS	`device=C:\windows\emm386.exe RAM`
EMS only	`device=C:\windows\emm386.exe`
UMB only	`device=C:\windows\emm386.exe NOEMS`

You must make sure this line is loaded immediately after the himem line, which should be the second line in `config.sys` after `DOS=High,UMB`.

To remind you, UMB, aka Upper Memory Blocks, is the name given to the memory area that can be addressed in real mode but is above the DOS 640 limit. Some of that is used for hardware ROM but usually 100 to 200 KB can be used to shoehorn in device drivers and resident programs that otherwise take memory space below 640 K. If UMB support is turned on, and you use **devicehigh** for device drivers and **loadhigh** for **autoexec.bat** resident programs, then these programs will go into the UMB area. Juggling programs into the limited space can be a bear but that's why it is called the penalty box (sigh!). EMS, aka Expanded Memory is used by a very few programs to store buffers and other data. If you turn on EMS, it takes 64 KB of valuable UMB space so it is usually not worth it to use EMS but that depends on your precise situation.

Basically, I expect most of you will want to have UMB-only support turned on, and a sizable minority will want both UMB and EMS. None of you will want only EMS turned on, which is precisely what the default check mark set up by Windows does. Oh, how I love a nice bug in the morning.

Dealing with CD-ROM Drives and Sound Cards For CD-ROM support, you need one or two lines in your `config.sys` and one in `autoexec.bat`. I can't tell you the precise syntax for the `config.sys` lines but on a typical SCSI system it reads:

```
device=C:\system\scsi\aspi7dos.sys /d
device=C:\system\scsi\aspicd.sys /d:aspicd0
```

Look at an old pre-Windows 95 `config.sys` for lines something like this. The CD driver will be a device line with the word CD in the name of the driver and usually a `/D:`*name* afterwards. Your old `autoexec.bat` should tell you what is after the `/D:`, as I'll explain. If your CD controller is SCSI (as are many controllers included on sound cards), you'll probably also have a device line in that old `config.sys` with `ASPI` in it; you want that driver also. A typical `autoexec.bat` has

```
C:\system\dos\mscdex.exe /v /D:aspicd0 /m:12 /l:g
```

It's no coincidence that this line has `/D:ASPICD0`, as does the device line. The names have to be the same, and you can use the `mscdex` line to help locate the driver.

To be explicit, here's how you figure out how to add CD support to a penalty box.

1. Try to locate an old matched `config.sys/autoexec.bat` that supported your CD. If you have dual boot under Windows 98, look for `config.dos` and `autoexec.dos`. Otherwise, look for `config` and `autoexec` files with extensions like `syd` or `001`.

2. In the old `autoexec.bat`, you'll find a line with `mscdex`. You want almost the identical line in your custom `autoexec.bat`. The only change will be the path in front of `mscdex,` which should read `C:\windows\command`. To add the line, open the old file in Notepad and cut and paste to the `.pif` dialog.

3. Using the name after `/D:` in the `mscdex` line, locate your CD driver in the old `config.sys` and also check for a driver with the string `ASPI` in its name. Copy those lines with no changes to your custom `config.sys`. You might check that the drivers are still where they are supposed to be.

4. After making sure all this works, make sure you've added UMB support and then experiment with putting a `loadhigh` in front for the `mscdex` command and `devicehigh` in place of `device` in the `config.sys` device line(s).

What's absurd is that the new Windows 98 StartUp disk does a pretty good job of loading generic CD drivers to give you access to your CD drive. I don't see why they can't give you the same support in the penalty box. If all else falls, you can try decoding the `config.sys` and `autoexec.bat` files on a startup disk to figure out what to try in the penalty box to get CD support.

For the sound card, try to locate the needed drivers in the old configuration files. They're usually in a directory that has something to do with the name of the card or the maker of the card. For example, old Sound Blaster Pro was in `\SBPRO`. Copy the driver load lines verbatim to your custom files if you need sound support.

If you have a computer that has seen only Windows 9X, you won't have old configuration files and maybe you won't even have the drivers. Check—maybe you lucked out and your vendor has arranged that the Figure 3-85 dialog has entries for CD-ROM and sound. If so, send them a love letter and tell your friends how wonderfully thoughtful they are. If not, you'll need to get on the phone or online service to them.

 You should be able to figure out how to start CD drives in Exclusive mode by making an Emergency StartUp Disk (ESD), as described in Chapters 6 and 7, that starts up your CD and seeing what drivers it uses.

DriveSpace

 One final tip about setting up penalty boxes. You may very well have **drivespace** loaded when you run in DOS Exclusive mode. Running **mem/c/p** should tell you. If you do, be sure to add UMB support and the line

```
devicehigh=C:\windows\command\drvspace.sys/move
```

to your **config.sys**. That'll move almost 60 K of memory-hogging space into UMBs.

 Don't assume that because you have no compressed hard drives you aren't loading **drvspace**. I've found that once a system has mounted a single compressed diskette, **drvspace** is there forever. At least I haven't figured out (short of a step-by-step boot) how to get rid of it.

Penalty boxes are the pits—a fitting punishment for the audacity to continue using unfriendly DOS programs. Keep cool and use my tips—on one of my systems, I had over 620 KB free at an Exclusive DOS prompt—that was with **drvspace** and CD drivers loaded into UMBs.

■ Mr. Rogers's Network

11th commandment: Covet not thy neighbor's Pentium.

—Heard on the Net

There isn't much to say about Network Neighborhood. If you're here to figure out how to stop it showing up on your desktop, you are in the wrong place— that's discussed in Chapter 9. (Hint to the Regedit literate: you'll need to add a DWord key to **HKCU\Software\Microsoft\Windows\CurrentVersion\ Policies\Explorer** called **NoNetHood**, give it the value **1**, and reboot.)

If you are on a large network, Network Neighborhood can be a wonderful tool in ferreting out resources, although trying to browse the entire network can take a long time. If your immediate workgroup is medium sized—large enough that you may not keep up with all the available computing resources but small enough that you needn't go out for lunch during a browse of all resources—Network Neighborhood can be exceedingly useful.

With a small network, say in a small office with fewer than five employees or in a home peer-to-peer network, Network Neighborhood is probably useless and even counterproductive. If you are in a situation where you know all the resources that are available, it is probably most efficient to set up a Desktop folder with these resources in it. You can add drive icons to network drives you often access and place them on the Desktop. Once you've done that, you can play the Registry game to blow NetHood away.

 When you set this up, I recommend you use UNC-type names rather than mapped drives as long as you're sure your programs will understand them. Mapped drives should be used merely as a convenience for aliasing very long UNCs.

■ Browsing the Net

When spider webs unite, they can tie up a lion.

—Ethiopian proverb

To do a comprehensive overview of all the elements of the Internet would take a whole book, but Windows and the Internet are so intertwined that I can't totally ignore the Internet tools. So here I give you MOM's top IE 4.0 tips and tricks, her favorite Web sites, and a discussion of Windows 98's e-mail client; I discuss other Internet tools in Chapter 4.

 You may wonder why we split things this way. Simple. The Web browser and e-mail are core components; the other tools are utilities.

MOM's Tip-Top IE Tip List

Here are MOM's ten favorite tips on getting the most out of Internet Explorer in no particular order.

- **Use Autocomplete on URLs.** If you type an address like **foobar1** into the address bar, IE will try in order to locate the addresses **foobar1**, **www.foobar1.com**, **www.foobar1.edu**, **www.foobar1.org**, **foobar1.com**, **foobar1.edu**, and **foobar1.org**. Then it will offer to search your preferred search site for sites related to **foobar1**.

 Ha. Netscape has done this for several years. I'm glad Microsoft finally caught on.

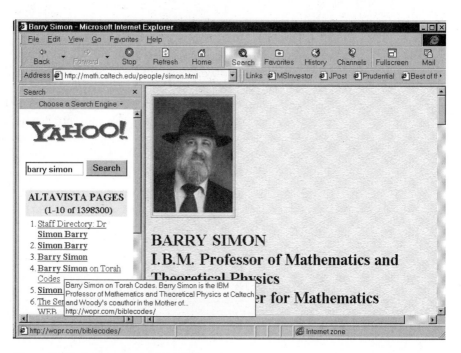

Figure 3-86. A Search panel ToolTip

- **Use the Search panel**. Don't forget to use the panel you open when you hit the Search button in the toolbar (Figure 3-86). This panel stays on screen as you click on various links in the search engine and look at the hits in the right panel. If the search engine supports it (for example Alta Vista does but Yahoo doesn't), as your mouse moves over various hits in the search hit list, you get a ToolTip with additional information (see Figure 3-86).

- **Use ? for quick searches**. If you type `Janet Reno?` into the Address toolbar (whether in Internet Explorer or one that is part of the Taskbar), IE will go to your preferred search site and search for "Janet Reno." It's important that you try to type in a phrase with a space in it because otherwise, IE first tries auto completion. If your kid needed to do a report on conifers and you typed in `conifers?`, IE will first try to locate `www.conifers.com` and all the other possibilities. This isn't terrible but you'll get a speedier response if you have a space in the search string!

Parents can use the History panel to check up on where their kids have been.

Ha, not once their kids find the setting in Tweak UI's Paranoia panel that clears IE history every time someone new logs on!

- **Use the History panel**. The History button brings up a panel that lets you see the names of all the sites you've visited for the past several weeks, allowing quick return to a site whose address you've forgotten.

- **Use the Back/Forward dropdowns**. The Back/Forward buttons have been part of the browser interface since the original Mosaic browser. Internet Explorer 4.0 has added dropdowns controlled by the little downward pointing arrows that list the last few pages. So instead of having to click Back four times (and perhaps overshoot), you can go to the dropdown and pick the exact page you want.

- **Use Help/Product Updates on a regular basis**. On the Help menu, there is a choice called Product Updates that takes you to the IE update page and allows you to check for updates. The page runs a program that checks what you currently have and compares it with what's available. Check this site at least once a month.

- **Shift to Thumbnail view of Favorites**. In the section "Fifth View: Thumbnails," I explained how to turn on Thumbnail view for any folder. If you turn it on for your Favorites folder, you'll get thumbnails of the Web pages for your favorite sites. You can access this via the Favorites/Organize Favorites . . . panel. Open that panel, right click, and pick View/Thumbnails. You'll get a view like that in Figure 3-87.

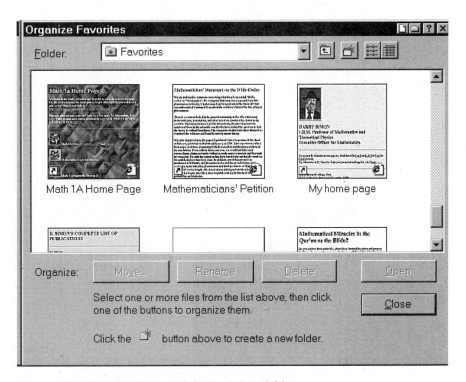

Figure 3-87. Thumbnail view of the Favorites folder

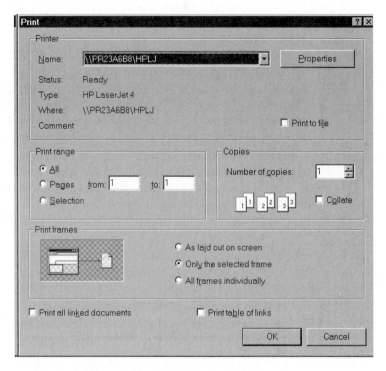

Figure 3-88. The Internet Explorer Print Dialog

- **Put an address toolbar on the Taskbar**. I mentioned this in the section on the Taskbar but it is worth mentioning again. Be sure to add an address toolbar to the Taskbar by right clicking a blank area on the Taskbar, picking Toolbars and making sure Address is checked.

- **Use the File/Print menu, not the Print button**. If you use the Print button on the toolbar, it uses some defaults and bypasses the dialog shown in Figure 3-88. That is sometimes good, but you'll often want some of the advanced options in the Print dialog, which include the ability to print only some of the frames, the ability to print a table of all the links on the current page, and the ability to print all the pages linked to the current page. (BEWARE!! That can be a lot!) To access this dialog, print through the menus.

- **Get Adobe Acrobat**. Adobe Acrobat is discussed in Chapter 2. Be sure to download the free plugin at **http://www.adobe.com/prodindex/acrobat/readstep.html**.

MOM's Tip-Top Web Sites

Here are MOM's ten favorite Web sites in no particular order. Limiting to ten means that they are all general interest and most are information oriented. The Web is so rich MOM could list a thousand.

- My favorite **search site** is still Yahoo at `http://www.yahoo.com`. Note that not only can you search for Web sites by topic, but it has e-mail address and phone number lookup and even maps.

- Alta Vista remains my favorite place to go when Yahoo comes up dry or the search is not topic related. Sure, it seems to be less good about having the latest pages because it may have become overwhelmed with the growth of the Web, but it still is amazing to be able to do a full text search on a significant fraction of the web. It's at `http://www.altavista.digital.com` and not at `http://www.altavista.com`.

- MS Investor at `http://investor.msn.com/home.asp` is my favorite site for **tracking stocks.** Its portfolio tracking is superb. Other people like `http://www.quicken.com` or any of the myriad sites with stock commissions under $30.

My full-service broker doesn't like the $19.99 commission sites.

Gee, do you think I could sell a coupla hundred million shares of Microsoft and pay a commission of only $19.99?

- MS Expedia at `http://expedia.msn.com` is my favorite **travel site**. Sure Microsoft is hoping you'll buy tickets there so they get the commission, but you don't have to and the flight lookup is fast and free.

I find it ideal to go to Expedia, figure out what I want, and then call my travel agent. Sometimes he gets a better price (and sometimes I tell him to look more because Expedia had a better price!), and more important, if there is a problem, I have an agent looking out for me.

It's remarkable that Microsoft has established a commanding presence in service-oriented sites, including Investor, Expedia, and Car Point.

- Of all the mainstream **news sources**, our favorite is CNN at `http://www.cnn.com`. Other people like msnbc or cbs or *Time* magazine's Pathfinder, but my top choice for succinct news clips attractively presented is CNN. For depth, check out the *New York Times* or your local newspaper. The *Jerusalem Post* (at `http://www.jpost.com`) appeals to those wanting news of Israel.

- The Drudge Report at `http://www.drudgereport.com` is surely my controversial choice. Matt Drudge stands for everything that is wrong with irresponsible Internet news reporting! I'm not suggesting you read the stuff he himself puts out, but the page has convenient links to oodles of

newspaper columnists and newspapers so I visit the page every week or so to catch up on my favorite columnists.

- Anchor Desk at `http://www.zdnet.com/anchordesk` is short, pithy opinion and news clips about **personal computer topics**. I try to visit it daily. Of course *PC Magazine* and *PC Computing* are also high on my list.

- CNET at `http://www.news.com` is my preferred source of more **detailed computer industry news.** A close second is ZDNet's new service at `http://www.zdnet.com/zdnn`, but Skinny DuBaud, CNET's rumor columnist, tips the balance in CNET's favor. These two megasites also fight over the bragging rights for the best source of shareware and freeware, CNET's download.com (`http://www.download.com`) and ZDNet's hotfiles (`http://www.hotfiles.com`).

- Zip2 at `http://www.zip2.com` is my favored site for looking up **addresses** and getting **travel directions** and **maps**. For local information a specialized local collection may be better—for example, Los Angeles has Pacific Bell's AtHand.

- **Internet commerce** is the little girl with a curl of the Internet—it either works very well or it is a disaster. Amazon.com, "the world's largest bookstore" at `http://www.amazon.com` does it all right from search to shopping cart to follow-up on ordering via e-mail. Of course, if you don't want books or audio CDs, you have to go elsewhere, but Internet commerce is blossoming.

 For computer purchases, I often check out prices on the Web (at several sites) and then call a vendor's 800 number to place the order. I tend to trust the *live person's* assurance that a product is in stock more than the Web's.

 And I'd like to invite you all to visit `http://www.wopr.com` for discussions in the Lounge, where guru of various stripes hang out and lend a helping hand.

■ Outlook Express

The e-mail of the species is more deadly than the mail.

—Heard on the web

Windows 95 shipped with the Exchange client, Microsoft's first crack at an e-mail client. Especially given Microsoft's reputation of never getting anything right until the third try, it was an impressive product, but it had lacks and a dearth of documentation. After that, Microsoft's e-mail offerings split into two tracks. The high end was Outlook 97 and then Outlook 98, part of Microsoft Office.

The low end were Internet mail-only offerings that shipped with several successive versions of Internet Explorer. IE 4.0 included Outlook Express (OE), which is therefore included with Windows 98. It has a much smoother interface than Exchange client and has greater power in some ways although it is missing some of the high-end features of Exchange client and Outlook itself.

 OE isn't half bad, but Outlook is better. At the time this book went to press, Outlook 98 was free for the download from Microsoft's Web site and Microsoft was giving the product away on CDs in magazines and at trade shows. They have been threatening to eventually limit the free version to owners of Office or Exchange Server, but you may qualify even if they limit it. So why futz around with OE when you can have the real thing?

 Like you, Woody, I use Outlook 98 as my main e-mail program, so I can't totally disagree with you. It is a much better program than OE, no doubt about it. But OE will suffice for many users and it's already installed if they have IE 4, so they should at least try it. Besides, Outlook uses OE for its newsgroup support, and if you have the corporate version of Outlook, OE is also used for e-mail address lookup (LDAP support).

OE's Basic Services

Outlook Express provides the following services.

- E-mail client that lets you collect and send e-mail over the Internet. Both the common POP3 protocol and the up-and-coming IMAP protocol are supported. You can have multiple e-mail accounts. The program supports encrypted e-mail.
- Address book for storing e-mail addresses plus postal addresses, phone numbers, and digital encryption data.
- Newsgroup reader for accessing the Usenet newsgroups.
- Applet for accessing publicly available e-mail address directory services using the LDAP protocol. It comes with seven well-known sites installed and you can add your own, for example, a company LDAP server.

Setting Up an E-mail Connection

Love letters, business contracts, and money due you always arrive three weeks late, whereas junk mail arrives the day it was sent.

—Aphorism

If you are going to use a dial-up connection to get your e-mail, you'll want to set that up first (see Chapter 4). Before you set up your e-mail account, you need to have in hand the following information.

1. Name you want to appear on your e-mail messages as the sender of the messages. This name doesn't have to have anything to do with your assigned e-mail address. It could be something as dull and boring as "Barry Simon" or it could be something like "One Cool Dude."

2. E-mail address you want to appear as the sending e-mail address, which will also be the one used when the recipient of one of your messages hits the Reply button in most programs. Normally this would be your regular e-mail address, the one associated with the account you are setting up, but there are several cases where it might not be. You might have several accounts and want to use a single e-mail address for replies. Or you might use a remailer.

An example of a **remailer** is Bigfoot for Life. It's a free address you register for at **www.bigfoot.com**. The e-mail address I give out is **bsimon@bigfoot.com**. But it's only a virtual mailbox. I tell Bigfoot where it should forward any mail that I get. This has a number of advantages—when I changed ISPs, I only had to make a single change at the Bigfoot site; others could continue to send to the Bigfoot address. When I was in Israel for four weeks with a local e-mail address, I repointed Bigfoot to it and collected my e-mail from a local address instead of having to use the Transatlantic lines from Israel, which can be painfully slow. Another use someone might want to make of a remailer would be to have personal mail sent to the remailer and redirected to a company account—if your company doesn't mind.

3. Names of the *POP* server and *SMTP* server on your *ISP*. The first is where you collect your mail and the second is the machine used to send it. The documentation from your ISP should clearly spell out the names of these two servers. They may have the same name and be called just "the mail server." The address will have no @ in it and will have a .com, .net, .org, .edu or something similar at the end. An example, is pop-server.myisp.com.

4. Your user name and password. This is the login information for the POP server and it must be precisely as your ISP has given it to you (unless you've changed the password). Passwords are often case-sensitive.

Notice that you need the password only for the POP server, not for the SMTP server. The lack of security built into SMTP is appalling. Most SMTP servers do not require a password, which means you can use any SMTP server you have the name of. Moreover, the protocol lets you use any name and return address you want without verification. So you could claim your name is William Jefferson Clinton and your return address is **president@whitehouse.gov** (although this could violate some federal law for all I know, so don't try exactly this if you want to test this thought).

5. "Friendly name" you want to give this account. If you have multiple e-mail accounts, you distinguish them with these friendly names.

6. Decision whether you want to have the account automatically dialed up. I say more about this in a moment.

Figure 3-89. Mail Account SetUp Wizard

Figure 3-89 shows how you use the six items of information in the Internet Connection Wizard.

 You invoke the Wizard the first time you pick Send or Send and Receive from the Tools menu in OE. Or you can invoke it at any time to set up a new account by picking Accounts . . . from the Tools menu and hitting the Add/Mail . . . button.

In the last panel, there are three choices. The middle one is what you use if you are on a LAN connected to the Internet or a system with a semipermanent phone connection. The first choice will automatically dial up the Internet any time a connection is needed and you aren't already connected. You must tell the Wizard which dial-up connection to use, so that's why you have to set it up beforehand. The last choice requires you to manually dial up by launching the dial-up connection.

 The choice between the first and third is not easy. You may want to switch back and forth and try each one. You can make that switch in the Connection tab of the Properties dialog I'm about to describe.

Before actually collecting mail the first time, you'll want to call up Tools/ Accounts, highlight the connection, and call up the Properties dialog (Figure 3-90). Here you can change any information you put into the wizard. That information is in the first three tabs (General, Servers, and Connection).

As I told you in item 2, the address you put in indicates the address the message came from and the reply address, but you can specify a different address for each function if you want in the General Tab. If the "Reply address" field is left blank, the "E-mail address" field is used for the Reply tab. Not all software is smart enough to use the reply address in incoming e-mail messages; some will use the sending address oblivious to the existence of a reply address. So my strong advice is to use only one address and make it the one you want replies sent to, even if that means you are technically lying about the sending address.

There are additional options on the Security and Advanced tabs. Security lets you set up digital signatures and encrypting messages using public key encryption.

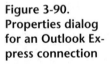 I've no doubt that encryption and digital signatures are in your future but I wouldn't urge you to be a pioneer here. If your need for encryption is so great that you want it now, you probably need a stronger version than can pass current U.S. export restrictions. You should be looking at PGP rather than this early Microsoft implementation.

Besides troubleshooting options, the Advanced tab (Figure 3-90) has a very useful option you should know about: "Leave a copy of message on server." By default (this box is not checked), OE deletes the messages from your mail server immediately after it collects them. "Leave a copy" tells OE not to do that now but to remove the messages after a time period you fix or when you delete them from your mail file. OE tracks which messages it has downloaded, so it doesn't download a second time messages you leave on the server.

Figure 3-90. Properties dialog for an Outlook Express connection

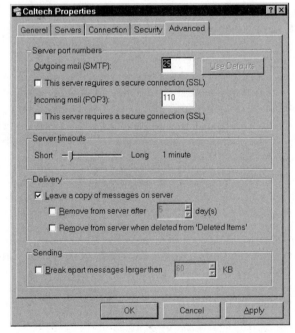

Here's a scenario where this option is valuable. You want to keep all your messages in your inbox in your office, but you'd like to be able to check the messages from home. If you set both the office and home versions of OE to leave messages on the server and tell one of them to delete the messages from the server after 2 or 3 days, you'll probably get exactly what you want!

Dealing with E-mail

Sending and receiving e-mail is fairly straightforward, but here are some tips for increasing your productivity with it.

- The program will read HTML mail both in its preview panel and when you open it (see Figure 3-91). That means you can subscribe to any of the sources of news that come with full HTML output, including pictures, like the CNN QuickNews shown in the figure.

- The default for sending messages is HTML, but I urge you to go into the Send tab of Tools/Options to change that to Plain Text. Your recipients may or may not have HTML mail, and you really don't need to waste time with layout. Do your recipients a favor and don't even think about using stationery. If you need to send a picture, send it as an attachment (just drag and drop into the Message/Compose panel).

- In Figure 3-91, the pane on the lower right is a preview pane. It can be turned on and off. You might expect to be able to do so via a check item on the View menu (as you can in Outlook 98), but they hid it. You have to pick Layout from the View menu and change a check box there (Figure 3-92).

**Figure 3-91.
Outlook Express
Inbox**

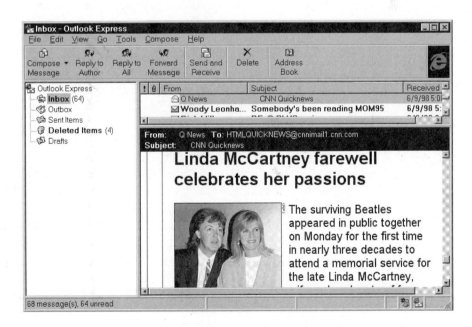

**Figure 3-92.
Outlook Express
Layout dialog**

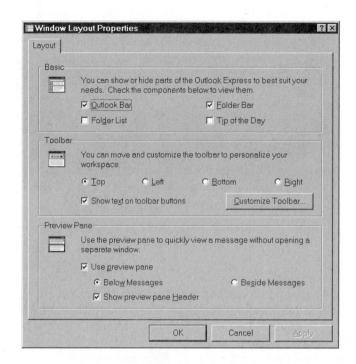

- From the View/Layout dialog, you can pick Customize Toolbar . . . (you can also do this by right clicking on the toolbar and picking Buttons . . .). Alas, you can add or remove only a limited choice of menu items and you cannot shift to small icons.

- You may want to use the Read/Unread status (which appears as boldface) to instead track which messages still require attention. If that is the case, you'll want to add Mark as Read and Mark as Unread buttons to the toolbar and uncheck the box in the Read tab of the Tools/Options dialog that says, "Message is read after being previewed."

- You should be warned that the default settings delete messages after they have been around for a while. You may want to look at the Advanced tab of the Tools/Options dialog to avoid being surprised by deleted messages.

- While reading a message (not in the preview pane but open in a separate window), you can right click on the sender or any of the recipients and choose to add them to your address book.

- You can set up group addresses that let you easily send messages to groups. Use the New Group button in the Address Book to set them up.

 Bah, humbug. Not only can't you change it easily via the menus, but it isn't an optional toolbar button.

Figure 3-93.
Outlook Express
with the folder
dropdown and
the Outlook Bar

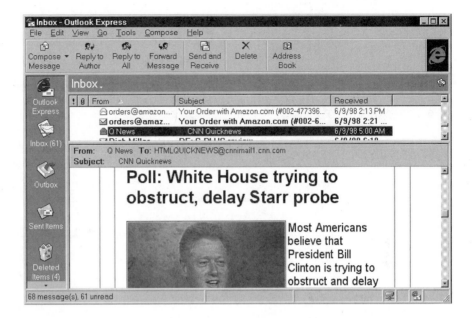

- The defaults in the Basic panel of the View/Layout dialog are to turn on the Folder List and Tip of the Day and turn off the Outlook Bar and Folder Bar. I suggest you do the opposite (Figure 3-92). This gives you a view like that in Figure 3-93 rather than the default view of Figure 3-91. The Folder drop-down doesn't take the space of the folder panel, but you can press on the current folder name to get a dropdown folder list from which to maneuver. The Outlook Bar is another way to maneuver between folders, and you can move items by dragging them from the message list pane to a folder on the Outlook Bar.

 Bah, humbug. Outlook Express's Folder and Outlook bars are pale imitations of their equivalents in Outlook 98. The Folder dropdown in Outlook 98 has a crucial thumbtack button that lets you keep it open temporarily if you want. The Outlook Bar has a Small Icons view, is easier to arrange, and allows multiple tabs, each containing exactly the buttons you want. OE's bar only lists all the folders.

- You can adjust the columns displayed in the view of a folder by using the View/Columns dialog that lets you reorder the columns and add or remove among nine possibilities.

- You can search for messages with full text search from the Edit/Find Message . . . dialog. By telling this dialog (Figure 3-94) to search all of Outlook Express, it will search across folders.

- You can save rather than send a message you are working on by using Save from the File menu or closing the message with the **x** button and answering

Figure 3-94.
Find Message
dialog

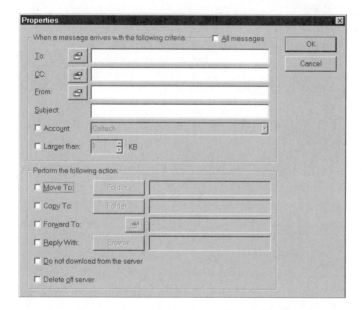

Figure 3-95. Outlook Express rules setup panel

Yes to the question you are asked. The message is saved in the Drafts folder. There is no AutoSave, though, of messages you've been working on for some time.

- Tools/Inbox Assistant lets you set up some very simple rules to automatically move, copy, and forward (you can delete by moving to the Deleted Items folder) messages based on their To/From/Cc lists or subject (Figure 3-95).

Again, OE is a pale imitation of Outlook 98, which supports multiple views per folder, column setting by a visual metaphor, powerful message search, AutoSave to the Drafts folder, and a truly sophisticated rules engine.

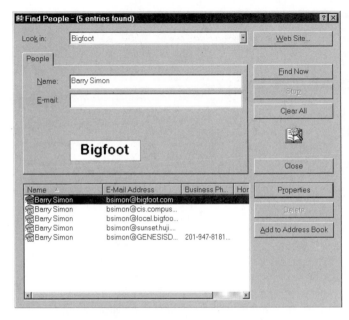

Figure 3-96. Finding people using LDAP search

Online Address Searches

Remarkably, you can search public databases for the e-mail addresses of people you'd like to contact. You may even find phone numbers for some of them. You can access the relevant panel either by going to the Find submenu of the systemwide Start Menu and picking People, by going to the Edit menu of OE and picking Find People. . . , or by clicking on the file card in a message panel and hitting Find . . . from the resulting Address Book view. You then type in a name or e-mail address and pick which of the address servers to try, and OE goes out to the Internet to search the public database and returns with the hits it finds (Figure 3-96).

Newsgroups

This is a test of the Emergency Broadband System. This is only a test. If this had been an actual emergency, your local newsgroups and mailing lists—in voluntary cooperation with state and local officials—would have posted alarmist spams announcing the imminent death of the Internet. This concludes this test of the Emergency Broadband System. Thank you.

—MALINDA MCCALL

Outlook Express also serves as a newsgroup reader, letting you read and send messages to the multitudinous Usenet newsgroups. You'll need the name of the newsgroup server that your ISP provides. The documentation from the ISP should have it, otherwise if the ISP domain is **someisp.net**, try using **news.someisp.net** for the newsgroup server name. If that doesn't work, get on the phone to your ISP.

With the news server name in hand, you set up News in much the way you set up an e-mail connection by picking Add News . . . from the Tools/Accounts dialog.

The first time you log on to News, you have a lengthy download of the full list of newsgroups, likely to be over 15,000 in all (unless your ISP does an awful lot of filtering). The list (left panel of Figure 3-97) can be searched. Once you pick a newsgroup, you'll download recent messages to a panel that looks a lot like the Mail view (right panel of Figure 3-97) except that the messages have an outline view with plus and minus that let you expand on threads of related messages.

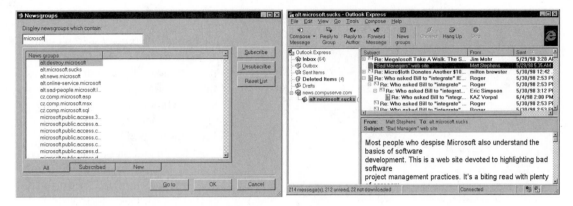

Figure 3-97. All the news that's fit to download

Usenet can be a huge time sink. The general interest groups tend to be made up of people venting. It's the way CompuServe forums could be when poorly managed except that on Usenet there is usually no one managing many of the groups. Moreover, almost any group winds up with spam from Internet sex sites. It's something of a mess that you may want to completely ignore.

While I can't disagree much, there are some specialized groups (like online support for certain diseases) that I'd consider a high point of the Internet. And I've occasionally found good tech support through company-sponsored newsgroups.

MOM's Tip-Top Mailing Lists

We do not talk—we bludgeon one another with facts and theories gleaned from cursory readings of newspapers, magazines, and digests.

—Henry Miller

Remember that mailing lists are very different from newsgroups. With newsgroups you use a special News-Reader mode and receive and leave messages on a public news server. Mailing lists use e-mail. Some lists allow discussions and have a little of the flavor of a newsgroup but others just send you information via e-mail. Often this mail is in HTML format with links to online sites with additional information. The mail may have banner ads to support it.

Think of e-mail information as push done right.

Herewith MOM's favorite ten informational mailing lists (all free and in no particular order).

- **WOW,** aka Woody's Office Watch. The best source of the straight dope on Microsoft Office put together by Woody (yeah, that Woody) and his gang of cohorts. Subscribe on the Web at `http://www.wopr.com/wow`.

You're probably thinking Woody put me up to this, but you're wrong. I use it myself to keep up with what's going on with Office. Invaluable!

Oh, so the fact that I promised to plug *WinMOM 98* on WOW if you plugged WOW here had nothing to do with it?

You know, Woody, I just had a thought. Let's put out WWW—Woody's Windows Watch. Our readers can go to `http://www.worp.com/mom98` to subscribe.

- **Infobeat.** You get to choose from oodles of options, including Reuters newsclips several times a day, daily summaries of stock activities, weather, sports news, and reminders. If you purchase a service from a Premium partner, you can get things like daily Doonesbury and Dilbert (one week old)! Subscribe at `http://www.infobeat.com`.

- **CNN QuickNews.** Subscribe at `http://cnn.com/QUICKNEWS/mail`. Get the HTML version if you are using Outlook Express.

- **Anchordesk.** This gives you essentially the home page of Anchordesk, ZD's service that MOM discussed when she talked about her favorite Web sites. Subscribe at `http://www.zdnet.com/anchordesk/whoiswe/subscribe.html`.

- **Wininfo.** Paul Thurrott's look at what's new with Windows and related issues. Subscribe by going to `http://www.wugnet.com/wininfo/subscribe.asp`.

- **Microsoft's mailing lists.** Sure, it's marketing propaganda, but sometimes it's useful marketing propaganda. Subscribe at `http://register.microsoft.com/regwiz/personalinfo.asp`. There are lots of different lists to choose from.

- **CNET News Dispatch.** CNET remains one of the premier sources of computer news on the Web. To get briefs daily with links to the full articles, subscribe at `http://www.news.com/Dispatch/Entry/0,65,,00.html?st.ne.nav.subscribe`. (If that has changed, try looking on the home page at `http://www.news.com`.)

- **ZDNN.** ZD's daily newsclips. Not as slick as CNET's but a useful counterpoint. You can subscribe to this (and other ZD mailing lists including AnchorDesk) at `http://www.zdnet.com/cc/email.html`.

- **This Is True.** An Internet success story, this is an online mailing list that went to newspaper syndication and a split-free and longer-pay subscription model. Each newsletter has truth-is-stranger-than-fiction newsclips with sardonic comments by list creator Randy Cassingham. I find this the funniest of the many humor mailing lists on the web. Subscribe at `http://www.thisistrue.com/subscribe.html`.

- **Arutz-7.** This is our example of a special interest list. Arutz-7 is a radio station in Israel founded by members of the settlers movement. Its daily newsclips provide a different slice of Israel news from the mainstream American or Israeli newspapers. You subscribe to this mailing list and many other Israeli mailing lists at Virtual Jerusalem (`http://www.virtual.co.il/city_services/lists`).

■ Microsoft Fax

Overview of Windows 98 Fax Software

Yessiree, we almost forgot to include fax software with Windows 98. We first included free fax software with Windows for Workgroups 3.1 and then with Windows 95, but it didn't link in well with Outlook Express, our new e-mail client, so we didn't include it with the early betas. We figured that would make Symantec (makers of WinFax) and Janet happy. But boy, did our users howl. So much that we included the Windows 95 fax components on the CD with no fanfare at all. You have to know where to look, but it's there.

Yeah, but it isn't integrated into e-mail, which is a pain and a half. Oh well, it's better than nothing.

If you have Outlook 98, the situation is a little complicated. If you installed the Internet-only version, it includes stunted fax software from Symantec as a teaser for its full WinFax product. If you install the Corporate version of Outlook 98, it has no fax, but you can install the fax-only stuff (see below) into Outlook 98.

If you *do* a lot of computer faxing, you'll probably want to invest in WinFax Pro; it really is a wonderful product.

You'll need a fax modem to use this software.

To get the free fax software Microsoft threw in, you install Windows Messaging, which uses MAPI. You then install the fax software. The resulting program allows you to send faxes either from within Windows Messaging or from any program you can print from. You can receive faxes and read them with Windows Imaging.

Windows Messaging looks and acts much like the Exchange Client that shipped with Windows 95. You can probably get an Internet Mail module for this program from the Microsoft site, but Outlook Express is probably a better choice than Windows Messaging for e-mail.

Nothing but the Fax

Figure 3-98. Fax software on the CD

Here's how to install the fax software on the CD. You'll want to be sure you've installed your fax modem into Windows 98 before you go through these steps.

1. Pop the Windows CD in and choose the Browse This CD option. Click to `\tools\oldwin95\message\us` (see Figure 3-98).

2. Double click on `wms.exe`. This will install Windows Messaging.

3. Double click on `awfax.exe`. This will install the fax software, after which you will need to reboot.

4. After rebooting, double click on the Inbox icon that has been added to your desktop. This will start a wizard.

5. In the first panel you get to pick from the services to include in this profile (Figure 3-99). Pick only Microsoft Fax.

 Although I don't recommend it, if you want Internet mail to be accessed with Windows Messaging, it'll be easier if you download the MAPI service before running this wizard, in which case it will appear on the list and you'll want to check it. The same is true if you want to access MCI mail this way.

6. In the next panel (Figure 3-100) you get to pick the modem you want to use.

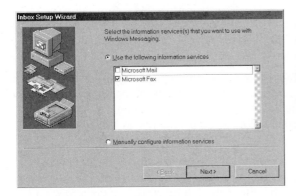

Figure 3-99. Step 1 in the Inbox Setup Wizard

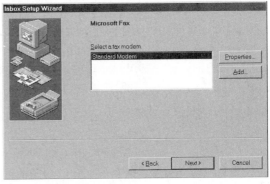

Figure 3-100. Step 2 in the Inbox Setup Wizard

Figure 3-101. Step 3 in the Inbox Setup Wizard

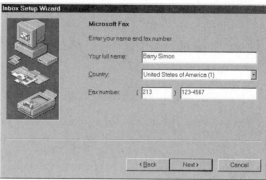

Figure 3-102. Step 4 in the Inbox Setup Wizard

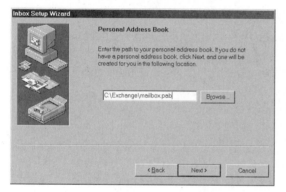

Figure 3-103. Step 5 in the Inbox Setup Wizard

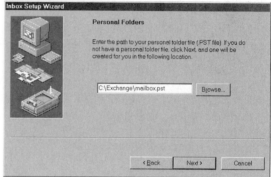

Figure 3-104. Step 6 in the Inbox Setup Wizard

7. In the third panel (Figure 3-101) you get to choose if you want the fax software to pick up the phone every time it rings. I explain later how you can change this if you want.

8. In the fourth panel (Figure 3-102) you put in your name and fax number. This is used on outgoing faxes and on outgoing cover sheets; again I explain later how to change it .

9. In the fifth panel (Figure 3-103) you pick the address book filename. This is where you'll be able to store fax numbers. It's what most fax programs would call your phone book. You can accept the default unless you already have a Personal Address Book from an earlier version of Windows Messaging or Exchange Client.

10. In the sixth panel (Figure 3-104) you pick the filename of the place your faxes, both incoming and outgoing, will be stored. Again, pick the default unless you already have such a file. After hitting Next, you get a final panel that says you're done and you are. You may want to adjust fax properties now or later; I describe how at the end of this section.

Installing Messaging adds two new Control Panel applets.

 Mail Loaded from `mlcfg32.cpl`. This is also accessible if you right click on the Inbox icon and pick Properties. This is the Windows Messaging Properties used to configure Messaging.

 Microsoft Mail Post Office Loaded from `wgpocpl.cpl`. Only relevant if you use Administer an MS Mail Post Office.

 You certainly shouldn't be using Microsoft Mail, so feel free to delete the files **wgpocpl.cpl** *and* **wgpoadm.dll** *from* **C:\windows\system**. *If you are using Messaging only for fax, you probably won't need to reconfigure it, but it pays to keep the Mail applet around just in case.*

 It is ironic that what is called "Mail" here was called "Mail and Fax" under the original Windows 95, because, for Windows 98 users, it is Fax only.

To customize the way fax works, you go through the Fax Properties dialog (Figure 3-105), which you get to by picking Services from the Tools menu, selecting Microsoft Fax in the resulting dialog, and clicking the Properties button. Or you can go to the Microsoft Fax Tools submenu of Tools and pick Options. . . .

There are four tabs in Properties. Messages has three subparts, which I discuss later. Dialing links up the standard TAPI locations, which I discuss when I talk about Dial-Up Networking in Chapter 4, and it lets you adjust the number of retries on outgoing faxes. Modem lets you change the Active Fax modem. User lets you add additional information about yourself that can be used in cover sheets if you want.

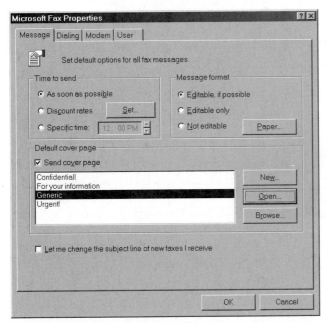

Figure 3-105. Fax Properties dialog

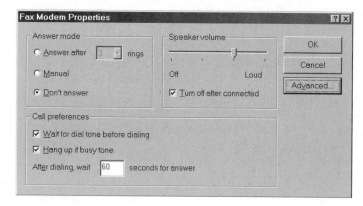

Figure 3-106. The well-hidden Fax Modem Properties sheet

 If the fax software and cover sheets are going to be used only by you, you may as well hardcode your information into them in the Cover Sheet Editor. Only if you are going to share cover sheets across a company do you want to fool with the User tab.

You're probably wondering where the heck you get to change your mind about whether the phone is answered on incoming fax or the number of rings. Microsoft has hidden it well, haven't they? The secret is to go to the Modem tab, highlight your fax modem, and hit Properties. You get the dialog in Figure 3-106.

Sending and Receiving Faxes

You have to have Inbox running to receive faxes.

 This is crazy, of course. There should be a way to just load the fax watch without the full Windows Messaging program.

Figure 3-107. Fax Status panel

After you start Inbox, you get a fax icon on the notification area that looks like [icon]. You can double click on it to get a panel that displays the fax status (Figure 3-107). From the Options menu in this panel, you can access the Fax Modem Properties (Figure 3-106) but not the main Fax Properties dialog (Figure 3-105).

 You'd have hoped that the panel and the ToolTip for the Notification Area icon would tell you the status of your autoanswer choice, but usually it will just display the word Idle.

If you have the fax software set to autoanswer, when a fax comes in, the Status panel pops up with the message saying Ringing..., as shown in Figure 3-107. You might expect that hitting Answer Now in that case would, er, answer now,

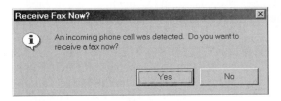

Figure 3-108. Manual fax option

but in our tests, it generated an error message, and the software answered on the ring you'd set it for with autoanswer. If you choose "Don't answer" in the Fax Modem Properties dialog, you can still answer if a fax call comes in by clicking the icon in the Taskbar and choosing Answer Now, which does work in that case. If you have chosen Manual for answer mode, you get a popup panel like that shown in Figure 3-108 if your fax line rings.

When a fax comes in it is stored in Inbox. If you open the fax by double clicking on it, it opens in Imaging for Windows, Kodak's superb fax bitmap program (Figure 3-109). If you get multipage faxes, you'll want to shift from the default Page view to the Thumbnail and Page view shown in the figure. From this program you can print faxes, annotate them, add scanned pages (if you have a scanner attached to your system) and resend them.

You might expect that to resend a fax (after annotating it, if desired), you'd use the Send command in the File menu, but that produces an error message. Instead, you use the Print . . . item in the File menu and choose the Microsoft Fax printer.

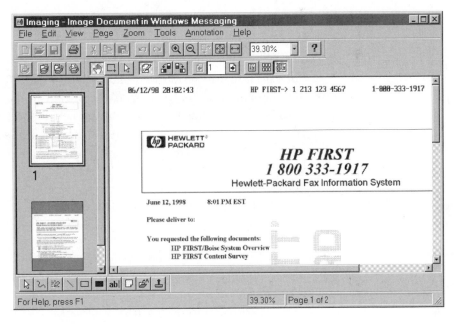

Figure 3-109. Imaging for Windows reads faxes

**Figure 3-110.
Important Send
options**

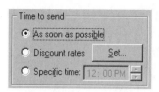

**Figure 3-111.
Faxes are waiting
to be sent!**

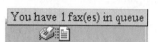

Before you send your first fax, call up the Fax Properties dialog and set the "Time to send" options (Figure 3-110). If you have any option other than "As soon as possible," the faxes are queued; the Notification Area icon adds a sheet of paper and its tooltip gives you information about the queue (Figure 3-111).

One way to send a fax is to use the new Fax Wizard, which you invoke from the Inbox's Compose/New Fax menu item. The Wizard lets you enter one or more fax numbers either by hand or from your phone book, choose a cover page (from the Compose/New Fax panel, the Options . . . button lets you override the default options for how soon the fax is sent), type in a brief note, and add file attachments if the fax is editable (see the section "Windows Secret File Transfer Program").

A second way to send a fax is to Compose a message whose recipients are either taken from your address book (with fax addresses) or by entering phone numbers in the To line of the message with the format (include the brackets and the explicit 1 in front!) **[1-201-123-4567]**. When you do this, you can compose long messages and paste bitmaps into the message (by loading them into Paint and using Copy and Paste).

The third way to send a fax is by using the fax printer as I'll discuss soon.

Windows Messaging Tips

Here are a few tips about using the Windows Messaging program.

- You can customize the toolbar from Tools/Customize Toolbar. . . .
- Shift from the Inbox-only view of Messaging to one that shows folders (click the second button on the toolbar or View/Folders on the menus).
- Queued faxes are in the Outbox and sent faxes in the Sent Items folder.
- You can create folders to store incoming and sent faxes by project, if you wish.
- You can print a fax without explicitly opening it by right clicking on it and picking Print. Imaging for Windows will open, print the fax, and exit.
- If a fax isn't sent because of no success after the specified number of tries or because you put in a wrong number, System Administrator puts a message in your Inbox. When you open it, there will be a Send Again button. That opens the message, and you can change the fax number from there, if you need to.

If you are on a network, I don't think the real System Administrator will be pleased that Windows Messaging is pretending to be her.

I've Got You Covered

The covers of this book are too far apart.

—AMBROSE BIERCE, one-sentence book review

There are some circumstances where you want a cover page for a fax or want a single-page fax that includes covering information and room for a note. Windows Fax includes a cover page editor that you invoke from **start menu/ programs/accessories/fax/cover page editor**. It's not the slickest program you've ever seen, but it serves its purpose well (Figure 3-112). There are four sample cover pages provided for you to use as templates. Each cover page is made up of regions where you can place simple objects, including vector graphics, using the program's primitive drawing tools, text areas, special fields, and (because the program is an OLE 2 in-place editing application) any object made by an OLE server—for example bitmaps using Paint. The fields can include the following information about the recipient: Name, Fax Number, Company, Address, City, State, Zip Code, Country, Title, Department, Office Location, Home and Office Telephone Numbers, To and Cc lists. Except for the last two items (which are taken from the names you put in at the time you send), the other items come from the Address Book entry for the recipient.

Fields can include Name, Fax Number, Company, Title, Department, Office Location, and Home and Office Phone Numbers for the sender. This

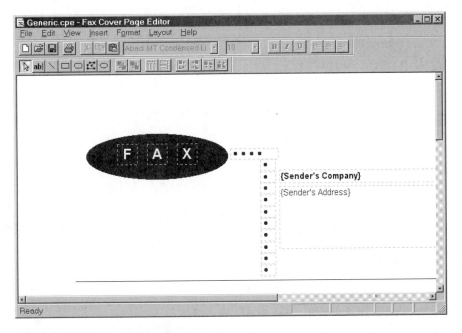

Figure 3-112. Cover Page Editor

information is obtained from what is filled in on the User tab in the fax property sheet. Obviously, if you are making a cover page for your use alone, you can just use your name, and so on, instead of the sender fields, but the fields are useful for cover pages made for workgroups or companies. If such a cover sheet is used, make sure that users fill in their User tab! Finally, you can provide the number of pages (including the cover page) and other message-specific information in fields.

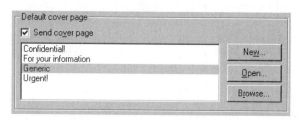

Figure 3-113. Cover me, partner

You get to decide on cover pages in many places. In the Message tab of the fax property sheet, there's a panel (Figure 3-113) that lets you choose whether to send a cover page with faxes composed without the Wizard and which cover page to use. You can change it in Send Options for messages created in the editor. If you use the Create Fax Wizard, you can choose the cover page. Only with this Wizard can you send a single-page fax with cover page including a brief note.

The So-Called Microsoft Fax Printer

E-mail is fax is for the computer savvy.

—The Mother of All Windows 95 Books

 Like Voltaire's bon mot about the Holy Roman Empire, the Microsoft Fax Printer is neither a printer nor is it a fax alone. But it *is* from Microsoft.

 Was Voltaire that guy in the Batman movie who kept shouting, "Holy Roman Empire, Batman"? I wonder how much it would cost to get Batman to use the word Microsoft instead of holy?

When you install the fax software, it installs a "printer" called Microsoft Fax. From a program that prints, you can tell it to print to this printer. It will then call up the Fax Wizard and help you send out a fax with the output from the program. You can add a cover page and include a note on the cover page.

 Oh, I get it. If you pick "Microsoft Fax" as your printer, and print from an application, then the file is faxed—it's sorta using the other guy's fax machine as a remote printer. Cool.

 If you just install the software from the installation disk, the Send menu items you find in lots of programs won't work. You need instead to use the Fax Printer.

Windows Secret File Transfer Program

Happens to me all the time. Someone needs to get a file to me urgently and I'm on the Internet while they are on AOL and they ask if we can't try a direct modem hookup. So I call up ProComm and go to host mode. Depending on their modem, it can go smoothly or roughly, but more often than not, we wind up having to try multiple Xmodem, Kermit, yeechy binary protocols. And its not only the hassle—I'm not happy that someone I don't know well gets some kind of direct access to my disk. So one of my favorite Windows 9X secrets is the really neat direct modem transfer that is built in.

Figure 3-114. Editable? Wazzat?

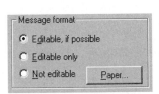

One of the reasons it is a secret is that it's not in networking where you'll find talk of direct cable connection and Dial-Up Networking, subjects I discuss in the next chapter. Rather, it's part of faxing!! The key is the panel in Figure 3-114 (part of the Message tab in the Fax Properties dialog) and the difference between editable and noneditable formats. Editable format is just a name for sending files instead of the usual bitmaps that fax machines use. If you pick "Editable only" or "Editable, if possible" and the Windows Fax software finds Windows Fax software on the receiving end, then instead of a fax bitmap, Windows sends a binary file.

Sending a fax in an editable format has three huge advantages. The first advantage involves the amount of data sent over the phone line. As a trial I sent the same seven-page Word document—straight text with a little formatting—between the same two Windows 9X machines with fax modem, but in one case I marked the message as "Not editable," forcing the file to be sent as a fax bitmap. I had the "paper" option set to "Best available," so it was sent as 300 dpi. The fax bitmap was 282 KB while the editable version was 27 KB. Not surprisingly, it took about ten times as long to send the fax bitmap.

The second advantage concerns text messages that are, er, editable, when sent in editable format. If you've prepared a message in Word, it'll arrive as a Word file with all its formatting and the text in a format that can be manipulated. To do that with a bitmap fax you'd need OCR and have some rate of errors.

The third advantage is that if editable format is chosen binary files can be sent. If someone who has Windows 9X wants to send you a bunch of files and you both have fax modems, have them zip them up using PKZIP or WinZip, have them address a fax message to you and drag the Zip into the message. Then you need to turn on fax autoanswer (manual is fine) and they phone you. The transfer is painless and rather quick given one restriction—even if your modems support higher speeds as modems, as faxes they will probably be limited to 9600 bps. In a test, it took almost exactly 3 minutes to transfer a 187-KB file, close to maximum efficiency for 9600 bps.

Believe it or not, Windows 98 offers some heavy-duty security options for binary fax transfers. Go to the Tools\Microsoft Fax Tools\Advanced Security . . . dialog. There are passwords, encryption, public key RSA encryption, digital signatures—the whole nine yards. In fact, one could say nine times nine yards. I didn't test any of this.

This is triply bizarre! Why is Microsoft putting RSA encryption—something sure to raise the hackles of the government snoops—into Windows 98, which is in part a consumer product? Why is there such heavy-duty stuff in a system whose password protection is so light, it can be overcome if you hit **Esc** at the login prompt? And, if Messaging is going to offer encryption, why of binary fax and not e-mail? Truly bizarre.

■ Helping Those Who Help Themselves

Historically, we've focused on documenting our products—that is, explaining how they work. . . . This motivated us to rethink our approach . . . . We realize that you have a job to do; you need to get from point A to point B. Our job is to provide you with a "map" and steer you in the right direction so that you can get there as quickly and efficiently as possible.

—PETE HIGGINS, Microsoft Group Vice President,
in *What Have We Done to Your Manual,*
an introduction to the Office 95 printed documentation

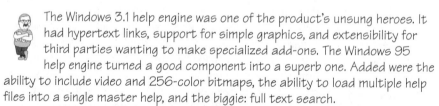 The Windows 3.1 help engine was one of the product's unsung heroes. It had hypertext links, support for simple graphics, and extensibility for third parties wanting to make specialized add-ons. The Windows 95 help engine turned a good component into a superb one. Added were the ability to include video and 256-color bitmaps, the ability to load multiple help files into a single master help, and the biggie: full text search.

Windows 98 has added an HTML-based help engine that Windows itself uses and that third parties are being encouraged to use. The shift will no doubt take some time, so it's worth talking about old-fashioned (Windows 95) help. I've got to agree that the Win95 help engine is a work of art—kudos to the help team, which, according to rumor, was a single, obviously smart programmer. But the Windows Help itself makes me very unhappy. There is a trend in all the help and documentation from Microsoft to task-based user assistance. The philosophy, as enunciated in the quote above from Pete Higgins, is to focus on "how-to?" for explicit tasks. This is often useful, but just as often, you find that the task in the Help is subtly different from the one you want to do and you have little recourse since the products don't come, as they used to, with documentation explaining how they work. This task-based frustration is what you'll find through most of the Help system for Windows itself.

Microsoft is a market-driven company. If users don't like this new format or want real documentation besides, they need to let us know loud and clear. We made the change because users complained that they needed task-based help. Besides Microsoft Press offers numerous books to fill in the gaps.

 Bah, humbug. The bottom line on this shift toward task-based help and documentation without any real explanation of how it works is, er, the bottom line. COGs, aka cost of goods, drove this decision. By far the most expensive part of the software packages from Microsoft is the printed documentation. Eliminate that and you save big bucks.

 Besides, think how many bugs were eliminated in one swell foop. It used to be that a user could point out that a program didn't work the way the documentation said it should. Now that there is no documentation to explain how it should work, there can't be as many bugs. Brilliant!

 As a book author, I should be pleased at the opportunities that Microsoft has given not only to Microsoft Press but to the computer book market in general. But I'm not. Users have gotten the shaft. I've no doubt that users have asked for task-based help, but I'm sure they didn't say they wanted it *instead* of real documentation rather than *in addition* to it. That was Microsoft's decision. If COGs are an issue, at least make real documentation available on disk as an option that users can install.

But enough of this philosophy. I first focus on the basics of the Windows 95 help engine that most of your applications will still use, most notably, the options on setting up full text search. Then I talk about less used help features like annotations. Next, I discuss some of the technical ins and outs about what kinds of files are part of the help system. Finally, I say something about HTML-based help.

I focus entirely on the ins and outs of the help engines (and the help files you invoke from the Help menu of applications), but you should be aware of and use the little **?** box in the upper right corner of the dialog boxes of most Windows 98 components and Windows 9X applications. It produces a **What's This?** mouse cursor—press that cursor on a part of the dialog box and a popup panel appears explaining what the component is. Some applications have a What's This? command if you right click on an object—you get a little help panel there. An example is the Windows Calculator.

Help Basics

. . . most programs are like Verdi operas. They communicate in a foreign language and require reading notes in advance to have any idea of what is happening.

—PAUL HECKEL

When you start up a Help file in stand-alone mode, one of four things is displayed.

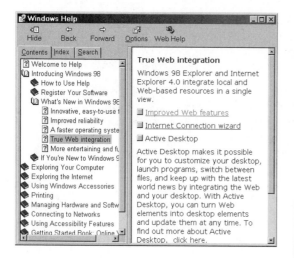
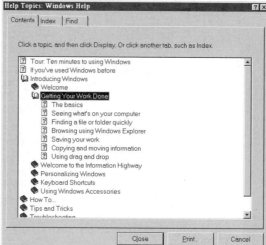

Figure 3-115. A tale of two Helps

1. If it is a Help made for the new IE4/Win98 engine, then you get a browser window like that shown at the left of Figure 3-115. There are three tabs shown as in the figure: Contents, Index, and Search.

2. If it is a Help file made for Windows 95 and it has a contents file, the Help Topics Window appears either with the Contents tab displayed (as at the right of Figure 3-115). There are three tabs shown as in the figure: Contents, Index, and Find.

 Notice that from Windows 95 Help to HTML Help, they changed "Find" to "Search." One wonders how many dollars of research went into a decision like that. You'd think they'd spend their time on more substantial issues.

 You'd think you'd spend your book space on more substantial issues!

3. If it is a Help file made for Windows 95 and there is no contents file (or one didn't get properly copied to your hard disk), the Help Topics Index tab is displayed (There are only two tabs, Index and Find).

4. If it is a Windows 3.1 Help file, the opening page of that file, often contents in the help window, is displayed. But you can get to a Help Topics window with Index and Find tabs by hitting the Search button on the Windows 3.1 Help window. One of the neat things about the Windows 95 help engine is that it adds full text search to Windows 3.1 Help files! A Windows 95 help system can be written so that the initial display is also a specific opening page for the Help file rather than the Index tab. If the Help author wants, by

doing that and not providing Help Topics, Index, Find or Search buttons, you can be locked out of doing a full text search.

 To avoid puzzlement, let me emphasize that I use the phrase "Windows 95 Help" to refer to any help system that uses the engine that was introduced with Windows 95. Of course, I'm not referring to the actual Help file that shipped with Windows 95 and that told you about Windows 95 itself.

If you access Help from within a program, it will either display the same initial window as if you ran stand-alone Help, or, if the Help is context sensitive, you'll get a Help window specific to the situation. That window should have a button called Search or Index that will take you to the main Help Topics screen. If there is a Contents button and if it is a Help file written for Windows 95, that button should also go to Help Topics. If you get the idea that Help Topics is the cockpit for accessing help features, you are right.

Contents, whether in Windows 95 or browser Help has a collapsible outline form—books indicate nodes that have subtopics and ? pages show topics you can open. Index lists the topics under keywords chosen by the author of the Help system. If the Help file is well made, the index and subindex topics are invaluable. The Search/Find tab is where you can search on individual words and phrases. You shouldn't assume that every Help Topic is accessible through the Contents—some can be accessed only through the other tabs.

 One difference between Windows 95 Help and HTML Help is that the help author can customize the icons used in the Contents pane, so you may not always see the closed and open books.

 The other big difference from a user perspective is the two-pane mode with synchronization between the topic chosen at the left and detailed help shown at the right.

 Because the Help panel is a full-fledged HTML page, it allows Active X controls, so the array of tools available for Web pages is also available for Help, which should lead to both some wonderful and some terribly gauche help systems. In fact, HTML Help is provided via an ActiveX control (**hhctrl.ocx**). As I explain later, you can call up Help with a wrapper program (**hh.exe**), and programs themselves can invoke the ActiveX control and avoid running a separate program. When this happens, you have the advantage that minimizing a program also minimizes its Help window.

The indices of HTML Help systems are normally precompiled and included with the Help file. Windows 95 Help systems need to have their indices and other extra files generated on your hard disk.

Before you can do a full text search on a Win 95 Help file, the help engine needs to make an index and save it to disk. The first time you access the Find tab, you invoke the Find Setup Wizard (Figure 3-116). If you want to change

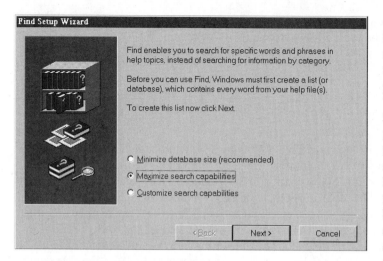

Figure 3-116. Find Setup Wizard

options, you can invoke it again by hitting the Rebuild . . . button on that tab. To illustrate the options and the sizes of the indices produced, let's consider the main Windows 95 Help, the one that is invoked when you pick Help from the Start Menu. It illustrates another feature of the Windows 95 help engine—it was built not from a single help but from 11 files totaling 1,071,163 bytes, namely `31users.hlp`, `access.hlp`, `common.hlp`, `expo.hlp`, `license.hlp`, `mouse.hlp`, `network.hlp`, `overview.hlp`, `server.hlp`, `windows.hlp`, and `winhlp32.hlp`. If they were present, several other Help files were added, including `plus!.hlp` (for the Plus! Pack), `oem.hlp` (for computer maker-specific help), and `pen.hlp` for pen-based machines.

 It seems to me to make sense to use the standard Windows 95 Help file as a benchmark even if you do want to compare it with some third-party program because I've no idea which third-party program you want to compare it with.

Returning to full text search, when you start the process of indexing (Figure 3-116) you have to make one of three choices: "Minimize database size," "Maximize search capabilities," and "Customize search capabilities." Windows recommends the first, but MOM recommends the second, if you have the disk space. What's the difference? I thought you'd never ask.

As a preliminary, you need to know that Help files are divided into topics—each panel or popup window is a separate topic. Some topics are assigned titles and some, which are usually accessed indirectly, are not. What fraction of topics have titles is a function of the Help file, but most files have mainly titled topics. If you choose "Minimize database size," then only topics with titles are indexed and all that is indexed is the individual words, not their position in the topic, so you cannot search on phrases. If you pick "Maximize search capabilities," then still only titled topics are included but three other capabilities are added:

1. You can search on phrases, that is, sequences of words in the exact order you type them.

2. You can have matching phrases typed in as you look for them.

3. You can turn on a Find Similar feature (described in a moment).

"Customize search capabilities" lets you choose which Help files are indexed for cases where there are multiple files (normally all of them are), pick which of the three extras just mentioned is included, and include untitled topics that then appear in lists as "Untitled topic #1," and so on.

 Except . . . except . . . there is this one buggy. If you have built the "Maximize search capabilities" index and then choose Rebuild . . . and pick all options including untitled topics, the help engine decides "Been there, done that," doesn't rebuild, so doesn't pick up the untitled topics. Oh, how I love a nice bug in the morning.

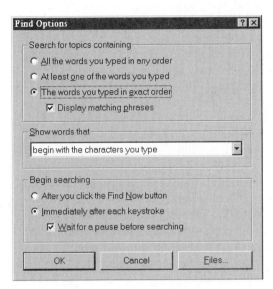

Figure 3-117. Find Options dialog

If you hit the Options . . . button, you get the dialog in Figure 3-117. The option currently chosen in the first group, viz. **"The words you typed in the exact order"** is not available if you chose the minimum option or customized and didn't choose to include phrase matching. The "Display matching phrases" check box is there because Windows claims that slow machines are even slower if "Displays matching phrases" is turned on.

It is important to note that unless you choose the "exact order" radio button in Options (and it is not the default!), typing in several words will start a search for those words in any location in the topic. The Files . . . button option on this dialog is another place to exclude files that would otherwise be included.

The Find tab indicates the current options in a text box just over the buttons; the first word, which is All, One+, or Phrase, indicates the first set of radio buttons.

If Find Similar . . . is turned on, and it is with the maximum choice I recommend, then each topic has a check box next to it. Check one or more of the topics and hit the Find Similar . . . button, and a list pops up of those topics with significant word overlap with the checked topics.

I did some tests on sizes. Recall that the combined `.hlp` files that make up the main Windows Help are about 1.1 MB. When I choose the Minimize Size option, the index files total 470 KB. The Maximize Capabilities option comes to 1.5 MB, and when untitled topics are included the index files are a whopping 2.9 MB. Even on a 486/66, it took only 30 seconds to make the index itself.

 If you pick the maximize option for a given Help file, be sure to go into Options . . . and check the "exact words" radio button.

Esoteric Win95 Help

What do *girls do who haven't any mothers to help them through their troubles?*

—Jo March, in Louisa May Alcott's *Little Women*

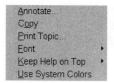

Figure 3-118. Topic context menu

Many of the Win95 Help extras involve the context menu (Figure 3-118) that pops up inside any individual topic (but not inside the main Help Topics window where there is no useful context menu). The menu is also accessible from the Options button in Windows 95 Help files. This menu pops up in Help files written for both Windows 95 and Windows 3.1. The Annotate . . . choice was an underused goody in Windows 3.1 Help. With it users can add comments and notes to any Help page. The page then shows a paper clip icon in the corner. Clicking on the paper clip brings back the comment.

Copy copies the selected text (or the whole topic if nothing is selected) to the clipboard. Print Topic . . . lets you print only an entire topic—not a selection—but it does let you choose which printer. While help authors can choose their own fonts, most help systems use default fonts. Despite what you might hope, the Font menu doesn't let you choose which font. The default font seems to be MS Sans Serif, a bitmapped (not TrueType) font included with Windows. There are three choices—large (10 point), medium (8 point), and small (8-point but with less leading). Keep Help on Top has three options—the default has the status determined by the help author who can specify some topic panels to keep on top and others not to. You can override this setting and globally determine what happens—for that particular Help file. The last item determines whether the Help Topic windows use the default color—motley-looking dithered yellow polka dots on white (yuck)—or the same color used by the system for the windows backgrounds. You can change the latter color in the Appearance tab of Display Properties by changing the Item to Window.

 The weird thing is that this Use System Colors choice is absent if you run with more than 256 colors. I guess big Bill's interior decorator must have approved the color that appears if a system has 64 K colors but then saw the color used when you have only 256 colors and exclaimed, "Yuck, you must give them a way to change it." Weirder still, there were undocumented but well-known ways to change the colors used by Windows 3.1 Help, but I haven't found in the Registry anything you can do for Windows 95 Help.

 Speaking of the Registry, I'm not sure the author of Windows 95 Help knows about it. Every bloody one of the context menus options is stored in the configuration file (**.gid**) for that help system and holds only for that system. There is no way to change the defaults used by all Help systems. Boo, hiss!

 Oy. It's two steps forward but one step back. If you run a Windows 3.1 help system under Windows 95, it uses the Help Topics dialog in place of the old Search. Otherwise, it uses the Windows 3.1 windows, which included two invaluable menu items that are no longer automatically included in Windows 95 help systems—indeed both are absent from the Help you invoke from the Start Menu! You could open a history window and look at where you've been and easily return. You could put a bookmark on any topic and later return there. But now Windows 95 Help seems to say, "Menus? We don't need no steenking menus," and those options are gone. Sigh.

Win95 Help Under the Covers

Self-help books are making life downright unsafe. Women desperate to catch a man practice all the ploys recommended by these authors. Bump into him, trip over him, knock him down, spill something on him, scald him, but meet *him.*

—FLORENCE KING, *Reflections in a Jaundiced Eye*

 Help under the covers!!! I knew it, I knew it. I knew you guys would figure out some way to bring Monica into this. This book has a mother on the cover, so it can pretend to be family fare. But the truth comes out, doesn't it?

 But Bill, didn't the Microsoft Network announce it would have adults-only areas? What's that? Chopped liver?

 Hey, that's entirely different. We have customers who want to pay for that stuff. Don't you want us to take their money? Don't we owe it to our stockholders to take their money? 'Course, we'll mark it so parents can keep kids out.

 The section title is there because I'm going to tell you some of the technical stuff behind Windows Help. But don't necessarily run away. I'll also tell you how you can combine several Help files into one with a common index and full text search, all by yourself.

Normally vendors ship two kinds of files for their Win95 help systems and Windows Help makes up to five more. Here's the lowdown.

Extension	Location	Purpose and Comments
`.hlp`	Home directory	Basic Help file(s)
`.cnt`	Home directory	Contents file in ASCII format
`.gid`	Home or Help directory but hidden	Help configuration file. Stores information such as which tab was active when the user last quit.
`.fts`	Home or Help directory	Index for full text search
`.ftg`	Home or Help directory	Information for FTS groups
`.ann`	`C:\windows\help`	Annotations are saved here.
`.bmk`	`C:\windows\winhlp32.bmk`	Bookmarks are saved here.

The basic files have the extension `.hlp`—they are documents associated with the executable file `winhlp32.exe` in the `C:\windows` directory. Help files written for Windows 95 should also have a contents file with the extension `.cnt`. If this file is missing, then when you start the Help file you'll get the Help Topics dialog with the Contents tab missing. If you run a Windows 3.x Help file, it normally has a contents built into the file, and that's what you see when you start up—as a separate panel, not as a part of Help Topics. Windows 3.x Help files do not have a separate `.cnt` file.

As we'll see, the Contents tab is built from the `.cnt` file. Normally, these are the only two files shipped with a help system. Up to three additional files are built during the basic help operations. They are normally put in the same directory as the `.hlp` and `.cnt` files—I call this the home directory in the table. If Windows can't put the files there, for example if you run a Help file from a CD or from a network drive where you don't have write privileges, then these files are put in `C:\windows\help`—which I call the help directory in the table.

The first time you run a Help file, you may see a message that Windows is preparing to run the Help file for the first time. What it is doing is making the `.gid` (the *Help Author's Guide*—the official documentation for help writers—is silent on what the letters GID stand for) file, which contains the following information.

- Binary representation of the `.cnt` file. This allows for faster loading and means that if you delete a `.cnt` file after running Help the first time, the Contents tab is still displayed.

- Names of all Help files referenced in the master `.cnt` file—as we'll see, a single running of Help can load multiple Help files.

- List of all the keywords for quicker loading of the Index tab.

- List of associated `.fts` and `.ftg` files

- Size and location of any other files, such as video or special dialog boxes, called by the Help file.

 It's the `.gid` file that allows for quick loading of the Contents and Index tabs. But that means that if you install a new version of the basic `.hlp` file without the `.gid` being updated, you won't have access to the new topics! When a program installs a new version of Help, it is supposed to regenerate the `.gid` file, but if it seems as if you can't get help on the new features in a new version of a program, the problem may be that the updating wasn't done. If you suspect that, just delete the `.gid` file. It will be regenerated the first time you run the corresponding Help file.

 You may think that because the information in it is stored in the `.gid` file, you can delete the `.cnt` file once the `.gid` is made. But that's dangerous if you ever need to regenerate the `.gid`. The `.cnt` files are small, so I say leave 'em where they are.

When you generate a full text search index, it is stored as a `.fts` file in the home directory, or, if that is unavailable, in `C:\windows\help`. Similarly, if you generate an index from a help system built from multiple `.hlp` files, an extra `.ftg` file is built.

Any annotations you make for a given Help file, say one called **name.hlp**, are stored not in the home directory but always in `C:\windows\help` in a binary file called **name.ann**. Bookmarks for all help files are stored in a single file **winhlp32.bmk** stored in `C:\windows`.

 Assuming you have Office 97, open up Explorer, go to the main Office folder (probably `C:\program files\microsoft office\office`), find **ppmain8.cnt**, and double click on it. In the Open With dialog, choose Notepad. Make sure that "Always use this program to open this type of file" is checked because `.cnt` files are text and you'll want to use Notepad. You'll see a text file that gives you considerable insight into how Windows 95 help can build help systems based on multiple `.hlp` files.

When you first look at **ppmain8.cnt**, skip past the lines that start with a `:`. You'll see a bunch of lines with numbers. They correspond precisely to the levels in the Contents tab you'll see if you pick Help from the PowerPoint menus.

Two of those lines with colons in front will concern us. `:Index` lets you add extra Help files to the Index and Find tabs and `:Include` lets you add extra entries to the Contents tab. Search through the file looking for `:Index` lines. `:Include` lines insert subsidiary contents entries into the middle of Contents.

You can use these lines to make your own combined Help files. For example, suppose you want to take two Help files and make a single combined one. You'll need to be sure the four basic files, call them **file1.hlp**, **file1.cnt**, **file2.cnt**, and **file2.hlp** are in a single directory. Load **file1.cnt** into Notepad and add the following line before the first entry without a `:` in front:

```
:Index My Help file=file2.hlp
```

and add

```
:Include file2.cnt
```

at the very end.

Now if you double click on **file1.hlp**, you'll get a contents pane that includes both of the Help files.

Beyond the Basics of HTML Help

HTML Help gives you much less control over configuration (although the help author gets more!), so there is a lot less to say about it than about Windows 95 help. The basic files in which help is kept have the extension `.chm` for compiled HTML file. The author gets to put together HTML pages, associated graphics files, index, and contents in a single Compiled and compressed binary file.

Most programs call up their `.chm` file directly, but if you ever want to start one independently of an underlying program, you can double click on it. The extension is associated with the program `C:\windows\hh.exe`. You could also use the Run box, typing in `hh <name of file>`, for example `hh C:\windows\help\windows.chm`.

The author can choose to make linked `.chm` files that in reality call several `.chm` files analogously to what a Windows 95 Help system can do. If you access the Index tab of such a `.chm` file the first time, it makes a combined index and stores it in a `.chw` file. For example, you will have an `iexplore.chw` file in your `C:\windows\help` directory if you ever accessed the index tab in help for IE4.

Chapter 4

Applets, Utilities, and More

PCs are the world's greatest medium for futzing around. They're computational catnip for obsessives, keyboard crack for neurotics, and seductive time sinks for ordinary folks who just want to make sure that they've reasonably examined all their options. Why do you think we call them "users"?

—MICHAEL SCHRAGE

 In this chapter, I cover all the parts of Windows 98 that didn't make it into the last chapter. The high points are the networking, the Internet components, and the new disk, scheduling and system information utilities. I faced a difficult decision on how to handle Plus! 98 which was built by the Windows team but isn't exactly part of Windows. It's a lot less essential than the Win95 Plus! Pack was, so I've banished it to Chapter 5. Similarly, I had a hard decision on the Windows Resource Kit Sampler, which ships on the Windows CD. I decided that it belongs with the full WRK in Chapter 5.

 Mom exaggerates when she says that all the parts of Windows 98 not covered earlier are here. Certain techie utilities come in the later, more technical chapters. Notable are the Control Panel applets in Chapter 8 and ScanReg in Chapter 9.

 Because of a certain logic, we've put the WRK Sampler in Chapter 5, but I want to be sure you don't miss it. You might think having sprung close to a hundred bucks for Windows 98 and a bit more for this book, you don't want to spend any more so you skip Chapter 5. But the Sampler is included on the Windows 98 CD you already have. In particular, you most definitely want to check out Tweak UI (discussed in detail in Chapter 8) and Microsoft File Information (MFI) (discussed in detail in Chapter 7).

 It's crazy. These tools are so essential they should have been automatically installed instead of hidden away. To make things worse, Tweak UI is mentioned in the WRK Sampler Readme file but isn't installed by SetUp (you have to install it separately—see Chapter 6) while MFI is installed by SetUp but isn't mentioned in the readme file.

■ Disk 'n Dat

It is a capital mistake to theorize before one has data.

—Sir Arthur Conan Doyle,
The Adventures of Sherlock Holmes

 In order to understand the function of Windows disk tools, you need to know a little bit about the system that DOS and Windows use to organize data on disk. For the full lowdown, you can read *The Mother of All PC Books*. Here's a brief summary.

Files are allocated space in units called **clusters** (ScanDisk calls them **allocation units**). A FAT16 disk is limited to 64 K of clusters while FAT32 can have a gazillion (well, up to 4 billion). Cluster size can be as small as 512 bytes (that's what it is on a diskette) and is always a power of two times this basic ½-KB unit. So cluster sizes are ½, 1, 2, 4, 8, 16, or 32 KB. You can find cluster size on FAT16 disks by dividing the size by 64 K and rounding up to the next possible cluster size. Thus, a 1-GB FAT16 disk will have 16-KB clusters but disks between 1 GB and 2 GB have 32-KB clusters. The maximum drive size supported by FAT16 is thus 2 GB = 64 K clusters × 32 KB/cluster. Above that, under FAT16, you must partition disks into multiple drives. FAT32 uses 4-KB clusters, at least if your disk is no more than 8 GB.

The operating system keeps a database called the **File Allocation Table**, aka **FAT,** of clusters. For each cluster, this database indicates one of three things:

- The cluster is not in use and can be assigned to a file if needed.
- The cluster is the final cluster in a file.
- The cluster is in use by a file, in which case the number of the next cluster in the file is indicated.

The directory entry for a file indicates the first cluster in the file. Then the FAT entries let the operating system successively figure out all the clusters in a file and their order. Notice that the clusters in a file need not be consecutive. This is useful—imagine you have a 10-MB file and add a few bytes that make the file need another cluster. If the very next cluster weren't available, the operating system would have to move the full 10-MB file if clusters had to be contiguous.

Of course, as files spread out over the disk in noncontiguous pieces, the drive has to do more to retrieve them and performance can plummet. A file that is in noncontiguous pieces is called "fragmented," and **defragmentation software** rearranges the clusters on which the data live (by physically moving the data) so that files are no longer fragmented.

 Actually, if you think about it, the best order for executable files is not in contiguous pieces. For as an executable loads, it calls other files, like `.dll`s. The ideal is to have the clusters of an executable file and the files it calls interspersed in the precise order that they will be needed. That's the idea behind the new Windows 98 defragmenter.

This idea originated with Intel and was licensed to Microsoft. The interface is essentially the same as that used by Windows 95 (developed by Symantec and Microsoft), so the defragger has copyrighted portions from all three companies.

Most of the logical ills that can befall a disk are sicknesses of the FAT. **Lost** or **orphaned clusters** refer to clusters that the FAT has marked as in use but which are not assigned to any file in any directory on the disk. **Cross-linked files** are situations where more than one file lays claim to the same cluster.

ScanDisk

A computer lets you make more mistakes faster than any other invention in human history, with the exception of handguns and tequila.

—Heard on the net

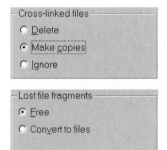

**Figure 4-1.
ScanDisk options**

You'll find the ScanDisk and Disk Defragmenter utilities on the Programs/ Accessories/System Tools menu, but it is probably easier to get them by selecting a drive in Explorer (or My Computer), asking for Properties and going to the Tools tab.

You should consider calling up the Advanced tab in ScanDisk and setting the options as shown in Figure 4-1. For cross-linked files, this makes copies of both files, even though it is certain that at least one of them is wrong. You should also turn on logging and one of the options that reports errors—either "Always" or "Only if errors found" in the Display summary panel—so that if you have a report of cross-linked files, you'll know to check them out. The "Lost file fragments" choice throws the information in the lost clusters away and frees up the clusters as unused.

 No doubt this advice to throw away lost clusters will cause howls in some quarters. I used to carefully save all such clusters to files and check them out, and under normal circumstances I never once found anything of any value whatever in these clusters. Nor has anyone else I know. Notice I said "under normal circumstances." I've had horrendous crashes (in the DOS days before Windows 3.x) that turned a directory into chopped liver. That meant that the lost clusters were associated with real files and saving them as such was invaluable. So, if you pick the Free option, you'll need to be sure to change it if there is a crisis. If you worry that you won't, better set it to "Convert to files" and delete the ones produced under normal circumstances by hand.

 Cross-linked files are a rarity and almost always indicate at least some lost data and perhaps more serious underlying problems. Lost clusters are fairly common, a symptom of some program that didn't properly close a temporary file. They aren't a cause for happiness, but if you get some occasionally with no apparent missing data, they aren't cause for much concern.

Several final remarks about ScanDisk:

1. The executable that runs ScanDisk for Windows is called **scandskw.exe**, not **scandisk.exe**. It resides in your Windows directory.

2. As a tool in case you have a disaster that prevents Windows from running, there is a program called **scandisk.exe** in **C:\windows\command**, which runs outside Windows as a DOS program. If loaded from Windows (whether from the Run box or at a DOS prompt in a DOS session over Windows), it loads **scandskw.exe** and exits. Its an interesting test to load it from the Run box, see a DOS session load, see ScanDisk for Windows pop up over it, and then see the DOS session close. The important thing is to remember that there is this DOS tool if complete disaster does strike.

3. You might consider including **scandskw** in your startup group so that your disk is checked every time you start up. If you do that, you'll be interested in the following command line parameters.

X:	checks drive X; can use multiple drives
/a	checks all drives
/p	reports errors but doesn't correct them
/n	closes ScanDisk when it is done (if there are no errors)

If you fear massive problems, use preview mode first so that you have an idea what you are up against before letting ScanDisk do its thing. In particular, if you have a lot of cross-linked files, you might want to first copy all of them to another medium.

4. If you fail to close down properly, the next time you start, Windows will run ScanDisk automatically on your drives. You can hit **Enter** to exit immediately or **Esc** to get an option to exit.

You might think that you can also use Tweak UI's Boot tab to totally skip this check since it has an option that seems to say you can do that. But it has no effect whatsoever. Windows seems to have hard-coded the desire to run ScanDisk when there is an abnormal shutdown.

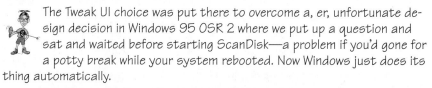
The Tweak UI choice was put there to overcome a, er, unfortunate design decision in Windows 95 OSR 2 where we put up a question and sat and waited before starting ScanDisk—a problem if you'd gone for a potty break while your system rebooted. Now Windows just does its thing automatically.

5. In the **C:\windows\command** directory, you'll find a file called **scandisk.ini** with options for further controlling the behavior of the DOS mode version of ScanDisk. The documentation for this **ini** file is inside the file itself. It affects how Scandisk runs only under DOS, not under Windows.

Oy. Not only is the printed documentation essentially nonexistent but the online help doesn't discuss this. The user is reduced to stumbling on an **.ini** file. And the **.ini** file refers to the OS as Windows 95, not Windows 98! Instead of behaving like a billion-dollar-a-year corporation, Microsoft is acting like a $100,000 garage operation.

You've got that wrong, Barry. The garage operation would have too much pride in its product to pull that kind of shtick.

Defragmenter

Under Windows 95, if you go to Disk Defragmenter from the **Tools** tab of a drive's property sheet and you ask to defragment now, you get a dialog like that at the left in Figure 4-2 that reports on the degree of defragmentation with advice on whether you need to run the program. Under Windows 98, you get the dialog at the right with Intel's name prominently displayed instead of information on how defragmented the drive is.

This is progress? Why the heck don't I get told not to bother to run the defragger?

Yes, Woody, it is progress. Because of our new strategy of defragging based on disk access by actual programs, the old degree of fragmentation isn't the right question to ask if you want to know if you'll gain by defragging. So we just run the defragger. Our idea is that you'll do this all via automatic scheduling using Maintenance Wizard, so this is no big deal.

When you run the program, you get a progress bar like that shown in Figure 4-3. If there is disk activity while this dialog is running, the process will seem to begin all over. But when it does start over, it quickly reads through the part of the disk it defragmented before the interruption. You can see this process in

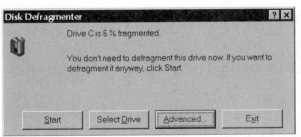

Figure 4-2. A tale of two defraggers

**Figure 4-3.
Defragmenter
running**

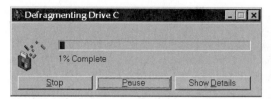

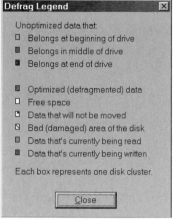

the dialog you bring up by
hitting the Show Details
button. You get a full-screen
display that is lovely to
watch although hard to
understand until you hit
the Legend button to get
an explanation of what is
going on (Figure 4-4). The screen shot in this book is gray scale, but the true
panel is color coded.

**Figure 4-4.
A Legend in its
own time**

You're probably wondering how often to run ScanDisk and Defrag. I'll discuss this when I talk about Maintenance Wizard below.

 Our new defragger really does improve application load times. The magazines report a decrease by a factor of about two. That's a real win for users.

 The new strategy of defragging depends on storing application startup information, which is stored in the directory `C:\windows\applogs`. The files are ASCII—you might open one and take a look. The defragger is storing information on the precise clusters read from disk and successive file opens. Neat!

 Be warned that the defragger is slow on big drives. The initial run on an 8-GB drive with about 3 GB of files took just over four hours! And don't trust the progress bar. It stuck at 10% for close to an hour, after two hours it said it was 10% done and after three hours 40% done, and it zipped to the end at four hours. The moral is to run defragger overnight, not while you sit there.

Aligning Segments and Intelligent Caching

A child of five would understand this. Send someone to fetch a child of five.

—Groucho Marx

Another disk-related improvement in Windows 98 concerns more intelligent disk caching. You don't need to do anything to benefit from this feature, so you can skip this section unless you want to understand the neat innovation you're getting when you install Win98.

Disk caching improves performance by keeping recently accessed disk data in RAM. Because RAM access is typically hundreds to thousands of times faster than disk access, this can make a big difference. Prior to Windows 98, the cache memory was used to store data for reuse but the data was not directly accessed from there. So the first time you loaded Word, Windows copied it from disk to cache and then from cache to the place in memory the program was run from. If you exited from Word and later reloaded Word while it was still in the cache from the prior use, Windows would happily just copy the code from the cache to the working area of memory.

You'll notice that with this scheme two copies of the Word code wind up in memory—one in the cache and one in the working set, the place it is actually run from. The new scheme involves using the copy in the cache to run from when possible. That means less copying from memory to memory and more important, less RAM usage. Less RAM usage means less disk swapping and improved performance.

 Our tests show that the RAM usage of Word is cut by close to 50%!

 There is, however, one small gotcha when it says, "Using the copy in the cache to run from when possible." The "when possible" indicates that it is only sometimes possible, and understanding that involves some background.

Windows executables are built in separate modules that are stored inside the **.exe** file as what are called **segments**. One segment of the file contains a road map to the other segments, including their locations within the file and which segments need to be loaded into memory initially.

Development packages that let programmers make **.exe** files have a linker that actually puts the modules together and sets up the list of the segment addresses. In doing so, the linker has to decide on what to use as a segment alignment size. Segments have to start at an integral multiple of an alignment size. This size has to be a power of two times 512 bytes, that is, 512, 1024, 2048, 4096. . . . Once the segment alignment size is picked, the linker pads all the segments to be an integral multiple of this size before packing the segment away.

Developers can set the segment alignment size but tend to use the default set by the maker of the programming tools. Traditionally, with disk space an issue, the segment alignment size was taken to be 512 bytes so that there would be as little padding as possible, and that was the old default.

But from the 386 onward, the RAM controlled by Intel CPUs organizes memory into 4-KB pages. Segments of running programs must start at an integral multiple of 4 KB. The cache has an exact image of the program on disk. If its segments are aligned on 4-KB boundaries, the program can be run from the copy in cache, but if not, the segments in the program have to be copied so that they each start on a 4-KB boundary.

So the new scheme works only with executables linked to have their segment alignment size set at 4 KB.

This is sooo cool. All we have to do is convince the leading programming tools maker to set the default segment alignment size to 4 KB and then convince the leading application maker not to change it.

But Billy, you are the leading programming tools maker and the leading application maker.

Oh, yeah. I've been told to stop thinking like that in case Janet subpoenas my brain waves.

In fact, Microsoft has set the defaults for segment alignment size in its C++ and other programming tools to 4 KB for some time, so quite a few programs are out there that can use the new scheme and new versions certainly will. Moreover, all the Windows `.dll` and `.exe` files use 4-KB segment alignment size.

The Windows Resource Kit includes a program called Winalign, which goes out to your disk and relinks all the executables to repad them to a segment alignment size of 4 KB so that all your executables can take advantage of the new scheme.

Take my advice. Don't even think about using this utility. Sure, any properly written program doesn't use absolute locations and the relinking should work, but the potential hassle when it doesn't is too great. Many of your programs will already be probably aligned, and let the others be fixed as you upgrade them.

Ha. It appears that Windows automatically install a Winalign task into the scheduler and schedules it to run once a month so Microsoft thinks it is safe. Maybe they are right.

There is one serious glitch caused by the fact that Windows restructures executable files. Patches for such files depend on the exact form of the executable file and they normally refuse to run if the executable file has changed. This is true for example of the so-called SR1 bug fix for Microsoft Office 97. The version you download from the web patches the Office files—it refuses to run on a Windows 98 system that has had Office files for a few days since Windows will have changed the files during that time.

Oy. That's yet another reason to avoid the online patch and get the full CD version that you can sometimes get for free from Microsoft.

One last remark on the 4 KB number. Presumably the default 4-KB cluster size that FAT32 uses for its cluster size (for disks below 8 GB in size) is chosen in part because of this 4-KB page size.

DriveSpace

Space isn't remote at all. It's only an hour's drive
away if your car could go straight upwards.

—FRED HOYLE, *London Observer*, September 9, 1979

FAT32 doesn't support disk compression, so only if you are still using FAT16 (or you want to use compressed diskettes) is DriveSpace relevant. Feel free to skip this section.

Disk compression is the closest thing the computer world has to a free lunch.

- The compression built into the operating system is best of breed.
- When running in Windows or DOS sessions over Windows, the memory cost of loading the software to handle compressed drives is negligible. If you have to use DOS Exclusive mode often, that isn't true, although you may be able to load the necessary drivers in UMB space.
- Processor speeds are now fast enough that there is virtually no performance penalty.
- The technology is now mature enough and tested enough that even many of us who were nervous with it early on are now quite comfortable with it.

 I don't agree with that assessment of performance penalty, at least with slower hard disks and very large files. My portable had a Pentium 100 and a 750-MB hard disk, which I doubled with the Windows 95 Plus! Pack (essentially the compression software included with Windows 98). I copied my 100-MB mail file to the portable. It took Outlook five minutes to open. I'm sure the decompression was the problem. It made the portable almost unusable for its main function—collecting mail.

 So did you drop the disk doubling?

 Nope, I got a new portable with larger hard disk, which, of course, is set to use FAT32, so I couldn't even think of disk doubling.

DriveSpace does its magic in using two tricks. First, behind the scenes, it allocates space to files in 512-byte sectors instead of clusters, which, as I explained earlier in the chapter, are (under FAT16)

256-MB to 512-MB hard drive	8-KB clusters
512-MB to 1-GB hard drive	16-KB clusters
1-GB to 2-GB hard drive	32-KB clusters

That means that a 768-byte icon file suddenly takes only 1 KB of space instead of 8 to 32 KB. Second, it uses a compression scheme based on the fact that bit patterns tend to repeat in files. The bottom line is that you should expect Drive-Space 3 to compress by a factor of about 2.5 if you choose the option that heavily compresses (at some performance cost).

An element of the magic is that the original drive becomes a host and the compressed drive appears as a huge file on the host. The compressed drive then acts as a virtual new drive. The operating system, in a masterful sleight of hand, then remaps the host to a new letter so that the compressed drive can take over the old drive letter. For example, you might have an uncompressed drive C on a portable. After the compression, what was drive C becomes drive D and the compressed drive is called C. From the user's point of view, D is irrelevant and may even get hidden; the drive that files are put on is still called C.

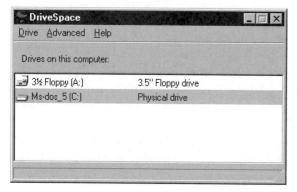

Figure 4-5. DriveSpace drive list

To compress a drive, you run DriveSpace from the Programs\Accessories\System Tools menu. The dialog that results (Figure 4-5) lets you choose a drive. If you then pick Compress from the Drive menu, it will offer to totally compress the drive. Another option is to only compress the free space on the drive to make a new compressed drive. You do that via Create Empty on the Advanced menu.

 I remind you that if you try to compress a FAT32 drive, all you get is a "No can do" error message.

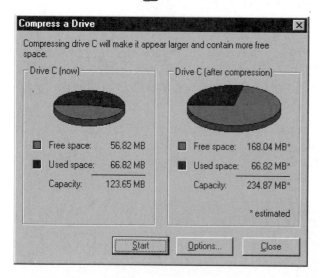

Figure 4-6. Compression before and after

If you go the File/Compress route, you are shown the current situation and estimates after the compression (Figure 4-6). The amount of free space afterward can be only an estimate because until you actually place files there, it cannot be known how effectively they can be compressed. You should at least look at the compression options dialog (Figure 4-7). It lets you determine to what letter the old host drive will remap. Normally, you'd take the choice made by the system (a complex algorithm), but you might choose to bump it higher if, for example, you planned to install a CD-ROM drive soon and wanted it to get the next letter.

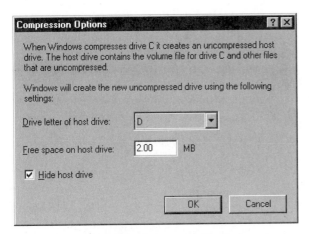

Figure 4-7. DriveSpace Compression Options

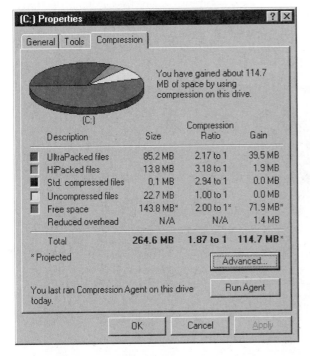

Figure 4-8. Compression tab

After you pick Start, Windows will reboot to a special mode. It can take several hours to do the initial compression, but it is a one-time operation.

DriveSpace 3 supports drives up to only 2 GB after compression (which means you'll need to create two drives if your uncompressed drive is over about 800 MB!). But if your drive is over 800 MB, you should probably be going the FAT32 route.

DriveSpace 3 supports two special compression schemes—HiPacked and UltraPacked. It doesn't automatically use them because there is a small performance penalty when accessing such compressed files and the compression times are lengthy. Indeed, on-the-fly compression of new files is always in Standard mode; the special modes require special processing. You get to pick these special modes in one of two ways. When using DriveSpace 3, the property sheet for a compressed drive picks up an extra tab called Compression (Figure 4-8). You can call the Compression Agent from here to change to better modes, or you can schedule the Compression Agent to do it overnight using Task Scheduler. You'll find the default choices on when to use which type of compression quite reasonable, although you can adjust them through the Advanced . . . button.

You can also compress floppy disks with DriveSpace 3. Even with DriveSpace 3, you can compress a floppy with DriveSpace only. You'll want to do that if you are sending the floppy to someone who has Windows 95 without the Plus! pack. You can configure DriveSpace (through the Advanced/Settings . . . menu item) to automatically read compressed floppies—and there is no reason you wouldn't want to once you are using disk compression.

If you use DriveSpace, Windows will copy **drvspace.bin** from **C:\windows\command** to the root directory twice, once as **drvspace.bin** and once as **dblspace.bin**. There are two copies there for compatibility with prior versions of DOS. These files provide access to the compressed drives only until Windows 98 itself loads. Then a protect mode driver called **drvspacx.vxd** in

`C:\windows\system\iosubsys` takes over. There is a file in the root directory called `dblspace.ini`, but it does not seem to be documented anywhere.

`Drvspace.sys` (or its copy `dblspace.sys`) is used only to move the Real mode driver into UMB space and is useful only for MS-DOS Exclusive mode (I discuss it in Chapter 3). The Resource Kit documents a lot of command line switches you can use with the Windows application `drvspace.exe`, which is run from the Start Menu.

 One warning. If you decide to look at the host drive, you'll find a huge hidden file there with extension `.cvf` (Compressed Volume File). That's your compressed drive. Fool with that file at your extreme peril.

Backup

Let's have the Union restored as it was, if we can;
but if we can't, I'm in favor of the Union as it wasn't.

—ARTEMUS WARD, *Artemus Ward: His Travels*

By the standard of previous DOS backup programs, the one that comes with Windows 98 is heaven—and it looks pretty good, too (Figure 4-9). DOS

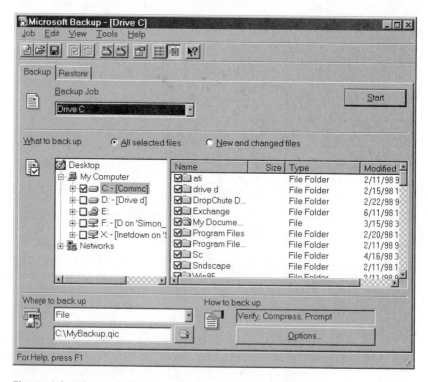

Figure 4-9. Microsoft Backup

Backup between the different DOS versions was incompatible, and until DOS 6 the command line interface was for the birds. And even when a decent interface was added in DOS 6 (by licensing the program from Symantec, makers of Norton Backup!), it supported backup only to floppies. Windows 95 Backup was a vast improvement, but it supported backup only to disk and QIC tapes and was limited in its ability to save named backups. Microsoft Backup, licensed from Seagate, is really wondrous, with one very big gotcha: you can't schedule totally unattended backups. That means it's virtually useless to schedule backups with Task Scheduler unless it's at a time you'll be there to get the process started.

 Whoa. You mean the one task people would most want to schedule can't be done, at least with the built-in Backup program? Crazy.

 Hey, Seagate had to hold something back to get folks to buy their full-fledged product, didn't they?

Some pointers on getting the most from the program:

- The wizards are well done but its as easy to set things up by hand as long as you know to go to the Options dialog (**Job/Options** in the menu or there is a button at the lower right). Even if you use the wizard, be sure to check out the options, which gives you more choices.

- Not all installs include Backup. You may need to run the Add/Remove Programs applet in Control Panel, go to the Windows Setup tab, and click on System Tools to add Backup.

- The program supports a large variety of backup media including DAT, QIC-80, and removable media like Jaz and SyQuest cartridges. QIC-40 is not supported.

- Since no command line parameters work, there is no way to use Backup with Task Scheduler short of writing a VB Script to pick the right menu and dialog options for you.

- You can restore Windows 95 backups but not those DOS backups.

 But by far the most important pointer about backing up is to do it! And often. It isn't a question of whether backup will ever save you but when. There are too many gremlins out there not to properly protect yourself.

Disk Cleanup

Disk Cleanup (Figure 4-10) lets you systematically delete five kinds of files from your disk:

- Temporary Internet Files (your IE cache)
- Downloaded Program Files. This does not mean files you've downloaded but Java applets and Active X controls. These are stored in `C:\windows\downloaded program files`.
- Recycle Bin
- Temporary Files, that is, files in the TEMP folder
- Windows Uninstall information, which typically takes over 100 MB.

By default, the first two are checked, but if you can afford the space, you should let IE handle those and instead check the last two within Maintenance Wizard (discussed in a minute). The More Options tab provides links to two tabs in the Add/Remove Programs applet.

 This is a pretty poor excuse for a disk cleanup tool. You can't set it up to, say, remove files from the Recycle Bin that are older than a week and similarly for the caches. And it won't look for .`tmp` files outside the TEMP directory. Close to useless.

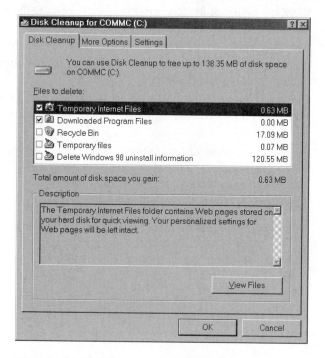

Figure 4-10. MOM says to clean your disk

Well, at least it didn't do what it threatened to. When I hit the View Files button on Downloaded Program Files, it showed the whole folder, but when I went ahead (it's a default), it did not delete the built-in Java applets without which Java would just stop working.

Disk Cleanup is not one of Windows 98's shining moments.

Plus! 98 includes an upgraded Disk Cleanup that includes extra modules from Cybermedia. It improves the cleanup considerably. I discuss it briefly in Chapter 5.

■ Undercover Agents

System Information

Disk Cleanup may not be one of Windows 98's shining moments, but Microsoft System Information (Figure 4-11) sure is. It's a techie user's dream come true. The basic program is a reporting module more thorough than a standard program like CheckIt, which used to cost more than the Win98 upgrade costs. It not only reports on the standard IRQ, DMA, and I/O port usage but on each Windows subsystem (for example, Printing and Display). Its list of running programs and modules, which includes both names and executable filenames, is the easiest way to find out all the stuff that's really loaded on your system. I'll bet you're surprised when you see it.

You can print out a complete report, but be warned— it will be over 100 pages! Or you can export it to a text file—it will be too big for Notepad but WordPad will handle it fine.

The jewels in System Information's crown are the items you can call from the Tools menu. Here they are in order. I've listed the executable name since you may want to add direct shortcuts

Microsoft System Information

File Edit View Tools Help

System Information
├─ Hardware Resources
│   ├─ Conflicts/Sharing
│   ├─ DMA
│   ├─ Forced Hardware
│   ├─ I/O
│   ├─ **IRQs**
│   └─ Memory
├─ Components
│   ├─ Multimedia
│   ├─ Display
│   ├─ Infrared
│   ├─ Input
│   ├─ Miscellaneous
│   ├─ Modem
│   ├─ Network
│   ├─ Ports
│   ├─ Storage
│   ├─ Printing
│   ├─ Problem Devices
│   ├─ USB
│   ├─ History
│   └─ System

IRQ	Device
0	System timer
1	Standard 101/102-Key or Microsoft Natural Keyboard
2	Programmable interrupt controller
3	Communications Port (COM2)
4	Communications Port (COM1)
5	ENSONIQ Soundscape
6	Standard Floppy Disk Controller
7	Printer Port (LPT1)
8	System CMOS/real time clock
9	All-In-Wonder PRO (atir3)
9	Adaptec AHA-294X/AIC-78XX PCI SCSI Controller
9	IRQ Holder for PCI Steering
9	IRQ Holder for PCI Steering
10	ENSONIQ Soundscape
11	(free)
12	PS/2 Compatible Mouse Port
13	Numeric data processor
14	Standard IDE/ESDI Hard Disk Controller
15	NE2000 Compatible

For Help, press F1   Current System Information

Figure 4-11. Microsoft System info

for some of them without having to start System Information first. In particular, you may want a separate shortcut for System Configuration Manager.

- **Windows Report Tool** (`C:\windows\winrep.exe`) lets you prepare reports for tech support. You can easily collect information from a variety of on-disk files and wrap them up as a `.cab` to go off to Microsoft or other vendors. You get to store user information and problem descriptions. The reports are stored in `C:\windows\helpdesk\winrep`.

- **Update Wizard Uninstall** (`C:\windows\upwizun.exe`) lets you undo any recent updates you've done via Windows Update.

 Sometimes it appears that things you grab from the update page register themselves in the Add/Remove Program uninstall rather than with Update Wizard Uninstall.

- **System File Checker** (`C:\windows\system\sfc.exe`) lets you restore files from the Windows install `.cab` files or other `.cab` files (see Chapter 7).

- **Signature Verification Tool** (`C:\windows\sigverif.exe`) allows you to check for digitally signed files and drivers and check out who the certificate issuer is. In particular, you can see if Microsoft Hardware Compatibility Labs has tested that latest driver you downloaded.

- **Registry Scan** (`C:\windows\scanreg.exe`) checks and backs up your Registry (see Chapter 9).

- **Automatic Skip Driver Agent** (`C:\windows\asd.exe`) reports on any drivers that Windows skipped after hardware failures. If you have several unsuccessful reboots followed by success, run this tool to see what the problem is.

- **Dr. Watson** (`C:\windows\drwatson.exe`) is Windows' crash reporting tool par excellence. I'll discuss it in the next section.

- **System Configuration Utility** (`C:\windows\system\msconfig.exe`) is first of all a place you can display and edit `config.sys`, `autoexec.bat`, `system.ini`, and `win.ini`. But it is much much more. You can selectively disable lines in any of these files. It also lists all programs that are automatically started when you run Windows (this comes from at least seven different places!) and lets you selectively disable their loading (see Chapter 6).

- **ScanDisk** (`C:\windows\scandskw.exe`) is discussed at the beginning of this chapter.

- **Version Conflict Manager** (`C:\windows\vcmui.exe`) tracks any `.dll` files that Windows 98 changes during its install (Chapter 7).

Dr. Watson

Elementary, my dear Dr. Watson.

—SHERLOCK HOLMES

Windows crashes have long been legion; talk of UAEs (Unexpected Application Errors) goes back to Windows 3.0. A program does something untoward and up pops a message telling you that. Windows then terminates the program giving you no chance to save anything.

 There are third-party products—most notably Norton's Crash Guard and Network Associates' Nuts & Bolts—that attempt to recover from a crash so that you can at least save your work. In real life they seem to work some of the time, but sometimes they only hose Windows worse. It's a tossup whether to run with them.

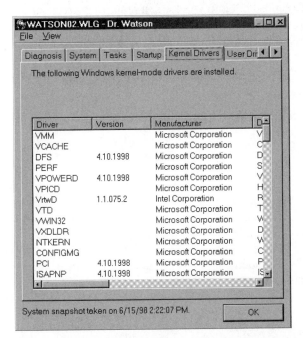

Figure 4-12. Dr. Watson's Advanced view

With Windows for Workgroups, Windows at least provided a tool for saving some information about the system at the time of the crash, but it wasn't much. Windows 95 continued the tradition—including not making it easy to save the crash information. Windows 98 finally gets it right. You can gather extensive crash information and automatically save it to a file.

The key is a program called Dr. Watson. It has to be running for it to catch a crash, and it is not run automatically when you install Windows. If you want, you can run it in your StartUp group, but my advice is to ignore it unless you have a program that crashes more than once. If it does, start loading Dr. Watson in startup.

Dr. Watson automatically saves crash information in logs that you can reload or forward to tech support. When you crash or reload a log, you normally get Standard view with a single panel with the name of the offending module. But go to the View menu and pick Advanced and the display blossoms (Figure 4-12).

 The logs are stored in the folder **c:\windows\drwatson** with the extension **.wlg**.

■ Let Me Work That into My Schedule

Ninety-Ninety Rule of Project Schedules: The first ninety percent of the task takes ninety percent of the time, and the last ten percent takes the other ninety percent.

 I talk first about Task Scheduler, but before you start setting it up by hand to run ScanDisk, check out the Maintenance Wizard, discussed in the second section. It automates some disk-related tasks.

Scheduled Tasks

There cannot be a crisis next week. My schedule is already full.

—HENRY KISSINGER

The best task scheduler I've seen is built into Windows. It replaces the System Agent program that was part of the Windows 95 Plus! Pack. If you had that program installed on a Windows 95 system and you upgrade to Windows 98, part of the upgrade process converts your System Agent tasks to the new Task Scheduler.

 By Task Scheduler, I mean something that schedules computer tasks, not something that manages your noncomputer projects or sets an alarm clock. Task Scheduler doesn't do that.

 Actually, you can set alarms with Task Scheduler; I'll tell you how at the end of this section.

On the Taskbar's Notification Area, you should see the 🖳 icon. Double clicking on it opens the Scheduled Tasks folder (Figure 4-13). You can also access this folder from My Computer, either by opening the My Computer icon and clicking on Scheduled Tasks or by opening an Explorer view and finding Scheduled Tasks on the tree side underneath My Computer. Notice the information displayed for each task—this view serves as a task summary.

Figure 4-13. Scheduled Tasks folder

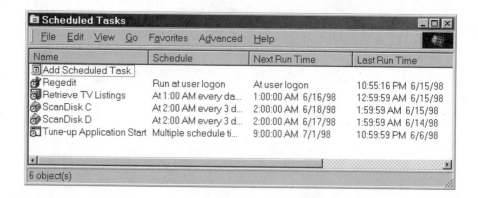

The Add Scheduled Task item runs the Add Task Wizard when you click on it.

 Talk about confusing interfaces. Why should the only way to add a task be through opening up a folder? Why doesn't task appear on the New menu? Why isn't there a menu item in the Start Menu hierarchy to add a new task? Alas, I tried in vain to find a way to invoke this wizard from a command line or VBScript so I could tell you how to add such a menu or Desktop icon yourself.

 And all these complaints apply just as much to the way you add a new dial-up connection, which also can only be done through an item in a special folder.

 At least I'll give you a backhand way to avoid the wizard if you want—and an elegant one—later in the section.

Here are the steps in this wizard.

1. The first panel (Figure 4-14 left) is for cosmetic purposes. I wish there were a "Don't show me again" check box on it.

2. The second panel (Figure 4-14 right) is where you get to pick the task. The list of applications displayed are precisely the items from the Start Menu. You can pick another program by hitting the Browse button.

3. The next panel (Figure 4-15 left) does double duty. You get to rename the item if you wish. This is the name that appears in the Scheduled Tasks view (and can later be changed in the same ways you can rename objects in folders). You also get to choose from three periodic schedules—daily, weekly, and monthly—or from three specialized schedules—one time, every time you start or restart Windows, or every time a new user logs in. In the latter case, the fifth-choice tasks are not run but the sixth-choice tasks are run.

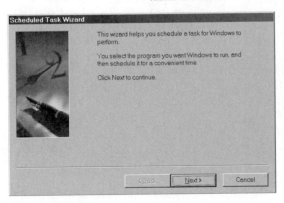 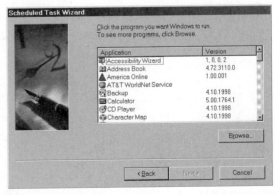

Figure 4-14. Add Task Wizard, Steps 1 and 2

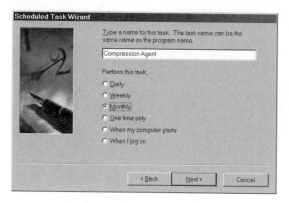
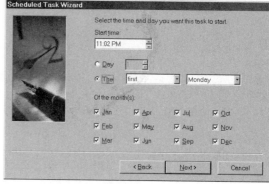

Figure 4-15. Add Task Wizard, Steps 3 and 4

4. The next panel (Figure 4-15 right) occurs only if you pick one of the first three scheduling options, and its possibilities depend on the choice. Seen here is the choice for monthly scheduling. Notice that it can be a fixed day of the month or weekday based. Notice also you can pick the month(s). So if you want a task to run only on April 15 each year, you say you want it monthly and then pick only the month of April.

5. The last panel (Figure 4-16) is also mainly cosmetic. The advanced properties that it refers to are the task Properties (Figure 4-17), which are also accessible by double clicking on the task in the Scheduled Tasks list.

 The ability to run a task when Windows starts up gives you yet one more way you can automatically start a program. Because Task Scheduler runs so early in the bootup sequences, programs loaded this way start before the programs in the StartUp group. Indeed, on a fresh boot they often appear before the Taskbar does!

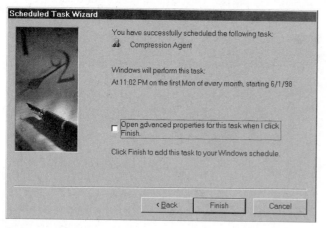

The panels on the Task property sheet (Figure 4-17) allow you to change the choices made in the wizard and also let you make a number of advanced choices.

Figure 4-16. Add Task Wizard, Step 5

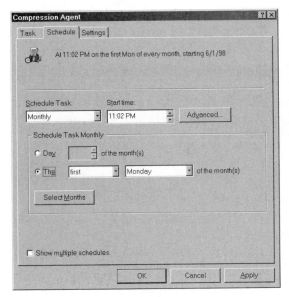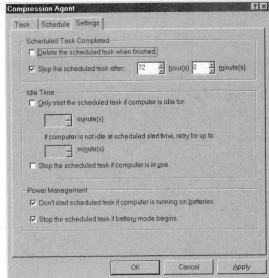

Figure 4-17. Task property sheet

- The Task tab (not shown) lets you change the program Run and Start directory. If a program is specifically Task Scheduler aware (Microsoft calls it SAGE aware, after the acronym for System AGEnt, the precursor of Task Scheduler), the Task tab will have a Settings . . . button that lets you change the way the program works according to how the program wants to let you. ScanDisk and Disk Defragmenter are both SAGE aware.

- Notice the "Show multiple schedules" check box on the Schedule tab. When you check it, you get a dropdown at the top of the tab that lets you set the task up to run on multiple schedules, say once at 10:00 A.M. and once at 2:00 P.M. daily.

- The Advanced . . . button on the Schedule tab lets you set up an end time for a task or repeat it every so many minutes.

- The Settings tab concerns options more advanced than the wizard. You can end the task after so many minutes if it hasn't finished, delay the task if the computer is idle, and most important, cancel the task if the computer is running on batteries.

 You shoulda heard the howls we got from the road warriors who turned on their computer at an airport check and then got a scheduled Compression Agent take over the machine so thoroughly that the machine wouldn't go into suspend mode. You fix that here.

The actual tasks are saved as files in `C:\windows\tasks`. The actual files have an extension of `.job`. This is connected with a caper that Barry will tell you about.

I figure I don't want no steenking wizards. I'd like to quickly create a new task and then call up its property sheet and change it there. No problemo, I figured. Select a task in the Scheduled Tasks folder, right click and pick Copy, then right click on a blank space and click **Paste**. But when I tried, I got an error message!

Of all the nonsense. On any other folder, if you take a file, say **foo.bar**, and go through this same process, you get an exact copy of the file with the name **Copy of foo.bar**. Why treat this folder differently.

Well, I found a way around it. `C:\windows\tasks` is a regular folder. If you try this copy-and-paste routine there, it works fine. After the copy, I clicked to rename the `.job` file and double clicked to adjust the properties.

Oy.

Actually, the Scheduled Tasks folder has at least one special feature that does work well and lets you make tasks without the wizard. If you drag an **.exe** file from an ordinary folder or Explorer view into an open Scheduled Tasks folder, it makes a **.job** file to run that **.exe**. This works for links too, but it runs the link rather than underlying **.exe**. It sets it to run at 9:00 A.M. every day, but you can double click the item and adjust it.

If you wish, `.job` files can be copied from one Windows 98 machine to another.

When Windows installs, it places exactly one Task in the Schedule. It is called **tune-up application start.job**. It doesn't have a program name, but it does have the single word "Winalign," even though (unless you install the WRK Sampler) your disk won't have any file with that name in it. Apparently, this task runs an internal **winalign**. I wonder why it isn't documented and why the WRK needs a separate **winalign.exe**?

Moreover, the file on the CD is called **winalign.job**, not **tune-up application start.job**.

You can use Task Scheduler for a very crude alarm system. Look in Chapter 3 at the section "Quick Install" for the VBScript `instmess.vbs`. It shows you how to pop up a message with VBScript. You could set up a task to run such a script and so pop up a message at a given time.

You can even play a wave file by running a script like the following (what appears to be three lines starting with **objWSHShell.Run** is one long line):

```
Set objWSHShell = CreateObject("Wscript.Shell")
objWSHShell.Run("C:\WINDOWS\rundll32.exe
   C:\WINDOWS\SYSTEM\amovie.ocx,RunDll /play /close
   C:\windows\media\tada.wav")
MsgBox "Send in your taxes",0,"MOM's Alarm"
```

Maintenance Wizard

By the time [the Leaning Tower of Pisa] was 10% built, everyone knew it would be a total disaster. But the investment was so big they felt compelled to go on. Since its completion, it cost a fortune to maintain and is still in danger of collapsing. There are no plans to replace it, since it was never needed in the first place. I expect every installation has its own pet software which is analogous to the above.

—KEN IVERSON

 What are the three programs you'd most like to run on a regular basis? We've got this neat utility that sets up the Scheduled Tasks to run them for you. Neat, huh?

 The three programs I'd most like to run on a regular basis are Backup, Backup, and Backup.

 Well, er, Microsoft Backup can't be scheduled to run unattended. What are the next three programs?

Maintenance Wizard, which is on Start Menu/programs/accessories/system tools, runs and makes tasks for three programs: ScanDisk, Disk Defragmenter, and Disk Cleanup. The tasks it makes have names like Maintenance-Defragment Programs. It is clever enough that if you already have a task that runs ScanDisk, it doesn't make another. You can let it pick the scheduling (Express SetUp) or you can do it yourself (Custom SetUp); see Figure 4-18. By default, it runs ScanDisk every three days, Defrag once a week and DiskClean once a month. It is probably adequate if you run them all once a month although given that ScanDisk can be an early warn-

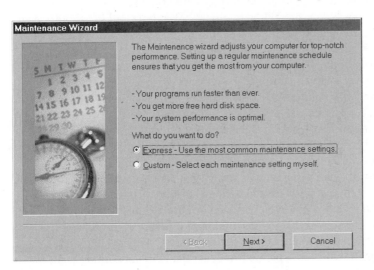

Figure 4-18. Maintenance Wizard

ing and only takes a few minutes to run, I'd suggest you run it at least once a week.

 With huge hard disks, ScanDisk can take more time to run than you might think. On one P90 with an 8-GB hard disk, it takes over half an hour.

 I leave my machine on overnight and have it configured to run a daily backup (third party) at 3:00 A.M., ScanDisk on all my drives at 4:30 A.M. and Norton Virus Scan on alternate mornings at 5:00 A.M., I run Defrag once a month.

 Plus! 98 includes an upgraded Maintenance Wizard that links to the extra Disk Cleanup modules from Cybermedia. I discuss it briefly in Chapter 5.

■ Gettin' It Together

A home theater would, within two decades, let people dial up symphonies, presidential speeches, and three-dimensional Shakespeare plays. . . . Novels, orchestras, and movie theaters would vanish.

—1912 prediction

In the mid-1980s, pundits kept predicting that "this year will be the year of the LAN," the year that local area networking finally took off. Just when the pundits began to seem silly repeating the same prediction, it became true in spades. Within the space of two or three years, most large- to medium-size corporations went from stand-alone to fully networked setups. Small businesses took a little longer but by the middle 1990s, almost all PCs in office environments are connected to LANs. The middle 1990s saw a dramatic explosion in the Internet both via network connections in the office and via dial-up connection from home. The designers of Windows 9X realized that networking is now a central part of computing. Network protocols are not only built into the system for computers on LANs but are part of Internet Dial-Up connections and even Laplink-style parallel cable connections between PCs.

Part of Windows Networking is the registration/installation of a network adapter in your hardware tree. If you are on a LAN via a physical connection, you have a hardware network adapter that is installed. If you are using one of the other forms of networking, you need a virtual adapter, which Windows calls a Dial-Up Adapter. The software and options for it are installed on your computer when you install Dial-Up Networking or Direct Cable Connection.

Networking is so vast that my discussion of it is spread throughout this book. General concepts, including the notion of UNC names, are found in Chapter 2. E-mail, which is separate from but related to networking is discussed in Chapter 3 under the discussion of Outlook Express. The Network applet in Control Panel and how to set up a simple peer-to-peer network is in Chapter 8. If you are here because you don't want to have to sign on when you start up your PC, here's what you do:

- In Control Panel (Start/Settings/Control Panel), double-click on the Network applet. Change the Primary Network Logon setting to Windows Logon. Click OK, and Windows will restart.
- Log on the usual way, then go back into Control Panel, double-click on the Passwords applet, and click Change Windows Password. Where it says, "Old password:" type your old password. Leave the boxes marked "New password:" and "Confirm new password:" blank.

That's it. Next time you restart Windows, your logon screen is gone.

 To bring the logon screen back, just pop into the Passwords applet and give yourself a password. That's all it takes.

 If you have to have a password, say to log on to a server, you can use Tweak UI (discussed in Chapter 8) to automatically log on. Do so advisedly, however, since it means anyone can log onto your system.

There's still lots to cover in this chapter. First, I discuss Dial-Up Networking (aka DUN)—the client that you're almost sure to use, the server you may not use, and the scripting language—then Direct Cable Connection, which should really be called Direct Parallel Port Connection since performance on the serial version is so awful, then the Briefcase. Next, I discuss the modem-based applets Hyperterminal and Dialer, several miscellaneous applications, and a word about online services. That leaves the Internet, something that has been the subject of acres of books. It's so important it gets two main sections after the one on networking.

Dial-Up Networking

Information networks straddle the world. Nothing remains concealed. But the sheer volume of information dissolves the information. We are unable to take it all in.

—GÜNTHER GRASS, *New Statesman & Society*, June 22, 1990

You'll need to setup a Dial-Up Networking connection before you can use DUN. If you're using the Connect to the Internet Wizard to make an Internet connection, it will set up the DUN connection for you (see the section "Internet Connection Wizard"). So you'll need to roll your own only if you are setting up a Dial-Up Internet connection manually or you are dialing in to a remote LAN.

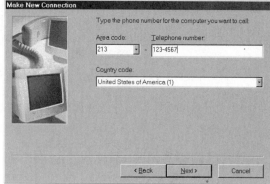

Figure 4-19. Dial-Up Make New Connection Wizard

To set up a DUN connection, open the Dial-Up Networking folder in My Computer (or find it under My Computer in Explorer) and click on New Connection to invoke the wizard shown here. You get to choose the name for the connection, the modem you'll use for the connection, and the telephone number you'll dial in to (Figure 4-19). When you're done, the DUN folder will show all the connections you've made (Figure 4-20).

 When you select the device in the dropdown in the panel at the left in Figure 4-19, one of the options will say Microsoft VPN Adapter. VPN is short for Virtual Private Network. It allows you to set up a highly protected virtual network over the Internet using very high levels of encryption and a protocol known as PPTP. VPN piggybacks on a standard Internet connectoid—you start that first, then the VPN connectoid, and you wind up with two icons in the Notification Area. VPN requires specially set-up servers, so the details are beyond the scope of this book, but this is an exciting development. We'll be hearing more about it over the years. DUN makes the setup easy.

When you double click on a DUN connection (or launch it from a shortcut) you get the login screen shown in Figure 4-21 (VPN login screens are slightly different). This lets you enter a User name and Password (why you aren't given an opportunity to enter this information in the Wizard—as you can in the Connect to the Internet Wizard—is beyond me). You can even tell the screen to remember your password—but bear in mind if you do that it blocks some of the protection that passwords offer.

Figure 4-20. DUNning agent

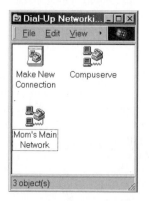

Under some circumstances, the Dial Properties . . . button on the login screen can be important. It brings up the dialog shown in Figure 4-22. This lets you define locations to dial from, especially useful if sometimes you are dialing up from one area code

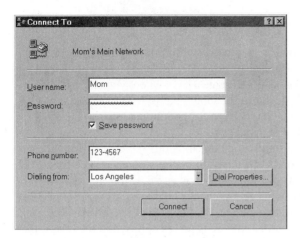

Figure 4-21. Connectoid login

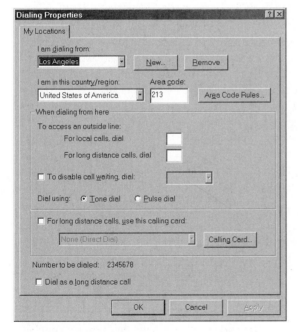

Figure 4-22. Dialing Properties

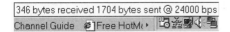

Figure 4-23. Dial-Up connectoid icon

and sometimes from another. This is also where you can automate credit card dialing—Windows understands many of the standard telephone credit cards and even has the 800 numbers for MCI and Sprint built in! You can set up your own credit card dialing strings with a primitive language available in help.

After you've dialed up, the connectoid will place an icon in the Notification Area whose tool tip will tell you the baud rate and some connect information (Figure 4-23). If you right click you can quickly disconnect from a choice on the context menu. Double clicking brings up a panel with additional information and a Disconnect button.

While you'll mainly dial in to an Internet service provider, if your LAN has a Dial-Up server, you can dial into that. Once you've made a Dial-Up connection to a LAN, you can do all the usual things you can do on a LAN including setting up shortcuts to programs and folders on the LAN.

If you double click on such a shortcut when you are not connected, you get a dialog inviting you to dial up. There will be a check box. If you pick it, forever afterwards when you click on the Desktop folder, Windows will pop up the DUN login screen and connect you, and, as soon as you are connected, it will open the folder or run the program that the shortcut was to. This is an elegant interface to Dial-Up Networking.

If you are connected to a corporate LAN, you may need to change the server type. If you right click on a connectoid and pick Properties, in the resulting dialog (shown later in Figure 4-25), the Server Type tab has the dropdown shown in Figure 4-24.

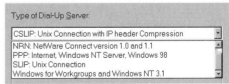

Figure 4-24. Dial-Up Server type

Most often you'll use DUN with an ISP or some corporate LAN with specialized servers that support remote access. But if you want to use it with a home machine or a small office network, you may want to use the Dial-Up Server. Microsoft has done a good job of hiding it. The DUN folder has an item called Dial-Up Server . . . on the Connections menu. That's where you can turn the server on and off and where you get to set a login password. An especially important option is invoked by the Server Type . . . button that leads to the drop-down that lets you choose PPP or Windows 3.1.

If the Dial-Up Server is a stand-alone machine or is a network with a Browse Master, you can choose what seems to be the obvious choice for server type—PPP: Internet, Windows NT Server, Windows 98. But if the server is on a small peer-to-peer network, you need to choose **Windows for Workgroups and Windows NT 3.1**. With that choice, the Dial-Up client will be able to access only the machine the server software is on (as opposed to the rest of the network); performance with the PPP choice is unacceptable at best and unreliable at worst when connecting to a peer-to-peer network.

 The underlying technology of DUN is neat and the ability to click on a remote folder and invoke remote dial-up login is wonderful, but much of the interface is confused and inconsistent. The Dial-Up Server is hidden, and the DUN SetUp Wizard doesn't let you put in a username and password. The Connect to the Internet Wizard does, even though that part of the Internet Wizard is setting up a DUN connection. The connection options are spread in two different places. Some you get to by double clicking the connection and hitting Dial Properties . . . in the DUN logon screen. Others you reach by selecting but not double clicking a connectoid and choosing Properties from the context menu (or the File menu) and then hitting Configure. . . . These last configurations are allowed to be modem dependent (for no good reason!), and the dialog that chooses them lists the modem name rather than the connection name. Finally, there is a third set of options involving how to redial if a line is busy under Connections/Settings in the menu of the DUN folder itself.

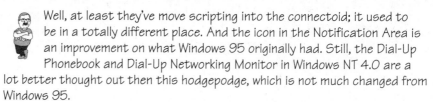 Well, at least they've move scripting into the connectoid; it used to be in a totally different place. And the icon in the Notification Area is an improvement on what Windows 95 originally had. Still, the Dial-Up Phonebook and Dial-Up Networking Monitor in Windows NT 4.0 are a lot better thought out then this hodgepodge, which is not much changed from Windows 95.

 I found a really strange gotcha on the "Save password" check box in Figure 4-21. If you have no Network client installed and haven't enabled multiple user profiles, then that check box is grayed out. If you either install a client (like Client for Microsoft Networks) or turn on multiple user profiles, then magically you have an enabled check box. Oh, how I love a nice bug in the morning.

That's not a bug. It was put there on purpose to punish someone so antisocial as to have neither a shared PC nor a network. Actually, the problem seems to be that there is no password file if neither of those options is available, and we weren't clever enough to make one if you checked that box.

Logon Scripts for CompuServe

A gent I know whose life is superfluidity
Took a job in CBS Continuity.
One night after too much Scotch paregoric,
He turned in a script just too prehistoric.
He was fired and said, as he read his doxology . . .
"I thought they would like my Paley-ontology."

—PAUL W. WHITE, Director of Special Events, CBS

Woody and I had a long discussion on whether to talk about scripting here or in the collection of sections on connecting to the Internet. We put it here since scripting is integrated into the connectoid property sheet, but it could be in either place. In this section, I tell you how to set up a PPP connection if you have a CompuServe account and want to use it as your general-purpose Internet provider. As you'll see, it's very easy. In the next section I tell you the more complicated things you need to do if you want to set up a more elaborate script for a third-party Internet provider.

Don't let the word "script" frighten you. Microsoft has included the script you need for CompuServe so you don't need to do any programming.

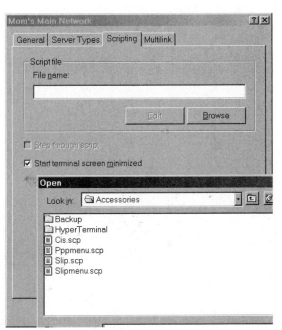

Make a Dial-Up connectoid for CompuServe as you would for any other ISP. But after you do, right click, pick Properties, and move to the Scripting tab (Figure 4-25). Click Browse and it should take you to the **C:\Program Files\ Accessories** folder where you'll be able to pick **cis.scp**, the script needed to log on to CompuServe as PPP provider.

Figure 4-25. Assigning a script to a connectoid

The Logon Scripting Language

If it's a good script I'll do it. And if it's a bad script, and they pay me enough, I'll do it.

—GEORGE BURNS, International Herald
Tribune, November 9, 1988

While it's true that most service providers have computers that are smart enough to log you on automatically when you dial in with Win98, in my experience some still make you type in your logon i.d., password, and usually a command like **PPP** or some such. That's why Win98 has a "Bring up terminal window after dialing" check box: Win98 has to step back after establishing the modem connection long enough to let you type in your i.d., password, and **PPP**.

You may wonder where Windows has hidden this darned option. You need to right click on the connectoid, choose Properties, hit the Configure button, choose the Option tab, and pick a check box. Pretty well hidden, eh, pilgrim?

Well, Windows 98 does away with all of this mumbo jumbo by allowing you to create automated logon scripts for any Dial-Up Networking connection, most particularly for dial-up access to the Net. The easiest way to set up a logon script is to right click on the connectoid, pick Properties, and go to the Scripting tab (Figure 4-25). In the filename location, first pick an existing script by browsing (to get the right directory—**C:\program files\accessories**) and then change the name and hit Edit. Notepad will offer to start a file and that's where you can type in your script. Here's the script I use for dialing in to my service provider. (My service provider prompts "Username:," then "Password:," then, after I'm logged on and the big computer says, "Annex:," I'm supposed to type in **ppp** and hit **Enter**.) Comments are proceeded by a semicolon.

```
; Woody's PPP logon script for Colorado SuperNet

proc main
   waitfor "username:" until 5 ;give it five seconds to
      stabilize
   if $FAILURE then
         goto BadConnection
   endif
   transmit $USERID + "^M"    ;the connection's userid +
      Enter
   waitfor "password:" until 5 ;another five seconds
      for pword
   if $FAILURE then
         goto BadConnection
   endif
```

```
      transmit $PASSWORD + "^M"
      waitfor "annex:" until 20  ;20 seconds to actually
          log on
      if $FAILURE then
              goto BadConnection
      endif
      transmit "ppp^M"
      goto Bye ;logged on
BadConnection:
              halt

  Bye:
  endproc
```

Basically, you create the script using Notepad, then attach it to a particular Dial-Up Networking configuration by using the Properties tab. If you're moderately comfortable with any Basic-type programming language, you'll find the Dial-Up scripting language easy to pick up—it's quite straightforward, with details in an eight-page file called **script.doc** in the **C:\windows** folder.

Four tips on using the scripting language:

1. If you want to look at more examples, check in the **\Program Files\ Accessories** folder for ***.scp** files. I found those samples to be a whole lot more complicated than I wanted, but you may find them useful.

2. After you type in your program, save it to the **\Program Files\ Accessories** folder with an **.scp** extension. That'll make it easier for the Properties sheet to find the script.

3. If you've been using the "Bring up terminal window after dialing" setting, remove it; it will only get in the way of your script. If you need to see what is happening, instead uncheck the box labeled "Start terminal screen minimized" in Figure 4-25.

4. The Dial-Up Scripting Tool has a great debug mode (Figure 4-26) you can invoke. Just check "Step through script" and uncheck "Start terminal screen minimized" in Figure 4-25. Debugging is pretty easy once you get the hang of it. Keep Notepad open with your **.scp** file showing, and try to log on. Rearrange the windows so that you can see what's going on. Step through the script by pushing the Step button. When the script bombs (and it will!), make changes to the script in Notepad, click File, then Save, and try to log on again. When it's all working right, remember to uncheck "Step through script," and check "Start terminal screen minimized."

Even if you're intimidated by the idea of writing a program, give it a shot. You'll get the hang of it in no time.

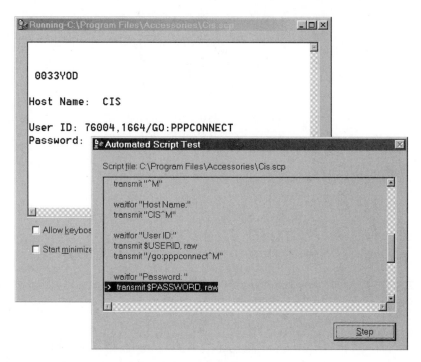

Figure 4-26. Script debugging

 Call up Windows Help, go to Index, click on **.scp** files and pick "Overview of scripting for Dial-Up Networking." It'll tell you to use the Dial-Up Scripting tool—which is gone with Windows 98 and replaced by property sheets. Oops!

Direct Cable Connection

A book is like a piece of rope; it takes on meaning only in connection with the things it holds together.

—Norman Cousins, *Saturday Review,* April 15, 1978

In the mid-1980s, when laptop computers were just coming into vogue, a program called the Brooklyn Bridge appeared, which let you use a parallel cable to transfer files between computers. One computer was the **slave**, and during the process, it had to be dedicated to the other computer, called the **master**. During the transfer, the slave couldn't be used for anything other than serving the master. The master had to be rebooted after it was connected to the slave and the slave was put into slave mode. It was an awkward procedure but useful enough that many purchased and used it. Since then, we've come a long way, baby!

The category was taken over by Laplink from Traveling Software, which over time became elegant and even supported serial linkups at respectable speeds. Some versions of DOS 6.0 had a pair of programs called Interlink that allowed transfers over cable, but they were very much in the slave/master mode of the original Brooklyn Bridge: one computer had to be totally dedicated to the link and the other had to be rebooted. It had a slightly prettier face than the Brooklyn Bridge, but it wasn't much more functional. And it was certainly no Laplink.

Windows 98 includes a program called Direct Cable Connection (DCC) that is finally a serious cable connection program—certainly competitive with Laplink. In one way, it is much worse than Laplink: its serial support is a joke, whereas Laplink's is pretty good (although even its serial speeds aren't as good as its parallel port speeds). But in another way, Windows 98's way is superior because it connects as a network using the Dial-Up Networking virtual adapter.

 The networking comes via the DUN virtual adapter but DCC is not run via the DUN folder! You use a menu item installed under Programs/Accessories/Communications in the Start Menu. You can of course place a shortcut to the executable (**directcc.exe**) on your desktop or assign a hotkey to it. If DCC isn't under your Start Menu, it probably isn't installed—go to the Add/Remove Programs applet of Control Panel, go to the Windows SetUp tab, highlight Communications, and hit Details. . . . You'll find Direct Cable Connection there. If you pick it and you don't already have DUN installed, it will install DUN as it installs DCC.

 You'll also need a cable to connect the two computers you want to talk to each other. You may lean toward the serial cable choice because you are more likely to have free serial ports than free parallel ports but DON'T DO IT! Serial port rates will be 1 to 3 KB/sec (a 1-MB file will take close to 15 minutes on a serial connection; the same file will take about 1 minute on a parallel connection); a simple parallel connection should be 10 to 20 times better than a serial connection.

 Using special enhanced parallel ports and a special cable called a Universal Cable Modem (sold for $70 by the supplier listed in Windows Help), there have been reports of speeds in excess of 100 KB/sec.

 You may have a suitable parallel cable left over from an earlier brush with file transfer software; if not, your local computer store should have them—they may refer to them as Laplink cables. Windows Help lists a supplier from whom you can order a cable for $20.

 New with Windows 98 is infrared support for DCC, so if your laptop and desktop have infrared ports, this may be the way to go.

If you transfer files a lot, you should consider setting up a real network. You can get a decent PCI Ethernet card for a desktop machine for about $30 and a PCMIA Ethernet card for a laptop for $90. Speeds are faster and the system is more reliable.

Before you start DCC, some things to keep in mind:

- Both machines need to have the Dial-Up Networking adapter installed with the same protocol on both sides (I'd recommend you install both Net-BEUI and IPX/SPX on both machines), and both need to have the Client for Microsoft Networks installed. See the discussion of the Network applet in Chapter 8 on installing Network protocols and clients.

- In a certain sense, the connection is one way: one machine (usually the portable) is designated the guest and the other the host. The guest computer can access the drives on the host but not vice versa. However, the guest computer can transfer files in either direction, so in that sense the communication is two way. Note that both the guest and the host can run DCC in the background.

- The host computer will need to have Printer and File Sharing turned on, and the drives the guest wants to access will need to have Sharing turned on for them explicitly. This is also discussed in Chapter 8.

First you need to decide which machine is going to be the guest and which the host. The guest is the machine you'll be using to do the file transfers. If one machine is a laptop, it is traditionally the guest. If you're transferring files from your old desktop computer to one you just bought, you'll probably want the new computer to be the guest.

You need to run DCC on both machines. Here I describe the guest setup (Figure 4-27). You need to tell the guest what ports to use (Figure 4-28). Of course, having read what I said earlier about ports, you pick parallel ports, don't you? The dialog says to plug in the cable at this point but, of course, you could have plugged it in before you began.

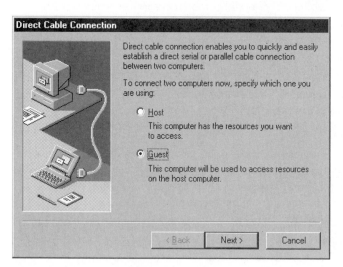

Figure 4-27. DCC setup, Step 1

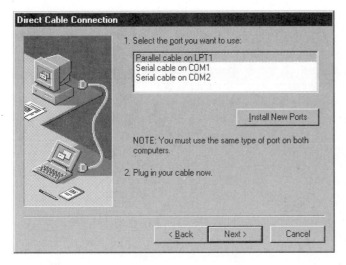

Figure 4-28. DCC setup, Step 2

After you get this far on each machine, hit Next on each. You should get a notice that the machines are trying to connect (Figure 4-29). You're then asked to type in the name of the host computer (Figure 4-30). And success (Figure 4-31)!!

Once you are connected, the host computer is accessible from the guest. Indeed, if you hit View Host . . . , a folder window should open on the guest with folders for each shared drive on the host. If it doesn't or you close it, you can access drives on the host using UNC pathnames. For example, if the host computer's name is **aye**, you could open its C drive by typing **\\aye\c** in the Run box. You can copy and move files via the standard Explorer methods.

 DOS commands understand UNC pathnames too, so once I've established a DCC connection, I often open a DOS box on the guest and use xcopy and move to transfer files.

 Because DCC is networking, it can be used to install software you have only on CD to a laptop without CD. Make the laptop the guest to a host that has a CD. You can then run the setup program on the CD, which will act like a drive—admittedly, a slow drive—on the laptop.

Figure 4-29. DCC setup, Step 3

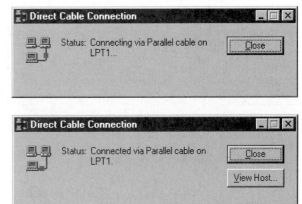

Figure 4-30. DCC setup, Step 4

Figure 4-31. DCC setup, Step 5

Figure 4-32. Subsequent sessions

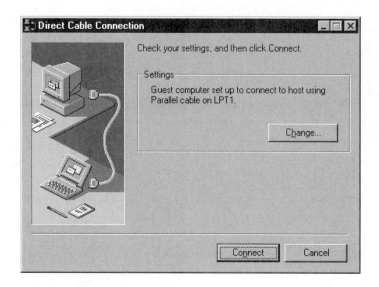

Because DCC is networking, all programs can use the host's drives. So for the Mom95 book, when I needed a screen shot from the portable, I used **PrtSc** and Paint to capture the screen and then used File\Save in Paint to save the file in **\\aye\c\windows\desktop** to save it on the Desktop of the, er, desktop machine.

Once you've set up a direct cable connection, the next time you try to run DCC, it offers to restore the connection last used so you don't have to pick guest/host and port type (Figure 4-32). Surprisingly, though, it doesn't remember the name of the host, which has to be entered each time.

Another disappointment is that it doesn't handle shortcuts to the host machine as slickly as DUN does. If you use a modem DUN connection, then, as I've explained, if you double click on a shortcut to the remote machine when you aren't connected, DUN offers to connect you. With DCC, if you make a shortcut to the other machine while connected and then double click it while you are not, you just get the error panel shown in Figure 4-33.

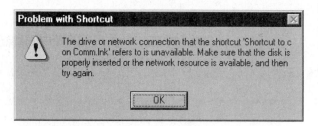

Figure 4-33. Disappointing error panel

Floppy Briefcase

A lawyer with his briefcase can steal more than a hundred men with guns.

—Don Corleone speaking in
Mario Puzo's *The Godfather*

 Windows provides a device for keeping files on two computers in synch. It's called a Briefcase, and it's just a special kind of folder.

 The idea behind a Briefcase is neat, but it never caught on. It may be that the implementation was too complex or that networks and other high-speed devices made them obsolete but I know no one who uses a Briefcase regularly. But Briefcase remains part of Windows, so I'll tell you about it in case you want to be the exception to the rule.

 There are two very different kinds of Briefcases, with two very different modes of operation. While their icons look the same and their technical guts are the same, their operations are different. One is floppy based and one is network based. Think of them as different, because if you don't, you'll use the methods for one in the context of the other and the files will lose synch. And except for one vague reference in Windows Help, Microsoft hasn't bothered to clearly explain the fact that there are two different modes.

 In the floppy-based mode, the Briefcase doesn't move, while in the network mode, it does. That is to say, in floppy mode, the floppy moves from one machine to another but the Briefcase doesn't move—it stays in one place on the floppy. In this mode, there are three versions of each file—one on each computer and one in the Briefcase on the floppy.

In the network mode, the Briefcase is moved to another location on the network and there are only two versions of the files, the one on the original machine and the one in the Briefcase, located somewhere on the network. It's important that in this mode, on machines other than the original, files be accessed directly from the Briefcase.

 The system knows that a folder is really a Briefcase because of two hidden files that are in the Briefcase folder—a text file called **desktop.ini** and a binary file called **Briefcase Database**. The first has a CLSID (CLaSs ID; see Chapter 9), the one assigned to Briefcases, and it's what tells the system what icon to use via information in the Registry under that CLSID. I'm not sure how the system distinguishes between what I'm calling the network and floppy modes—it may be that if it finds a Briefcase on a moveable medium, it assumes it is a floppy Briefcase.

 Even if you have told Explorer to display hidden files, it doesn't display these two when showing you a Briefcase. But a **dir /a** at the DOS prompt shows them.

Here's the basic idea. You make a Briefcase on a floppy disk. The briefcase cannot span floppies, but you can obviously have multiple floppies, each with its own Briefcase. If you prefer, you can make the Briefcase on your desktop, copy some files there, and then move the Briefcase to the floppy. But once you've got the Briefcase on the floppy, you shouldn't move the Briefcase to another location.

Windows is pretty intelligent about the defaults for dragging to Briefcases and for dragging Briefcases. If you drag a Briefcase to a drive icon, the Briefcase is moved (copied and deleted from the source). If you drag a file to a Briefcase, even from the same drive, it is copied. This is different from the behavior of any other kind of folder.

I'll imagine using a floppy-based Briefcase to move files between computers you have at the office and at home. Each file has three copies, (1) one in the Briefcase. (2) the one on the office machine, and (3) the one on your home machine. You set this up by creating the file on the office machine and dragging it to the Briefcase. Then when you get home, you drag it from the Briefcase to a convenient folder on your home machine. Once you have these three copies in place, do not drag them to or from the Briefcase. That's so important I'll shout it: **With floppy-based Briefcases, you drag files to and from the Briefcase only during the initial setup.** Once the three copies of files are in place, you don't even think about dragging them to/from the Briefcase or, for that matter, dragging them between folders on your office or home PC, since the Briefcase will then lose track of them! Of course, if you've been using a given file (in three copies) for months and need to synch another file, you can do the create and drag routine on that new file without affecting the existing files.

Once set up, the key command for Briefcase is called Update. If you open a Briefcase in Folder view or view it in Explorer, an extra Briefcase menu appears between Favorites and Help. It includes commands to update all or to update selected files (Figure 4-34). Alternatively, you can right click on a closed Briefcase and pick Update All from the context menu. If there are no files out of synch, you get a message saying that. Otherwise you get the dialog in Figure 4-35—although if you've done everything right, the recommendation will al-

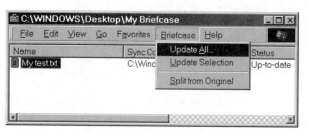

Figure 4-34. Briefcase menu

ways be a replace arrow rather than the skip arrow shown here. If you right click on a line you can override the recommendation as shown here. Once you've checked all the recommendations, you just click Update. This means that if you want to do some work at home on some files from the office, and you've already set up the three copies, you'd do the following sequences of steps.

Figure 4-35.
Update dialog

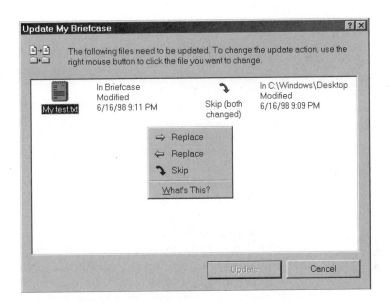

1. Before leaving the office, put the floppy Briefcase(s) into your floppy drive, open the floppy in Folder view or Explorer, right click on the Briefcase, and pick Update All. Take the floppy out of the drive and put it in whatever you'll be using to take it home—most likely your, er, briefcase.

2. Before starting work at home, put the floppy in the drive, right click on the Briefcase inside the floppy folder, and Update All. The three copies of the file are all now in synch.

3. After finishing your homework, do another Update All.

4. After you get the floppy back to the office, again do an Update All. All three copies will again be in synch.

Network Briefcase

The network Briefcase is even simpler in concept than the floppy Briefcase. You want to lend some of your files to someone else or take them elsewhere in a situation where the elsewhere is accessible via the network at least via Dial-Up Networking or Direct Cable Connection. The procedure is simple.

1. Make a Briefcase on your system. It's easiest to do this on your desktop, but it can be anywhere you want. There's a New Briefcase command on the Desktop context menu.

2. Drag the files you want to synch to the Briefcase—Windows will make copies there.

3. Move the Briefcase folder to some other location on the network, for example to a laptop currently connected via a docking station.

Figure 4-36.
Replicated
databases and
Briefcase

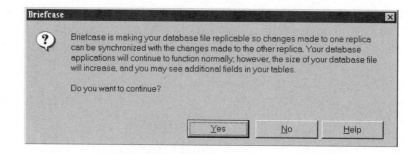

4. The files in the Briefcase can be accessed and changed by the person working at the location of the Briefcase, for example on the laptop, which is now out on the road. But here's the important proviso—the files have to be accessed from the Briefcase. **In network Briefcase mode, while in the secondary location, do not move or copy files into and out of the Briefcase.** So if you've dragged `budget.xls` to Budget Briefcase and then moved Budget Briefcase to `C:\` on the laptop, then on the laptop, you'd tell Excel to open `C:\budget briefcase\budget.xls`.

5. Once the Briefcase is on the network in a place where the originals are accessible, you right click on the briefcase and do an Update All and it will put things back in synch. If you've used Dial-Up Networking to move the Briefcase, it will offer to make the call for you when you do an Update All.

Briefcases work well if you've changed only one of the pair of files involved in an update. If you've changed both, you'll normally get the message in Figure 4-35 warning you that both have changed and you'll need to resolve the changes by hand. But programs can register a merge procedure with Briefcase. For example, if you drag an MS Access 97 database to a Briefcase, you get a message (Figure 4-36) offering to set up a replica (in my test, 2.5 MB blossomed to 3.6 MB after replication). Then if you change both, Briefcase offers to merge them and Access has a Resolve Conflicts menu item to complete the merge.

Hyperterminal

Like everyone else, I hate modems. They are infuriating, complicated, obscure, etc., etc. But mostly, they are slow. No matter how fast they are, they are slow. And slowness is the ultimate crime in computing.

—Stewart Alsop

Hyperterminal is, in the spirit of Windows 3.x Terminal, a fairly bare-bones modem communications program. It does poorly on most magazine roundups, although it does better than Terminal did since it does support Zmodem transfers and ANSI-BBS terminal emulation (the two biggest lacks in Terminal).

You save connections as icons in the Hyperterminal folder. These include a name and phone number and settings obtained from various dialogs. These are set in the property sheet of the connection. Don't overlook the button that says Configure . . . on the Connect To tab. That's where you set communication parameters. Despite the implication that these settings are for the modem, they are for a specific connection.

There is no CompuServe B protocol and no scripting language at all.

 I take the position that because of the advent of Internet, this program is becoming irrelevant. It was already true that to access online services, you wanted or even were required to use a service-specific program. But a terminal program was important for vendor bulletin boards and for accessing the vast BBS culture out there. But that's changed. Vendor BBS are being replaced by Web sites or newsgroups and some general-purpose BBS have Telnet access.

 The Windows 98 version of Hyperterminal has several improvements over the Windows 95 version. The top of the list is Telnet support and support for restarting interrupted Zmodem transfers from where you left off.

 The Telnet support is transparent—you tell a Hyperterminal connection to use TCP-IP and (after starting a Dial-Up connection if need be) the connection makes a Telnet link to the IP domain you specify.

 You can go to **http://www.hilgraeve.com/htpe.html** and download an upgrade called HyperTerminal Private Edition (HTPE) from Hilgraeve, the makers of Hyperterminal. HTPE is free for personal, non-commercial use. Hilgraeve also sells HyperAccess, their full-fledged comm program.

Dialer

The Englishman's telephone box is his castle. Like the London taxi, it can be entered by a gentleman in a top hat. It protects the user's privacy, keeps him warm, and is large enough for a small cocktail party.

—MARY BLUME, *International Herald Tribune*, August 30, 1985

Phone Dialer is a fairly simple way of dialing your phone through the modem but with more functionality than you might think. It is a TAPI dialer, which means that other programs can link to it.

The program has eight speed-dial tabs, a number pad to enter numbers with, and a dropdown of recently dialed numbers (Figure 4-37). When you dial, Dialer pops up a box where you can tell it the name of the person you are calling and let it know when you stopped. It is then supposed to store this name, the number, and the date, time, and duration of the call in a log.

The log is an ASCII text file (**C:\windows\calllog.txt**). You can turn off call logging by first picking Show Log from the Tools menu in Dialer and then Log/Options from the menu in the log window that results.

Figure 4-37.
Roll your dex

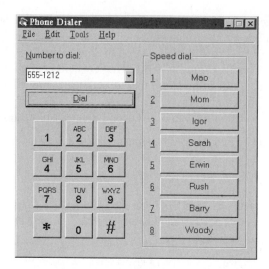

 The logging feature was in the Windows 95 version and worked fine. It was dropped from the NT 4.0 version. It appears on the menus and the dialog asking who you called under Windows 98 but no log was kept in our test directly with Dialer. When Dialer was used indirectly from Windows Messaging, a log was kept. Ah, well, they broke it and it appears not a single beta tester noticed. Must be a very important feature, mustn't it?

The true importance of Dialer comes from the check box in the dialog of Tools/Connect Using . . . in the main menu system. It says, "Use Phone Dialer to handle voice call requests from other programs," and it is enabled by default. If enabled, Dialer is the TAPI voice provider, which means, for example, that the Dial button on the Phone tab of items in Windows Messaging's Address Book will invoke Dialer, passing it names as well as phone numbers. Dialer is functional as is but will be more important because of these links.

WinChat and WinPopup

Many of the quests for status symbols—the hot automobile, the best table in a restaurant, or a private chat with the boss—are shadowy reprises of infant anxieties. . . . The larger office, the corner space, the extra window are the teddy bears and tricycles of adult office life.

—DR. WILLARD GAYLIN, The Rage Within

 I get a big kick out of WinPopup (Figure 4-38). Any time I want to send a note to somebody on the network, I just push the button and away it goes. The trick with WinPopup is that both you and the person you are sending to have to have it running—typically, by putting it in your StartUp folder—before it responds to messages. If you installed either Client for Netware Networks or Client for Microsoft Networks from a CD, you'll find

**Figure 4-38.
WinPopup in
action**

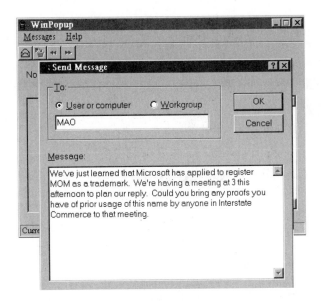

winpopup.exe in your **\windows** folder. If not, click Start, Settings, Control
Panel. Double-click Add/Remove Programs, and bring up the Windows SetUp tab,
click System Tools, and add it by clicking WinPopup.

 Kinda weird to put it on System Tools; I looked first at Accessories and
Communications.

Add it to your StartUp group if you plan to use it.

 Windows for Workgroups had a similar program called Chat, and it worked
better than WinPopup. It was included on the Windows 95 CD, but alas, it
is gone from Windows 98. Too bad. Hmm; actually I prefer ICQ; see Chapter 5. You chat via the Internet, but if both your machines have hardwired
Internet connections, ICQ will work fine.

Online Bazaar

 You may wonder why the other books tell you about the Microsoft
Network (MSN) and I don't. It's because I object to Microsoft using
Windows 98 to push its online service. Using a monopoly in one part
of the business to benefit another is something I don't cotton to.

 Right on, MOM. The Department of Justice shoulda made 'em pull MSN
from the box when they were looking at the MSN/Win95 links in August
of 1995. And at times since.

Hey, it's a check box during install. The user can choose not to install MSN. So where's the beef?

Nonsense, Billy. Even if the user says no, there is still an icon that's installed that tells you to click there to install MSN. And according to press reports, Microsoft requires hardware vendors to install MSN when they install Windows.

■ Gettin' Hitched to the Net

Always marry a short woman;
Her clothes will cost you less.

—Moroccan proverb

What I keep telling Janet is that the Internet is so integrated into computing that one can't separate it out into little pieces independent of the rest of Windows, and Barry and Woody prove that in spades. Their discussion of the Internet is spread throughout this book.

Billy's right; it is all over the place. An overview of the services on the Internet is in Chapter 2 and Chapter 3 discusses IE (Internet Explorer 4.0) and OE (Outlook Express). The guts of the Internet applet in Control Panel are in Chapter 8. But that leaves a lot for here. First I talk about how to connect up to the Net, then the many Internet tools that Windows 98 has—including a little more on IE that goes beyond the tips list of Chapter 3.

Net 101

Net: Anything reticulated or decussated at equal distances, with interstices between the intersections.

—Samuel Johnson, *Dictionary*, 1755

First, a little tutorial. I promise to keep this painless, even if you're a Net Newbie. The Internet, as you probably know, is a network that connects computers all over the world. If you're running Win98 and have a modem, you already have almost everything you need to get on the Net. The one part that's missing is a "service provider," and (unless you have a cushy deal with a university or a research group) service providers are not free.

A service provider has a computer that's connected to the Net. Your PC dials into the service provider's computer and is thus connected to the Net. You pay the service provider for use of their computer, for the fee they pay for access to the Internet, and (in theory anyway) for their help and support when your attempts to connect to the Net are thwarted. A few providers may try to sell you a so-called "shell" account, which essentially turns your PC into a big, dumb monitor connected to their UNIX machine—with a "shell" account your only access is through a series of character-mode menus. Bleccch. What you want for full-fledged Net action—and the only type of connection supported by Internet Explorer, Outlook Express, and the rest of the Win98 goodies—is a Point-to-Point Protocol (PPP) account. There is an older kind of direct net access account called a SLIP account, but these days most accounts are PPP accounts. You want PPP, not SLIP.

 Roughly speaking, Internet service providers (ISPs) are divided into two groups: the big four—America Online (AOL), CompuServe, the Microsoft Network (MSN), and Prodigy Internet—and "local" ISPs.

 Some of the local ISPs, like EarthLink and MCI, are really national and the distinction from the big four is a little less clear. But basically the big four provide services that aren't accessible from the Internet or that are accessible from the Internet only if you are logging in through them. They also tend to have special software.

 My advice is to concentrate on what you get with a generic PPP connection and to access it with generic tools. You can do that with three of the big four (although it requires some fiddling!) but not with AOL, which is why I recommend against AOL. AOL does not yet use POP mail.

 So if you don't travel a lot, pick a local ISP based on price, on what you hear about (lack of) busy signals, and on what you hear about service. If you do travel, pick one of the big three (the big four minus AOL) or one of the national ISPs.

 No matter what, look into one of the remailers (Bigfoot for Life at **www.bigfoot.com** is my favorite). They'll forward to any standard Internet mail address. You give out your address at the remailers and then redirect the forwarding if you change ISPs.

 This is critical to avoid becoming a hostage to the ISP. Both Barry and I do it. Barry's standard address is at Bigfoot; mine is at WOPR, essentially a private remailer.

 If you want to use one of the big four, they have paid big bucks, er, scratch that. If you want to use one of the big four, I've graciously arranged for Windows 98 to show icons that make signing up easy for you (Figure 4-39). And you'll find a national "local" ISP there—AT&T WorldNet. I've put an icon for MSN on the Desktop itself, and the boys have added a shortcut to the Online Services folder so you can see all the possibilities laid out.

 If you want to use one of these five services, you can sign up and set them up on your Windows 98 machine just by clicking on an icon. But it isn't much harder to use a generic ISP if you have the right information, as I'll tell you in the next section.

Internet Connection Wizard

Whatever befalls the earth befalls the sons of the earth. Man did not weave the web of life: he is merely a strand in it. Whatever he does to the web, he does to himself.

—SEATTLE, Indian chief, *Letter to President Franklin Pierce*, 1854

Got that? If you're going to use one of the five "built-in" service providers, you can run the Wizard now. If you already have an account with a service provider (and have the tech support line's phone number!), you can run the Wizard as soon as you get some simple information together. But if you don't want to use one of these five and you don't already have an account with a service provider, you have to get yourself set up with one before you continue.

Don't get the willies. The Internet Connection Wizard really is the simplest Internet setup routine I've ever seen—and I've sweated through a bunch of 'em. Start by checking your documentation or calling your service provider for all of the following information:

- Telephone number you dial to get into their computer
- Whether you have an explicit IP address and, if so, what the address is (four numbers, each up to three digits—each always 255 or less). If you have an explicit IP address, find out if you also need a subnet mask. These days, you'll probably be told they assign it dynamically and you don't have to have an explicit IP address.
- Your provider's DNS (Domain Name Server) address (four numbers); if there's a Secondary DNS, get its address, too (another four numbers). Again, you'll probably be told they do this dynamically.
- Name of your provider's mail system (something like **daemon.microsoft.com**); the mail server is also commonly called a POP server, but don't tell MOM that, OK? Also find out if there is a different SMTP server.
- If you want to access Usenet newsgroups, you'll need the name of the ISP's news server.

There are a few other things you'll need to know but probably won't be able to get over the phone. With a little luck, you can find them in the material the provider sends to you. You need your logon user name and password (the ones you use to log on to the provider's computer) and your e-mail address, if you have one (like, oh, billg@microsoft.com).

For a LAN setup, you'll need a Gateway Address instead of a phone number and you may have hardcoded IP and DNS numbers.

Let's step through the Wizard now and take a look at the things you'll need to figure out. If you have an icon on the Desktop called Connect to the Internet, click on it. That'll start the Internet Connection Wizard. Otherwise, you should have an icon called The Internet that will invoke the Wizard. Right click on that, pick Properties, go to the Connection tab and hit the Connect. . . button (Figure 4-40). Or you can pick Programs/Internet Explorer/Connection Wizard on the Start Menu.

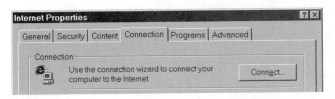

Figure 4-40. Getting to the Internet Connection Wizard

The first few steps branch into all sorts of possibilities. I'm going to take you through the scenario where you've signed up with a "local" ISP.

In the first step (Figure 4-41 left) you pick among three choices.

1. You want to set up a new connection including signup. The computer asks for your area code and dials an 800 number to retrieve a list of possible ISPs for you to choose from.

 Grumble. Guess who gets to charge ISPs for the privilege of being on this referral list?

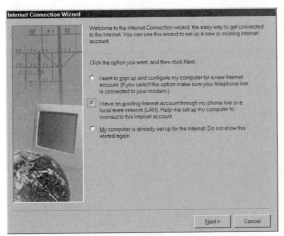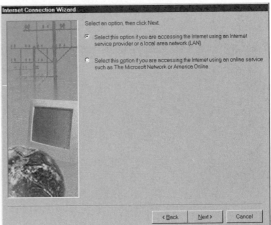

Figure 4-41. First two steps in the Internet Connection Wizard

2. You already have an account (the scenario we are following).

3. Banish the wizard from the Desktop, because you are already set up, thank you.

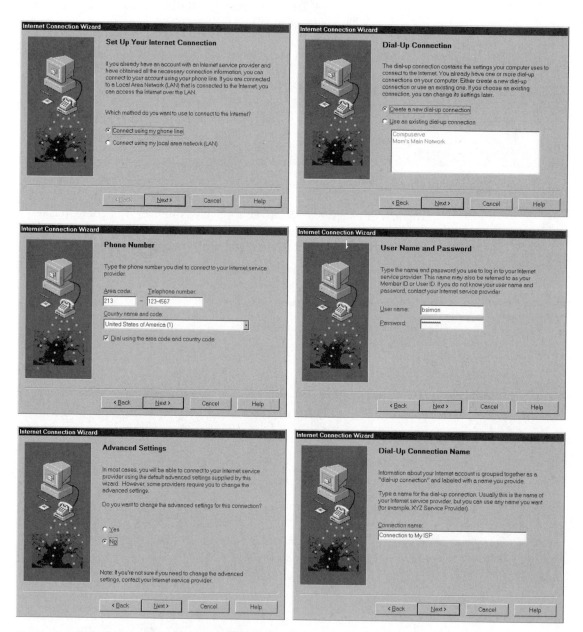

Figure 4-42. Setting up the Dial-Up connectoid

In the second panel (Figure 4-41 right), you choose either

1. Local ISP or LAN
2. National ISP. If you pick this, you are told to start in the Online Services Folder, not the Wizard—something I told you already!

 If Microsoft were elegant, it would open the folder for you!

The next steps set up the Dial-Up Networking connection. (As you read the steps, follow along in Figure 4-42.)

1. Pick a phone connection (the branch we'll follow) or LAN. If you pick the LAN, you fill in Gateway and/or Proxy Server information. Your system administrator will probably give you exactly the information you need.
2. Unless you've already set up some Dial-Up connectoids, you won't even see this screen. If you have, pick an existing connectoid and skip the next three steps.
3. Give the ISP's phone number.
4. Fill in your user name and password.
5. Deal with some Advanced settings. You can probably say No here; you want to say Yes only if you are dealing with one of four special situations: SLIP rather than PPP, the need for a login script, a hardwired IP address, or a hardwired DNS address.
6. Name the connectoid.

Congratulations, you've set up the connectoid! Onward, brave one.

You can now set up accounts for Mail, News, and LDAP directory service (Figure 4-43). If you answer Yes for any of these, you invoke appropriate account setup wizards for Outlook Express. I describe what happens if you ask to set up an e-mail account in the section "Setting Up an E-mail Connection" in Chapter 3. My guess is that you'll want to set up mail and news (assuming you have a news server name from your ISP). You probably won't set up any LDAP accounts other than the built-in ones.

Behind the scenes, the Internet Connection Wizard installs Dial-Up Networking and/or TCP/IP support and **winsock.dll** for your Dial-Up Networking adapter or for your LAN adapter if needed.

Bear in mind that all this Wizard does is set up a DUN if not already in place, a Dial-Up connectoid, and possible OE accounts. You can do the former by picking Make New Connection in the Dial-Up Networking folder and the latter with the New Account Wizard in OE. You may need to do this if you want to set up only one of these accounts, say an extra connectoid when you are on the road or an additional e-mail account.

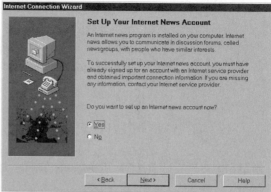

Figure 4-43. Setting up accounts

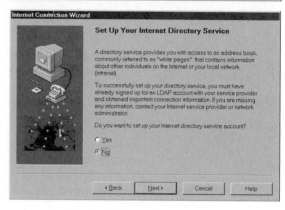

Can't Get Connected

The most common interconnection problem is a phone line that just sits there and does nothing. You double click on The Internet, wait a minute or two, hear the modem being dialed and the other end picking up, they squeal for a bit, and then absolutely nothing happens. After a while you may get a message saying that you were disconnected or that the computers were unable to establish a compatible protocol. That's all hogwash.

If you got all the entries in the Wizard right and you can log on to your service provider manually (you should double-check both, of course), the most likely source of the problem lies *with your service provider's computer* and its inability to automatically log on Win98 users. Here's how you can check to see if that's what's keeping you from getting on (Figure 4-44). Double click on My Computer, double click on Dial-Up Networking. Right click on the name of the connection you typed into the Wizard and pick Properties. Click Configure. Click on the Options tab and check the box marked "Bring up terminal window after dialing." Click OK all the way back out. That check box tells Win98, "Go

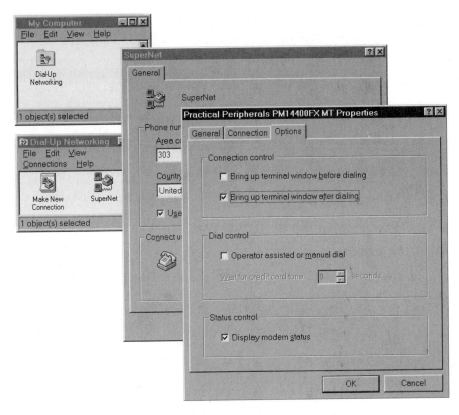

Figure 4-44. Bringing up a terminal window

ahead and dial the phone, but when the computer on the other end asks for a logon user name and password, let me type them in."

Now double click on The Internet on your Desktop. You hear the modem dialing and the squeal that typifies happy cyberconnections. As soon as the connection is established, a window pops up and you go through your usual logon sequence. You probably have to enter your logon user name and password and some sort of command like **ppp** or **slip**; your service provider can give you the details. When the screen starts to spout gibberish, hit **F7** to see if the two computers can sort out their differences and connect.

If that solves the problem, get on the phone with your service provider and yell bloody murder: they'd better get with the system according to Windows 98, or they're gonna lose your business! Or figure out how to make a script to automate the process.

If that *doesn't* solve your problem, call your service provider. They should be quite accustomed to Win9X questions by now. And remember that Microsoft charges $35 a pop (or $1.95 a minute) to answer Network questions.

Can't Get Your Mail

 The second most common problem occurs when you can log on, the Internet browses the Web just fine, but for some unknown reason Outlook Express won't retrieve your Internet mail. Again, if you got the settings in the Wizard right and you can retrieve your mail with some other program (double check both), the fault may lie with your service provider—but in this case, it really isn't their fault.

Some service providers require a separate Internet e-mail user name and password, different from your usual logon user name and password. That's not necessarily a bad thing, but it does require some extra effort on your part to get Windows to use it. Most likely, you typed in the same user name and password in two places the Wizard asked for them.

Start by finding out what your Internet e-mail user name and password are. You may have to rummage through the settings of your current e-mail package; you may have to call your service provider once again. When you have the user name and password, start Outlook Express, go to the Tools/Accounts . . . menu item, click on your mail account, click Properties and check out the Servers tab to make sure you have the account name and password right. Of course, the password will be stars, so reenter it and see if that solves the problem.

■ Internet Tools

A successful tool is one that is used to do something undreamed of by its author.

—S. C. JOHNSON

The Internet Applet

I think it is truly a wonderful thing that, through the Miracle of Computing, millions of people can read my column instead of leading productive lives.

—DAVE BARRY, commenting on
the online posting of his column

I discuss most aspects of the Internet applet in Chapter 8 but deal with one aspect here because it is central to Internet connectivity. I've explained how to set up a proper PPP signon to the Internet and I'm about to explain how to use various Internet applications. But how do you link the signon and the applications? One way is manual. You can start any Dial-Up connection by double clicking its icon in the DUN folder. Or you can drag the icon to the Desktop or a Start Menu subfolder to make a shortcut and launch it that way. If you have multiple Internet Dial-Up connections, even if you've chosen a preferred provider by the method I come to momentarily, you can override that choice

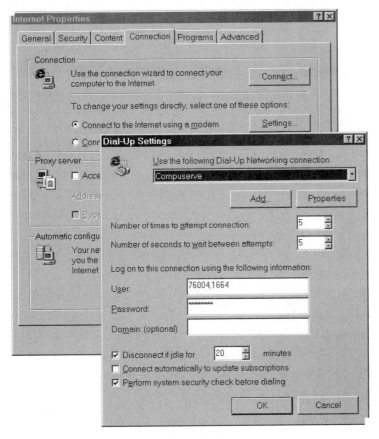

Figure 4-45. Choosing a preferred provider

by just starting some other provider and letting the logon finish before you start the Internet application.

The Wizard should have set up the connection you made for autodial, but if it didn't or if you set up the connectoid by hand, here's how you set up the connection yourself. It's also how you change the preferred provider (the one used for automatic dialing). Call up the Internet Control Panel applet—from Control Panel, or as the Properties of the Desktop's The Internet, or as View/Internet Options in IE itself.

Hop to the Connection tab and make sure that "Connect to the Internet using a modem" is chosen. Hit the Settings button (Figure 4-45). At the top is a dropdown where you pick the connectoid that is used for autodial. That's where you change it.

If you don't want autodial, simply use "Connect to the Internet using a local area network" in the Connections tab.

Do this even if you don't have a LAN—this choice doesn't mean what it says. What it really means is "Don't use autodial, use a connection that exists before you connect."

 But that would be lying to Windows. What's become of our high moral standard when computer books advise their readers to outright lie to their computers?

 Autodial is so convenient that I urge you to think hard before disabling it. Consider the intermediate mode I discuss at the end of the section.

I emphasize knowing about the choice of radio buttons, "Connect to the Internet using a modem" and "Connect to the Internet using a local area network." I visited a friend in a corporation with a fast T3 connection to the Internet and wanted to use my laptop, which is set up for Dial-Up connections. My friend's office had an extra Ethernet port, I had a dual Ethernet/Modem card, and the network folks in his office said I could connect. I knew enough to call up the Network applet and configure the TCP/IP protocol for the Ethernet adapter using the IP address, gateway address, and DNS addresses the net folks gave me. But that didn't work. I could not access the net or their LAN through Network Neighborhood. Then I remembered those radio buttons. I switched to "Connect to the Internet using a local area network" and things worked perfectly. Even Network Neighborhood suddenly worked!

 Notice the other options in the Dial-Up Settings panel in Figure 4-45. If you don't want to disconnect automatically, uncheck the first check box at the bottom. Think hard before you enable autodial for subscriptions— do you really want the computer dialing out at three in the morning?

If you configure this applet to autodial, then whenever you start any Internet application, it first checks to see if you are connected to the Internet and if you are, it uses that connection. Otherwise, it requests that Windows 98 start up the provider you choose in the dropdown, and the Dialing Progress dialog appears (Figure 4-46). It's all sort of magical.

 Adding to the appearance of magic are the smarts that are built into Dial-Up Networking (Figure 4-47). If an Internet application has invoked an autodial connection, then if that connection is lost while the application is still running, it autodials again. When you exit the application that initiated the connection, you get the dialog in Figure 4-47.

There is an intermediate mode between requiring a previously set-up connection and totally automated Dial-Up. If you hit Cancel in the dialog in Figure 4-46, you are greeted with the dialog in Figure 4-48. If you uncheck the box "Connect automatically," you are shifted to a mode where every time a program wants to access the Internet,

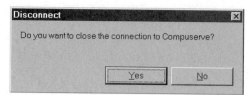

Figure 4-46. Autodial now

Figure 4-47. Smart connections

Figure 4-48. The Dial-Up semiautomatic dialog

you get the dialog in Figure 4-48 (but with the box unchecked). You can then choose to Connect or to Work Offline.

Browsing the Web with Internet Explorer

That devilish Iron Horse, whose ear-rending neigh is heard throughout the town, has muddied the Boiling Spring with his foot, and he it is that has browsed off all the woods on Walden shore, that Trojan horse, with a thousand men in his belly, introduced by mercenary Greeks! Where is the country's champion, the Moore of Moore Hall, to meet him at the Deep Cut and thrust an avenging lance between the ribs of the bloated pest?

—HENRY DAVID THOREAU, *Walden*

The basic browsing metaphor is one I'm sure you are familiar with so I'm not going to dwell on it. Instead I want to talk about three of the aspects of IE 4 you might miss: Web page context menus, offline browsing, and foreign language display. This supplements the tips I gave in Chapter 3 in the section "MOM's Tip-Top IE Tip List."

You'll want to check out the right-click context menus that are active when you are viewing an HTML document (whether online or local) in Internet Explorer (Figure 4-49). You get different menus for the page as a whole, for links, and for graphics.

Especially noteworthy are the Link command Open in a New Window and the Background command View Source; they can give you a quick lesson in

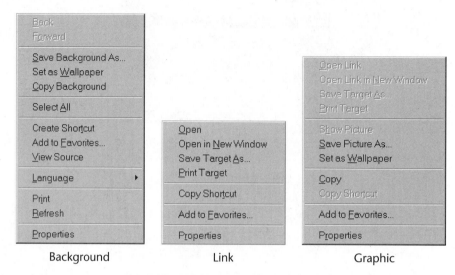

Background   Link   Graphic

Figure 4-49. Web page context menus

what HTML is all about. Notice the Set as [Desktop] Wallpaper items in each context menu. This saves the graphic (typically a **.jpg** or **.gif** file) as the Windows bitmap **C:\windows\internet explorer wallpaper.bmp**. Each time you save, the file is overwritten, so if you want to save a wallpaper, be sure to rename the file.

You can directly access the ability to save a file as **.bmp** by using the Save Background As . . . or Save Picture As . . . items and choosing Bitmap **(*.bmp)** from the "Save as type" dropdown. Since you can load any **.jpg** or **.gif** file from disk using Internet Explorer's File/Open dialog, the program can serve as a file conversion utility.

 The Background wallpaper referred to is the tiled effect under the text and graphics on some sites. The tiles tend to be freely grabbed from one site to another even though it may be a copyright violation.

Note Create Shortcut in the Background context menu. It places a shortcut to the current page on your desktop. Copy Shortcut on the Link menu places a shortcut to the link on the clipboard where you can paste it. I wonder why the designers made the two behaviors different?

An especially useful mode for IE on a laptop is the use of offline browsing. When the dialog in Figure 4-48 appears (either because you hit Cancel in Figure 4-46 or you have unchecked autodial), you can pick Work Offline. In that mode you can browse any pages in the cache. These pages might be there because you used subscriptions or you did a quick look while connected to the Net. So you can grab pages before that plane ride and then browse offline. While in offline mode, Windows 98 stops trying to connect to the Internet.

 You may wonder how to turn off offline mode. If you ask to refresh a page (or click on a link not in the cache), Windows pops up the dialog in Figure 4-50. If you hit Connect, you turn off offline.

Figure 4-50. Going back online

Another nook fraught with potential problems is display of non-Latin alphabets in IE. We illustrate with Hebrew. Look at Figures 4-51 and 4-52 to see the difference between a good and a bad setup.

The difference is the use of the right fonts. The reason that the bad setup looks so strange is that traditionally, Hebrew is encoded in ASCII codes just above 128, which are used for accented Latin characters in the IBM scheme. The right fonts have Hebrew characters at the right positions. The right fonts don't come with Windows 98, but they are available for free on the Web; a good place to get more information and the fonts themselves is `http://www.snunit.k12.il/heb_new.html`. I got Figure 4-52 using the font ElroNet. After downloading the fonts and extracting them, I copied them to the `C:\windows\fonts` folder, thereby installing them as Windows fonts. Then I called up the Internet Properties dialog, and on the General tab I hit the Fonts . . . button. In the resulting dialog (Figure 4-53), I picked the ElroNet fonts. Voilà, the Hebrew displayed properly.

 Microsoft has Cyrillic and other Eastern European fonts available for download on its Web site.

 This solves the problem, but in searching for solutions, I came across a number of puzzles that are tantalizing. These involve the Language button and the Language submenu.

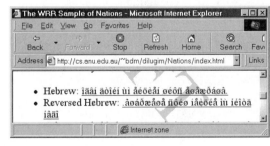

Figure 4-51. Huh?

Figure 4-52. That's more like it!

Figure 4-53. IE Fonts dialog

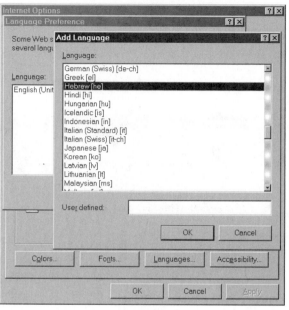

Figure 4-54. IE Language dialog

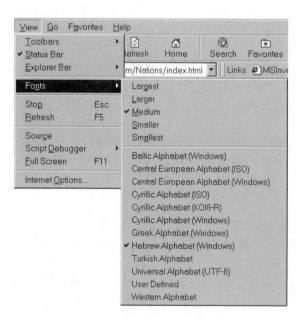

Figure 4-55. Language submenu

On the same panel of Internet Properties that has the Fonts . . . button is a Languages . . . button that leads to the dialog shown in Figure 4-54. But adding Hebrew there or deleting it had no effect whatsoever on the display with or without the ElroNet font installed and it had no effect on the Fonts submenu. I have no idea what the heck it does.

In IE itself, there is a submenu of the View menu called Fonts (Figure 4-55). Notice that Hebrew Alphabet is checked. That would seem to be what we need, and indeed, on the system this menu was taken from, when it is checked, Hebrew displays in the standard New Times Roman font with no special ElroNet fonts loaded. The problem is that this menu is taken from an NT system. On our test Windows 98 system, the menu is the same except that no Hebrew Alphabet item appears. Darned if I can figure out how to get it.

Push, Active Channel Bar, and Subscriptions

The promotion of Push is the silliest piece of puffery to waft along in several seasons.

—JAMES GLEICK, *New York Times Magazine,* March 23,1997

In early 1997, prime planning time for Windows 98, Push was all the rage in the computer magazines, at the computer shows, and in the general buzz at computer companies. The idea was that rather than users browsing the Web looking for information, information would go to them, arriving on their desktop. This was a silly idea, but it had a few pure nuggets. For one of the few voices of reason, see James Gleick's "Push Me, Pull You," which originally appeared in the *New York Times Magazine* and is now at **http://www.around.com/push.html**.

The expectation that this model would be a huge success had two sources. First, the phenomenal feat of PointCast impressed the industry. Second, the desire gave birth to the perception. Let me explain.

PointCast was a free program that went out to the Net and grabbed news-clips, stock quotes, sports scores, and so on and presented them to you in a somewhat clunky but still useable form including a screen saver with headlines and scores. It made money with the little ads it included in the corner. Millions started using the product, and the frequent updates that PointCast scarfed off the Web brought more than one corporate LAN to its knees.

But the pundits misunderstood the reasons. This was in the early days of the Web. Sites like the current **cnn.com** and the current plethora of stock quote sites did not exist. People were taken by the content, not the delivery mechanism.

And the industry began to think about how nice Push would be: Web browsing is controlled by the user; Push is controlled by the pusher.

 Hmm. Pushers and users! Quite a statement about the technology isn't it? Hmm.

To the content providers, Push was wonderful. But not to users who had gotten the hang of browsing. Push bombed. It's almost passé. But it's built it into Windows 98 (or rather IE 4). I think most of you can ignore it.

If you have a really fast Internet connection—a corporate T1 or a cable modem at home—you don't need Push to leave what you want on your hard disk. You just add a few sites like CNN and MS Investor to your Favorites, and that beats Push any day. If you have a slow dial-up connection, do you really want Push clogging it at any old time of day or night? Push via e-mail (look at the description of Infobeat in the top mailing lists in Chapter 3) does make sense. Straight Push is a solution in search of a problem.

Figure 4-56.
Channel
Bar

 I have one system connected via a 55-K modem more or less all the time. My phone company hates people like me, as does my ISP, but I pay the same flat rate to both whether I dial in as needed or stay connected. So on that system, I've subscribed to PointCast, and it is downloaded—but to tell the truth, I hardly ever use it!

So maybe you want to use a little pit of Push—for example, Windows 98/IE 4 subscriptions?—but I'll bet not much. If subscriptions are minimally useful, you certainly won't want to waste Desktop real estate with the glitzy subscription agent called Channel Bar (Figure 4-56). Get rid of it! For example, you can right click the Desktop, pick Active Desktop/Customize my Desktop . . . , and uncheck Internet Explorer Channel Bar.

If you want to experiment with subscriptions, one route is to look at the Active Channel Guide (Figure 4-57) online. You reach this by opening IE, clicking on the Go menu and choosing Channel Guide. Or if you want to see the exact list of channels that the Active Channel Bar would give, hit the Channels button on the IE button bar. The resulting view (Figure 4-58) has a list of channels you

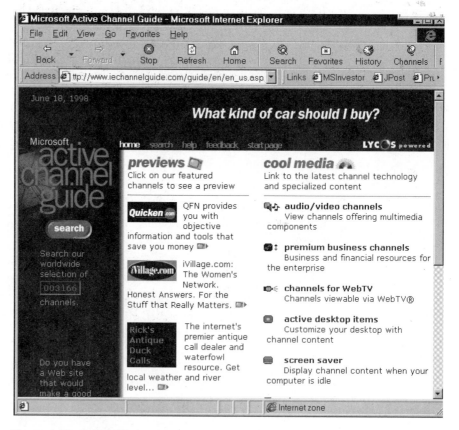

Figure 4-57. Active Channel Guide

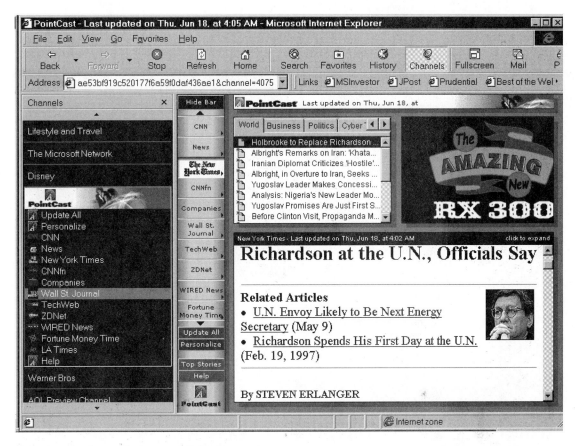

Figure 4-58. Channel pane and PointCast

can access at the left and displays signup information or the channels themselves at the right.

 In Figure 4-58, the right side displays PointCast inside IE—if you've ever run the stand-alone program, you'll recognize it.

Here's how you install a new channel (Figure 4-59).

1. In the Channel Guide, look for the button to Add Active Channel and click it.

2. When you get the Add Active Channel panel, decide if you only want the channel added to the Active Channel Bar and panel, want e-mail notification, or want it pushed (downloaded).

3. If you want Push, I suggest you pick Customize . . . . The first step in this Wizard lets you decide to download only the home page or all the content specified by the site.

Step 1

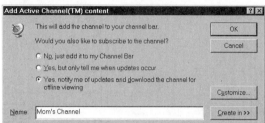

Step 2

Step 3

Step 4

Step 5

Figure 4-59. Installing a new subscription

4. You can choose e-mail notification.

5. You can pick the schedule.

When you add a site to your Favorites, you get a dialog similar to the one in Figure 4-59, Step 2, and the customization is then similar to Steps 3–5.

 It's neat to set up a Favorite so that you are notified by e-mail whenever the page changes. You can also subscribe to your favorite sites for later offline viewing on a laptop on an airplane.

 The way notification by mail works is that, behind the scenes, IE compares the creation date of the page to what it has stored as the last change date. If IE determines that the page has changed, it sends e-mail to you. In essence, your computer is sending e-mail to itself. A little weird.

 Once you've set up channels and/or subscriptions, two folders are important. `C:\windows\favorites\channels` shows the actual channels (Figure 4-60) while `C:\windows\subscriptions` shows information on the subscriptions (Figure 4-61). If you bring up the property sheet for a subscription, you get to change the precise properties that you set up in the Customize Wizard when you made the Channel.

 The items in the Channels folder are a bit weird. They are actually directories (!) with a single file `desktop.ini`. That file is ASCII with a CLSID, url for the Channel definition, and names for logo and icons that are typically stored in `C:\windows\web`.

Figure 4-60. Channels folder

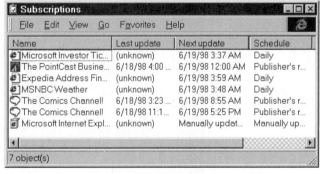

Figure 4-61. Subscriptions folder

FrontPage Express

Outlook Express is a very pale imitation of Outlook and Write a pale imitation of Word. But FrontPage Express (FPE), the HTML editor included with Windows 98 (Figure 4-62) is more than a pale imitation of FrontPage 98. It's true that FrontPage 98 is awesome at managing whole Web sites and has style sheets and oodles of goodies. But as an HTML editor, FrontPage Express is wonderful. In fact, it is basically the HTML editor from FrontPage 97.

- Its main mode is totally WYSIWYG, so you don't have fiddle with raw HTML codes.
- It has a color-coded viewer/editor if you want to use raw HTML.
- It has a table editor, which is a vast improvement over raw HTML table creation.
- It supports marquees and background sounds and colors.
- It allows you to place form fields and various controls (for example, buttons) in the middle of the text.
- You can add a control that displays the last time the page was edited.

 The Help that comes with FPE, though, is just about the worst I've seen in any computer program. Skimpy hardly describes it. Just awful.

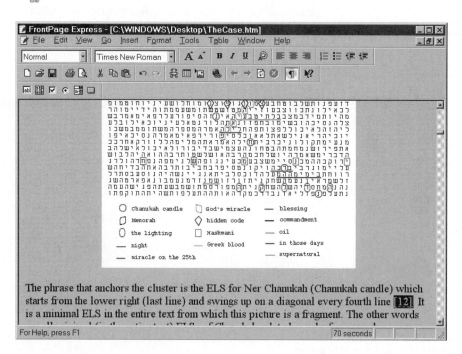

Figure 4-62. FrontPage Express

Figure 4-63. It was called Comic Chat for a reason

Microsoft Chat

Before Microsoft purchased it, the product was known as Comic Chat (Figure 4-63). It's the front end of a chat room with comic characters that can have expressions and gestures. You can run it in a pure text mode, but the comic strip mode is what appeals to potential users.

 If you're into the chat room scene, this may appeal to you; if not, you can uninstall it.

NetMeeting

NetMeeting (Figure 4-64) is a substantial application. By using it, you and someone else on the Internet can exchange voice, video, text, files, and more. Microsoft and **411.com** have set up public Internet Locator Servers (ILSs) that you can use to set up a connection with the other party. Your system administrator can also set a private ILS on an Intranet—details are available at **http://www.microsoft.com/netmeeting/ils**.

With NetMeeting you can do the following.

- Make voice calls, if you and the other party have standard audio hardware, including a decent microphone. When NetMeeting is started the first time, it runs an Audio Tuning Wizard to test and configure this hardware; you can run it any time from the Tools menu.

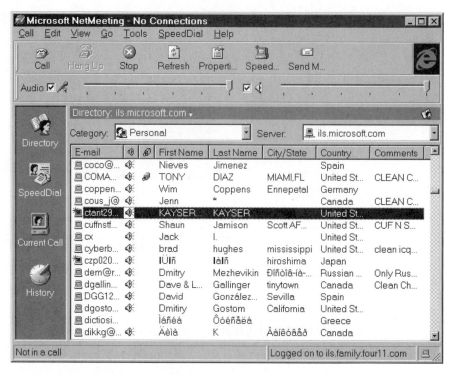

Figure 4-64. Microsoft NetMeeting

- Make video calls, if you have video camera attached to your computer.
- Go into chat mode where you type messages to each other. This is especially useful for multiple-person meetings, which are possible.
- Open a special white board application, where you can draw in a common shared area.
- Share applications over the Internet. Each application can be controlled by only one person at a time.
- Send files to each other.

 Especially if you are connected via a corporate LAN or Intranet, Net-Meeting deserves a very close look. It is now in version 2.1, and many of the glitches in earlier versions are gone.

NetShow

Ain't much to say about NetShow. It's Microsoft's answer to Real Video. Both programs attempt to send video in real time over 28.8 or at least 55-KB modems. If you go to a site that has a NetShow video, it will start up in the browser as an ActiveX control. Why you'd want the stand-alone player is beyond me. You can remove it from your Start Menu.

Yo, Billy, can you tell me who *is* using NetShow?

Well, there's the Microsoft site. And there's the site that Microsoft runs. Oh, and did I mention the Microsoft site?

Microsoft hasn't put a big push behind NetShow and has even invested in the makers of Real Video. But I wouldn't count them out. They may change their minds, and then who knows.

Personal Web Server

A desktop user needs a personal web server like a fish needs a bicycle.

—MOM's list of aphorisms

Used to be that Web server software was a thousand-dollar proposition. We throw one in, admittedly a somewhat limited one, free with Windows 98.

Only one type—well one and a half types—of users need to consider installing Personal Web Server. Web developers will find a Web server incredibly useful. That's why the full-blown FrontPage has long included Personal Web Server. The developer can test pages without installing them on a production system.

The second set of users who will find PWS useful is the SOHO market with a purely peer-to-peer network—they can set up an intranet with PWS on one of the workstations.

Yeah, but the SOHO types should bite the bullet and spring for Microsoft's Small Business Server, which includes NT Server and its full-blown Web Server.

You install PWS by popping the Windows CD in, browsing to **\add-ons\pws** and running **setup.exe**. Depending on how much online documentation you load, it will take from 35 to 170 MB of disk space. For example, PWS supports Active Serve Pages. The documentation for them is 60 MB!

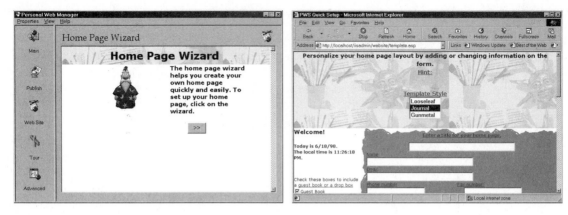

Figure 4-65. PWS Home Page Wizard

Of course the main component of PWS is the server itself, but included are a Personal Web Manager with a wizard to make your site's home page (Figure 4-65) and Microsoft Transaction Server (MTS).

 I can't believe they've included MTS. I first saw it in December of 1986 just before it shipped as a multithousand dollar add-on for NT Server. I was blown away. Before MTS, you needed highly specialized (and highly paid) programmers to build transactional databases—ones that wouldn't lose data if they crashed in midstream. After all, you wouldn't want to take someone's order and then lose it. MTS encapsulated it and made transactional databases easy to make. I thought at the time that I could imagine a company president saying to her CIO: "I don't care if we are a UNIX-only shop— deploy some NT Servers so they can run MTS." And now it's bundled on the Windows 98 CD!

Other Internet Tools

While the main Internet tools are Outlook Express and Internet Explorer (or some other mail program and browser), some other minor tools are included with Windows 98. They aren't installed on the Start Menu, so you need to put them there or else enter them at the command line.

Telnet   Telnet means `C:\windows\telnet.exe`. This is a Windows application (Figure 4-66) that presents a fairly dumb terminal mode where you type in text commands and get text responses. It's important because there are still an awful lot of dumb terminal interfaces out there.

As you can see (Figure 4-67), there are some very simple options available via the Terminal/Preferences . . . menu choice. You can change the background color and, through the Fonts button, the foreground color. The terminal

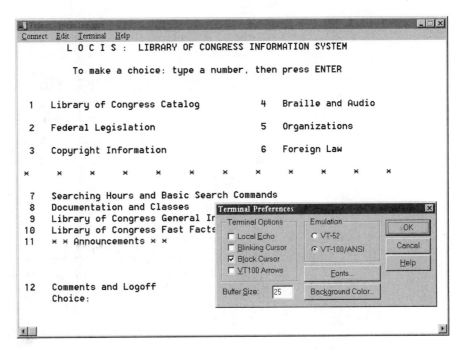

Figure 4-66. Telneting to the Library of Congress

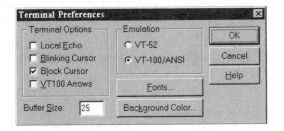

Figure 4-67. Telnet options

emulation is limited; most notably, what is often called ANSI BBS (which gives colors and other fancy BBS screens) is missing.† With the advent of Telnet-accessible BBS, this limitation will be important for some.

There is no support for keyboard translation, and in particular on systems that don't understand **Backspace** but use **Del** for **Backspace**, you can't redefine **Backspace** to send a **Del**.

 All the fonts available under the Fonts button are fixed pitch since terminal programs often assume you have fixed-width characters.

---

† ANSI = American National Standards Institute. While the ANSI BBS spec is related to the ANSI spec for VT-100 terminals, they are distinct and the ANSI there doesn't mean that ANSI BBS colors are supported—they are not.

The most important setting is buffer size, which is given in lines. The default is 25 lines, but I've run it under some circumstances at 500 lines and the scrollback was wonderful. But this is a setting you need to change with care. Some terminal mode UNIX programs go bananas if they think your screen size is more than 25 lines. Telnet would be much more useful if you could assign a buffer size on a per-connection basis, but you can't—it's global and you'll have to change it by hand.

The Windows 98 Telnet program is barely adequate for the occasional user of Telnet services. Now that Hyperterminal allows Telnet connections you should use it instead.

FTP

Real men don't eat quiche, and I guess they must feel they have to use command line FTP utilities that show them raw UNIX-style directory listings and make them worry about the difference between mode binary and mode ascii. I can't imagine why anyone would use this utility instead of using a browser to do FTP. But if you like to demonstrate your machismo, its there as **C:\windows\ftp.exe**. Run it if you get nostalgic for the **C>** prompt.

Check out FTP Voyager in Chapter 5 if you do a lot of FTP work.

Miscellaneous Here are one-line descriptions of little Internet applets you'll find in **C:\windows**.

- **ARP** Displays and modifies the IP-to-Physical address translation tables used by address resolution protocol (ARP), whatever that is.
- **Ping** Diagnostic tool that sends packets to an IP address and waits for them to echo back.
- **Route** Manipulates the network routing table. Keep your hands off this unless you are a network guru.
- **Tracert** Traces the connection route; more later.
- **Winipcfg** The only GUI program of the five, this displays the IP configuration in a window.

If you want to be awed at how the Internet works, open up a DOS window when you are connected it an Internet provider and type **tracert whitehouse.gov** at a DOS prompt. You'll be amazed at what a long route of nodes is taken.

Two uses of Ping. If you want to see if you are connected to a TCP/IP network, find the numeric IP address of at least one node on the LAN and **ping** it. If it replies, at least your hardware is working. Second, if you suspect your DNS service isn't working but you want to confirm that you are really on the Internet, type **ping 198.137.241.30**. That's the IP address of **whitehouse.gov**. If it pongs back, you know the connection is working.

In *Windows 95*, we used **ftp.microsoft.com**, but the Microsoft site is so busy that these utilities are likely to time out trying to interact with it!

■ Your WordPad or Mine?

Quotation . . . A writer expresses himself in words that have been used before because they give his meaning better than he can give it himself, or because they are beautiful or witty, or because he expects them to touch a cord of association in his reader, or because he wishes to show that he is learned and well read. Quotations due to the last motive are invariably ill-advised; the discerning reader detects it and is contemptuous; the undiscerning is perhaps impressed, but even then is at the same time repelled, pretentious quotations being the surest road to tedium.

— Henry W. Fowler, *A Dictionary of Modern English Usage*

Oh, wow, I'm impressed by how well read and learned you are to have found that quote. But I find the quote kinda tedious, maybe even repulsive.

ASCII files are ones that store pure text together with characters that indicate the ends of lines. No formatting information is stored. Examples of ASCII files are your basic pre-Windows 95 configuration files (**autoexec.bat**, **win.ini**, etc.), **.ini** files for most Windows 3.x programs, and batch files.

Language source code (except for many flavors of BASIC) is also ASCII. That means that the ASCII file editor market is broken into two parts editors intended for mere mortals and the programmer's editors with macro languages to warm the heart of a true code aficionado, compile-from-within options, and other goodies.

So you need an ASCII editor to change your ASCII files. Windows 98 comes with, count 'em, four different programs that can manipulate ASCII files.

You may be a mathematician, Barry, but you can't count. Everyone knows that Windows comes with two such programs: Notepad and WordPad.

Besides Notepad and WordPad, Windows 98 has a specialized program called System Configuration Utility for editing your standard ASCII system files and there is a DOS-based editor called **edit** that is by far the best of the bunch!

Notepad will edit a single file at a time as long as the file isn't too large—once it is too large you get a message offering to load WordPad, which has no limit on the size files it will load. I tried a 20-MB ASCII file with WordPad and it did load, although **Ctrl+End** to get to the bottom of the file took a *long* time. System Configuration Utility (SCU) loads four files but those are hard-coded as the four system files: **config.sys**, **autoexec.bat**, **win.ini**, and **system.ini.** I discuss SCU in Chapter 6.

The limit for Notepad is about 50 KB—it is clearly related to the 64-KB data segment limit for 16-bit programs, so it shows Notepad is still not 32 bit.

Notepad's Print command lets you put in date, time, and filename into headers and footers using the following special codes.

&d	Current date
&p	Page numbers
&f	Current filename
&l	Text (following the code) to be aligned at the left margin
&r	Text (following the code) to be aligned at the right margin
&c	Text (following the code) to be centered between the margins
&t	Current time

To have a header with the date at the left margin, filename centered in the middle, and page number at the right, you would type **&l&d&c&f&rPage &p** in the header entry of the File/Page Setup menu dialog. These strings can now be found in the Notepad online Help, but they also appear if you press **?** in the File/Page Setup . . . dialog and point at the word Header, which is where you need them.

Notepad lets you add the date and time to a file from Time/Date item on the Edit menu. Even more interesting, if you put **.LOG** on the first line of a file (it needs to be the only thing on the line, it must be the first line, it must start at the right, and it must be in ALL CAPS), Notepad will append the date and time to the bottom of the file every time you open it.

On Notepad's Edit menu is a toggle called Word Wrap. It wraps long lines at the word break closest to the right edge of the window, adjusting breaks as you resize the Notepad window. Use it with care, because you can forget it is on and save a file missing line breaks where you thought they were! And don't print with it on because Print does not wrap lines, and you won't realize what won't print if Word Wrap is on.

So what's missing? Here's a partial list.

- Ability to open several files at once. It sure would be nice to have an MDI interface available in Notepad.
- Most recently opened file list—for example, have the file menu display the last three files you opened and let you reopen by just picking, à la the word processing programs
- Search and Replace as well as Search
- Ability to handle very large files—at least to 300 K
- Goto line number command and a status bar showing line numbers
- Multilevel undo
- Ability to insert a file
- Word count
- Memory via dropdown lists of previous choices of print headers and previous search strings

Not a long list, but the features are significant.

 Check out Notepad+ in Chapter 5. It avoids a lot of these limitations.

There is also a DOS (!) program introduced with Windows 95 called **edit**. There has been an MS-DOS editor by that name since DOS 5, but that **edit** was a backdoor to a special mode of Qbasic where only the editor was active. This is a brand-new program that at least avoids some of the above deficiencies—you can load up to nine files, there is Replace, it loads files with up to 65,280 lines, and line numbers are displayed in the status bar. But there is no Undo at all, no file insertion (although you can load a second file and cut and paste), no GoTo, no recently opened list, no word count. Edit is undoubtedly the best tool Windows provides to edit ASCII files, but it is still nothing to rave about.

 Millions of Windows users edit ASCII files each day. Is it too much to ask for a tool that is halfway decent?

Write, Windows' venerable word processing applet, has been retired and replaced by WordPad. In some ways, WordPad is an improvement. It reads Rich Text and Word **.doc** files. It's got a button bar and a ruler, and through the View/Options . . . dialog, you can turn them on or off independently for the four file types WordPad supports: Text, RTF, Word, and Write. Just as Write was a showcase for OLE 1.0, WordPad is a showcase for OLE 2.0—you can embed an object and have the native menus for the object appear when you are editing it. You can drop OLE scrap onto the Desktop.

But when it comes to word processing features, WordPad is a step backwards. The only supported tab stop is left, you can't justify paragraphs, and you can't insert page breaks, for example. WordPad will do for the occasional one-page informal letter, but you need a real word processor if you intend to produce printed documents often.

 WordPad's so-called support for Word **.doc** files is rather lacking. It is royally confused by tables, doesn't show colored text, and otherwise is something of a mess.

 Another Write feature missing in WordPad is the ability to load binary files. Write would load them, display their ASCII strings, and let you change them.

 That was hardly a feature in Write—it was giving users a gun that tended to explode in their face if they pulled the trigger. The relative positions in a binary file are critical to the proper working of that file. With Write you could easily edit a string and inadvertently change its length, turning the binary file into junk or worse.

■ Draw, Pardner

Vigorous writing is concise. A sentence should contain no unnecessary words, a paragraph no unnecessary sentences, for the same reason that a drawing should have no unnecessary lines and a machine no unnecessary parts.

—WILLIAM STRUNK, JR., AND E. B. WHITE, *The Elements of Style*

 Here we'll look at the two bitmap editors that come with Windows. Paint is pretty poor. Imaging is wonderful as a fax reader but not outstanding as a bitmap manipulator. If you need this stuff much, you'll want one of the many $50 photo editors on the market or one of the higher-end products like PhotoShop and Picture Publisher.

 If you have Office 97, you have Photo Editor, Microsoft's lower-end bitmap manipulator. Some might prefer Adobe's low-end product, Photo Deluxe, although I prefer Photo Editor. But the bottom line is that either is vastly better than the bitmap products that ship with Windows.

 If you convert a lot of images to **.jpg** for the Web, you'll want to invest in PhotoShop—it does the best job on that process by far.

Painted into a Corner

Microsoft Paint is a bitmap editor that is an improvement over the Paintbrush program included with Windows 3.1, but it is still pretty limited (Figure 4-68). There are three functions one wants to use bitmap manipulation programs for: file conversion, bitmap editing, and bitmap creation. Paint is limited in all three areas!

Figure 4-68. Microsoft Paint

The native format for Paint is Windows Bitmap (`.bmp`). Indeed, it can save only in this format. In principle, this is a loss from Widows 3.1's Paintbrush, which allowed saving in `.pcx` format, but in practice it isn't, since that save was problem prone! Paint can load five formats—`.bmp`, `.gif`, `.jpg`, `.pcx`, and `.tif`.

 I wonder why the Open dialog makes it appear that Paint will only load `.bmp` *and* `.jpg`.

All you need to do is choose All Files in the Open dialog dropdown and pick one of these types and it gets converted to `.bmp`. This is useful if you have a file in one of these formats that you want to use as wallpaper—you can save the file as a Windows Bitmap and use it as wallpaper—Paint even has a menu choice to make it easy. You can reduce 24-bit color bitmaps to 256 colors by using File/Save As, but there is no way to convert from color to gray scale images.

Bitmap editing is the weakest of the elements of Paint. You can resize, skew, rotate, and mark a block to move it. But there are no serious selection tools and nothing you can do with a selected area except move it or copy it to the clipboard. In particular, you cannot crop a picture. There are no filters, not even a simple brighten/contrast.

By using the size command, you can crop the right and/or bottom off a picture.

Note the resize. Because it requires you to resize separately in the horizontal and vertical directions and uses percentages, it's a pain to work with, but you can use it to resize wallpaper. Note that 640 x 480 to 800 x 600 is 125%, 640 x 480 to 1,024 x 768 is 160%, and 800 x 600 to 1,024 x 768 is 128%.

On the creation/annotation side of things, there is a pretty good text tool (see Figure 4-68; you right click on the text entry box and pick Text Toolbar to invoke the font change dialog), and there is a curve tool and tools to draw a polygon, rectangle, circle, and oval with the ability to draw a border only, a filled area, or an area with border. But anyone who has ever used a program like Fractal Painter will know that the creation tools are woefully limited.

So Paint does what it does with panache, but it is a pretty limited tool from any point of view.

C'mon, guys, gimme a break. Of course Paint isn't serious competition for Hijaak on file conversion, Picture Publisher on bitmap editing, or Fractal Painter on bitmap creation any more than WordPad is a competitor for Word. It's intended as a tool for users who want to futz a little with their wallpaper and little more. Oh, and it's part of the free screen capture program built into Windows 98, which you guys describe in Chapter 2 in the section "Keys to the Kingdom."

Imaging for Windows

Microsoft licensed Imaging for Windows from Wang, which then sold its software division to Kodak. It was included in Windows as a fax reader, and that's what it primarily is (see Chapter 3). But it can also serve for image manipulation in a pinch.

Its bitmap conversion tools are better than Paint's but still limited. You can open files in the following formats—`.tif`, `.awd`, `.bmp`, `.jpg`, `.pcx`, `.xif`, `.gif`, and `.wif`—and save as any of the three native formats, the first three in the list.

`.awd` is a fax format used by Messaging to save faxes. `.xif` is a Xerox modification of `.tif` used by its scanning software (Pagis Pro). I've no idea what the heck `.wif` is. The others are all the major standard bitmap formats.

But Imaging won't even change color depth. Its only conversion capability is to rotate an image—the manipulation most relevant to the fax recipient whose fax comes in upside down!

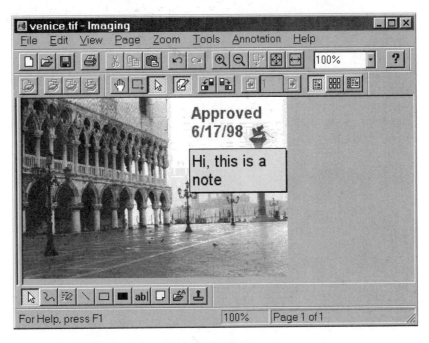

Figure 4-69. Imaging for Windows

Its bitmap editing and creation abilities are minimal and motivated by its roots as a fax manipulator. You can annotate with stamps and notes, as can be seen in Figure 4-69, but that's about it.

 The bottom line if you have Office is to remove Paint from your Start Menu and replace it with Photo Editor. Unless you get a lot of straight fax files, you can also remove Imaging from the Start Menu—that won't affect Messaging's ability to use it for fax rendering.

■ Little 'ns

Listen to me, little fetus,
Precious homo incompletus,
As you dream your dreams placental
Don't grow nothing accidental!

—Anonymous prospective father

The miscellaneous applications I discuss here are small little applets, but each is useful in its own way.

In fact Magnifier, if you are sight impaired, can be the most essential tool on your machine.

Calculator

It is wonderful when a calculation is made, how little the mind is actually employed in the discharge of any profession.

—SAMUEL JOHNSON

The Windows Calculator in its normal mode (Figure 4-70) is simplicity itself, but for a quick calculation, it can be very handy because Edit/Copy instantly places the result of the calculation on the clipboard. The base Calculator has four functions with square roots and one memory location. It supports up to thirteen-digit numbers. It will shift into scientific notation if numbers get larger, but in this mode there is no way to enter numbers in scientific notation.

If you go to the View menu and switch from Standard to Scientific, you are switched to the impressive mode shown in Figure 4-71. This is both a programmer's calculator with binary and hex (even octal!) modes and a scientific calculator. For programming purposes, there are functions like **Xor**, and the scientific part has the basic trigonometric and hyperbolic functions and their inverse functions. You can enter a number in scientific notation in this mode: enter the mantissa, hit the **Exp** button or the letter **x** and then enter the exponent.

There is also a way to enter a series of numbers and get their average, sum, and standard deviation. You hit the **Sta** button, which opens a statistic box that displays the data. Then you click on the calculator and enter the data. After each entry, you hit the **Dat** button or the keyboard's **Ins** key. You can clear an

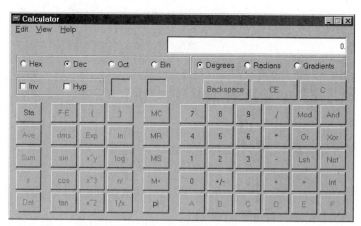

Figure 4-70. Mild-mannered Calculator

Figure 4-71. Calculator on steroids

Scientific							
sin	**s**	Arcsin	**is**	sinh	**hs**	arcsinh	**his**
cos	**o**	arccos	**io**	cosh	**ho**	arccosh	**hio**
tan	**t**	arctan	**it**	tanh	**ht**	arctanh	**hit**
cot	**tr**	arccot	**rit**	coth	**htr**	arccoth	**rhit**
Exp(N)	**Nin**	ln	**n**	log	**l**	n!	**!**
1/N	**Nr**	square	**@**	sqrt	**i@**	cube	**#**
pi	**p**	2*pi	**ip**	N^M	**NyM=**		

Memory		Statistics		Programmer's Functions			
MC	**^L**	STA	**^S**	And	**&**	RSH	**i<**
MR	**^R**	DAT	**<Ins>**	Or	**|**	int part	**;**
MS	**^M**	Ave	**^A**	Xor	**^**	frac part	**i;**
M+	**^P**	Sum	**^T**	Not	**~**	mod	**%**
		StdDev	**^D**	LSH	**<**		

Figure 4-72. Calculator keyboard shortcuts

entry from the statistic box by highlighting it and hitting the CD button on the statistic box. The **Ave**, **Sum**, and **s** buttons will then display the average, sum, and standard deviation.

The Calculator has keyboard shortcut entries for a wide variety of functions (Figure 4-72). Remarkably, until Windows 98, this information did not appear in a table in the Help or documentation but had to be gleaned a key at a time from the context menu of the buttons! There are now two Help panels, but they aren't as clear as the table here.

In the table, the roman columns list functions and the boldface columns list keystrokes—to compute the arctanh of a displayed number, you hit the three keys **h** and **i** and **t** in that order. In the table, **^L** means **Ctrl+L**. **<Ins>** means the single Insert key. Text font cap N and M stand for entered numbers; to compute N^M (N to the power M), you first enter N, then hit **y**, then enter M and hit **=**.

 Those are the keystrokes for Scientific mode. Remarkably, the designer of the Calculator made the decision that while **@** computes the square in Scientific mode, it computes the square root in Standard mode.

 Folks are so used to seeing the number buttons on the screen they tend to hit them with the mouse, but keyboard entry works, too—use the numbers (on either the keypad or top row keys) or the letters A–F for hex digits. Indeed, the apparently strange choice of **o** for cos is to avoid the conflict with the hex digit C.

The Calculator is basically unchanged from Windows 3.x—the panel is now a solid gray, but otherwise, in the Windows 95 version, there was only one change—a bug fix! The only change from Windows 95 to Windows 98 is that the font on the button is less bold and some names have been spelled out, for example **Back** has become **Backspace**.

 If you have the old Windows 3.1 Calculator somewhere, run it (it'll run fine in Windows 98) and compute 2.01 – 2.00. Are you surprised that the answer is 0.00? Yeah, me too. This bug was apparently first pointed out to Microsoft during the early beta test phase of Windows 95 (then called Chicago) by a tester who thought it was a new bug. The reply he got was that the problem was already in the Windows 3.x Calculator. They'd try to fix it but since millions of 3.x users hadn't reported it, it wasn't terribly high priority and might not get fixed. Then the Pentium coprocessor bug hit, and in the aftermath, the *Wall Street Journal* mentioned the Windows Calculator bug on its front page. Whaddya know—it was fixed in a day.

Charmap

The analysis of character is the highest human entertainment.

—Isaac Bashevis Singer, *New York Times,* November 26, 1978

Charmap (Figure 4-73) displays the full character set of any font. You pick the font from the dropdown. You can press on a character to enlarge it for a better view, as I did here with the bomb. Double clicking copies the characters to the copy box on the upper right. Hitting the Copy button then copies it to the clipboard. A simple but elegant application.

Under Windows 95 there was a problem with the way other Windows applications handled pastes from what Charmap put on the clipboard. The characters are copied as straight text but also as RTF text, which includes font information.

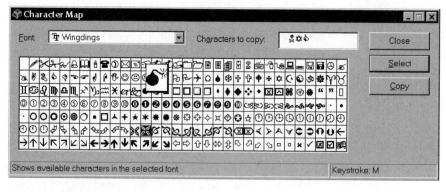

Figure 4-73. A great judge of character

Word 7 passed in flying colors but WordPad and other programs didn't get the font right. That's been fixed with Windows 98. Hurrah for Microsoft!

Charmap is installed as **C:\windows\charmap.exe**. It is not on the Start Menu. You can do so or you can always run it from the Run box.

Clipboard Viewers

A viewer who skips the advertising is the moral equivalent of a shoplifter.

—Nicholas Johnson, FCC member

Included with Windows is not one but two programs for viewing the clipboard—Clipboard Viewer and Clipbook Viewer , each with its own icon. But Clipbook isn't installed on your disk.

Despite spending hundreds of million of dollars in development costs and listing hundreds of people on the team, the situation with clipboard shows that in some of the obscure corners of the product, things are—how can I put this delicately?—a bit of a mess. Clipbook was introduced with Windows 3.1 and required a separate install under Windows 95. It's on the Windows 98 CD, but is it hidden! The WRK says you'll find it and an install script in the **\addons\clipbook** folder on the CD, but there is no such folder. It also tells you to consult Windows Help on Clipbook, but that turns up dry. The Clipbook Help file, **clipbook.chm**, is installed on your system, but it's pretty bare bones and worthless without the program.

The program files are on the CD inside **Win98_40.cab**. But the situation is worse; you'll also find the Win95 Help files for Clipbook there, in another **.cab**. Wotta mess!

To install Clipbook, you need to grab two files from the Windows CD, **clipbook.exe** and **clipsrv.exe**; may as well put them in **C:\windows**. There are two ways to do this.

1. You can use the System File Checker (Figure 4-74, discussed in Chapter 7). Run Programs\Accessories\System Tools\System Information from the Start Menu and pick System File Checker from the Tools menu (or try typing **sfc** in a Run box). Choose "Extract one file from installation disk," type in **clipbook.exe**, and hit Start. Fill in the fields where your Windows CD cabs are (probably **x:\win98**, where **x** is the letter of your CD) and the destination folder. Now repeat the process with **clipsrv.exe**.

2. Since there are two files, it may be easier to do it by hand. Open the CD's **\win98** folder, locate **Win98_40.cab**, and double click on it. In the resulting window, select **clipbook.exe** and **clipsrv.exe**, right click, and pick Extract. Tell it where to put them (see Figure 4-75).

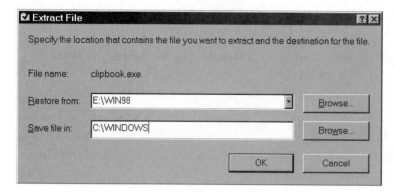

Figure 4-74. Using System File Checker

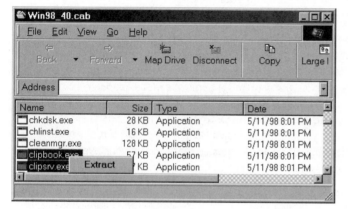

Figure 4-75. Extracting from a cab

Either way, you'll need to add the program to your Start Menu or else run it from the Run box.

Both programs display what is currently on the clipboard. Both have menus (called Display in Clipboard and View in Clipbook) that display the formats currently on the clipboard in black and the formats the supplying application has promised it will supply if requested in grayed out. You can display the black (but not the grayed-out) formats by choosing them from the menu. Both programs have File menus that allow you to save the contents of the clipboard in a file with the extension of **.clp** and later open a saved **.clp** file. Both have a Delete command in the Edit menu that lets you clear the Clipboard.

That's about as far as Clipboard Viewer goes. Clipbook Viewer goes further in two ways. First, it lets you save clipboard material into extra book pages that are always accessible to the program. These pages can be given names and later put back on the clipboard from within the Clipbook program. To put it back on the clipboard, you merely select the page and choose Edit/Copy. The juggling is a bit much, but it can be helpful if you have several large pieces of text or several bitmaps you want to reuse.

The second feature is that you can share Clipbook pages over a network. When Barry started the research for this section, he found he couldn't get Clipbook to work. The Clipbook Help describes how to use the Connect item in the File menu to access remote Clipbooks. But Barry couldn't get a Connect item on his File menu no matter what he tried. Then he ran into Woody in the hall and mentioned that it didn't work.

 Mine works great. I use it to send Justin parts of my Hearts Tips books all the time.

Figure 4-76.
You gotta have
Hearts

Button bar and File menu
without NetDDE

Button bar and File menu
with NetDDE running

 Hearts!! Games, games. If you didn't play so many games, we might actually learn something around here. Get back to work!

 Now, Barry, I am doing research for the games part of the book. Besides, I seem to have learned how to get Clipbook to work over a network. Just run Hearts first.

Woody's right. Running Hearts will make the File menu and Button bar for Clipbook blossom (Figure 4-76).

But of course we couldn't tell serious business users that the way to run Clipbook over a network is to first load Hearts! There is another way besides running Hearts and an explanation of why Hearts works: both Hearts and Clipbook require Network DDE to work.

 Under Windows for Workgroups, NetDDE was loaded in the StartUp group, but because not that many users actually use NetDDE, it is not automatic in Windows 98. We modified Hearts so that when it is loaded, it looks for NetDDE, and if it isn't there, it loads it. But, er, we forgot to fix Clipbook.

 Bravo! Shows the right sense of priorities to put Hearts ahead of Clipbook.

 Well, our scientific surveys show that a lot more users play Hearts over the network—on their lunch hour, of course—than use Clipbook.

You certainly fooled the Microsoft Product Support Services folks. They have a knowledge base article where they say that while this feature works in Windows 3.1, it doesn't in Windows 9X. Gack—if even Microsoft Support can't get it right . . . . I guess they need to play Hearts more.

So you need to run the program **netdde**, which is in the **C:\windows** directory. If you are using Clipbook over the network all the time, place a shortcut to **C:\windows\netdde.exe** in your StartUp folder. Otherwise, I'd suggest you place a shortcut in the Start Menu that invokes Clipbook by running a batch file with the lines

```
start C:\windows\netdde
start C:\windows\clipbrd
```

Once you got the network stuff running, choosing File\Connect or clicking the correct button asks the name of the computer whose Clipbook you want to access. Once the connections are established, getting stuff from the remote Clipbook pages is as easy as getting stuff from your local Clipbook. And whenever you run Clipbook, it will try to reestablish its prior connections.

 If you need to share stuff across a network and don't want to start futzing with NetDDE, you can save a **.clp** file on a shared network drive and have the recipient open it in their own Clipboard or Clipbook Viewer.

Packager

Adam and Eve ate the first vitamins, including the package.

—Squibb Pharmaceutical ad

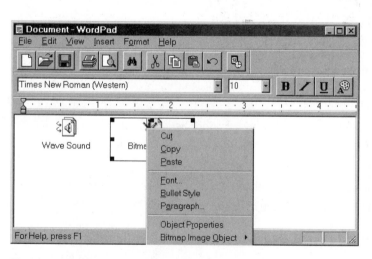

Figure 4-77. Object context menu

OLE data is most often embedded in documents as editable information viewed in its native format, but sometimes it is displayed as an icon instead. For example, you can drag a shortcut (Windows **.lnk**, DOS **.pif**, Internet **.url**, or Microsoft Network **.mcc**) to a document or e-mail message and have it embedded as an icon. This embedded icon and action is called a **package**.

The program Object Packager lets you edit the contents of a package or create a custom package yourself. It is still on

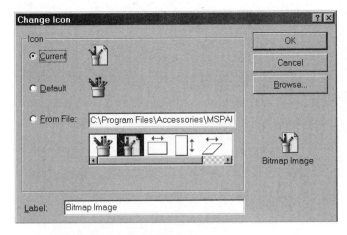

disk and some books may tell you about it, but it has become a relic of the past: OLE itself now does what you used to need Packager for. If you right click on an embedded OLE object (whether displaying data or an icon), you get the context menu shown in Figure 4-77. Pick Object Properties and the View tab lets you switch between display of data and an icon. If you choose "Display as icon," the Change Icon . . . dialog, shown in Figure 4-78, does what Packager used to do and does it better.

Figure 4-78. Packager's replacement

Resource Meter

"Resource-constrained environment" [are] fancy Pentagon
words that mean there isn't enough money to go around.

—GEN. JOHN W. VESSEY, JR., Chairman,
Joint Chiefs of Staff, *New York Times*, July 15, 1984

 My favorite little applet is the Resource Meter, a little stepladder thing that sits in the Notification Area and keeps track of free system resources, those little fixed-size pools of memory that, when stressed, can bring all sorts of trouble. As long as the ladder is green, I'm in good shape. When I pass my mouse over the ladder, Resource Meter pops up a reading of the percentage of space left in each of the three free system resource pools, as you can see in Figure 4-79.

Figure 4-79. The Resource Meter in action

Resource Meter is automatically installed on your Start Menu's Program/Accessories/System Tools menu. If it is not, it must have been removed and can be reinstalled in under the Details panel of the System Tools item of the Windows SetUp tab of the Add/Remove Programs applet (in that panel it is called System Resource Monitor, even though "System" doesn't appear in the menu item or application caption). See Chapter 3 for instructions on how to install it in your StartUp group, my recommended place for it.

Two other related applets (available if you have the CD) are System Monitor and NetWatcher, both installable under the Details panel of the System Tools item of the Windows SetUp tab of the Add/Remove Programs applet. System Monitor gives you reports in real time on all sorts of techie information while NetWatcher displays information on which users are opening which files on your machine.

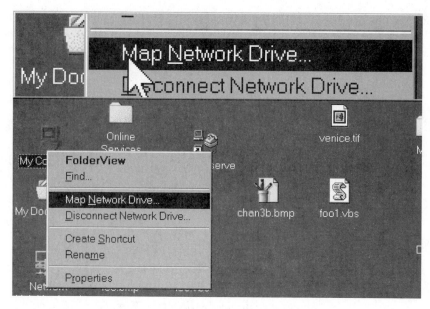

Figure 4-80. Magnifier

Magnifier

While it's intended as an accessibility tool (discussed in Chapter 8), Magnifier is so cool, you may use it for other purposes. When loaded (it's on the Start Menu under Program\Accessories\Accessibility; you may need to install it from the Accessibility submenu of the Windows SetUp tab, Add/Remove Programs), you get a magnified view of the neighborhood of your mouse cursor displayed in a strip at the top of the screen (Figure 4-80).

■ Multimediaaaaahhhhh

Television: a medium, so called because it is neither rare nor well done.

—ERNIE KOVACS

 There are five applets that appear on the Programs/Accessories/Entertainment submenu of the Start Menu. Three of them you may never need to start explicitly. Media Player and Active Movie more or less duplicate each other in their ability to play MIDI video and audio files. CD Player starts automatically when you place an audio CD in the drive.

Sound Recorder is what you'll use if you have a microphone or want to manipulate **.wav** files. If you've plugged a microphone into your sound card but it won't record, check out the section on the sound mixer.

 That leaves two other items on the Entertainment menu: Interactive CD Sampler and Trial Programs. These are ads for Microsoft products. Other than noting that Janet should be yelling about them, we have nothing to say about them.

 You may have WebTV there also (see Chapter 1).

Multimedia Player

The media have just buried the last yuppie, a pathetic creature who had not heard the news that the great pendulum of public consciousness has just swung from Greed to Compassion and from Tex-Mex to meatballs.

—BARBARA EHRENREICH, *The Worst Years of Our Lives*

Media Player is a powerful but simple application with the magical quality that it can play media formats that didn't even exist when it was written. Basically, it is a shell around MCI commands. I discussed the MCI spec in Chapter 2 in the section "Media Control Interface—Do You Mean Mike McCurry?" You can load files with MCI drivers (for a default setup that means video in **.avi**, **.mpg**, **.mov** and other Active Video formats, sound in **.wav** format, and MIDI in **.mid** and **.rmi** formats) and then play them. Under Windows 95, Media Player was the open command for Video and MIDI files, so you called up Media Player if you double clicked on an **.avi**, **.mid**, or **.rmi** file. Under Windows 98, all videos, MIDI, and **.wav** files open in Active Movie, but you could use File Types (see Chapter 3) to change the default or at least add an extra right click to open in Media Player.

The Media Player controller (Figure 4-81) has eleven buttons on it, many of them standard VCR-type controls. The first three ⏸ ⏹ ⏏ are play/pause, stop, and eject (works only if you have CD audio picked). The next four ⏮ ⏪ ⏩ ⏭ return what is being played to the start, take it a macro step backward and forward, and advance it to the end. What I call a macro step is precisely $\frac{1}{16}$ of the total amount from start to finish. The start and end buttons do that only if there is no selected region. If there is a selected region, then the buttons stand for four "marks"—file start, selection start, selection end, and file end; and the outermost two buttons go to the previous and next mark.

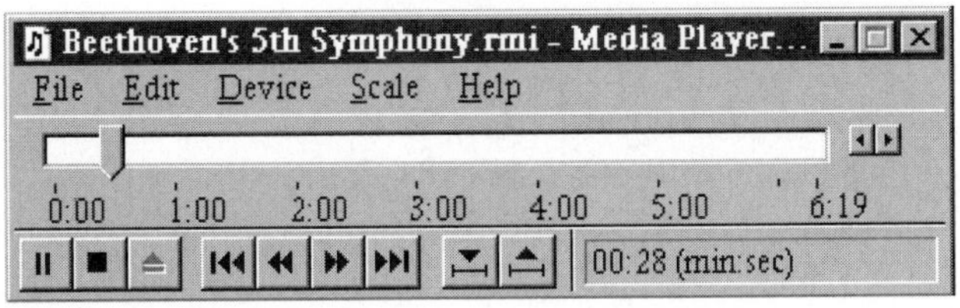

Figure 4-81. Media Player

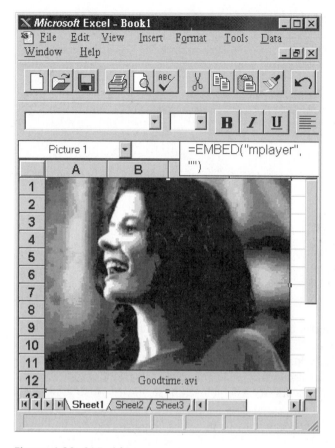

Figure 4-82. OLE videos

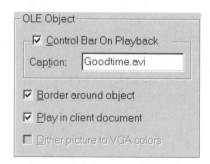

Figure 4-83. Controlling playback

The last two buttons are for marking the start and end of a selection. The tiny buttons to the right of the slider area move a single video frame or $\frac{1}{128}$ of the total amount for sound files.

By using the Edit/Copy Object command, you can copy a media file to the clipboard and embed it in an application by pasting it in. Figure 4-82 shows a video clip embedded in Excel. Double click on the embedded video and Media Player plays the clip. Unlike my tests with Windows 3.1 applications several years ago, all the major applications properly supported this feature.

You can control how the OLE clip appears and plays by setting some options in the Edit/Options menu of Media Player (Figure 4-83). You have to make the choices before you copy the clip to the clipboard. You choose whether there is a simple slider control on playback. If there is, when not playing there is a caption, and you choose that.

Note that if you drag a multimedia file from Explorer to Media Player, it will load and start playing. A more ideal way to check out the `.avi` files on a CD-ROM or a bunch of `.wav` files is to place Explorer and Media Player side by side and drag the files over. If you drag over a file while another is playing, Media Player will stop the first and play the second.

Finally, if pasting a video clip as a full-size picture as in Figure 4-82 seems a bit much, remember that you can use Object Properties to have it appear instead as an icon (see the discussion of Packager earlier in this chapter).

Sound Recorder

One of the greatest sounds of them all—and to me it is a sound—is utter, complete silence.

—ANDRÉ KOSTELANETZ, *New York Journal-American*, February 8, 1955

If you're here because you've plugged a mike into your sound card and you can't record, you're in the wrong place. Jump forward two sections to the discussion of the Mixer.

Sound Recorder, as its name implies, is an applet that will record sound to a **.wav** file. But it serves four other purposes.

- It provides information from the header of any **.wav** file—sample size, sample rate, and number of channels (mono vs. stereo). I describe the meaning of this header data in "Riding the Perfect Wav" in Chapter 2.
- It is a comprehensive sound conversion module.
- It can be used as an OLE server for **.wav** files and is often a better alternative than Media Player for embedding sounds.
- It is a rudimentary sound editor.

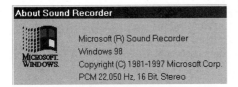

Figure 4-84. About Sound Recorder

Let's take them one at a time. You record sound by clicking the button with a red dot on it, but there is no menu option and no way of using the keyboard to record sound except repeatedly hitting **Tab** and **Spacebar**.

The strangest use by far is getting header information. To get the header information on a sound file, load it into Sound Recorder and choose Help/About from the menu. The important part of that box is shown in Figure 4-84. Notice the fourth line, which says, "PCM 22,050 Hz, 16 Bit, Stereo." There it is, the header information.

This has to rank as one of the weirdest tidbits in the Windows applets. Who had the idea of putting that information in the About box? Who'd normally expect to look there? Unlike Windows 3.1, though, there is a more reasonable way of accessing information on the file. Go to the Properties item on the File menu and you get a panel like that shown in Figure 4-85. Notice the Convert Now . . . button. It leads to a dialog (Figure 4-86) where you can choose new properties and even a compression format to use. Obviously converting from lower to higher quality won't magically improve the quality of the recording, but it will let you trade quality for file size, and if you use compression, the loss in quality may not be that severe. This conversion is pretty neat—too bad 99.9% of users won't have the foggiest idea it is here.

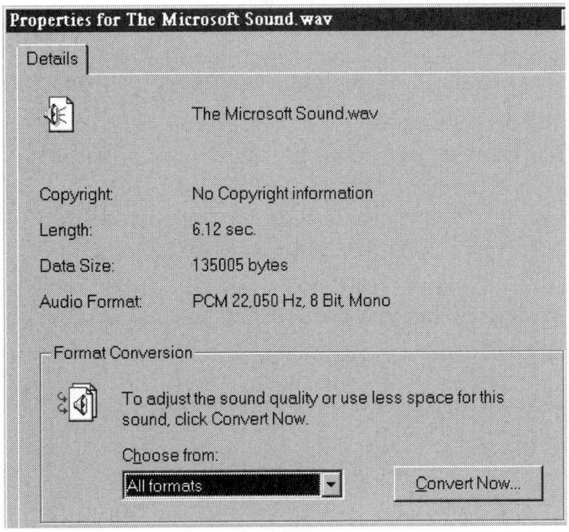

Figure 4-85. File/Properties in Sound Recorder

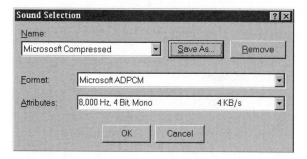

Figure 4-86. It's a sound conversion

To get OLE to work, just choose Edit/ Copy from the Sound Recorder menus and paste it into the client application. You'll see a loudspeaker icon. Clicking on that will play the sound with no direct sign of Sound Recorder loading.

Sound editing is fairly limited. You can insert one `.wav` file in another, mix two, increase or decrease volume and speed, reverse, and add echo. It's amusing to play some sounds in reverse—try it on The Microsoft Sound. What's missing from sound editing? The ability to deal with stereo channels, fade in and out, smoothing, and noise filtering to name a few. Take a look at Sonic Foundry's Sound Forge (`http://www.sfoundry.com`) to see what a full-fledged sound editor can entail. Or get their $50 light Sound Forge XP.

 What happens if you play **tada.wav** in reverse? Do you get "data"?

 No, you get "adat," of course!

 Nope. It *is* data, after all!

 For sound conversion and recording, Sound Recorder lets you give names to a combination of compression types and the other characteristics of the `.wav` file. It comes with three predefined types, all using standard uncompressed (PCM) format: CD Quality (44 KHz, 16-bit stereo), Radio Quality (22 KHz, 8-bit mono), and Telephone Quality (11 KHz, 8-bit mono). These schemes and any you may define are stored in the Registry key **HKEY_CURRENT_USER\software\microsoft\multimedia\audio\ waveformats**.

CD Player

One gets tired of the role critics are supposed to have in this culture: It's like being the piano player in a whorehouse; you don't have any control over the action going on upstairs.

—ROBERT HUGHES, *Publishers' Weekly*, December 12, 1986

While you can use Media Player to play audio CDs, Windows 98 includes a more flexible and powerful CD Player applet (Figure 4-87). Unless you change the option in the File Types dialog (see Chapter 3), the CD Player will pop up and start playing automatically when you place an audio CD into any drive on your system.

 Phooey! Just install the Power Toys FlexiCD and ignore this piece of, er, this fine utility.

 Plus! 98 has an enhanced CD Player with interesting Internet links.

Figure 4-87. CD Player

The controls to the right of the time display are of VCR type and similar to those in Media Player. I recommend displaying the button bar (no, its not under Options but under View). ToolTips will tell you about their functions, but I want to note one of them.

pops up a Play List where you can choose to play only some of the tracks and the order of play. Here you type in Artist, CD Title, and Track names. These get stored in the file **cdplayer.ini** in the **C:\windows** directory in a section whose name is a seven-digit hexadecimal number. Every audio CD has a unique number (a sort of digital ISBN for audio CDs), so once you've entered the information, it is remembered for ever after. Audio CDs using the new CD Plus format will have these fields on the CD so you won't even need to fill them in once. The format of the **.ini** file is so simple that it may be easier for you get the CD IDs by adding, say, a Title and then putting the other information in an ASCII editor.

 The Windows 95 version had a multiple player feature for those with juke boxes. But it has been dropped. Too bad.

We wanted to provide proper support for multiple disk changers in the OS, but it didn't make it. When it does, we'll fix CD Player.

You can configure the CD Player so that the time displayed is the time elapsed on the track, the time remaining on the track, or the time remaining on the CD.

Sound Mixer and Volume Control

Political image is like mixing cement. When it's wet, you can move it around and shape it, but at some point it hardens and there's almost nothing you can do to reshape it.

—WALTER F. MONDALE

Windows comes with a volume control that works with most sound cards. Buried in the control is the input mixer; you may need it to be able to record with your microphone!

You'll find Volume Control on the Programs/Accessories/Multimedia submenu of Start Menu. More important, there is a check box labeled "Show volume control on the taskbar" on the Audio page of the Multimedia applet in Control Panel. If that's checked, a loudspeaker icon appears in the Notification Area. Double clicking that will bring up the Volume Control applet, which looks a lot like the applet in Figure 4-89 but is labeled Volume Control instead of Recording Control. That control is pretty much self-explanatory. There is a slider for master volume and, typically, separate sliders for CD, Wave, and MIDI (called Synthesizer).

Now pick Properties from the Options menu. That will bring up a dialog like that in Figure 4-88 except that the radio button will be on Playback. If your mike isn't working, you may be tempted to check off the Mic/Line box in the Playback list that appears when you first call up this control. Instead, you need to click on the Recording radio button and then hit OK. That will bring up the Recording Mixer seen in Figure 4-89. This determines what input device is used, and for the mike to work, you need to be sure that the check box labeled Mic/Line is checked.

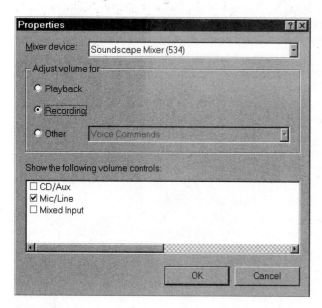

Figure 4-88. Accessing the Recording Mixer

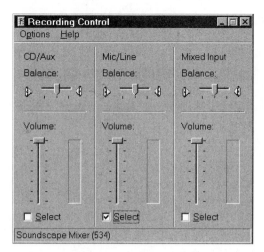

Figure 4-89. Recording Mixer

You won't need the mixer often, so it is probably just as well that whenever you invoke the Volume control it pops up showing the Playback options.

One weird thing is that you can show a Mic/Line slider on the usual Volume Control (in Playback mode). Despite what you might think, it does not affect how you record. It affects only what would happen if you sent output through the mike jack (don't ask me how you do that!). To control the input volume, you need to shift to the Recording Control and adjust the slider there.

Active Movie Control

 There isn't much to say about the Active Movie control. It does have a hidden menu that you can access by right clicking on the panel surrounding the time, but the menu doesn't really have much of interest. You can shift from showing time to showing frame number (big deal).

Figure 4-90. My favorite newsgroup is
`alt.barney.dinosaur.die.die.die`

You can call up a property sheet from this hidden menu and add controls much like those for Media Player. Don't forget to consider maximizing the screen. You'll probably get something grainy, but you may like it.

 One wonders about the need for a separate Active Movie Player when Media Player handles videos about as well as Active Movie does. But Microsoft likes it so much that Active Movie is the default for opening various files that used to be assigned to Media Player.

■ Da Games

 You forgot the games.

 Maybe I forgot the games, but Microsoft sure didn't. Each time a new version of Windows comes out they keep the old games and add a game. Well, they didn't add a game this time, but there are plenty from prior versions of Windows. Must give the State of Virginia (which banned Mine Sweeper from the offices of state employees) apoplexy.

- **Solitaire** (`C:\windows\sol.exe`)   The original Windows 3.0 game. Not a great game but wizzy graphics.
- **Mine Sweeper** (`C:\windows\winmin.exe`)   The most habit-forming game known to humanity ('scuse me while I play a quick one). First introduced with Windows 3.1.
- **Hearts** (`C:\windows\mshearts.exe`)   Lets you set up multiple-player games over the network. Introduced as a demo of what NetDDE could do with Windows for Workgroups 3.11. Not the greatest computer hearts implementation; Card Shark Hearts is a lot better.
- **FreeCell** (`C:\windows\freecell.exe`)   The second-most habit-forming game known to humanity. Introduced with the Win32s libraries but made a little slicker for Windows 95.

 Hover and Pinball from Windows 95 are gone. Boo, hiss. Not that they were very good games, mind you!

FreeCell sure is addictive after an initial "This game is impossibly hard." I had a lot of fun with Barry over this 'un, with a little help from MOM's guru Sarah. I ran into Barry one day in the hall at MOM's, and he says to me, "Well, Grasshopper, I finally understand what you find so fascinating about games. For a coupla weeks there I could hardly get any work done because I was sneaking in FreeCell games. I play sets of 50, resetting the statistics after each set. I seem to have no trouble getting to about 5 in 50 but can't push that down further very often." So I says, "Why would you want to push the number of wins down?" He explained that 5 was the number of losses and he was regularly winning at least 45 out of 50 games. I think he sensed I was suspicious, so he took me to his office to show off his current statistics—25 straight—very impressive (Figure 4-91).

 But I figured as a games player, I could do a lot better than that. Boy, did Barry's jaw drop when I took him into my office a week later and showed where I was at (Figure 4-92). He'd finally met a serious games player!!

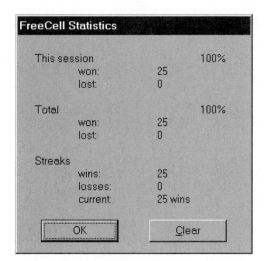

Figure 4-91. Barry's FreeCell score

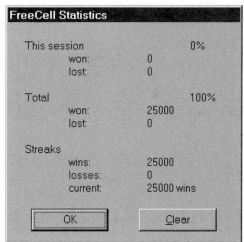

Figure 4-92. Woody's FreeCell score

Hehe. What I didn't tell him is that when I went to Sarah, she told me about the Registry key **HKEY_CURRENT_ USER\Software\ Microsoft\Windows\CurrentVersion\Applets\FreeCell** and showed me how it all worked. I used calc to figure out that 25,000 was 61A8 in hex, which I needed, but it was easy. The complete set of keys is shown in Figure 4-93. Barry still treats me with respect. Hehehe.

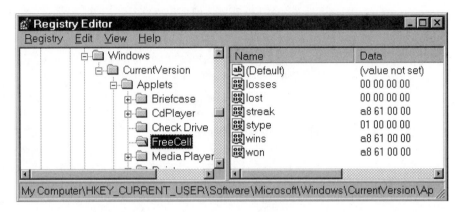

Figure 4-93. Woody's secret

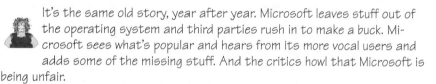

Chapter 5

Add 'em On

. . . don't assume that just because a utility or add-in program is available, it's worthwhile. Utilities are meant to be problem solvers. If there's no problem, chances are pretty good you don't need a solution.

—BARRY OWEN

 It's the same old story, year after year. Microsoft leaves stuff out of the operating system and third parties rush in to make a buck. Microsoft sees what's popular and hears from its more vocal users and adds some of the missing stuff. And the critics howl that Microsoft is being unfair.

 Well, not quite the same old story, MOM. The critics are at a new level. Janet and the grasshoppers have a field day on some of this stuff.

 But it is hard to claim that users lose when the OS picks up functionality they used to have to pay extra for. Some of the vendors do lose, but they have to realize that when you dance in the shadow of an elephant, you have to be nimble or risk being stepped on.

 As usual, Microsoft has left stuff out. You owe it to yourself to get the tools that make your computer interaction safe, pleasurable, and fun. Microsoft has done a remarkable job of putting together a great set of tools in the base operating system, but that doesn't change the fact that there are still lots of places for other vendors to add value. I'm going to tell you about the best of these tools. No doubt others will appear. I first talk about utility add-ons from Microsoft and then turn to some third-party products.

You'll find no antivirus programs in our capsule reviews. That's because it's hard to choose between them—they all do their job very well, thank you. So flip a coin between Norton, McAfee, and the others. But put antivirus support at the top of the list. If you get Plus! 98, be sure to use the included McAfee antivirus software.

Absolutely. There are too many jerks out there for you not to protect yourself with a program. Now that they offer signature upgrades over the Internet be sure to update those at least once a month. Use Task Scheduler to do a virus scan at least weekly and daily if you've ever had a problem. I'd just recommend running the scanner. The resident programs can be pretty heavy-handed, so unless you're in a high-risk group, I'd avoid loading the resident watcher program.

■ Microsoft Presents

The premier "third party" is Microsoft itself. There are too many opportunities to make a buck for them not to try, so Windows 3.1 had a Font Pack and Windows 95 and Windows 98 have a Plus! Pack. After discussing the parts of the Windows Resource Kit (WRK) that are included on the Windows CD, I discuss the Plus! Pack for Windows 98. Then comes the full WRK utilities and finally the Power Toys.

The Power Toys cost the least (free for the download) and are just wonderful. Be sure to check them out.

Resource Kit Sampler

A few of the WRK items are on the Windows CD in the form of a Sampler. You load them by popping in the CD, browsing to **\tools\reskit**, and running **setup.exe**.

At the risk of repeating it too often, don't miss the Tweak UI utility. **Readme.doc** says it is installed by SetUp but it isn't, so switch to **\tools\reskit\powertoy**, right click **tweakui.inf**, and pick Install. I tell you all about this wondrous applet, which installs into Control Panel, in Chapter 8.

Here's what the WRK Sampler includes.

- **Resource Kit Online Book**   A 3-MB compressed HTML file contains the entire 1,766-page book in searchable format!

- **Microsoft Management Console**   Also known as the Tools Management Console, this is a shell (Figure 5-1) that provides access to the other tools, which are not on the Start Menu although you can add shortcuts to them.

- **Code Page Changer**   Adjusts the character set that DOS uses for users outside the United States. Yawn.

- **Time Zone Editor**   You edit or create the time zones that Windows understands when you call up the Date/Time applet (Figure 5-2). Yawn.

**Figure 5-1.
Tools Manage-
ment Console**

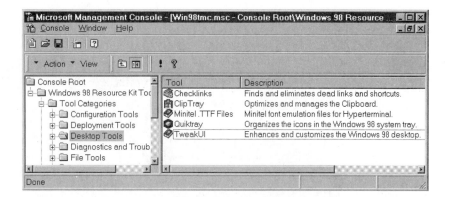

**Figure 5-2.
Time Zone editor**

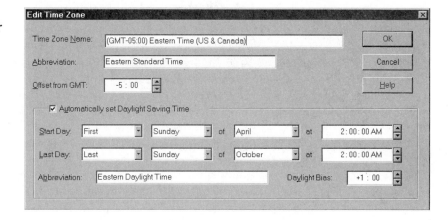

- **FAT32 Conversion Information Tool**   Tells you how much space conversion will save you.
- **Checklinks**   Finds shortcuts on your disk that point to nonexistent programs.
- **ClipTray**   Lets you define some named text snippets and places an icon in the Notification Area. When you right click the icon, you get a list of names; picking one lets you place that snippet on the clipboard.
- **Quiktray**   Lets you place some icons in the Notification Area that launch applications. Given the Quick Launch Toolbar, this seems pretty redundant.
- **Microsoft File Information** (Figure 5-3)   Gives a description of every file in the Windows distribution CD and diskettes and the precise CAB file they are in. The information is in an access database called `Win98.mfi`, so you can copy it to a filename with an `.mdb` extension and use Access to manipulate it. This is discussed further in Chapter 7.
- **TextViewer**   Does what it says but doesn't even have a search. Pretty useless.

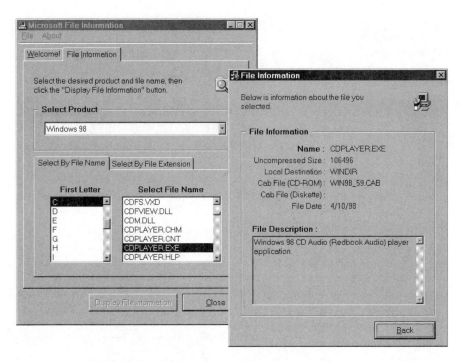

Figure 5-3. Microsoft File Information

- **WinDiff** Text file difference analyzer (discussed in Chapter 9). It's a useful program.
- Miscellaneous additional tools and help files, some of special interest to system administrators.

Plus! Pack

Think of the earth as a living organism that is being attacked by billions of bacteria whose numbers double every forty years. Either the host dies, or the virus dies, or both die.

—GORE VIDAL, *Observer of London,* August 27, 1989

On balance, the Windows 95 Plus! Pack was worth the price but I'm not so sure about Plus! 98. Still, if the past is a guide, pretty soon new machines will ship with Plus! 98, so we'll give a quick look. Note that the full install takes a whopping 200 MB of disk space.

 With hard disks at 5 GB or more, 200 MB is not exactly whopping any more.

Figure 5-4. Plus! 98

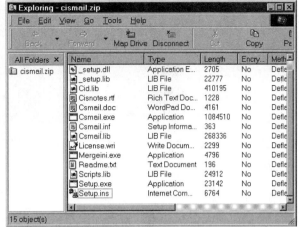

Figure 5-5. Compressed folder

Here's what's there (Figure 5-4).

- **Compressed Folders**   Much like the built-in CAB viewer. Zips appear with a folderlike icon next to them, and when you double click they open in what looks like a folder or an Explorer view (Figure 5-5). You extract by dragging from the window and compress by dragging in.

   But it's not really a folder. It doesn't appear in the folder side of the Explorer tree, nor can you access its insides from an open dialog. You can't run programs from it, nor is QuickView available on the context menu.

   Mijenix ZipMagic makes zips really appear like folders so Explorer or any other program can access the files within. Compressed Folders is a program just like WinZip but with a different, less flexible, but prettier interface.

   And the compression/decompression is much slower than what we've seen in other products. Typical of Microsoft—a pretty face but not as good a program as the competition. Still, for occasional use, it fills the bill fine.

- **Deluxe CD Player**   Audio CD player (Figure 5-6) that when you put a disk in offers to dial the Internet where it grabs the artist, title, track names, and times. Really neat technology.

   The Internet lookup depends on the fact that the CD has an ID number, which can be read.

 Yeah, it's neat, and the technology is grand, but I prefer the Power Toys
FlexiCD player myself. Still, I wish FlexiCD would grab info from the Net.

- **19 Desktop Themes**   Additional to the 17 that Windows ships with. Included are Doonesbury, Garfield, and some professionally laid-out themes
  like World Traveler (Figure 5-7).

- **Disk Cleanup**   Replaces the built-in module and adds an extra module
  (Figure 5-8) from Cybermedia (the makers of First Aid 9X) that erases
  what it calls "non-critical files." Unlike the automated mode of the built-in
  program, this extra module is interactive (Figure 5-9).

- **New version of Maintenance Wizard**   Adds to the built-in virus scan
  list, and cleans up temporary setup files, old ScanDisk save files, and dead
  Start Menu entries.

Figure 5-7.
World Traveler
Desktop Theme

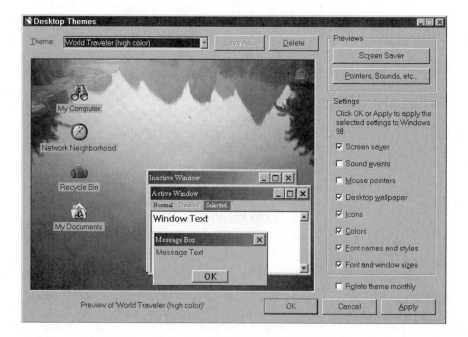

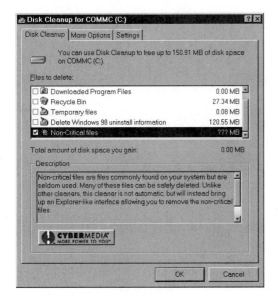

Figure 5-8. The added cleanup module

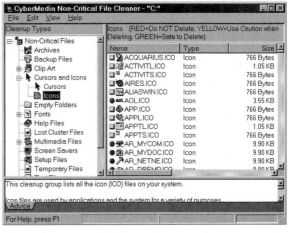

Figure 5-9. Non-critical files

- **Organic Art Screensaver**   Lets you cycle through several screensaver possibilities. It's no After Dark.

- **Picture It! Express**   Yet another image editor. It's made to work well with digital photos. As an image editor it's a lot better than Paint but not as good as Photo Editor, the program that comes with Office 97.

- **McAfee VirusScan for Windows**   Includes both the scanner and resident guard program. When you run the scanner it prompts you to download the latest virus definitions files if they are out of date. And it grabs them over the Internet.

- **Three games: Golf Lite 98**, **Spider Solitaire,** and **Lose Your Mind** Golf refuses to run with Large Fonts and the other two are not in the outstanding Windows games tradition.

 Yup—that's the button line. You'll have to lose your mind to buy this collection of warmed-over modules.

 I dunno, Woody. There's nothing that leaps out and grabs you by the lapels and screams, "Use me or you're a fool." But there's a lot of stuff for the $35–$45 you can expect to pay. The virus product is excellent, zip manipulator is workable albeit not outstanding, and the themes are fun. Still, if you have a zip manipulator and an antivirus product already, you shouldn't give 98 Plus! a second look.

Full Resource Kit

Like many businessmen of genius he learned that free competition was wasteful, monopoly efficient. And so he simply set about achieving that efficient monopoly.

—MARIO PUZO, *The Godfather*

 The Windows 98 Resource Kit is a $70 monster book that is the official docs for Windows 98. It includes a CD with a lot more goodies besides those on the Sampler on the Windows CD.

 I got the book from Amazon.com for $56 plus shipping!

As well as the Sampler programs, the WRK utility collection includes

- **Boot Editor**   Lets you disable some of the boot sequence options.
- **ScanReg Information File Editor**   Gives a GUI interface to the editing of `scanreg.ini`. I discuss ScanReg and its `.ini` file in Chapter 9.
- **Animated Cursor Editor**   Edits animated cursors (Figure 5-10). Micro-angelo, discussed later in this chapter, is a lot better.
- **Image Editor**   Edits bitmaps and cursors. Its sterling Windows 3.1 interface, er, makes you want to puke. At least you have a tool for touching up cursors.
- **Quick Launch Express**   Puts up a single icon to launch Windows system utilities (Figure 5-11), user-defined "Favorite Programs," and other tools.

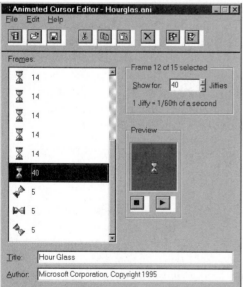

Figure 5-10. Animated Cursor Editor

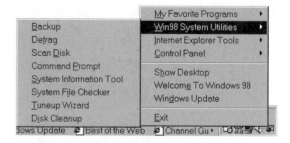

Figure 5-11. Quick Launch Express

Figure 5-12. Techie heaven

 This is a really neat applet especially given what a pain it is to launch a program like System File Checker from the default Start Menu.

- **DupFinder**   Locates and deletes duplicate files.
- **OLE/Com Object Viewer** and **Dependency Walker**   Two of several incredible techie but useful tools (Figure 5-12).
- Nine DOS command line programs that work like a UNIX user's favorite commands, including `cat` and `qgrep`. Oh, wow, like how could I live without this?
- **Regina REXX**   Windows version of the REXX scripting language. This is actually a Microsoft pass-on of a free program.
- A bunch of DOS batch file utilities like Waitfor and Choice.
- Lots of other miscellaneous stuff.

Besides the utility pack, the WRK CD includes

- **Imagination Engineer LE**   Technical drawing package from Integraph. It isn't nearly as good as Visio, but it's on the CD.
- **Microsoft Dictation** and **Microsoft Speech Suite 3.0**   The first is marked as a "Research Demonstration," and it shows where Microsoft is heading. It's no Dragon Naturally Speaking, but it would make me awfully uncomfortable if I were the Dragon CEO. The second installs a Text-to-Speech Engine (labeled as a Technology Demonstration), Microsoft Voice (a command dictation module), and the Speech SDK.

 Did you ever notice that computer text-to-speech voices sound like the Swedish chef from *The Muppets Show*?

- **NetShow Resource Kit** and **NetMeeting Resource Kit**

Too many of the offerings in Plus! and on the WRK CD are LE (Limited Edition), "Express," or "Lite." That's stuff some vendor is willing to give out for free as a come-on.

Power Toys

Put down the book and run to your machine, get online and jump to **www.microsoft.com**, and search for Power Toys, or do the same at **hotfiles** or **shareware.com**. I can't tell you exactly what will be there for Windows 98 but I can tell you what is there in the Windows 95 version, which you should still be able to get.

 The CAB file viewer and Screen Res product are now built into Windows 98—don't install them and don't use the full package install. The other products you can install by right clicking on the **.inf** files and picking Install.

Here are some of the goodies (in order of how highly MOM ranks them).

- **Tweak UI**   You should have already gotten it from the Windows CD and installed it!

- **SendTo Extensions**   Adds various extensions to the Send To menu including Send To Clipboard as Name and the Any Folder . . . Other Folder item, which lets you pick one or more files and call up the dialog, shown in Figure 5-13, to pick the destination. There is a dropdown of recent destinations and a browse button.

- **FlexiCD**   CD player that sits inconspicuously as an icon in the Notification Area.

- **Find Extensions**   Adds items to the Find submenu of the Start Menu.

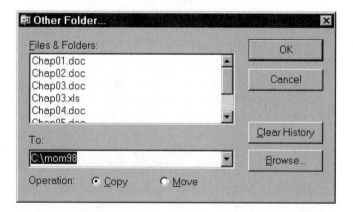

Figure 5-13. Power Toys Any Folder Copy/Move utility

- **Target** Adds an extra submenu to a shortcut that lets you access the context menu of the target of that shortcut.
- **Xmouse** Makes the mouse work like it does in UNIX's X Windows. It's kinda hard to describe—I suggest you load it and decide if you like it or not. This is part of the new Tweak UI. Do not install it separately.

 There are also Kernel Power Toys, which are kinda techie. I'd pass on 'em until there is an official collection for Windows 98. The UI-based ordinary Power Toys for Win95 should work fine with Windows 98. I urge restraint with the Kernel Power Toys.

■ File Utilities

Quick View

Inso software controls viewer technology for Windows. Virtually any third-party product with viewers has licensed them from Inso, Microsoft's Quick View included, so you may as well get Quick View Plus from Inso (**http://www.inso.com**) if you want serious file viewers.

 I was aghast when I heard that Inso purchased the old MasterSoft from Adobe. That was its only serious competition in the viewer space. Was the Justice Department asleep at the switch, or is Janet so obsessed with big Bill she doesn't think about any other software monopolies?

The text viewer (Figure 5-14) lets you search and copy to the clipboard. There are also oodles and oodles of graphics and database and spreadsheet viewers. There is even a zip viewer that lets you extract files from zips.

Figure 5-14. Quick View on a text file

WinZip

I have not had major experience of talking with people once pronounced brain-dead, but I think we could be safe in saying he did not have great zip.

—Sir Howard Smith, *The Times* of London, September 8, 1988,
talking of Leonid Brezhnev

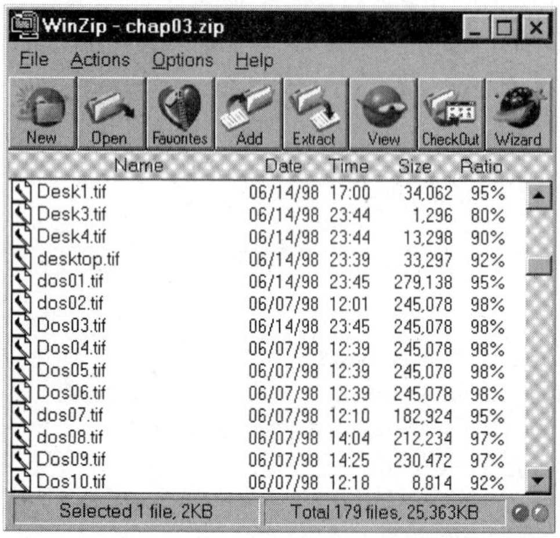

The PKZIP file format has become a standard for compressed libraries of files. Compression is typically 2 to 1 for text files, less for executable files, and much more for uncompressed multimedia/graphics files and certain other files. For example, during the preparation of this book, where files had to be sent via e-mail between MOM's branch offices, we dealt with graphic-heavy WinWord docs and typically had compression factors of at least 10 to 1 by zipping. As you can see (Figure 5-15), some files had a compression factor of 30 to 1. You need a tool to unzip files that you download, but even more, you need to compress files if you often send them by modem or on diskette.

Figure 5-15. Winzippity-doo-dah

The standard tool for dealing with zips among MOM's minions is WinZip (`http://www.winzip.com/winzip`). This is well integrated into Windows 98. Once you've installed WinZip, you can select any set of files in Explorer, right click, and choose a menu item called Add to Zip, which WinZip has added. And when you double click on a `*.zip` file extension, the file opens in WinZip.

The interface is simple and intuitive. You have lots of options, such as the ability to use supercompression (which typically decreases zip files by 10% and takes several times longer to compress). You do not need PKZIP to run WinZip—the zip compression and decompression is built in. Winzip also supports other compressed file formats, such as those used by UNIX.

PowerDesk

Mijenix PowerDesk (`http://www.mijenix.com`) is a utility collection that includes a desktop enhancement, zip support, and a file manager (Figure 5-16). The file manager can replace Explorer some of the time you use it. One of its nicest features is the three-panel display that includes a viewer panel (using viewers from Inso, of course!). Its zip capability is close to par with WinZip, so it's a less expensive route than QuickView and WinZip.

 What makes this product essential to me is its dialog helper, which adds two buttons to the standard File Open/Save dialog. The buttons give you a dropdown. One lets you switch to recently accessed folders (Figure 5-17) and one lets you pick recently opened files.

Figure 5-16.
PowerDesk file
manager

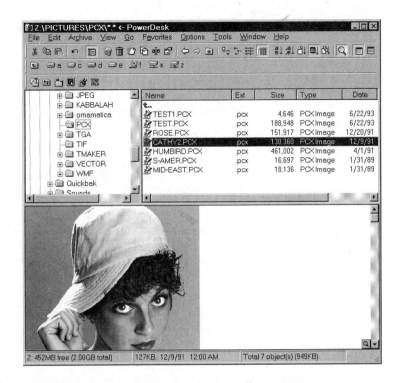

Figure 5-17.
PowerDesk dialog
helper

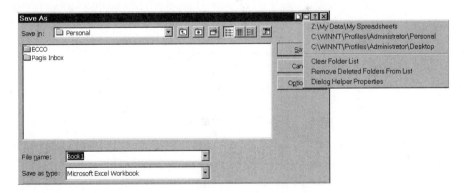

■ Internet Tools

FTP Voyager

If you do much in the way of FTP file transfer, especially if you manage an FTP site, you owe it to yourself to get the shareware FTP Voyager (Figure 5-18). It displays three panels—an Explorer-like view of the FTP site, an Explorer-like view of your local hard disk, and a window showing the automated commands

Figure 5-18.
FTP Voyager

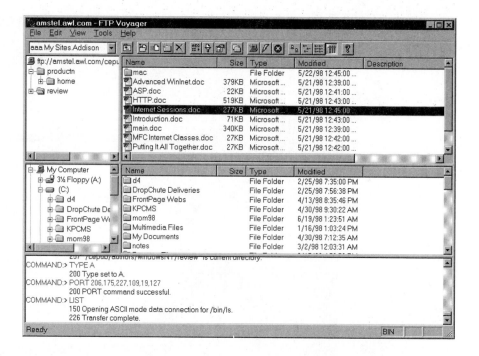

Figure 5-18.
FTP Voyager

that Voyager sends to log you in and to display directories, download, upload, and so on. Transfers are done by drag and drop not only between Voyager's windows but also from its windows to Explorer windows, including the Desktop. You can even double click on a file on the remote site and have Voyager download the file and open it in the associated program and then, after you save the file, Voyager will upload it. The program is available at its maker's Web site: **http://www.ftpvoyager.com.**

ICQ

Chatting over the Internet one on one works wonderfully. The slickest and most popular of the Internet chat programs is ICQ (**http://www.icq.com**). It's free for the download.

Figure 5-19.
ICQ's status icons

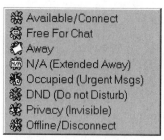

As long as you are connected to the Internet, anyone whom you have authorized can send you a message. The ICQ icon that sits in the Notification Area changes to a note and you get an optional sound effect. You can track all your messages to/from a single person. Millions of people use this program and you can reach any of them. Great for anyone connected to the Net regularly.

ICQ = I Seek You. Get it? Oy.

 AOL thought so much of the program that it purchased the company for almost $200 million!

 ICQ gets roughly 50,000 new subscribers each and every day. The Internet is an amazing place, isn't it?

Netscape Navigator and Netscape Communicator

You really should try out Netscape. Sure, maybe you're happy with IE. But shouldn't you at least try what remains the most popular browser around? It's free for the download at **www.netscape.com**. You can get either the browser alone—it's called Navigator (Figure 5-20)—or the full suite—Communicator—with e-mail, scheduler, and more.

You know, when IE 1.0 shipped, Netscape had over 85% market share. Why, that's a monopoly isn't it? Shows how tenuous market share is in the computer world, doesn't it?

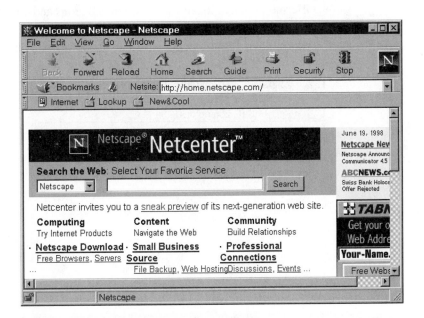

Figure 5-20. Netscape Navigator

At least if Microsoft is after your market. Tell me, Billy, can you name a single market Microsoft controlled and later lost?

■ Other Goodies

Microangelo

I'd asked around 10 or 15 people for suggestions. . . . Finally one lady friend asked the right question, "Well, what do you love most?" That's how I started painting money.

—ANDY WARHOL, *Manhattan Inc,* October 1984

Windows 98 supports and uses several new formats beyond the 32×32 pixel, 16-color icon that was the Windows 3.x standard. That means that Windows 3.1 icon editors won't work on all icons and they won't read the 32-bit libraries that many icons are now packed in. Impact Software (**http://www.impactsoft.com**) hasn't merely ported some Windows 3.1 tools—they've produced a powerful package of five programs you can use to organize all aspects of icons and cursors.

- **Microangelo Browser**   Lets you look through directories for icon libraries.
- **Microangelo Librarian** (Figure 5-21)   Lets you view icons and make your own libraries with keywords assigned to icons.
- **Microangelo Studio**   Icon editing and creation tool.
- **Microangelo Engineer**   Lets you install icons and cursors for the various places the shell uses them.
- **Microangelo Animator**   Animated cursor browsing and editing tool.

Figure 5-21. Microangelo Librarian

This is a well-put-together, functional package. There are several special tools for editing 256-color icons that make what would be a complex task a pleasure. The Microangelo package is shareware. They also have tools for making and editing animated gifs.

Figure 5-22. ATM

ATM

Adobe's ATM is a font manager for Windows (**http://www.adobe.com**). You'll need it if you want to use Post-Script fonts with Windows or if you want to organize oodles of fonts—for example, making them into sets that you turn on only as needed.

Notepad on Steroids

Notepad+ (which you can download from **http://www.hotfiles.com** or **http://www.download.com**) is a free 32-bit Notepad replacement from Rogsoft (there are other programs out there with similar names). It allows loading of multiple files (Figure 5-23), search and replace, insert file, and a re-open list. It opens files of essentially arbitrary size.

Figure 5-23. Notepad+

Chapter 6

Crank 'er Up

Kirk: What's going on in the engine room, Mr. Scott?

Scott: I dunnae know, Captain, but I'm giving her all she's got!

Kirk: Wrong line, Scotty. We're orbiting on impulse power.

Scott: The dilithium crystals are drained, Captain.

Kirk: There's nothing wrong with the crystals, Scotty. What have you been drinking?

Scott: It'll take at least a week, Captain.

Kirk: Mr. Scott, must you always speak in clichés that rarely pertain to the topic at hand?

Scott: If we push her any harder, sir, she'll blow!

Kirk: What does it take to get a straightforward answer to a simple question, Engineer?

Scott: I cannae lie to ye, sir. Microsoft hired me to write user manuals.

This chapter tackles SetUp and startup, two terribly underdocumented parts of Windows 98. SetUp refers to the entire installation process, from preparing your machine for a new Win98 installation to cleaning up the mess that Win98 so often leaves behind, as well as finding, installing, and deleting portions of Win98 as your predilection (or abject fear) may dictate. Startup refers to all the things that happen—and can and do go wrong—between the time you turn on your machine and the point when Windows' smiling face, the Desktop, appears.

I decided to put the instructions for upgrading from Windows 95 to Windows 98 back here in the middle of the book because the SetUp and startup topics overlap so much they really need to be discussed together. And, since you need to know a lot about Win98 before you can see how startup really works, the only logical approach was to wait until all the pieces fell into place.

■ Installation Blues

With a bit of luck, you'll have to install Windows 98 only once or twice. Some of you who were fortunate enough to have Win98 preinstalled on your PC won't ever install it at all. Still, it's worth your while to step through this chapter because some day disaster may strike, and you may find yourself staring at the SetUp Wizard.

Microsoft's Windows Resource Kit goes to extreme lengths to explain all the details of Setup. But most of the nitty-gritty is for network administrators. For example, the WRK covers "Push" server installation in amazing detail. What they've omitted is a straightforward, cookbook description of how the majority of us Windows users should approach SetUp and what we should do when things don't quite run to textbook perfection.

 Be strong and of good faith. The Windows 98 installer is incredibly robust: in fact, it may be singularly the most bulletproof program I have ever used. So try not to jump outta your gourd when you get an awful error message and want to cry and curse the Redmondians at the same time. Even if you do succumb to crying, follow the instructions on the screen (or in this book) while the tears flow.

If you've already installed Win98 and never expect to go through *that* experience again, skip down to the section "Checking the (Emergency) StartUp Disk." The latter part of this chapter contains lots of important information, including a bunch of tips for making Win98 work better. Don't miss it.

■ Deciding How to Install

*Let men decide firmly what they will not do, and they
will be free to do vigorously what they ought to do.*

—Mencius, *Discourses,* ca. 300 B.C.

Spend a little time up front deciding *how* you're going to install Windows 98, and you'll avoid a lot of last-minute panic decisions that might land you in hot water—or irreversibly create the kind of Win98 SetUp you don't really want.

Up-front decisions fall into six categories:

- Which version of Win98 you should get
- Whether you should install it from DOS or an earlier version of Windows
- Where you should install to
- How much of Win98 you really need
- If you want to use FAT32 for all your disks
- Whether you should wipe out all vestiges of Windows 95 while you're doing the upgrade

The decisions are pretty straightforward for most people once they're presented without the obscure terminology.

Which Win98?

First things first. Which flavor of Win98 should you buy? That's easy. Unless Win98 comes preinstalled on your PC, you almost certainly want to buy the Win98 upgrade, since it "upgrades" almost any version of DOS, Windows, or OS/2. In other words, unless you assembled your PC from a kit, you'll want the upgrade.

If you're buying a new PC with Win98 installed, insist on getting the Win98 CD. If you're upgrading and you have a CD drive, get the CD version of Win98: list prices for CD and 3.5-inch floppy versions are the same, so why spend all that time shuffling diskettes? Besides, the CD has extra goodies. The CD also includes an abbreviated version of the Windows Resource Kit and many, many additional files that you'll find useful, sooner or later.

 If you have the CD version of Win98 and an extra 170 MB of free space on your hard drive, consider transferring all of the installation files from the CD—the ones in the **\drivers** and **\win98** folders—to your hard drive. Once they're all copied, you can install from the hard drive and futz around with settings and adding/removing components of Win98 until you're happy with your installation. Then you can simply delete all the files. Transferring all the files is easy: using DOS or your current version of Windows, create a new folder (called, say, **\winstall**), then copy all the files in the Win98 folder from the CD to that directory. Then, when you run SetUp, do so from that directory.

 I'd suggest keeping the **\winstall** directory there if you can afford the space. It'll make life easier if you need a file when installing some new hardware or if you need to reinstall.

Where From?

Once you've got the goods and you've ascertained that you have at least 200 MB of free disk space (the amount of space necessary for a typical install over Windows 3.1 or Win95), you need to decide from where you will install. Uh, from whence you shall install. From. (Pardon my dangling preposition.) It all boils down to a question of what operating system is running on your computer when you kick in the Win98 installer. You have five options.

- Install Win98 from DOS. To use this option, start by reading the rest of this chapter, then get DOS cranked up, switch over to the drive that holds the Win98 CD (or diskette or **\winstall** directory), type **setup**, and hit **Enter**. (*Note*: You can't install from a DOS box in Windows 3.1 or Windows 95!)

- Install Win98 from Windows 95, Windows 3.x, or Windows for Workgroups 3.11. If you have Win95, Windows 3.x, or WFW 3.11 working on your machine, this is the way to go. Most upgraders will choose this option, and for good reason. As you'll see in a minute, it's probably the best way to make sure all your hardware works under Win98 the first time around. To install from Win3.1, read the rest of this chapter, then quit all your Windows programs and use File Manager to run `setup` on the CD (or diskette or `\winstall` directory); or in Program Manager, click on File, then Run, navigate to `setup`, and click OK. To install from Win95, simply put the Win98 upgrade CD in your CD-ROM drive, and the installer should kick in automatically.

- Install Win98 from Win98. Already have Win98 running on your machine, but you're afraid that some of the system files are hosed? This might be the way to fix the problem. Run `setup` from the CD (or diskette or `\winstall` directory), and specify that you want to reinstall Win98 to the same directory, the one that currently contains Win98. The installer will automatically verify all the Win98 system files and restore any that have been clobbered. Note that you can't use Win98 to install a brand-new copy of Win98 into a different directory; the installer won't let you. If you want to create a brand-new copy of Win98 in a new directory, you have to install from the DOS prompt. (To get there from Win98, click Start, then Shutdown, click the Restart Computer in MS-DOS Mode? button, and OK.)

- Install Win98 from Windows NT to create a multiboot (WinNT, DOS, Win95) system. Since Win98 won't recognize NT File System (NTFS) partitions on your hard disk, and NT 4 won't recognize FAT32, you need to set up at least one FAT16 partition and format it. Read the rest of this chapter. Then make sure WinNT is set up to dual boot between NT and DOS. Use the dual boot to get into DOS. (Do *not* boot to DOS from a floppy; if you do, you'll wipe out WinNT!) Switch over to the drive with the Win98 CD (or diskette or `\winstall` directory), type `setup`, and hit `Enter`. Note that the Win98 installer isn't smart enough to pick up WinNT settings, so expect a rocky ride with any moderately unusual hardware. Also note that once you've installed Win98, running DOS from the WinNT multibooter is a bit convoluted: pick DOS from the multiboot menu, hit `Ctrl` when the Windows 98 splash screen appears, then pick Command Prompt Only (option 6) from the Windows 98 Startup Menu.

- The fifth type of install is called a Push install because it involves a network server "pushing" Win98 onto a networked machine. It's a topic unto itself, well beyond the scope of this book. If you're a network administrator struggling with a Push install, read the rest of this chapter, rub your lucky rabbit's foot, pore over Chapters 4 and 5 of the Windows Resource Kit, stockpile a couple gallons of latte, and (*please!*) tread lightly on your users by implementing as few system policy restrictions as possible. Remember that preventing users from choosing their own Windows wallpaper is as dumb as preventing office workers from putting family pictures in their cubicles. And remember what the movie *Easy Rider* had to say about Pushers.

 If you want to be able to continue to easily boot into Win95 or Win3.1 for a while or want to double-boot into OS/2 or Windows NT, look into System Commander, a well-done generic multiboot program from V Communications. Check **www.systemcommander.com**.

Where To?

The next question is, Install *to* what? Your new copy of Windows 98 has to live somewhere, and your choice of location can have many interesting—even devastating—ramifications. You have four options.

- Install Windows 98 on top of your current Win95, Win3.1 (or Windows for Workgroups 3.11) folder. Windows 98 removes a whole bunch of old Windows and DOS files and sticks the new Win98 files in the old **\windows** folder. This isn't quite as final or as fatal as it may sound. Windows 98 actually compresses all the old files and saves them in two files called **winundo.dat**, and **winundo.ini**, stored in the root of your boot disk. If you should decide to uninstall Windows 98—and you haven't done something drastic like change your hard drives over to FAT32—the old files are restored. When you install this way, all the settings you have in old Registry and Windows **.ini** files are reflected in the Win98 Registry and all your old Program Manager groups are converted, so they appear on the Start/Programs menu in Win98.

- Install Win98 to a new folder. If you want to start with a clean slate and have enough room on your hard drive, this option holds several advantages. It creates a new Registry from scratch, so old Registry settings aren't carried forward. None of the old garbage floating around in the **\windows** folder and in **win.ini** and **system.ini** is brought forward. The Start Menu starts out fresh. And you effectively have a dual-boot system. (To boot to the old Win95, first boot to DOS, then switch to the old Win95 folder and type **win**.) On the downside, Win98 may not be able to identify some hardware, you'll have to reinstall almost all your programs, and you'll lose any customizing in those programs—settings, passwords, everything. To install Win98 into a new folder, you have to install from DOS (see the preceding section "Where From?").

- Install Win98 to a freshly reformatted hard drive. We'll cover this at the end of the SetUp section. This is similar to installing to a new folder, but it ensures that Win95 is well and truly gone from your PC. It's a drastic approach, best suited for advanced Windows users. We've come up with an interesting way to perform a "virgin" install like this, with a minimum of hassle, that we'll discuss at the end of the SetUp section.

- Install Win98 on top of your current version of Win98. This isn't so much an install as a refresh: Win98 scans the current system's files and replaces any that appear to be damaged.

 My advice is to do what Microsoft recommends, which is to install Windows 98 on top of an existing Windows system's files and you'll be able to uninstall Windows 98 if the urge should strike you. Reformatting your hard drive during an installation can be hugely traumatic, and if something goes wrong you can really be left up the creek. In addition, you'll have to reinstall every bloody Winapp and most of your fonts, and you'll lose your program groups and any other customization you did. That's a bunch of powerful reasons for going with the default.

 While that's the best advice for 95% of our readers, the heavy experimenters are advised to start from scratch once a year to get rid of the junk their experimenting accumulates.

How Much 98 Do You Need?

So by now you've probably decided you're going to install Windows 98 from Windows 95, and if you're a power user you'll probably install to a clean hard drive. (If you're a bit sheepish, though, you might've decided to install on top of Windows 95. That's cool. *De gustibus non est disputandum,* eh wot?)

The last thing you must decide is *how much* of Windows 98 you want to install. The bare-bones size of Win98 will vary, depending on whether you are installing on top of an existing Windows installation or to a brand new folder. Table 6-1 lists the base sizes.

Table 6-1. Hard Disk Space for a "Typical" Install	
Upgrade from Windows 3.1 or 95	195 MB
Install to a new, reformatted disk (FAT16)	225 MB
Install to a new, reformatted disk (FAT32)	175 MB

If you install from DOS, the Windows 98 SetUp Wizard will present you with three prefab options (Typical, Compact, and Portable), plus the opportunity to pick and choose from a list of the options you might want (Custom). Table 6-1 shows the size of a Typical installation. You have to add all the additional space required by any options you choose.

Table 6-2 shows you how much room each of the Win98 options requires and whether those options are included in a Compact, Portable, or Typical installation.

Table 6-2. Win98 Installation Options

Option	Compact	Portable	Typical	Size
Accessibility				
Keyboard, Sound, and Mouse Options	Yes	Yes	Yes	0.5 MB
Magnifier Tool, Mouse Pointers				2.3 MB
Accessories				
Briefcase		Yes		0.0 MB
Calculator			Yes	0.2 MB
Desktop Wallpaper				0.6 MB
Document Templates			Yes	0.2 MB
Games				0.6 MB
Imaging (Image Viewer, TWAIN support)			Yes	4.4 MB
Mouse Pointers				0.7 MB
Paint			Yes	2.3 MB
QuickView				4.2 MB
Screen Savers (additional savers 0.2 MB)			Yes	1.1 MB
Windows Scripting Host		Yes	Yes	0.9 MB
WordPad		Yes	Yes	1.5 MB
Communications				
Dial-Up Networking	Yes	Yes	Yes	1.0 MB
Dial-Up Server				0.1 MB
Direct Cable Connection		Yes		0.4 MB
HyperTerminal		Yes		0.7 MB
MS Chat 2.1				4.6 MB
MS NetMeeting			Yes	4.3 MB
Phone Dialer		Yes	Yes	0.1 MB
Virtual Private Networking		Yes		0.1 MB
Internet Tools				
MS FrontPage Express		Yes	Yes	4.2 MB
MS VRML 2.0 Viewer				3.2 MB
MS Wallet				0.9 MB
Personal Web Server		Yes	Yes	0.1 MB
Real Audio Player 4.0				2.4 MB
Web Publishing Wizard				1.1 MB
Web-Based Enterprise Management (for remote system administration)				3.2 MB
Outlook				
Outlook Express	Yes	Yes	Yes	4.5 MB

Table 6-2. Win98 Installation Options

Option	Compact	Portable	Typical	Size
Multilanguage Support				
Baltic Languages				2.3 MB
Central European Languages				2.4 MB
Cyrillic				2.3 MB
Greek				2.3 MB
Turkish				2.2 MB
Multimedia				
Audio Compression	Yes	Yes	Yes	0.2 MB
CD Player	Yes	Yes	Yes	0.2 MB
Macromedia Shockwave Director			Yes	1.5 MB
Macromedia Shockwave Flash			Yes	0.2 MB
Media Player		Yes	Yes	0.2 MB
MS NetShow Player 2.0				3.9 MB
Multimedia Sound Schemes				5.8 MB
Sample Sounds				0.5 MB
Sound Recorder		Yes	Yes	0.2 MB
Video Compression		Yes	Yes	0.5 MB
Volume Control		Yes	Yes	0.2 MB
Online Services				
America Online	Yes	Yes	Yes	0.1 MB
AT&T WorldNet	Yes	Yes	Yes	0.2 MB
CompuServe	Yes	Yes	Yes	0.1 MB
Prodigy Internet	Yes	Yes	Yes	0.4 MB
MSN (The Microsoft Network)	Yes	Yes	Yes	0.1 MB
System Tools				
Backup				4.3 MB
Character Map				0.1 MB
Clipboard Viewer				0.1 MB
Disk Compression Tools	Yes	Yes		2.0 MB
Drive Converter (FAT32)		Yes	Yes	0.4 MB
Group Policies				0.1 MB
Net Watcher				0.2 MB
System Monitor				0.2 MB
System Resource Meter				0.1 MB
WinPopup			Yes	0.1 MB
WebTV for Windows				
WaveTop (requires WebTV for Win)				10.00 MB
WebTV for Windows				24.00 MB

In addition, there are 17 Desktop Themes you can install, for a total of 22.6 MB.

Actually, the options aren't quite as simple as they might appear. The installer is quite clever in figuring out what kinds of hardware you have installed and modifying the default options accordingly. For example, if you choose the Compact option and Win98 determines that your machine has a modem installed, it will probably pick up Dial-Up Networking and Direct Cable Connection, whereas modem-less machines won't get those on a Compact installation. There appear to be dozens, if not hundreds, of combinations, so use MOM's numbers as a guideline, not as a definitive statement.

By the way, if you look at the official published list from Microsoft (in the Windows Resource Kit), you'll see that the numbers in Table 6-2 are different, over and over again. Our guess is that Microsoft put the numbers in the WRK during one of the early beta test cycles and didn't bother to update it before Win98 shipped. Try it for yourself. You'll see.

I'm surprised that Typical installation doesn't include QuickView, the Clipboard Viewer, and Backup, which almost everybody can use. I wouldn't even think of running Win98 without Net Watcher and the System Resource Meter, and the System Monitor helps, too.

You forgot the games! Why doesn't the Typical installation include Microsoft's games? Free Cell, Hearts, Minesweeper, and Solitaire may not be the most awesome games on the planet, but they're all quite good . . . and they're free! Besides, they take up less than 1 megabyte of space, and even Windows novices—people who would have a hard time installing the games—would get a big kick out of them. They might improve their mousing skills while they're at it.

It's easy to claim your free games, even if you're still scared of blowing up your computer. Click on Start, then Settings, then Control Panel. Double click on Add/Remove Programs. Click on the Windows SetUp tab. Click Accessories, then the Details button. Make sure Games has a check mark beside it, and click OK. Click OK again. Now Windows 98 will ask you to insert a diskette or the CD in the appropriate drive. Do so. There. You just paid for this book!

It's more than just games. The Multimedia Sample Sounds include righteous MIDI files of excerpts from "Bach's Brandenburg no. 3," "Beethoven's Fifth," and "Für Elise," "Dance of the Sugar-Plum Fairy," "Claire de Lune," "Hall of the Mountain King," and "Mozart's Symphony no. 40." (If you explicitly elect to install them, they get copied to the Win98 **\windows\media** folder.) If you have a MIDI card, you really need to listen to these files.

Hey, wait a minute, fellas. You guys in the press have been roasting us 'Softies mercilessly for "program bloat"—the increased size of our programs and how much disk real estate they demand. Now you're jabbing us for not including all your pet components in a Typical install! You can't have it both ways, guys.

Well, you've got a point, but it's not that simple. Some of the components that get installed are so poorly documented that most people probably don't even know they have 'em! For example, on a Typical install, if Win98 detects a network card, you'll automatically get a little "accessory" called WinPopup. That WinPopup is so cool I can hardly stand it: with it I can send little messages to any person on my network, any machine, or all machines in a "broadcast." But to make it work, you have to make WinPopup start automatically every time Windows starts—and there's no documentation on WinPopup anywhere in the online Help file!

I prefer WinChat because it traces the entire conversation, WinChat and WinPopup are described in Chapter 4. I can understand your frustration. WinChat, too, is not covered in the Win98 Help, and since it's not automatically copied from the Win98 CD to your hard disk, the contortions you have to go through to install it are pretty bizarre, too.

My advice? If you have 100 MB of extra free disk space, just go ahead and install everything. Think of it this way: hard disk space costs less than a nickel per MB. If installing all of Win98 takes up an extra 140 MB, that's seven bucks' worth of disk space. Big highfalutin' deal. Install everything. Live dangerously.

FAT32?

Next you need to consider whether you're going to convert your PC's hard drive(s) over to FAT32 (we talked about FAT32 and its implications in Chapter 4). Basically, almost everybody will benefit from converting to FAT32, but you need to keep these potential problems in mind.

- Once you've converted to FAT32, there's no way (short of reformatting the drive and losing all your data) to go back to FAT16. Microsoft provides a converter to go from FAT16 to FAT32, but there's no analogous converter to take FAT32 disks back to FAT16. So, for example, if you convert to FAT32 and later decide you want to uninstall Win98, to go back to the original version of Win95 you'll lose all the data on the FAT32 drive.

- You may not have enough room. If you're using DriveSpace or one of the other commercial disk compression programs, you'll have to uncompress the data before you can convert the drive to FAT32. You may not have enough room on the hard drive to uncompress all the data. If that's the case, you'll have to move enough data off the hard drive or delete enough files to uncompress what's left before converting to FAT32. In addition, the FAT16 to FAT32 converter will need an extra 100 MB or so on the drive—extra shuffling room—to make the transition.

- DriveSpace and other disk compressors work only on FAT16 drives. While file access under FAT32 is much faster than that under DriveSpace, there's no denying that DriveSpace gives you more room on a specific hard drive. If you're up to 80% full using DriveSpace, you may not have any room left after converting to FAT32—even if you use the tricks described later in this chapter to get over the initial conversion hump.

- FAT32 is not supported on drives smaller than half a gigabyte (less than 512 MB).

- None of your FAT16 disk utilities will work with FAT32. You'll have to upgrade them. Some antivirus products may have problems, too, although the latest versions of all the commercial AV products will work fine. In addition, if your portable has a "suspend" mode that writes to disk, check with the manufacturer to make sure that function will work with FAT32.

- Only Windows 98, a late version of Windows 95 called OSR2, and Windows NT 5 or later can work with FAT32 disks. So if you have a dual-boot system, the data on the FAT32 drives won't be accessible unless you're running Win98 (or NT 5). Similarly, if you like to boot to older versions of DOS from time to time, the files under FAT32 won't be accessible.

- If you try to convert a FAT16 drive with *just one* cluster containing a "bad cluster" mark, Win98 will refuse. There's nothing you can do about it; Win98 was designed that way.

Unless you fall into one of these high-risk categories, you should definitely plan on spending an extra hour or two during Win98 installation to convert your drives to FAT32.

Get Rid of Win95?

Do you have a funny feeling that your old Windows 95 or 3.x setup is so screwed up it's clobbering your PC? Are you worried that whatever demons haunted your old setup may reappear in Win98 if you install Win98 on top of your old Win95/Win3.1 folder? Are you concerned that installing Win98 to a totally new folder may not fully exorcise the demons? It may sound overly paranoid, but to tell the truth, we at MOM's place worry about such things all the time.

 If you install on a freshly reformatted hard drive, it is a virgin install. As you've used Windows, you probably installed some stuff and got rid of it, but you were unable to do thorough uninstalls. So you probably have extra DLLs around, whole sections of your Registry and **win.ini** that are junk, and lots of flotsam and jetsam in your **\windows\system** directory. A fresh start is often the best thing—although, yes, there is the cost of reinstalling your applications.

The only way you'll know for sure that all vestiges of your old Windows 95 (or Windows 3.x) setup has disappeared for good is if you completely reformat your hard drive prior to installing Windows 98. It's a difficult decision, one that shouldn't be taken lightly, but for advanced Windows 95 users, the benefits may well outweigh the considerable difficulty.

Also, if you have large hard drives with partitions and you want to get rid of the partitions so that you can take advantage of FAT32's large drive capabilities, you have two choices: either use FDISK and destroy all the data on the hard drive or buy a product like Partition Magic, which can rearrange partitions without messing up all the files. (More information about both options is in the section "Nuking Win95," later in this chapter.)

If you currently have Windows 95 installed on a partitioned hard drive and you want to unpartition that drive—and you don't want to spend the $70 or so for Partition Magic—*you have no choice* but to obliterate Win95 and everything else on the drive.

Our bottom-line advice is to do a clean install on a freshly formatted hard drive if

1. You've run Windows for more than two years or have a complicated setup.

2. You can make good backups of all the data on your hard drive.

3. You don't mind reinstalling all your applications, resetting all your customizing, and have a record of all of your passwords!

For those willing to take the plunge, we have a little trick that may mitigate the trauma a bit. Look at the "Nuking Win95" section for details.

■ Preparing for Installation

To lead an untrained people into war is to throw them away.

—Confucius, *Analects*, ca. 500 B.C.

Be prepared. That's where it's at. If you follow all eight of Barry's steps, covered in the next several pages, *before* you install Windows 98, you'll save yourself untold headaches during the installation process. An ounce of prevention is worth a pound of cure. Better safe than sorry. Look before you leap. In fair weather prepare for foul. Beware of Greeks bearing gifts. Ooops. Wrong aphorism.

Make that "Beware of Geeks bearing gifts," and it's apropos.

Step 1: Double-Check the Minimum Requirements

One last time, make sure your system is up to Win98 snuff, both in terms of processor power and available hard disk space. See Chapter 1 for a list of minimum requirements and Table 6-1 for additional details on hard disk space. In short, figure you need at least a Pentium 90, 32 MB of RAM, and 200 MB of free disk space.

Step 2: Make a DOS Emergency Boot Disk

 This one could save your PC's life, so listen up! If you don't have a boot disk, stick a clean diskette in the **a:** drive and make an emergency system disk *before* you upgrade. Here's how.

- If you're running DOS, type **format a: /s**. Copy across **autoexec.bat** and **config.sys** from your hard drive's root directory and at a least **edit.com** and **qbasic.exe** from your **\dos** directory. You'll probably want to pack the diskette with **himem.sys** and **mouse.com** and any other programs that appear in **autoexec.bat** and **config.sys**. Some older versions of DOS don't automatically copy **command.com** when you do a **format /s**, so make sure there's a **command.com** in the root directory of the emergency diskette.
- If you're using Windows 3.x, exit to DOS and follow the above instructions.
- If you have Win95, go into the Control Panel's Add/Remove Programs applet, click the StartUp Disk tab, and create a new startup disk. Then get a fresh disk and copy onto that disk **config.sys** and **autoexec.bat**, if either or both exists, from the hard drive root directory and every file mentioned in either of them. You don't necessarily want **autoexec** and **config** on your boot disk, but it'll be helpful to have them handy if worse comes to worst.

In most cases that will give you all the pieces you need to get your system going again, should something go horribly wrong with the upgrade.

If you already have an emergency boot disk, make sure it works! Stick it in your **a:** drive and hit your PC's Reset button. Make sure you know how to get DOS and Windows started.

 If you find that Windows boots instead of the boot diskette, you've probably set your BIOS to skip the diskette drive and go directly to the hard drive. While that has some real advantages in general, during the Win98 install, I'd recommend that you switch to the mode where it tries to boot first from diskette and then hard drive.

Step 3: Win 3.x Users Prep

Windows 95 users can skip to Step 4.

The first hurdle Windows 3.x users must clear to effect an easy Win98 installation is to clean up your **autoexec.bat** and **config.sys** files. If you're relatively comfortable with those two Files from Hell, hum a happy tune: once Windows 98 is installed, you may never need to touch them again. If you're a bit unsure of those two relics from a far sadder time, just follow along here and we'll teach you enough to go in and skin them alive.

As the commercial says, "They're germs. They deserve to die."

- Start by making backup copies. Using Windows 3.1 or DOS or whatever is handy, move over to your boot drive (normally **c:**), make a copy of **autoexec.bat** called, oh, **autoexec.mom**, and make a copy of **config.sys** called **config.mom**.

- Now make sure Win98 doesn't get pointed in the wrong direction. Win98 is usually smart enough to find itself; but if there are vestiges of old Windows 3.1 flimflammery hanging around, Win98 can get confused. Open up **autoexec.bat** using Notepad in Win3.1 or Edit in DOS. If your **autoexec.bat** has either or both of these lines at the very end:

  ```
  cd \windows
  win
  ```

  stick **REM** and a space in front of either or both lines, turning them into comments, effectively zapping them out. If they existed before, they should end up looking like this:

  ```
  REM cd \windows
  REM win
  ```

  If you do **REM** out these lines but are installing to a new directory because you want to double-boot, be sure after the install to edit the file you'll find called **autoexec.dos** and remove the **REM**s. That'll be the **autoexec.bat** used when you dual boot to your old DOS.

- If the last line of your **autoexec.bat** calls another **.bat** file that contains those two lines, go into the other **.bat** file and **REM** the lines out.

- Close **autoexec.bat** (and any other open **.bat** files) and save changes.

- Using Notepad or Edit, open up **config.sys**. We need to get rid of EMM386's **highscan** parameter. If you have a line that looks like this,

  ```
  device = emm386.exe 512 highscan
  ```

  remove the **highscan** on the line. There may be many more parameters and worse-than-senseless things before or after **highscan.** Don't worry about them. Just zap the **highscan** and leave single spaces between the parameters.

- DOS 6.x lets you specify multiple "configurations" in **config.sys**, using something called a **[Menu]** command, and lets you choose among them when DOS is started. Windows 98 still supports multiple configurations, but we've had nothing but headaches with them getting tangled up in Win98 setup. More than that, we can't think of one good reason to keep multiple DOS configurations in Windows 98. If your **config.sys** has a **[Menu]** command, pick the configuration you most often use and pare back **config.sys** to that single configuration.

- Finally, you'll want to get rid of your last drive setting. If your **config.sys** has a line that looks like this,

    ```
    lastdrive = e
    ```

    remove the whole line. The letter on the end may be an **f** or a **z** or just about anything. Don't worry about it. Zap the entire line.
- That's it for **config.sys**. Close it and save changes. Then reboot your machine entirely to make sure you didn't screw up anything. You should be able to get into Windows 3.1 just as you normally do, except that you might have to type **win** and hit **Enter**. If there are problems, copy **autoexec.mom** back to **autoexec.bat** and **config.mom** to **config.sys**, and try again.

If you are running a third-party memory manager (for example, QEMM or 386max), consider removing it before you try to install Windows 98. Otherwise, Win98 may set things up so that it loads that manager for you every time you start Win98, but you don't want to do that! Running a Win3.1 version of QEMM or 386max isn't likely to produce any problems, but you'll get no benefit and may lose memory.

The easiest way to remove QEMM, if you are using it and DOS 6.x, is to run DOS's **memmaker**. Just pop out to DOS and type **memmaker**. Don't even try to do anything fancy—optimize upper memory or anything like that. Win98 will take care of everything later on. When **memmaker** is done, you should double-check **autoexec.bat** and remove QEMM's **dosdata** and **dos-up** programs by hand, if necessary.

Step 4: Win95 Users Prep

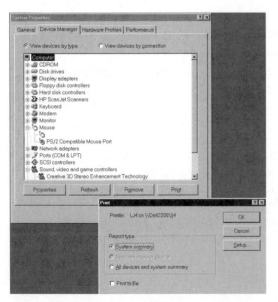

Take a minute before you run Win98 SetUp to record all the hardware settings you currently have. Win98 is supposed to respect those hardware settings, but it never hurts to have a hard copy backup!

To print out a current list, click Start, Settings, and Control Panel, then double click the System applet. Click once on the Device Manager tab, then Print, System summary. You should see something like Figure 6-1.

Tuck that summary away, just in case something goes bump in the night.

Figure 6-1. Win95 users should print a system summary

That summary will list IRQ, I/O ports, and DMA channels. If Windows 98 gets some of those wrong (and I've seen it happen), it is invaluable for you to know the settings that used to work.

Step 5: Check Your Hard Drives

If you run Windows 98 SetUp from DOS, it's going to check your hard drives before it starts, looking for cross-linked files and the like. If Win98 SetUp finds errors, it's going to tell you that you need to run ScanDisk, and then it will stop running so that you can comply. You may as well do it yourself before you run SetUp for Windows 98.

To do so from Win3.1, go out to DOS and run ScanDisk. From Win95, click Start, Programs, Accessories, System Utilities, ScanDisk.

Run it on every one of your hard drives, not just the one that you are going to install Windows 98 to—because that's what Windows 98 SetUp is going to do.

It's probably a good idea to give your disks a real workout and just generally get your spinning platter house in order before the big Win98 installer hits. You can wait to defragment them, though. Win98 has a nifty defragmenter, far superior to the ones in earlier versions of Windows.

Step 6: Back Up, Back Up, Back Up

 Ninety-nine times out of a hundred the Win98 installer works just fine. You may have to boot and reboot and cuss and kick your machine a few dozen times, but genuine data loss is so rare that you can safely ignore it, except . . .

Except when it happens to you, eh?

Don't be a chump. Back up. Back up. Back up. Every single file. Go out and buy a $150 tape drive if you have to: this is the perfect excuse to do what you should be doing every day anyway. Or, if you are on a network and can get enough space elsewhere on the network, just do a straight copy of all your files to that network location.

Step 7: Gather the Stuff You'll Need

Like most installers, the Windows 98 SetUp routines require you to enter some information. You'll need to know, uh, your name ("Spiff, Citizen of the Univers" works just fine). You can also enter a company name ("Spacely Sprockets," anybody?). If your PC is connected to a network, you'll need a logon ID and password—and if it's a Netware network, you can save yourself a lot of headache by entering your Netware ID and password correctly the first time.

Some of the other information is a bit more subtle. If you're connected to a network, you need to know your network workgroup name, and that name has to match your coworker's workgroup name precisely. You'll also need a unique code name for your PC. And you should know the manufacturer and "official" model name or number of every single piece of hardware in or attached to your PC. Dig out the old user manuals or receipts if you aren't absolutely sure; as a last resort, look for labels on the hardware itself.

Finally, you'll need one diskette that will fit in your **a:** drive. Everything on it will get wiped out, so don't use last year's tax return. That's about it.

Step 8: Brace Yourself

Whether you're installing from DOS, Windows 3.1, or Windows 95, you must first make sure all of your peripherals are working and that you're connected to the network, if you have one. So reboot your machine afresh; bring up Windows 3.1 if you're going to be installing from it, or Win95 if that's the beast that bears you; test every single peripheral, including every disk drive, your modem, your printer, and especially your CD-ROM drive; then make sure your network connections are all working right.

Then disable any antivirus software you may have running and anything else that remotely looks like a program. Hit **Ctrl+Alt+Del** to bring up the Task Manager and "End Task" for all the programs you see there except Explorer and Systray. If your PC has some sort of antivirus routine built into its BIOS, disable that, too.

Most important: turn off your screen saver and any power management utilities that might kick in while you're doing the upgrade. There's nothing worse than a crazy screen saver springing to life or a hard drive spinning down when you're trying to determine if your machine is frozen.

Now, hold your breath, pilgrim. It's time to take the big dive.

■ SetUp Vérité

It is no disgrace to start over. It is usually an opportunity.

—GEORGE M. ADAMS

 I have gone through gazillions of Win9X installs on many different machines and, while it can get a bit scary at times, invariably Windows has installed correctly. Every single time. Some of our family members and associates can't say the same thing, but they tried to install before this book was ready and thus didn't have the advantage of MOM's sage advice and chicken soup.

In a nutshell, the Windows 98 SetUp Wizard takes a look at your system, figures out what parts of Win98 you need, then copies files and establishes preliminary hardware settings. After that it reboots, sets up some general items like Control Panel, and reboots a final time. During that final reboot, additional hardware drivers may be added. Often after the first or second reboot,

Windows appears to get into deep doo-doo. There may be a shift to text mode with a message about a fatal error. Or the hourglass pops up and stays and stays and stays, while Win98 drifts off to La-La Land. But invariably, when you reboot—by turning the PC off, then back on again, as specified in the Wizard screens—SetUp recovers and goes further in its process. On one machine the SetUp Wizard crashed four times, and on each occasion we figured we'd bit the dust for good. But after those four extra reboots, SetUp finished and the machine worked perfectly.

My worst Win98 install happened on my main working PC, a couple of weeks before this book was due. Most of the installation went fine, until I got to the Setting Up Hardware step. Suddenly, I got a General Protection Fault ("This program has performed an illegal operation and will be shut down") on something called **msgsrv32**. I turned the PC off, waited 30 seconds, and turned it back on again. Win98 went through its ScanDisk routine, seemed to be going OK, and then I got a message saying, "Do you want to restart your computer?" I said Yes. Win98 rebooted again, went through a couple more gyrations, then froze on the dread Blue Screen of Death ("Fatal Exception OE"). I hit Enter a few times, and it cascaded—one Blue Screen after another, each with different problems. Finally, I hit the Reset button. When Win98 came back up, it went into the Control Panel SetUp routines, all the way through the following restart, then it crashed with a GPF in **ie4uinit** while setting up Outlook Express. I restarted again, as recommended, and got another Blue Screen of Death, this time while in the System Configuration phase. Restarted one more time, it went back to the Control Panel SetUp and seemed to complete.

The installation left a lot of my customizations totally screwed up—my Internet Explorer settings were gone, the shortcuts in my toolbar were deleted, even Outlook 98 reverted to settings I hadn't seen in months. When I finally got around to using various applications—and these are standard, everyday, MS Office applications—I hit GPFs every few minutes. The whole system was so unstable it was virtually unusable.

So I went back to the drawing board. Booted to DOS, using the Win98 Emergency StartUp Disk, ran SetUp off the Win98 CD from DOS, and had the Win98 SetUp Wizard install Win98 in the same folder I had been using for Win98 and, before that, Win95. That install went all the way through. I booted Win98 again, and all of a sudden it was usable. I could go 20 or 30 minutes without a GPF.

Know what the problem was? I had installed a large hard drive in an old PC, and it required a special program to "map" the drive so Win98 could use it. Solution? Install a new BIOS. Cost $50, took ten minutes, and it works like a champ.

Anybody who tells you that all Win95 to Win98 upgrades go smoothly just hasn't tried hard enough . . .

It's like we said at the beginning of the chapter. Be strong and of good faith. The Windows 98 SetUp Wizard is incredibly robust: in fact, it may be singularly the most bulletproof program we have ever used.

The key to the Win98 SetUp Wizard's excellent non-self-destructiveness lies in several files that it creates and maintains as it's looking at your system. If the installer crashes once, it's smart enough to take a look at the log of its previous incarnation and skip over the step that hosed it the last time around. While it's true that this try-and-crash-but-live-to-try-again process can put gray hairs on the head of any PC user, it's a marvelously robust way to run an installer.

In fact, Microsoft learned so much from this piece of software that they built a similar routine into Windows 98 itself, so Win98 is smart enough to bypass a particularly vexing piece of software when it tries to boot. That's how the Automatic Skip Driver feature originated.

Let's step through a typical (which is to say, hassle-free) Win98 installation, one screen at a time, and see what's really going on. We ran this installation from Windows 95, using the CD version of Win98, installing on top of the current **\windows** folder. Follow along as we take a look at the ins and outs of what appears on the screen.

■ A Perfect Installation

Start Windows 95, and put the Win98 upgrade CD-ROM into the CD drive. When asked, tell the CD that you want to install Win98.

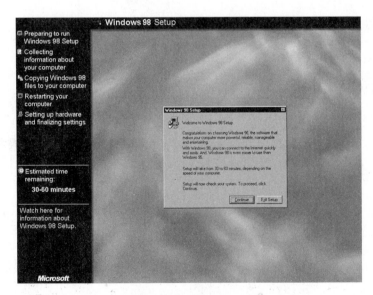

Figure 6-2. The feel good Win98 SetUp screen

Up pops the Win98 Feel Good SetUp screen (Figure 6-2). Yeah, yeah, yeah. You're cool, wired, and very good looking—not to mention intelligent—because you bought Win98.

If you're very lucky, SetUp will take a half hour. In most cases, we'd allow a leisurely afternoon (or a hectic evening) to get the beast installed and configured, convert your disk(s) to FAT32, and get a good jump start on the Windows tour and tutorial.

If you installed from the DOS prompt, as you must if you're going to put Win98 in a different folder from Win95, the installer goes through a ScanDisk run, then launches the Win98 SetUp Wizard.

The Wizard won't be able to update any files that are in use, so it would behoove you to close everything down. In practice, we've run some small programs while the Wizard was running, but we wouldn't make a habit of it.

At this point the Wizard starts keeping a log of all the choices you make, and the actions it takes in response to those choices, in a hidden file called **setuplog.txt**, which is stored in the root directory of your boot drive (e.g., **C:\setuplog.txt**).

You'll be asked to accept the Microsoft End User Licensing Agreement (or EULA). It's a typical, unenforceable, one-sided "contract" that says you will only use one copy of Win98 on one machine, you won't rent it out, and if your company goes bankrupt as a result of bugs in Win98, Microsoft owes you only the amount of the purchase price. You know. The usual. (This is a personal—not a legal—opinion. If you have any questions, ask your lawyer, but be braced for the possibility that s/he will turn catatonic in laughter and later sue you for loss of work time.)

Next you have to enter the product key from the sticker on the back of the jewel case your upgrade CD came in. While you're thinking about it, now is a good time to take a permanent marker and write the product key on the top (that is, the printed side) of the CD. That way, if you ever need to use the CD again, you won't have to go scrambling for the possibly long-departed jewel case.

If you install from the DOS prompt, the Wizard will present you with a dialog labeled Select Directory (Figure 6-3).

For the DOS installer, this is the single most important decision you will make during the installation. If you leave the top button checked, Win98 is installed on top of your existing copy of Windows 95 (or Windows 3.1). If you click the lower button, Win98 is installed to a new directory, and you'll be prompted in the next message to type in a folder name. For a detailed discussion, see the earlier section "Where To?"

The Wizard checks to make sure that there's enough room in the Windows folder to hold everything. You can still cancel at this point and return to your old Win95 setup without fear of being tossed into a weird half-Win95, half-Win98 twilight zone. (It can happen. Trust us. You don't want to be there.) We'll let you know when we reach the point of no return.

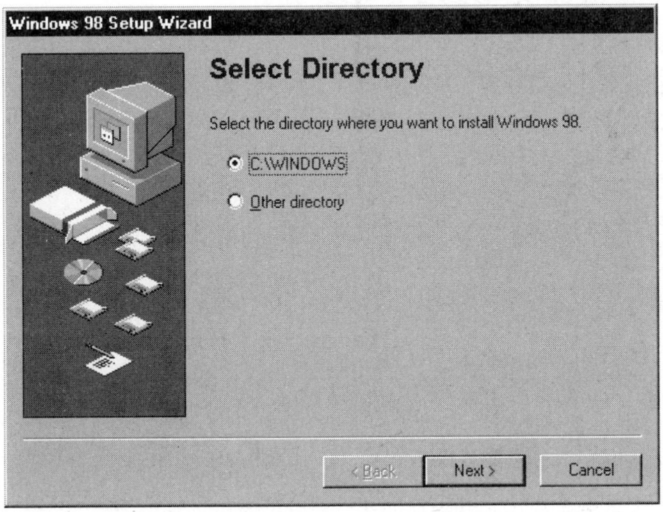

Figure 6-3. If you install from DOS, the Wizard asks where you want to put Win98

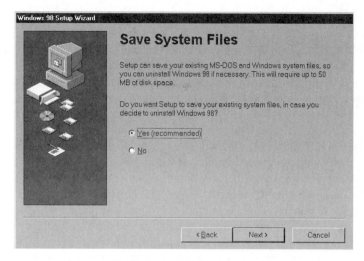

Figure 6-4. The ultimate safety net

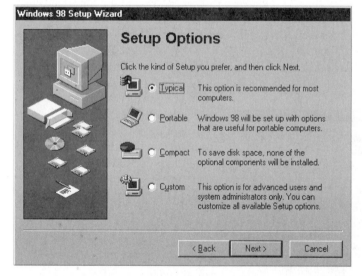

Figure 6-6. The Wizard wants to know how much Win98 you can stand

Figure 6-5. Choose a location for `winundo.dat` and `winundo.ini`

Since you're installing on top of the existing Win95\\`windows` folder, the Wizard asks if you want to save your system files (Figure 6-4).

If you click Yes, the Wizard packs up the files `winundo.dat`, `winundo.ini`, and `winlfn.ini` and puts them in the root directory of the drive you choose in the next dialog, Figure 6-5. Microsoft says `winundo.dat` can "be up to 50 MB in size," and that's simply wrong: we've seen them over 75 MB.

If the Wizard can determine which components you have installed, it assumes that you want to update those components and not add any new ones. But if you're installing from DOS, you'll see a screen that looks like Figure 6-6.

Now it's down to the nitty-gritty. If you're short on disk space, pick Portable or Compact. Otherwise, pick Custom. *Never choose Typical.* Why? Because all the Typical choices are automatically selected when you choose Custom plus Disk Compression, which is selected in Custom but not in Typical. By choosing Custom, then clicking Next>, you can see (later in the installation procedure) what Win98 wants to install on your system, then adjust the automatic choices as you see fit.

Figure 6-7.
The Wizard wants
your name

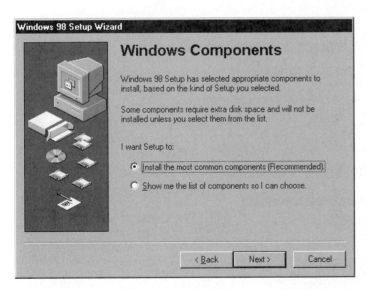

Time for a little breather. Once you've chosen your SetUp option, the Wizard asks you for your name and your company's name (Figure 6-7), unless it can find them on your PC. Make sure you use something for your name and your company's name that you can live with—those names can show up in the most embarrassing places.

With that formality out of the way, the Wizard gets serious about nailing down precisely which components of Win98 you want to install. Again, if it has scanned your Win95 system and thinks it knows what you need, you won't be asked. But if you're installing from DOS, you'll see the Windows Components dialog, as in Figure 6-8. If you tell Win98 that you want to see the list of components, so you can choose, you get the Select Components dialog shown in Figure 6-9.

At this point, if you're connected to a network and the Wizard can't determine the name of your computer or the workgroup (e.g., if you're installing from DOS), you see a dialog box asking for that information. If you don't know your computer's name, don't panic: pick a short name composed of random letters and numbers.

Figure 6-8. If you want to specify which pieces of Win98 to install, choose the second option

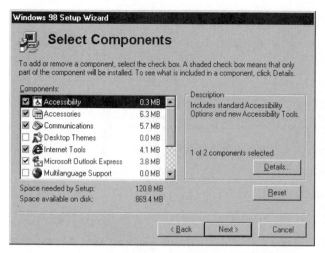

Figure 6-9. Here's where you can pick and choose the components described in Table 6-2

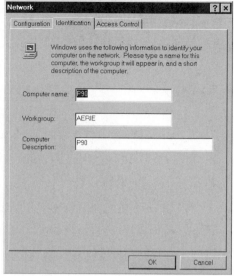

Figure 6-10. A coworker can retrieve the workgroup name from the Network applet

Unfortunately, you can't fake the workgroup name: if it isn't right, you won't be connected to the network. Check with your network administrator, or ask a coworker on the same network to look in the Control Panel Network applet's Identification tab (Figure 6-10), and copy the workgroup name from there. The computer name must be unique within the workgroup. Be careful! You may be able to enter a computer name or workgroup name with spaces and odd characters, but some programs may go haywire trying to use them. Stick to simple names: letters and numbers.

Next the Wizard asks you where you're from, primarily for Web site content and getting the keyboard settings right (Figure 6-11).

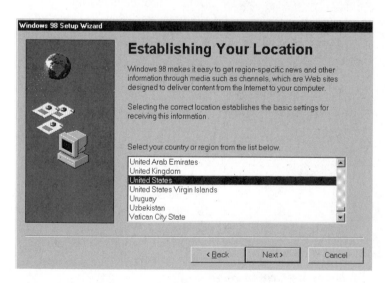

Figure 6-11. Tell the Wizard where you live

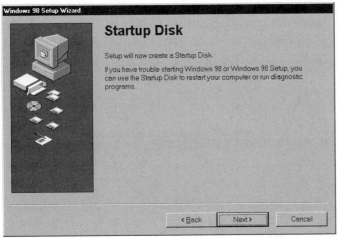

Figure 6-13. The ESD gets completely reformatted, so don't lose any worthwhile data

Figure 6-12. The Wizard wants to create an Emergency StartUp Disk

As the final preliminary step, the Wizard creates a StartUp Disk (Figure 6-12). Almost everybody in the Win98 realm calls this an Emergency StartUp Disk (ESD) or an Emergency Boot Disk, but we'll bow to Microsoft's sensibilities. The ESD is a rather remarkable beast (we talk about it in Chapter 7). For now, get a diskette ready, and make sure you use one that doesn't have any important data on it (Figure 6-13).

Figure 6-14 shows the key dialog for the whole Wizard because *if you click Next> here, you go beyond the point of no return.* (Well, there is a return, but it involves uninstalling all of Windows 98.) Make sure your computer isn't going to hit a power glitch in the next half hour or so—don't let the kids run near the power cord—and when you're feeling sufficiently adventurous, click Next>.

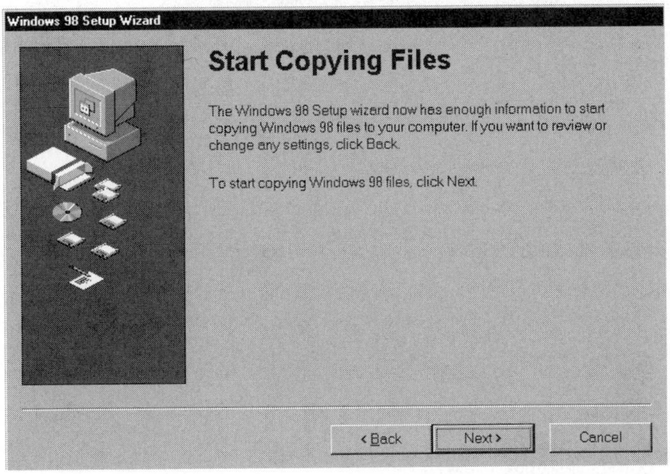

Figure 6-14. The Wizard starts obliterating Win95 as soon as you click Next>

Now the installer switches from asking you for information to analyzing the psyche of your PC itself. While what you see on the screen (Figures 6-15 and 6-16) appears quite innocuous, the installer is in fact churning overtime underneath. The Wizard creates several files along the way (all these files are discussed Chapter 7). For example, the **setup.log** file contains information on everything you've chosen or typed up to this point.

Figure 6-15. Underneath this placid façade, the Wizard is gathering all sorts of information

Figure 6-16. And when this dialog appears, the Wizard is copying Win98 files onto your machine

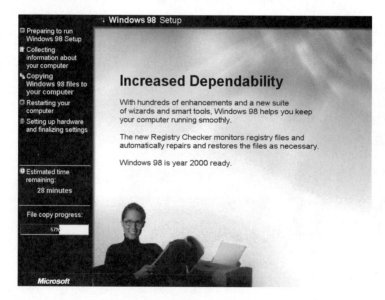

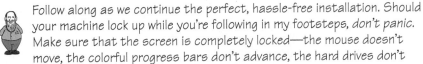Follow along as we continue the perfect, hassle-free installation. Should your machine lock up while you're following in my footsteps, don't panic. Make sure that the screen is completely locked—the mouse doesn't move, the colorful progress bars don't advance, the hard drives don't whirr, absolutely nothing happens—for a full five minutes. Time it with a watch. Only after you're completely sure the machine is toast should you follow the instructions on the screen to effect a recovery. (That means you physically turn off the machine—don't press **Ctrl+Alt+Del**. Wait a minute or two, turn the machine back on, rerun SetUp, go through the rigmarole of getting the Installation Wizard going again, then click "Use Safe Recovery (Recommended)" on the Safe Recovery screen, if it's presented to you.) We continue with the scary part of the discussion in the next section, "What Can Go Wrong?".

When the files have been copied, the Wizard restarts the machine. You can tell you've reached this point because the splash screen says, "Getting ready to run Windows for the first time." Even if you've run Windows a zillion times before.

The Win98 SetUp Wizard then goes through two hardware detection phases, first covering Plug 'n' Play devices, then looking for non-Plug 'n' Play hardware. The results of its exploration are logged to a file called `detlog.txt`, which is in your boot drive's root folder. A separate file called `detcrash.log` contains detailed information about each installer attempt to reach out and touch something. That file is used if the Wizard locks up and you have to restart your machine—for if the installer's going to get hosed, this is where it's most likely to happen. (We go into great depth on these and other files in Chapter 7.)

Don't trust that progress bar. It can hop from 15% to 40% in a split second, then spend three or four minutes going from 96% to 97%.

If all goes well, Win98 restarts again and, when it comes back, flashes a message about setting up hardware. Then you'll be informed of Win98's progress as it sets up the Control Panel, adds programs to the Start Menu, installs Windows Help, goes through a fairly lengthy period called "Tuning up Application Start," and finishes with something mysteriously called System Configuration.

Frequently Win98 restarts yet again, lets you log on to the network (if you have one, and it was correctly detected), comes up and builds a driver database, may restart yet one more time, and finalizes the shortcuts and various personalized settings.

Whew.

If Win98 seems to be working (take it around the block once or twice, and restart it on your own at least once), you can get down to business, cleaning up and fixing the many weird default values that Win98 insists on establishing. Skip the next section, "What Can Go Wrong?", and continue with the section "Postpartum Blues, Part 1."

Would that all installs were this hassle-free!

Hey, if all installs were this easy, y'all wouldn't need us. . . . Remember the Full Employment Act of 98?

■ What Can Go Wrong?

Success generally depends upon knowing how long it takes to succeed.

—C. L. DE MONTESQUIEU, *Pensées,* ca. 1750

Boot, Boot, and Boot Again

Far and away the most common installation problem is a lockup when the Win98 SetUp Wizard is trying to detect hardware devices, both Plug 'n' Play and non-Plug 'n' Play. If you suspect that the Win98 installer has dozed off, following a very simple series of steps will maximize your chances of resuscitating your PC. Follow them carefully.

- Make sure the machine is frozen but functioning. Move the mouse around and see if the pointer on the screen goes anywhere. Watch that progress bar and see if another color block appears—it's entirely possible for an additional color block to appear long before the percent status number increments. Look at the hard drive activity light and listen for any sign of life from your hard disk. And be aware of the fact that a screen saver (you *did* turn off the screen saver, didn't you?) can make the screen appear to be frozen while the installer is doing just fine, thank you.

- Once you're absolutely convinced that the machine has frozen, go get a clock or watch and *time it* for an additional five minutes. We've seen that screen sit there for three or four minutes without a breath of discernible activity, then suddenly start running like hell afire.

- If you're absolutely, totally convinced that the machine has passed into another realm, follow the instructions on the screen. To wit, turn the machine off. Don't hit **Ctrl+Alt+Del**. Don't push the Reset button. Don't collect $200. Turn the power off.

- Wait a couple of minutes, then turn the power back on. About 90% of the time, you're still in the hardware detection phase—and this time you'll get at least a little bit farther than you did the last time.

It's not unusual for a machine to freeze two or three times during hardware detection. That means it isn't unusual for you to have to switch the PC off and back on several times.

Figure 6-17.
Entrance to Safe
Recovery mode

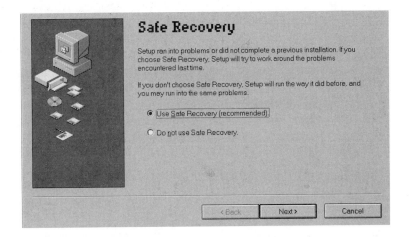

Safe Recovery Mode

In certain unusual situations the Win98 SetUp Wizard does fail, and when you reboot, you find yourself either back in Windows 95 (or 3.x) or in DOS. If that should happen to you, click File, then Run, type `D:\setup` (using the appropriate drive letter), and run the SetUp program again. If you're installing from DOS, turn the PC back on and run SetUp from there.

- Sometimes you get weird text-only screens that warn you of all sorts of dire problems. If you see them, just navigate back out to DOS or choose from the screen menus to restart your machine. Then run SetUp again. In every situation we've encountered, the installer comes up with a screen that looks like Figure 6-17.

- It's hard to imagine a situation where you'd want to bypass Safe Recovery. In every case we've encountered, Safe Recovery has worked, sooner or later. (Yes, one machine did take four rounds of freezing and Safe Recovery. But such is life, eh?)

At this point, the installer goes back to detecting hardware, and while it may fail again, it will undoubtedly fail further down the road towards completion. The lockups during hardware detection may put a few gray hairs on your head, but they always seen to come up aces.

Safe Mode

 The kinds of problems that really scare me are the ones that typically come at the end, when the installer is trying to reboot. They're unusual, and they make it sound as if I've done irreparable harm to my machine. Fortunately, that's never been the case. I've seen a couple of different categories of problems, er, opportunities, that end in something called Safe mode.

- Sometimes when the installer is trying to reboot, you'll hear a beep and then a text screen pops up with several options, among them Safe mode, which is usually option 3 (take a peek ahead at Figure 6-57, if you're curious). If you're given the choice, that's the one you want.

- Sometimes you aren't given any choice at all, and Win98 starts in Safe mode. (In spite of the similar names, starting Win98 in Safe mode and re-running the installer in Safe Recovery mode are two entirely different things.) You know you're in Safe mode because the Desktop has "Safe mode" in all four corners and may or may not show any icons (see Figure 6-18). It can take ten minutes or more for Win98 to come up in Safe mode and, when Win98 is in Safe mode, it runs slower than a snail in mud, so don't panic if things don't spring up quite the way they should.

- No matter how you got into Safe mode, there's at least a 90% chance that simply clicking on Start, clicking on Shutdown, picking the Restart the Computer button, then clicking Yes will bring you back up in Windows 98. Something else they didn't tell you in Win98 school, eh?

- If you end up in Safe mode again, you might have to play around with the settings in the Control Panel (click Start, then Settings, then Control Panel). The most likely suspect is your hardware configuration, so double click on the System applet and bring up the Device Manager tab. Then, one at a time, bring up the properties for each hardware component and compare them to the printout you made before you started installing. (You *did* print the system settings, didn't you?) If you can find any obvious sources for your problem, you may be able to change the driver using the **\drivers** folder on the SetUp CD. If that doesn't work, it's time to punt: you need to get Microsoft on the horn and plead your case. Pray for mercy.

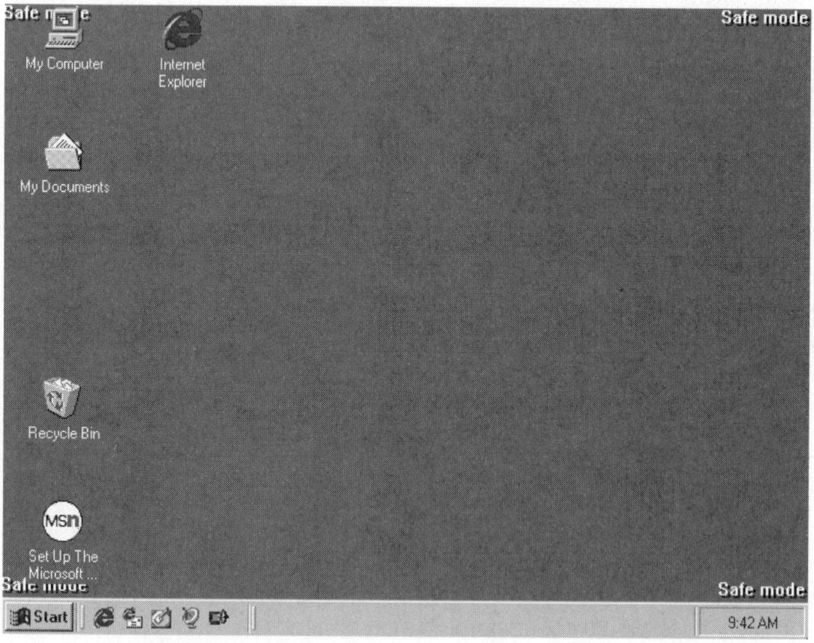

Figure 6-18. Safe mode

I've actually come across one PC that wouldn't go into Safe mode, no matter how hard I tried. Never did figure out why—or what to do if the time ever came when I needed to go into Safe mode.

Missed My CAB

Another problem you'll frequently encounter is a message from the installer that looks like Figure 6-19. It sounds so much more, uh, official, than "You have a dirty CD," doesn't it? Nine times out of ten that's the problem, though. Take the CD out of the drive, blow on it or wipe it on your sleeve, or do whatever you usually do to clean a CD, stick it back in the drive, and click OK. If that doesn't solve the problem, get a can of compressed air and blow out the innards of the drive, then click OK again. If *that* doesn't work, get a CD drive cleaning kit, even if you have to wait overnight to use it.

Figure 6-19. CAB File Error

I've seen some people who share their CD drive from their Windows for workgroup machines and then attempt to install over the network from that shared drive. When this happens, sometimes they get random failure cases during the copying of the files. It seems that some versions of MSCDEX and/or CD drive firmware simply can't keep up with the constant reads that the Win98 SetUp Wizard attempts. In every case I've seen so far, it works to manually copy all the files in the **\win98** directory from the shared CD drive over the network to the local machine and then run the SetUp locally.

This is one of many reasons that I recommend copying files to your hard disk and running SetUp from there.

The High Price of Nonsuccess

So what happens if you get this far and you can't solve the problem? Start by reading the long file called **setup.txt** that's in the root directory of the Win98 CD. It may help. If that doesn't work, it's time to get on the phone to Windows' tech support. (Their phone number is in the Win98 box.) Make sure you're sitting in front of your PC and that you're prepared to talk civilly to somebody whose only purpose is to resolve your problem.

Microsoft will give you ninety days of free telephone support, as long as the support doesn't cover networking. As soon as a tech support person decides that your Win98 problem is really a Win98 networking problem, you'll be given the choice of hanging up and punting, or paying a robust $1.95/minute or $35 an incident to stay on the phone.

Hey, don't look at me that way. Tech support for these complex networking questions gets mighty expensive. We could do what IBM did, and sell an extra-cost package to add networking to the operating system. Instead, we gave it all away as part of Win98 and only charge people who need telephone support to get it working. Most of the time, the problem ends up being some other vendor's bug—so why should we swallow the expense?

 Whooooooa. Wait a minute. You aren't just talking about Netware bugs bringing down Win98 networking. The official Microsoft spokesperson also said that users will be charged from day 1 to resolve peer-to-peer Win98 networking problems, even when no software other than Win98 is involved. They even said they'd charge to resolve connection problems with The Microsoft Network!

 I can't believe they're charging $35 for hookup support for The Microsoft Network. Users faced with that will just jump to CompuServe or America Online.

 I can't believe we're charging $35 for hookup support for The Microsoft Network. Users faced with that will just jump to CompuS . . . , er CompuS . . . , er someplace else.

■ Postpartum Blues, Part 1

Right away after the install is done, you've got a bunch of recommended tasks.

Checking the (Emergency) StartUp Disk

The very first thing you should do after Win98's installation appears to have succeeded is to double-check and make sure your new Emergency StartUp Disk (ESD) works. Most of all, you need to make sure that you can boot with the ESD and be able to use your CD-ROM drive. Here's how to check.

- Shut down Win98: click Start, Shutdown, choose Shutdown, and click OK.

- Put your new ESD (the one created during Win98's installation) in your **A:** drive.

- Hit the Reset button on your PC. You'll eventually get the Win98 Startup Menu (Figure 6-20).

**Figure 6-20.
Windows 98
Startup Menu**

```
Microsoft Windows 98 Startup Menu
==================================

1. Start computer with CD-ROM support
2. Start computer without CD-ROM support
3. View the Help file.

Enter a choice: 1   Time remaining: 30
```

Figure 6-21. Verification that your CD-ROM drive is working

```
MSCDEX Version 2.25
Copyright (c) Microsoft Corp. 1986 - 1995. All rights reserved.

        Drive E: = Driver MSCD001 Unit 0

To get help, type HELP and press ENTER.

A:\
```

- Choose 1, boot with CD-ROM support. You'll see quite a few messages on your screen, but the very last one should look something like Figure 6-21. The drive letter may be different (your CD-ROM drive may be **`F:`** or **`D:`**), but the CD should be accessible. That's important because some day you may need to boot from the ESD, and your only recourse may be to reinstall Win98 from the CD.
- If you don't get the message in Figure 6-21, you desperately need to fix the ESD so that your CD-ROM drive is accessible.

If the CD-ROM drive isn't accessible, it's because Microsoft's general-purpose CD-ROM driver, **`oakcdrom.sys`**, doesn't work with your CD. In our experience 4X and faster CD-ROM drives work fine with Microsoft's generic driver, but some older 2X and 1X drives don't make the cut. Also, CD drives connected to sound cards are more likely to need special drivers.

```
Config.sys - Notepad
File  Edit  Search  Help
[CD]
device=himem.sys /testmem:off
device=oakcdrom.sys /D:mscd001
device=mtmcdae.sys /D:mscd001 /I:10 /P:310 /T:7
device=btdosm.sys
device=flashpt.sys
device=btcdrom.sys /D:mscd001
device=aspi2dos.sys
device=aspi8dos.sys
device=aspi4dos.sys
device=aspi8u2.sys
device=aspicd.sys /D:mscd001
```

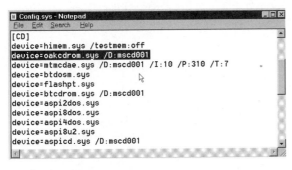

Figure 6-22. Microsoft's generic CD-ROM driver, `oakcdrom.sys`

To get rid of the Microsoft generic driver, use Notepad to open **`config.sys`** on the ESD. You'll find a line invoking the **`oakdcdrom.sys`** driver, as in Figure 6-22.

You need to replace that line with one recommended by your CD-ROM manufacturer. Look at the documentation that originally came with the drive, or check the manufacturer's Web site. One of our machines, for example, has an older Mitsumi CD-ROM drive. It doesn't work with the **`oakcdrom.sys`** driver. We scrambled around a bit to find the old documentation and discovered that this particular drive requires a line that looks like this:

```
device=mtmcdae.sys /D:mscd001 /I:10 /P:310 /T:7
```

So we stuck that line in **`config.sys`**, as you can see in Figure 6-22, deleted the old **`device=oakcdrom.sys`** line, and stuck a copy of the **`mtmcdae.sys`** file on the ESD. We plopped the ESD back in the **`A:`** drive, hit Reset, and the CD-ROM drive worked fine.

You need to keep at this until you get the right combination of driver and inscrutable settings to make your CD-ROM work. It may seem like a lot of work right now, but it sure beats waiting until your PC is dead in the water and your only hope is restoring a file (or a system!) from the CD-ROM drive.

Be sure to check out the section "Emergency StartUp Disk" in Chapter 7 to find out how to improve your ESD.

Uncompress Hard Drives

Are any of your hard drives compressed with Microsoft's Drive Space? You can tell by clicking Start, Programs, Accessories, System Tools, and then choosing DriveSpace. (If there's no DriveSpace listed, none of your drives are compressed.)

If none of your drives are compressed, skip down to the next section, "Nuking Win95." But if any of them are compressed, you should seriously consider uncompressing them and then converting them to FAT32. As discussed in Chapter 2, compressed drives cannot be converted to FAT32.

It's true that changing a DriveSpace compressed drive over to FAT32 will increase the amount of space your files occupy: DriveSpace reduces file sizes, on average, by 30% to 40%, where FAT32 increases drive capacity by only 20% to 30%. So your files are going to take more room on a FAT32 drive compared to a DriveSpace drive.

On the other hand, FAT32 is much faster and more reliable than DriveSpace.

Unless DriveSpace's additional 10% of hard drive space efficiency rates as a make-or-break feature for you, there's no question that FAT32 is the better way to go.

With Win98 installed and working and a usable ESD in hand, you're ready to uncompress your hard drives. Here's how.

- Run DriveSpace: click Start, Programs, Accessories, System Tools, Drive-Space. (Again, if you can't find DriveSpace listed under System Tools, you don't have any DriveSpace-compressed drives!) Up comes the dialog in Figure 6-23.

- Click on the drive you want to uncompress, then click Drive, then Uncompress. Wait a few seconds to see if you have enough hard disk room to run the uncompress routine, then sit back for a long wait. We've seen uncompress runs take two hours or more.

- If there isn't enough room to uncompress the drive, you get the message in Figure 6-24.

- If you don't have enough room, you'll have to delete what you can and move files off the indicated drives, probably onto backup media. The uncompress routines won't proceed until you've removed enough data from the drives to make uncompression possible.

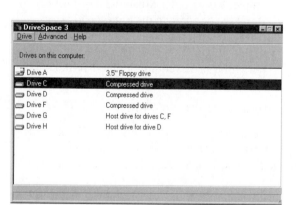

Figure 6-23. DriveSpace tells you which drives are compressed

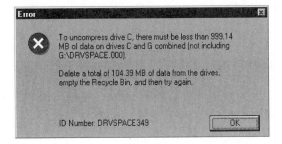

Figure 6-24. Not enough room at the inn

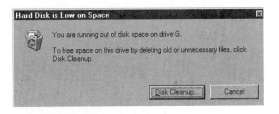

Figure 6-25. The "host" DriveSpace drive can run out of space, too

- If you're cutting very close to the line on available disk space, you may get the message shown in Figure 6-25. If this happens to you, click the Disk Cleanup button and follow the instructions as best you can.

- After a prolonged amount of time, DriveSpace pops up with the message shown in Figure 6-26, telling you that it has succeeded in uncompressing the drive.

- While Figure 6-26 may make it seem as if there's absolutely no space available on the drive, reality may not be so dire. Go out to Windows Explorer, right click on the drive, and pick Properties. You may find that there's a little bit more space there than first meets the eye (Figure 6-27).

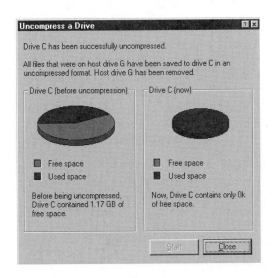

Figure 6-26. Uncompressing complete

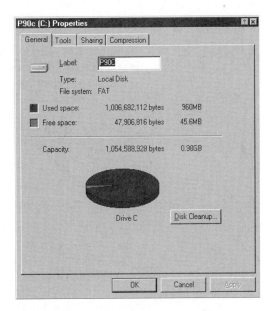

Figure 6-27. While Figure 6-26 may make you think there's no room, in fact there's a little bit

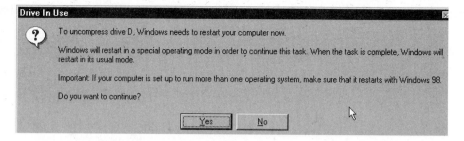

Figure 6-28. To uncompress the \windows drive, Win98 has to restart

Win98 has to go through one extra step when uncompressing the drive that includes the **\windows** folder. It'll restart the computer, per Figure 6-28. If you see that message, don't worry—it's normal.

Nuking Win95

Now let's take a look at how you can get rid of Win95 completely—by reformatting your hard drive—while safely installing Win98. This is strong medicine, but for the advanced Windows 95 user who has installed and uninstalled applications till the cows come home, it's a bit of castor oil that can leave your system working better than ever.

If you have any large hard drives that have been partitioned into smaller logical drives and you want to get rid of all those little partitions in preparation for converting to FAT32, you can follow the instructions here. But you might also want to consider buying a program called Partition Magic (**www.powerquest.com**), which can rearrange partitions without destroying all the data on your hard drive.

I know it sounds like throwing out the baby with the bath water, but I strongly recommend that people who use Windows hard—day in, day out—reinstall Windows, from scratch, at least once a year. When I say "from scratch" I mean all the way, from the very beginning, including the scorched earth step of reformatting your hard drive. It's the only way you'll restore stability to your system. And, even though it's traumatic, your PC will love you for it.

I think it's overkill. Windows 98 has more provisions than ever to keep aberrant programs from overwriting key system files and more fail-safe protection points than ever to make this kind of drastic action unnecessary. If your current **\windows** folder is on a partitioned drive, you won't lose that much by leaving it partitioned. What I'm trying to say is that Microsoft does not recommend this approach.

Ya pays yer money and ya takes yer chances . . .

If you want a "virgin" Windows 98 system, there's no better time to delete the old operating system than right now, while you're in the middle of installing Win98.

It may seem a bit backward to talk about nuking Win95 *after* installing Win98, but we've found that the Win98 Emergency StartUp Disk makes it much easier to ensure a (relatively) safe nuking experience. We also recommend that you uncompress your drives before you try this technique so that FDISK doesn't completely discombobulate your PC.

WARNING: If you have the Windows 98 upgrade CD (and you probably do), you'll need to have your old Windows 95 (or 3.x) installation CD or *all* of the diskettes in the installation stack to make this work. Make sure you have 'em on hand before you start, as Win98 will ask for it as "proof of ownership" for the upgrade.

If you're serious about wiping all vestiges of your old Windows system off the face of your PC, here's how you do it.

- Make sure Win98 is working and that your ESD boots with full CD-ROM support.

- Carefully go through all your applications. Make sure you have either install disks for all of them or copies of the applications someplace handy. Remember that many applications have supporting files stored in weird places—`\windows` and `\windows\system` are two of the favorite hiding places. You need all the files, including the supporting files. Fonts, too.

- Write down any important settings. Remember, reformatting your hard drive means never having to say you're sorry—it's all gone, and it all has to be replaced.

- Pay particular attention to passwords. If you can't remember a password, there's a utility called Revelation that will "reveal" the password sitting behind the asterisks that appear on the screen (Figure 6-29). Revelation is a free utility from SnadBoy Software; it can be downloaded from `www.snadboy.com`.

Figure 6-29. SnadBoy's Revelation will show you the password behind the ****** on the screen

- Shut down Win98 (Start, Shutdown, Shutdown, Yes): Stick your ESD in drive **A:** and punch the Reset button on your PC. When you get the Win98 Startup Menu (Figure 6-20), type 1.

- Double-check and triple-check to make sure you can get at your CD-ROM drive. Put the Win98 CD-ROM in it, move over to the drive (by typing, for example, **E:** and hitting **Enter**), and make sure you can see everything on the CD (by typing, for example, **dir** and hitting **Enter**). The drive letter for your CD-ROM drive may be different than it usually is inside Win98. Don't worry about that. But be very, very sure you have access to your CD before you go beyond this point.

- Time to blast away your hard drive. Type **fdisk** and hit **Enter**. You'll get the FDISK screen shown in Figure 6-30.

- **WARNING**: Before you change the partitions on your hard drive(s), you should make sure that your system BIOS and hard drive controller will support the larger partition sizes. In addition, if you have software that makes large drives accessible to earlier versions of Windows and DOS (e.g., Ontrack, EZDrive), make sure that software won't interfere with your repartitioned drives under Win98. Contact your PC and/or drive manufacturer for details.

- Follow the screen in Figure 6-30 to delete partitions on all your hard drives (or at least all the hard drives you're going to reformat). Set the active partition—it will almost undoubtedly be the only partition on your **C:** drive—if need be. Then hit **Esc** to exit FDISK. Be sure to tell FDISK to use FAT32.

- Format all the hard drives you've repartitioned using the format **C:** (or **D:**, or **E:**) command. That can take a while.

- Once all the hard drives are in good shape, move over to the CD-ROM and run SetUp. The Win98 SetUp Wizard will pop up, and you'll have to go through all the installation steps we discussed earlier in this chapter. Early in the process, the Wizard will ask you to insert a Windows CD or diskette to prove that you're "upgrading." You'll have a chance to specify what kind of install you want—Typical, Custom, Portable, or Compact—and set all the other options that may have eluded you the first time you installed.

```
                   Microsoft Windows 95
                  Fixed Disk Setup Program
            (C)Copyright Microsoft Corp. 1983 - 1995

                       FDISK Options

Current fixed disk drive: 1

Choose one of the following:

1. Create DOS partition or Logical DOS Drive
2. Set active partition
3. Delete partition or Logical DOS Drive
4. Display partition information
5. Change current fixed disk drive


Enter choice: [1]




Press Esc to exit FDISK
```

Figure 6-30. FDISK will wipe out your disk's data in a heartbeat

Rather than run SetUp from the CD, I recommend you copy the files to your hard disk as I discussed earlier.

Congratulations. You now have a fresh, virgin copy of Win98, and all your hard disks are set up for FAT32 so you don't have to worry about a FAT32 conversion. Now all you have to do is re-install and reconfigure every single application on your PC. Aren't you the lucky one?

Check Out Your Hardware

Make sure all your hardware is working. Play a **.wav** and a **.mid** file in Media Player, read a CD and diskette, try to print a test page on each of your printers, call up Phone Dialer and make sure you can dial through your modem, and check out your network.

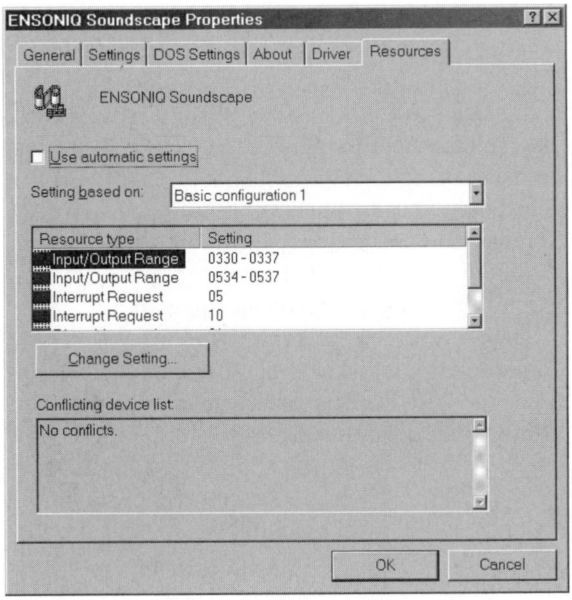

Ninety-nine times out of a hundred, it'll all be hunky-dory, but if it isn't, the first thing to do is to call up Device Manager (right click on My Computer, pick Properties, and shift to the Device Manager tab). Is the hardware even indicated as installed? If not, you'll need to open Control Panel and run the Add New Hardware applet. You may as well try the automatic hardware detect, but if Windows missed it the first time, you'll probably need to do a manual install.

If the hardware is listed, click on it, right click, and pick Properties. Look at the Resource tab (Figure 6-31), which lists IRQs, I/O ports, and DMA channels. Check the System Summary printout I told you to make before you began the install. If the printout has different resources, pick Change Settings . . . and fix it.

Figure 6-31. Resource tab for a device

When I did the reformat and install Windows 98 routine, my sound card didn't work. I discovered Windows had gotten the wrong DMA channels. I fixed that and hit OK. Instantly, the Found New Hardware message popped up, Windows installed the drivers, and the card worked.

In extreme cases, you can delete the device in Device Manager, run Add New Hardware, and hope it installs properly the second time around. It happens.

If these steps don't work, you'll have more trouble. If the network isn't working, try adding extra protocols in the Network applet. Look in Windows Help for a troubleshooter to see if it can help out. If all else fails, get on the horn to your hardware maker or to Windows' tech support.

Register

'E isn't one o' the reg'lar line, nor 'e isn't one of the crew;
'E's a kind of a giddy harumfrodite—soldier and sailor too.

—RUDYARD KIPLING, *Soldier an' Sailor Too,* 1892

You gotta register, OK? We know you don't like the idea of becoming another bit in Microsoft's bucket. (They call the repository of all user information the "Regbase," short for "Registered User Database.") But it's for your own good. You'll get tech support over the phone only if you register. And you're likely to receive notices of bug fixes—cleverly disguised as upgrades—only if you're in the Regbase.

In addition, you'll be able to use the Windows Update Wizard (described later) only if you've gone through all the steps to register.

The easiest way to register is by using the online Registration Wizard available at the end of Win98 installation or by pushing the Online Registration button on the Welcome screen that pops up every time you start Windows (Figure 6-32).

What's that, you say? You got tired of the Welcome messages and unchecked the box that says, "Show this screen each time Windows 98 starts," and now you want to do the online registration? No sweat. Click on Start, then Run, and type in **welcome**. Hit **Enter**. Voilà—the Welcome screen appears and you can proceed with online registration (Figure 6-33).

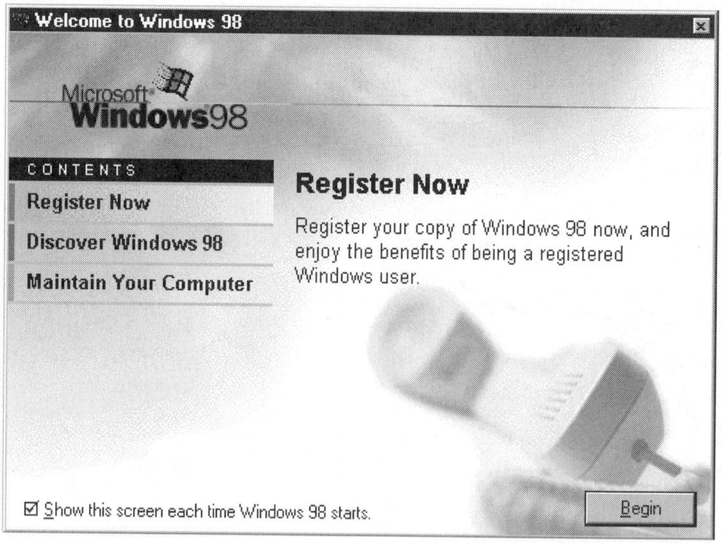

Figure 6-32. Register by modem

Figure 6-33. `reginfo.txt` information destined to be sent to Microsoft

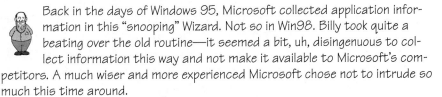

```
reginfo.txt - Notepad
File  Edit  Search  Help
Product Identification = 79878-005-9847867-24768
Processor = GenuineIntel, Pentium(r) Processor
Math co-processor = 1
Total RAM = 48664 KB
Total Disk Space = 5522736 KB
Removable Media = GENERIC NEC  FLOPPY DISK,Mass Storage
Display Resolution = 1024 x 768
Display Color Depth = 256
Pointing Device = PS/2 Compatible Mouse Port
Network = Intel EtherExpress 16 or 16TP ISA
Modem = Sportster 56000 Voice Internal
Sound Card = Creative Sound Blaster 16 Plug and Play
CD-ROM = SANYO CRD-256P
Operating System = Microsoft Windows 98, Ver.4.10.1998
Include System = 1
Include Products = 0
Application Name = Microsoft Windows 98
OEM Manufacturer =
Version = 3.0.0000
Company Name = Microsoft
ResultPath = Software\Microsoft\Windows\CurrentVersion
Date = 06/10/1998
Language = 1033
```

The Registration Wizard collects information on you and your machine. You can choose to include or exclude the machine information when you register. If you choose to send that information to us, we can use it to tailor offerings specifically for you, your hardware, and your software; we can also use it to help you if you call with a tech support question. The whole thing is put in a file in your Win98 **\windows** folder called **reginfo.txt**. When you give the OK, the Registration Wizard dials the phone and uploads the registration info—and only the info that you have approved—to Microsoft's computers.

Back in the days of Windows 95, Microsoft collected application information in this "snooping" Wizard. Not so in Win98. Billy took quite a beating over the old routine—it seemed a bit, uh, disingenuous to collect information this way and not make it available to Microsoft's competitors. A much wiser and more experienced Microsoft chose not to intrude so much this time around.

I still think this is a whole lot of fun. What's to keep you from hacking **reginfo.txt** before sending it off? Notepad does a nifty job. Just wait until after the Registration Wizard has gathered all its information, then tackle **reginfo.txt** with Notepad before you click the button to dial the phone. Microsoft might be surprised to find a few lines like these in their database:

```
Application Name = None Of Your Business 98
Product Inventory 1 = Kicking Grasshoppers
Product Inventory 2 = Secret DOJ Snooper
Product Inventory 3 = Java Rules, VC++ Drools
Product Inventory 4 = Crash MS Regbase Virus
```

Just don't tell 'em where you got the idea, OK? Hehehe.

Convert to FAT32

Ready to convert your hard drive(s) to FAT32? Before you start, a few things to keep in mind.

- You may already have FAT32 on your drives, if you're running a newer version of Windows 95 (the so-called SR2 release). To see whether a particular disk is using FAT32, go into Windows Explorer, right click on the drive, and pick Properties. The File System entry (see Figure 6-27) will tell you if it's a FAT32 drive.

- You cannot convert compressed drives to FAT32. Uncompress them before proceeding.

- FAT32 eliminates all the need for and most of the advantage of partitioning drives. If you have any partitioned drives, consider removing the partitions.

- Some PCs won't support larger partition sizes: older BIOSes are particularly problematic. Make sure your PC will be able to handle larger partitions by contacting the manufacturer. Also, if you have special software (e.g., Ontrack, EZDrive) that makes larger drives available to earlier versions of Windows and DOS, check with the manufacturer to figure out if the software will get in the way of Win98's FAT32 access.

- If your drive has any bad clusters, even one, the converter won't run. But the FDISK/format route will work.

To convert a drive to FAT32, use the Drive Converter Wizard (Figure 6-34).

- To bring up the Drive Converter Wizard, click Start, Programs, Accessories, System Tools, Drive Converter (FAT32).

- Click Next> and the Wizard takes a look at your drives, letting you know which ones can be converted (Figure 6-35).

- Pick the drive you want converted and click Next>. When converting the drive that contains the **\windows** folder, the Wizard has to flip into DOS mode (Figure 6-36).

- Although the Wizard warns (Figure 6-36) that converting to FAT32 might take a few hours, we've never had a conversion take more than about fifteen minutes.

It's really that simple. Win98 has all sorts of fail-safe and fallback routines built into the Drive Converter Wizard, but we've never had to rely on any of them. The whole conversion goes painlessly.

**Figure 6-34.
The Drive Con-
verter Wizard**

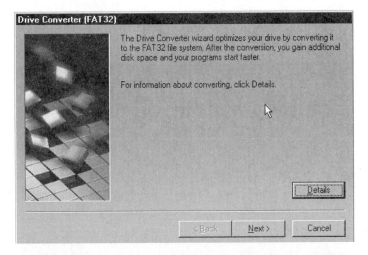

**Figure 6-35.
Click on the drive
you want to
convert**

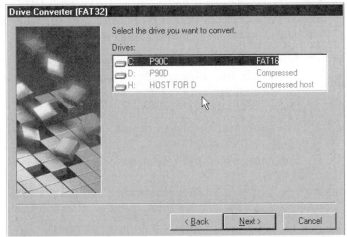

**Figure 6-36. The
Wizard goes into
DOS Mode to
convert the drive
with the
\windows folder**

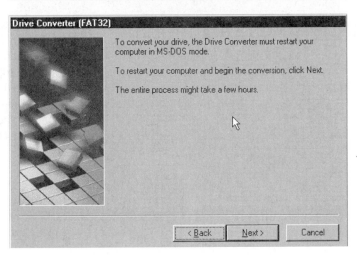

■ Tooling Along

Next, there's a bunch of extra tools on the CD to install.

Windows Resource Kit

All looks yellow to the jaundiced eye.

—ALEXANDER POPE, *Essay on Criticism,* 1711

We'll never know why Microsoft pretends that this is a separate package. The Windows Resource Kit Tools Sampler is distributed on the Win98 CD, and you'd be absolutely crazy to pass up the opportunity to install and use all its tools, including the WRK itself.

To install the WRK, reinsert the Win98 CD in your CD-ROM drive. When the screen comes up, click on "Browse this CD," move to the `\tools\reskit` folder, then double click on `setup.exe` (Figure 6-37).

These are the key components of the Tools Sampler:

- **Windows 98 Resource Kit**   Yes, the entire 1,800-page book is on the Win98 CD, free, in (searchable) Help format. After you install the Tools Sampler, click Start, Programs, Windows 98 Resource Kit, Resource Kit Online Book. There. You just saved $70.

- **Microsoft Management Console**   Gives you a quick and easy way to use all of the Tools Sampler tools (Figure 6-38). To use the MMC, click Start, Programs, Windows 98 Resource Kit, then Tools Management Console. This is an extensible product, so don't be too surprised if more Microsoft products in the future use it.

- **Microsoft File Information**   This great little utility lets you look up any Windows 98 system file and read the Properties information for the file. It'll tell you where the file is located on the Win95 install CDs and where the file gets put on your hard drive. This one little utility replaces most of the information we put in Appendix E of *The Mother of All Windows 95 Books*—thirty pages of dense text that we don't have to include in this book. Awright!

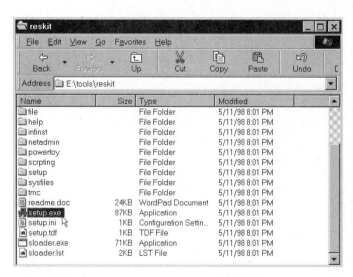

Figure 6-37. The `setup.exe` you need to run to get the Resource Kit tools

**Figure 6-38.
Microsoft Man-
agement Console**

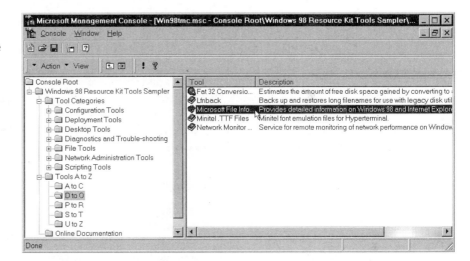

Figure 6-38.
Microsoft Management Console

- **Checklinks, Cliptray, Quicktray**   Tools to check for missing DLLs, beef up the Windows Clipboard, and improve the System Tray; discussed in Chapter 5.
- **Netmon**   For monitoring network performance; covered in Chapter 5.
- **USB Viewer**   To watch what your USB peripherals are doing.

All these little utilities come free, straight off the Win98 CD. You just have to know where to find them!

 Pardon me for kvetching, but why aren't most of these utilities stuck in Control Panel? At the very least, the MMC should go on the Desktop. It's hard finding all the cool utilities—so hard that many initial reviews of Win98 missed them completely! And if the reviewers can't find the bloody things, how are normal people like you and me supposed to discover them? And while I'm griping anyway, why are the MMC and the System Informa-tion Utility two separate products? At least 80% of both of them are adjuncts to what currently sits in Control Panel applets. Why make us search over hell's half acre for these things?

Tweak UI

Tweak UI is an indispensable part of Windows 98 that lets you configure vari-ous parts of Win98 that you can't get at through normal means. We talk about it in Chapter 8.

Since Tweak UI is part of the Windows Resource Kit Tools Sampler—some would say the single most important part—you'd assume that installing the WRK Tools Sampler also installs Tweak UI, right?

Wrong.

Even though Tweak UI is sitting under the **\reskit** folder on the Win98 CD, *and* even though the WRK Tools Sampler **readme.txt** file clearly states that Tweak UI is installed along with the rest of the WRK Tools, *and* even though Tweak UI is listed in the Microsoft Management Console, you still have to dig into the bowels of the CD and specifically install it, manually.

To install Tweak UI, navigate to the **\reskit\powertoys** folder on the Win98 CD, right click **tweakui.inf**, and pick Install. (Yes, you read that right. There's no setup or install program. You right click and pick Install. It's the only way you *can* install Tweak UI.)

Windows Update Wizard

Quite possibly the most important new wizard in Win98 is the Windows Update Wizard. It sits on top of the Start Menu (Figure 6-39), as a constant reminder.

It's important that you use the Update Wizard frequently, because it will constantly refresh your system with new versions of important files, particularly the latest drivers. Instead of your having to run out and pick up your favorite video driver of the week—video drivers in particular can change that frequently—the Update Wizard brings the driver to you and downloads and installs it, with little or no hassle.

Figure 6-39. Windows Update Wizard

Figure 6-40. The Update Wizard connects to Microsoft's Windows Update page

We recommend you use the Update Wizard immediately after installing Win98 and once a week thereafter. While you'll occasionally get a bad update file, most of the time the update will be well worth your while. Connect to the Wizard just before lunchtime, and you'll give it more than enough time to bring your system up to date.

To use the Wizard, click on Windows Update. You end up on Microsoft's Update Wizard home page (Figure 6-40).

Click Product Updates and the Wizard runs a program that figures out precisely what software is installed on your PC and whether the Update site has new files, drivers, and so on that would apply to your system. If the Wizard finds any such files, it downloads them and then offers to install them for you.

Sometimes the update doesn't work any better than the original—in fact, occasionally they work worse. For such situations, there's a Rollback option, which returns your PC to the state it was in before the Update Wizard did its thing. You can get to Rollback both from this site and from the System Information Utility (Start, Programs, Accessories, System Tools, System Information); see Figure 6-41.

 At the time we went to press, there was a great deal of controversy over the Update Wizard—most of it centering around the question of whether Microsoft will do a good job of controlling which drivers appear on the Update page. At this point, it's still too early to tell. Keep an eye on the newsweeklies and Web sites to see if Microsoft does indeed post drivers that really work.

**Figure 6-41.
To roll back an Update Wizard action, click Tools, then Update Wizard Uninstall**

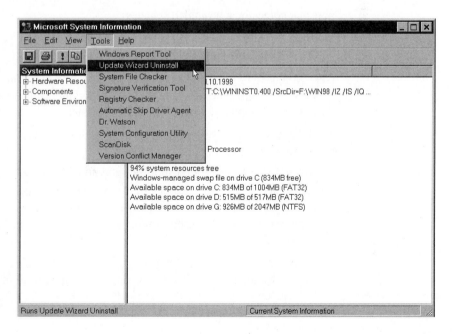

If you're on a network, the network administrator can block your access to the Update Wizard, so if you can't use this particular feature, complain to your network administrator!

■ Postpartum Blues, Part 2

Who would be free, themselves must strike the blow.

—Byron, *Childe Harold,* 1812

There's a final sequence of steps you should take after installing Win98—steps that can make a big difference in how well Win98 works and how stable your system will be. While none of these rate up there with the big steps covered earlier in this chapter (checking the ESD, uncompressing, reformatting hard drives, registering Win98, converting to FAT32, checking the Windows Update Wizard for the latest), they're all important and can make a big difference in the way Win98 works for you, day in and day out.

Print System Information

Now that you have Win98 installed and your drives converted to FAT32, it's a good time to print out a full system report to file away for a rainy day.

Simply bring up the System Information Utility (Start, Programs, Accessories, System Tools, System Info) and click the print icon on the toolbar.

Make sure you have enough paper. A good-sized system can generate a report that comes in at around 100 pages.

Start Maintenance Wizard

Next, you need to get the Maintenance Wizard working. Win98's new Maintenance Wizard will schedule runs of three important utilities—all of which are described in Chapter 4, where the Task Scheduler is also discussed.

- **Disk Cleanup**   Wipes out temporary Internet files and several other kinds of files that just clog up your drives.
- **ScanDisk**   Looks for corrupt files and knits them back together, if possible.
- **Disk Defragmenter**   Moves files around on your hard drive so that they occupy contiguous locations—thereby speeding up file access—and moves your most frequently used programs to spots where they can be accessed more quickly.

To get the Maintenance Wizard going, click Start, Programs, Accessories, System Tools, Maintenance Wizard. Up comes the dialog in Figure 6-42.

Figure 6-42. Maintenance Wizard main options

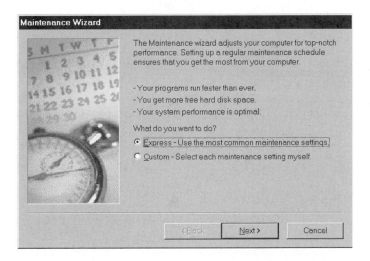

Figure 6-43. Pick a general time of day and the Wizard will work out a schedule

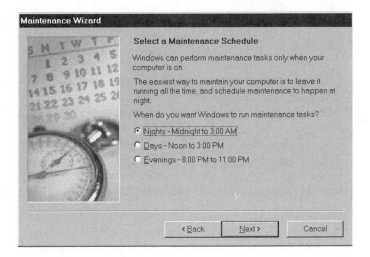

Express SetUp will do for most Win98 fans. Click Next> and you'll be asked to give a general time slot for Maintenance to run (Figure 6-43). We generally recommend that you run maintenance activities in the middle of the night, leaving your PC on to accommodate the schedule.

Click Next> one more time and you can tell the Wizard to run all the maintenance steps for the first time. Be cautious when you select this option, though (Figure 6-44), because running all three utilities the first time can take an hour or more, depending on how much data you have on how many drives.

Figure 6-44. Careful! Running all three tasks for the first time can take an hour or more

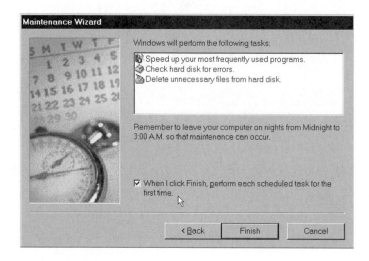

Fix Weird Settings

When Win98 installs itself, it leaves behind several settings that are . . . strange. Billy98 says many of them are set that way to help novice users. That may be the case, and we're sure he has Usability Lab numbers to back up his conclusions, but any user who spends much time at all with Win98 is bound to get confused and/or clobbered by some of this stuff. There are also a couple of things you can do that will make Win98 much easier to use.

Some of these changes are detailed elsewhere in this book, but we want to bring them all together here in one place so you have a simple checklist for what to do every time you install Win98 or break in a new system. Here's our list of the most important things you should change immediately, before you try to get any work out of Win98.

- **Power** Win98's power-down settings drive us nuts. If you don't use your PC for fifteen minutes, the default power-down setting turns off your monitor. If you don't use your PC for an hour, all your hard drives get cut off. Restoring the monitor can take an aggravating minute or more; getting the hard drive platters to spin again can take several minutes—and all the while, you're sitting there, twiddling your thumbs, wondering why the PC won't do anything. To make your own power-down settings, click Start, Settings, and Control Panel, then double click on the Power applet and adjust the two dropdown lists at the bottom of the Power Schemes tab (Figure 6-45). We usually set them at 1 hour and 3 hours, respectively.

- **Explorer** If you use Windows Explorer much, you're going to gag when you start working with Win98's version. Bring up the Windows Explorer by right clicking on My Computer and picking Explore. Get rid of the "cute" picture in the right pane of the Explorer by clicking View and unchecking the line marked "as Web Page" (Figure 6-46). (Win98 tries its hardest to put a pretty airhead face on this quintessential Windows tool.) Now tell Win98 that you want to see file statistics by clicking on View, then Details (Figure 6-47). Finally, tell Win98 that you want to see all the information about all your files by clicking on View, then Folder Options, and the View tab, unchecking the box marked "Hide file extensions for known file types," clicking the button that says "Show all files," and then clicking the button marked "Like Current Folder" (Figure 6-48).

Figure 6-45. Win98's default power-down settings are just too intrusive

Figure 6-46. Lose the cutsie picture in the right pane

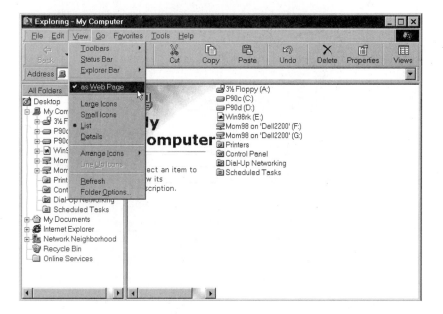

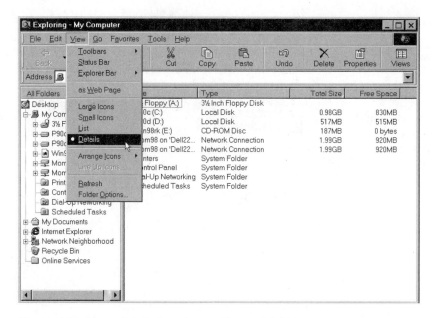

Figure 6-47. Show details for all your files and folders

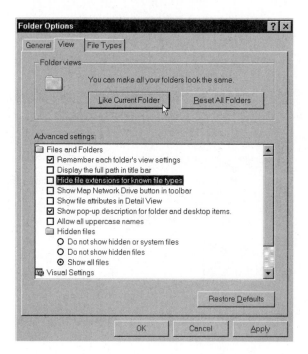

Figure 6-48.
Bare minimum
settings you need
to see what's go-
ing on

**Figure 6-49.
Windows Ex-
plorer—at last, in
a usable state**

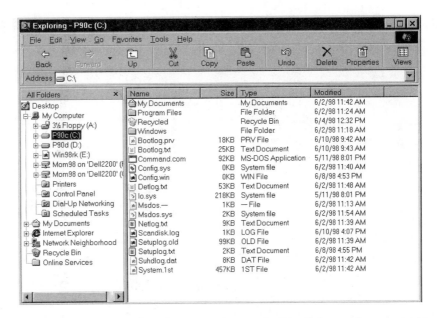

 Or you can make a few more changes in this dialog, as I suggested in
Chapter 3.

If you did everything as described, the Windows Explorer should now look like
Figure 6-49.

- **Printer** Win98 may not have installed your printer properly, particularly if you're using a networked print server. To set it up, click Start, Settings, and Control Panel, double click
  on the Printers applet, and double click
  on Add Printer. The Printer Wizard
  takes over (Figure 6-50). You may
  need your Win98 CD to complete the
  installation.

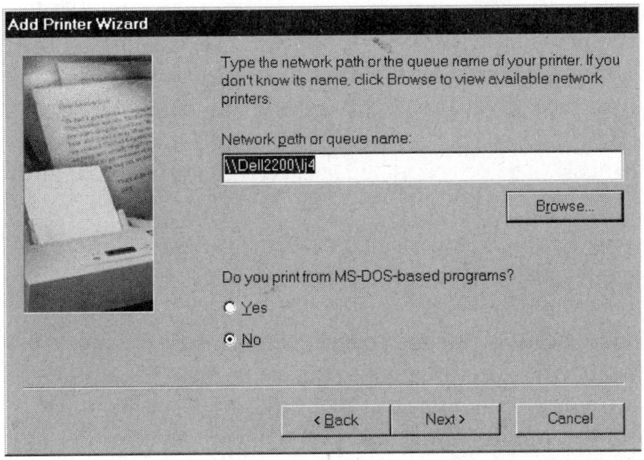

**Figure 6-50. You may need to set up your printer manu-
ally, particularly if it's networked**

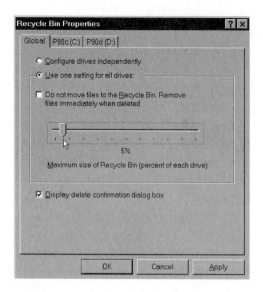

Figure 6-51. Set the Recycle Bin size to a more rational 5% (or less) of the hard drive

Figure 6-52. Don't let your "subscription" Web pages call indiscriminately

- **Recycle Bin**   By default, Win98 sets aside 10% of the size of each drive for the Recycle Bin. For most people that's a bit excessive. Turn it back to 5% and you'll be just fine. Right click on the Recycle Bin on your Desktop, pick Properties, and bring up the Global tab (Figure 6-51).

- **Autodial**   If you have a permanent, free connection to the Web, we salute you. But if you try to keep your online time down to a manageable level, it may surprise you to know that when you "subscribe" to a Web page, possibly through the Active Channel Bar, the page may trigger periodic phone calls to connect to the Web. To cut those off at the knees, click Start, Settings, and Control Panel, double click on the Internet applet, click the Advanced tab, and uncheck "Enable scheduled subscription updates" (Figure 6-52).

- **Address Bar**   If you use the Web very much, you may be pleasantly surprised to know that you can put Internet Explorer's Address Bar—the thing you type Web addresses into—directly on Win98's Taskbar. Simply right click on the Taskbar, select Toolbars, and check the one marked Address (Figure 6-53). Any time you want to go to a Web page, just type its address in the Address Bar. If you are running at $1,064 \times 768$, consider the three-row Taskbar SetUp, with Address Bar, Links, and Quick Launch, that I suggested in Chapter 3.

Figure 6-53. Internet Explorer's Address Bar goes on Win98's Taskbar

 Finally, I think everybody should use the trick mentioned in Chapter 3 of putting a cascading list of all Control Panel applets on their Start Menu. And add the System Resource Meter, as described in Chapter 4.

Get Rid of Real Mode Drivers

The worst antagonists to your Win98 system's performance fall in the general category of real mode drivers. There's nothing particularly real about them: they were written to work with Windows 3.1 or earlier—or even DOS. Captive to the lower regions of memory below the 640-K line, they can't adapt to the greater freedom Win98 offers. Since they can't break free of their lower memory chains, Win98 has to handle them specially, and that special handling extracts a significant performance and stability penalty.

There are cases where real mode drivers are necessary, particularly for older networks. Those network drivers are usually loaded in **autoexec.bat** so that they can kick in before Win98 takes over. If you discover a real mode network driver in **autoexec.bat** after the Win98 installer does its things, you need to tread carefully when trying to get rid of it. Keep plenty of backups, and make only small, incremental changes, testing as you go along.

Real mode drivers are usually loaded in either **config.sys** or **autoexec.bat**. You can tell if you have any real mode drivers infesting your Win98 system by clicking on Start, Settings, Control Panel, double clicking on the System applet, and bringing up the Performance tab (Figure 6-54). If you have a real mode driver showing under the Performance tab, there's a quick, easy way to see if the Win98 installer goofed and left the driver in when it isn't absolutely necessary: try booting with completely empty **autoexec.bat** and **config.sys** files. In the root directory of your boot disk (typically **c:**), rename **autoexec.bat** to **autoexec.mom** and **config.sys** to **config.mom**. Then click Start, double click Shutdown, and click OK, and

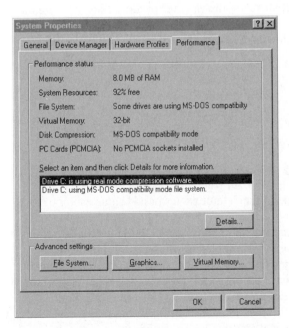

Figure 6-54. Real mode drivers gumming up the works

when Win98 says, "It is now safe to shut off your computer," hit the PC's Reset button. When Win98 comes back up, take a look and see if everything is working. Pay particular attention to CD-ROM drives, scanners, and any oddball hardware. If everything works, thank your lucky stars and forget the old, now obsolete files.

If everything goes to hell, get running in DOS mode (use your Emergency Startup Disk) and type these two lines, hitting Enter at the end of each:

```
ren autoexec.mom autoexec.bat
ren config.mom config.sys
```

Then hit **Ctrl+Alt+Del** to restart Win98. Ah, well. It was worth a try.

 In fact, that trick is a good idea for everybody, whether they have real mode drivers showing on the Performance tab or not. Why? We're trying to get rid of those old dinosaurs! If you can make your system work with no **autoexec.bat** or **config.sys**, you're in the best of all possible situations. I strongly suggest that every first-time Win98 upgrader try to boot with no **autoexec.bat** or **config.sys**. Strike a blow for progress.

Note that the Win98 installer automatically makes a copy of your old **autoexec.bat** and calls it **autoexec.dos**; it also makes a copy of the old **config.sys** as **config.dos**. If you push **F8** when booting and choose to "Run Previous Version of MS-DOS," the **.dos** files are used to get the machine going.

If you can get Win98 to work without those hellish files, you can gradually add just a line or two to each to solve very specific problems. What kinds of problems? Well, if you're well versed in the vagaries of those files, here are the kinds of things to look out for.

Win98 establishes the following defaults for settings that DOS used to get from **config.sys**:

```
dos=high                      files=60
device=himem.sys              lastdrive=z
device=ifshlp.sys             buffers=30
device=setver.exe             stacks=9,256
shell=command.com /p          fcbs=4
```

Win98 doesn't really need any of those values. They're of interest only because some (lousy, old) programs require them when running in DOS mode.

If you need to override one of the default values or add some esoteric switches to them, put a line in **config.sys**. For example, a **files=90** statement in **config.sys** will force Win98 to allocate ninety file handle buffers in DOS sessions. The setting is ignored completely when you're running Windows—it comes into play only when running DOS sessions under Windows.

Another example: if you have a (lousy, old) program that requires **emm386** with the **NOEMS** switch, put a **device=emm386.exe noems** line in your **config.sys**. (Note that Win98 is smart enough to figure out that you're loading **emm386** and automatically includes the equivalent of a **dos=umb** setting when it sees you loading **emm386**.)

Hey, I thought Win98 would get rid of all this DOS mumbo jumbo. I mean, who cares if you're running **emm386**? And why should I have to futz around with a dumb text file to get a memory manager going? PCs these days are supposed to be smarter than that.

PCs are smarter than that. Unfortunately, people aren't. They're still running programs that were written five, even ten years ago—and those programs aren't so forgiving. All of these weird settings are in the interest of backward compatibility. If you don't want to bother with ten-year-old settings and obscure ten-year-old DOS concepts, don't use ten-year-old software!

If you're going to tackle a custom **config.sys** job (talk about living in the past!), the Windows Resource Kit contains a long list of files that should've been removed by the Win98 installer. In particular, Share, Smart Drive and any other disk caches, Mirror, and Fastopen should've been removed automatically. Don't put any of them back in. You should also manually remove any mouse-related **device=** entries; Win98 ignores them anyway.

If you're the kind of DOS junkie who loves to tweak the **command.com** command line, **config.sys** is child's play. Don't even bother with it. The real mother lode of **command.com** settings is in the Properties dialog. Look in Chapter 3.

Over on the **autoexec.bat** side, Win98 during StartUp automatically sets the variables **tmp** and **temp** to point to your Win98 **\windows\temp** folder and variable **comspec** to point to the Win98 **\windows\command.com** file. (*Note:* The Windows Resource Kit is wrong here, too.) The **prompt=** is set to **pg**. Finally, it automatically adds the Win98 **\windows** and **\windows\command** folders to your **path=** statement.

If you should be possessed by an overwhelming desire to manually edit your **autoexec.bat** file, make sure that the first two folders to appear on your **path=** are the Win98 **\windows** and **\windows\command** folders. You can add just about anything after that. Dosshell, Fastopen, Mirror, Share, Smart Drive (and any other disk caches), virus-checking software, and the command **win** should've been removed automatically. Don't put them back in. You should also manually remove any mouse-related entries.

Microsoft warns against adding your Win3.1 and Win95 **\windows** and **\windows\system** directories to the **path=**, if those directories still exist, but I had the Win3.1 directories on my path for years with nary a problem. Microsoft also advises that you leave your old DOS directory in the path. I don't, and it hasn't bitten me, either. Yet.

Set Up Sharing for Your Drives

If you're on a network, check that you can access shared resources on other machines. That takes care of you getting out, but if you want to let other people on

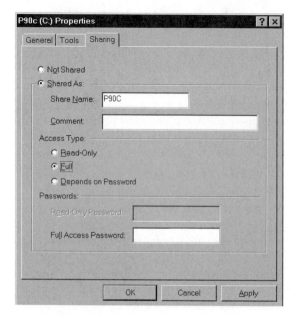

Figure 6-55. You know that sharing is working if the Sharing tab appears

Figure 6-56. Turn on File and Printer Sharing

your network into your machine, you may need to do a little more work. In some cases you'll need to go in and explicitly turn on Sharing for resources that you want to share. Highlight the drive or directory you want to share in Explorer, right click, and pick Properties. There should be a Sharing tab (or pick Sharing . . . from the right click menu). See Figure 6-55.

If there is no Sharing tab in the Properties dialogs for Drives and Directories, File and Printer Sharing is not turned on. You do that by clicking the Network applet in Control Panel and clicking on the File and Printer Sharing . . . button in the Configuration tab (Figure 6-56). To turn on Sharing for a Printer, find it in the Printer's folder and pick Properties or Sharing . . . from its right-button menu.

You can tell if a drive is set to be shared by looking at it on the tree side in Explorer. Sharing is on for the drive if and only if there is a hand underneath the drive—sort of handing it off to someone!

■ How Win98 Starts

The secrets of success are a good wife and a steady job.
My wife told me.

—HOWARD NEMEROV, *Writer's Digest,* December 1988

It's very important that you understand the Win98 StartUp sequence, both to avoid and to recover from all sorts of very painful problems. Surprisingly, we've never seen the startup process described succinctly in any books or manuals. So let's approach the sequence a little bit at a time.

BIOS Bootstrap

Win98 relies on the good old-fashioned BIOS bootstrap routine to get things going—if you don't have a Plug 'n' Play BIOS, the routine is identical to the one you've been using for years, whether you knew it or not. "BIOS bootstrap" is just a fancy way of saying that there's a program inside your computer that runs whenever you turn it on. The program is responsible for checking memory (you'll see it counting off chunks of memory when you start the machine), possibly moving some system functions from slower to faster parts of memory (called "shadowing"), then verifying the existence and identity of your major peripherals. When it's done with the very low-level stuff, the bootstrapper looks for a boot diskette and, failing that, hands over control to a file called **io.sys**, which is essentially the DOS 7 part of Windows 98. (Microsoft calls **io.sys** "the Real Mode Operating System that replaces MS-DOS" which, as far as we're concerned, is the same thing as "the DOS part of Windows.")

 Most BIOSes can be configured in their SetUp to skip the diskette drive and go directly to the hard disk. That's an extra precaution against getting a boot virus from a diskette you left in the drive by mistake, so I recommend it.

If you do have a Plug 'n' Play BIOS, it kicks in after the low-level check and resolves any configuration conflicts before loading and handing off control to **io.sys**.

If you have DoubleSpace or DriveSpace compressed hard drives, either **dblspace.bin** or **drvspace.bin** or both, as needed, are "preloaded" from the root folder of the boot directory. They're the real mode (old-fashioned DOS mode) drivers but are ultimately replaced by analogous VxDs, when Windows 98 is ready to run in protected mode.

Real Mode

Now **io.sys** takes control of your machine. The first thing **io.sys** does is read a file of settings called **msdos.sys**. If you're an old DOS maven (or even a young one), you probably remember **msdos.sys** as one of those strange hidden files that's copied onto a diskette when you format it as a system diskette—and in the old days, that was true. Nowadays, though, **msdos.sys** is just a text file. It—like **io.sys**—sits in the root folder of your boot drive. And it's "hidden," so you may have to go into Explorer's View/Options/View tab and check Show Hidden Files to see it. If you want to see what's inside it, double click on it in Explorer and pick Notepad from the list that pops up (we recommend that you make sure the "Always use . . ." check box is *not* checked since there are so many other **.sys** files floating around, not all of them text files).

The action **io.sys** takes next depends entirely on the contents of **msdos.sys**. I'm going to assume that you installed Win98 to a clean, new directory, and that you therefore have settings in **msdos.sys** that look much like mine (in particular, that you have a setting of **BootMulti=1**). The implications of this and other **msdos.sys** settings are covered in Chapter 7.

io.sys causes your PC to beep. From the moment you hear that beep until the moment the "Windows 98" splash screen appears, you can hit **F8** if you want to pick a nonstandard way of starting (say, going into Safe mode or booting to a DOS prompt). See the details in the next section, "Nonstandard Ways of Starting."

 Back in Windows 95 days, **io.sys** put a message on the screen that said, "Starting Windows 95 . . . ." Apparently somebody at Microsoft felt it wasn't politically correct to advertise the fact that DOS had taken over the machine and was about to start Windows. That message is gone. Now all you get is a beep.

 Ah, but there's more! In Win95 you could use only the F8 key to bring up the Windows Startup Menu—and thus start Windows in a nonstandard way. Now, you can press and hold the left **Ctrl** and get much the same effect. As long as you're holding down **Ctrl** when the "Windows 98" splash screen appears, you'll see the Windows Startup Menu and be allowed to start any which way.

There's one subtle difference between **F8** and **Ctrl**, by the way. When you use **F8** to bring up the Windows Startup Menu, there's no timer. But if you use **Ctrl**, there is a timer, which starts counting down the moment the screen appears.

In the normal course of events, **io.sys** next grabs the Windows 98 splash screen and sticks it on your monitor. It first looks in the root folder of your boot drive for a Windows bitmap (one that usually has the extension **.bmp** but not in this case!) called **logo.sys**. (Amazing how many different kinds of files are called **.sys**, eh?) Assuming the file is the right size (320 dots × 400 dots × 256 colors), **io.sys** uses it for the splash screen; otherwise **io.sys** uses a built-in bitmap—which just happens to be the "flying windows" splash screen you're probably used to. Windows itself doesn't come with a **logo.sys** but the Plus! Pack installs one. We'll talk about this and other splash screens in Chapter 7.

Then comes the ScanDisk run. If you didn't click Start, Shutdown, then Restart or Shutdown the last time you exited Win98, **io.sys** runs ScanDisk for a scan of your boot drive. When the scan is over, the splash screen goes back up and processing continues.

Next, **io.sys** sets up the Registry (described in Chapters 2 and 9) from files **user.dat** and **system.dat** in the Win98 **\windows** folder. **io.sys** then looks in the folder specified by **WinBootDir=** in **msdos.sys** and loads the drivers **himem.sys**, **ifshlp.sys**, and **setver.sys** from that folder, if they exist. **himem.sys** and **setver.sys** have their traditional roles as memory manager and adjuster of DOS-version calls in older programs. The **ifs** in **ifshelp.sys** stands for "installable file system" and indicates the role of this driver as the first step in support for Windows 98 file architecture.

io.sys next scans the **config.sys** file, if there is one, in the root directory of the boot drive. Settings in **config.sys** may override the settings already established by **io.sys**.

After establishing and then modifying **config.sys**-style settings, **io.sys** starts acting like **autoexec.bat**. If you're on a network, it runs the equivalent of a **net start** command, then sets up all these DOS environment variables, using the Win98 **\windows** directory as established by the **windir=** setting in **msdos.sys**:

```
TMP=C:\WINDOWS\TEMP
TEMP=C:\WINDOWS\TEMP
PROMPT=$p$g
winbootdir=C:\WINDOWS
PATH=C:WINDOWS;C:\WINDOWS\COMMAND
COMSPEC=C:\WINDOWS\COMMAND.COM
windir=C:\WINDOWS
```

 Note the capitalization here, which is documented incorrectly in the Windows Resource Kit. Also note that the Windows Resource Kit shows the wrong value for **COMSPEC=**.

Next, **io.sys** checks to see if there's an **autoexec.bat** file in the root folder of the boot directory. If there's an **autoexec.bat**, it loads the DOS command interpreter (the program that handles DOS commands: **command.com**), which better be in the location specified in **COMSPEC=**. **io.sys**, then runs **autoexec.bat** with the results showing on the monitor—that is, if something in **autoexec.bat** writes to the monitor, the splash screen is yanked and the output from **autoexec** is displayed; if nothing in **autoexec** writes to the monitor, the splash screen stays up. **autoexec.bat** runs as it always does, possibly modifying the DOS environment variables established earlier and possibly loading real mode drivers. **command.com** is then unloaded.

 If you run a lot of DOS windows under Windows you might want to add the line

```
C:\windows\command\doskey
```

to your **autoexec.bat**.

Automatic Skip Driver

A new Win98 technology called Automatic Skip Driver lurks in the background of all this activity. Windows Startup tries to bring up each of your pieces of hardware in turn. Sometimes either the hardware device fails to "wake up" or the software driver controlling the hardware crashes and burns. In either case, your machine won't be working right when Win98 sees the light of day.

This major irritation can turn into an all-out disaster if the failing hardware or driver hangs up your system completely. In earlier versions of Windows, there was no way to bypass individual failed components short of running a manual startup (and even that wouldn't always work, particularly for PnP devices).

Using a method very similar to the Windows SetUp Wizard's approach to detecting hardware, Win98's Automatic Skip Driver detects when there have been two consecutive failed attempts to bring on a hardware device or driver. From that point on, it skips the problematic process, so, at least in theory, you should never have to boot more than three times to get your machine running again.

All this would be a bit esoteric if it weren't for the fact that Windows 98 lets you take a look at the log of what devices are skipped and why. Click on Start, Programs, Accessories, System Tools, then System Information. Inside the System Information applet, click Tools, then Automatic Skip Driver Agent. If you find a failure that interests you, click on it, then click Details.

Windows 98 Emerges

When **autoexec.bat** finishes, **io.sys** puts the splash screen back up on the monitor. (If there is no **autoexec.bat**, the splash screen never went away.) It then enters its cocoon phase—**io.sys** enters the phase as an ugly real mode caterpillar and Windows 98 emerges at the end, a full protected mode butterfly.

 Or a vicious, horned Doom II incubus spitting hellfire. Perceptions vary. Take your pick.

Then **io.sys** loads a real mode program called **win.com**, which then assembles the components of Windows 98 itself. The beginning of **win.com** is something of a bellwether point. You can tell Win98 to start in Command Prompt mode (which looks and acts just as you would expect a DOS 7 to act, with a **c:>** and the whole nine yards), then type in the command **win**, and get precisely the same behavior from that point onward that you'll see if you simply let **io.sys** load and run **win.com** all by itself.

 Actually, the command prompt ain't the whole nine yards, because there is no support for long filenames—which can be a problem if you are trying to use the command prompt for some subtle troubleshooting. I'd say about six and a half of the whole nine yards.

Among other things, **win.com** sets in motion a program called **vmm32.vxd,** which is charged with loading virtual device drivers (so-called VxDs—the programs that connect Win98 to the outside world). **vmm32.vxd** is a mashed-together bunch of VxDs that the Win98 SetUp routine builds for each machine.

Next, **vmm32.vxd** looks in the Registry key **HKEY_LOCAL_MACHINE\ System\CurrentControlSet\Services\VxD** and loads any VxDs it finds listed there. Then it scans the Registry for any other **StaticVxD=** entries and loads those virtual device drivers.

Next, **vmm32.vxd** opens up **system.ini**, if it exists in the Win98 **\windows** folder. It then loads any **device=** VxDs it finds in the **[386Enh]** section, overwriting any existing VxDs with the same name. Finally, **vmm32.vxd** looks in the Win98 **\windows\system\vmm32** folder for any **.vxd** files, overwriting any previously encountered, similarly named VxDs with the files it finds there.

> And you thought you were done with **system.ini**! No way. Don't throw out those old Windows 3.1 books. The best source of unbiased info on **system.ini** and **win.ini** is the original *Mother of All Windows Books*, of course, ISBN 0-201-62475-3. If you can find it. The next best source of info is Microsoft Press' *Windows 3.1 Resource Kit*. Good luck. You'll need it.

One crucial component loaded by **vmm32.vxd** is the I/O Supervisor, which controls all input and output under Win98, including initialization of the devices during startup and ongoing file activities while Win98 is running. The I/O Supervisor sets up shop by looking in the Win98 **\windows\system\iosubsys** folders for drivers. Port drivers reside in **.pdr** files; Windows NT-style miniport drivers are **.mpd**s; other drivers may either be **.386** files (the designation used by Windows 3.1 drivers) or **.vxd**s designed to run with the I/O Supervisor.

Another crucial component loaded by **vmm32.vxd** is the Configuration Manager, which works with Plug 'n' Play devices and Registry entries to figure out what is attached to your PC. As it sorts out the various conflicts, it has the I/O Supervisor initialize the peripherals, and your machine is almost ready to start.

Somewhere in here any real mode device drivers that aren't needed any longer—such as **drvspace.bin**—are taken over. Their memory is reclaimed and made available again for the system to use elsewhere.

> For you network buffs, the network redirectors are loaded at this point and initialize the lower-level network ("Ring 0") code on your machine. At this point they also asynchronously broadcast a machine addname to each of the protocols you have requested to be loaded. The system then pauses to wait for the acknowledgment of the addname (or a timeout occurs, whichever comes first). If you are running TCP/IP against a DHCP server, a dynamic IP address is assigned to your machine from the pool of available IP addresses at this point. Once your machine is available on the Net (at these lower levels), any machine-level policies are downloaded from the appropriate secure Windows NT or Netware servers.

Then the main Windows components, the WinOoze, are loaded: **kernel32.dll**, **krnl386.exe**, **gdi.exe**, **gdi32.exe**, **user.exe**, and **user32.exe**. Notice that both the old 16-bit and the new 32-bit versions make an appearance. Windows then checks the Registry entries for fonts. It then looks for additional fonts and other entries in **win.ini**, if it exists in the Win98 **\windows** folder, and updates the Registry accordingly.

Windows looks for a file called **winstart.bat** in the **windows** folder of the boot drive (usually **C:\windows**). If it exists, Windows takes the splash screen off the monitor, loads **command.com**, and runs **winstart.bat**, just like any other **.bat** file, with the results displayed on the monitor. If it doesn't exist, Windows looks for a file called **winstart.bat** in the *root* folder of the boot drive (usually **C:**). If it exists, Windows runs it just like the other kind of **winstart.bat**. Then **command.com** is unloaded. **win.com** does all the command interpretation in Windows outside the DOS boxes. (If there is no **winstart**, the splash screen stays up and **command.com** is not loaded.)

 This **winstart.bat** stuff is very confusing, and it's going to get more confusing when we talk about the System Configuration Utility—where it ties in to a bug. So remember: **C:\windows\winstart.bat** runs if it exists. If it doesn't, **C:\winstart.bat** runs.

 Commands in **winstart.bat** are different from commands in **autoexec.bat** in that programs loaded in **winstart.bat** are available for the Windows Desktop and for Windows applications, but they are unloaded for any DOS session run over Windows.

The multiprotocol network route module **mprexe.exe** looks at the Registry's **HKEY_LOCAL_MACHINE\SOFTWARE\Microsoft\Windows\CurrentVersion\ RunServices** key to see if there are any programs that need to be started up before the user logs on and then finally presents the logon screen to the user.

 At that point, if you have enabled multiple-user logon, Win98 asks for your logon user name and password. This is another choke point: all paths lead here, and then many things happen immediately after the user name and password are validated. Let me try to get them in the right order.

- After you enter your user name/password combo, the system verifies the password, unlocks the master password file, and then attempts to log you onto each of the various networks you have loaded. Network authentication then occurs against any secure Windows NT and/or Netware servers you have on your network. If all is OK, you are granted access to the appropriate network resources the system administrators have arranged for you— disks, printers, and whatnot.

- Any user-level policies that a system administrator has entered are placed in effect. Then any network user-level Registry entries (the **user.dat** hive) are downloaded, merged in your PC's Registry, and placed in effect.

- Next, Win98 processes any Netware logon scripts you might have.

- Now Win98 looks in your Registry for the **HKEY_LOCAL_MACHINE\ SOFTWARE\Microsoft\Windows\CurrentVersion\RunOnce** key. It runs any programs found there and *waits for the programs to finish* before it proceeds. If a **RunOnce** program requires user interaction, the program will sit on a completely blank screen—nothing else running, no Desktop, no Taskbar, nothing—waiting for the user to provide input.

- It's a little hard to say precisely which of the following programs run in what order, but as far as we can tell, Win98 next runs any programs listed in **win.ini**'s **[windows]** section, **load=** line. (The **load=** programs run minimized.) Then it runs any programs on **win.ini**'s **run=** line. (The **run=** programs run "restored," or partial screen.) Then it runs any programs listed in the Registry's **HKEY_LOCAL_MACHINE\SOFTWARE\Microsoft\Windows\CurrentVersion\Run** key. The Desktop is created and the Taskbar appears on the screen. All these programs are run normally, in that they are started and allowed to multitask. They could complete in almost any order; that's why it's hard to tell exactly which ones run first.

- Next Win98 looks in the Registry's **HKEY_CURRENT_USER\Software\Microsoft\Windows\CurrentVersion\Run** key and runs any programs listed there. Then it looks in the **HKEY_CURRENT_USER\Software\Microsoft\Windows\CurrentVersion\RunOnce** key and runs any programs listed. Unlike the **HKEY_LOCAL_MACHINE RunOnce** programs, the **HKEY_CURRENT_USER RunOnce** programs run just like any other program; they don't hold the machine hostage until finished, and they multitask with everything else.

- Next, Win98 runs any programs located in the **\Windows\Start Menu\Programs\Startup** folder.

- Finally, Win98 runs any programs located in the **\Windows\All Users\Start Menu\Programs\Startup** folder. It brings back up most folder windows that were open the last time Windows shut down and hands control over to the user.

 Nawww, it isn't that complicated, is it? Couldn't be. Hmmmmm . . . maybe it is . . .

Note that there are two **Run** keys in the Registry and two **RunOnce** keys. The paths to them look similar, but one pair starts from **HKEY_LOCAL_MACHINE** and is thus systemwide, affecting all users on that machine. The other pair starts from **HKEY_CURRENT_USER** and so is user-specific on systems with multiple user profiles. The **RunOnce** keys are called that because after the system finishes running the commands, they are removed from the Registry.

The two **RunOnce** keys behave very differently for a good reason. The one in **HKEY_LOCAL_MACHINE**, which prohibits any other programs from running until it is done, is there to allow an install program to reboot the system and be sure of regaining control. The one in **HKEY_CURRENT_USER** is there to allow a program to save its state when it is told Windows is shutting down, and then to restore that state upon a reboot.

Cool.

So Windows loads Windows programs each time you start (as opposed to RunOnce) from the following places: **win.ini**'s **Run=**, **win.ini**'s **Load=**, HKLM's **Run** key, HKCU's **Run** key, the regular StartUp group, and the All User's StartUp group. If some crazy program keeps loading automatically because some install made it and you can't figure out where the heck it is loading from (so you can stop it loading), you now know where to look. You'll need to use Notepad on **win.ini**, Regedit on the two Registry keys, and Explorer on the two StartUp groups.

Lest you think that the parts that load the VxDs only load a VxD or two, I'd like to tell you about the logged boot I ran on my machine. The log file that resulted was 24 K bytes and more than 600 lines; 60 VxD, 7 **.drv**, 6 **.exe/.dll**, and 8 **.fon** (bitmapped fonts) files were loaded. Wait a minute—60 VxDs? What a complicated architecture! Gotta be something wrong here.

Au contraire. Think of all the subsystems that need to be loaded. There are VxDs for keyboard, mouse, vfat, vcache, comm driver, disk stuff, network stuff, memory management, and a lot more.

That, as best we can tell, is the precise sequence of steps Win98 takes to get itself up and going in the morning. And to think, all you have to do is drag a comb across your head, scrape your teeth with a brush, walk downstairs, and pour some hot java.

■ Nonstandard Ways of Starting

When two do the same thing it is never quite the same thing.

—PUBLILIUS SYRUS, *Sententiæ*, ca. 50 B.C.

Shifty Starts

Throughout Win98, holding down **Shift** while you start a program (sometimes even when you open a file!) usually means the typical startup sequence gets bypassed. Win98 itself is no exception. There are, in fact, two different times during the startup sequence when holding down **Shift** will work.

If you hold down **Shift** either before that initial startup beep or shortly after, and you keep it held down, you get a message flashed on the screen that says, "Windows is bypassing your startup files." (It may go by so fast you can't see it.) Startup progresses normally, but neither **autoexec.bat** nor **config.sys** are run. Similarly, **winstart.bat** is bypassed. You'll end up (after five minutes or so of heavy disk activity) in Safe mode.

The other time **Shift** comes into play: If you hold down **Shift** immediately after the network logon screen appears, Windows bypasses your **\StartUp** group.

Holding down **shift** at any other point in the startup process doesn't appear to have any effect.

F Key Express

As mentioned in the previous section, "How Win98 Starts," you can hit **F8** shortly after the initial startup beep, and be confronted with a large number of alternative ways of starting parts of Win98. Ends up that **F8** isn't the only option. Let's take a look at all the F keys you can use, which options you have, and what they all accomplish. We're going to assume your **msdos.sys** file looks as it would if you installed Win98 to a clean subdirectory—and that you haven't gone out of your way to delete any of the system files that Win98 creates. We'll have much more to say about all those files in the next chapter.

If you hit **F8** shortly after the initial startup beep, you get the Win98 Startup Menu, Figure 6-57.

If option 7 doesn't appear in your Startup Menu, it probably means that you installed Win98 on top of Windows 95, so it can't boot to your previous version of DOS (without a boot diskette, anyway). We go over the many flavors of **msdos.sys** in Chapter 7.

1. **Normal** is the choice you want to make if you accidentally got into the Startup Menu and want to get the hell out. It just tells Win98 to start the way it usually does.

2. **Logged (\BOOTLOG.TXT)** tells Win98 to start normally but log each startup activity as it proceeds. The log is written to the file **bootlog.txt** in your boot drive's root folder. We look at **bootlog.txt** extensively in Chapter 7. A more complicated way of accomplishing the same thing is to choose option 5 from the menu, wait until you get the **C:>** command prompt, and type **win /b** to start a boot log.

3. **Safe mode** forces Win98 to start in, uh, Safe mode, that weird quasi-Windows state (see Figure 6-18) that may or may not let you repair what ails your Windows. Safe mode's greatest achievement—the fact that it will run just about any time, even if your machine is on its last legs—is also its greatest shortcoming. In order to run in a crippled state, almost everything you might want to look at either doesn't work or works minimally. For example, the Control Panel System applet's Device Manager will tell you

Figure 6-57.
Windows 98
Startup Menu

```
Microsoft Windows 98 Startup Menu
====================================

    1. Normal
    2. Logged (\BOOTLOG.TXT)
    3. Safe Mode
    4. Step-by-step confirmation
    5. Command prompt only
    6. Safe mode command prompt only
    7. Previous version of MS-DOS

Enter a choice: 1

F5=Safe mode Shift+F5=Command prompt Shift+F8=Step-by-step confirmation [N]
```

that, on every device, "Status is not available when Windows is running in Safe mode." Hardly a comforting situation.

Safe mode runs with generic mouse and keyboard drivers and standard VGA. That's about it. Your CD, for example, may not spin, your printer won't print, your network connection won't work, and your modem won't mo. Dem. While Safe mode doesn't use many (if any!) settings from the Registry, you can get at Regedit while in Safe mode to modify aberrant Registry values.

 Safe mode for Windows 95 had a network connection option, but it no longer exists.

 Little-known fact: if Windows tries to boot twice in succession and the Automatic Skip Driver detection isn't good enough to allow a full boot, Win98 kicks into Safe mode and lets you deal with the problem manually.

The hard way to get to Safe mode is to choose option 5 on the Startup Menu, wait for the `C:>` prompt, and then type `win /d:m`. The easy way to get into Safe mode next time is to reboot, listen for the startup beep, and hit **F5**. Safe mode has a more restrictive variant called Safe Mode Without Compression that bypasses the usual disk compression routines, for those of you still using DriveSpace. The only way we found to get into that mode was by rebooting, waiting for the beep, then hitting **Ctrl+F5**.

4. **Step-by-step confirmation** boots into normal Windows 98, but it gives you the option of including or skipping just about every step of the startup process—not just the traditional lines in `config.sys` and `autoexec.bat`. That can be very valuable if you've narrowed a startup problem down to one offensive component. It can also be very dangerous if you elect to exclude a crucial part of Win98. There is a much easier way to accomplish the same thing, without doing it all manually, by using the System Configuration Utility, which we discuss in the next subsection.

 I ran a test on step-by-step confirmation and was quite impressed by the thoroughness of the choices offered. It really does seem to hit every component of the startup process, giving you the opportunity to run the command or pass it by. Here is a log of what Windows said.

```
Windows will prompt you to confirm each startup
    command
Process the system registry?
Create a startup log file (\BOOTLOG.TXT)?
Process your startup device drivers (Config.sys)?
Device = d:\windows\himem.sys?
Device = d:\windows\dblbuff.sys?
Devicehigh = d:\windows\ifshlp.sys?
```

Then it asked to run each line in **config.sys**:

```
Process your startup command file (Autoexec.bat)?
```

Then it asked to run each line in **autoexec.bat**:

```
WIN?
Load all Windows drivers?
```

If you choose no, Win98 starts in Safe mode. If you choose yes, you get

```
Vnetsetup.vxd?
ndis.vxd?
ndis2sup.vxd?
javasup.vxd?
C:\windows\system\vrtwd.386?
C:\windows\system\vfixd.vxd?
vnetbios.vxd?
vredir.vxd?
dfs.vxd?
vserver.vxd?
msmouse.vxd?
```

There's one odd part of step-by-step confirmation that, uh, bugged me. It always seemed to run **winstart.bat**, no matter which choices I made. While it's true that few Windows users have a **winstart.bat** file, it's also true that those who do (often network users with weird connection problems) may need the step-by-step process more than the average Win user. You can't even bypass **winstart.bat** using the System Configuration Utility (I talk about that in the next subsection).

If you want to run Step-by-step confirmation without going through the Startup Menu, reboot. When you hear the beep, hit **Shift+F8**.

5. **Command prompt only** you diehard DOS fans! This option puts you in what amounts to DOS 7 mode, with a bare **c:>** prompt, on a wing and a prayer. It runs **config.sys** and **autoexec.bat** and does everything else noted in the discussion about **io.sys** earlier, except the variable **windir=** is no longer in the DOS environment. Precisely as it should be.

   Surprisingly, there doesn't appear to be an accelerator key combination to get directly at the command prompt after the initial startup beep. You have to hit **F8**, wait for the Win98 Startup Menu to appear, then type 6. That's an odd oversight, because speed demon DOS types seem to be the most likely to demand obscure key combinations to cut directly to their hallowed **c:>**.

6. **Safe mode command prompt only** is just about as bare-bones as you can get. Or would want to. This mode is a bit like Command Prompt mode, except Win98 doesn't even look at your **config.sys** or **autoexec.bat** files. You get a **c:>** prompt, the same environment variables as in Command Prompt mode, with **msdos** taking up 77 K of lower memory,

drvspace (if you have compressed drives) taking another 109 K, and **command** its 10 K.

There *is* a quick combination into Safe mode command prompt, though. When you hear the initial startup beep, hit **Shift+F5**.

7. **Previous version of MS-DOS** works slick as could be, providing you installed Win98 to a clean directory. When you choose this option, Win98 does the following in the root folder of the boot directory.

- Renames **autoexec.bat** (the current Win98 **autoexec** file) to **autoexec.w40**. Renames **autoexec.dos** (the copy of your original **autoexec.bat**, created when you installed Win98) to **autoexec.bat**.

- Renames **config.sys** (the current Win98 **config** file) to **config.w40**. Renames **config.dos** (the copy of your original **config.sys**, created when you installed Win98) to **config.sys**.

- Renames **command.com** (the Win98 command interpreter) to **command.w40**. Renames **command.dos** (the version of **command.com** that existed when you originally installed Win98, typically from DOS 5 or DOS 6) to **command.com**. Similarly, **mode.com** is renamed **mode_dos.w40** and **mode.dos** is renamed **mode.com**.

- Renames **msdos.sys** (the Win98 text file with startup settings) to **msdos.w40**. Renames **msdos.dos** (the program—*not* a text file—**msdos.sys** that existed when you originally installed Win98, typically from DOS 5 or DOS 6) to **msdos.sys**.

- Renames **io.sys** (the Win98 workhorse that gets Win98 started in the first place) to **winboot.sys**. Renames **io.dos** (the DOS 5 or DOS 6 program that existed when you originally installed Win98) to **io.sys**.

- Hands over control to the newly named **io.sys**, which in turn gets your old version of DOS running.

The accelerator key combination for running your previous version of DOS is to reboot, wait for the initial beep, then hit **F4**. Note that you have to be set up for dual booting (the mentioned files have to exist, with their proper names, and **msdos.sys** must contain the line **BootMulti=1**).

Once you're done with your DOS 5 or DOS 6 session, simply reboot the way you always have. All the files are renamed to their initial states, and Win98's shining face will greet you.

 The Windows Resource Kit says that Win98 **io.sys** is renamed to **io.w40**. T'ain't true. If you go looking for it, you won't find it . . . and therein lies a story. We'll take a look at it in the section "How Win98 Really Boots."

 If you compare Figure 6-57 with the same menu in Windows 95, you'll find that "Safe Mode with Network Support" is missing. Too bad—it saved my bacon once when I got some badly needed files over the network.

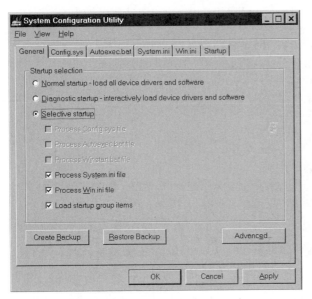

Figure 6-58. System Configuration Utility

System Configuration Utility

Windows 98 sports a brand-new program called the System Configuration Utility. It basically puts a GUI face on many of the Win98 Startup Menu options we just discussed.

You can't use it all the time—for example, if you can't get Win98 to boot, the System Configuration Utility won't be available. But you can (almost) always get to the Win98 Startup Menu by pushing **F8** after the initial startup beep. If you can get into Win98, you'll find this utility much simpler (and less error-prone) than stepping through a step-by-step startup.

On the General tab (Figure 6-58), you can specify, in advance, whether you want a step-by-step startup and, if so, whether `config.sys`, `autoexec.bat`, `system.ini`, `win.ini`, or programs in the `\windows\Start Menu\Programs\ StartUp` folder (and a few other places, discussed in a minute) are to be processed.

 Yes, I know I didn't mention `winstart.bat`. Hang on a second.

The System Configuration Utility is even smart enough to look and see if this particular PC has `config.sys`, `autoexec.bat`, or `winstart.bat` files and reflect its finding on the General tab. In Figure 6-58, you can see that this particular PC doesn't have any of those three files: all three choices are grayed out.

If you choose to process `config.sys` and `autoexec.bat` (assuming they exist), you can click on those tabs in the System Configuration Utility and choose line by line which parts of each file you want to include or exclude. Very cool, and much less error-prone than the step-by-step method described earlier.

Similarly, if you choose to have `system.ini` and `win.ini` processed, you can flip over to those tabs and pick which parts of those files to include or exclude (Figure 6-59).

In fact, you can even select which startup programs you want Win98 to execute, using the list on the Startup tab (Figure 6-60), but (in spite of what you've read on the General tab) these are not solely programs in the `\StartUp` folder.

Figure 6-59. Choose individual groups, or lines, within `system.ini`

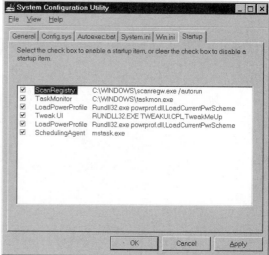

Figure 6-60. Include or exclude programs in the `\StartUp` folder

 We've found seven different places these Startup tab items can come from.

- The usual **StartUp** group—**C:\windows\Start Menu\Programs\ StartUp**. If you uncheck the box in front of a program that's in this **StartUp** folder, the program is moved to the folder **C:\windows\ Start Menu\Programs\Disabled Startup Items** (Figure 6-61).

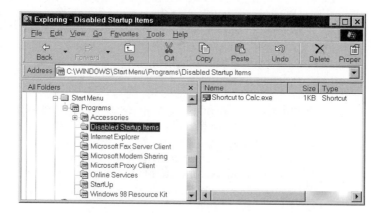

Figure 6-61. Startup folder items disabled by the System Configuration Utility get shuffled to a newly created folder called Disabled Startup Items

- The weird StartUp group—`C:\windows\All Users\Start Menu\Programs\StartUp`. If you uncheck one of these programs, it's moved to `C:\windows\All Users\Start Menu\Programs\Disabled Startup Items`.

- The `load=` line in the `[windows]` section of `win.ini`. If you uncheck these programs in the System Configuration Utility, Windows turns the line into a `noload=` line (Figure 6-62). Note in particular that the whole line is treated as one unit: either all the `load=` programs run or none of them do.

- The `run=` line in the `[windows]` section of `win.ini`. Similarly, if you uncheck these critters, Windows puts them in with the line `noload=` (Figure 6-62). And, just like `load=`, all the `run=` programs are treated as a single unit: either all of them run or none of them do.

Figure 6-62. In `win.ini`, loads turn to noloads (some brokers should get excited about that) and runs turn to noruns

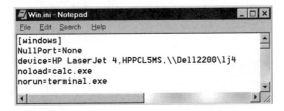

- The Registry key `HKLM\Software\Microsoft\Windows\CurrentVersion\Run`. If you uncheck a program that's stored in that key, the System Configuration Manager moves it to the equally tongue-twisting `HKLM\Software\Microsoft\Windows\CurrentVersion\Run-` (see Figure 6-63). (We have much more to say about these keys in Chapter 9.) Note the minus sign added after "Run."

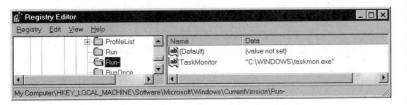

Figure 6-63. `HKLM\. . .\Run turns to \Run-`

- Similarly, anything in the key `HKLM\Software\Microsoft\Windows\CurrentVersion\RunServices` also appears in the System Configuration Manager list. If you uncheck a program's box, it's moved to `HKLM\Software\Microsoft\Windows\CurrentVersion\RunServices-`.

- Likewise, anything in the key `HKCU\Software\Microsoft\Windows\CurrentVersion\Run` appears and if unchecked goes to `HKCU\Software\Microsoft\Windows\CurrentVersion\Run-`.

 There's one important subtlety here. The Scheduling Agent in Figure 6-64 is really the Task Scheduler (sometimes called the Task Manager), the one we discussed in Chapter 4. It's the one you can get to by double clicking on the Task Manager icon in the tray. If you leave this box checked, the Task Scheduler will run. And inside the Task Scheduler, you can schedule a task to run at system startup or at login. So it's kind of a cascading series of events: let the Task Scheduler run and all those tasks will run, too.

Figure 6-64. Scheduling Agent—better known as the Task Scheduler

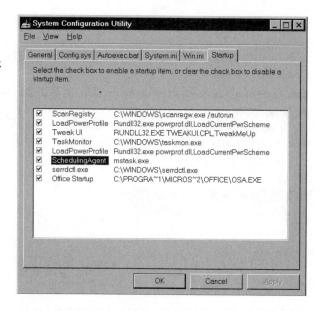

Finally, the "Load StartUp group" items on the General tab (Figure 6-65) are all the items on the Startup tab. If you uncheck that box on the General tab, all these programs—including the Task Scheduler—are disabled.

 In case you're curious, no, the programs in the **\RunOnce** Registry keys don't appear in the System Configuration Utility list.

 This really is a neat utility—but there's one teensy, tiny problem. There's a bug. Remember how I complained that you couldn't bypass processing of **winstart.bat** while going through the Win98 Startup Menu's step-by-step confirmation option? Guess what. You can't do it with the System Configuration Utility either. Try the following experiment. Make a **C:\windows\winstart.bat** that says

```
echo hi from Mom
pause
```

Now restart Windows to see this run. Next run System Configuration Utility and uncheck the box that says Process Winstart.bat. Restart again and you'll find that it is still running. Bug. Bah, humbug.

 So that means that neither step-by-step confirmation nor the System Configuration Utility check box prevents **winstart.bat** from running. You can prevent it from running only by using Safe mode or by renaming it.

Figure 6-65.
System Configu-
ration Utility
doesn't even see
`C:\winstart.bat`

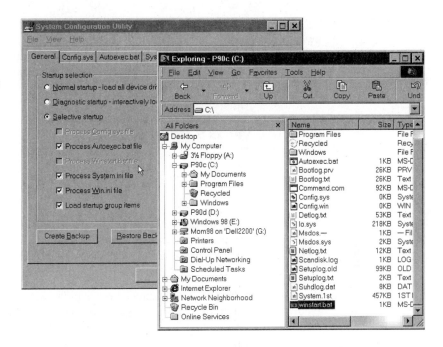

 But wait! It gets worse! The System Configuration Utility doesn't even recognize `C:\winstart.bat`, the version of **winstart** that sits in the root folder of the boot disk. (As mentioned in the earlier section "How Win98 Starts," Win98 first looks to see if there's a `C:\windows\winstart.bat` and, if there is, runs it. If there isn't, Win98 looks for a `C:\winstart.bat` and runs that.) If you have a `C:\winstart.bat` (Figure 6-65), the System Configuration Utility doesn't even bother to un-shade the box in the General tab.

System Recovery Wizard

Certainly the most nonstandard way of starting, hands down, has to be via the Windows 98 System Recovery Wizard.

If you make a complete backup of your system using Microsoft Backup, you can actually restore the full backup from the DOS command line. Though it's not for the faint of heart, it may save your skin some day. It will work only if you have a full system backup, made via MS Backup, and the device that backup resides on is accessible from your Emergency StartUp Disk.

Start Win98 from the Emergency StartUp Disk and choose CD-ROM support. Then put your Win98 installation CD in the drive. Go over to `\tools\sysrec` on the installation CD, and run the program called `pcrestor.bat`.

There are detailed instructions in the file `\tools\sysrec\`
`pcrestore.bat`. Make sure you read it and the Help window on the Wizard.
In particular, make sure you understand under what circumstances you want to
check the box marked "Restore hardware and system settings to the registry."

■ How Win98 Really Boots

When you want to fool the world, tell the truth.

—Otto von Bismarck

Does this multiple boot stuff have you all confused? Yeah. Me, too. Like,
how does Win98 mysteriously reappear after you've multibooted to
DOS 6 and then restarted the PC? Something has to go in there and
swap out the DOS 6 `io.sys` with the Win98 `io.sys`, doesn't it?

When a PC boots from a hard drive, it reads in the first record (called a **boot
record**) on the hard drive and hands control to the little program—the bootstrapper—located on that boot record. The bootstrapper, in turn, passes control
over to a specific place on the hard drive that must contain all the programs
necessary to bring the PC to life. The bootstrapper don't know nuthin' about
filenames or any of that stuff. It just knows locations on the disk.

In good ol' DOS, the boot record would always hand control over to a file
called `io.sys`, which was always in the first data sector of the disk. When you
made a boot disk, you essentially put `io.sys` in the first data sector, thus en-
suring that when the boot record handed off control, `io.sys` in particular and
DOS in general would take over.

But Win98 got tricky—it had to, if it was going to keep the ability to boot
either to Win98 or to the previous version of DOS. Win98 has a file that can
have either of two different names—`winboot.sys` or `io.sys`—depending on
whether Win98 is running (when it's known as `io.sys`) or the previous version
of DOS is running (when it's known as `winboot.sys`). The trick is that the file
doesn't move.

When Win98 installs itself, it creates a new boot record that points to this
file-with-two-names. That means whenever your PC boots off the hard drive,
control is passed to this file—whether it's called `io.sys` or `winboot.sys`
doesn't matter.

When it comes to life, this program looks at one of the files that is renamed to see if DOS or Win98 was the last to run. It probably looks at the first file on the disk. (At least that would be one reasonable way to do it.) If the first file on the disk is called **io.dos**, the program knows that Win98 was the last operating system to run, that all is hunky-dory, and that processing can continue. But if it discovers that the first file is called **io.sys**, it knows that a previous version of DOS was the last operating system to run, so it has to rename a whole bunch of files before it proceeds: **config.sys** has to be renamed **config.dos**; **config.w40** has to be renamed **config.sys**; similarly with **autoexec**, **command**, **msdos**, and **mode**.

Wait a minute! It can't be that simple, Billy. What if there's no older version of DOS on the PC? The first file on the disk could be almost anything. Oh, but you could get around that by . . .

Details, details, details. Now you know how Win98 *really* wakes up in the morning: with an Excedrin-class headache.

Chapter 7

Techie Files, Techie Programs

As he knew not what to say, he swore.

—Byron, *The Island*, 1823

As you wend your way toward the Registry—and I just *know* that's what you're doing, reading these chapters sequentially in spite of all the warnings—the going gets tougher when you start talking about the files Win98 uses to store things, what's put in those files, and how certain fancy programs interact with the files.

In this chapter we tackle files you can play with and programs that will inevitably go kablooey when you do. The crazy part is that you may be forced to dig into these files some day whether you want to or not. And at that point, I'll certainly understand if you use a word or two generally reserved for, oh, barroom brawls—or TV talk shows.

This is where you find out how to change the splash screens that Windows 98 uses—how to replace the Windows logo that hogs the screen during bootup with a picture of your significant other . . . or MOM.

We also tackle three new Windows 98 utilities, the Microsoft File Information program, System File Checker, and Version Conflict Manager. Nothing better than managing conflict, eh?

It's also where you'll learn how to create your own Active Desktop, even to the point of writing your own VBScript programs to control the Active Desktop. We won't go into a lot of detail on VBScript—that would take another book this size—but with a little bit of luck, we'll get you started and pointed in the right direction. And with VBScript, that's not easy.

■ SetUp

Doceo insanire omnes.
(I teach that all men are crazy.)

—Horace, *Satires,* ca. 25 B.C.

The key to the Windows 98 SetUp Wizard's wonderful robustness—or its infuriating inability to install on your machine, should you be so unfortunate—lies in the files SetUp creates and uses to guide itself through the installation process. These files can generally be divided into three types:

- Log files, which keep track of each step in the installation
- `.inf` files, which try to guide the installer, typically pointing it to correct drivers for identified hardware
- A whole bunch of miscellaneous files, some of which are totally inscrutable (to us anyway) and some of which can save your posterior if it becomes exposed

Let's take a look at each of them.

Log File Anatomy

Most log files and all INF files are simple ASCII text files, arranged like a Windows 3.1 INI file. Open up one of them and you'll find entries like this:

```
[Section]
Key1 = value
Key2 = value
```

Within a given section, there should be no duplicate keys. The ordering of sections within the file is not significant, nor is the ordering of keys within a section. For many other details on the precise way `.ini` files and their values are (generally) interpreted, see Chapter 8 of the original *Mother of All Windows Books,* ISBN 0-201-62708-6. If you've never dissected an `.ini` file, not to worry. You'll catch on real quick.

setuplog.txt

As the Win98 SetUp Wizard progresses through its steps, it maintains several log files. The first one to be created is called `setuplog.txt`. It resides in the root folder of your boot drive and serves several purposes. First, it's the repository of information for the Windows 98 SetUp Wizard—if you push a <Back button in one of the Wizard dialogs, the Wizard can retrieve earlier information from `setuplog.txt`. Second, it provides a record of the early steps in installation—the part that comes before hardware detection—and then the later

parts of installation, primarily the copying of files and booting of Win98 for the first time.

If SetUp crashes during the early or late stages, it's usually smart enough to read **setuplog.txt**, merge that information with the Registry if it exists, carry your good settings forward to the safe recovery stage, and avoid whatever it was that made SetUp crash the first time. (We talk about hardware detection crashes when we discuss **detlog.txt** later.)

Finally, and most important to us, **setuplog.txt** is designed to let *you* look at the results of SetUp running on your machine—most likely for the purpose of isolating a SetUp problem so that you can bypass the problem spot during a hellacious installation.

 The Win98 SetUp Wizard maintains one level of backup of the **setuplog.txt** file. If you've set up Windows twice on the same machine, **setuplog.old** is a copy of the previous install's **setuplog.txt**.

Although the beginning of **setuplog.txt** looks more or less like an **.ini** file (with sections, keys, and values), the parts at the end are simple log entries, recorded when certain tasks have begun or ended. It's almost as if the Windows 98 SetUp Wizard programmers started out intent on building a real **.ini** file, then got lazy midway through. The log entries at the end are created sequentially—as things happen, the Windows 98 SetUp Wizard adds entries to the end of the file, some of the section names repeat (which would never happen in a well-behaved **.ini** file), and the entries start getting sloppy.

A few notes about **setuplog.txt**:

- The Windows 98 SetUp Wizard runs a check on your system's CMOS before it starts to copy files onto your PC. It's looking to see if your PC has antivirus protection running in CMOS. If you don't disable the antivirus program, you may get bogus warnings about changes to the Master Boot Record. The results of that check are in a section called [ ] (yep, it's blank).

- **[Started]** holds info about the Win98 version: the entry **version= 262154,1998** means you *are* running Win98; that's just the funny way Windows stores the version number, which (as you'll find by typing **ver** inside a DOS box) is 4.10.1998.

- If you installed from a network server, the Win98 SetUp Wizard starts digesting entries from a file called **msbatch.inf**. Chances are pretty good the **msbatch.inf** file is in the **\windows** folder on the server. The original contents of the sections **[Setup]**, **[System]**, and **[Optional Components]** come either from **msbatch.inf** or defaults built into the setup routine itself, and get modified as you make choices in the Wizard.

- References to the "EBD" are for the Emergency Boot Disk (better known as the Emergency StartUp Disk (ESD) or, as the Marketing folks prefer to call it, the StartUp Disk).

- There's a log of `.inf` files—hundreds of them—that get copied to `C:\windows\inf`. These `.inf` files are "real" `.inf` files: they help detect and install myriad types of hardware and support software.

 If you want to get a feel for the enormous amount of work involved in Windows 98 SetUp—both computer work and programmer work—take a quick glance at `setuplog.txt`. It's a humbling experience.

system.1st

At the beginning of the Copy Files phase, the Windows 98 SetUp Wizard starts building the Registry, based out of two files, `system.new` and `user.new`, in the root directory of the boot drive. They're both hidden, read-only files. If Win98 SetUp runs through to completion, these files are copied to the `\windows` folder and renamed `system.dat` and `user.dat`, which you may recognize as being the files that make up the lion's part of the Registry (see Chapter 9).

Setup then creates the Emergency StartUp Disk. Or Emergency Boot Disk. Whatever.

On successful completion of the Copy Files phase, the SetUp routine loads the Registry with its RunOnce program (the one that does the final configuration—setting Time Zones, moving Windows 3.1 groups to the Start Menu if appropriate, building the initial Windows Help files, and the like; there's a description of RunOnce in Chapter 9). At this point, the SetUp routine copies the Registry file `system.dat` (in the `\windows` folder) to the root of the boot drive, marking it hidden, read-only, and system, and naming it `setup.1st`.

`system.1st` is as close to a clean Registry as your machine will ever see: if you somehow clobber both the Registry `.dat` files and their backups or if Win98 SetUp hangs when running the RunOnce program—a dilemma we encountered on a bone-stock 486—you may need `system.1st` to restore things. Using `system.1st` is *not* easy. You have to reboot with **F8** (see Chapter 8) and get into the Command Prompt mode. Then you need to use the `attrib` command to change the hidden and read-only attributes on `system.1st` and `\windows\system.dat`, e.g.,

```
attrib -h -r c:\system.1st
attrib -h -r c:\windows\system.dat
```

Let's hear it for the DOS 7 command line, eh?

Finally, you need to copy `system.1st` on top of `\windows\system.dat`. When you reboot into Win98, Windows will start in with the SetUp RunOnce program, and you can proceed from there.

detlog.txt

While `setuplog.txt` is a real working file, `detlog.txt` can best be thought of as just another pretty face. The SetUp routine uses `setuplog.txt` for all sorts of things, but **detlog.txt** exists only for humans to look at. And swear over. None of the hardware detection routines use any of the entries in **detlog.txt**. Amazingly, **detlog.txt** is marked by Win98 as hidden, so you have to futz with Explorer or the **attrib** command before you can look at it.

Windows creates a **detlog.txt** every time it runs its Automatic Hardware Detection program, known to techies as **sysdetmg.dll**.

 If you look at the **detlog.txt** file and all the **.inf** files in your **\windows\inf** folder, you get a feel for how much effort goes into detecting every bit of hardware that's ever gone into anything remotely resembling a PC. **Sysdetmg.dll** does a good (but not perfect) job of detecting hardware and getting it to work. Much better, though, is Plug 'n' Play, where the hardware responds to a "request for enumeration." Put simply, Windows says, "Who are you?", and the hardware comes back and says, "I'm a PnP sound card, and I'm using IRQ 3, DMA 7, and I/O area 320-33F." We don't need **sysdetmg.dll** for most kinds of PnP hardware or for PCI-based or PCMCIA cards, and you won't find those well-behaved devices listed in **detlog.txt**.

The Windows 98 SetUp Wizard runs automatic hardware detection shortly after the first time it reboots your PC. You can also run it if you pick Automatic Detection while using the Control Panel's Add/Remove Hardware applet (discussed in Chapter 10). This **detlog.txt** makes no pretensions to being an **.ini** file or anything else. It's a straight, sequential ASCII text file that keeps a blow-by-blow log of all the steps **sysdetmg.dll** takes in trying to find and identify all your hardware.

The auto hardware detector maintains two generations of **detlog** files: **detlog.txt** and **detlog.old**. If the auto hardware detector discovers when it starts that it is running from inside the SetUp routine while the SetUp routine is in Safe Recovery mode (see Chapter 6), it merely appends new hardware detection entries to the end of the existing **detlog.txt**. But if the auto hardware detector comes to life and finds it's running outside Safe Recovery mode, and it sees that there's an existing **detlog.txt** in the root directory of the boot drive, it renames that file **detlog.old** before creating a new, clean **detlog.txt**.

That means, in general, if the auto hardware detection routines freeze, you can open up **detlog.txt**, take a look at the final entry (see Figure 7-1 for an example of a crash during detection of a CD-ROM drive), and have a pretty good idea of what was happening when the detector went belly-up. *You* can. The *computer* doesn't; after all, **detlog.txt** is for human consumption only.

Instead, every time **sysdetmg.dll** is about to try something the least bit likely to cause your system to lock up, it updates **detlog.txt**, then creates a binary file called **detcrash.log** in the root directory of the boot drive that

Figure 7-1.
detlog.txt logs
a crash

```
NewDanger: *:DETECTMITSUMI was crashed by *:DETECTSONYCD

LogDangerRes: new crash func. *:DETECTSONYCD

IO=310-313
```

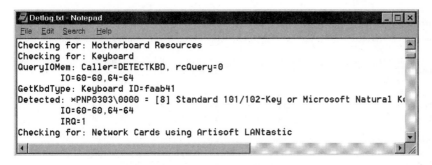

Figure 7-2. `sysdetmg.dll` searches for a keyboard

says something like, "I'm about to try to find such-and-such hardware at thus-and-so location." If your system hangs during the detection and you restart in Safe Recovery mode, `sysdetmg.dll` immediately looks for a `detcrash.log` file.

If one exists, `sysdetmg.dll` is smart enough to fast forward to the detection point that caused the hang, *skip over* the bad detection step—the one that locked up the machine—and continue with the next attempted detection in its list. That's the brilliance of hardware autodetection and the core of Win98's Automatic Skip Driver technology.

Would that the documentation were so brilliant. Don't trust what the Windows Resource Kit says about `detcrash.log`. It's wrong, repeatedly.

 Funny how the WRK keeps saying that `detcrash.log` is created if the hardware detection procedure locks up the machine. Kinda hard to create a file after your machine is locked up, eh?

When the hardware autodetection completes successfully, it deletes any existing `detcrash.log`, but it preserves `detlog.txt` in case you should ever need it.

If you're interested in a detailed definition of `detlog.txt` entries, look in Chapter 5 of the Windows Resource Kit, but to give you a taste of what's up, let's try this entry from a `detlog` on for size (Figure 7-2). We trace it all the way back to its origins, a key step missing in all the existing documentation.

As you can see, `sysdetmg.dll` gives you a full, almost-English-language analysis of what it is trying to find, and when it finds the hardware it's looking for, it tells you precisely what it found. (Bravo, Redmond!) In this case, it's looking for the keyboard by querying I/O locations 60 and 64. It detected a keyboard of the type PNP0303, which is a standard keyboard, using I/O locations 60 and 64, and IRQ 1. Cool.

You might think `sysdetmg.dll` is smart—but wait, it's even smarter than you think! This hardware detection stuff isn't hardcoded into the program. Instead, Microsoft designed it to be spoon-fed by a file called `msdet.inf`, which is located in your Win98 `\windows\inf` folder. For example, the line in `msdet.inf` that tells `sysdetmg.dll` to go out and search for a keyboard looks like Figure 7-3.

The **BUS_ALL** value says that **DetectKbd** should be run for any (ISA, EISA, or MCA) bus machine. The **RISK_VERYLOW** value tells `sysdetmg.dll` that the chance of hanging the PC when running **DetectKbd** is, uh, very low.

Figure 7-3.
DetectKbd in
msdet.inf

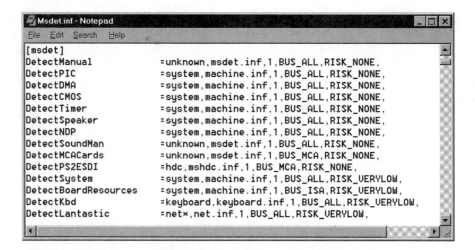

```
Msdet.inf - Notepad

File  Edit  Search  Help

[msdet]
DetectManual            =unknown,msdet.inf,1,BUS_ALL,RISK_NONE,
DetectPIC               =system,machine.inf,1,BUS_ALL,RISK_NONE,
DetectDMA               =system,machine.inf,1,BUS_ALL,RISK_NONE,
DetectCMOS              =system,machine.inf,1,BUS_ALL,RISK_NONE,
DetectTimer             =system,machine.inf,1,BUS_ALL,RISK_NONE,
DetectSpeaker           =system,machine.inf,1,BUS_ALL,RISK_NONE,
DetectNDP               =system,machine.inf,1,BUS_ALL,RISK_NONE,
DetectSoundMan          =unknown,msdet.inf,1,BUS_ALL,RISK_NONE,
DetectMCACards          =unknown,msdet.inf,1,BUS_MCA,RISK_NONE,
DetectPS2ESDI           =hdc,mshdc.inf,1,BUS_MCA,RISK_NONE,
DetectSystem            =system,machine.inf,1,BUS_ALL,RISK_VERYLOW,
DetectBoardResources    =system,machine.inf,1,BUS_ISA,RISK_VERYLOW,
DetectKbd               =keyboard,keyboard.inf,1,BUS_ALL,RISK_VERYLOW,
DetectLantastic         =net×,net.inf,1,BUS_ALL,RISK_VERYLOW,
```

Figure 7-4.
PNP0303 entry
for an enhanced
keyboard

```
Keyboard.inf - Notepad

File  Edit  Search  Help

[MS_KBD]
%×PNP0300.DeviceDesc%  = PC_XT_83_Inst,×PNP0300         ;PC/XT (83-Key)
%×PNP0301.DeviceDesc%  = PC_AT_84_Inst,×PNP0301         ;PC/AT (84-Key)
%×PNP0302.DeviceDesc%  = PC_XT_84_Inst,×PNP0302         ;PC/XT (84-Key)
%×PNP0303.DeviceDesc%  = PC_AT_Enh_Inst,×PNP0303        ;PC/AT Enh(101/102-Key)
%×PNP0304.DeviceDesc%  = Olivetti_83_Inst,×PNP0304      ;Olivetti (83-Key)
%×PNP0305.DeviceDesc%  = Olivetti_102_Inst,×PNP0305     ;Olivetti (102-Key)
%×PNP0306.DeviceDesc%  = Olivetti_86_Inst,×PNP0306      ;Olivetti (86-Key)
%×PNP0309.DeviceDesc%  = Olivetti_101_102_Inst,×PNP0309 ;Olivetti (101/102-Key)
%×PNP030a.DeviceDesc%  = ATT_302_Inst,×PNP030a          ;AT&T 302
%×PNP030b.DeviceDesc%  = PC_AT_Enh_Inst,×PNP030b        ;Default keyboard
%×CPQA0D7.DeviceDesc%  = PC_AT_Enh_Inst,×CPQA0D7
```

Moreover, the **keyboard.inf** value instructs **sysdetmg.dll** to look for details about detecting a keyboard in the file **keyboard.inf**, located in the Win98 **\windows\inf** folder. Buried down in **keyboard.inf**, you'll find an entry that looks like the PNP0303 line in Figure 7-4. Then, later in the file, you'll get the reference in Figure 7-5, which apparently tells **sysdetmg.dll** which VxD virtual device driver to use for this particular keyboard (it gets mashed into

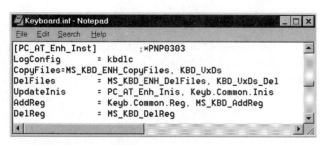

```
Keyboard.inf - Notepad

File  Edit  Search  Help

[PC_AT_Enh_Inst]        ;×PNP0303
LogConfig       = kbdlc
CopyFiles=MS_KBD_ENH_CopyFiles, KBD_UxDs
DelFiles        = MS_KBD_ENH_DelFiles, KBD_UxDs_Del
UpdateInis      = PC_AT_Enh_Inis, Keyb.Common.Inis
AddReg          = Keyb.Common.Reg, MS_KBD_AddReg
DelReg          = MS_KBD_DelReg
```

\windows\system\vmm32.vxd) and which entries to apply to the Registry. If you've ever wondered how the hardware autodetection routine figures out which VxDs and Registry entries are associated with a particular device, it's all buried here, down a couple of levels in huge **.inf** files.

Figure 7-5. Nitty-gritty on PC_AT_Enh_Inst

Ever wonder why there are hundreds of `.inf` files? Consider. It takes all this to detect the most common kind of keyboard. Then think about what's necessary to find and properly hook up an obscure, buggy, old network interface card!

netlog.txt

As you might imagine, a big, tough part of hardware autodetection lies in figuring out what kind of network devices are attached to your computer and which network protocols should be installed. The initial detection of network cards occurs during normal hardware detection, triggered by lines like this in **msdet.inf** that prompt **sysdetmg.dll** to look for an Intel EtherExpress 16 network interface card:

```
DetectEE16 =net,net.inf,BUS_ISA,RISK_DELICATE,
```

which, tied in with a **net.inf** line like this

```
*pnp812d=netee16.inf
```

to link to entries like this in **netee16.inf**

```
[*PNP812D.ndi]
AddReg=*pnp812d.ndi.reg,EXP16.ndi.reg
LogConfig=*pnp812d.LogConfig
```

can result in a **detlog.txt** entry that looks like the one in Figure 7-6.

```
Detlog.txt - Notepad
File  Edit  Search  Help
Checking for: Intel EtherExpress 16 or 16TP Network Adapter
NCD: detecting net card ×pnp812d
QueryIOMem: Caller=DETECTEE16, rcQuery=0
        IO=300-30f
NetAvoidIO: 300-30f
QueryIOMem: Caller=DETECTEE16, rcQuery=0
        IO=300-30f
DetFlags: 100000
Detected: ×PNP812D\0000 = [9] Intel EtherExpress 16 or 16TP ISA
        IO=300-30f
        IRQ=9
```

Figure 7-6. sysdetmg.dll finds an Intel EtherExpress 16 card

Figure 7-6 correctly identifies an EtherExpress 16 card, its I/O address, and IRQ. But wait! We aren't done yet. Network configuration is so hairy that when the hardware autodetector encounters a network card or a modem, it starts (are you ready for this?) *yet another* log file, called **netlog.txt** located in your boot drive's root directory, that records the details of installing services and protocols on the network card and dial-up adapter.

This makes absolutely no sense, but while **detlog.txt** is marked as a hidden file and thus takes some effort to peek at, **netlog.txt** has no restrictions at all. Why? Who knows.

**Figure 7-7.
Writing to** `p.ini`

```
Netlog.txt - Notepad
File  Edit  Search  Help
NETDI:  Wrote p.ini:DriverName=EXP16$, sect: EXP16$
NETDI:     GenInstallDriver, C:\WINDOWS\INF\NETEE16.INF,exp16.ndis2
```

**Figure 7-8.
The mysterious**
`p.ini`**, aka**
`protocol.ini`

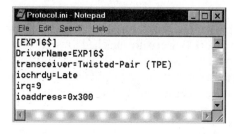

```
Protocol.ini - Notepad
File  Edit  Search  Help
[EXP16$]
DriverName=EXP16$
transceiver=Twisted-Pair (TPE)
iochrdy=Late
irq=9
ioaddress=0x300
```

Much as **msdet.inf** in the hidden \windows\inf folder provides information for detecting hardware, **netdet.ini** (note: not .inf!) in the wide-open \windows folder supplies information for identifying Netware installations and network programs such as WinFax Pro for Networks.

If you're curious about the meaning of the various lines in **netlog.txt**, or if you're stuck with a network configuration problem that has you scanning **netlog.txt** for some insight, there's a very brief explanation of some of the entries in the Windows Resource Kit, Chapter 5.

 I ran through my **netlog.txt** and found quite a few lines with undocumented actions, including several like the ones in Figure 7-7 I was mighty perplexed—there's no **p.ini** on any of my machines.

 Then one day I noticed a few entries in the **\windows\protocol.ini** file on one of my machines that looked very suspicious (Figure 7-8). I'm convinced that these are the result of actions referred to by the **Wrote p.ini** entries in **netlog.txt**. Note that **protocol.ini**, much like **system.ini** and **win.ini**, can contain values that override Registry settings.

autoexec.bat and config.sys

 The Windows 98 SetUp Wizard uses and modifies several other files. We talked in Chapter 6 about its modifications to **autoexec.bat** and **config.sys** specifically to make those files peacefully coexist with Win98. But there's one modification I didn't mention then, just to keep from confusing an already cloudy situation.

Have you been wondering how the Win98 SetUp Wizard figures out if it's starting out new or if it's been restarted after the PC locked up? In the latter case, the Wizard asks if you want to proceed in Safe Recovery mode, thus bypassing whatever glitch caused SetUp to fail in the first place. How does it know? The trick lies in modifications the SetUp routine makes to **autoexec.bat** before it starts mucking around with your system.

To help manage all sorts of temporary SetUp-only files, SetUp creates a temporary directory on your boot drive called **\wininst0.400**. If you've crashed and seen a strange directory sitting around with that name, it was left there by the SetUp routine. When you start SetUp, it sticks a DOS batch program called **suwarn.bat** in that temporary directory. **suwarn.bat**'s only purpose in life is to start SetUp with a prompt asking the user if he or she wants to continue in Safe Recovery mode.

The trick? Once **suwarn.bat** is in place and before it does anything at all significant to your system, SetUp puts these two lines at the beginning of your **autoexec.bat** file (each of these is a single line in the batch file although it is wrapped in the text below):

```
@if exist c:\wininst0.400\suwarn.bat call
c:\wininst0.400\suwarn.bat

@if exist c:\wininst0.400\suwarn.bat del
c:\wininst0.400\suwarn.bat
```

Those lines say, simply, if **suwarn.bat** exists, run it and then delete it. If you restart your PC because it froze during a hardware detection phase, those two lines zip you back into SetUp's Safe Recovery mode. Ingeniously simple.

Chapter 6 in this book and Chapter 5 in the Windows Resource Kit cover most of the rest of the changes made to **autoexec.bat** and **config.sys** during SetUp.

system.ini and win.ini

If you installed Win98 on top of Windows 3.1, your **system.ini** and **win.ini** files are bound to be a jumbled mess. Chapter 5 of the Windows Resource Kit will tell you which entries are altered by the SetUp routine. The rest of the garbage in those files may date back to three weeks before the beginning of time, and there's precious little you can do about it.

On the other hand, if you installed Win98 to a new directory or a clean hard drive, your **system.ini** and **win.ini** should look pretty much like typical Windows 3.1 versions. (At the risk of flagellating an expired equine, the original *Mother of All Windows Books,* ISBN 0-201-62475-3, covers these topics at length.) **system.ini** has sections marked **[boot]**, **[keyboard]**, **[boot.description]**, **[386Enh]**, **[drivers]**, **[mci]**, and **[NonWindowsApp]**, all of which look like their Win3.1 brethren. **[Password Lists]** and **[drivers32]** are new but self-explanatory.

In **win.ini**, **[windows]**, **[Desktop]**, **[intl]**, **[FontSubstitutes]**, **[Compatibility]** (ten times its old size with a similar purpose but—surprise—none of these entries are migrated to the Registry; they're read on startup and somehow stored internally, outside the Registry), **[mci extensions]**, **[MCICompatibility]**, **[Extensions]**, **[Ports]**, **[embedding]**, **[PrinterPorts]**, **[Devices]**, and **[colors]** look much as they did under Win3.1. **[Compatibility32]**, **[Compatibility95]**, and **[ModuleCompatibility]** are new sections, but they're self-explanatory, too.

There's one change that isn't obvious. In `win.ini` (whether you installed Win98 on top of Win95 or Win3.1 or into a new directory), there's a new entry that looks like this:

```
[Pscript.drv]
    ATMWorkaround=1
```

No, it isn't a secret Microsoft plot to take over what little is left of the Adobe Type Manager (ATM) world. It's just a flag that keeps earlier versions of ATM from clobbering the print driver. Apparently older versions of ATM write over a previously unclaimed part of the print driver. Win95 reclaimed that real estate as its own, and Win98 wants it, too. `ATMWorkaround=1` lets the two live in détente.

 Drat! And here I thought I had another good Microsoft conspiracy theory.

 You know, if this were a fix of a Microsoft product, you guys would be all over me, but since it's an Adobe product, I'm a great guy. The fact that I've added a fix for an Adobe product in `win.ini` should mean that there is nothing wrong in the Office fixes you complain about later, shouldn't it?

■ Startup

I saw "Hamlet, Prince of Denmark" played,
but now the old plays begin to disgust this refined age.

—JOHN EVELYN, *Diary,* November 26, 1661

Another morass of files surrounds Win98's startup sequence. Two of the files are particularly important, one for diagnosing problems, the other for allowing you to change some of Win98's startup behavior. Though this be madness, yet there is method in't . . .

bootlog.txt

When you start Win98, you can tell it to produce a boot log by pressing **F8** immediately after the initial startup beep and then choosing option 2 from the Windows 98 Startup Menu. The boot log, a simple text file called **bootlog.txt** (marked hidden and located in the root directory of the boot drive), contains hundreds of lines of detail about the Win98 startup process. A boot log is also produced automatically when you first boot Win98, at the tail end of the SetUp sequence.

Actually, Windows maintains two generations of boot logs. If you tell Windows 98 that you want a boot log and it discovers there's already a file called **bootlog.txt** in the root directory, that file is renamed **bootlog.prv** before Win98 creates a new **bootlog.txt**.

 Why **bootlog.prv**? I mean, all the other cycled-out files are called **.old**. I guess **.prv** must mean *previous*. Certainly is a strange inconsistency. And why on earth are both **bootlog.txt** and **bootlog.prv** marked hidden? Their only possible reason is to inform prying eyes of the progress of a Win98 boot.

The boot log contains a blow-by-blow description of what gets loaded and when and if any problems were encountered in the process. If something goes seriously wrong when you try to start Win98, creating a boot log and then scanning the tail end of **bootlog.txt** may provide some insight into what went awry.

The boot log starts by telling you if the real mode drivers—typically **himem**, **ifshlp**, and **setver**—loaded properly. Then it tells you, one at a time, whether each of the dozens of virtual device drivers loaded correctly and whether they initialized properly. After that, the boot log notes loading of the system files, like **gdi.exe** and **user.exe**, sound and communication drivers, system fonts, mouse, keyboard, and the like and finally any installable drivers.

If your system starts acting very flaky—you can't get Win98 to boot from a SCSI drive, the mouse stops dead in its tracks, you start getting SHARE violations, or the print spooler suddenly croaks—it would be worth the effort to run a boot log and scan for the string "fail." Usually VxDs that fail to load do so for a good reason (they aren't needed or won't work on your machine), but occasionally a bit gets flipped in the **.vxd** file causing a load failure. You may be able to revive a failed component by reconfirming the entire Win98 installation (just run Setup from diskette or CD) or by decompressing an appropriate file (see the later section "System File Checker"). Sometimes the fail is only because the VxD was loaded earlier. If you see a "Load Failed" line, check earlier in the log file and you'll probably find that the load succeeded.

msdos.sys

This is the first-level hacker's file, the one dangled for tire kickers and weekend PC mechanics to modify. It contains a handful of settings that produce moderately interesting effects in the Win98 startup process. It's a simple **.ini**-style file, with sections, keys, and values—a far cry from the old DOS 6 (and earlier) **msdos.sys**, which was an impenetrable binary file.

All the kick-butt Win98 power is in the Registry, of course. If you get a minor jolt out of rigging your **msdos.sys**, you're in for the rush of a lifetime when you twiddle the bits in your Registry. Patience. That's Chapter 9.

Let's start by taking off the training wheels. Right click My Computer, pick Explorer. If you haven't already rigged Explorer to show all your files, click on View, then Options, make sure the "Show All Files" button is checked,

Figure 7-9.
Bone-stock
msdos.sys, from
a clean install

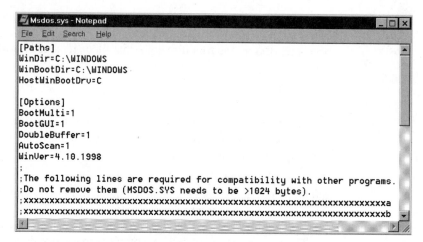

and uncheck the "Hide MS-DOS File Extensions for File Types That Are Registered" box. Now go into the root directory of your boot drive (probably **c:**), right click on Msdos.sys, and pick Properties. Clear the Read-only button. Click OK.

Back on the Explorer menu, click Edit, then Copy. Next click Edit, then Paste. If you scroll down to the bottom of the file list, you'll find a file called Copy of MSDOS.SYS. Right click on it, pick Rename, and change the name to **msdos.mom.** Good. You now have a backup copy of **msdos.sys** with a short filename that's easy to get at from the DOS command line—just in case you screw up. A simple DOS command like

```
copy c:\msdos.mom c:\msdos.sys
```

will return all your Win98 startup settings to their original upright positions.

Time to see what you have to play with. Right click on Msdos.sys, pick Open With, make sure the "Always Use This Program To Open This Kind of File" box is unchecked, scroll down, and double click on Notepad. You should see some entries like those in Figure 7-9.

Don't play around with the entries in the **[Paths]** section. Pointing **io.sys** (see Chapter 6) to the wrong directories for fundamental WinThings can lead to a severe case of indigestion—yours, of course. Think Hannibal Lector, *sans* fava beans.

 The Windows Resource Kit documents seventeen settings for the **[Options]** section. Unfortunately, it doesn't get all of them right—and all the books and articles I've seen merely parrot the incorrect official documentation. Let me see if I can set the record straight. As best I can tell, this is exactly how the Win98 startup routine[†] handles settings in **msdos.sys**.

[†]It's really **io.sys**, but I'll call it the startup routine so I don't sound so pretentious.

Step 0   Startup reads the entire **msdos.sys** file from beginning to end, figures out which settings are in the file, and keeps track of all the settings. This is very different from the way typical **.ini** files are used—programs usually look up **.ini** file values only when they need 'em. If startup doesn't like one of your settings, it'll give you an error message.

Step 1   Startup beeps.

Step 2   Startup looks at the **BootMenu=** entry. If **BootMenu=1**, it immediately brings up the **Microsoft Windows 98 Startup Menu** and jumps down to Step M1 (after Step 8). (One variation of the Startup Menu is shown here as Figure 7-10.)

Step 3   If there is no **BootMenu=** entry or if **BootMenu=0**, startup looks at the **BootKeys=** entry. If **BootKeys=0**, startup bypasses the normal monitoring for the user to hit **F8** or **Ctrl** and jumps down to Step 5.

 If you can't get **F8** or **Ctrl** to work, chances are good some furshlinger system administrator or software vendor decided to make your PC "more secure" by adding the line **BootKeys=0** to your **msdos.sys**. You can flip 'em an electronic bird by simply modifying **msdos.sys** to get rid of the offensive line. (If Win98 has been jimmied so you can't edit **msdos.sys**, just boot from a floppy and edit the sucker in DOS mode.)

Step 4   If there is no **BootKeys=** entry or if **BootKeys=1**, startup begins monitoring for key presses. If it detects an **F8** or **Ctrl** (or any of the other shortcut keys that change the startup sequence, including **F4, F5,** and several **Shift+** combinations; see Chapter 6), startup brings up the **Microsoft Windows 98 Startup Menu**, per Figure 7-10, or performs whatever action is dictated by the startup shortcut keys and skips to Step M1.

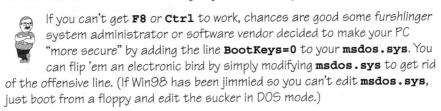

```
Microsoft Windows 98 Startup Menu
==================================

   1. Normal
   2. Logged (\BOOTLOG.TXT)
   3. Safe Mode
   4. Step-by-step confirmation
   5. Command prompt only
   6. Safe mode command prompt only
   7. Previous version of MS-DOS

Enter a choice: 1

F5=Safe mode Shift+F5=Command prompt Shift+F8=Step-by-step confirmation [N]
```

Figure 7-10. Windows 98 Startup Menu corresponding to the msdos.sys in Figure 7-9

 There used to be a setting called **BootDelay**, which, in the Win95 days, controlled how long Windows would "delay," waiting for **F8** to be pressed. (It's even documented in the Windows Resource Kit.) I'm here to tell ya, **BootDelay=** doesn't work in Windows 98, and any book or article that tells you it does is just cribbing straight from the WRK. Try it yourself. You'll see.

Step 5   Startup looks at the **Logo=** entry. If **Logo=0**, startup does not put the startup logo (see the section "**logo.sys**") on the screen. If there is no entry or **Logo=1**, the logo goes up.

 This one's really bizarre. If **Logo=0**, Windows doesn't show the splash screen, but it puts the message **Starting Windows 98 . . .** up on the screen! In several places the WRK says Windows no longer has the **Starting Windows x . . .** message. ('Course in several other places, it refers to the message as if it still existed.) Another truly strange inconsistency. My small mind is hobgoblined.

 I'm not sure why, but one of the most-often-asked questions about earlier versions of Windows was "How do I disable the startup screen?" (Remember **win :?**) Some folks felt that splashing the screen on the monitor somehow slowed down Windows' loading—when in fact the screen made at most a fraction-of-a-second difference. If you really want to disable the startup screen in Win98, it's as easy as editing **msdos.sys** and putting the line **Logo=0** in the **[Options]** section. Before you do that, though, keep in mind that Win98 does take a substantial amount of time to load, and many people—myself included—get antsy when they don't see anything but a dumb blinking cursor.

 The Windows Resource Kit says that setting **Logo=0** "also avoids hooking a variety of interrupts that can create incompatibilities with certain memory managers from other vendors." I don't know firsthand if that is true, but if it is, you gotta ask yourself why people don't get rid of their incompatible memory managers! Dumb, dumb, dumb.

Step 6   Startup runs through **config.sys** and **autoexec.bat**, then checks the **BootGUI=** entry. If **BootGUI=0**, startup dumps you out at the DOS 7 command prompt. As best I can tell, the net result is exactly the same as if you had hit **F8** or **Ctrl**, then chosen **Command prompt only**. (DOS environment variables and memory allocations appear to be identical.) When you're at the command prompt, you can type **win** to get Win98 started.

Step 7   Next, startup looks to see if you shut down Windows 98 "properly" the last time you ran it. "Properly" in this case means clicking Start, then Shutdown, then Shutdown. If you didn't shut down in the prescribed manner— say, Windows 98 hit a GPF and locked up, or the cat chewed through your power cord—startup looks in **msdos.sys** for an entry called **AutoScan=**.

If you have **AutoScan=0** in **msdos.sys**, startup skips down to Step 8. In most other cases, startup runs ScanDisk, admonishing you to not shut down so carelessly in the future. (As if it were your fault!)

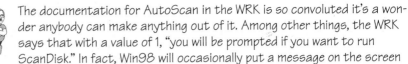

The documentation for AutoScan in the WRK is so convoluted it's a wonder anybody can make anything out of it. Among other things, the WRK says that with a value of 1, "you will be prompted if you want to run ScanDisk." In fact, Win98 will occasionally put a message on the screen saying it's going to run ScanDisk and you can push any key to continue. (Not exactly a prompt, asking if you want to run ScanDisk, eh?) We got this preliminary warning message only sporadically—it most certainly does not appear on every machine every time there's an aborted shutdown and **AutoScan=1**.

The WRK also talks about a value of 2. Every time we used an AutoScan value of 2 and there was an aborted shutdown, ScanDisk ran without any preliminary warning message.

What triggers the message remains a mystery to me.

Step 8   That's all she wrote; **msdos.sys** is done. Startup continues in the usual way, loading things, running **winstart.bat**, and the like, finally bringing up the Desktop and stepping out of the way to let you go at it.

Several settings in **msdos.sys** control the way the startup routine handles the Startup Menu. If you find yourself in the Startup Menu—whether by hitting **F8** or **Ctrl** at the right time or using **BootMenu=1** in **msdos.sys**—these are the steps startup takes.

Step M1   Startup figures out if it needs to put a timer on the Startup Menu screen. (The timer controls how long startup will show the screen, waiting for the user to type something before taking off with the default action.) If startup determines that it got to this point by pressing **F8**, there's no timer, and the Startup Menu will wait until hell freezes over for the user to type something. If startup determines that it got to this point in any other way (typically, **Ctrl** or **BootMenu=1**), it looks at the **BootMenuDelay=** setting and uses the indicated number of seconds for the timer. If there's no **BootMenuDelay=** setting, startup uses 30 seconds.

Step M2   Startup determines which Startup Menu options are valid. Six options are always available: **Normal**, **Logged**, **Safe mode**, **Step-by-step confirmation**, **Command prompt only**, and **Safe mode command prompt only**. If **BootMulti=1**, the option **Previous version of MS-DOS** is added to the end of the option list, providing Win98 can find the old version of DOS. (If **BootMulti=0** or there is no **BootMulti=** entry, there's no such option.) The result is a list of six or seven options.

Win95 had another entry, named **Network=**, which controlled something with an option called **Safe Mode with Network Support**. For whatever reason, MS doesn't offer that option any more.

Step M3 Startup determines whether the user pushed an invalid shortcut key. If you pushed **F4**, which is the shortcut key for **Previous version of MS-DOS** and **BootMulti=0**—thus disabling the option—the startup routine jumps back up to Step 5 and continues with a normal startup. It's not nice to fool Mother Nature.

Step M4 The options are numbered sequentially (from 1 to 6 or 7, depending on the entries constructed in Step M2), and the Startup Menu appears on the screen, with a timer if appropriate (as determined in Step M1). Refer to Figure 7-10.

Step M5 Startup looks for a **BootMenuDefault=** entry and highlights the indicated number on the Startup Menu as the default choice. If the **BootMenuDefault=** number is less than one or if there is no entry, option 1 is used as the default. If **BootMenuDefault=** is greater than the maximum number of options, the last option is used as the default.

Step M6 The user makes a choice or the timer expires with a default option, and startup continues as explained in Chapter 6. If option 1 is chosen, startup effectively jumps back up to Step 5.

 The Windows Resource Kit documents a setting called **BootFailSafe=**. Hey, maybe it works on all the machines in Redmond, but I can't get it to work on any machine around here. I consistently receive **Invalid Entry in MSDOS.SYS** error messages whenever I try. Most of the documentation on **BootMenuDefault=** is all wrong, too.

 The WRK also documents a setting called **BootWarn=**. Based on the description in the documentation, I thought it might control the message you get when you boot into Win98 in Safe mode—you know the one, **Windows is running in Safe mode. This special diagnostic mode of Windows . . .** etc., etc. I also thought it might toss up a warning when you try to go into Safe mode from the Startup Menu. No dice. Couldn't get it to do anything.

 There are several other documented settings shown in Chapter 5 of the WRK. **BootWin=** is supposed to disable Win98 as the operating system. I decided I'd rather drink hemlock than give that one a try and recommend you do likewise. **DblSpace=** is supposed to disable Double-Space; similarly for **DrvSpace=**. **Double-Buffer=** is supposed to be useful with double-buffered SCSI drives. And **LoadTop=** is supposed to disable loading DOS in upper memory, presumably for Netware compatibility. If you need any of those, consult the official documentation—and good luck.

ios.ini, ios.log

Several additional files control your startup destiny.

The startup routine, **io.sys**, uses the file **\windows\ios.ini** (also known as the "Safe Driver List") to determine if it can replace "safe" real mode drivers with protected mode drivers. If it decides to boot out a real mode driver and replace it with a protected mode driver, it writes a log of that action in **\windows\ios.log**. If you're getting strange driver problems, check the Windows Resource Kit for a description of the Safe Driver List entries.

Logon Password

If you don't see a network logon screen every time you start Windows 98, you can safely skip this section and go on down to "Other Files and Programs."

 Wish I had a nickel for every time I've been asked about logon passwords. While it's true that passwords help provide a more secure computing environment, it's also true that passwords provide the single simplest way to shoot yourself in the foot. If your PC is located in an area where just anybody can saunter in and log on and you're connected to a network with sensitive data that isn't protected, you probably need a password. Otherwise . . . well, think about it.

 If you want to know how to avoid logging on, see the discussion in Chapter 4.

Note that you can set up separate users on one machine—ideal for a home, where several family members want to use the same machine but maintain their own preferences for wallpaper, icons, and the like; or for an office with shared PCs—*without requiring passwords.* Simply make sure each user has a unique logon user name and Win98 will take care of the rest (see Chapter 3).

 Hey, my middle name is security. I know all about this game. Wherever there are passwords, you find that the single most common complaint is "I forgot my password. How do I set it to something I'll remember?" Fortunately, Win98 comes with its own picklock. You bypass logon security by deleting the **username.pwl** *file. For example, if your logon user name is woody, deleting the file* **\windows\woody.pwl** *and rebooting will let you log onto the machine as woody, and then you can change the password to anything you like. It's really that simple, although you may have to use the* **F8** *Win98 startup trick to get to a command prompt and delete the file. The* **.pwl** *file isn't even marked hidden or system, so a simple* **Del** *command will zap it out. No wonder they call Win98 insecure . . .*

Or consider this scenario. By booting to a DOS prompt, someone can move **woody.pwl** to another directory, muck around as you described, and then move **woody.pwl** back, so when you reboot, password problems won't alert you to what's happened.

The file **username.pwl** contains all your system passwords stored in a one-way encrypted format. ("One-way encrypted" means that there's a validation program that takes the password you type into the computer, scrambles it, then compares the results of the scrambling with what's stored in the **.pwl** file. You can't go backward; that is, you can't figure out the original password by looking at the scrambled entry in the **.pwl** file.)

If you delete **username.pwl**, you delete not only the logon password but other system passwords that aren't set up on your domain as well, possibly including the passwords you need to get onto disk drives or printers on connected Windows machines, passwords for Internet Explorer, Exchange (for example, to log onto Microsoft Network), Netware passwords, and the password on Windows NT servers.

While we're on the subject of passwords, do you know how to bypass the screen saver password? We talk about it more in Chapter 8, but the trick is that you have to hit the Reset button on your PC (or turn the power off, then back on again), log on with your user name and password, and before the screen saver kicks in, right click on the Desktop, pick Properties, then the Screen Saver tab, and uncheck the Password Protected box.

■ System Files

None cuts a diamond but a diamond.

—JOHN WEBSTER, *The Malcontent*, 1604

Windows 98 contains an extensive set of tools for keeping track of the family jewels—the system files that make Win98 work. If Win98 begins to act oddly and you think it may be because one of the key files has been clobbered, this is the place to look.

System File Checker

Have you ever wished that Windows could take a look at its key files and tell you if any of them are damaged? Well, with Windows 98, your wish has come true.

The only problem with the System File Checker? It's tucked away in a backwater location you'd never find unless you knew about it. To start the System File Checker, you have to run the System Information Utility (Start, Programs, Accessories, System Tools, System Information), then click Tools and System File Checker.

There's a much faster way to start SFC. Just click Start and Run, type **sfc**, and hit **Enter**. Or, if you have the full WRK, run Quick Launch Express, which puts an icon in the Notification Area that pops up a launch menu for a variety of system tools including System File Checker.

Figure 7-11. System File Checker set to scan

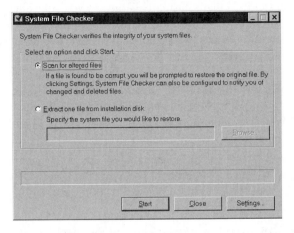

In fact, System File Checker looks at all your **.dll, .exe, .sys, .vxd** and other files—including file types and locations you can specify—to see if any of them have become corrupt.

The System File Checker (Figure 7-11) actually looks inside all the indicated files and constructs something called a CRC (Cyclic Redundancy Check number). If any part of the file changes—just one little bit gets flipped—the CRC changes as well. By comparing a "known good" CRC with the CRC that's calculated, the System File Checker can tell if the file has been altered (Figure 7-12). The "known good" CRCs are stored in a file called **default.sfc** in the **\windows** folder.

There are several options you can set for System File Checker's efforts by hitting the Settings . . . button (Figure 7-13). To pick additional file types and locations, click the Search Criteria tab, and System File Checker adds those files to the list of the ones it scans.

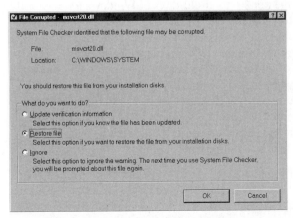

Figure 7-12. Options for a file that doesn't match the "known good" CRC

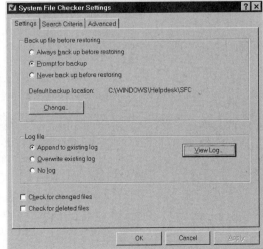

Figure 7-13. Options for running SFC

If the CRC for a given file doesn't match the "known good" CRC that's been stored away—most often because some problem with your hard drive wreaked havoc on one of the files—the System File Checker offers you three options.

- **Update verification information.** If you know for a fact that the version of the system file that's currently sitting on your machine is a good one, you can tell the System File Checker to replace the "known good" CRC information in **default.sfc** with the CRC that was just calculated. Use this option sparingly and only if you know for a fact that the file in question is valid.

- **Restore the file.** If the CRCs don't match, the System File Checker helps you restore the original version of the system file by pulling it off the original Win98 installation CD using another utility called Extract File. We go into more detail on that in the next section.

- **Ignore.** If you don't know what to do and your machine seems to be working well enough, it's probably best to click Ignore. That gives you a chance to try your system for a while, see if things are working well, and if so, re-run the System File Checker.

It's important to realize that the System File Checker really does look inside every single system file and every additional type of file you specify on the Search Criteria tab, and that it will identify a single changed bit.

 If you ever elect to "Update verification information" and later decide that it was a mistake, you can restore the list of CRCs to its original state. Replace **default.sfc** with a file called **default.sf0** and run the System File Checker again.

Extract File

What if one of your system files has gone belly-up? How do you get back a good version of the file? In the not-so-good-old-days of Windows 95, your only choice, in many cases, was to manually extract the original file from the installation CD—a very difficult task, as you had to know where the original file was located, and you had to use an inscrutable DOS command called **extract**.

Windows 98 takes care of all that. If you click the lower button in the System File Checker dialog, type the name of the file you want to retrieve from the Win98 installation CD (Figure 7-14), and click Start, Win98's Extract File utility kicks in. The Extract File utility scans the contents of all the compressed (**.cab**) files in the folder you specify (Figure 7-15) and if the indicated file is found, copies the file to the location you provide.

 There's a very important trick to using Extract File: you have to point to the precise folder that contains the **.cab** files you want to have scanned. Thus, if you're trying to retrieve a system file from the Win98 installation CD, you have to go all the way into the **\win98** folder.

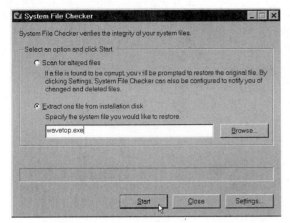

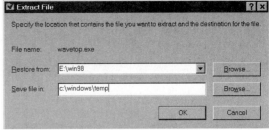

Figure 7-15. Extract File will pull individual files out of `.cab` (compressed) libraries

Figure 7-14. Specify which file you want to extract, and click Start

Figure 7-16. Extract File won't let you accidentally overwrite an existing file

Even though the Extract File utility is accessible only through this convoluted series of steps, it works fine on any `.cab` files—it isn't limited to Win98 SetUp files. But you have to give it a folder with at least one `.cab` file: if you tell it to look in a specific `.cab` file, it won't work!

If you try to extract a file out of a CAB and overwrite an existing file, the utility will warn you (Figure 7-16), offering to make a backup copy in the location of your choice. That's a very reassuring feature.

 Wait a minute. What if I don't know the precise name of the system file I want to restore? I mean, these filenames can get pretty goosey, and if I don't know the exact filename, Extract File doesn't do any good.

 Ah, for that you need the wonderful new Windows 98 program called the Microsoft File Information utility.

 Yep, FileInfo is a dandy little utility. But you won't find it here. To get it working, you have install the WRK Sampler on the Windows CD (browse to **\tools\reskit** and run **setup.exe**), launch the Tools Management Console, er, Microsoft Management Console, then you have to look under "M" for "Microsoft," and then . . . check out the install details in Chapter 5.

OK, OK, I get the picture. It's another one of those enormously useful hidden utilities, just like Extract File, only this one is in a completely different location and unless you knew it already existed, you'd never be able to find it.

Precisely.

Windows File Information

This enormously useful utility, part of the Windows Resource Kit Tools Sampler, gives you important details about every single file included in Windows 98. If you hit a system file and want to know what it does—or if you know something's gone wrong with a program but can't figure out what the program's filename might be—this is the place to go spelunking.

To bring up the Microsoft File Information utility, go into the Tools Management Console, aka the Microsoft Management Console, by clicking on Start, Programs, Windows 98 Resource Kit, Tools Management Console. Click the "D to O" folder at the left, and you'll see something like Figure 7-17.

Hey, Barry! You weren't kidding. This really is filed under "M" for "Murder," uh, "Microsoft."

Yep. Oh. Didja notice how this entry lists "Windows 98" and "Internet Explorer" as if they're two different products? Guess the Political Correctness Committee at Microsoft missed this one.

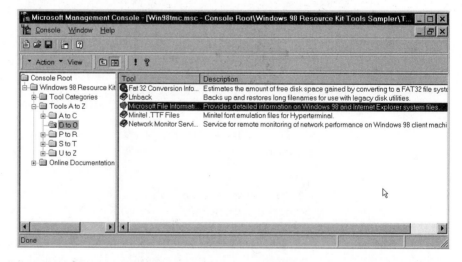

Figure 7-17. Tools, er, Microsoft Management Console—the easiest way to File Information

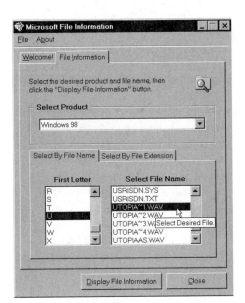

**Figure 7-18.
Pick a file that
piques your
curiosity**

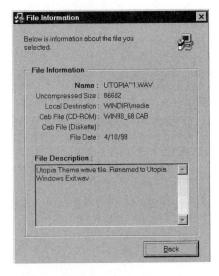

**Figure 7-19. File Information tells
you not only where the file is located but where it extracts to**

Double click Microsoft File Information on the right and the FileInfo utility
magically appears (Figure 7-18).

The Welcome tab is nothing more than a commercial for Microsoft's Tech-
Net, an additional-charge source of technical information about Microsoft's
products. The guts of FileInfo sit on the File Information tab.

FileInfo lets you look up filenames in two different ways: either alphabetized by filename or based on the filename extension (e.g., **.dll**, **.exe**,
.sys). Simply click on a file that you're interested in and click Display File
Information.

The information includes the following (Figure 7-19).

- Filename in old DOS 8.3 form
- Size of the file when it's decompressed and the location where the in-
  staller will place the file (**WINDIR = C:\windows**)
- Which CAB file contains this file, both on CD and on diskette (if there's no
  entry for Diskette, that means this file isn't available on the diskette version
  of Win98)
- Creation date for the file
- Description—usually accurate

Given all that information, you can usually figure out which file you're looking for.

Figure 7-20.
If you have
Microsoft Access,
you can get at
the FileInfo data
directly

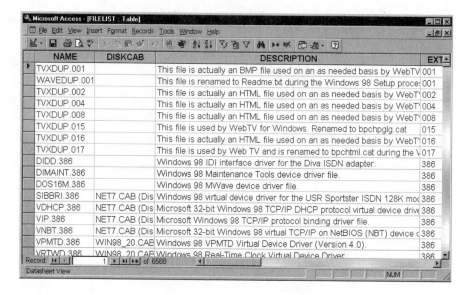

NAME	DISKCAB	DESCRIPTION	EXT
TVXDUP.001		This file is actually an BMP file used on an as needed basis by WebTV	001
WAVEDUP.001		This file is renamed to Readme.txt during the Windows 98 Setup proce	001
TVXDUP.002		This file is actually an HTML file used on an as needed basis by WebTV	002
TVXDUP.004		This file is actually an HTML file used on an as needed basis by WebTV	004
TVXDUP.008		This file is actually an HTML file used on an as needed basis by WebTV	008
TVXDUP.015		This file is used by WebTV for Windows. Renamed to bpchpglg.cat	015
TVXDUP.016		This file is actually an HTML file used on an as needed basis by WebTV	016
TVXDUP.017		This file is used by Web TV and is renamed to bpchtml.cat during the V	017
DIDD.386		Windows 98 IDI interface driver for the Diva ISDN adapter.	386
DIMAINT.386		Windows 98 Maintenance Tools device driver file.	386
DOS16M.386		Windows 98 MWave device driver file.	386
SIBBRI.386	NET7.CAB (Dis	Windows 98 virtual device driver for the USR Sportster ISDN 128K mod	386
VDHCP.386	NET7.CAB (Dis	Microsoft 32-bit Windows 98 TCP/IP DHCP protocol virtual device drive	386
VIP.386	NET7.CAB (Dis	Microsoft Windows 98 TCP/IP protocol binding driver file.	386
VNBT.386	NET7.CAB (Dis	Microsoft 32-bit Windows 98 virtual TCP/IP on NetBIOS (NBT) device d	386
VPMTD.386	WIN98_20.CAE	Windows 98 VPMTD Virtual Device Driver (Version 4.0).	386
VRTWD.386	WIN98_20.CAE	Windows 98 Real-Time Clock Virtual Device Driver	386

Ah, but you can do better! You needn't limit yourself to searching based on the first letter of the filename or the filename extension. In fact, you can search for any text in any of the fields—if you have Microsoft Access and you know the trick!

The Microsoft File Information utility is driven by a data file called **win98.mfi**, located in the **C:\Program Files\Win98RK** folder. Guess what? It's a simple Access **.mdb** database, and if you have Access on your machine, you can get at all the data directly.

Make a copy of **win98.mfi** and call it, oh, **win98.mdb**. Then double click on the new file. Double click the FILELIST table, and you'll see all the FileInfo data, as in Figure 7-20. Want to search for the phrase "extract"? Simply click the Find button on the toolbar (it looks like a pair of binoculars), type **extract** in the Find What? box, and set Match to "Any part of field." Click Find First, and Access will look in all the data fields for **extract**.

So, you can search for filename or filename extension—and you can also search for text in the description field, CAB filename, file date, size, destination, or any other data that appears in the records. You can also sort the records to come up with, say, a list of all the files that normally get copied into **C:\windows\command**. Very cool.

Version Conflict Manager

 Oy! This utility had so much promise—and it ends up being nothing but a stunted, nearly useless shadow of what could have been. Based on its name and the press hype about VCM that surrounded Windows 98's release, I just naturally assumed that the Win98 Version Conflict Manager managed conflicts in various versions of system files. It doesn't. Not even close.

Here's what really happens:

- When the Windows 98 SetUp Wizard installs Win98, it goes in like a steamroller, replacing any like-named files it may find on your PC. So, for example, if you have a file called **cspman.dll** installed on your PC in Win95 and you run the Win98 SetUp Wizard, the file is replaced by the Win98 file of the same name. Period.

- When the Win98 SetUp Wizard hits a situation where a like-named file already exists on your PC, it compares the version number of the existing file with the version number of the file installed on your PC. If Win98's version number is larger—generally indicating that the version on the Win98 CD is more recent than the one on your PC—the SetUp Wizard overwrites the old file with the one that ships on the installation CD. Period.

- On the other hand, if the version number of the file on the Win98 CD is smaller—indicating that Win98 has an older version of the file than the one already installed on your PC—the Wizard makes a copy of the "newer" file (the one on your PC) and puts it in **C:\windows\vcm**.

That's it. There's no warning. You don't have a chance to choose if Win98 should overwrite the (presumably) newer file with the older version. All you get is a copy of the (presumably) newer file and this utility called the Version Conflict Manager—tucked away safely in an obscure corner of the Win98 world.

 That may sound draconian—and we've taken some heat in the press for it—but there's a good reason why we replace "newer" versions with "older" ones. We know Win98 is stable with the "older" versions—and we have no control over the newer ones. So, while some journalists give us a hard time about VCM—one even said we made it this way to delete "competitors'" drivers! That isn't true. VCM will even overwrite newer versions of our own drivers. This isn't a case of big, bad Microsoft zapping out the little, poor competitors' drivers. It's a simple effort to make the upgrade experience better for more users.

 It's also a marvelous example of how Microsoft doesn't think through how one of its "features" will work three, six, or twelve months down the line.

**Figure 7-21.
Version Conflict
Manager deals
only with files
overwritten by
the Win98 SetUp
Wizard**

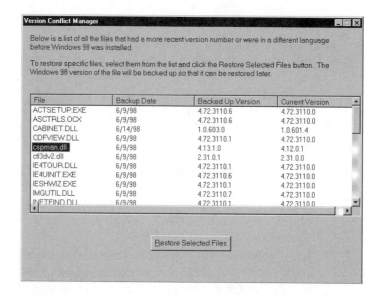

To start the Version Conflict Manager, bring up the System Information utility (Start, Programs, Accessories, System Tools, System Information), then click on Tools, then Version Conflict Manager. You'll see a report like that in Figure 7-21. Pick the file you want to restore, click Restore Selected Files, and Win98 dutifully replaces the files its installer wiped out with the version you've chosen.

 At least when the Version Conflict Manager restores a file, it remembers to change the entry in **default.sfc**, so that the next time you run the System File Checker, it'll skip over the newly restored file.

 Think how wonderful it would be if Windows tracked all overwrites of **.dll** files in Version Conflict Manager!

Sysbckup

One of the most brilliant innovations introduced in Windows 95 was contained in a rarely noticed, hidden folder called **\windows\sysbckup**. That's where Win95 kept copies of its most vulnerable system files, the programs and drivers that are so often clobbered by stupid application installation programs. You know the kind of installation program we're talking about—the ones that insist on replacing vital Windows system files with older versions without warning or even as much as a nod at the user.

Windows 95 would detect the replacement when Windows rebooted and would prompt you to copy the original version of the file, contained in **\sysbckup**, back over the version that had been installed by the renegade application's installer. In fact, Win95 had some really advanced built-in smarts to prevent those renegade programs from overwriting the family jewels in the first place. Win95 monitored certain types of installation programs to see if the installer clobbered any of the files in **\windows\sysbckup**. If Win95 found that the installer had overwritten one of those files, it actually jumped in and automatically tried to change the file back to the original version by copying from **\windows\sysbckup**. In those cases where it couldn't get the old versions re-installed, it tried to warn the user to use the Win95 SetUp disks to verify all files.

 The Windows Resource Kit says that Win98 is supposed to behave similarly: "Windows 98 restores its original DLLs after every setup application runs and for the first three startups thereafter." But for the life of me I couldn't trigger any restorations from **\sysbckup**. Hey, maybe I'm overlooking something obvious—or maybe all my test systems just fell into some sort of time warp—but it sure looks as if this is one feature we've lost in the transition from Win95 to Win98.

■ Other Files and Programs

The physician can bury his mistakes, but the architect
can only advise his client to plant vines.

—FRANK LLOYD WRIGHT, *New York Times*
Magazine, October 4, 1953

There's much more to the "techie files, techie programs" story. Here's a grab bag of insights we've gleaned.

An INI Still?

Old sacks want much patching.

—THOMAS FULLER, *Gnomologia*, 1732

Hard to believe in this brave new world of Win98 that Windows itself continues to use old-fashioned **.ini** files. Microsoft has exhorted the programming troops to move on to the Registry and leave the **.ini** files behind, all the while keeping a bunch of **.ini** files in its own closet. While some of them—notably **win.ini** and **system.ini**—have obviously been maintained for backward compatibility, and others are apparently used because Microsoft was too lazy to update old Win3.1 applications, a disturbingly large number of **.ini** files are attached to brand-new applets.

 What amazes me about several of these files is that they appear to be simple *replacements* for working with the Registry, as all "good" Windows 98 programs should. In some cases it's unavoidable. But in other cases there isn't any apparent reason for it.

ScanDisk, for example, uses **\windows\command\scandisk.ini** to store settings for use when it's run in command prompt mode (in other words, out in DOS). The Registry isn't really available at that point, so it makes sense to store the settings in an **.ini** file. If you ever wondered what kinds of settings you can make for ScanDisk, take a look at **scandisk.ini**. It's packed full of options, values, and very complete documentation on using the **.ini** file.

Similarly, **scanreg.ini** needs to be available when the Registry isn't.

 But why on earth is there a **wordpad.ini**? Or a **telephon.ini**? Not to mention all the **.ini** files associated with brand-new Windows 98 utilities: **fpxpress.ini** (for FrontPage Express), **htmlhelp.ini**, various **ie*.ini**s for Internet Explorer, even **mmc.ini** for Microsoft's all-new Management Console!

 Some of those old files are still hanging around because other people have written Windows applications that scab off the old Win3.1 files to pick up settings. In other words, we have to keep the old files around so that the Win3.1 programs don't break. A good example of that is the old Control Panel information file, **\windows\system\control.inf**, or **\windows\control.ini**. We also kept the old Program Manager info file, **\windows\progman.ini**, and the old File Manager info file, **\windows\winfile.ini**, for precisely the same reason: if we did away with them, some old programs wouldn't run any more.

 Two Windows 98 **.ini** files really boil my blood: **msoffice.ini** and **powerpnt.ini**. A clean, virgin Windows 98 install—with freshly reformatted hard drives (I even disconnected the network!)—left behind those two files. Undoubtedly, they've been included to make Office run better. But, hey, can you give me a more dramatic, simple example of how Microsoft is using its monopoly in one area (operating systems) to smooth over rough edges and thus gain a competitive advantage in another area (office suites)?

 I remember a similar bit of skulduggery years ago. Let's see. Oh yes, here it is, on page 261 of the original (Windows 3.1) version of *The Mother of All Windows Books*. Igor found a setting in **win.ini** that Microsoft slipped in to the Windows 3.1 SetUp routine:

```
[Microsoft Word 2.0]
HPDSKJET=+1
```

Its sole purpose was to force Word 2.0 to use the proper settings when printing envelopes on HP DeskJet printers.

 I've defended Microsoft for years and years on the old "Chinese wall" subject. Remember the Chinese wall? Supposedly a mythical wall erected between the Windows and the Office groups prevented the Office people from gaining inside information about Windows. The wall (since repudiated by Microsoft management) ensured that Microsoft's monopoly position in one area wouldn't be used to unfair advantage in another area. Except for a few examples we found in Windows 3.1, I've always felt pretty comfortable that Microsoft's competitors had good—if not superb—access to important details about Windows.

No, I'm not overly naive. A good friend of mine used to work for Microsoft, and his sole job was to provide Windows support for one of Microsoft Office's biggest competitors. He was a real straight shooter, and we talked about this subject many times. He worked hard to provide the competitor with the same information the Office team received, and I'm convinced that (at least back then) Microsoft management was committed to a level playing field in the applications arena.

 Well, guess what? This discovery blows the wall away. It demonstrates, incontrovertibly, that the playing field is not level. Here we have clear, indisputable evidence that Microsoft is using its monopoly in operating systems to improve its competitive position in applications.

And to think that Microsoft blew it over a couple of tiny files with settings that don't mean much to anybody.

Recycology

Where the Devil can't go he sends his grandmother.

—German proverb

 As far as I know, nobody has documented what the Recycle Bin really entails. It took a while to figure out the details, but in the end Win98 Recycology is pretty simple. And some of the details might come in very handy should you ever attempt to reconstruct a file that was accidentally deleted when you emptied the Recycle Bin.

As you know from Chapter 3, the Recycle Bin contains all deleted files from local hard disks. (Files on floppy are not placed in a Recycle Bin. Nor are files deleted from network drives. Diskette and network files are both "deleted" using the old-fashioned DOS tricks; for more details, see *The Mother of All PC Books*.) To restore a recycled file, simply double click on the Desktop's Recycle Bin. To well and truly delete all the files in the Recycle Bin, go into the Recycle Bin, click File and then Empty Recycle Bin. That's the easy part.

Here's what's going on behind the scenes. Each logical hard drive on your system (including partitions on partitioned drives and hosts for compressed drives) contains a hidden system folder called `\recycled`. Any time you delete a file on a particular drive—that is, send a file to the Recycle Bin—Windows actually moves the file to the `\recycled` folder on that drive.

When it's moved, the filename extension is retained, but the initial part of the name is changed to **dd**, followed by a number. For example, if the first file "deleted" on the **c:** drive is called **mydoc.doc**, it's moved and renamed to **C:\recycled\dd1.doc**. If the second "deleted" file is called **Some Program.lnk**, it's moved and renamed to **C:\recycled\dd2.lnk**. Note that the "deleted" files are not compressed or manipulated in any other way: they're simply moved to the appropriate **\recycled** folder and renamed— a very fast operation, as only a few bytes need to be rewritten on the disk.

So where does Win98 store the original filenames? Good question. There's a file in every **\recycled** folder called **info2**. That's it, just **info2**. We didn't dig far enough into the structure of the file to figure out its precise format, but if you look at **info** with a hex viewer, you'll see that all the original filenames and their paths are stored in **info**, in the event that Win98 needs the information to restore a recycled file. Win95 stored similar information in files called **info**.

Don't bother trying to find these folders or files with Win98's Explorer. As soon as you get into the **\recycled** folder, Explorer tosses a facade on the screen—much as it does with fonts—to hide all the inner workings from you. If you get as far as the **\recycled** folder in Explorer, you'll see a consolidated list of *all* "deleted" files in *all* the **\recycled** folders on your PC. It appears that Explorer looks in a file called **\recycled\Desktop.ini**, which has two lines like

```
[.ShellClassInfo]
CLSID={645FF040-5081-101B-9F08-00AA002F954E}
```

then uses the **CLSID** to look in the Registry for general Recycle Bin programs and settings.

The only way you'll be able to see what's really happening in your Recycle Bin is by using the DOS prompt to get into each drive's **\recycled** folder, removing the "hidden" attribute with a command like

```
attrib *.* -h
```

and then using an editor like DOS's Edit to look inside the appropriate files.

How can this information help you? Win98 "empties" the Recycle Bin by doing a plain old-fashioned DOS delete—in other words, it leaves the data intact but changes the File Allocation Table. (Again, for details, see *The Mother of All PC Books*.) If you've emptied the Recycle Bin accidentally and you're trying to restore a deleted file by using the old DOS undelete command, the files you want to look at are called **dd*.***, where the filename extension matches the extension of the file you accidentally clobbered. The "emptied" Recycle Bin files are located in the appropriate drive's **\recycled** folder, uh, subdirectory. That should get you pointed in the right direction. Happy spelunking!

Changing the Splash Screens

Vision is the art of seeing things invisible.

—JONATHAN SWIFT, *Thoughts on Various Subjects,* 1706

YO, READER! THIS IS THE PART YOU'RE LOOKING FOR!

 This is where you learn how to change the startup splash screen. I *know* that's the only reason why you're reading this chapter. Well, I've got some good news for you. Not only is the screen easy to change, but you have all the tools you need to play around with it—draw your own, bring in scanned images, modify existing screens, touch up, and paint to your heart's content, the whole ball of wax—right there on your disk, in bone-stock Win98. Complete details follow.

The Windows startup screen has become something of a geek Rorschach test. Some people report that they can see a rampant horse in the vibrating blue clouds. Others claim it's big Bill himself, striking a pose that would make Frank Zappa proud. Most of all, the screen Rorschach proves one thing: if you can see something in those clouds, you desperately need to get a life.

When Win98 starts, it looks in the root directory of your boot drive (typically, **C:**) for a file called **logo.sys**. Win98 is very picky about that file: it has to be a bitmap and 320 dots wide by 400 dots high by 256 colors. If it finds a file matching those specifications, the file is used as the splash screen. If it doesn't find any file called **logo.sys**, it uses a file stored internally in **io.sys**, the one you're probably accustomed to seeing as the Win98 splash screen. If it does find a file called **logo.sys** but that file doesn't match the $320 \times 400 \times 256$ specifications precisely, no splash screen will appear.

Chances are good that you don't have a **logo.sys** file in your root directory unless you've installed Plus! 98, which copies its own **logo.sys** file into the root directory when you install it.

When Win98 shuts down, it uses two different exit screens, both of them the standard 320 dots wide by 400 dots high by 256 colors. The first one, called **logow.sys**—the "Windows is shutting down" screen—must be located in the **\windows** folder (Figure 7-22). The second one, called **logos.sys**—"It's now safe to turn off your computer"—has to be in the **\windows** folder, too (Figure 7-23). If Win98 can't find those files or they are of the wrong size, it puts a blinking cursor in the upper left corner of a blank screen for the duration of time the screen would normally occupy. It's a very disconcerting image.

As you can see, the Microsoft Paint application that ships with Windows 98 is reasonably suited for editing these **.sys** files. These are very odd-shaped files—they're taller than they are wide, whereas every screen you're likely to use is wider than it is tall. Win98 stretches the pictures in the files horizontally when they appear as splash screens.

Figure 7-22. `logow.sys` available for editing in MS Paint

Figure 7-23. `logos.sys`, also in MS Paint

 Here are my top tips for using Microsoft Paint to edit the splash **.sys** files.

- Make backup copies of the **logo*.sys** files before you start. (If worse comes to worst and you obliterate one, you can retrieve it from the Win98 installation **.cab** files; just use the Extract File utility described earlier in this chapter.)

- You may find it easier to start with **logow.sys** (or possibly **logos.sys**) and modify it, instead of trying to draw from scratch. Both those files are already trimmed to 320 dots by 400 dots, so you don't need to worry about stretching or cropping.

- If you are working with a scanned image or any lifelike artwork, start by using the Image/Stretch and Skew menu to scrunch the drawing by about 50% horizontally (or stretch it vertically by 200%). That maintains fairly lifelike proportions. Remember, the picture you see in Microsoft Paint is *not* the image that ends up on the splash screen.

- If you don't start with **logow.sys** or **logos.sys**, you can adjust the drawing to the correct size by clicking on Image/Stretch and Skew to stretch or scrunch it. Once the drawing is approximately the right size, use Image/Attributes to trim it down or enlarge it to 320 by 400 dots. Remember that the Attributes setting crops—it lops off the right or the bottom of the picture to match whatever size you specify.

Figure 7-24.
MOM's splash
screen

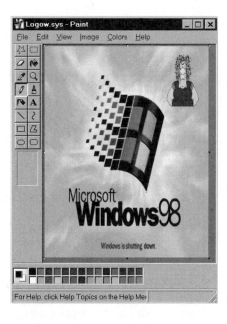

- Try pulling in clip art or any image that MS Paint will accept. When you get the image scrunched the way you like it, select the image, use Edit/Copy to copy it to the clipboard, open up the `.sys` file, use Edit/Paste to paste the image on the splash screen, then immediately use the four-headed arrow to drag the image wherever you want to place it (Figure 7-24).

We never did figure out a way to get the animated right-to-left crawler at the bottom of the splash screen to work; editing animated bitmap files is a real black art. Even copying it from the bottom of the Plus! Pack's `logo.sys` (which is animated) didn't help. There's a bit of undocumented magic going on behind the scenes. So if you create your own screen, don't expect to see it move unless you start with a screen like the one from the Plus! Pack that does move.

 Ah! You guys never did take a hex editor and change byte 32 (hex) to 0xEC, didja?

Emergency StartUp Disk

They that are booted are not always ready.

—GEORGE HERBERT, *Outlandish Proverbs,* 1640

When you originally install Win98, you have an opportunity to make an Emergency StartUp Disk (ESD; sometimes called an Emergency Boot Disk, EBD). In addition, any time you feel like it, you can go into the Control Panel's Add/Remove Programs applet, select the **StartUp Disk** tab, and make an identical ESD.

In less squeamish days, DOS manuals and books would contain dire warnings, emphasized in neon red, that every user *needs* an Emergency Boot Disk—preferably two—and that the disks should be kept handy in case the system goes crashing about the user's knees. Well, this disk is an Emergency Boot Disk, and you do need one, just in case your system heads south in a hurry.

I must emphasize strongly that you must try out the ESD after you make it. You don't want to wait to find it has bad sectors or the wrong drivers when that disaster strikes.

With small differences, the StartUp Disks Windows 98 makes are the same on all machines, so if you forget to make one and have a crisis, you can make one on another machine.

We covered the user-side view of booting with the ESD in Chapter 6, "(Emergency) StartUp Disk." Here's what really happens, from the system's point of view:

```
Microsoft Windows 98 Startup Menu
=====================================

1. Start computer with CD-ROM support
2. Start computer without CD-ROM support
3. View the Help file.

Enter a choice: 1  Time remaining: 30
```

Figure 7-25. Win98 Startup Menu, implemented in `config.sys` with a `[Menu]` command

- When you boot from the ESD, the file **`config.sys`** on the ESD uses the **`[Menu]`** command—the old DOS "multiple configurations" trick—to present you with three options (Figure 7-25).
- **`config.sys`** loads the DOS high-memory manager, **`himem.sys`**. In addition, if you choose **`1. Start computer with CD-ROM support`**, **`config.sys`** tries to load its generic CD-ROM driver (from Oak Systems), followed by its BusLogic and Adaptec SCSI board and CD-ROM drivers.
- Finally, **`config.sys`** creates a RAMdrive, a fake "drive" that sits in upper memory.
- **`autoexec.bat`** kicks in after **`config.sys`** finishes and, no matter which option you choose, runs a program called **`setramd.bat`**.

`setramd.bat` has to be the worst example of DOS command line spaghetti code I've seen in a Microsoft product in ages. (No, I'm not blaming the programmer: DOS commands just seem to demand spaghetti treatment.) Anyway, its purpose is a simple one: **`setramd`** looks for the highest assigned drive letter—which also happens to be the drive letter for the RAMdrive that **`config.sys`** just created. So, for example, if you have two hard drives (or two hard drive partitions), **`setramd`** will return the letter **`E`**—since **`A:`**, **`B:`**, **`C:`**, and **`D:`** have been taken—and **`config.sys`** must've just created a RAMdrive with the letter E.

For you inveterate techies: **`setramd.bat`** works by calling a program, **`findramd.exe`**, that returns a DOS errorlevel that identifies the drive. **`setramd`** then translates the number in errorlevel to a drive letter, which it puts in the DOS environment variable **`%RAMD%`**. (There's also a bogus variable called **`%CDROM%`**, but don't get me started.)

- **autoexec.bat** then copies **command.com**, **extract.exe**, and **readme.txt** to the RAMdrive. All of them are placed there so that they'll run much, much faster than they would if run from the diskette.

- Next, **autoexec.bat** looks to see if the file **ebd.cab**—a compressed Microsoft CAB format file containing various system utilities—is on the diskette. If it isn't, **autoexec** puts a very strange message up on the screen (**Please insert Windows 98 Startup Disk 2**) and loops until the user sticks a diskette containing a file named **ebd.cab** into the **A:** drive.

 That's strange, of course, because there is no Windows 98 StartUp Disk 2!

 *The EDB, er, EBD is extensible and can include more files than you found. If there isn't room for everything on one disk, we move **ebd.cab** to a second diskette. That's why the batch file says that.*

- **autoexec** extracts all the files in **ebd.cab** and puts them on the RAM-Drive. When that's done, it writes the message **The diagnostic tools were successfully loaded to drive xx** on the screen.

- Way back in the Win98 Startup Menu (Figure 7-25), if you choose **3. View the Help file**, **autoexec.bat** calls a batch file named **help.bat**, which in turn cranks up the Edit program, **edit.com**, loaded with the file **readme.txt**. When you leave Edit, **autoexec.bat** reboots using the program **restart.com**. It's a very convoluted approach to something simple—showing the **readme.txt** file on the screen.

- If you choose **2. Start computer without CD-ROM support**, **autoexec** exits at this point, and you're at the DOS **A:>** prompt.

- If you choose **1. Start computer with CD-ROM support**, **autoexec** loads the Microsoft CD Extensions library, **mscdex.exe**, and—providing the correct driver was loaded in **config.sys**—brings your CD-ROM drive to life. Then it exits to the sweet strains of **A:>**.

 What's wrong with this approach? Two things, far as I can tell. First, it takes a lot of time to go through all these machinations—running off a diskette is slow business and dealing with all these possibilities takes forever. I'll show you how to streamline your ESD later in this section. Second, the inclusion of a RAMDrive bumps the letter of your CD-ROM drive up by one. So if you normally see your CD as, oh, drive **F:**, this process will make it drive **G:**. That's a monumental PITA should you install Windows after booting from the ESD. Win98 "remembers" the installation drive, and you'll have to manually override the drive letter every time you want to add programs or restore files from the CD.

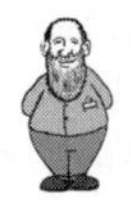

There is also the KISS—Keep It Simple, Stupid—principle. This Rube Goldberg scheme makes me uneasy.

Before we start monkeying with the ESD, let's take a look at which files are on the ESD. Whether you create the ESD during Windows 98 SetUp or from the Add/Remove Programs applet, Figure 7-26 lists the files that are placed on your ESD. And in Figure 7-27 you can see the contents of the compressed CAB file, **`ebd.cab`**. The Windows Resource Kit has a nasty habit of calling this file "edb.cab" (with the b and d transposed). It isn't, and if you scan the online WRK for "ebd" you'll miss the main section discussing this file. EBD = Emergency Boot Disk, no matter what WRK says.

Name	Size	Type	Modified
Aspi2dos.sys	35KB	System file	5/11/98 8:01 PM
Aspi4dos.sys	15KB	System file	5/11/98 8:01 PM
Aspi8dos.sys	37KB	System file	5/11/98 8:01 PM
Aspi8u2.sys	40KB	System file	5/11/98 8:01 PM
Aspicd.sys	29KB	System file	5/11/98 8:01 PM
Autoexec.bat	2KB	MS-DOS Batch ...	5/11/98 8:01 PM
Btcdrom.sys	22KB	System file	5/11/98 8:01 PM
Btdosm.sys	31KB	System file	5/11/98 8:01 PM
Command.com	92KB	MS-DOS Applic...	5/11/98 8:01 PM
Config.sys	1KB	System file	5/11/98 8:01 PM
Drvspace.bin	68KB	BIN File	5/11/98 8:01 PM
Ebd.cab	266KB	Cabinet	5/11/98 8:01 PM
Ebd.sys	0KB	System file	6/9/98 2:17 PM
Extract.exe	92KB	Application	5/11/98 8:01 PM
Fdisk.exe	63KB	Application	5/11/98 8:01 PM
Findramd.exe	7KB	Application	5/11/98 8:01 PM
Flashpt.sys	63KB	System file	5/11/98 8:01 PM
Himem.sys	33KB	System file	5/11/98 8:01 PM
Io.sys	218KB	System file	5/11/98 8:01 PM
Msdos.sys	1KB	System file	6/9/98 2:17 PM
Oakcdrom.sys	41KB	System file	5/11/98 8:01 PM
Ramdrive.sys	13KB	System file	5/11/98 8:01 PM
Readme.txt	16KB	Text Document	5/11/98 8:01 PM
Setramd.bat	2KB	MS-DOS Batch ...	5/11/98 8:01 PM

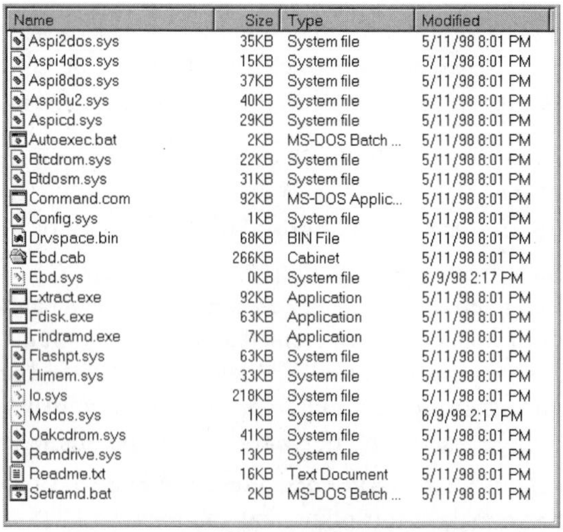

Figure 7-26. Contents of the Emergency StartUp Disk

Name	Size	Type	Date
Attrib.exe	15 KB	Application	2/13/98 12:47 AM
Chkdsk.exe	28 KB	Application	2/13/98 12:48 AM
Debug.exe	21 KB	Application	2/13/98 12:49 AM
Edit.com	69 KB	MS-DOS Application	2/13/98 12:56 AM
Ext.exe	13 KB	Application	2/5/98 4:55 PM
Format.com	49 KB	MS-DOS Application	2/13/98 1:22 AM
Help.bat	1 KB	MS-DOS Batch File	2/5/98 4:55 PM
Mscdex.exe	25 KB	Application	2/13/98 12:52 AM
Restart.com	1 KB	MS-DOS Application	2/12/98 8:47 PM
Scandisk.exe	141 KB	Application	2/13/98 1:16 AM
Scandisk.ini	8 KB	Configuration Settin...	7/18/97 6:33 AM
Sys.com	19 KB	MS-DOS Application	2/13/98 12:54 AM
Uninstal.exe	77 KB	Application	2/12/98 8:28 PM

Figure 7-27. Contents of `ebd.cab`

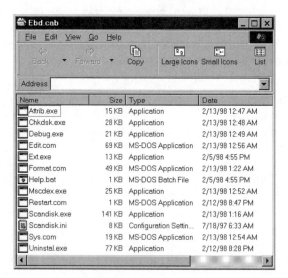

There seem to be slight variations between ESDs. For example, on a machine where Windows 98 was installed in a new directory, **uninstal.exe** is included.

These files fall into three major groups. First, the files that the ESD needs to get itself going (we've already discussed most of these).

- **config.sys** and **autoexec.bat**, of course
- System files needed to make it all run: **io.sys** (which is the Win98 DOS program), **msdos.sys** (the text file), **himem.sys** (for loading the RAM-Drive into high memory), **ramdrive.sys** (to create the RAMDrive), **extract.exe** (to extract **ebd.cab**), **restart.com** (to reboot), **command.com** (for interpreting DOS commands), **mscdex.exe** to let you get at your CD-ROM through DOS, and **drvspace.bin** (the DriveSpace disk compression routines, just in case you have any DriveSpace disks)
- All the little ancillary files that tie the ESD together: **findramd.exe** (to find the last assigned drive letter), **setramd.bat** (to change the number created by **findramd** into a drive letter), **readme.txt** (which is the "help" displayed when you choose "Help"), and **help.bat** (which calls **edit.com** to display **readme.txt**)

Then there are all the drivers that are necessary to get most CD-ROM drives to work.

- A bunch of SCSI drivers, just in case your CD-ROM drive is attached to a SCSI card—**Aspi*.sys** is for Adaptec SCSIs; **Bt*.sys** and **Flashpt.sys** are for BusLogic SCSI cards. There are also CD-ROM drivers for each.
- Generic CD-ROM driver from Oak Systems, **oakcdrom.sys**, that lets you run a very large percentage of all existing CD-ROM drives from the ESD.

Finally, there's a whole bunch of additional files that you might want to use directly, once the ESD boots. Some of them go on the RAMdrive, others stay on diskette. Those of you who are old enough to remember DOS 6 will recognize almost all of these files (and commands) immediately.

- **attrib.exe** lets you change the hidden, system, and read-only attributes of files.
- **chkdsk.exe** is the old, familiar check disk utility.
- Hard to believe that Microsoft would include the old byte-level editor **debug.exe** on a fancy twenty-first century emergency system disk, but they do.

 Hey, it isn't as if they included Edlin! I recall one time a program wiped out the boot sector on my hard drive and I used Debug to write a new one to the drive. So it isn't crazy to include that 21-KB file for the few guru who can use it when flying blind in a situation where you can't get to your hard disk!

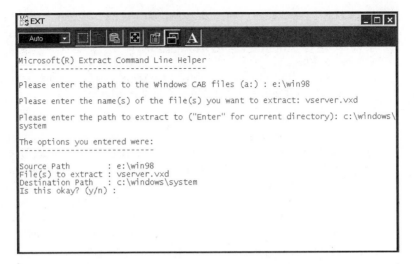

Figure 7-28. New EXT command, which helps run **extract.exe**

- **edit.com** is used to display **readme.txt**, but don't forget that it's here! Edit's a full-screen text editor that has the look and feel of the old DOS 6 **edit.com**. Edit's features are discussed in detail in Chapter 4.

- **ext.exe** puts a new face on the old **extract.exe** utility. Where **extract.exe** is unforgiving—it has a half-dozen command line parameters, and they all have to be typed precisely or the whole thing goes belly-up—**ext** can actually be useful. Most of all, with **ext** you don't need to know the precise name of the CAB file that holds the file you want to extract; it's enough to simply point to a folder holding a bunch of CAB files that you want to have searched. Type **ext** and you'll be prompted for the information extract needs (Figure 7-28).

 Note that like the Extract File utility that System File Checker calls, EXT searches all CABs in a folder, so you don't need to know what CAB a file is in.

- **fdisk.com**, perhaps the most dangerous utility ever created, is capable of partitioning (read: destroying) your hard drives with a slip of the fingers.

- **format.com** similarly lets you blast away an entire disk in nothing flat.

- That old DOS standby **mode.com** lets you not only set the colors on your monitor, but manage serial and parallel ports and do a whole lot more—albeit through a cryptic, ancient text interface.

- **scandisk.exe** and **scandisk.ini** are the reliable, relatively modern DOS mode disk scanning utilities you've no doubt come to love and their **.ini** files. Don't confuse this DOS ScanDisk with the full-blown Windows ScanDisk, which lives in a file called **scandskw.exe**.

- **sys.com** will transfer **io.sys**, **msdos.sys**, and **command.com** to a disk. If you really bollix up your system, you might have to use this program to transfer copies of those files from the ESD to the hard disk.

- **uninstal.exe** is apparently the Win98 uninstaller. Running it should restore your old version of Windows.

Actually, I didn't have the guts to try it, and I would recommend strongly that you follow my lead in the chicken department.

O ye of little faith. Don't you trust Microsoft to warn you before zapping you? **Uninstal.exe** *is put on the ESD only if you installed Windows 98 on top of Windows 95, and its purpose is to restore Windows 95. In Figure 7-29, you can see the virtually identical warnings that the program gives you when run outside Windows (at the top) and inside Windows.*

Oh, and lest we forget . . . there's a funny little zero-byte file called **ebd.sys** *that doesn't do anything in Win98. Not a thing. In Win95, it was supposedly used to identify "genuine" ESDs, but I have my doubts about that, too.*

Figure 7-29. Uninstall warnings

```
Windows 98 Uninstall
Copyright (c) 1985-1998 Microsoft Corp.

Uninstall removes Windows 98 from your computer
and restores your previous version of Windows.

If you uninstall Windows 98, any programs you
installed while running Windows 98 will have to be reinstalled.
You may also have to reconfigure your swapfile.

WARNING: Do not uninstall Windows 98 if you
compressed your hard disk(s) or converted to FAT32 after setting up Windows 98.

Restoring disk partition table
Restoring master disk partition table
WARNING: Uninstall should be run from within Windows 98
to insure that all the information on your disk(s) is properly restored.

Are you sure you want to continue? (Y/N)
```

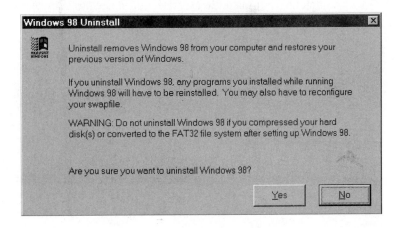

And—do I need to repeat this?—whatever you do, don't trust the Windows Resource Kit on any of this ESD material, either. They're wrong over and over again.

MOM's Better ESD

The ESD is fine, as far as it goes, but it could do so much more—with so much less!

 I started down this path after reading Ed Bott's tips in the "Windows Superguide" published in the October 1998 issue of *PC Magazine*. (An amazing article, by the way, even if I do say so myself. I did write a little bit of it.) It's really amazing how much you can do to make the ESD better, and I want to thank Ed for pointing me in this direction.

Before we start, a simple admonition: if you don't know DOS commands, couldn't care less about seeing another **config.sys** or **autoexec.bat**, or really don't care how well your ESD works, skip on down to the next section, "Bad Programs." What's here rates as an advanced course, not for the faint-hearted.

If that didn't scare you away—ah, there are still some real hackers out there!—you can have an ESD that works much faster and more reliably than the original and one that doesn't screw up your CD-ROM drive letter. It's really rather easy, if you don't mind getting your fingers dirty with **config** and **autoexec**.

 Let's face it. When you boot with your ESD, you're going to want your CD-ROM drive working, and you want it to have the drive letter the way it normally appears. All this RAMdrive garbage only gets in the way. So let's put together a MOM-worthy ESD, one that you can use quickly and easily any old time you want to boot to DOS.

The only real trick: you have to know which drivers your CD-ROM requires (we go into great detail on the drivers, how to identify and retrieve them, in Chapter 6). For this little exercise, you'll need to know which drivers "kick in"—and you can identify that by simply running your ESD once, making notice of which drivers produce a response. If there's no response from your PC, you don't need the driver.

Chances are good you'll need one of these sets of drivers.

- Most people will require only **oakcdrom.sys**. If you have a CD-ROM drive connected to your IDE controller (by far the most common setup these days) and the CD-ROM drive is a fairly recent one, **oakcdrom.sys** is all you need.

- If you have a BusLogic/Mylex SCSI card or compatible and your CD-ROM drive is attached to it, you'll need one of the BusLogic SCSI drivers (**btdosm.sys** or **flashpt.sys**) plus the **btcdrom.sys** CD-ROM driver.

- If you have an Adaptec SCSI card or compatible and your CD-ROM drive is attached to it, you'll need one of the Adaptec SCSI drivers (**aspi2dos.sys**, **aspi4dos.sys**, **aspi8dos.sys**, or **aspi8u2dos.sys**), plus the Adaptec CD-ROM driver, **aspicd.sys**.

- If you have an old, weird, or off-brand CD-ROM drive or controller, you'll need the driver(s) that shipped with the drive. These are the same drivers you had to dig out in Chapter 6 to get your CD-ROM drive working with the ESD.

Just to make things interesting, we'll use the toughest case—where none of the generic drivers work—for this example.

Step 1 Start Windows 98 and format a clean, new system diskette by sticking an expendable diskette in drive **A:**, going into Windows Explorer, right clicking on **A:**, and choosing Format. You'll get the Format dialog (Figure 7-30). You can go for a quick format, but make sure the "Copy system files" box is checked. Pull the diskette out of the drive and mark it "MOM's Quickie ESD" or some such.

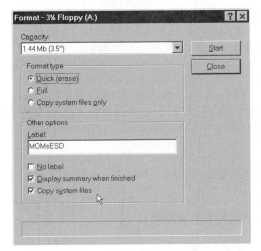

Figure 7-30. Start by creating a clean, new system diskette

Step 2 Use Notepad to create a bare-bones **config.sys** file that runs **himem.sys**, loads DOS high (just in case you need to do some work with large real mode programs after an emergency boot), and then loads your CD-ROM driver(s). The one we used is in Figure 7-31. Most of you will use a much simpler final line in place of the relatively complex **mtmcdae** line shown in Figure 7-31. (We talk about **mtmcdae**, the real mode CD-ROM driver for older Mitsumi CDs, in Chapter 6.) In most cases this will suffice:

```
device=oakcdrom.sys /D:mscd001
```

But if you have one of the Adaptec SCSI drivers, for example, you may need two lines, like this:

```
device=aspi2dos.sys
device=aspicd.sys /D:mscd001
```

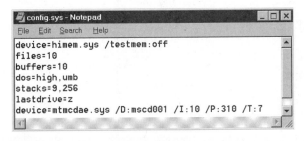

Figure 7-31. MOM's bare-bones
config.sys

Figure 7-32.
MOM's minimal
autoexec

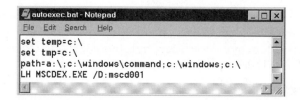

Step 3 Create a bare-bones **autoexec.bat** that loads **mscdex.exe** into high memory. The one in Figure 7-32 will work in every case we can imagine. Yes, it really is this easy.

Step 4 Make sure the Quickie ESD sits in your **A:** drive, and copy over **autoexec.bat**, **config.sys**, and any special CD-ROM drivers you may need that aren't on the standard ESD. Move to **C:\windows\command\ebd** (Figure 7-33), and copy these files onto the **A:** drive: **extract.exe**, **fdisk.exe**, and **himem.sys**, plus the drivers that are necessary for your CD-ROM drive. Double click on **ebd.cab** and copy these files onto **A:** as well: **attrib.exe**, **chkdsk.exe**, **edit.com**, **ext.exe**, **format.com**, **mscdex.exe**, **scandisk.exe**, **scandisk.ini**, and **sys.com**. If you're old and gray and don't care what people think about you, consider copying **debug.exe**, too. If you still have a DriveSpace, doubled hard disk, after asking yourself why you haven't upgraded to FAT32, copy **drvspace.bin** there also. If you are on a network, consult your system administrator to see what software you can install to start your network in DOS mode.

That's it. Your Quickie ESD should be complete. Stick MOM's Quickie ESD in your **A:** drive, click Start, Shutdown, Restart. Betcha it works the first time.

Figure 7-33.
Copy files from
C:\windows\
command\ebd to
your A: drive

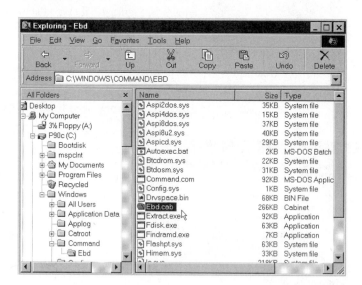

Here's the amazing part. MOM's Quickie ESD boots in one quarter the time of the old ESD. It leaves the CD-ROM with the drive letter that the Windows gods intended. And you'll have about 450 K of leftover space on that diskette to hold anything you want!

At this point you might want to load the diskette with other programs you can use. Since the **path=** statement in **autoexec.bat** automatically points DOS to **\windows\command** and **\windows**, think about any programs you might want if your hard drive isn't working.

Personally, I've put a bunch of files on my Quickie ESD: **xcopy.exe**, and **xcopymod.exe** from **\windows\command**; my mouse drivers, so I can use the mouse with Edit (I had to change **config** and **autoexec** to load the drivers); and a handful of programs that can come in real handy if the hard drive conks out. I even put **scanreg.exe** there, so I can restore the Registry if the version of **scanreg.exe** on the disk gets screwed up. There's a lot of extra room on MOM's Quickie ESD.

Bad Programs

DOS always says, "Bad command or filename." That's so negative!
Why can't Windows say, "Most excellent command or filename, dude"?

—Heard on the Net

One of Win95's most brilliant capabilities, brought across intact to Win98, lies in the trapping of old Windows applications known to cause problems under Win98 and *letting you do something about them.* The source of this magic lies in the Registry, in a key called (take a deep breath) **HKEY_LOCAL_MACHINE\System\ CurrentControlSet\Control\SessionManager\CheckBadApps** and **\CheckBadApps400.** If you crank up the Registry (click Start, then Run, type **regedit**, hit **Enter**) and scan down to those keys, you'll find a list of hundreds of programs that are known to cause problems with Win98. (Note that **SessionManager** is all one word—if you go down to **\Session Manager** you'll end up in the wrong place.)

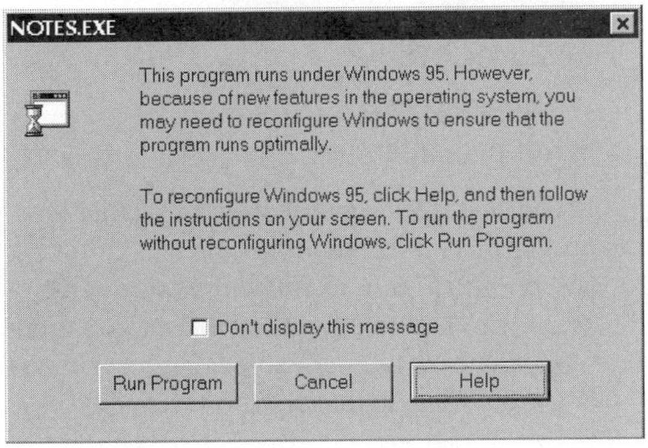

If you try to run a program with one of the indicated names (there's also a version number check going on behind the scenes), you get a warning message like that shown in Figure 7-34. If you click on Help at that point, you'll see a full description of the known problems with that application, as in Figure 7-35. The Help message is tailored to this specific program, and following the tips in Help should get you going with the program (or at least should clue you in on its Win98 shortcomings!) in no time.

Figure 7-34. Notes has a compatibility problem

NOTES.EXE

This program runs under Windows 95. However, because of new features in the operating system, you may need to reconfigure Windows to ensure that the program runs optimally.

To reconfigure Windows 95, click Help, and then follow the instructions on your screen. To run the program without reconfiguring Windows, click Run Program.

☐ Don't display this message

[Run Program] [Cancel] [Help]

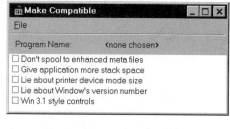

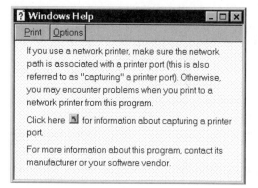

Figure 7-35. There's even a diagnostic tool to help solve the problem

Figure 7-36. The easy ways Win98 can lie

Speaking of bad programs and their reformation, Win98 ships with an application called `mkcompat.exe`, which lets you tell Windows how to fake out an older program that may have problems working with Windows 98. To run `mkcompat.exe`, just click Start, then Run, type `mkcompat`, and hit **Enter**. You'll see the screen in Figure 7-36. Click on File, then Choose Program, and open whichever program has been giving you problems. Try clicking on some (or all!) of the boxes, clicking File, then Close, and running the application again. Win98 intercepts the program and applies whatever sleight of hand you specify. If you want to look at all the options available in `mkcompat`, click on File, then Advanced Options. You'll get a list that looks like Figure 7-37.

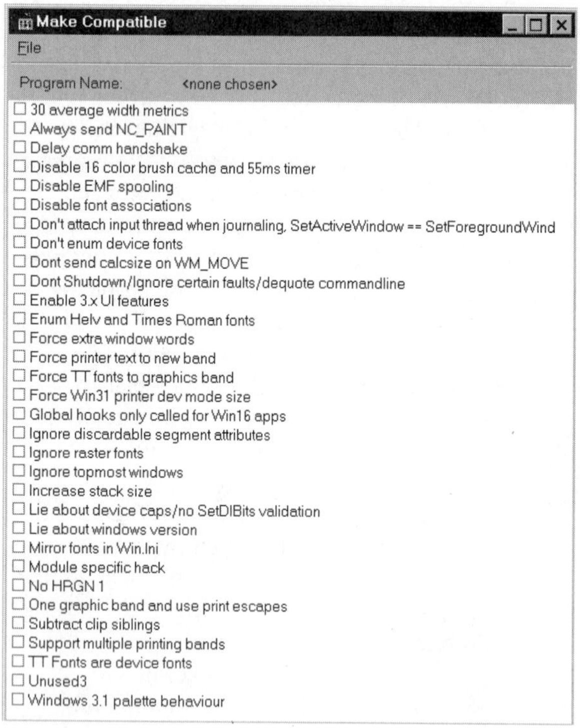

How does it work? You won't believe it. Win98 stores a compatibility flag in `win.ini`! You'll get an entry that looks something like this:

```
[Compatibility]
AIRUUE=0x200000
```

If you scan the Registry, you'll find that the program is never mentioned there. `mkcompat` simply manufactures `win.ini` `[Compatibility]` entries and merges them with whatever internal table Win98 generates at startup to keep track of those flags.

Figure 7-37. All the options to force compatibility

Cleaning Up

'Tis much, among the filthy, to be clean.

—Robert Herrick, *Hesperides,* 1648

This section is only for those who, in spite of our suggestions in Chapter 6, installed Win98 on top of Windows 95. While Windows 98 is pretty good at cleaning up after itself, it still leaves behind the Win95 Undo files, and you can reclaim 30 MB to almost 100 MB of space by getting rid of them. Those of you who followed our suggestions and installed Win98 to a new, clean disk can skip down to the section "Yet More Files."

If you've installed Win98 and lived with it a while and have no intention of undoing the install to permanently return to your previous version of Windows, you may be able to reclaim an enormous amount of space by removing two files, **winundo.dat** and **winundo.ini**. On one machine we used for testing— a veteran Win95 machine—those two files took up *more than 80 MB* of space. Take a look at your files. They're hidden, read-only files in the root directory of your boot drive, typically **c:**. They're created by Win98's installer if you install Win98 on top of Win95 *and* you specify during the installation that you want to be able to remove Win98. If you have Explorer set up to show hidden files (click Tools/Options/View), you'll be able to see those big suckers.

Resist the temptation to click on each file and hit the **Del** key. Instead, use the politically correct method: click Start, Settings, Control Panel, double click on Add/Remove Programs, click "Delete Windows 98 uninstall information," and click Add/Remove.

Remember, this is an irreversible decision. If you delete these files and then decide to give up on Win98 some time in the future, you'll have to wipe out most of your hard drive and reinstall Windows 95 from scratch.

 Note, though, that removing the files won't interfere with your ability to boot to DOS with your ESD (or MOM's Quickie ESD), or using the Windows 98 Startup Menu. They're compressed archive files, so they don't enter into the equation at all. Even with **winundo.dat** and **winundo.ini** long farmed out to the bit bucket, you can still hit **Ctrl** on-startup and boot to "Previous version of MS-DOS." I have no idea why, but this fact doesn't seem to be mentioned in the Win98 online Help, the Windows Resource Kit, or any of the magazine articles I've seen. Odd.

Yet More Files

Moderation is a fatal thing;
nothing succeeds like excess.

—Oscar Wilde, *A Woman of No Importance,* 1893

Windows 98 uses dozens—maybe hundreds—of additional files to go about its daily business. We couldn't begin to list them all or define their functions. But a

---

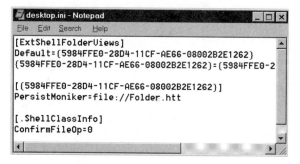

Figure 7-38. Default `desktop.ini` stored in `C:\windows`

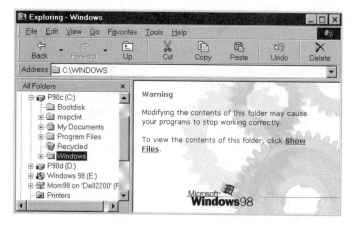

Figure 7-39. `desktop.ini` causes Windows to display this warning when viewed as Web page

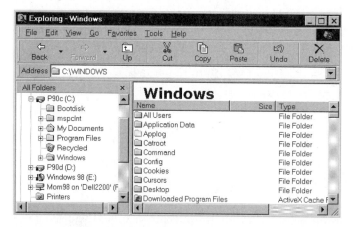

Figure 7-40. The same folder, also in Web page view, without `desktop.ini`

handful of files that don't fall into earlier categories could prove important to you, depending on your circumstances and position on the Win98 life cycle.

In Chapter 3 we talked about `desktop.ini` files, stored in folders as you enable thumbnail view. Look for `desktop.ini`s and you'll find quite a few (Figure 7-38). The files contain settings apparently related to viewing the folders as Web pages. (Surprisingly, for you geeks, the `{5984FFE0-...}` guid's are not registered CLSIDs.) Take a look at how `C:\windows` looks in Web page view with `desktop.ini` intact (Figure 7-39). Compare that with how the same folder appears in Web Page view without `desktop.ini` (Figure 7-40).

Many of the more widely used system folders also contain files called `folder.htt`, the file referred to as `PersistMoniker=`. Although they may sound mysterious, in fact they're just HTML files (Figure 7-41), which contain JavaScript (not VBScript!) programs.

The JavaScript programs in the `folder.htt` files are the ones that display the Warning dialog you see in the right pane of Figure 7-39. If you remove `folder.htt`, you'll get the Figure 7-40 appearance if Explorer is set to View as Web page.

Figure 7-41.
A folder.htt
file is just an
HTML page

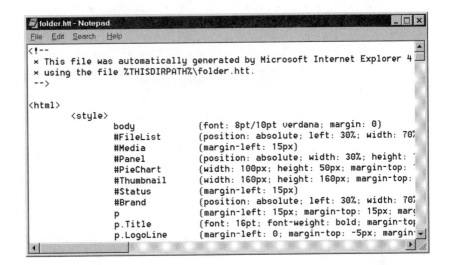

Oh, I get it. **desktop.ini** apparently tells Explorer where to look for the JavaScript program that displays that Warning message. The program sits in a file called **folder.htt**. So if you remove (or rename) **desktop.ini**, the link is broken, and Explorer can't find the program that shows the Warning. Similarly, if you remove (or rename) **folder.htt**, the program itself disappears, and the Warning can't appear. How 'bout that.

Ever wonder where Windows stores all the overlay files for Web view, the ones that say, "Use the settings in Control Panel to personalize your computer" and the like? They're all in the **C:\windows\web** folder, in **.htt** files—JavaScript programs—just like **folder.htt** (Figure 7-42).

Then, there are **\windows\ShellIconCache** and **ttfCache** (both without filename extensions), two more interesting oddball files. As their names imply, Windows stores the most recent icons that the shell uses—like those for disk drives—in **ShellIconCache** and the most recently used TrueType fonts

Figure 7-42.
The .htt files in
C:\windows\web
that make Web
view overlays
work

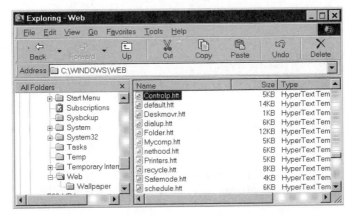

in `ttfCache`. The files' sole purpose seems to be to speed up reboot of the system. If you delete the files, Windows 98 will gladly recreate them the next time it starts; it just takes a little extra time. If some of your basic Desktop icons seem screwy, `ShellIconCache` may have become corrupted; try deleting it and rebooting. Also, if you've made a change that should've taken effect but didn't—for example, if you edit a `.dll` with icons in it and the changes don't "take" on the Desktop—try deleting `ShellIconCache` and see if the problem goes away.

Surprisingly, `ShellIconCache` also includes information about Desktop hotkeys. If you associate a hotkey with a Desktop icon and then delete the icon, Win98 won't let you re-use the hotkey! To reclaim the hotkey (and lose all your other hotkey assignments in the process), delete `ShellIconCache` and reboot.

My favorites are the `\windows\system\color\*.icm` files, the ones that implement Image Color Matching. Although you shouldn't play around with these files manually, they're used to match colors when switching media: a red coming in from a scanner will look the same on the screen and then look the same on paper or film when you print it out. It's a technology created by Kodak and licensed by Microsoft that translates among different devices' "color spaces" (and you thought computer geeks used weird terminology). Anyway, high-end image processing applications use these `.icm` files. Keep your hands off!

MOM asked me to track down a few other techie things, but we couldn't get the 'Softies to talk. They wouldn't take a carrot or a stick. Tough guys. We never did find out what the `suhdlog.dat` and `suhdlog.bak` files hold, although Ed Bott swears they're associated with `winundo`, and they certainly appear to be "SetUp Hard Drive Log" files. Maybe they're logs for checking hard drive read/write compatibility? Oh, well. I guess any lady as classy as Win98 deserves to have a few secrets left.

The fewer the better, as far as I'm concerned. This feminine mystique crap is way overblown.

■ Active Desktop

*We have to understand the world can only be grasped by action, not by contemplation.
The hand is more important than the eye . . . . The hand is the cutting edge of the mind.*

—JACOB BRONOWSKI, *The Ascent of Man*, 1975

Internet Explorer 4 introduced the concept of an active desktop to a skeptical world. Now, with its latest incarnation in Windows 98, we remain skeptical—but intrigued.

The simple fact is that an active desktop takes way too much computer power, it's far too fragile—with frequent crashes and odd behavior—and it's distracting. But, oh, when this technology grows up, it's going to be killer.

The concept behind the Active Desktop couldn't be simpler: instead of having a Windows Desktop that just sits there, we're going to use a genuine HTML page (or, if you prefer, a Web page, which is the same thing) as the Desktop. By making that simple switch, anything that can be done on a Web page can also be done on the Desktop. With a few exceptions.

OK, OK. Quite a few exceptions. Still, it's going to be great when it finally works—and you can prepare yourself for the future by following along in this final "techie" section.

Turn It On

That which the fool does in the end, the wise man does in the beginning.

—R. C. TRENCH, Archbishop of
Dublin, *Lessons in Proverbs,* 1853

Windows 98, as it ships straight out of the box, doesn't set up the Active Desktop. Which is just as well, given Active Desktop's instability and appetite for computer cycles.

In the earliest beta, IE 4.0 had the Active Desktop turned on, but beta testers howled so loudly that Microsoft backed down.

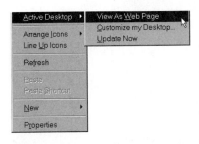

Figure 7-43. Switching to the Active Desktop

To switch on the Active Desktop, simply right click on any empty part of the Windows Desktop and choose Active Desktop, then View as Web Page (Figure 7-43). Make sure you stand back from the monitor when you switch over. The blinding blue flash can be a bit overwhelming (Figure 7-44).

The actions going on behind the scenes here are pretty amazing. Your old, single-colored wallpaper (or the static picture you used as wallpaper) has been discarded, replaced by a genuine HTML document—a Web page, if you will. This HTML document, consisting of a blue background and that strange Microsoft logo in the upper right corner, is actually the file `C:\windows\web\wallpaper\windows98.htm` (Figure 7-45). You can verify that by using Explorer to find the file and double clicking on it. Internet Explorer comes up with the page loaded.

Figure 7-44.
The Active Desktop springs to life

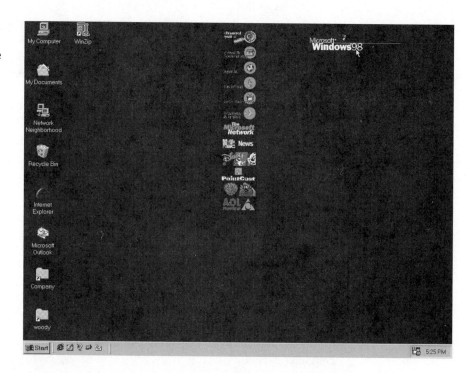

Figure 7-45.
The new wallpaper is just an HTML file

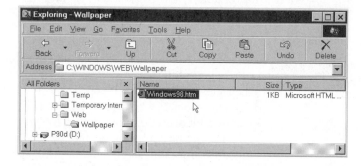

Figure 7-46.
MAW, MOM's Active Wallpaper, installed and ready to go

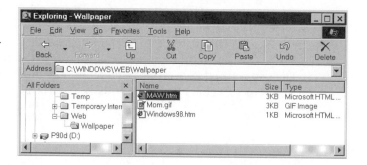

Figure 7-47.
Choosing MAW
as your Active
Desktop

 If you have a chance, and you want to follow along here closely (particularly in the VBScript programming parts), drop by MOM's home page, **www.wopr.com/mom**, and download **MAW.zip**. That's MOM's Active Wallpaper. Unzip the two files **MAW.htm** and **Mom.gif** and put them in **C:\windows\web\wallpaper** (Figure 7-46). Then switch over to MAW by right clicking on the Active Desktop, choosing Active Desktop, then Customize My Desktop, clicking the Desktop tab, and picking MAW from among the offered wallpaper choices (Figure 7-47). Click OK, and MOM's Active Wallpaper appears as your Active Desktop (Figure 7-48). Note how the Desktop tab gladly shows any HTML file (or picture file, for that matter), in **C:\windows\web\wallpaper**.

If you're not interested in learning about how to program Active Desktop wallpaper or writing VBScript programs to execute inside Windows 98, skip to the section "Adding Active Cool Stuff." Those who do dare to tread the programmer's path need to be reasonably conversant with Visual Basic and its constructs—for example, you should have an idea of what an "event" entails from the VB point of view and why that might be important to a VBScript program.

We give you programmers and programmer wannabes a whirlwind introduction to VBScript in Windows 98 divided into four sections:

- "HTML for VBScript Programmers" covers the **<HTML>** tags necessary to get a VBScript program running inside a Web page or Active Desktop wallpaper.

- "VBScript for Everyman" takes a closer look at the VBScript language itself. We skip the basics (variable types, control statements) and go directly to the meat of the subject.

Figure 7-48.
MAW appears
as the Active
Desktop

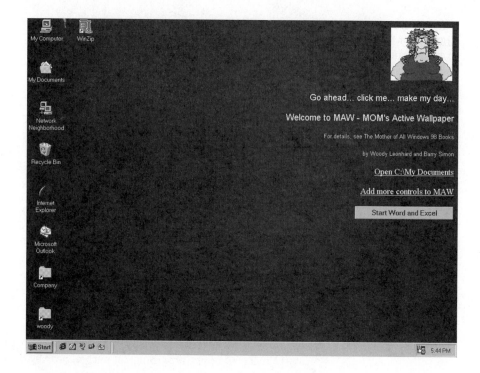

If you're going to skip the Basics, does that mean you'll use Java instead? Groan!

- "MAW's Start Word and Excel" shows you how MOM's Active Wallpaper manages to get both Word and Excel going when you click the appropriate button. MAW uses a rather advanced VBScript program, and we'll step through it to show you how you can modify it for your own uses.
- Finally, "Windows Scripting Host" concentrates on running VBScript inside Windows in general—not necessarily tied to a Web page or the Active Desktop.

There's just no way we can do justice to a huge subject like VBScript in the few pages available here. But we can get you started—in fact, we think we can give you a better start here than you'll find in any VBScript programming book, simply because we stay focused on getting VBScript programs to work, first on Web pages, then in Win98 itself.

Both Active Desktop and Windows Scripting Host understand JavaScript (which hasn't a particularly close relation to Java!) as well as VBScript. We'll use VBScript because we're both dyed-in-the wool VB programmers and prefer to limit our Java to what comes in cups.

By the way, if you have VB or VBA installed on your PC (for example, if you use Office or have downloaded Microsoft's free VB Control Creation Edition), you may find it easier to do your VBScript programming in VB. When the code works, you can just copy it into your HTML file.

HTML for VBScript Programmers

The chief virtue that language can have is clearness, and
nothing detracts from it so much as the use of unfamiliar words.

—GALEN, *On the Natural Faculties,* ca. 175 A.D.

HTML—the language behind Web pages—has evolved almost exponentially in the past five years. No, we aren't going to try to turn you into an HTML expert. That'd take another book this size—and everything would have changed by the time you finished reading it anyway. Instead, we're going to focus on a few key HTML language elements (HTML "tags") that have a direct bearing on Active Desktop wallpaper and the VBScript programs that can propel the tags.

Using only the tools that ship with Windows 98, by far the easiest way to work with the HTML in Active Desktop wallpaper (and simple Web pages in general) is via FrontPage Express. That's what we'll do.

I've already given you a brief introduction to FrontPage Express in Chapter 4 and won't duplicate that material here. But you need to see a few different kinds of HTML tags and understand how HTML works behind the scenes so that you know how you can hook VBScript programs into your Active wallpaper.

VBScript programs in Web pages appear inside a specific kind of HTML tag called a Script tag. Here's an example of a simple VBScript program:

```
<SCRIPT LANGUAGE="VBScript">
  MsgBox "Hello World!"
</SCRIPT>
```

Here is a simple VBScript subroutine:

```
<SCRIPT LANGUAGE="VBScript">
  Sub DoNuthin
   A = B + C
  End Sub
</SCRIPT>
```

And this is a simple VBScript Function:

```
<SCRIPT LANGUAGE="VBScript">
  Function IsBig(Number)
   If Number > 10000 Then
    IsBig = True
   Else
    IsBig = False
   End If
  End Sub
</SCRIPT>
```

Note how the initial **<SCRIPT>** tag identifies the language as VBScript. Other than that, there really isn't much to putting together a genuine VBScript program. You can stick as many Subs and Functions between the **<SCRIPT>** and **</SCRIPT>** tags as you like, and you can have zillions of **<SCRIPT>** tag pairs in any particular document. The Subs and Functions don't need to appear before they're used, so you can stick a program that refers to the DoNuthin subroutine up in the **<HEAD>** of a document but put DoNuthin way down at the bottom. Or vice versa.

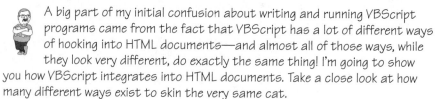 A big part of my initial confusion about writing and running VBScript programs came from the fact that VBScript has a lot of different ways of hooking into HTML documents—and almost all of those ways, while they look very different, do exactly the same thing! I'm going to show you how VBScript integrates into HTML documents. Take a close look at how many different ways exist to skin the very same cat.

VBScript programs hook into HTML documents in one of four ways.

- They can just appear in the document. Since Web browsers go through an HTML document sequentially from beginning to end, any **<SCRIPT>** tag sitting in the **<HEAD>** or the **<BODY>** of a document is executed as soon as the browser comes across it. If there's a program in the **<SCRIPT>** tag, it runs. (Note in particular that Subs and Functions aren't programs—if the browser hits either a Sub or a Function, it just compiles the code and tucks it away, without running anything.)

- Subroutines can be explicitly attached to events that occur to **<INPUT>** tags, **<A>** anchor tags (**<A>** tags typically put pictures on your HTML pages), and **<AREA>** or **<BUTTON>** tags. For example, if you have a command button defined this way:

```
<INPUT TYPE="button" NAME="cmdButton1" VALUE="Don't
  push MOM's button">
```

this VBScript subroutine will run when that button gets clicked.

```
<SCRIPT LANGUAGE="VBScript">
 Sub cmdButton1_OnClick
  MsgBox "I told you not to push MOM's button!"
 End Sub
</SCRIPT>
```

Again, location doesn't matter: the Sub can appear inside a **<SCRIPT>** tag before or after the **<INPUT>** tag.

- There's a very similar way to write exactly the same kind of routine using something called a **<SCRIPT FOR>** tag. Using the preceding **<INPUT>** button, this VBScript subroutine does exactly the same thing as the **Sub cmdButton1_OnClick** routine:

```
<SCRIPT FOR="cmdButton1" EVENT="OnClick" LANGUAGE=
   "VBScript">
 MsgBox "I told you not to push MOM's button!"
</SCRIPT>
```

There's absolutely no difference in how the two routines run.

 While you VB and VBA fans may cringe at the **"OnClick"** event in VB-Script, as opposed to the much more familiar **"Click,"** the concept remains the same.

- You can turn the tables around a bit and specify in the **<INPUT>** or **<A>** tag which subroutine you want to run in response to a recognized event. For example, this **<INPUT>** tag:

```
<INPUT TYPE="button" NAME="cmdButton1" VALUE="Don't
   push MOM's button" OnClick="SomeSub">
```

combined with this subroutine:

```
<SCRIPT LANGUAGE="VBScript">
  Sub SomeSub
   MsgBox "I told you not to push MOM's button!"
  End Sub
</SCRIPT>
```

does exactly the same thing as the preceding two examples.

- Finally, you can call a subroutine or invoke a function from another program, subroutine, or function, just as you would with any VB or VBA program. For example, if you put the IsBig() Function described at the beginning of this section on an HTML page, this program would produce a message that says True, because the argument sent to IsBig() is over 10000.

```
<SCRIPT LANGUAGE="VBScript">
  MsgBox IsBig(10001)
</SCRIPT>
```

VBScript has all sorts of limitations you might not expect. For example, except in very specific circumstances (for example, the Submit button on a Form), you can't "fire" an event programmatically. So even though you'll see lines like

```
Document.SomeForm.Button1.Click
```

in some VBScript programs, you'd be well advised to avoid trying it until you're more conversant with Submit buttons.

 Speaking of things that don't work, you can't automatically assume that all the tags that work in HTML will work on Active Desktop wallpaper. For example, I can't get the **<REFRESH>** tag to work. That's the one that forces the browser to "refresh" or reread the page. I complained about it during the Windows 98 beta, but Microsoft never responded. Without the **<REFRESH>** tag, it's impossible (far as I can tell) to build an Active Desktop wallpaper that has a clock. Microsoft has a long, long way to go before the Active Desktop becomes more than a curiosity. It's the little details that drive wallpaper designers like me up the wall.

 That concludes this quick lesson on the part of HTML that directly affects VBScript programming. It's by no means complete, but it should give you a fighting chance at deciphering most of the VBScript programs you'll see.

VBScript for Everyman

Let every man practice the art that he knows best.

—CICERO, *Tusculanae disputationes*, 45 B.C.

Before you try to do anything with VBScript, you need to get on the Web, head over to **www.microsoft.com/scripting**, and pick up the latest version of four files.

- **VBScript documentation** (such as it is), in a file called **vbsdoc.exe**. You should run that file on the PC you'll be working on to install the documentation. At first it looks like the installer is unpacking many hundreds of HTML files in the current folder, but not to worry: ultimately it asks where you want the files to go, and you can create a folder just to hold them (Figure 7-49). After installation, the documentation is available by clicking on Start, Programs, and VBScript documentation and choosing either the Tutorial or the Reference.

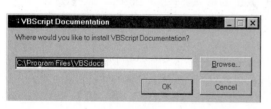

Figure 7-49. The VBScript documentation installer lets you pick a location for the files

- **Microsoft Script Debugger,** in a file called **ie*dbg.exe** (the * version number, currently 401, will probably change by the time you read this). Run the file and the Debugger installs itself in your copy of Internet Ex-

**Figure 7-50.
IE 4 Script Debug-
ger, working on
MAW.HTM**

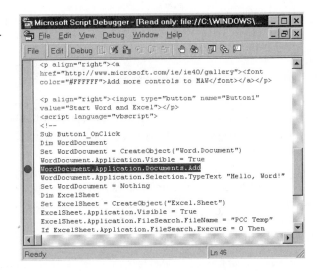

plorer. Unfortunately, the debugger won't run in FrontPage Express, but it still beats trying to debug a VBScript program manually. Once installed, simply open the HTML file that contains the VBScript program you're trying to debug, then click on View, Script Debugger, Open (Figure 7-50).

- **Windows Scripting Host Programmer's Reference**, file **wshobj.exe**. It contains specific information about the objects available to stand-alone VBScript programs, designed to run directly under Windows 98 (which is to say, VBScript programs that don't sit inside HTML documents). These VBScript "macros" live inside **.vbs** files; we discuss them in the section "Windows Scripting Host."

- **VBScript examples,** written as stand-alone **.vbs** files. Since you're in the right place on the Web anyway, download the file **samples.exe** (Figure 7-51), extract it, and put the resulting VBScript files someplace convenient, like in the **C:\Program Files\VBSDocs** folder.

 I'm not going to try to point you to specific online locations for each of those three files because they move all the time. But you will find them under **www.microsoft.com/scripting**. Somewhere.

**Figure 7-51.
Download and in-
stall the VBScript
samples**

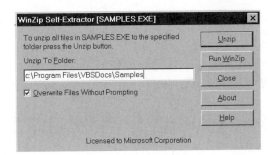

Notice that Microsoft licensed WinZip for this one—they must share MOM's high opinion of the program (see Chapter 5).

You're going to discover, quickly, that each of these tools has serious limitations.

- The VBScript documentation (at this point anyway) is so incredibly lacking it doesn't even discuss events! We've looked for reliable information on events in HTML pages and haven't come up with much beyond some very technical documentation about DHTML.

- While the IE 4 Script Debugger allows you to set breakpoints, view values, and set variables (via an immediate window—called a Command Window here), *it won't let you edit the VBScript program!* Yes, you read that correctly. You can watch—but don't touch.

- Solid working samples—the core of any decent tutorial—are sadly lacking.

 We have a wonderful model for a superb development environment for macro languages—VBA! Its autocompletion environment makes writing programs a pleasure and its debugger is great. The Office team, Visio, Adobe, and dozens of other vendors have shown enough respect for their users to license this environment; but apparently the Windows team hasn't been willing.

 No doubt about it—I want VBA for WSH and VBScript. How about an e-mail campaign to big Bill to tell him you want it too?

Until Microsoft gets its VBScript support act together, you'll have to rely on third-party books. Our number-one recommendation (although it's dated, at least as we went to press) is *Learning VBScript* by Paul Lomax (O'Reilly & Associates, ISBN 1-56592-247-6). VBScript changes as quickly as anything else running on Internet time, but Lomax's book remains timeless in its treatment of the foundations of VBScript programming.

Let's try a couple of relatively interesting VBScript programs and put them in Active Desktop wallpaper. The first program is a nascent clock—one that would be a lot better if the Active Desktop would recognize `<REFRESH>` tags. Anyway, try this.

Step 1   Go into Windows Explorer, and navigate down to `C:\Windows\Web\Wallpaper`. Right click on `windows98.htm` and pick Edit (Figure 7-52).

Step 2   FrontPage Express pops up. Click on File, Save As, and As File, and save a copy of `windows98.htm` as, oh, `momtest.htm`.

Step 3   Click on View, then HTML. You should see a screen like Figure 7-53. We're going to put this program just above the `</body>` tag, so go down there and hit `Enter` a few times.

Figure 7-52.
Start with windows98.htm—home of the vibrant blue background

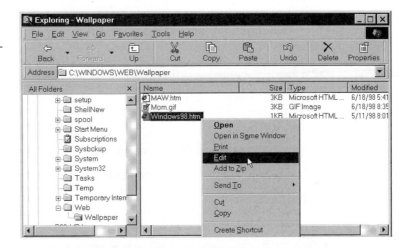

Figure 7-53.
Put the program just above the </body> tag

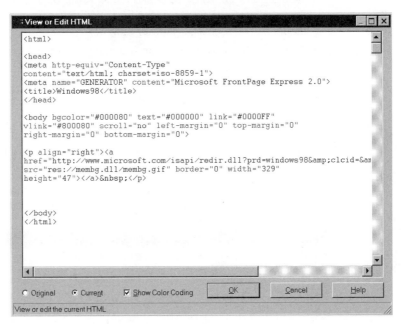

Step 4 Type this program:

```
<font color="#FFFFFF">
<script language="vbscript">
document.write "<p align=" & Chr(32) & "right" &
    Chr(32) & ">"
If Hour(Now) < 12 Then
    document.write "Good morning. "
ElseIf Hour(Now) < 18 Then
    document.write "Good afternoon. "
```

```
Else
    document.write "Good evening. "
End If
document.write "You last booted on " & Date & " at " &
    Time
document.write "</p>"
</script>
</font>
```

Here's a quick description of how the program works (Figure 7-54).

- First, before you start the VBScript program, you have to switch the text color over to white; otherwise, it won't show on the screen!

- The first line inside the program puts the text `<p align="right">` in the current document. That `<p>` tag right aligns all subsequent text.

- The big `If/Then/Else` construct, as you probably figured out, writes different text on the screen depending on whether the current hour is before noon, before 6:00 P.M., or after 6:00 P.M.

- The next line puts the current date and time on the screen. Since this is going to become wallpaper, the "current" date and time are really the date and time you last booted. If Windows 98 had a working `<REFRESH>` tag, we could set this HTML document up to "tick" or refresh every minute. But `<REFRESH>` doesn't work, so we're SOL.

- Finally, the program closes off the paragraph with a `</p>` and shuts down. Then, just to be nice, we reset the default font color to its ghastly low-contrast black.

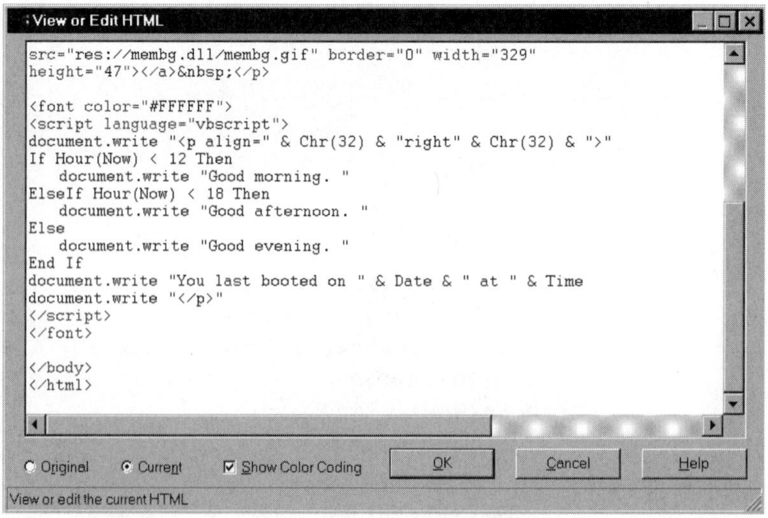

**Figure 7-54.
Program in
`momtest.htm`**

```
View or Edit HTML                                      _ □ ×
src="res://membg.dll/membg.gif" border="0" width="329"
height="47"></a> </p>

<font color="#FFFFFF">
<script language="vbscript">
document.write "<p align=" & Chr(32) & "right" & Chr(32) & ">"
If Hour(Now) < 12 Then
    document.write "Good morning. "
ElseIf Hour(Now) < 18 Then
    document.write "Good afternoon. "
Else
    document.write "Good evening. "
End If
document.write "You last booted on " & Date & " at " & Time
document.write "</p>"
</script>
</font>

</body>
</html>
```

◯ Original   ⦿ Current   ☑ Show Color Coding   OK   Cancel   Help

View or edit the current HTML

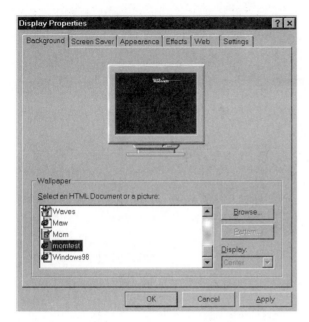

Figure 7-55. Using momtest as Active Desktop wallpaper

Click OK to get out of FrontPage's HTML view, then click File, Close, and Yes you want to save changes. **momtest.htm** should be sitting on your disk in **C:\windows\web\ wallpaper**, ready to do battle.

To get this Web page, er, HTML document working as Active Desktop wallpaper, right click on the Desktop and pick Properties. On the Background tab, pick **momtest** and click OK (Figure 7-55). If you aren't using Active Desktop, Win98 asks if you want to switch. Assuming you do, you should end up with a desktop that looks like (Figure 7-56). Try restarting Windows a few times and you'll see how the clock stays "frozen" on the time you booted. Congratulations. You've not only created your own Active Wallpaper, you've also bumped into one of the many bugs that plague the current implementation of Active Desktop.

For our second demonstration of skill and legerdemain, let's write an Active Desktop VBScript program that Microsoft says can't be done.

Figure 7-56. momtest takes over the Desktop

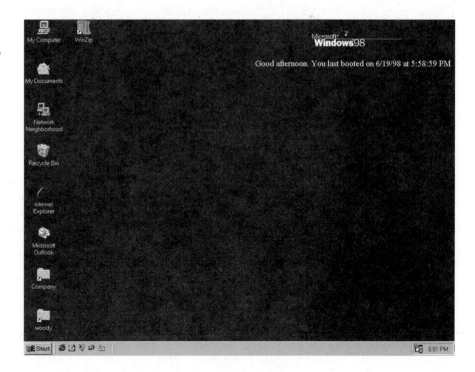

One of my favorite lies on the Microsoft Web site goes like this. I've taken the following text straight from Microsoft's VBScript FAQ page.

Q: How does VBScript compare to Visual Basic and the Visual Basic language in the Microsoft Office applications (Word, Excel, and so on)?

A: Microsoft® Visual Basic® Scripting Edition is a subset of the Microsoft® Visual Basic® for Applications language used in Microsoft® Excel, Microsoft® Project, Microsoft® Access, and the Microsoft® Visual Basic® 5.0 development system. VBScript is designed to be a small and lightweight interpreted language, so it does not use strict types (only Variants). Also, because VBScript is intended to be a safe subset of the language, it does not include file I/O or direct access to the underlying operating system.

No matter how you slice it, that's simply a lie. VBScript includes all sorts of file I/O and some access to the underlying operating system, if you just know how to do it.

Traditionally there are lies, damn lies, and statistics. I think we need to add a fourth category: Microsoft marketing lies. That's what you see here.

Step 1   Open **momtest.htm** in FrontPage Express.

Step 2   Click View, then HTML, move down just above the **</script>** tag, and type in this program:

```
document.write "<p align=" & Chr(32) & "right" & Chr(32) & ">"
Set objFileSys = CreateObject("Scripting.
    FileSystemObject")
Set objDrives = objFileSys.Drives
document.write "Available drives: <BR>"
    For Each drive in objDrives
        document.write drive.DriveLetter & ": ("
    Select Case drive.DriveType
            Case 0: document.write "Unknown)<BR>"
            Case 1: document.write "Removable)<BR>"
            Case 2: document.write drive.VolumeName & ")<BR>"
            Case 3: document.write drive.ShareName & ")<BR>"
            Case 4: document.write "CD-ROM)<BR>"
            Case 5: document.write "RAM Disk)<BR>"
        End Select
    Next
document.write "</p>"
```

Figure 7-57.
Drive Listing code

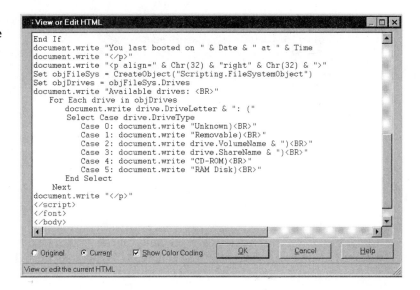

```
: View or Edit HTML                                          _ □ ×
End If
document.write "You last booted on " & Date & " at " & Time
document.write "</p>"
document.write "<p align=" & Chr(32) & "right" & Chr(32) & ">"
Set objFileSys = CreateObject("Scripting.FileSystemObject")
Set objDrives = objFileSys.Drives
document.write "Available drives: <BR>"
    For Each drive in objDrives
        document.write drive.DriveLetter & ": ("
        Select Case drive.DriveType
            Case 0: document.write "Unknown)<BR>"
            Case 1: document.write "Removable)<BR>"
            Case 2: document.write drive.VolumeName & ")<BR>"
            Case 3: document.write drive.ShareName & ")<BR>"
            Case 4: document.write "CD-ROM)<BR>"
            Case 5: document.write "RAM Disk)<BR>"
        End Select
    Next
document.write "</p>"
</script>
</font>
</body>
```

○ Original   ◉ Current   ☑ Show Color Coding   OK   Cancel   Help

View or edit the current HTML

It should appear like Figure 7-57.

Here's what that VBScript code does.

- First, it right aligns the coming paragraph. Yawn.

- Next, it creates a new "File System" object called **objFileSys**. You have to dig deep in the documentation to see exactly how to use it, but the File System object basically gives you full access to any files or drives on the PC.

- Based on the File System object, the program creates a Drives object, which can get at all the drives accessible to this particular PC.

- Stepping through each available drive, one at a time, the program puts the drive letter and drive type on the wallpaper page. In the case of local and shared drives, it also includes the volume name or the share name. Note the use of the **
** tag to get a line feed: VB programmers will be tempted to use the **vbCrLf** constant—which doesn't work in HTML documents.

- Finally the program closes off the paragraph.

Step 3   Click OK to get out of HTML view, then File, Close, Yes you want to save changes. Now, if you already have **momtest.htm** set up as your Active Desktop wallpaper, simply reboot Windows 98.

As it comes back up, the page will appear, and then you'll get the warning shown in Figure 7-58. Believe me, this is a good sign. Windows 98 is warning you that there's a program (er, an "ActiveX object") lurking behind that fancy wallpaper of yours, and the program could be very dangerous (uh, it could "initialize and be accessed by scripts"). In fact, if you wrote the program right it won't hurt anything. But it's conceivable that somebody could screw up and write a very destructive program—one you might never be

Figure 7-58. Win98 warns you that the program in `momtest` could mess up your system

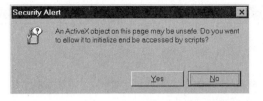

able to recover from. So take this very poorly worded admonition seriously; it may be couched in so much nonsense jargon that no normal human being could ever understand it, but its heart is in the right place. Click Yes.

 Their hearts may be in the right place but their heads sure aren't! What "page"? How do I know if this is a warning about my Desktop wallpaper, about some ActiveX control that is downloading from the Web, or about an alien invasion from outer space? And what ActiveX control? There sure ain't any of those here.

With any luck at all, **`momtest`** will appear in all her Figure 7-59 glory.

Congratulations. You're well on your way to learning how to use VBScript effectively inside Web pages—and you did it all on your Windows 98 (Active) Desktop!

 Fingers never leave the hands . . .

Figure 7-59. `momtest` with a full active drive list

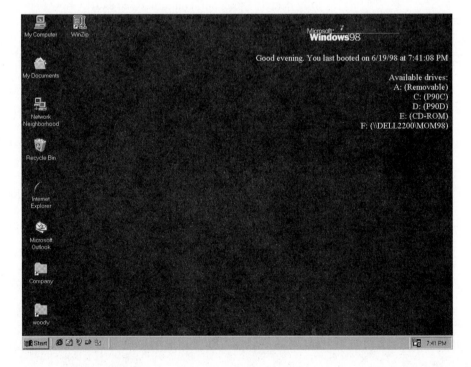

MAW's Start Word and Excel

When the harlot reforms it is only to become a procuress.

—Arab proverb

There's one more VBScript program we'd like you to step through. Think of it as an advanced course in how to make Active Desktop wallpaper reach out and touch your system.

 I originally demo'd this idea for Active wallpaper in the Windows Super-guide that appeared in the October 1998 issue of *PC Computing*. Unfortunately there wasn't enough room in the article to go into detail about the hows and whys of the VBScript program that ran the beast. So the important gory details appear here for the first time.

 If you download **MAW.htm** from MOM's Web site, **www.wopr.com/mom**, you'll be able to follow along here without typing anything. I'd definitely recommend that. It's very easy to miss a comma here or a colon there, and VBScript—with its look-but-don't-touch debugger—is one unforgiving, uh, bugger.

Most of the MAW components (see Figure 7-48) were assembled quite simply with FrontPage Express: click here, drag there, type in a hot link, and it's done. The one part that took a long, long time was the VBScript program that sits behind the button that says Start Word and Excel. Here's the HTML and VBScript subroutine that go along with Start Word and Excel:

```
<p align="right">
<input type="button" name="Button1" value="Start Word
    and Excel">
</p>
<script language="vbscript">

Sub Button1_OnClick

Dim WordDocument
Set WordDocument = CreateObject("Word.Document")
WordDocument.Application.Visible = True
WordDocument.Application.Documents.Add
WordDocument.Application.Selection.TypeText "Hello, Word!"
Set WordDocument = Nothing

Dim ExcelSheet
Set ExcelSheet = CreateObject("Excel.Sheet")
ExcelSheet.Application.Visible = True
ExcelSheet.Application.FileSearch.FileName = "MOM Temp"
If ExcelSheet.Application.FileSearch.Execute = 0 Then
    ExcelSheet.Application.Cells(1, 1).Value = "Hello, Excel!"
```

```
        ExcelSheet.Application.ActiveWorkbook.SaveAs "MOM Temp"
    End If
    ExcelSheet.Application.Workbooks.Open "MOM Temp"
    Set ExcelSheet = Nothing

    End Sub
    </script>
```

At first blush that may appear pretty straightforward, but it isn't. Guaranteed.

The idea's pretty simple: by clicking one button, we want to be able to launch both Word 97 (or later) and Excel 97 (or later), get them to do something innocuous—and (here's the hard part) *have them stay up on the screen.* Word's a pussycat, behaving precisely as an experienced VB programmer would expect. Excel, on the other hand, has atrocious manners. You'll see why.

Here's how the Word part of that VBScript program works.

- The program creates an object called WordDocument, which, as you might imagine, is a Word document.

- Then the program makes Word visible—Word shows up on the screen.

- Next, it creates a new Word document. You can see that document on the screen.

- Now the program "types" the text "Hello, Word!" in the new document.

- Finally, the magic link is broken, the object destroyed—and Word sits up there on the screen with a new document containing the text "Hello, Word!" Very simple (at least, once you figure out how to use CreateObject, which is far from trivial). Almost elegant—if it weren't so slow in actual operation.

You might imagine that the Excel part of the program would behave similarly. But you'd be wrong. Excel doesn't work at all like Word.

- The program creates an object called ExcelSheet. In fact, the object is an Excel Workbook, but Excel doesn't seem to mind, so we won't either.

- Then the program makes Excel visible. You see it appear on the screen.

- Here's where it gets dicey. If we continue using the Word method—create a new worksheet, put some data in it, then destroy the object—*Excel disappears!* As soon as this VBScript program stops running, Excel heads for the hills, and it takes the new worksheet along with it—there's absolutely no indication that the worksheet ever existed. It's very disconcerting behavior and so unlike Word that we have to wonder if the Excel folks really understood what they were doing when they made it behave this way.

- So we finally found a way around the problem—a kludge, pure and simple, but it works. There's a little routine at this point to see if there's already a file called **MOM Temp.xls** in the current directory. If not, the program creates a new worksheet, puts "Hello, Excel!" in the first cell, and saves the worksheet as **MOM Temp.xls**.

- Finally the program makes Excel open the file **MOM Temp.xls**. Here's the truly bizarre part: Excel *doesn't* disappear when this VBScript program ends, because it has a "real" worksheet open!

 I guess that's another one for the "ActiveX Files." I can't even begin to imagine why it works this way, but it does—and if you want to control Excel from your Active Desktop wallpaper, you need to be aware of this truly bizarre bug.

 The truth is out there, eh, Mulder?

Windows Scripting Host

A host is like a general: it takes a mishap to reveal his genius.

—HORACE, *Satires,* ca. 25 B.C.

Now that you know, ahem, all there is to know about VBScript buried inside HTML documents, let's widen our horizon a bit.

You may have heard that Windows 98 includes support for a new "macro" language, VBScript, via something called the Windows Scripting Host. Although that's certainly literally true, the actual implementation may give you pause. WSH is still in its infancy, and you'll find it difficult to get information, examples, or help. And, of course, there's no development environment, debugger, or any of the other civilized amenities experienced VB and VBA programmers have come to expect.

The Windows Scripting Host comes built into Windows 98 and (as of this writing anyway) is expected to be in Windows NT 5. It's also available as a free download from **www.microsoft.com**, and it will install into either Windows 95 or NT 4.

At its heart, a VBScript macro designed to run in Windows 98 is just a text file with a **.vbs** filename extension. (Yes, there are other ways to invoke WSH, but if you're just trying to knock off a quick macro, the **.vbs** file is the way to go.)

From a superficial (which is to say, working) point of view, there are two other main differences between VBScript programs designed for HTML documents and VBScript programs designed to run on Windows 98 itself:

- VBScript programs, subroutines, and functions inside an HTML file have to be surrounded by **<script>** and **</script>** tags. There are no tags (much less **<script>** tags) in **.vbs** files.

- Most of the interesting commands available to Windows 98 VBScript programs have to use the Wscript objects.

That last point probably sounds like voodoo, but it's pretty simple when you see an example. Let's put one together.

Figure 7-60. Using the Wscript object in a stand-alone VBScript program

Figure 7-61. Most of the Wscript repertoire

Step 1 Create a new text file on your Windows Desktop. Call it, oh, **momtest.vbs**.

Step 2 Type this line into **momtest.vbs**:

```
MsgBox Wscript.Name
```

Step 3 Save the changes to the file, then double click on **momtest.vbs**. You should see something like Figure 7-60.

There's a handful of very uninteresting information available from the Wscript object. Figure 7-61 covers about half of them.

This would be a very boring exercise if it weren't for one simple fact: the Wscript object also includes the CreateObject command. And that opens an enormous world to explore. Just for starters, it means you can get at all the **"Scripting.FileSystemObject"** goodies.

Try putting this program in **momtest.vbs**.

```
Set objFileSys =
    Wscript.CreateObject("Scripting.FileSystemObject")
Set objDrives = objFileSys.Drives
sMsg = "Available drives - "
For Each drive in objDrives
    sMsg = sMsg & drive.DriveLetter & ": ("
    Select Case drive.DriveType
        Case 0: sMsg = sMsg & "Unknown) "
        Case 1: sMsg = sMsg & "Removable) "
        Case 2: sMsg = sMsg & drive.VolumeName & ") "
        Case 3: sMsg = sMsg & drive.ShareName & ") "
        Case 4: sMsg = sMsg & "CD-ROM) "
        Case 5: sMsg = sMsg & "RAM Disk)"
    End Select
Next
MsgBox sMsg
```

Figure 7-62.
Using the WSH in a stand-alone VB-Script "macro" to list available drives

```
momtest.vbs - Notepad
File  Edit  Search  Help
Set objFileSys = Wscript.CreateObject("Scripting.FileSystemObject")
Set objDrives = objFileSys.Drives
sMsg = "Available drives - "
For Each drive in objDrives
    sMsg = sMsg & drive.DriveLetter & ": ("
    Select Case drive.DriveType
        Case 0: sMsg = sMsg & "Unknown) "
        Case 1: sMsg = sMsg & "Removable) "
        Case 2: sMsg = sMsg & drive.VolumeName & ") "
        Case 3: sMsg = sMsg & drive.ShareName & ") "
        Case 4: sMsg = sMsg & "CD-ROM) "
        Case 5: sMsg = sMsg & "RAM Disk)"
    End Select
Next
MsgBox sMsg
```

```
Visual Basic
Available drives - A: (Removable) C: (P90C) D: (P90D) E: (CD-ROM) F: (\\DELL2200\MOM98)
              [ OK ]
```

Run it and you'll get a result that looks like Figure 7-62.

Pretty remarkable, eh? In the same way, you can get at Word 97 (or later), Excel 97, or any other program that can be used in a CreateObject statement.

The WSH adds all sorts of objects you might want to play with—WSHShell, WSHNetwork, WSHCollection, WSHEnvironment, WSHShortcut, WSHSpecialFolders, and WSHUrlShortcut. All of those are created using the CreateObject() command. Try a simple example, something like this:

```
Set objWSHShell = Wscript.CreateObject("Wscript.Shell")
ObjWSHShell.Popup "Hello Windows!"
```

WSHShell and all the other WSH objects are covered thoroughly in the Windows Scripting Host documentation. You'll find commands there that you can use all the time.

 One last hack that really had me up in arms. I think of it as the Holy Grail of Web page VBScript hacking. Say you want to run a Windows 98 program—any Win 98 program—from an HTML document, aka a Web page. How do you do it? By burrowing through the WSHShell object!

Want to run, oh, the Windows calculator, whenever somebody looks at your Web page? If they're running Windows 98, it couldn't be easier—if you know the trick. Simply add this VBScript routine

```
<script language="VBScript">
Set objWSHShell = CreateObject("Wscript.Shell")
ObjWSHShell.Run("calc")
</script>
```

to any HTML document and the calculator appears on the screen, summoned by a rather circuitous path through the Windows Scripting Host Shell object. You can hook it up to run when a button is clicked, of course, or using any of the other myriad VBScript "hooks" that tie programs to HTML tags. Similarly, you can put it on an Active Desktop wallpaper. Or even in an HTML message. The only requirement is that the viewer must have the Windows Scripting Host installed—and if they're using Windows 98, WSH is a given.

 This two-step approach to running applications is of course very useful in writing **.vbs** files.

Adding Active Cool Stuff

He who hath not a dram of folly in his mixture hath pounds of much worse mattter.

—CHARLES LAMB, *All Fools' Day,* 1820

 OK, OK. So much for programming. Let's get back to the other things readers might want to do with their Active Desktop wallpaper.

Where Windows 95 let you put only one picture on the desktop, using Active Desktop lets you stick any number of pictures on your wallpaper. Although you can do that using FrontPage Express and modifying the HTML file you use as wallpaper, there's a much simpler way.

Make sure you have an Active Desktop wallpaper on your screen, then right click on it and pick Active Desktop, Customize My Desktop. The Web tab of the Display Properties dialog should appear. Click New (Figure 7-63). Click

Figure 7-63. First step in adding multiple pictures to an Active Desktop

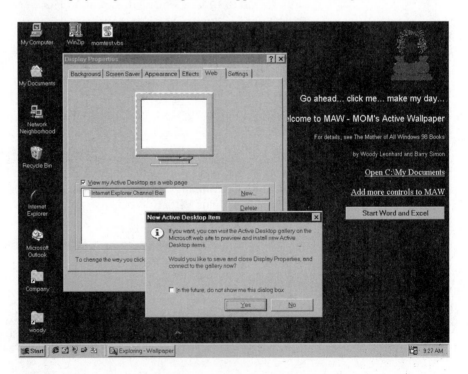

No—you don't want to go onto the Microsoft Web site just yet—and browse to whatever picture you want to put on your Active Desktop (Figure 7-64). Click OK and the picture gets picked up and a check box is established for it so that you can turn the picture off easily, if you want to (Figure 7-65). Click OK and the picture appears on your Desktop (Figure 7-66).

In fact, in spite of appearances, the picture doesn't go into the wallpaper at all. You can open **MAW.htm** and see for yourself. In fact, the picture is placed on a floating "layer" that sits above the wallpaper. Once there, it can be clicked and dragged anywhere you like—and the wallpaper HTML document won't be touched.

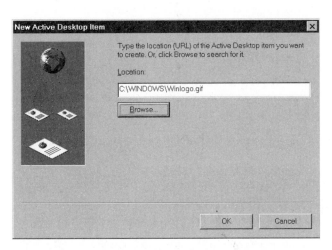

Figure 7-64. Locate the picture on your disk, your network, or the Web

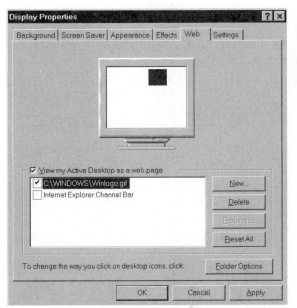

Figure 7-65. The picture gets a check box

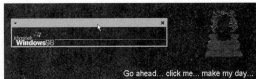

Figure 7-66. The picture appears on the Desktop—sorta

Hmmmm. . . . Come to think of it, the program-launch shortcut icons must not be inside the wallpaper either, eh? They must be floating in the "layer" on top of the wallpaper.

 True. In fact, you can turn off the icons, if you should be so inclined. Just right click on the Desktop, pick Properties, and click the Effects tab. There you'll find a check box that will turn the icons off if you're viewing your Desktop as a Web page (Figure 7-67). Click OK, and the Active Desktop only shows your HTML document, plus whatever pictures you've manually placed on top of it (Figure 7-68).

 Now that you know how to call Windows 98 programs with the WSHShell object, you don't really need any icons any more, do you? Heh heh heh.

Finally, Microsoft has set up a Web page that includes some truly amazing ActiveX controls that you can place on your Active Desktop. One very popular control provides twenty-minute delayed stock quotes. To place a Microsoft-designed control on the "layer" above your Desktop, right click on the Active Desktop, click Active Desktop, Customize My Desktop, then New. When you see the dialog box in Figure 7-63, click Yes.

 MOM has a little trick up her sleeve, if you've installed MAW. Instead of going through all those machinations, just click "Add more controls to MAW" and you'll be transported directly to Microsoft's ActiveX download site.

Figure 7-67. Icons, be gone!

Browse around Microsoft's download site and pick up any controls that interest you. To add them to your Active Desktop, simply click the Add to Active Desktop button that appears on the bottom of each screen (Figure 7-69). The final result, on your Desktop, seems nothing less than magical (Figure 7-70).

If you're connected to the Web most of the time—or all the time—this kind of instant information feed can be very helpful or very distracting, depending on your predilection. And Microsoft doesn't have a stranglehold on the technology: any ActiveX control can be placed on the "layer" above your Active Desktop. As time goes by, expect to see more useful (and useless) choices from all sorts of sources.

**Figure 7-68.
Desktop devoid of
icons**

**Figure 7-69.
Click Add to Active Desktop and
the control appears on your
Desktop**

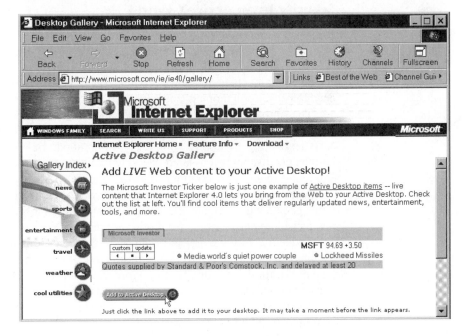

Figure 7-70.
MAW with a cus-
tom stock ticker
and news crawl

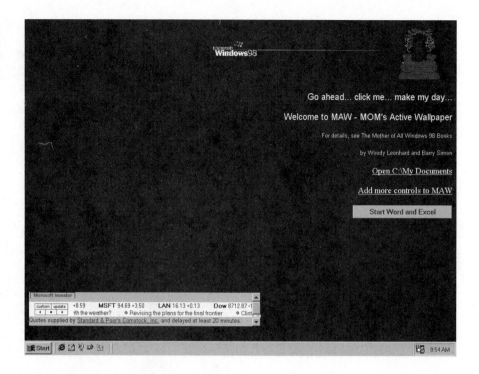

Security in an ActiveX World

The way to be safe is never to feel secure.

—H. G. Bohn, *Handbook of Proverbs,* 1855

As the components of Windows become ever more closely knitted together, you need to pause for a moment and consider the security implications of all this.

The simple fact is that we're rapidly approaching a time—if we aren't there already—when a program (or a macro) written in one part of Windows can have devastating effect on a completely different part of Windows. We won't go into the details, but rest assured that your exposure to viruses, Trojans, and general malware will only continue to grow by leaps and bounds.

A few years ago, it was pretty hard for your system to be infected with a virus: people who exchanged dubious diskettes were most at risk, and only a few picked up nasty critters from other sources.

Suddenly, with the arrival of the Word Concept virus in July 1995, that all changed. Within a year most Word users were at risk, and many had been infected. Within three years, writing Word viruses had turned into an industry—a major growth industry, at that—with thousands of known, identified, and replicated viruses. What happened with Word is about to happen with the rest of Windows. Mark MOM's words.

The antivirus industry is already straining under the load of all these Word viruses, and the viruses are becoming much more sophisticated. Now that VB-

Script is built into Windows itself and can hide inside any Web page or any HTML e-mail message, it's only a matter of time before the malware writers (heinous miscreants that they are) start exploring all the new commands at their disposal. And when a few of them figure out how to put all of it together, all hell's going to break loose.

I still have a lot of enemies inside Microsoft because I demanded that the Windows 98 developers improve their security settings before Win98 shipped. I went so far as to create a "demo" Web page for Microsoft's consumption and threatened to take those destructive discoveries to the mainstream press if the 'Softies didn't change Win98. Fortunately, they did—just days before Win98 went to the duplicators.

I think Microsoft should have people inside their development groups specifically charged with playing devil's advocate—figuring out devious ways to misuse the products, then insisting on changes to make things more secure. Right now, security seems to be a catch-as-catch-can topic, way down on the list of priorities.

In fact, Microsoft is very concerned about malware—and not just viruses targeted at Microsoft products. We've taken several significant steps in the past year to improve our working relationships with anti-virus software manufacturers, and we have many more initiatives under way. I can't talk about them, of course, but I assure you they're ongoing. People have to realize that the antisocial miscreants who create viruses and Trojans and worms are using the tools we built based on users' demands. The fact that those tools can be used for both good and evil shouldn't surprise anyone: that's been true of computers since they were first created.

And true of most human-made tools.

At this point, MOM's crew has four strong recommendations, which should be understood by anybody installing Windows 98.

- First, keep it all in perspective. While it's true that destructive viruses do exist and do infect some peoples' machines, they aren't nearly as common as some companies' PR departments would have you believe. You're still much, much more likely to clobber your own data accidentally or screw up a document or spreadsheet under your own power than to fall victim to some destructive virus.

- That said, you need to realize that the rules are changing. Rapidly. Before Windows 98 arrived, it was (for all intents and purposes) impossible to get infected by surfing to a Web page, or viewing an e-mail message. (The fine print: if you are running Internet Explorer 4 and have downloaded and installed the Windows Scripting Host on a Win95 or NT 4 machine, yes, it is

**Figure 7-71.
Windows 98's se-
curity settings are
all in the Internet
applet**

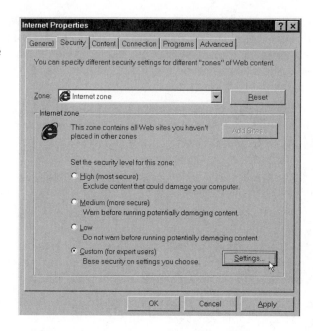

possible to get infected.) With Win98, though, you're exposed: the WSH and all its VBScript capabilities come built into Win98. It most certainly *is* possible to get infected by merely viewing a Web page or reading or even previewing an e-mail message, unless you follow the steps below.

- **Don't screw around with your security settings**. Windows 98, as it comes straight out of the box, has a good, solid collection of security settings. Mess with them at your own peril. If there's a chance you have changed a security setting, click Start, Settings, Control Panel, then double click on the Internet applet. Click the Security tab (Figure 7-71), and make sure the Internet Zone is selected. ("Internet Zone" covers security settings for all Web pages—unless you've given them special status—as well as all your e-mail messages, when viewed in Outlook or Outlook Express.) Click the Medium security button.

   If you can't live with the restrictions imposed by the Medium security level, click Custom, and then Settings. Use the Reset button (Figure 7-72) to reset to Medium security and work from there—but make very sure you understand the implications of every single item you change!

- Finally, when you see the horribly inscrutable message shown in Figure 7-73, **JUST CLICK NO!**

 At least, click No unless you know for sure—I mean, absolutely, totally, with no doubt whatsoever, for sure—that whatever is running won't hurt your PC.

Figure 7-72. At the very least, reset the Internet Zone to Medium security and work from there

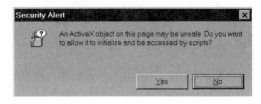

Figure 7-73. A message straight from Win98's security department

That message can appear in all sorts of strange places—when you open an HTML document (as you saw earlier in this chapter), when you're surfing the Web, even when you *preview* a message in Outlook Express or Outlook 98. You may not understand what the message means—heaven knows, nobody at MOM's place can make heads or tails of it—but it's telling you something important. It says that the program that is running (and you may not even know there's a program running!) can clobber your system.

Be careful!

■ ■ ■ ■ ■ ■ ■ ■

Chapter 8

Control Panel

So was their jolly whistle well y-wet.

—GEOFFREY CHAUCER, *The Canterbury Tales,* 1386

This chapter concerns itself with the parts of the Control Panel that have not already been discussed. In particular, we look at adding new hardware; Display properties and other settings (for the mouse, keyboard, and joystick, for example) that directly alter Registry values; and a handful of additional settings.

Woody and Barry take on each of the 22 standard Control Panel applets, in turn—plus Tweak UI—and show you how each one works. Oh, in case you've forgotten, to get at the Control Panel, click Start, then Settings, then Control Panel. Even better, check out the section "Advanced Start Menu Tips" in Chapter 3 to find out how to add a dynamic Control Panel submenu to the Start Menu.

We want to encourage you to start poking around your Registry, if you haven't done so already. This is a nice, low-anxiety place to start learning Win98 brain surgery. To see the effect of Control Panel changes in the Registry, click on Start, then Run, type **regedit** and hit **Enter**. Then follow along in this chapter as we look at how Control Panel applets do their thing, and—halfway through the chapter, in the Screen Saver section, if you're brave enough—we actually go in and change a real live setting. All together now: *Oooooooh. Aaaaaaaah.*

Chapter 3's first brush with Control Panel included the name of the `.cpl` file that each applet comes from. You need this name for shortcuts that launch a particular applet, even a particular tab on a particular applet. The syntax for such shortcuts is at the end of the section "A Fistful of Applets" in Chapter 3.

Let's take a look at each of the 22, er, 23 Control Panel applets in alphabetical order. Note that Windows can install some other applets, depending on the hardware included in your system (for example, Infrared, PC Card, and Scanners and Cameras). We don't cover them here because, for most people, they're pretty esoteric. You're also likely to have other Control Panel applets from applications—Find Fast (from Microsoft Office) being a prime example.

Abbreviations in the Belfry, er, Registry

In order to speak short on any subject, think long.

—H. H. BRACKENRIDGE, *Modern Chivalry,* 1792

We're going to be seeing a lot of the Registry in this chapter. Just to get you in the mood, we're going to start using two common abbreviations for Registry keys—they'll not only save us tons of typing, they'll save a few trees, too. If you look in the Registry, you'll find two keys used all the time: **HKEY_CURRENT_USER** and **HKEY_LOCAL_MACHINE**. Yep, they're always written in CAPITALS_LIKE_THAT. Well, our two time-saving, eye-saving, tree-saving abbreviations are these:

```
HKCU = HKEY_CURRENT_USER

HKLM = HKEY_LOCAL_MACHINE
```

These abbreviations are commonly used by programmers, including the ones who wrote the technical documentation for Microsoft. We think you'll get accustomed to them both very quickly. We thank you. Your eyes thank you. Our 20 blistered fingers thank you.

 ## ■ Accessibility Options

Adversity reminds men of religion.

—LIVY, *History of Rome,* ca. 10 A.D.

The Control Panel Accessibility applet represented one of Microsoft's greatest achievements in Windows 95, and there are just a few minor changes in Win98. While few people use the options here, those who do soon learn that somebody in Redmond cares about making computers usable by those with minor disabilities. Bravo.

Options include (see Figure 8.1)

- StickyKeys, the ability to make Ctrl, Alt, and Shift "sticky," so you don't have to hold down one key while pressing another
- FilterKeys, which tells Win98 to "forgive" brief, presumably accidental, keystrokes
- ToggleKeys, which make the PC beep with different tones when Caps Lock, Num Lock, and Scroll Lock are turned on and off
- SoundSentry, which flashes the Windows title bar whenever the built-in speaker beeps
- SerialKeys device support for those who can't readily use a keyboard
- MouseKeys, which let you use the number pad's arrow keys to move the cursor (described in Chapter 2)

**Figure 8-1.
MouseKeys in the
Registry**

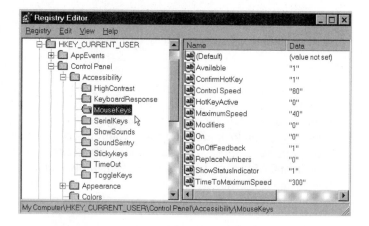

Other settings are meant to feed information to applications, rather than to change Windows itself: Win98 controls a setting in the Registry, and programs are supposed to read that setting and respond to it. Show Sounds, for example, tells applications to substitute on-screen actions for sounds; HighContrast turns on a large-format, white-on-black mode that makes the screen easier to read for those with eyesight problems.

If you've installed any of the Accessibility options, these settings are stored in the Registry key called **HKCU\Control Panel\Accessibility**. (Remember, **HKCU** = **HKEY_CURRENT_USER**.) If you've never poked around with the Registry before, now's a good time to try it: click **Start**, then **Run**, and type **regedit**. See the values called "On," "Enable," or (as in Figure 8-1) "Available." They're the ones that change when you turn on and off the various options that appear in the Accessibility applet.

You can go back and make changes in the Accessibility applet, then flip to Regedit and see the effect of those changes. Just remember to hit **F5** while you're in Regedit so that the program will "refresh" by rereading the contents of the Registry.

 I had a pretty rough time with High Contrast. Word 95, in particular, wouldn't go back into anything resembling normal condition when I turned off High Contrast. Fortunately, rebooting cleaned things up, but if Microsoft itself can't implement the options, it kinda makes you wonder, no?

 C'mon, Woody. This is an option that is intended to be turned on and left on. Users are likely to turn it off either never or one time. And you want to make a big deal about the need to reboot after turning it off. Gimme a break.

■ Add New Hardware

Omnia mutantur, nihil interit.
(All things change; nothing perishes.)

—OVID, *Metamorphoses,* ca. 5 A.D.

Installing new hardware used to be such a joy. You had to check the vendor's documentation to see what IRQ settings were allowed, which I/O addresses would be taken, how many DMA channels were required, and which ones they might be. Then you had to take an inventory of what was in your computer and (usually in a process of divination) figure out which IRQs, I/O addresses, and DMAs were available. If your new hardware needed a setting already taken by an installed component, you had to pull out *that* component and see if it could be changed.

Nowadays, things are a little bit easier. The hardware manufacturers are slowly getting their act together (although those of you with PCMCIA cards may violently disagree—and with good reason). Win98 has some native smarts that, when they work, can make installing new hardware a snap. When they don't work, though, you're back in the same old stew of IRQs, I/O addresses, and DMAs—although Win98 *will* give you an accurate inventory of occupied settings—a far more detailed (and accurate) inventory than the one available in Win95.

 The obvious solution is to throw away all your old hardware and get nothing but the newest Win98-logo'd Plug 'n' Play everything. Then, when you start swearing because your favorite piece of new hardware won't install right, you can cuss Microsoft, too. That should make you feel better. Lots.

Windows 98 offers two different ways to install new hardware. In one case, you tell Win98 what kind of hardware you're going to install, and it tells you which settings to use. You figure out how to get the settings straight on the new hardware, then physically install it. Win98 boots up, recognizes the hardware, and has it going in no time flat. That approach is good—in fact, I would say it's "preferred" for any hardware that isn't Plug 'n' Play—if you understand IRQs, I/O locations, DMAs, and how to play with jumper switches, and if futzing around with things doesn't drive you nuts.

 If you're a little rusty on IRQs, I/O, and DMAs, there are plenty of books that will bring you up to speed. I'd be remiss if I didn't mention that *The Mother of All PC Books* has more than enough information on those topics to take you through just about any bout of Install Depression.

The other way to install new hardware—and *the* way to go with Plug 'n' Play hardware—is to simply open up your computer and stick it in. Either Win98 will realize that it has a new piece of hardware or it won't. If it does realize there's something new, Win98 will bring up the Add New Hardware Wizard and step you through the configuration as best it can. In all cases with PnP hardware (at least in theory), and in some cases for non-PnP hardware, it'll recognize the hardware and install it for you without asking any questions. You should see some reassuring messages, though, telling you that it recognizes and is installing the new hardware.

If it doesn't realize there's something new on board, you can kickstart the Add New Hardware Wizard by clicking Start, then Options, then Control Panel and double clicking the Add New Hardware applet. Whether Win98 realized it had new hardware or not, by using the Add New Hardware Wizard you stand a very good (but not perfect!) chance of getting the hardware installed properly and working in fairly short order. This is the better method for installing hardware if you don't care to learn about IRQs and all those senseless things, or if the thought of opening up the back of your computer makes you break out in a cold sweat. The upside: if it works, it's easy. The downside: if it doesn't work, you're probably best off returning the new hardware and getting your money back.

We're going to step you through the Add New Hardware Wizard twice, once using the "guru" method, once using the "naive" method. In both cases we're going to install a Sound Blaster AWE-32 sound board—a board that's far from the snarliest around, but one that nonetheless doesn't support Plug 'n' Play or anything resembling Plug 'n' Play. If you're installing a new non-PnP board, or a board that claims to be PnP but isn't recognized as such by Windows 98, this should be pretty typical.

 While the AWE-32 board we discuss here to illustrate non-PnP hardware is not PnP, the more recent and currently more common AWE-64 board is PnP.

Let's start with the guru.

Guru Installation So you just bought a shiny new SoundBlaster AWE-32 board and you're going to install it into your Windows 98 machine. You can tell an IRQ from a DMA (even if you aren't exactly sure what they are or why they matter), you know that no two hardware devices can have the same IRQ number or use the same DMA channel, and you aren't intimidated by those little plastic and metal thingies called jumpers.

Well, the first good news is that the AWE-32 doesn't have any jumpers you need to play with to get the sound going. So you can put away the needlenose pliers. Fewer and fewer boards these days require you to make manual adjustments; most of them are software adjustable.

Take a few minutes to look at your new board. Pet it (from outside the protective plastic wrapper, of course). Think good thoughts. Open up the manual and read about how good it's going to be. But don't crack open your PC just yet. Get Win98 running. Click Start, Settings, and Control Panel and double click Add New Hardware.

Figure 8-2.
Add New Hardware Wizard

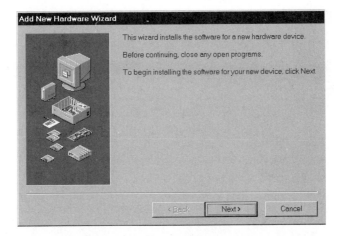

Figure 8-3.
The Wizard wants to scan

The Add New Hardware Wizard springs to life (Figure 8-2). Don't take that graphic on the left too seriously—your PC should be safely closed, Windows 98 should be running (note the conspicuous lack of sparks!), and the only entrails on your desk should be the new card, still in its protective wrapper, with the detritus from inside the box strewn out appropriately.

The Add New Hardware Wizard offers to detect new Plug 'n' Play hardware for you (Figure 8-3). Since the Wizard isn't clairvoyant, actually finding your new sound board would be a little difficult, but you need to go through this step anyway. Click Next and watch as Win98 looks for something that doesn't exist.

Having discovered no new PnP devices, the Wizard asks if you want to have it look for non-PnP devices. If you tell the Wizard No at this point (Figure 8-4), you'll have the opportunity to pick drivers for the new hardware before it's physically installed. You end up in the Wizard's lair for manually choosing new hardware (Figure 8-5). Sometimes the choices in this window aren't so obvious. For

Figure 8-4.
For a guru's instal-
lation, don't let
Win98 scan for
your hardware

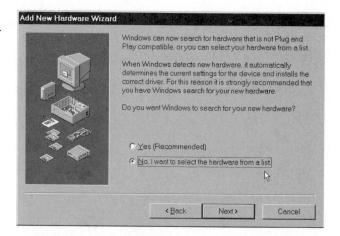

Figure 8-5.
Manually picking
the type of new
hardware

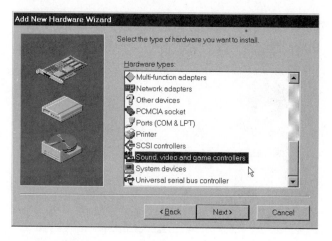

example, "Memory technology drivers" includes Flash memory and SRAM cards; "Multi-function adapters" includes combo COM/LPT port cards, Sound/SCSI cards, and the like. If you can't figure out the category, pick something reasonable and click Next. ("Other devices" actually lists all the available hardware.) You'll have an opportunity to backtrack with no untoward effect. We chose "Sound, video and game controllers," of course.

Pick the manufacturer in the left pane (Figure 8-6), and then pick the specific model in the right pane. If you don't find your hardware on the list, click Back and try to find a better category. If you still can't find the hardware listed, look in the box your hardware came in. If it has a diskette clearly marked Windows 98 Driver (or Windows 95 Driver), stick it in your diskette drive and click Have Disk. If there's no such diskette, or the only diskette in the box contains a Windows 3.1 driver, call the manufacturer and gripe. Real loud.

If Win98 detects no IRQ, I/O, or DMA conflicts, you get the message in Figure 8-7 as an all clear. If you get a screen like this, rejoice! You needn't futz

**Figure 8-6.
Choosing the
AWE-32**

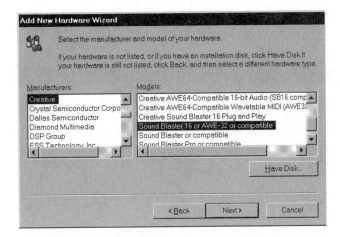

**Figure 8-7.
No conflicts iden-
tified, ready to
proceed**

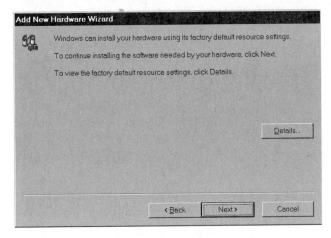

with any settings at all—just install the card the way it came from the factory,
and it should work right the first time. (Click Details if you're hopelessly curious—or if the factory settings have somehow become jumbled and you need to
figure out what needs to be set to get 'em back.)

On the other hand, if Win98 detects a conflict (in Figure 8-8, an IRQ overlap that we artificially induced by changing another card while you weren't
looking), it warns you that you're going to have to change the hardware away
from its factory default. More than that, though, it tells you exactly which settings you need for a clean installation. With these settings and the hardware's
manual in hand, it should (*should!*) be relatively easy to preconfigure the board.
When you click Next, Win98 proceeds to copy any drivers it needs from the
Win98 installation CD (Figure 8-9).

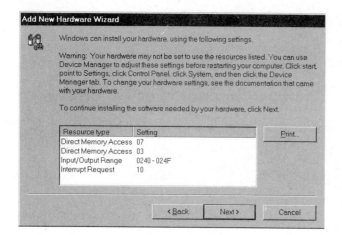

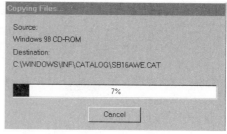

Figure 8-9. Drivers are installed

Figure 8-8. Conflict detected, and your work is cut out for you

 OK, OK. I *know* you really wanted me to show you what's under the Details button in Figure 8-7. I was surprised to find that the factory default DMA settings (channels 1 and 5), which are both open on this machine, are good enough for the "all-clear" panel (Figure 8-7), but they aren't the ones used in the "You gotta change the settings" panel (Figure 8-8). Somehow the Wizard doesn't find that the default DMA channels are both wide open—and thus it tricks you into changing DMA channels on the card when it isn't absolutely necessary.

With the final screen (Figure 8-10), the Wizard is telling you that all you have to do is click Finish, shut down your machine, install the hardware per the manufacturer's instructions (possibly modifying the default settings, if the Wizard found any conflicts), and turn the machine back on. With a little bit o' luck,

Figure 8-10. Ready to rock 'n roll

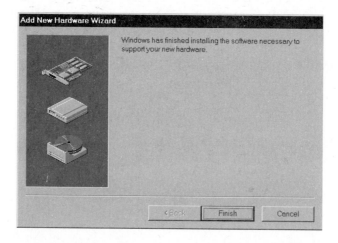

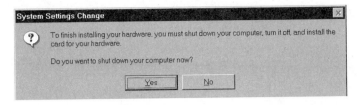

System Settings Change

To finish installing your hardware, you must shut down your computer, turn it off, and install the card for your hardware.

Do you want to shut down your computer now?

Yes   No

Figure 8-11. Final step

Win98 will detect the presence of the new hardware on startup and suddenly it'll be working—with no further effort on your part. But just in case you're a little slow on the up-take, Win98 finishes with a flourish, telling you precisely what you need to do to get the hardware working (Figure 8-11). Bravo.

This precise installation worked like a charm on my machine. I stuck the card in my PC without modifying a thing. When I rebooted, Win98 informed me that it had detected new hardware, and a few seconds later it was all working.

What happens if you can't get your hardware to match the settings the Add New Hardware Wizard demands? Good question. We saw it happen once. Windows 98 Help has a good troubleshooter that covers many possibilities, including the situation where the hardware you're installing can't conform to the Wizard's recommendation and the possibility that you've run the Wizard twice for the same piece of hardware, creating two different entries in the Device Manager for one single physical piece of hardware. To get to the troubleshooter, click Start, then Help. Pick the Index tab. Type **hardware conflict**. Click as indicated to start the hardware conflict troubleshooter, and follow the bouncing WinBall . . .

Naive Installation Now let's try to install the same board, in the same machine, by just sticking it in and seeing what happens.

I put the board in the PC and turned it on. Win98 didn't detect anything, so I clicked Start, Settings, and Control Panel and double clicked Add New Hardware. I was greeted by the same Add New Hardware Wizard used in the guru installation (Figure 8-2).

Figure 8-12. Let Win98 do the dirty work

Add New Hardware Wizard

Windows can now search for hardware that is not Plug and Play compatible, or you can select your hardware from a list.

When Windows detects new hardware, it automatically determines the current settings for the device and installs the correct driver. For this reason it is strongly recommended that you have Windows search for your new hardware.

Do you want Windows to search for your new hardware?

◉ Yes (Recommended)

○ No, I want to select the hardware from a list.

< Back   Next >   Cancel

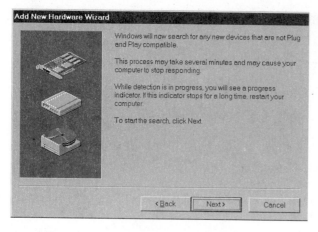

I got the same spiel about automatically detecting new hardware, except unlike the guru installation, I clicked Yes, I really do want Win98 to take care of all this IRQ, DMA, and I/O crap for me. PDQ. UC? I clicked Next (Figure 8-12). After a "fair warning" dialog box (see Figure 8-13), Win98 takes off. I'm sitting there watching the lights flash and listening to the hard drives whir. That progress bar faked me out a couple of times—it goes real fast for a while, then sits forever in the same spot—but I remembered MOM's Second Law of Progress Bars: don't panic unless they freeze for a full five minutes. MOM's First Law of Progress Bars? Don't believe 'em, period. Forget the Second Law.

Figure 8-13. Detection proceeds slowly

 Finally the Wizard popped up and said it had identified the new hardware. I pushed the Details button (Figure 8-14) so I could see the proof, but was there really any doubt? I clicked Finish, Windows went away for a few seconds, I rebooted once, and the AWE-32 board was working fine.

 Most (modern) hardware I've tried to install has really gone just that easily. It's rare that I have to think about any of the old bugaboos: many of the demons that used to keep me from installing new hardware have somehow been exorcised. Quite a refreshing change.

 One exception is an Ensonique Soundscape sound card, which was released while Win95 was in beta. Whenever I reinstall Windows, it doesn't properly set up the card until I go into Device Manager and change the DMA settings by hand to the right ones. As soon as I do, the PnP dialogs pop up, and Win98 installs the sound drivers.

Figure 8-14. Hardware recognized and ready to install

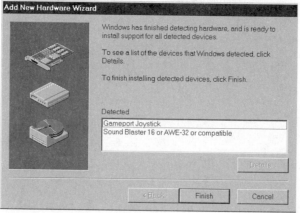

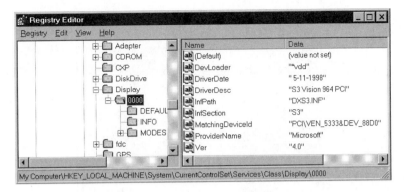

Figure 8-15. Where your display device driver lives

When Win98 performs a hardware autodetect, it maintains a file called `detlog.txt` with all the detection information. See Chapter 6 for details.

 Many of the hardware settings are stored in and around Registry key `HKLM\System\CurrentControlSet\Services\Class`; for example, look at Figure 8-15. (Remember, `HKLM` = `HKEY_LOCAL_MACHINE`.)
Again, feel free to use Regedit to poke around there, but don't touch anything! I don't think *anybody* knows how all those entries are interconnected with the rest of the Registry.

■ Add/Remove Programs

The Add/Remove Programs Wizard is covered at length in Chapter 3 in the section "Software Installation."

Since you've made it this far in the book, it probably won't surprise you to realize that the uninstall information maintained in the Control Panel's Add/Remove Programs applet actually resides in the Registry.

For example, the uninstall information you see in the Wizard in Figure 8-16 owes its existence to the `HKLM\Software\Microsoft\Windows\CurrentVersion\Uninstall` key shown in Figure 8-17. The DisplayName value shows up on the Add/Remove Programs list, and the UninstallString value tells Win98 where the uninstall program for that particular application resides. See how it works?

 Sometimes a program uninstalls and leaves behind its entry in the Add/Remove Programs tab. Although you can remove it in the Registry, it is easier to use Tweak UI, which will also let you drop an entry from the list but restore it easily later.

**Figure 8-16.
Uninstall
information**

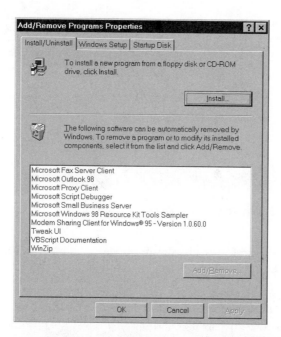

**Figure 8-17.
Corresponding
Registry entries**

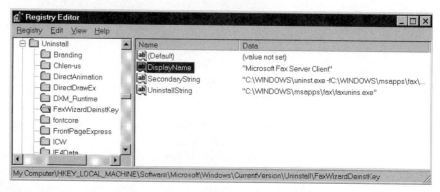

■ Date/Time

*Lost time is never found again,
and what we call time enough always proves little enough.*

—BENJAMIN FRANKLIN, *Poor Richard's Almanac,* 1757

By now you know all about that clock down in the lower right corner of your
Win98 screen. Hold your mouse over the top of it and the ToolTip shows the date.
Double click on it and you get the Control Panel's Date/Time Properties dialog,
just as if you picked the Date/Time applet from the Control Panel itself. From

Figure 8-18.
The ho-hum clock

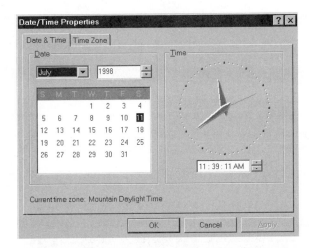

Figure 8-19.
The geographical ho-hum clock

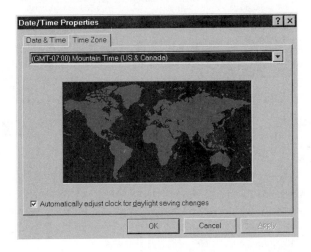

there you can set the time and date (Figure 8-18) and the time zone (Figure 8-19). No biggie.

Now, let's take a look at some things we bet you *didn't* know.

 Windows 95 tried to highlight locations in the time zone map, showing graphically which time zone was currently in effect. That was before Microsoft discovered India, China, and a number of additional countries with hotly disputed border areas—places where a misplaced pixel in the map could engender calls for massive boycotts of Microsoft products or even lead governments to block the distribution of the old Windows. Hey, we learned. It's too bad, though—the original Win95 version was *très* cool.

Win98 supports 62 different geophysical locations with their own time zones; you can see them in the Registry key **HKLM\Software\Microsoft\Windows\ CurrentVersion\Time Zones** (Figure 8-20).

**Figure 8-20.
Registry entry for
the Mountain
time zone**

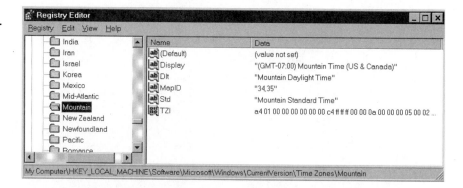

**Figure 8-21.
Where the
currently active
time zone
information lives**

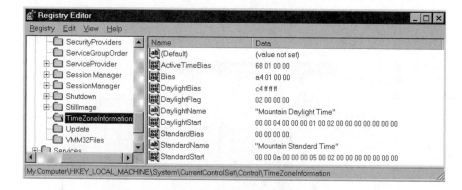

 With all the care that's obviously been lavished on the political sensibilities of various countries—including, for example, six different entries for GMT + 2 hours, which crosses the volatile Middle East—Win98's creators somehow missed Nepal, which has a unique time zone. The oversight may seem like small potatoes from the comfort of a Redmond office desk, but believe me, in Nepal it's a big deal.

While it's apparent that the time zone information stored in **HKLM\Software\ Microsoft\Windows\CurrentVersion\Time Zones** makes its way into **HKLM\System\CurrentControlSet\Control\TimeZoneInformation** (see Figure 8-21)—you can actually see the TZI value in the former migrate to the **DaylightStart** and **StandardStart** keys in the latter, for example— trying to change any of these keys by hand is an invitation to disaster.

 If for some strange reason you need to add a time zone or modify one, the WRK Sampler on the Windows CD (and discussed in Chapter 5) includes a Time Zone Editor.

 If you want to change the format of the date and time (say you want a military-style 24-hour clock or you want the date to appear as YY/MM/DD), you're in the wrong place. Take a look at the Regional Settings applet, described later in this chapter.

If you set the time with the Date/Time applet, your PC's motherboard clock will be set, too.

 ■ **Desktop Themes**

In the Windows 98 milieu, a Desktop theme is a collection of wallpaper, screen saver, active and inactive window formatting—colors, fonts, and the like—sounds, mouse pointers, and icons all pulled together into one family. At least in theory each individual theme is supposed to hang together, presenting a pleasing melange of settings that somehow "looks right." Your opinion may vary, of course.

Figure 8-22. Choosing a specific Desktop theme

Win98 itself ships with 18 themes, but none of them is installed in a "Typical" installation. (Desktop Themes were included in the Windows 95 Plus! Pack, and all the themes that shipped with that package are among the 18 now included in the Win98 base product.) The Windows 98 Plus! Pack includes an additional 19 themes. Third parties, like Gizmos 98, can have additional themes. If you can't find a Desktop Themes applet in the Control Panel list, it's because you didn't explicitly install Desktop Themes when you installed Win98.

To remedy the situation, click Start, Settings, and Control Panel, double click the Add/Remove Programs applet, click the Windows SetUp tab, click Desktop Themes, and click Details. You're presented with the choices shown in Figure 8-22.

Pick any theme that might interest you and click OK. Put the Win98 distribution CD in your CD-ROM drive, and a few minutes later your themes should be available for the choosing via the Desktop Themes applet in the Control Panel.

 On the reasonable assumption that the themes themselves are useless without the program to install them, if you choose one, Windows will insist on installing Desktop Themes Support.

To select a Desktop theme, click Start, Settings, and Control Panel and double click on the Desktop Themes applet. You'll get the Desktop Themes window shown in Figure 8-23. Pick a specific theme in the Theme box (in Figure 8-23 we've chosen the theme "Windows 98 (256 color)"), and follow the instructions on the screen. Clicking the Screen Saver button in the upper right of the screen shows you how the theme's chosen screen saver will work; moving the mouse or typing on the keyboard stops the screen saver preview and sends you back to the Figure 8-23 screen.

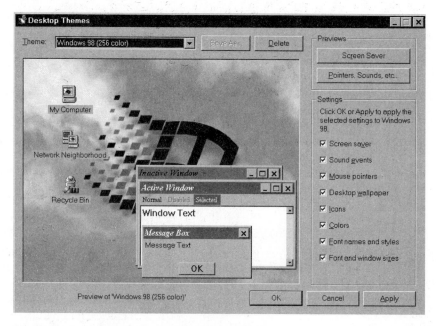

Figure 8-23. Details of the "Windows 98" theme

The Pointers, Sounds, etc. button in the upper right gives you a thorough preview of all the other pieces that make up the selected theme. Click that button and pick the Pointers tab (Figure 8-24) to review the pointers in this theme.

Figure 8-24. Pointers for the "Windows 98" theme

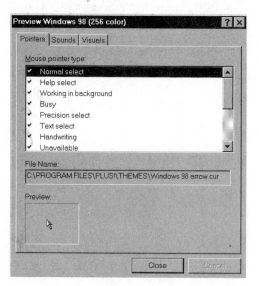

A check mark in front of a particular pointer type indicates that it is included in the specific theme (not all themes have pointers of all types).

The existence of a filename box in the Pointers screen might lead you to believe that you can change a specific pointer in a theme by changing the pointer name right here. Unfortunately, it doesn't work that way. The box is "dead"—you can't make any changes to it. Once you've installed a theme using the Desktop Themes applet, you can go back and change individual pointers using the Mouse applet, which we discuss later in this chapter.

 Ah! But there is a way to change settings for a specific theme—you just have to be a little tricky. No, surprisingly, the key isn't in the Registry. Take a look at the ***.theme** files in the **C:\Program Files\ Plus!\Themes** folder. Yeah, you read that right. Even if you don't have the Plus! Pack, as long as you've installed Desktop Themes from the Win98 distribution CD, you have a folder with that name. Open the ***.theme** file that corresponds to the theme that interests you. In Figure 8-25, I've opened the file **Windows 98 (256 color).theme**. If you want to permanently change a specific cursor for the indicated theme, scroll down to the section marked **[Control Panel\Cursors]** and change the filename to the right of any of the entries, then save the changes and close the file. That new cursor will not only appear the next time you bring up the Desktop Themes applet, it will take over as the installed cursor when you select and "apply" the theme in the Desktop Themes applet.

 In putting in your own filenames, please note that in pathnames for files you must replace each **** by a **%**.

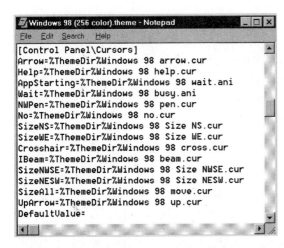

Figure 8-25. **.theme** file that defines the "Windows 98 (256 Color)" theme

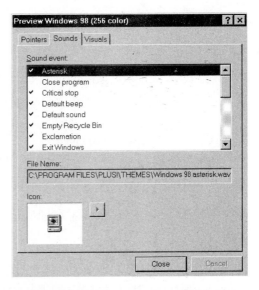

Figure 8-26. Built-in "Windows 98" theme sounds

Figure 8-27.
Sounds in a
Desktop theme

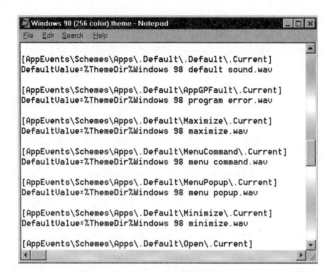

Similarly, the Sounds tab in the Desktop Themes applet identifies the sounds that have been chosen for that theme for certain system events. You can play the sound, but once again, you can't change it in this dialog box. Once you've installed ("applied") the theme, you can change an individual sound by using the Control Panel's Sound applet, which we discuss later in this chapter.

 If you want to permanently change a sound associated with a given theme's system event, you're in for another surprise. Start by crawling into the **.theme** file for the theme that interests you, just as I did with the cursors. There you'll find a whole bunch of sections that dictate which sounds will be played (see Figure 8-27).

As you'll see in the sounds discussion later in this chapter, each of the section names corresponds to a different Registry key. You have to match the key name with the sound and then change the filename here to force Win98 to recognize a different sound in one of its themes. Bizarre, no? And completely different from the way you change cursors!

 No, I don't know why these are implemented so differently. Yes, the programming teams did talk to each other while they were writing Windows 98. Oh, well. A small inconsistency, eh?

Finally, the Visuals tab on the Desktop Themes preview dialog contains a hodgepodge of settings assigned to a specific theme; it's basically an "other" category listing. Oddly, the wallpaper doesn't show up in the Picture preview box—nor does the screen saver.

 Why is that odd? The wallpaper is previewed in the basic Desktop Themes choice dialog, which has an explicit separate button for previewing the screen saver (since our testing shows that's what users most care about!); see Figure 8-28.

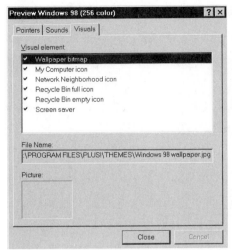

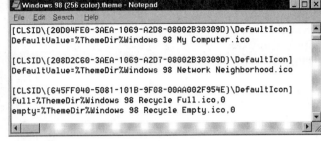

Figure 8-29. Theme settings for icons

Figure 8-28. "Windows 98" theme Visuals

Once you've installed a theme, you can change the My Computer, Network Neighborhood, and Recycle Bin icons via the Effects tab in the Control Panel's Display applet (see the next section of this chapter). Wallpaper and screen saver are also changed in the Display applet, of course.

 To change one of the Visuals permanently for a particular theme, open up the associated `.theme` file as we did before. The four icons are stored in three sections, each associated with a specific Registry key. (See Figure 8-29; we talk about the Registry entries for the Recycle Bin at length in Chapter 9.)

Settings for the wallpaper and screen saver appear at the end of the `*.theme` file in the `[Control Panel\Desktop]` and `[boot]` sections, respectively.

 ■ **Display**

The sense of sight is the keenest of all our senses.

—Cicero, *De oratore*, ca. 80 B.C.

The Control Panel's Display applet is accessible from two different locations: you can start up the Control Panel and double click on Display, or you can right click on a blank part of the Desktop and choose Properties. Either way, you get the screen shown in Figure 8-30. In this section we take a look at the Background, Screen Saver, Appearance, Effects, Web, and Settings tabs.

**Figure 8-30.
Display applet,
also known as the
Display Properties
dialog**

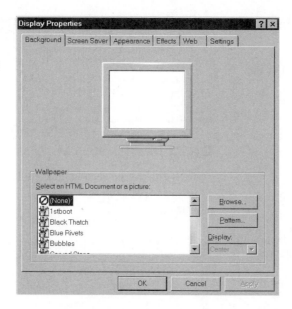

Background Tab

 I always get confused by the difference between pattern and wallpaper—two rather meaningless terms for similar WinThings. Fortunately, the preview offered under the Display applet's Background tab makes the differences pretty obvious when you're actually trying to put them to use. I finally figured out how they differ conceptually when I looked at the Registry entries.

When you first bring up the Display applet, Win98 runs out to your `C:\windows` folder and looks for all the `.bmp`, `.dib`, and `.rle` files that sit there. It lists those at the beginning of the Wallpaper box. It then looks in `C:\windows\web\wallpaper` and adds to the bottom of the list any `.htm`, `.gif`, `.jpg`, `.bmp`, `.dlb`, or `.rle` files it finds there. (Oddly, no `.gif` or `.jpg` files in `C:\windows` get listed.)

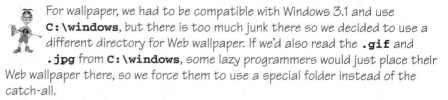 For wallpaper, we had to be compatible with Windows 3.1 and use `C:\windows`, but there is too much junk there so we decided to use a different directory for Web wallpaper. If we'd also read the `.gif` and `.jpg` from `C:\windows`, some lazy programmers would just place their Web wallpaper there, so we force them to use a special folder instead of the catch-all.

You're then invited to choose from the offered files (Figure 8-31). If you click the Browse button, Win98 lets you go out and pick any `.bmp`, `.dib`, `.rle`, `.gif`, `.jpg`, or `.htm` file.

The Display box in Figure 8-31 controls whether the wallpaper image will be centered on the Desktop, stretched all the way across the screen, or repeated—"tiled"—from the upper left corner.

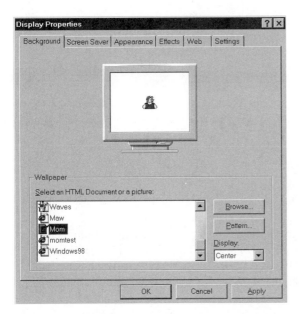

Note that there's no way to get the Wallpaper box at the bottom of Figure 8-31 to show you the filename extensions for all the listed files, so you have to rely on the icons in front of the filenames for visual cues. For example, in Figure 8-31 Waves is a **.bmp** file, MOM is a **.gif**, and Maw is an **.htm**.

If you choose an **.htm**, **.gif**, or **.jpg** file as wallpaper and you aren't running Active Desktop, Win98 asks you if you want to switch over to Active Desktop (Figure 8-32). That's necessary because the only way Win98 can display an **.htm**, **.gif**, or **.jpg** file on the Desktop is to treat it as a Web page. Choosing Yes is identical to right clicking on the Desktop, choosing Active Desktop, and putting a check mark alongside View as Web Page. Both of those are *also* equivalent to clicking the Web tab in the Display applet and checking the "View my Active Desktop as a Web page" box—three different ways to accomplish precisely the same thing, with at least two wildly different descriptions.

Figure 8-31. Choosing a centered `C:\windows\` `web\wallpaper\mom.gif` **as the wallpaper**

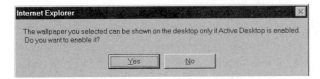

Figure 8-32. Requisite for using an .htm file as wallpaper

If you want to add a pattern to appear "behind" the wallpaper, click the Pattern button, and the Pattern dialog appears (Figure 8-33). A pattern is a collection of eight numbers, each between 0 and 255. The numbers correspond to the pixels. An easy way to see what's going on is to bring up the Desktop tab, click Pattern, pick a pattern, then click Edit Pattern. You get the Pattern Editor, as shown in Figure 8-34.

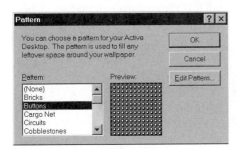

Figure 8-33. Apply a pattern for the entire Desktop here

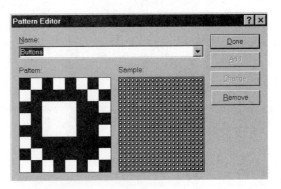

Figure 8-34. Pattern Editor, working on the Buttons pattern

Take a look at the black and white squares in the Pattern box. Those squares define the pixels that make up the pattern. You can think of the Buttons pattern shown in Figure 8-34 like this:

1	0	1	0	1	0	1	0
0	1	1	1	1	1	0	1
1	1	0	0	0	1	1	0
0	1	0	0	0	1	1	1
1	1	0	0	0	1	1	0
0	1	1	1	1	1	1	1
1	0	1	1	1	1	1	0
0	1	0	1	0	1	0	1

Each of the eight lines is interpreted as a binary number. The first number, 10101010 binary, is 170 in decimal. The second number, 01111101 binary, is 125. Then comes 198 (take my word for it), 71, 198, 127, 190, and 85. If you look at the Pattern value in Figure 8-35, you'll see how the Buttons pattern is stored in the Registry. Neat, huh?

 Believe it or not, the built-in Windows patterns are tucked away in your Win98 **C:\windows** folder, in an old-fashioned **.ini** file called **control.ini**. There you'll find the entries shown in Figure 8-35. Too bad Windows uses such a weird hodgepodge of places to store information.

If you want to distribute your own patterns, simply edit **control.ini** to add your favorites, and give the new **control.ini** to your circle of friends. The Registry contains no mention of any of the built-in patterns—the Registry (see Figure 8-38) concerns itself only with the currently installed pattern (as a set of eight numbers), regardless of where it came from—so customizing your own **control.ini** is an easy, safe way to pass your patterns around.

Patterns are rather monotonous, single-color beasts, although it *is* rather surprising what can be done with a monochrome 8 × 8 bit array. Want to change the color of your pattern? You don't do that here. Look at the Desktop setting under the Appearance tab.

Putting the wallpaper and pattern together, as in Figure 8-36, produces a Desktop that looks like Figure 8-37.

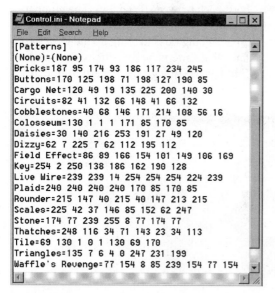

Figure 8-35. Patterns available in control.ini

**Figure 8-36.
Using mom.bmp
as wallpaper and
the Button
pattern . . .**

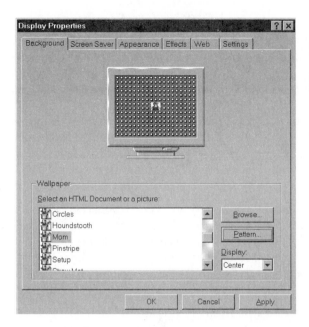

**Figure 8-37. . . . creates
a Desktop that looks like
this**

Apparently when Win98 draws the Desktop, it goes through a procedure
something like this. First, it figures out if you've turned on the Active Desktop.
(Or, equivalently, if you've chosen to "View my Active Desktop as a Web
page.") If so, it uses the Web page viewing engine in Internet Explorer to put
the page up on the screen. We talk more about Active Desktop later in this section, in the discussion of the Web tab.

If there's no Active Desktop, Win98 looks at the Pattern value in
HKCU\Control Panel\Desktop and interprets the set of eight numbers
there as a bit pattern (Figure 8-38). If you've chosen no pattern, the Registry
value is set to "(None)", and it's interpreted as if all the eight pattern numbers
were zeros.

**Figure 8-38.
Registry entry
that controls a
non-Active Desk-
top's appearance**

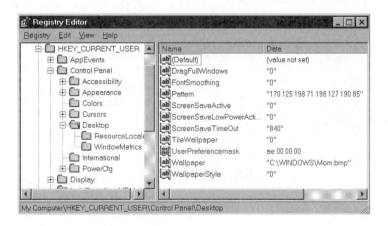

Next, if there's no Active Desktop, Win98 looks at the wallpaper value to see if you've chosen a valid picture (`.bmp`, `.dib`, or `.rle` files all work; `.pcx` and `.wmf` files do not). If you haven't chosen a wallpaper, the value is simply " ".

Then Win98 looks at the TileWallpaper and WallpaperStyle values. If both are 0, the wallpaper is centered on top of the pattern. If TileWallpaper is a 1, the pattern is discarded completely and the wallpaper is duplicated so that it covers the entire Desktop ("tiled"), starting with an image in the upper left corner. If WallpaperStyle is a 2, the image specified in the Wallpaper key is stretched to fit the entire screen. Next, Win98 draws the icons, Taskbar, windows, and the like on the Desktop. Finally, if you have Active Desktop turned on, Windows draws any ActiveX controls or simple pictures that you've added to the Active Desktop.

 Some folks who like to use scanned-in pictures as their wallpaper have bemoaned the fact that they couldn't use multiple pictures. Now they can, since you can add individual pictures in the Web tab of the Display applet. On my portable's Desktop I've got separate pictures of my grandchildren taken with my digital camera, a lovely Nikon Coolpix 900.

Screen Saver Tab

The Screen Saver tab not only allows you to choose a screen saver, it also lets you set up password protection for screen savers in general. There's also a "tunnel" from the Screen Saver tab to the Power Management applet, which we discuss later in this chapter.

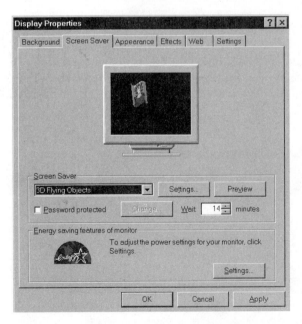

Figure 8-39. MOM as texture on a Flying Objects flag

When you bring up the Display applet's Screen Saver tab (Figure 8-39), Win98 scans the Win98 `c:\windows` and `\windows\system` folders for any `*.scr` files. The names of those files (without their extensions) are presented in the Screen Saver Scroll-down box. Win98 makes no allowances for screen savers located in other folders. If the `.scr` file you choose is a valid Win98 screen saver, the Preview button will work. If, in addition, the screen saver has user-adjustable properties, the Settings button comes to life. If the screen saver supports Win98 password protection—and many old Windows 3.1 screen savers do not—the "Password Protected" box becomes active.

If you click on the Settings button in the panel labeled "Energy saving features of monitor," you'll be transported to the Control Panel's Power Management applet. We talk about that in a bit.

Figure 8-40.
Screen saver set-
tings in the Reg-
istry

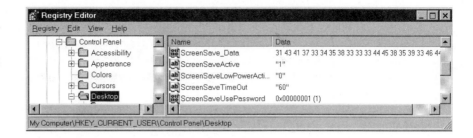

 While they may have some minor value as password protection devices, screen savers, of course, do absolutely nothing beneficial for your monitor. They're just for fun. Back in the days when screens were green and advanced screens were amber, monitor burn-in was a problem. But ever since the late 1980s or so, monitors haven't been prone to burn-in.

One of the weekly trade magazines made a big deal of the fact that typing **Ctl+Alt+Del** would bypass password "protection" on Windows 3.1 screen savers running under Windows 95 and Win98. While that's literally true, at least for the screen savers that still work in Win95 and Win98, the Win3.1 screen saver password "protection" was a joke to begin with. And if they had bothered to look here at the Screen Saver tab, where such things come to roost, they would've discovered the "Password Protected" box grayed out. The moral of the story: don't rely on Win3.1 screen savers, particularly not for password protection. The **.scr** file format changed between Win3.1 and Win95, and programmers have had to rewrite their screen savers to take advantage of all the hooks in the new Win95/Win98 world.

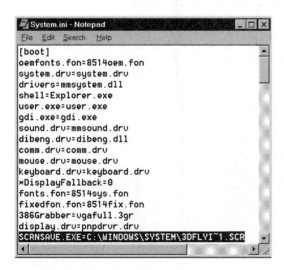

Win98 stores the settings you would expect (screen saver active, password required, time delays, and the like) in the Registry's **HKCU\Control Panel\Desktop** key (Figure 8-40). Even the password itself, one-way encoded in the value ScreenSave_Data, is here. Except the one thing you would most expect to be stored in the Registry—the name of the screen saver **.scr** file! To find the name of the current screen saver, you have to pop over to the Win98 **c:\windows** folder and look in **system.ini**'s **[boot]** section for a line called **scrnsave.exe=** (Figure 8-41). Bizarre!

Figure 8-41. The name of the Screen Saver file
is stored in system.ini, in DOS 8.3 format

Not bizarre at all, gentlemen. That's where the name of the screen saver was stored in Windows 3.1. If we had moved it, millions of people would've been disappointed (or worse!) when their favorite old screen saver or screen saver program didn't work. You don't understand how attached people become to their flying toasters.

The Time-Out settings under the Screen Saver tab are all measured in minutes, and if you play with them, you'll discover that none can be set to less than 1 minute or more than 60 minutes. Bummer. Some days wouldn't you really like to set your screen saver to kick in quickly? Well, guess what? You can do it. The time-out values in the Registry (**ScreenSaveTimeOut**, **ScreenSavePowerOffTimeOut**, and **ScreenSaveLowPowerTimeOut**) are measured in seconds. All you have to do is change the setting manually in the Registry—and, subsequently, avoid using the Screen Saver tab, which (if you click Apply or OK) will reset the numbers.

 This is an excellent opportunity to edit your Registry if you've never done so before: the setting is easy to find, and if you screw up, you need only call up the Display applet's Screen Saver tab to make everything right. Start by bringing up the Screen Saver tab, picking a screen saver, and setting the wait time at 1 minute. Click OK. Now start Regedit, the Registry editor, by clicking Start, then Run, typing **regedit**, and hitting **Enter**. At the left, double click on **HKCU** (that's **HKEY_CURRENT_USER**, remember?), then **Control Panel**, then **Desktop**. At the right, double click on the value you want to change, in this case **ScreenSaveTimeOut**. You should get a box like Figure 8-42.

Replace the old value of 60 (seconds) with 10, and click OK. Congratulations. You've just performed the Win98 equivalent of brain surgery. Now, restart your computer by clicking on Start, then Shutdown, pick the Restart button and click OK.

When you reboot, just wait about 10 seconds and all of a sudden your screen saver will kick in. Boom. Play with it a bit and you'll see that the screen saver does, indeed, work with a 10-second fuse. To restore everything to its old status, just right click on the Desktop, pick Properties, bring up the Screen Saver tab, and make any changes you like.

You can run any Windows screen saver, even one that isn't your current one, by double clicking on it in Explorer. The quickest way of checking out a bunch of screen savers is to run a Find (Start, Find, Files, or Folders) for ***.scr** files and double click on 'em one at a time.

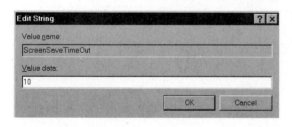

Figure 8-42. Changing the `ScreenSaveTimeOut` value to 10 seconds

**Figure 8-43.
Creating a Boss
Button**

 Be sure to check out and use the right-click context menu for screen saver files. Not only is there the default test item that double clicking brings up but there is a configure choice and an Install choice that whisk you directly to the Screen Saver tab of the Display applet.

 My favorite Stupid Desktop Trick has to be the screen saver hotfoot, er, hotkey—better known as the Boss Button. You know the scenario: the boss suddenly drops by and you're playing Leisure Suit Larry. If you have the Boss Button set up, a quick key combination gets rid of all the incriminating evidence, and before the boss has a chance to say, "Beach Blanket Babes from Beyond," you're sitting in front of a completely innocuous screen.

Go into Explorer and right click and drag any `.scr` file (such as, oh, `C:\windows\system\3D Flying Objects.scr`) onto the Desktop. When you let go of the mouse button, pick "Create Shortcut Here." Right click on the new shortcut, pick Properties, bring up the Shortcut tab, click on the "Shortcut key" box, and hit whatever key combination you like (say, **Alt+F10**), as in Figure 8-43. Click OK. Now hitting that key combination will bring up the screen saver.

 I put the Boss Button on the Desktop because it cranks up faster when located there—it takes about 2 seconds, on my vintage Pentium 90, for 3D Flying Objects to take over when I'm running Word 98. (Other, less complex screen savers start faster.) I could've put it in **\Windows\ Start Menu** or any folder in **\Start Menu** (or **\Desktop** for that matter), but the hotkey doesn't work as fast from those locations.

Now that you've read almost everything there is to know about Win98 screen savers, there's one little detail you've probably been wondering about: how to disable password protection on Win98 screen savers. Chances are pretty good you've been to a store with PCs on display—and all of the PCs are running password protected screen savers. No matter what you try, you can't get around the password prompt—and with the screen saver on the screen, you can't do anything but stare at a bouncing ball or morphing geometric patterns.

Bypassing the screen saver password "protection" is so easy that it's embarrassing. Simply restart the PC (say, hit the Reset button), and after Win98 comes up, quickly right click on the Desktop, click Screen Saver, and clear the "Password Protected" box you see in Figure 8-39. You'll then have full access to the PC.

Appearance Tab

The Appearance tab lets you choose colors and fonts for just about everything that has to do with the Desktop, windows, and, uh, Windows. Settings that you choose under the Display tab (Figure 8-44) are stored in a shorthand form in the Registry's **HKCU\Control Panel\Appearance** key (Figure 8-45), with the actual working settings scattered more extensively in other parts of the Registry.

A large collection of Appearance settings is stored in Schemes. A scheme, in this case, is just a collection of settings for everything from the Desktop color to the Active Title Bar's font size—it's roughly analogous to a Desktop theme—except themes involve collections of what are stored in schemes. Typically a scheme involves a collection of closely related settings while a theme involves most of the settings you can change in the Desktop interface. Windows comes with a predefined collection of 33 different Desktop schemes. You can see them by scrolling down the Schemes list on the Appearance tab or (easier) by looking at the Registry's **HKCU\Control Panel\Appearances\ Schemes** key. There are also schemes for mouse cursors and sounds.

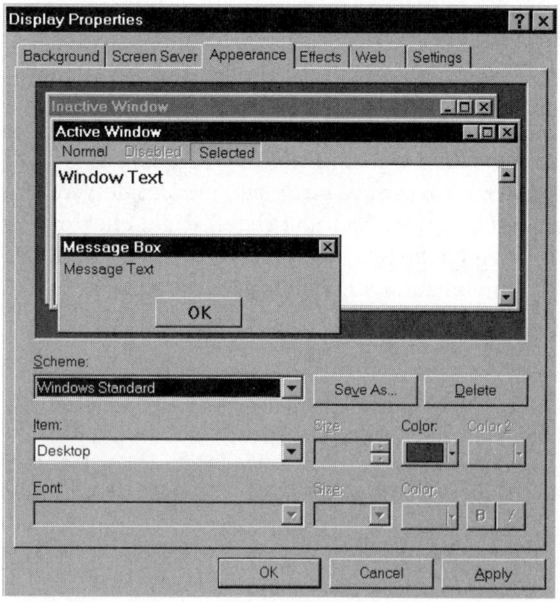

Figure 8-44. Display applet's Appearance tab

Figure 8-45. Appearance settings in the Registry

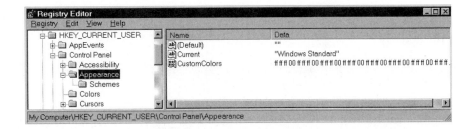

Figure 8-46. MOM's Favorite Color Scheme, created in the Appearance tab

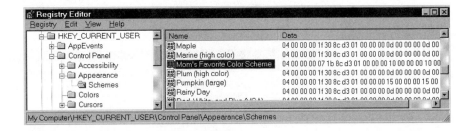

Figure 8-47. MOM's Favorite Color Scheme details

As you create new schemes with the Save As button on the Appearance tab (or delete them, for that matter, with the Delete button), the collection under the **\Schemes** key grows (or shrinks). In Figure 8-46, for example, I've created a new Appearance scheme called MOM's Favorite Color Scheme by using the Save As button. See how it appears under **\Schemes**?

There's nothing particularly magical about schemes. At its core, an Appearance scheme is really just a 520-byte collection of settings. You can see the odd assortment of numbers and ASCII characters that make up a scheme by double clicking in the Registry on the scheme of your choice to bring up the Registry's edit box (Figure 8-47).

The Item list on the Appearance tab contains 18 Desktop items—from 3D Objects to Desktop to Window—that you can adjust from the Display applet. It probably won't surprise you to discover that these 18 settings are just a small subset of all the Desktop settings maintained in the Registry.

**Figure 8-48.
\WindowMetrics
in the Registry**

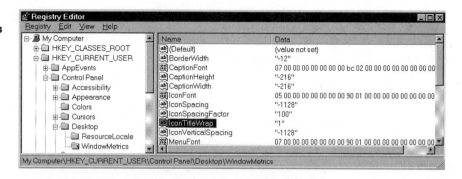

**Figure 8-49.
\Colors in the
Registry**

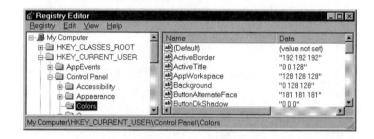

 I'll tell you what surprised me. I thought a scheme would hold a setting for each of those 18 items. By choosing a scheme, I figured, all the 18 items would be set to values defined by the scheme. Not so. It ends up that a couple of the items work independently of schemes: you can change the scheme till you're blue in the face but never touch these items' values. Weird.

Let me tell you what surprised me. This schemes and items folderol doesn't really mean anything. All they amount to is a pretty face painted on the top of the real, working settings: when Windows 98 or a Win98 application goes to draw a screen, it couldn't care less what you've chosen for, say, the Desktop item or the 3D Objects item. The real Appearance settings are in the Registry, stored in **HKCU\Control Panel\ Desktop\WindowMetrics** (Figure 8-48) and **HKCU\Control Panel\ Colors** (Figure 8-49) keys. These are the settings that actually affect how your screen appears—schemes and items are mere biological window dressing for the binary-inhibited. You can control the appearance of your screen much more accurately by ditching the Display applet's Appearance tab and editing the Registry entries by hand!

To see how changes in the 18 Appearance tab items rippled down to the real working settings in the Registry, I started by looking at those Registry settings with a pristine installation of the Windows standard scheme—the default settings. Here's what I found for the **\WindowMetrics** settings.

Registry key	Default value
BorderWidth	-12
CaptionFont	*
CaptionHeight	-216
CaptionWidth	-216
IconFont	*
IconSpacing	-1,128
IconSpacingFactor	100
IconTitleWrap	1
IconVerticalSpacing	-1,128
MenuFont	*
MenuHeight	-216
MenuWidth	-216
MessageFont	*
ScrollHeight	-192
ScrollWidth	-192
Shell Icon BPP	16
Shell Icon Size	32
SmCaptionFont	*
SmCaptionHeight	-216
SmCaptionWidth	-180
StatusFont	*

* All default fonts are MS Sans Serif; the first two bytes are the font size, in hexadecimal

While most of those values are primarily of interest to C programmers, the identity of the fonts can come in handy. The **CaptionFont** is what most people would call a window title font. For some unknown reason, though, it's also the font used in the Taskbar and for the time in the Taskbar's Notification area. (**CaptionHeight**, for what it's worth, controls not only the height of the window title area, but it also controls the height of each line in the Taskbar area.) The **IconFont** is not only the font used for icon captions, as you might expect; it's also the internal font used for identifying folder contents, and by Explorer, Regedit, and other Windows apps. The **MenuFont** controls menus, including entries on the Start Menu (but not Start itself, which is in the **CaptionFont**). **MessageFont** controls the text in only a very few messages: most applications seem to ignore it. The only place we could find **SmCaptionFont** was in Microsoft Office's Shortcut Bar, where it's used for a very brief time as the Shortcut Bar is loaded. And the **StatusFont** not only controls the status bar in several Win98 applications; it's also used for ToolTips! Only Redmond knows why

StatusFont is not used for the status bars in the MS Office applications. What's good for the goose, eh?

If you go into to hack, uh, examine the Registry entries for these fonts, you'll find that the first two bytes are always the font's point size, expressed in hexadecimal (base 16). To change a 7-point font to 16-point, for example, change the first two bytes from 07 to 10 (since, of course, 10 base 16 is 16 decimal).

Since Win95 uses the scalable Marlett font for the Minimize/Maximize/ Close buttons in the upper right corner of every window (see Chapter 2), those three buttons can automatically adjust their size, depending on changes in **CaptionHeight**. That's pretty cool and sure beats the unscalable bitmaps used in Win3.1 and its ancestors.

 To get our bearings before we started really messing up the Registry, I took a look at the **\Colors** settings. These all consist of a set of three numbers, representing red, green, and blue color intensities: 0 0 0 is black; 255 0 0 is bright red; 255 255 255 is white; and so on (color RGB values are discussed in Chapter 2).

 To get you up to speed on RGB values, I'll tell you the default colors inside parentheses for the first few items.

Registry key	Default value	Determines the color of:
ActiveBorder	192 192 192	Thin line inside border of resizable window with focus; thin line around Taskbar (default = light gray)
ActiveTitle	0 0 128	Title bar of window with focus; this setting is ignored by MS Office applications (default = dark blue)
AppWorkspace	128 128 128	Background color in some applications (the "client area," for example, if there is no open document in Word or if all documents are minimized; this is not the color behind Word documents in Page View) (default = medium gray)
Background	0 128 128	Desktop color; also primary color in pattern (default = cyan)
ButtonAlternateFace	181 181 181	Presumably a darker version of **ButtonFace**, but we couldn't find it used anywhere in the major Win98 applications (default = light gray).
ButtonDkShadow	0 0 0	Extreme right and bottom of button (default = black)
ButtonFace	192 192 192	Used all over Win98: face of buttons; dialog backgrounds; top and bottom areas of many Win apps; status bar background; Taskbar background; highlight around edges of menus; toolbar backgrounds; scrollbar "thumb" (or "slider"); dithered with **ButtonHilight** for faces of "pushed" buttons and for scrollbar itself

Registry key	Default value	Determines the color of:
ButtonHilight	255 255 255	Extreme top and left of button; secondary color for Win app buttons and common dialog buttons; also used on dialog text boxes; many more less obvious uses
ButtonLight	223 223 223	Just below ButtonHilight on buttons
ButtonShadow	128 128 128	Just above ButtonDkShadow on buttons
ButtonText	0 0 0	Text on buttons; text on status bars; Taskbar icon captions; Taskbar time text; arrows on dropdown lists and scrollbars; primary color on Win app buttons and common dialog buttons
GradientActiveTitle	0 0 128	End color for a gradient-filled title bar with focus. ("Gradient-filled" title bars change color as you move from left to right.) I discuss gradients at the end of this list. Note how the default value is the same as ActiveTitle, which means no gradient effect.
GradientInactiveTitle	128 128 128	End color of a gradient-filled title bar without focus. The default is the same value as InactiveTitle; again, no gradient.
GrayText	128 128 128	Some old Windows 3.1 apps use this color to indicate unavailable menu selections, but in Win98 unavailable menu selections use a ghosted font; primary use of GrayText in Win98 is for the lines connecting folders in the tree side of Explorer-style windows
Hilight	0 0 128	Background of selected item in menu or in some Win apps; background of selected text in a text box and other Windows controls; dithered with icon caption background color when icon has focus
HilightText	255 255 255	Text of selected item in menu or in some Win apps (e.g., Explorer); color of selected text in a text box and other Windows controls; also color of icon caption on Desktop when icon has focus
HotTrackingColor	0 0 255	Controls the highlighting color Win98 uses when you choose "Single click to open an item" in the Explorer View/Options menu. Icon on the Desktop or folder or file in Windows Explorer turns this color when the cursor passes over it.
InactiveBorder	192 192 192	Thin line inside border of resizable window without focus; also used on Taskbar
InactiveTitle	128 128 128	Background of title bar of window without focus
InactiveTitleText	192 192 192	Text on title bar of window without focus
InfoText	0 0 0	ToolTip text in Win98 and the text of tips on buttons in such applications as Explorer, Paint, WordPad, and the Toolbar tips in the MS Office suite

Registry key	Default value	Determines the color of:
InfoWindow	255 255 225	Tooltip background in Win98 and the background color of tips in Explorer, Paint, WordPad, and Office
Menu	192 192 192	Background of menu bar; background of menu items (including the Start Menu but not the Start button)
MenuText	0 0 0	Text on menu bar and menu items (including the Start Menu but not the Start button)
Scrollbar	192 192 192	Some old Win3.1 programs use this for the main part of the scrollbar; I couldn't find it used anywhere in Win98. The main part of Win98 scrollbars are constructed by dithering ButtonFace and ButtonHilight.
TitleText	255 255 255	Text on title bar of window with focus (although the MS Office apps ignore this setting)
Window	255 255 255	Background of most Win apps and Explorer-style icon windows; color of "page" in MS Office apps; background color for Windows controls, e.g., text boxes and list boxes, even radio buttons!
WindowFrame	0 0 0	Outermost right and bottom lines on some (not many) windows; outline for default buttons; outline for Tooltips in MS Office apps.
WindowText	0 0 0	Text within most applications; text and + and – boxes in Explorer; text in Windows dialog boxes; unselected text in text boxes and list boxes

WARNING: You must restart Windows (at least "Log on as a Different User") to see the effect of changing these settings!

Gradient title bars are new with Windows 98. If you have a 256-color setup, don't even think about them because they require at least High Color. If you have High Color and you set the item dropdown in Figure 8-44 to Active Title Bar or Inactive Toolbar, the button marked Color 2 (which stays Gray under 256-color setups) becomes live and allows you to pick a second color. This second color, not surprisingly, is stored as **GradientActiveTitle** or as **GradientInactiveTitle**, and the title bar starts with Color on left and Color 2 on the right with a smooth interpolation in between. It's a striking effect—be sure to try it if your display supports High Color or True Color.

Armed with a guidebook of how the Registry settings start out, let's step through each of the 18 Appearance tab items in turn and see what changing them does to Windows. By the way, very little of this stuff is documented anywhere, as far as we know—and the little documentation we have seen is wrong, over and over again. Odd, considering how much interest there is in "personalizing" the Desktop.

This is a good time to go ahead and play with the Registry, if you like, although you'll have to reboot after making changes so they'll take. ("Log on as a

Different User" will do it.) If you bollix everything up, not to worry: bringing back the Display applet's Appearance tab and picking a scheme will reset all the settings. Well, almost all of them. I'll show you the two that stay "stuck."

Many of these settings were hopelessly screwed up in Win95. It's good to see that Microsoft has taken a hint—probably from MOM!—and put its house pretty much in order.

We aim to please.

3D Objects The 3D Objects item defines the background color (in the upper Color dropdown box) and the text color (in the lower Color dropdown box) of any standard Windows 3D control. Yes, both those boxes are hot; make changes to them and you'll see. Since Win98 pretty much lives and dies with 3D objects—they appear everywhere from the Taskbar to the background of popular Windows applications—these settings can make a huge difference in Windows' appearance.

Behind the scenes, changing the 3D Objects background item really changes settings for 12 different Registry entries: **Scrollbar**, **InactiveTitle**, **Menu**, **ActiveBorder**, **InactiveBorder**, **AppWorkspace**, **ButtonFace**, **ButtonAlternateFace**, **ButtonHilight**, **ButtonLight**, **ButtonShadow**, and **GrayText**.

I found the most wonderful thing when working with 3D Objects and background colors. The dropdown Color box has 20 entries, as usual. The first 16 colors (reading left to right) in the dropdown list box are the standard RGB colors used since the very first PC descended from the Boca Raton heavens. The last one is fixed at almost-gray with RGB = 160, 160, 164. But colors 17, 18, and 19 change depending on which color you've chosen for the 3D Objects background! Once you've chosen a color—which will become the **ButtonFace** color—Win98 automatically recalculates the 12 other colors and sticks them in the Registry. If you click on the Color dropdown box again, the **ButtonShadow** color is presented in the dialog as the new color 18, and the **ButtonHilight** color is offered as color 19.

Because it takes over these three colors (recall that the 20 colors in the dropdown box are the 20 solid system colors on 256-color systems, Win98 can let you choose a dithered color (see Chapter 2) for 3D Objects backgrounds. If you pick a dithered color, the color 17 in the dropdown box becomes the solid color with RGB values identical to the color that used to be dithered! This is the only situation I know about where the Control Panel changes system colors on the fly.

If you change the font color in the 3D Objects item, then in the lower box on the Appearance tab, Win98 will change **IconFont** in addition to all the Registry settings mentioned above that were modified with the background change.

Active Title Bar The Active Title Bar item on the Appearance tab, as you might imagine, changes the color, size, and font of the Active Title Bar. Not unexpectedly, it changes the Registry `\WindowMetrics` entries for `CaptionFont`, `CaptionWidth`, `CaptionHeight`, and `smCaptionFont` and the `\Colors` entries for `ActiveTitle` and `TitleText`. Ho-hum. As I already noted, changing Color 2 (not possible with only 256 colors) changes the `GradientActiveTitle` color.

Active Window Border The Active Window Border item changes the `BorderWidth` (each unit of 1 on the Appearance tab seems to correspond to 5 pixels' thickness) and the `ActiveBorder` color, as expected.

Application Background The Application Background item on the Display applet's Appearance tab changes `AppWorkspace`. No surprises there.

CaptionButtons The CaptionButtons item on the Appearance tab not only lets you adjust the height of the Minimize/Maximize/Exit buttons in the upper right corner of every window; it also controls the height of each line in the Taskbar and the size of the icons in the Taskbar. It affects the Registry settings for `CaptionWidth` and `CaptionHeight`.

Figure 8-50.
Icon with gray Desktop color, no wallpaper, no pattern

Figure 8-51.
Same icon, tiled wallpaper, no pattern

Figure 8-52.
Same icon, no wallpaper, Buttons pattern

Desktop The Desktop item controls the color of the Desktop (Registry entry `Background`), but it's a little more complicated than that. Each icon gets the Desktop color as a background to the caption: the color fills a small rectangular area surrounding the icon's text. If there's no wallpaper and no pattern, what you'll see is something like Figure 8-50. If there's a tiled wallpaper (see the section "Background Tab," earlier in this chapter) or wallpaper fills the whole screen, the Desktop color appears only as background to the icons' text, as in Figure 8-51. If the wallpaper doesn't fill the whole screen and there's no pattern (see "Background Tab"), the Desktop color fills the Desktop, except for areas occupied by icons and the Taskbar. If there's a pattern, the Desktop color is used for the "white" color in the pattern, with black filling the other squares, as in Figure 8-52. Changing the Desktop item changes the Registry `\Colors` value for `Background`.

Icon The Icon item lets you pick the size of your icons and the font and size of the icons' captions. Changing the item under the Appearance tab changes Registry entries `IconFont`, `IconSpacing`, `IconVerticalSpacing`, and `Shell Icon Size`. As noted earlier, `IconFont` is the font used not only for Desktop icons but also for displaying folder contents and in Explorer, Regedit, and other Windows applications.

Want to change the color of your icon font? Well, as best I can tell—and, believe me, I tried—there's no way to do it! The font for a Desktop icon that doesn't have focus seems to be either white or black, depending on the **Background** color, and Windows appears to control the font's color, automatically, internally. When you click on an icon and it takes focus, it takes on the color called **HilightText**. That's the only human-adjustable icon caption color control I could find, either in the Control Panel or buried within the Registry itself. Considering how much control you have over every facet of Desktop appearance, this oversight seems bizarre.

Win98 generally has 32 × 32 pixel icons stored away for most applications, although it also has 48 × 48 pixel icons, should you select them under the Effects tab. If you choose a size of 32, you'll get good icons. Size 48 creates good icons, too. Choose any other number, though, and what you'll see is an (usually ugly) automatically clipped-down version of what the icon should look like. Stick to size 32 or 48 and you'll be in good shape. Also, note that changing the size of the icon changes spacing in weird places—including the items on the Start Menu.

Icon Spacing The Icon Spacing (Horizontal) and Icon Spacing (Vertical) items adjust the grid Win98 uses to rearrange icons on the Desktop. (They also adjust the grid used by Explorer windows with large icons.) The icons "snap to" the nearest grid location whenever you right click on the Desktop and choose Line Up Icons; they fill in missing spots in the grid (from top to bottom, then left to right) if you click Arrange Icons or leave Autoarrange Icons checked.

If you increase the (Horizontal) number, icons get more space stuck between them from left to right. If you increase the (Vertical) number, they space out more from top to bottom. Unfortunately, when you get beyond that simplistic explanation, it isn't quite as simple as it sounds. And in spite of what you may have read, these numbers have nothing to do with pixels or anything else that makes logical sense.

 The problem lies in the way Windows measures distances on the screen. The Win98 Software Development Kit defines four different ways of measuring distances—and the fourth method, called Physical Device Space,[†] can in fact encompass many more ways of measuring distances. Personally, I don't pretend to understand it—and I'm not sure I trust people who say they do . . .

[†] Yes, Windows programming geeks talk that way: "Hey, Brad, hand me that quarter-physical-device-space-inch wrench. The one with the dented-logical-uh-page-space end." And you thought Ozzies talked funny. Here's a quick little test for hotshot Win98-space programmers: I am using Large Fonts (125 pixels/inch) and set the Appearance tab's Icon Spacing (Horizontal) to 60 and (Vertical) to 50. I then change to Small Fonts (96 pixels/inch) and reboot. What are the final values in the Registry for **IconSpacing** and **IconVerticalSpacing**? And, based on those settings, how many icons will appear on my 1,024 × 768 Desktop grid? *Bzzzzt.* Nope, you're wrong. Try it. You'll see.

I sure wish Microsoft would find a way to present values to the user (or at least to me!) that bear some relationship to reality. When I'm working with the screen, I understand pixels. When I'm working with printed output, I understand inches—and, if coerced, will put up with centimeters and points. Anything more complicated than that falls into the category of "stuff the computer should figure out." These settings are among the worst offenders. Why doesn't Windows just let me pick how many icons I want to show on the screen? For years Word has had a sliding Insert Table toolbar button that accomplishes the same thing. If I change resolutions, I should be asked if I want to change the grid. Why must such simple things be so difficult?

Anyway, the (Horizontal) and (Vertical) numbers you pick here under the Appearance tab are scrunched together with the Windows 98 Zoom factor (which we talk about later under "Settings Tab"), and the result is stuck in the Registry settings **IconSpacing** and **IconVerticalSpacing**.

 I've found that my 1024 × 768 screen, running with Large Fonts, can pack 10 icons across the screen with (Horizontal) set to 70. It will fit 11 icons across at 60 and 12 icons across at 50. With the (Vertical) number at 60, I get 8 icons up and down; at 50, I get 9; and at 40 I get 10.

If I switch over to Small Fonts, I see one or two more icons across and one more icon up and down. If I run a custom font (see the section "Settings Tab") at 150% zoom, I generally get one fewer icon in each direction than with the Large Fonts setting.

If your (Horizontal) and (Vertical) numbers get screwed up, make sure you have the size of font you want in the Settings/Advanced/General tab, then flip over to the Appearance Tab. Start with 60 for (Horizontal) and 50 for (Vertical), then right click on the Desktop and pick Line Up Icons. Adjust the numbers until you get an icon arrangement you can live with.

These numbers are not stored in the scheme. You can pick a new scheme and (Horizontal) and (Vertical) will not change. Similarly, you can change (Horizontal) and (Vertical) without changing your scheme. But (Horizontal) and (Vertical) numbers *do* change if you switch from Small Fonts to Large Fonts or pick some custom Zoom factor under the Settings/Advanced/General tab.

Inactive Title Bar The Inactive Title Bar item on the Appearance tab changes a whole lot more than the color of the title bar of inactive windows (those without focus). For reasons known only to Redmond, when you change Inactive Title Bar, the Registry's **SmCaptionWidth** value changes. In the **\Colors** section, it changes the **InactiveTitle** color and the **ButtonAlternateFace** color.

Inactive Window Border The Inactive Window Border item changes the **InactiveBorder** color.

Menu One of the few Appearance tab items that really does what it says it does, the Menu item adjusts the Registry's **MenuWidth** and **MenuHeight**, the **MenuFont**, and the colors for **Menu** and **MenuText**. Remember that the Start Menu is a menu, too, and is thus affected by this setting. The Start button itself is considered part of the Taskbar and escapes any Menu item changes. Let's hear it for Control Panel settings that do what they say they'll do. It's the American way.

Message Box In direct contrast, the next item, Message Box, changes all sorts of things—but probably not the things you were expecting! You might think that Message Box would change the font used in message boxes. Well, it does, sorta. When you change the Message Box item, the Registry **\WindowMetrics** value for **MessageFont** changes. As noted earlier, that doesn't do much—very, very few Windows messages use the **MessageFont**.

 It also changes the **\Colors** entry for **WindowText**, and that changes the color of just about everything inside Win98: text in Explorer and the other Win98 applications; the "default" color of text in MS Office applications, fer heaven's sake; the text in every standard Windows control (list boxes, text boxes, and the like); the body of Properties dialogs; and so many more things we couldn't begin to list them all. This is one duplicitous setting.

Palette Title

 Sheeeesh. You want a duplicitous Appearance tab item, take a look at Palette Title. What the setting has to do with palettes is way beyond me. The setting just changes the Registry's **\WindowsMetric** values for **SmCaptionWidth** and **SmCaptionHeight** (which are always both set to the same number!) and **SmCaptionFont**, which, as noted earlier, is used almost nowhere.

Scrollbar

We're on a roll here. The next Appearance tab setting, called the Scrollbar item, changes only the *size* of scrollbars. (To change the color, you have to experiment with 3D Objects item. Good luck.) It affects the **\WindowsMetric** values for **ScrollHeight** and **ScrollWidth**— both always set to the same value—which in turn affect the size of scrollbars and the down arrows for dropdown list boxes and spin boxes, and at least a few MS Office toolbar buttons!

Selected Item The next Appearance tab item is called Selected Item, and it changes stuff all over the place. It's supposed to control how selected menu items appear on the screen, but it changes the Registry's **MenuHeight** and **MenuWidth** settings and the **MenuFont**—thus affecting all menus, including the Start Menu, whether anything is selected or not. It also changes **SmCaptionWidth**, heaven knows why. It changes **Hilight** and **HilightText**, thus doing what it's supposed to do with selected menu items, and the color of icons with focus on the Desktop.

ToolTips Talk about weird side-effects. Changing the ToolTips item on the Appearance tab changes the Registry's **StatusFont**. While **StatusFont** is used for the font in Win98 Desktop ToolTips and the tips attached to buttons in WordPad and Paint, among others, it is also used as the status bar font in many applications. The ToolTips item also affects the Registry's **InfoText** and **InfoWindows** color settings, which are picked up in some applications and ignored in others.

Window Finally, the Window item on the Appearance tab lets you choose both a background color (in the upper box) and a foreground color (in the lower box) for nearly all applications in Windows 98. The upper box changes the Registry's **\Color** value for **Window**; the lower box changes **WindowText**. The **Window** value controls the default background color in most Windows applications—the "page" in MS Office applications, for example—as well as the background color in My Computer-style icon boxes. It also controls the background of virtually all Windows built-in controls, like check boxes, text boxes, unselected items in list boxes, and just about everything else except buttons. **WindowText** controls the default color of text in most applications, the color of text in dialog boxes, and unselected text in virtually all Windows built-in controls except buttons.

So much for the Appearance tab.

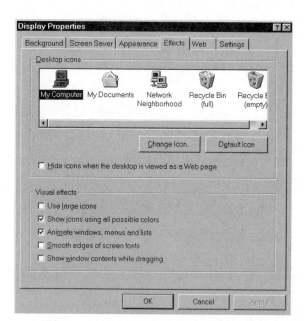

Figure 8-53. Settings available on the Effects tab

Effects Tab

The Windows 98 Effects tab holds a number of worthwhile improvements to the old Windows 95 way of working (Figure 8-53).

The Desktop icons box lets you change the pictures associated with five of Win98's standard Desktop icons. Click on the picture you want to change, then click Change Icon, and look for a picture in any convenient file by using the Browse button (Figure 8-54). In the **C:\windows** folder, you'll find large icon collections in these files: **explorer.exe**, **moricons.dll**, and **progman.exe**. In the **C:\windows\system** folder, look for **awfxex32.exe**, **cool.dll**, **iconlib.dll**, **pifmgr.dll**, **setupx.dll**, **shell32.dll**, **syncui.dll**, and **wmsui32.dll**.

Figure 8-54.
Browsing for icons

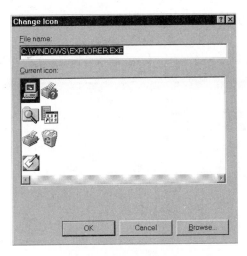

Check the box marked "Hide icons when the desktop is viewed as a Web page" if you don't want Win98 to show icons on top of your Active Desktop wallpaper. (There's an extensive discussion of Active Desktop wallpaper in Chapter 7.)

The "Use large icons" box is a particularly well-implemented one. If you check this box, you tell Win98 that you want to use 48 x 48 pixel icons on the Desktop. This setting changes the number in the Appearance tab's Icon Size box in a very clever way. If you specify 32 as an icon size on the Appearance tab, this box on the Effects tab is unchecked. If you pick 48 in Appearance, this box is checked. If you choose any other size, the box is checked and grayed.

It works the other way, too. If you check this box on the Effects tab and flip over to Appearance and pick the Icon item, you'll see that you have set a size of 48. Uncheck the box here in Effects, and Appearance turns to 32. Whoever programmed this did an admirable job.

The "Show icons using all possible colors" check box refers to Win98's attempts to render a fancy 256-color icon in all its glory. Uncheck the box, and all icons are reduced to 16 colors. Check it and the full 256 colors will appear—for icons that are so endowed.

"Animate windows, menus and lists" just adds a little sliding screen graphic. You've probably seen them: click on a Taskbar button, for example, and the associated program appears to "glide" open. Some people like it, some people hate it, but there's almost no performance penalty.

"Smooth edges of screen fonts" refers to antialiasing, a topic discussed at length in Chapter 2 in the section "That's a Cockroach of a Different Color."

"Show window contents while dragging" affects the "ghost" Win98 can put on a window that's being dragged.

Figure 8-55.
The Web tab col-
lects many Active
Desktop–related
settings

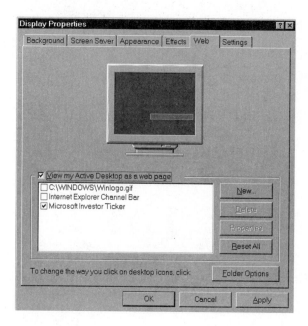

Web Tab

The Web tab brings together a bunch of settings related to the Active Desktop, or using an **.htm** file as wallpaper (Figure 8-55). There are a few surprises, so be careful as you poke around here.

If you click the box marked "View my Active Desktop as a Web page," Win98 turns on Active Desktop, the same as if you had right clicked on the Desktop, chosen Active Desktop, and checked the box marked View As Web page. When that happens, Win98 does three things.

- In most cases Win98 brings up the most recently used Active Desktop wallpaper and sets it up as the current Active Desktop wallpaper, as described in Chapter 7 in "The Active Desktop" section. We've hit some situations where the most recently used Active Desktop wallpaper didn't come up— and can't figure out how or why. The MRU wallpaper's name is not stored in the Registry anyplace we can find, other than the **HKCU\Software\ Microsoft\Windows\CurrentVersion\Explorer\Recent Docs** key, nor is it in any file we've been able to discover.

- On top of the Active Desktop wallpaper, it puts a floating layer that's meant to hold ActiveX controls along with any picture files you wish to add. The ActiveX controls and pictures that have check marks on the Web tab are placed in that layer.

- Finally, if you haven't checked the box on the Effects tab marked "Hide icons when the desktop is viewed as a Web page," Win98 puts the Desktop icons in that floating layer.

The means and strategies for adding new pictures and ActiveX controls to the floating layer are discussed at length in the section "Adding Active Cool Stuff" in Chapter 7.

Settings Tab

The final tab proffered by the Display applet is one marked, uh, Settings. (See Figure 8-56. They *pay* somebody to come up with these mnemonic terms, don-cha think?) The Settings tab lets you alter your display: the drivers for your monitor and video card; the pixel resolution to be displayed on your screen; the maximum number of colors that can be displayed on the monitor simultaneously (commonly called the "color depth"); and the Win98 Desktop Zoom factor.

The Colors dropdown list lets you choose the maximum number of colors your monitor can display simultaneously, from 16 to 256 colors and—if your video card can support it—High Color (16 bits) or True Color (24 bits). Once upon a time, using a larger palette would seriously reduce your video performance and effectively drag Windows to its knees. Nowadays, if you have an accelerated video card (and almost all new Windows machines do), the performance penalty for more on-screen color generally isn't all that great.

 With most screen drivers, you have an icon in the Notification Area (![icon]) that provides a quick way to change resolution and color depth. Right click on it and it will list the supported combinations of resolution and color depth and let you change them by merely picking from the list.

Why would you want more color depth? It makes your display more lifelike and lively. Pictures that contain more than 256 colors are becoming increasingly common—Windows 98 contains several wallpaper images in High Color, for example—and if you display those pictures with a palette of 256 (or, worse, 16) colors, the results are mighty underwhelming. See Chapter 2 for the definitive discussion of color palettes.

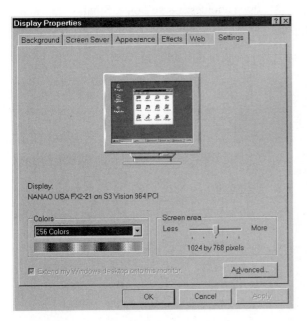

Figure 8-56. Display applet's Settings tab

The next box, marked "Screen area," controls the resolution you see on screen. The minimum size (which results in the largest objects on screen) is 640 × 480 pixels—effectively, Win98 generates 480 lines of 640 dots each, and those lines are more or less evenly plastered on your monitor. Most people try to put at least 800 × 600 pixels on their 15-inch or larger screens, simply because that lets them stuff more legible things (Desktop icons, Taskbar buttons, toolbar buttons, text) on the screen. If you have a 17-inch screen, try 1,024 × 768 pixels. And if you have a 21-inch or larger screen, the last thing you need is me trying to tell you what to do . . .

 There's a trade-off here. The amount of memory on your video card limits the color depth you can display at any particular resolution. If you move the slider to turn resolution up to 1,024 × 768 and suddenly the color depth flips from High Color to 256 colors, you know you've hit a limitation of your video card. Add more memory to the video card (*not* main memory inside your computer, video memory!) to allow improved resolution and/or greater color depth.

Click on the Advanced button and you'll be greeted by the video card Properties box (Figure 8-57). Win98 tries to make you think that the "properties" here are attached to the video card (note the "S3 Vision 964 PCI" in the title bar of Figure 8-57), but in fact you'll find pretty much the same settings available for all video cards, give or take a few on the Adapter tab.

That brings us to the Settings tab's advanced properties Font Size box (at the top of Figure 8-57). If you click the Font Size dropdown arrow, you'll find three choices: Large Fonts, Small Fonts, and Other. Choosing Other leads to the dialog in Figure 8-58.

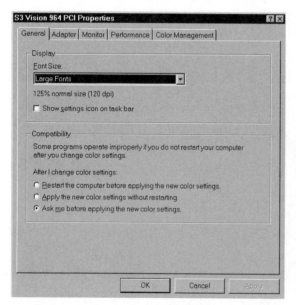

Figure 8-57. Advanced video settings live here

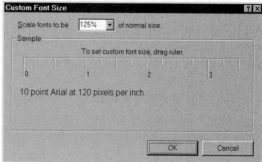

Figure 8-58. Custom Font Size dialog

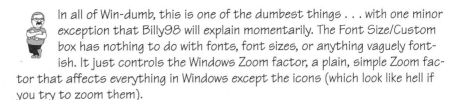

In all of Win-dumb, this is one of the dumbest things . . . with one minor exception that Billy98 will explain momentarily. The Font Size/Custom box has nothing to do with fonts, font sizes, or anything vaguely font-ish. It just controls the Windows Zoom factor, a plain, simple Zoom factor that affects everything in Windows except the icons (which look like hell if you try to zoom them).

My guess is that Win98's designers were trying to avoid the concept of "zoom," figuring it was too complex for, uh, dummies. Pardon me if I borrow one of Billy's favorite sayings, but that's *really stupid*. If you've ever used a moderately capable word processor, paint program, spreadsheet, or just about any Windows application, you've learned to work with Zoom. It's an easy concept to grasp and use. But Win98's creators felt Zoom was too complicated, I guess. In its place Microsoft concocted this grandiose story about font sizes and rulers that bears no relation to reality. (Hold a ruler up to the "ruler" shown on your screen in Custom Font Size box and you'll see what I mean.) The Large Fonts and Small Fonts and "pixels per inch" have absolutely nothing to do with real inches, the kind you measure with a real ruler. It's artifice from beginning to end.

Sure, it's really sexy to click on the ruler and drag it left and right—but Microsoft got the metaphor completely ass-backwards. There is no "inch" on a monitor. There're just pixels. What they *should* be showing you is how big or how small typical Desktop items will look as you change the Zoom factor: at a higher Zoom, dialog boxes look bigger; Desktop icon captions swell; the Taskbar holds fewer and taller buttons; 11-point text, say, in WordPad is larger—as is text in everything else, from Explorer to the MS Office applications. As I mentioned in the Appearance tab discussion, the "snap-to grid" also adjusts itself, depending on the Zoom. Why not show all of that happening, instead of an expanding ruler juxtaposed on a slice of text that always measures, more or less, "two"? Oy.

OK, OK. Put down the brickbat. Dragging on the ruler is pretty intu-itive—until you stop to think about it. Just like the scrollbar behavior you talked about in Chapter 2. We couldn't call it Zoom because the icons *don't* zoom—they really deteriorate if we try to scale them to any size other than their hand-tuned original size. You guys are partially right, though. We showed the user our internal way of scaling things, instead of con-centrating on stuff the user is interested in—how icon text fits into the Desk-top grid, how big objects will appear in non-zoomable applications, things like that. That ruler with the text line that's always "two" wide, with no indication of two *what*, was a master stroke, though. What can I say?

Well, you can start by 'fessing up about what's really happening with Large Fonts and Small Fonts. Those settings don't have anything to do with fonts, do they, Bill? Man, you've managed to fool me for a long, long time. The Large Fonts setting is just shorthand for "125% Zoom," isn't it? The Small Fonts is just shorthand for "100% Zoom." If you click the Custom button, you can pick from 75%, 100% (Small Fonts), 125% (Large Fonts), 150%, and 200% Zoom settings. That's all there is to it, right?

 Not quite, although I'll admit you're pretty close. The Zoom factor you choose in the Custom Font Size dialog is translated into a number that we call Physical and Logical Dots Per Inch—a fancy term for "Zoom," if you will. Those settings are stored in the Registry key **HKLM\Config\ 0001\Display\Settings** as **DPILogicalX**, **DPILogicalY**, **DPIPhysicalX**, and **DPIPhysicalY**. (All four numbers are identical.)

 That's weird. All the **\WindowMetrics** settings we've seen so far are in **HKCU\Control Panel**. These Zoom factor Registry entries in **HKLM** are machine-wide settings and don't change if a different user logs onto the same machine.

 Anyway, the one place where you're not quite right, guys, is that we *do* change the font based on the Zoom factor, although the visual consequences are admittedly small. If the user picks a Zoom factor of 100% or less (or, equivalently, chooses Small Fonts), Windows uses the VGA resolution fonts for MS Sans Serif (file **sserife.fon**). Since MS Sans Serif is the default font for all the Appearance tab settings, that effectively changes the font size, providing the user hasn't chosen a different font for things on the Desktop. So, even though our real reason for replacing the **.fon** file was to get a better-looking hand-tuned font on the screen, in fact, the Settings tab Font Size/Custom box does change fonts.

 Ach! Caught by a technicality! In fact, MS Serif is changed to VGA resolution, too, at Zoom factors of 100% or lower, as are Symbol and the font called "Small Fonts." All those settings are in the Registry key **HKLM\Config\0001\Display\Fonts**. The DOS fonts are changed, too, with a swap to VGA resolutions for **fonts.fon**, **fixedfon.fon**, and **oemfonts.fon**, which are all in **HKLM\Config\0001\ Display\Settings**. Finally, there's a small change in the **DisplayParams** value in **HKLM\SOFTWARE\Microsoft\Windows\CurrentVersion\ MS-DOS Emulation**, presumably to change the appearance of the Lucida Console font in the DOS box.

The remaining General tab settings are pretty self-explanatory.

On the Adapter tab (Figure 8-59), Win98 lists settings that are specific to your particular video card. If Win98 has misidentified your video card, click Change to change it or feed Win98 a new driver.

Figure 8-59. The Adapter tab

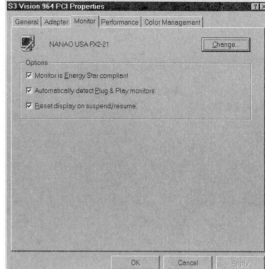

Figure 8-60. Monitor settings

 The only real problem I've had with this tab is in the choice of refresh rate. I'm not sure if it's Win98 or the driver itself, but whenever I change the resolution on the screen or the color depth, this box is reset to Adapter Default—and at least in my case, the default looks like it's a 20-Hz refresh rate, interlaced. I always have to go back to this tab and reset it to the highest refresh rate available.

Not everyone has a monitor that will support the ultrafast refresh rates made possible by the latest video cards. It's at least theoretically possible to burn out a monitor by driving it at too fast a refresh rate. So be sure you check the manual that came with your monitor to ensure that it can keep up with whatever refresh rate you specify here.

The Monitor tab (Figure 8-60) carries information that pertains to your monitor. Unless you have a Plug 'n' Play monitor, there's a fair chance Win98 hasn't identified it properly. If that's the case, click Change and pick the correct one.

Once in a very blue moon, your video card won't be able to keep up with Win98: it may freeze, or your mouse pointer may go ballistic. In those cases, you can use the Performance tab (Figure 8-61) to slow Win98 down. The Performance tab isn't really about performance—as is usual in Windows, it's a troubleshooting tab, which lets you throttle back Win98 if your hardware can't take it. Click and drag on the slider to see a simple explanation of the effect of each throttling-down notch.

Figure 8-61. Slow Win98 down here if it's too fast for your video adapter

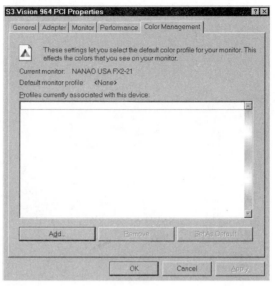

Figure 8-62. ICM color profiles go on the Color Management tab

Figure 8-63. Win98's default ICM files

Image Color Matching (ICM) comes into play in the final tab, marked Color Management (Figure 8-62). ICM helps to ensure color accuracy: if you scan a picture into your PC, you want to make sure that the colors of the scanned image match the original colors, regardless of the biases of your scanner. Similarly, if you look at a picture, you want your monitor to give "true" colors—and the same can be said for printing.

To add Image Color Matching for a peripheral connected to your system, click Add and choose from one of the offered **.icm** files (Figure 8-63).

 ■ **Fonts**

The Control Panel's Fonts applet just opens a, uh, window onto Explorer's font routines. Fonts were discussed in Chapter 2. If you're getting your feet wet with the Registry, take a look at **HKLM\Software\Microsoft\Windows\CurrentVersion\Fonts**.

■ Game Controllers

Windows 98 has been billed as a gamer's delight, and you can see why right here. While Win95 could simultaneously handle only two joysticks, flight yokes, or similar devices, such as digitizer tablets, Win98 can take a virtually unlimited number. Most *applications* work with only one, but that sad state of affairs seems to be improving. Win98 also accommodates 3D motion and up to four buttons on each joystick, plus all the fancy feedback tricks. In short, Win98 can take almost anything current state-of-the-art game controllers demand, although it remains to be seen if Win98 will be up to handling VR helmets and other exotica.

The Game Controllers dialog (Figure 8-64) appears when you crank up the Control Panel's Joystick applet. To add a new joystick (yoke, whatever), click the Add button, and either choose from the list of devices or insert a diskette and choose your own.

Once the joystick has been added in this dialog and physically attached to the PC, click Properties. The Test tab in the Game Controller Properties dialog (Figure 8-65) gives you a chance to move your joystick around and see the effect in the Axes box (3D controllers will also show up in the Point of View Hat box). Click the buttons on the joystick and see which of the numbers in the lower box light up. You might be surprised—sometimes the buttons on the joystick don't correspond to the numbers the way you think they will.

Figure 8-64. Main dialog for the Game Controllers applet

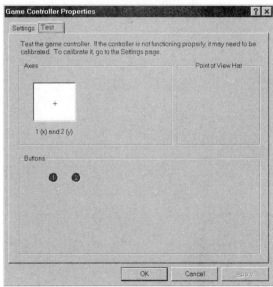

Figure 8-65. Test your controller here

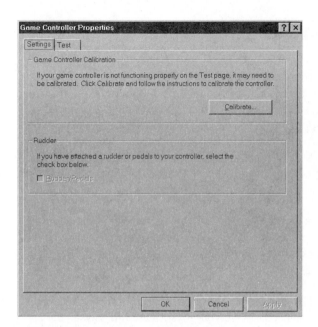

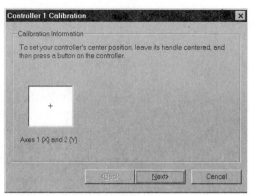

Figure 8-67. Start calibration by pushing a button

Figure 8-66. The Calibration Wizard is launched from the Settings tab

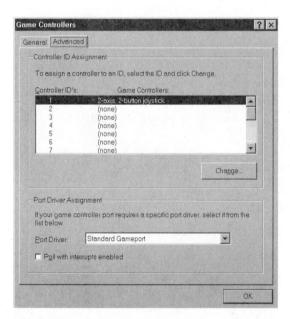

Figure 8-68. Assign ID numbers to controllers on the Advanced tab

Calibrate your joystick by clicking on the Settings tab (Figure 8-66) and clicking Calibrate. Everyone with a joystick should go through the Calibration Wizard at least once. The Wizard starts by having you center the joystick and push a button, as in Figure 8-67. (If all your buttons are on the stick itself, it can be a bit difficult to push the button without wiggling the stick. Good luck.) You're then instructed to move the joystick in full circles a few times and hit a button again. Finally, you confirm the calibration by centering the stick again and pushing the button one last time.

At the end of the calibration, you should go back to the Test tab (Figure 8-65) and test the stick. You want to make sure the calibration worked correctly, that the cross-hairs sit in the middle of the Joystick box, and that you get a full range of movement with the stick.

Finally, if you have more than one joystick, you can assign and reassign controller IDs in the Game Controller dialog's Advanced tab (Figure 8-68).

Joystick settings are scattered throughout the Registry; the major repository of information about a stick's capabilities and calibration is the key `HKLM\System\Current ControlSet\Control\Media Resources\joystick`.

It doesn't hurt to recalibrate fairly often. Large swings in room temperature can affect stick calibration.

 ## ■ Internet

The Internet applet is identical to what you see when you go into Internet Explorer and click View/Internet Options. It's also what you get when you right click the Internet Explorer icon on the Desktop and pick Properties.

With a few very important exceptions—security settings and automatic dial-up—this applet doesn't really control your access to the Internet. It's quite specific to Internet Explorer. If you use, oh, Netscape Navigator (or Communicator), making changes here won't accomplish anything.

General Tab The first tab, marked General (Figure 8-69), controls a wide variety of settings. In the "Home page" box you can pick which Web page will first appear when Internet Explorer launches. You should change this to whatever page you like to access first (or most), simply to avoid going to Microsoft's infamous home page, `home.microsoft.com`.

 Wait a minute. What's wrong with `home.microsoft.com`?

Figure 8-69.
General tab on
the Internet
applet

Nothing, really, except you set things up so people go there automatically, and don't tell people right off the bat how to change things so they won't go there automatically.

We have to send them somewhere, don't we? Why not send new users to a world-class, customizable home page, where they can get news, weather, stock market reports, all sorts of things—all absolutely free?
Netscape does the same thing—except their home page strategy is a big part of the company's financial plan for keeping the company alive. And the current beta of Navigator 4.5 tends to send you to their home page when you type in a variety of what they call keywords.

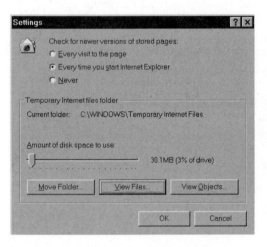

Figure 8-70. Temporary Internet files can take an enormous amount of space

The next box, marked "Temporary Internet files," deals with, uh, temporary Internet files, which, as explained in Chapter 2, are stored in the `C:\Windows\Temporary Internet Files` folder. Internet Explorer uses these files to minimize the amount of data it pulls down from the Web. If the browser needs a picture or even an `.htm` file, it checks in that folder first to see if a copy exists locally. If you keep hitting the same pages over and over again—and most of us do—this feature saves all sorts of online time.

If you click the Settings button in the "Temporary Internet files" box, you see the Settings dialog in Figure 8-70. Here sit the controls in the ever-raging battle between disk space and Web access speed. You can adjust the slider in the Settings dialog to limit the amount of space used to cache Web files— but before you constrain Internet Explorer too much, be aware of the fact that throttling back here too much can slow down your Web surfing substantially.

On the other hand, don't go overboard. I set the slider to 30% of a 1-GB drive. After a while, IE 3.0 started crashing something awful. I tried reinstalling, but that didn't help, so I made one of my few calls to Microsoft tech support. They decided my problem was too many files in the cache. I emptied it and set it to only 10% and the crashes went away. I'd aim for a cache of no more than 50 MB.

It's true that if you really want to save speed, you can set "Check for newer versions of stored pages" to "Never," but pages change, so I urge you to leave that setting at the default "Every time you start Internet Explorer."

If you are ever suspicious that the page in your browser is from the cache and is out-of-date, you can hit the button marked "Refresh."

Figure 8-71.
Internet Explorer's
complete history
of every URL
you've visited

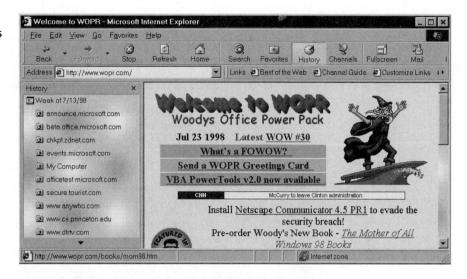

Internet Explorer also keeps a list of all the URLs you've visited, so if you click the History button—as I have in Figure 8-71—it knows which URLs to list along the left side of the screen. You control the limits of Internet Explorer's historical memory by the third box in Figure 8-69, the one marked, appropriately, "History."

Not surprisingly, the push buttons at the bottom of Figure 8-69 let you change the colors used by Internet Explorer; the default fonts (that is, fonts not specified within the HTML page itself), character sets, and size; the default language; and accessibility options for those who have a difficult time reading the screen.

 I discuss using non-Latin alphabets and the Font and Language buttons in the section "Browsing the Web with Internet Explorer" in Chapter 4.

Security Tab The settings under this tab are among the most important settings in all of Windows (Figure 8-72). If you screw them up, you can leave your machine open to attack by viruses, Trojans, and all manner of mean, nasty programs. So if you don't understand precisely what's going on, leave these settings alone.

If you decide to take your security into your own hands, make sure you read the last section of Chapter 7—"Security in an ActiveX World"—and understand it before you proceed.

 You might wonder why we get so worked up about security—after all, there haven't been any major outbreaks of mayhem caused by bad Web pages or infected e-mail messages (as we went to press anyway). The reason is very simple: for the first time, with Win98, it's possible to be

**Figure 8-72.
Security settings—not
just for Internet
Explorer**

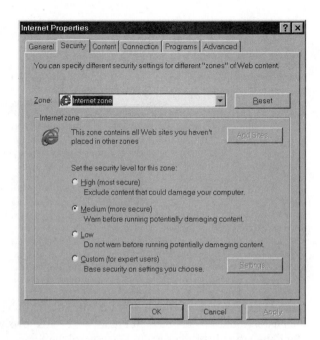

infected or have your data wiped out while merely *viewing* a Web page or *reading* an e-mail message. At the end of Chapter 7, I went into a lot of detail about how VBScript works in HTML files. Those techniques can be used to build viruses (programs that replicate themselves and may contain destructive payloads) or Trojans (programs that simply ruin things). It's vital that you keep your security settings at high levels and that you heed messages like the one in Figure 8-73.

 As I mentioned at the end of Chapter 7, I was involved in a big controversy with Microsoft just before Win98 shipped that all boiled down to one very poor setting in this applet. Believe me, people who understand security very, very well—and I mean people *outside* Microsoft, as well as inside—have been over these settings with a microfine-tooth comb. Many of the outsiders feel that the phrase "Microsoft software security" is an oxymoron—and they tore this part of the Internet applet to pieces before they

put it back together again. The net result: even people who don't think much of Microsoft software's security capabilities grudgingly admitted that these settings were adequate. Thus if you're going to change anything on this tab, make sure you make the settings *more* stringent, not less.

The Security tab settings (Figure 8-72) not only control the way Internet Explorer behaves; they also dictate what kind of security warning messages you see whenever you look at an HTML page; for most

Figure 8-73. If you ever see this message, click No!

Win98 users, that means when you're using Outlook Express or Outlook (any version) to view an HTML e-mail message or if you have an HTML file ("Web page") serving as Active Desktop wallpaper.

If you use a non-Microsoft product (or anything other than Outlook or IE) to view HTML files—whether they're masquerading as e-mail messages, under development with an HTML editor, on a local disk, an intranet, or the Web— you need to check with the manufacturer to see if these settings will be used. If they aren't, make sure you understand the manufacturer's security scheme—or you may suffer the consequences.

Microsoft's implementation of Internet security hinges on the concept of "zones." It's a reasonable approach that recognizes the fact that you might trust some sources of information—say, a corporate intranet—while you don't trust the wild, wild Web, no way no how. The Security tab allows you to set security warning levels for four zones.

- The **Local intranet zone** is supposed to include sites you access via your company's intranet. Unless you click the Add Sites button and add specific URLs to the list of Local intranet zones, this zone includes local intranet sites, any site that bypasses the proxy server (if your company uses one to control Web access), and all network paths specified by UNCs.

- The **Trusted sites zone** contains only specific URLs you have entered by hand using the Add Sites button. I would recommend that you not put any sites in the Trusted sites zone under any circumstances. The sites you might be tempted to trust the most—say, **www.microsoft.com**—are also the sites most likely to be attacked and altered by miscreants.

- The **Restricted sites zone** also contains just the specific URLs you have entered by hand. I never use it, but if you hang out around sites that feature creeps who like to write viruses and Trojans and the like—well, you deserve what you get.

- Almost everything should go into the **Internet zone**, including all the URLs except those subsumed by the rules for the Local intranet zone and those you've entered by hand into one of the two other zones. In particular, e-mail messages should be treated as coming from the Internet zone—even if they've physically arrived on your machine via a corporate mail server.

That's an important point. Unless you've taken very definite steps to move a specific URL into a special zone—everything (including HTML files viewed as e-mail and HTML pages used as Active Desktop wallpaper) should default to Internet zone.

You might think there should be a special setting for your own machine because you shouldn't need security for the VBScripts you write and run locally. But think again, because by the time you read an e-mail message, it's normally in a file on your local machine, and e-mail represents the most worrisome source of VBScript infection.

There are more than a hundred specific security level settings accessible by choosing the "Custom (for expert users)" button and hitting Settings. We won't go into them here for two specific reasons. First, some of them are quite complex. Second, if we described them, you'd be more tempted to change them! Take our advice and stay out. Leave the Internet zone at Medium security, don't manually put any URLs in the Trusted sites zone, and always click No if you see the message in Figure 8-73. It's that simple.

Content Tab   This tab (Figure 8-74) is jammed with four unrelated settings—applications in their own right, as a matter of fact. First and foremost, the Content Advisor is designed to restrict Web access according to rules you set. While it isn't in the same league as, oh, Net Nanny and commercial Web site blockers, the RSAC (Recreational Software Advisory Council) rating system and Content Advisor give you a great deal of flexibility—on sites with RSAC ratings.

Click Enable in the Content Advisor box, and the Content Advisor will ask you to establish a password. Anybody with this password can override the settings in Content Advisor, so make sure you store it in a secure place.

The Advisor itself (Figure 8-75) lets you choose separate threshold levels in each of four different categories: Language, Nudity, Sex, and Violence. If you don't make any changes, Content Advisor defaults to the least offensive setting in each of the four areas—thus even mildly charged sites are deemed off-limits.

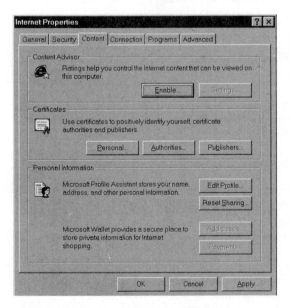

Figure 8-74. Content tab with its four applications

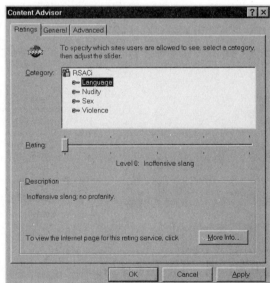

Figure 8-75. The Advisor has detailed definitions for RSAC categories

Figure 8-76. Almost all Content Advisor users keep the top box unchecked

Figure 8-77. Specify non-RSAC rating systems here

Unfortunately, not every Web site has an RSAC rating. Generally, those concerned enough to employ the Content Advisor won't want unrated Web pages to be accessible, but that decision can be overridden on the General (Figure 8-76) tab.

The Advanced tab allows you to change rating systems so that you aren't bound by the RSAC (Figure 8-77). Access to a secondary rating system involves an additional Web "hit" for each page you browse, so make sure you really want to take the performance hit before you invoke a different rating system.

 When I tried to get the Content Advisor working, I kept bumping into the warning message you see in Figure 8-78. All I know for sure is that nobody tried to tamper with Content Advisor—the message seemingly appeared out of nowhere. If you should have the same problem, get out of Internet Explorer and rename the file `C:\Windows\System\Ratings.pol` to `Ratings.sav`. Then bring up the Internet applet, click the Content tab, and click Settings. As soon as you provide the password, all will be well—the Figure 8-78 message magically disappears.

Figure 8-78. Content Advisor is on the blink

Figure 8-79.
When Content
Advisor is work-
ing, the Disable
button can turn it
off

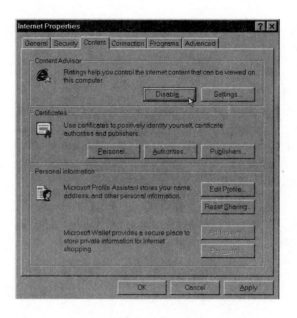

If you get tired of Content Advisor, just bring up the Content tab again and click Disable, as in Figure 8-79.

The Certificates panel handles a variety of digital certificates. Under the Personal button, you can install the certificates you'll need if you want to start using encrypted e-mail or digital signatures. Occasionally, you'll be browsing and a certificate for a software publisher will pop up and you'll be allowed to tell the browser to always trust software from XYZ publishers, for example, from Microsoft. Under the Publishers button, you get to change your mind and remove some approvals you've already given.

The theory behind Personal information panel and the Microsoft Profile Assistant is that you can use them to avoid typing in all sorts of information at multiple sites when you register.

 Until there is some kind of decent Internet privacy specification in place, I'd suggest you ignore this panel.

Connection Tab

 I discussed the Connection panel on this tab at length in Chapter 4, "The Internet Applet."

The other parts of this tab are normally activated only under the direction of your Network Administrator.

 A proxy server redirects your requests for Web pages through a special program, usually on another machine, called, er, a proxy server. The proxy server then fetches the page and sends it to you. Why would any-one want such indirection? A corporate site might want it to control what pages you access or to track what pages you visit—like xxx.hotgirls.com. Another advantage is that all individuals share a common Web cache, so a lot of people checking CNN on their lunch hour won't bring the Internet gateway to its knees.

Finally, a proxy server is a way to allow you to access resources from off site that check your domain name. For example, Caltech has a subscription from the American Math Society to access certain databases. When you try to access them, the site checks that you are accessing them from a **caltech.edu** address. That means that I can't access them from home—or I couldn't until Caltech set up a password protected proxy server I could use instead. My browser accessed the proxy server, which requested the page, and it did have a **caltech.edu** address.

Programs Tab Internet Explorer relies on outside programs for many capabilities. On the Programs tab (Figure 8-80), you tell Internet Explorer which outside programs to use.

 I'm always amused by the News setting on this tab. If you install Office, the installer takes it upon itself to change News to point to Microsoft Outlook. That's a bit of puffery—Outlook 97, 98, and 2000 do not have news readers. Outlook just goes and calls Outlook Express, the only member of the Outlook family capable of reading newsgroup missives. I'd recommend you eliminate the middleman and change this entry to Outlook Express.

 I like the little button that says "Internet Explorer should check to see whether it is the default browser." This is the anti-Netscape button. If you keep it checked, every time Internet Explorer starts it looks to see if it's the one associated with **.htm** and **.html** files—in other words, if it's the program that will spring to life if you double click on a file with an **.htm** or **.html** filename extension. If Internet Explorer isn't the one associated with **.htm** and **.html** files, it asks if it's OK for it to take over the assignments.

Of course, Netscape does exactly the same thing.

Figure 8-80. Ancillary programs go here

**Figure 8-81.
Turn off sched-
uled updates on
the Advanced tab**

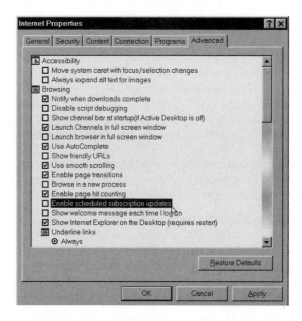

Advanced Tab Finally, the Advanced tab (Figure 8-81) holds dozens of settings for the minutiae of Internet Explorer's operation.

 The only setting that Microsoft really got wrong is the one called "Enable scheduled subscription updates." If you keep that box checked,
your PC can connect to the Web at weird and often unpredictable times.
I strongly recommend that you turn it off.

■ Keyboard

The Keyboard applet in the Control Panel is used to set not only keyboard response characteristics—repeat rate and delay until autorepeat begins—but also
the insertion point blink rate (yeah, this applet calls it a cursor, but the official
term is **insertion point**, the point at which text is inserted if you start typing),
and the language settings for multikey character composition support.

The Keyboard applet brings up the Keyboard Properties dialog, set on the
Speed tab (Figure 8-82). Though it may be a little hard to tell from this dialog,
you have a choice of 4 different preset delay values and 32 different preset repeat rate values. There is no finer tuning: if "Short" is too short but the notch
immediately to its left is too long, you're outta luck.

Sometimes these settings get "stuck" (especially when you first install
Win98), so before you go hog-wild making adjustments, try nudging the slider
one notch in either direction. See if you can live with the change you make by
practicing in the indicated box. Remember, these settings apply to every well-
behaved Windows application, including DOS boxes running under Windows 98.

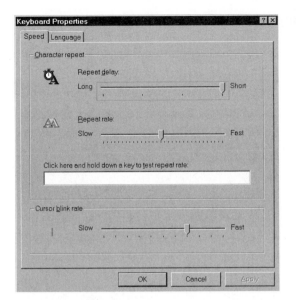

Figure 8-82. Keyboard applet's Speed tab

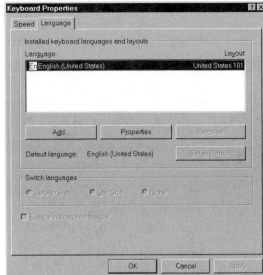

Figure 8-83. Alternate language support

The Language tab (Figure 8-83) lets you specify alternate languages: if you commonly use different languages, this box and the ability to specify hotkeys for switching languages can be a godsend. (If you want to change keyboard layout without changing languages, e.g., to specify a Dvorak layout for your U.S. English keyboard, click the Properties button.)

 ¡Cuidado! Achtung! Don't count your multilingual chickens before they're hatched. Some applications are notorious for not recognizing all valid key combinations in all languages, while others "swallow" keystrokes unexpectedly. Extensive testing is in order.

If you have more than one keyboard language installed and you check the "Enable Indicator on Taskbar" box, an icon appears in the Taskbar's Notification Area telling you which language is active. Click on that icon and you can switch languages without using the hotkey.

 Keyboard repeat rates are stored in Registry key **HKCU\Control Panel\Keyboard**. (That key doesn't exist until you make a change in the Keyboard applet.) The entry **KeyboardSpeed** ranges from **3** (which is shown as Long on the Speed tab) to **0** (which is Short). The entry **KeyboardDelay** takes on values from **0** (Slow on the Speed tab) to **31** (Fast). The cursor blink rate is in **HKCU\Control Panel\Desktop**, where the entry **CursorBlinkRate** goes from **1,200** (which appears as Slow on the Speed tab) to **200** (Fast). Manually adjusting the repeat rate entries beyond their prescribed bounds can have an unpredictable effect on the rates (in other words, on reboot, Win98 changes them in ways I don't understand). Manually adjusting **CursorBlinkRate**, on the other hand, works fine.

Want to see the insertion point flicker like a firefly in heat? Try setting **CursorBlinkRate** to **50**. You'll have to restart your machine for the setting to take effect. Talk about Stupid Desktop Tricks.

 ■ **Modems**

We are in great haste to construct a magnetic telegraph from Maine to Texas, but Maine and Texas, it may be, have nothing important to communicate.

—H. D. THOREAU, *Walden*, 1854

If you don't have any modems currently installed and you crank up the Modems applet in the Control Panel (or try to do just about anything that requires a modem, from running the Welcome screen's On-Line Registration to sending a fax), you'll be rocketed to the Install New Modem Wizard. This Wizard is pretty simple, so I won't bore you with the details. Basically, Windows has to figure out what AT command set your modem recognizes—an **AT command set** being the language your modem speaks when talking to your computer. So if you don't find your specific modem listed, pick one that's compatible with your modem or pop over to the "Standard Modem Types" list and pick one that runs at the same speed. (*Hint:* Almost all modems claim to be "Hayes-compatible" and that's equivalent to "Standard" in this list.)

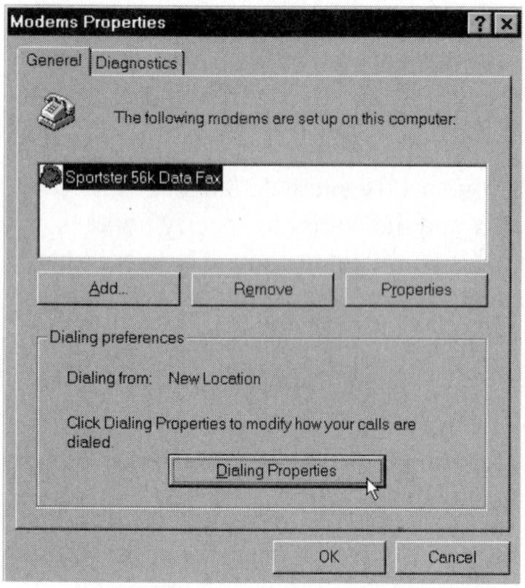

Once a modem is installed, the Modems applet in the Control Panel will bring up the Modems Properties dialog (Figure 8-84). You can get to the same screen from Control Panel's System applet. Click on the Dialing Properties button here if you need to change your calling card number, outside access numbers, tone/pulse dialing, and the like. Most of these change only if you're on the road.

Figure 8-84. Modems applet

 There's one reason you might want to dig into Dialing Properties even on a desktop machine. Many local phone companies are moving to ten-digit dialing as a way to relieve the pressure on area codes. With ten-digit dialing, you're forced to dial an area code for every phone number—even if the number's area code is the same as your own. I know. Colorado went through the trauma in September.

If you need to set up your machine for ten-digit dialing, click Dialing Properties. The Dialing Properties dialog is shown in Figure 8-85. In the Dialing Properties dialog, click Area Code Rules and up comes the Area Code Rules dialog in Figure 8-86. Then click the box marked "Always dial the area code (10-digit dialing)," and you'll be ready for your phone company's switch to ten digits.

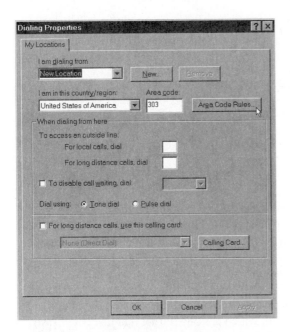

Figure 8-85. Dialing Properties, usually needed only if you move around

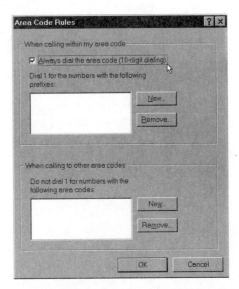

Figure 8-86. Area Code Rules—the key to ten-digit dialing

Figure 8-87. Change the modem's characteristics here

Back to the Modems Properties dialog in Figure 8-84. If you click on the Properties button, you'll get the Properties dialog shown in Figure 8-87. It's important that you take a close look at the "Maximum speed" box here. Back in the days of Win95, Windows had a nasty habit of setting the maximum speed to the rated speed of the modem—28,800, say. This box doesn't have anything to do with the rated "baud" speed of your modem. It limits the speed of the connection between your modem and your PC!

This box once saved my hide. I was on the road and needed desperately to connect to CompuServe to collect my e-mail, but the phone line was so bad, I'd get disconnected moments after logging on. I finally used this box to force a connection at 14,400 bps, and that kept up long enough to let me pick up my e-mail.

You should crank this baby up as high as you can put it—115,200—if Windows hasn't already done so. Back off the high setting only if some communications program starts griping about bad packets—the telltale sign of a comm link trying to run too fast.

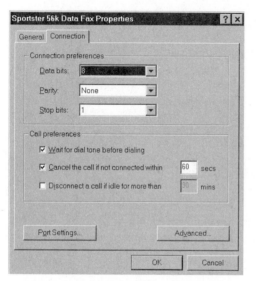

Figure 8-88. Modem connection settings

The Connection tab (Figure 8-88) isn't very interesting. It's highly unlikely you'll want to change the 8N1 Data/Parity/Stop setting. You might turn off the "Wait for dial tone before dialing" box if you got stuck in a hotel room that was impossible to automatically dial out of. (You'd uncheck this box, dial the phone manually, then get the modem going.)

The interesting part of the Connection tab lies behind the two buttons at the bottom: Port Settings and Advanced, which has one setting that just could save your tail some day.

The Port Settings button leads to the dialog box in Figure 8-89, called Advanced Port Settings (confusing the way they mixed the two buttons' names, eh?), that lets you control the effective size of the 16550's buffers. All modern PCs have something called a 16550-compatible UART, which is a chip that controls the flow of data between your modem and your PC. The PC, being much faster than a modem, looks for data only at predefined intervals. The modem (actually, the UART that sits between the PC and the modem) needs to be able to store ("buffer") incoming and outgoing data, to fill in the time gaps when the PC itself isn't looking. If the modem receives more data than it can store while the PC is away, you get a "buffer overrun" and the data are lost.

While there's no problem jacking up the Transmit Buffer size, be cautious with the Receive Buffer. Experiment, and back off if you get too many errors.

Figure 8-89. Advanced Port Settings controls the size of the UART buffer

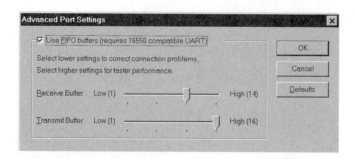

Beneath the Advanced button is the Advanced Connection Settings dialog shown in Figure 8-90. You should change the Error Control and Flow Control settings only if a knowledgeable system administrator, who is obviously in full possession of his faculties (truly a *rara avis*), holds a gun to your head. Anything you type in "Extra Settings" is sent to the modem after the AT command. The important check box, "Append to log" causes Win98 to append a detailed log of modem commands and responses to **ModemLog.txt**, in the Win98 **\Windows** folder. Good debug information, if you speak AT.

The Diagnostics tab in the Modems applet (Figure 8-84) contains a button marked Help (which brings up the Modem Troubleshooter) and another button mislabeled More Info (Figure 8-91).

More Info actually runs a full local-loop test of your modem. Push that button and you get a complete run of the AT command set, and the results of the test are displayed in a box for you to compare with what your modem manual says should be valid results. Wonder if the modem is responding correctly to all the commands? This tells you.

I have no idea why a diagnostic routine this handy is buried down here in Mudville and why it's accessible only through this torturous route.

Information about the currently active modem is stored in the Registry key **HKLM\System\CurrentControlSet\Services\Class\Modem\0000**, with much of the important information crammed inscrutably into an entry called **DCB**. The Windows Resource Kit and Device Developer's Kit both have long, boring discussions of values listed under the **\Class\Modem** key.

Figure 8-90. Other Advanced Connection Settings

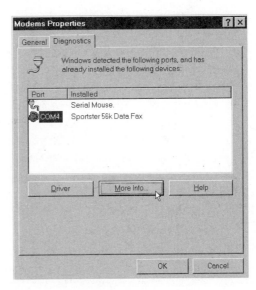

Figure 8-91. Valuable modem diagnostics

■ Mouse

Quod movetur ab alio movetur.
(That which moves is moved by another.)

—Thomas Aquinas, *Summa theologicæ*, ca. 1265

Every Win98 user can take advantage of animated mouse cursors—and if you didn't install any Desktop themes, this is where you'll find them.

When you double click on the Mouse applet in Control Panel, you'll be greeted by the Buttons tab of the Mouse Properties dialog (Figure 8-92). At the top you can swap the functions of the left and right mouse buttons. At the bottom you tell Win98 how quickly you want to click the mouse button to make two button clicks a "double click." Test by clicking on the jack-in-the-box.

The Pointers tab (Figure 8-93) lets you replace the built-in Windows pointers for everything from simple pointing to selection, the busy hourglass, resizing, and just about anything else you've ever seen.

> Note that the Text Select pointer is not the same thing as an insertion point. As far as I can tell, the insertion point is implemented in hardware and can't be changed manually. Many stationary pointers (***.cur** files) and animated pointers (***.ani** files) await under the Browse button. Even if you (*sniff!*) wouldn't dream of putting something frivolous on your computer, consider using the Animated Hourglass mouse pointer scheme. Often a frozen hourglass will be your first hint that the entire system has gone south.

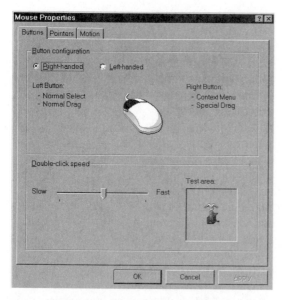

Figure 8-92. Mouse central, in the Mouse applet

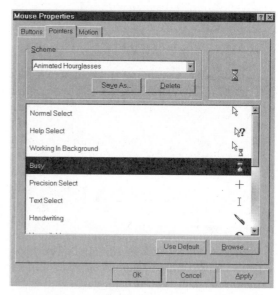

Figure 8-93. Customize mouse pointers on the Pointers tab

Actually, you needn't use the whole Animated Hourglass scheme. The animated hourglasses, if you have them, are in files **\Windows\ Cursors\appstart.ani** and **hourglas.ani**, and you can use them in any scheme by pushing the Browse button.

If you ran a typical install of Windows 98, you may be able to add more pointers and schemes (in particular, the 3D Pointers scheme, Standard [Large], and Standard [Extra Large]) by going into Control Panel's Add/Remove Programs applet, Windows Software tab, Accessories check box, and picking Mouse Pointers.

Especially if you are running at a high screen resolution, like 1024 x 768, you owe it to yourself to check out the Large and Extra Large schemes. Your eyes will thank you.

Note also that the themes available via the Control Panel's Desktop Themes applet contain complete sets of mouse pointers—some good, some bad, most just ugly.

When is a scheme not a scheme? Good question. Windows 98 has four different official schemes that I could find: the Desktop scheme, used in the Display applet; the Mouse Pointer Scheme, used here in the Mouse applet; Power schemes, used in the Power Management applet; and the Sound scheme, used in the Sound applet. (There are many more parts of Win98 that look and behave much like schemes—Desktop themes or the Country/ Language choices in the Regional Settings applet, for example—but Microsoft doesn't call them schemes.) While all four are called schemes, they all behave very differently—and the differences have stung me more than once.

When you're using a Desktop scheme and change one of the items in the scheme (say, the Desktop's background color), Win98 responds by turning the box that holds the scheme name blank. That's great. It's a warning that you've changed something, and the scheme is no longer in full effect. The changes you made are put in the Registry, and all of it stays the same until you open the Display applet again. If you change to a new scheme, you're prompted that the current scheme (the homegrown one you created) hasn't been saved and will be overwritten if you don't save it. You can actually redefine the built-in Desktop schemes by clicking Save As and carefully typing in the name of the scheme you want to overwrite or by clicking on a built-in scheme and hitting Delete. That's all working the way it should. This method of handling schemes gives you a lot of flexibility, eliminates unnecessary constraints (for example, it doesn't require you to give a name to a scheme you may not want to save), and protects you from yourself.

The Sound schemes SetUp behaves the same way as Desktop schemes—a big improvement over Windows 95.

The Mouse scheme is a completely different breed of vermin. If you change just one item in this scheme, the whole scheme is overwritten, unless you're very, very careful to assign it a new scheme name. There's no warning about it: change one pointer and click OK, and the built-in scheme is nuked, with nary a squeal of protest.

 We used big Bill for our model of schemes. He has all sorts of different schemes at any time so we figured you should, too.

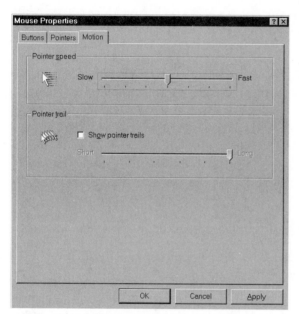

Figure 8-94. Mouse motion controls

The Motion tab lets you set the pointer's speed (actually, its sensitive to how you physically move your mouse) between Slow and Fast (Figure 8-94). It also lets you show pointer trails (for improved visibility, typically on portables) and adjust them from Short to Long. Straightforward stuff.

There are also several mouse-related settings available on the first tab of the Tweak UI applet. Yet another bit of user-friendly engineering—you have to run all over hell's half acre to get all the settings put together.

The Registry settings that correspond to Mouse applet values are scattered around. On the Buttons tab, changing to a left-handed mouse puts the value **SwapMouseButtons=1** into the Registry key **HKCU\Control Panel\Mouse**. The "Double-click speed" is in **HKCU\Control Panel\Mouse**, where the setting Slow corresponds to a **DoubleClickSpeed** value of 900, which in turn means that Win98 will let you spend up to 900 milliseconds between clicks. The setting Fast corresponds to a **DoubleClickSpeed** value of 100, or at most one-tenth of a second between clicks. (Don't know about you, but we can't click that fast!)

 Here's a fun undocumented setting. In addition to the time restrictions on a double click—you have to click twice within the **DoubleClickSpeed** amount of time for the click to be considered double—there are also space restrictions, which correspond to values for **DoubleClickHeight** and **DoubleClickWidth**. The rule is pretty simple: you must click twice within the **DoubleClickSpeed** amount of time within a rectangle that is **DoubleClickHeight** pixels tall by **DoubleClickWidth** pixels wide. The odd part is that the two space restriction values are located in Registry key **HKCU\Control Panel\Desktop**, not in **\Mouse**.

Figure 8-95.
Desktop key in
the Registry

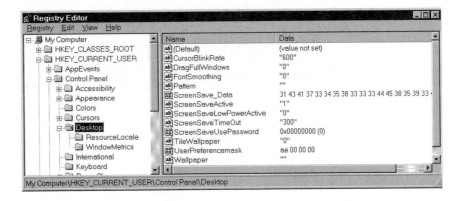

Tweak UI changes these settings, but we haven't reached that applet yet in this chapter. That gives us more than enough incentive to urge you to try changing the settings manually in the Registry. If you're still wet behind your Registry ears, try this little change. (Don't worry, you won't hurt anything. If you screw up, the settings will just be ignored.) Start by double clicking in and around the Mouse applet's jack-in-the-box, shown at the bottom of Figure 8-92. Move the "Double-click speed" way down to Slow, and see how far you can move the mouse and still have a double click "take." Not very far, true?

OK. Let's change it. Get out of the Mouse applet. Click Start, then Run, type **regedit**, hit **Enter**. Double click **HKCU** (remember, that's shorthand for **HKEY_CURRENT_USER**), then double click Control Panel, and then double click Desktop. Now look at Figure 8-95. We want to add a string value, so click Edit, then New, then String Value. Type **DoubleClickHeight** (no spaces, upper-case letters where shown) and hit **Enter**. Double click **DoubleClickHeight**

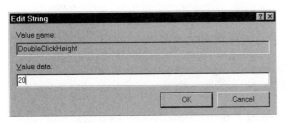

Figure 8-96. **DoubleClickHeight** goes into
the Registry

and type in the value **20** (no quotes), as in Figure 8-96. Hit **Enter**. Replicate those steps (Edit, New, String Value, type the name, **Enter**, double click the name, type the value, **Enter**) to put in a value name called **DoubleClickWidth** with value data of 20.

Want to see the effect of what you just did? Restart Windows. Go into the Control Panel's Mouse applet. See how far you can move the "Double-click speed" down and still have a double click "take." See that? You've just expanded the double-click area to 20 × 20 pixels, a square roughly the size of the front panel of the jack-in-the-box's box. Congratulations. You're on your way to becoming a Registry pro.

To get rid of all the new stuff, just click once on **DoubleClickHeight** and hit **Del**, then click once on **DoubleClickWidth** and hit **Del**.

The cursor files used under the Pointers tab are stored in **HKCU\Control Panel\Cursors**. The cursor files used in the Windows Standard Scheme are apparently stored internally in Windows itself, as this key lists only cursors that differ from those used in the Windows Standard Scheme.

The schemes themselves appear in the **HKCU\Control Panel\Cursors\Schemes** key. Apparently somebody at Microsoft took the admonition in *The Mother of All Windows 95 Books* to heart and turned this key—which was a pathetic mess in Win95—into something that can be understood by mere mortals. Good job, Redmond.

 The Motion tab has its own . . . idiosyncrasies. Registry settings for the mouse sensitivity (which the Motion tab calls Pointer Speed) are stored in the key **HKCU\Control Panel\Mouse** in three separate values: **MouseSpeed**, **MouseThreshold1**, and **MouseThreshold2**. (The key itself isn't created until you change the pointer speed.) The interaction of the three values can get pretty complicated.

Your mouse generates a hardware interrupt from time to time, and the interrupt tells your PC how far the mouse has moved and in what direction. Microsoft discovered long ago that if you move your mouse slowly, you expect the cursor to move on the screen with great precision; conversely, if you move your mouse quickly, you expect some sort of acceleration to kick in, so the cursor flies across the screen much more rapidly. These three Registry entries control the amount of acceleration and how fast your mouse has to be moving—equivalently, how far it travels between hardware interrupts—before the acceleration kicks in.

If **MouseSpeed** has a value of **0**, there is no acceleration. That's easy.

If **MouseSpeed** has a value of **1**, Windows looks to see how many pixels your mouse has traveled between interrupts. If that number exceeds the value of **MouseThreshold1**, the first level of acceleration kicks in and distances are doubled. For example, if your mouse has traveled 8 pixels since the last interrupt—**MouseSpeed** is **1** and **MouseThreshold1** is, say, **6**—Windows doubles the distance and tells your applications that the mouse has actually traveled 16 pixels.

If **MouseSpeed** has a value of **2**, again, Windows looks for the number of pixels traveled between interrupts. Just as in the previous case, if the number exceeds **MouseThreshold1**, the first-level accelerator kicks in and the distance is doubled. In addition, if the number exceeds **MouseThreshold2**, the second accelerator kicks in and the distance is doubled again—so the application is told that the mouse moved four times as far as it actually did.

For example, if **MouseSpeed** is **2**, **MouseThreshold1** is **4**, and **MouseThreshold2** is **12**, a movement of 2 pixels is reported as 2 pixels; if the mouse goes 8 pixels, the application thinks it went 16; and if the mouse really traveled 14 pixels, Windows treats it as 56 pixels.

Table 8-1. The Truth on Mouse Acceleration							
Pointer Speed slider location	*1*	*2*	*3*	*4*	*5*	*6*	*7*
MouseSpeed	0	1	1	1	2	2	2
MouseThreshold1	N/A	10	7	4	4	4	4
MouseThreshold2	N/A	N/A	N/A	N/A	12	9	6

 I talked about moving the mouse by pixels to give you a graphical feel for what's involved. But the mouse movement really involves how far the ball underneath rolls and is measured in a unit called a Mickey. No, really, it's true—not a joke.

Of course, the Motion tab (Figure 8-94) doesn't mention anything about **MouseSpeed** or **MouseThreshold**s. The Pointer Speed box just has a little slider that stops in seven different positions, from Slow to Fast.

 The only way you can understand the seven positions and how they behave is by seeing the underlying Registry entries and correlating them with some idea of how the mouse accelerators kick in. For example, the jump from position 4 to position 5 is huge because the secondary acceleration afterburner kicks in, whereas the transition from position 3 to position 4 is pretty subtle. The real scoop on Pointer Speed is in Table 8-1.

 The Pointer Trails setting, a number between 2 and 7 that specifies the number of "ghosts" the mouse pointer generates—corresponding to the six slider positions in the Pointer Trail box, where 2 is Short and 7 is Long—sits in Registry key **HKLM\Config\0001\Display\Settings**, the **MouseTrails** value. I have no idea why they stuck it there in the low-rent district with the resolution settings and system fonts.

 # ■ Multimedia

Our sweetest songs are those that tell of saddest thought.

—P. B. SHELLEY, *"To a Skylark,"* 1819

The Control Panel's Multimedia applet adjusts the settings for sound and video. Windows 98 contains a host of new multimedia capabilities, and most of them sit in this applet.

When you start the Multimedia applet, the Audio tab presents itself (Figure 8-97). The Playback box simply specifies the sound card you want to use for everything except MIDI sound (see Chapter 2 for definitions). The Recording box determines the device you'll use to record—typically the recording part of your sound card.

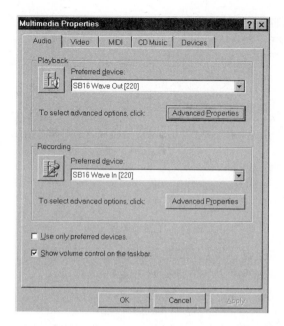

Figure 8-97. Multimedia applet

Figure 8-98. Pick the speaker system that best matches yours

 You may be puzzled by this preferred device stuff because most folks don't put several sound cards in one machine but instead consider a voice-enabled modem. Some voice-enabled modems can record sounds and play them back over a phone speaker—for example, I have a telephone handset as part of a special computer telephone. The handset mouthpiece and earpiece install their own recording and playback drivers, so my system does have several devices installed.

Those icons with sliders in the back, to the left side of the Playback and Recording boxes, bring up sound mixers. That's where you adjust the volume, for play and record, respectively. I discuss the mixers in detail in the section "Sound Mixer and Volume Control" in Chapter 4.

Click the Playback Advanced Properties button and Win98 gives you a chance to specify the kind of speakers you're using—from pedestrian desktop speakers to surround sound (Figure 8-98).

 I didn't find any appreciable difference between the speaker settings, and I'm usually pretty good at picking out such nuances. Your mileage may vary, of course, but don't tell Win98 that you have a surround sound system and expect it to greatly improve the sound coming out of the speakers. Even if you have a surround sound system attached to your PC.

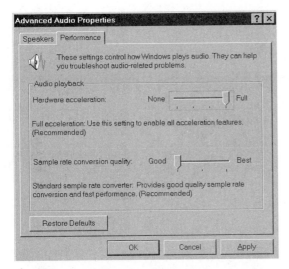

Figure 8-99. Performance tab, for scaling back performance while troubleshooting

The Performance tab on the Advanced Audio Properties dialog (Figure 8-99) as usual isn't about performance at all—it's a troubleshooting tab.

If playing a sound off your hard drive leads to skips, squeaks, or squawks, try moving back the "Hardware acceleration" slider. (Note that this doesn't apply to sound files on CDs—which are more likely to be zapped by slow CD drive reads.)

If you play back a voice recording and it sounds as if it originated on Edison's original wind-up music box, you can try increasing the sample rate conversion by moving the lower slider to the right. (The sample rate is discussed in the section "Ride the Perfect Wav" in Chapter 2.) Changing this setting probably won't help—you'll start getting dropped-out segments of the conversation unless you have a very powerful PC—but it's worth a try.

 Leave it to Microsoft marketing to come up with a slider that runs from Good to Best. Nothing in Windows can be less than Good, eh?

The Advanced Properties button in the Recording box leads to the Advanced Audio Properties dialog shown in Figure 8-100.

As with the Advanced settings for Playback, the upper slider lets you reduce Hardware acceleration in case your recordings come out garbled; the lower slider allows you to adjust the Sample rate. For more details about recording, check the section "Sound Recorder" in Chapter 4.

The Video tab in the Multimedia applet (Figure 8-101) controls the size of the video playback window. It lets you pick full-screen or partial-screen ($1/16$, $1/4$, or $1/2$) playback.

The MIDI tab (Figure 8-102) contains settings for MIDI devices. Surprisingly, Windows 98 may not pick the best MIDI synthesizer available on your machine. You can change the synthesizer, er, instrument here under the MIDI tab. In the particular instance shown in Figure 8-102, Win98 chose the Creative Music Synthesizer—which pales

Figure 8-100. Make a better recording via the Advanced Audio Properties dialog

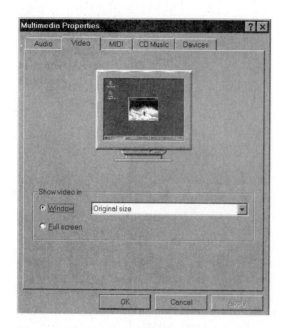

Figure 8-101. Change the size of your screen's video playback window here

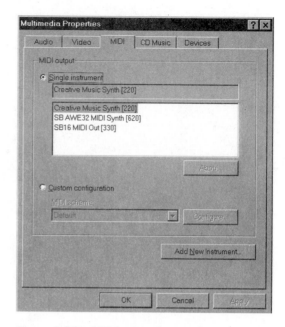

Figure 8-102. MIDI control central

in comparison to the AWE32 MIDI Synthesizer. Pick a synthesizer, click Apply, then play a `.mid` or `.rmi` file by double clicking on it. Choose the synthesizer you like best.

If you have a new MIDI instrument that you want to connect to your PC, click Add New Instrument and follow along with the MIDI Instrument Installation Wizard (Figure 8-103). Once you have new instruments defined, you can patch through to those instruments on specified MIDI channels by clicking Custom configuration (in Figure 8-102), then Configure, choosing the channel, clicking Change, and picking the instrument.

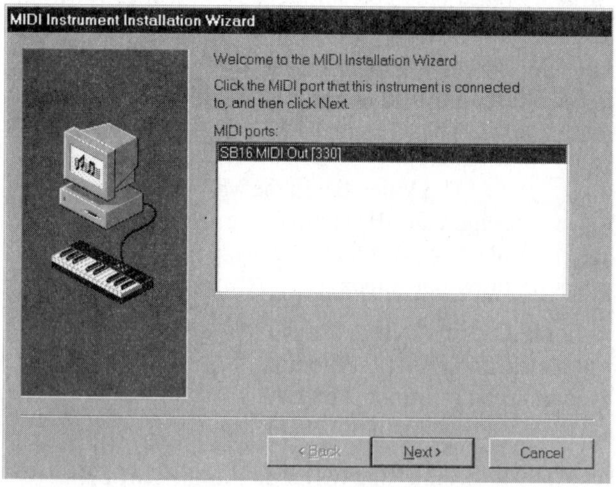

The CD Music tab (Figure 8-104) tells Windows where to find your CD-ROM drive and lets you adjust the volume of music played on the CD-ROM drive. This volume control is totally independent of the overall audio volume control.

Figure 8-103. MIDI Instrument Installation Wizard—specifically for MIDI instruments

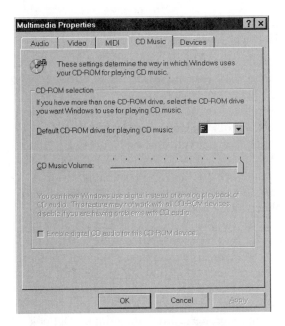

Figure 8-104. CD Music tab in the Multimedia applet

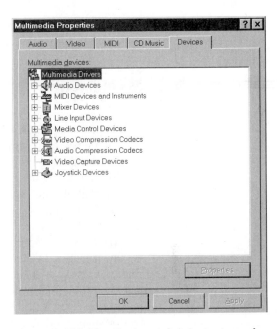

Figure 8-105. The Devices tab is just a tunnel

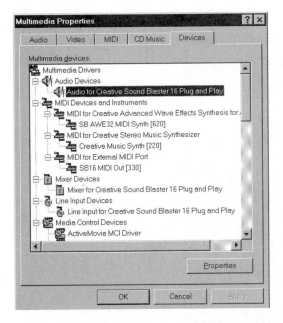

Figure 8-106. Each individual multimedia component appears in the Devices tab

Finally, the Devices tab (Figures 8-105 and 8-106) contains dozens of entries, each associated with a specific multimedia capability. You can explore all of your multimedia components—including video and audio codecs—from this tab. Most components can be turned on or off individually, and the relative priorities of the various audio codecs can be adjusted here, too.

Strangely, though, many of the driver-related activities you'd normally associate with a list like this can't be performed here. To change drivers or add new drivers, you have to work with the Control Panel System applet's Device Manager.

General multimedia information is stored in Registry key **HKCU\Software\Microsoft\Multimedia**, with basic sound card information in **\SoundMapper**. Volume settings are in **HKCU\Software\Microsoft\Windows\CurrentVersion\Applets\Volume**

`Control` with a key name equal to the name of the sound driver. There are other settings scattered throughout the Registry.

■ Network

This applet is available from the Control Panel, of course (Figure 8-107). You may find it easier to get here, though, by right clicking on Network Neighborhood and choosing Properties.

Want to know the most common use for the Network applet? It's to *turn off* that blasted logon screen. If you have a stand-alone PC—one that doesn't ever connect to a local network—you're probably tired of seeing that stupid logon screen every time you boot Windows 98. Get rid of it.

WARNING! Before you try to get rid of the logon screen, look for folders underneath `C:\windows\profiles`. If there is anything in any of those folders, remove it or make backup copies now! Although we couldn't replicate the problem, I swear that I once lost all the data in these folders while making changes to the Passwords applet's User Profiles tab. In particular, Outlook has a nasty habit of putting `outlook.pst`—the primary Outlook data file—in `C:\windows\profiles\username\Application Data\ Microsoft\Outlook`. If you have such a file, copy it someplace handy before you make this change!

**Figure 8-107.
Network applet's
Configuration tab**

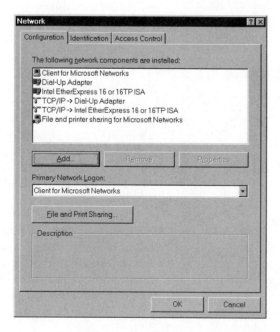

- In the Network applet's Configuration tab, click on the box marked Primary Network Logon and pick Windows Logon. Click OK, and Windows will restart.
- Log on the usual way, then go back into Control Panel, double click on the Passwords applet, and click Change Windows Password. Where it says "Old password," type your old password. Leave the boxes marked "New password" and "Confirm new password" blank. Click OK.
- Then shift over to the User Profiles tab and click the button that says "All users of this computer use the same preferences and desktop settings."
- That's it. The next time you restart Windows, your logon screen is long gone.

To bring the logon screen back, just pop into the Control Panel's User applet and set up a new user.

 Even simpler than this method of getting rid of the logon screen is to use Tweak UI's automated logon option which will also work if you are on a network where you have to log on. I discuss it later in the section on Tweak UI.

If you're looking at the Control Panel's Network applet for anything other than getting rid of that pesky logon screen, you probably want to do one of four things:

- To set up a simple network cheap, read on.
- To figure out how to dial up your office PC from home or while you're on the road, look in Chapter 4. The PC at home (or on the road) just needs to be able to speak the right language over the modem. That's easy: if you don't have an entry on the Network applet's Configuration tab (Figure 8-107) that says TCP/IP → Dial-Up Adapter, click Add, click Protocol, click Add, on the left pick Microsoft, on the right pick TCP/IP, and click OK to back out. If there's still no TCP/IP → Dial-Up Adapter line, click once on the Dial-Up Adapter line, click Properties, click the Bindings tab, and check the TCP/IP box. Click OK all the way back out. There. You're now ready to dial into your office computer. (If your office computer doesn't support TCP/IP—and most of them now do—you might want to install NetBEUI. Talk to your network's administrator.)
- To figure out why your simple network isn't, uh, networking, go over the steps in this section, but don't get hung up on it. If you can't find the answer easily, click Start, then Help, bring up the Find tab, and type **network trouble**. You want the network troubleshooter. If that doesn't give you enough information, cross your fingers and dive into the Windows Resource Kit. Good luck.
- To get your PC to work with the big network at the office, contact the netdroids at the office. Troubleshooting Netware networks and Windows NT client/server networks falls way beyond the scope of this book . . . not to mention the fact that you're traveling in shark-infested waters that require very specialized navigation.

There are two different kinds of networks: peer-to-peer, where each PC is equal to all the others, and client/server, where one PC is the "server" and all the other PCs attach themselves as subordinate "clients." We'll concentrate on peer-to-peer networking here, because that's the kind you're most likely to be setting up yourself.

Setting up a peer-to-peer PC network has never been simpler than it is with Win98. It can literally take you less than an afternoon to put together a two-PC network and share all the disk drives and printers between the two—if you know what you're doing. And there's the rub.

Start by getting the right hardware. Talk to somebody you trust at your local computer shop, or call a company like Cables To Go (voice 800-826-7904, Web **www.cablestogo.com**) that sells lots of computer cables and networking equipment. Tell them you need a cheap but 100% Intel EtherExpress-compatible setup to daisy-chain together two (or three or four . . .) Win98 (or Win95) PCs. They'll sell you a ThinNet rig, with a Network Interface Card (NIC; pronounced "nick") to go into each PC, a hunk of special coaxial known as ThinNet cable, T connectors to connect the cable to the NIC, and terminators to cover the bare ends of the T connectors, one each at the beginning and end of the cable.

 An alternative to ThinNet and T connectors is Twisted Pair, which looks a lot like phone cable and connectors, although the plugin is somewhat larger than with standard phone cable. The downside of Twisted Pair is that you need to purchase a little box called a hub, but they cost only about $40. With Twisted Pair, each computer gets plugged into this box and you don't need to worry about T's and ends. Moreover, the hub allows longer distances between machines because it amplifies the signals, and its flashing lights can be very useful while troubleshooting a problem. Basically, with two nodes or maybe three, ThinNet is the preferred choice. With more nodes, you'll want Twisted Pair. In any event, if you are going with ThinNet for now, make sure that the NICs you get also support Twisted Pair (the connectors are called 10BaseT for ThinNet and 10Base2 for Twisted Pair) in case you want to upgrade later.

 Try to get NICs that are Plug 'n' Play. If they are, the hardware and software installation I'm about to describe will be done automatically, but be sure to read the parts on file and printer sharing and on machine identification, because you'll still need that!

When the package arrives, install the NICs in the PCs using the Add Hardware applet described earlier in this chapter. You can pick the guru or the naive method, as befits your technological self-image. Just install the cards; don't expect any heroics. Don't bother with any software that ships with the cards unless it's specifically designed for Windows 95 or Windows 98 (and if the cards are 100% Intel EtherExpress-compatible, you won't need those diskettes anyway). Once the cards are installed, turn off the machines and daisy-chain the cable to the NICs, following the instructions that come in the package. When the cable is installed and you have the machines turned on, get on each PC in turn and pop into the Control Panel's Network applet. If you get a message saying "Your network is not set up properly," ignore it. Of course it isn't working properly . . . yet.

Start with the Configuration tab (Figure 8-107). It's important that you have four "components" installed; if any of them are missing, click Add and continue with the next panel.

- Client for Microsoft Networks is a computer program that lets you communicate with the other Windows 95, 98, and NT PCs on your network.

- File and printer sharing for Microsoft Networks is another program that lets other people look at your disks or print on your printer.

- Your NIC should have an entry with a weird green P next to it.

 Ahem—that isn't a weird green P. It's an icon of a green adapter, with a gold attachment at the right and some electronics on the board. It only looks like a weird green P.

- Finally, you should have one of those loop-the-loop plug entries with TCP/IP → pointing to the name of your NIC.

Once you have all this installed (clicking Add as necessary), make sure Primary Network Logon shows Client for Microsoft Networks; that forces Win98 to log you onto the network whenever you reboot your machine.

Any missing pieces in the Configuration tab are added by pushing the Add button there and working with the dialog shown in Figure 8-108. The descriptions at the bottom are confusing, so ignore them. At the very least you need one Client (for Microsoft Networks), one Adapter (whichever NIC you have installed), one Protocol (TCP/IP hooked up to the NIC), and one Service (file and printer sharing for Microsoft Networks). That's all.

When you get back to the Configuration tab, don't forget to click the File and Printer Sharing button and make sure both of the boxes in Figure 8-109 are checked. These boxes just hook up your disks and printer to the network: they don't allow anybody in particular to use them. We'll cover that base in a bit.

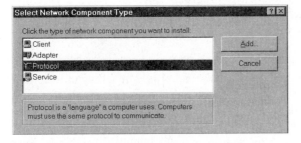

Figure 8-108. Add network components as necessary

Figure 8-109. You have to check the boxes here to share your files and/or your printers

**Figure 8-110.
Giving the PC a
name for the net-
work**

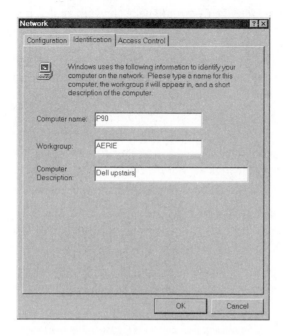

Once you have the Configuration tab complete—and it pays to spend some
time on that tab to make sure you get all the details right—move on to the Identification tab (Figure 8-110). The Computer name box here has to have a name
that's unique on the network: if you have two computers attached to the same
network, they must have two different computer names. This is the name other
people will use to get at the disks and printer attached to your computer. Avoid
the temptation to be verbose; this name is typed a lot. Also, limit yourself to
simple letters and numbers—no spaces or other weird characters.

 *Note carefully the advice to avoid spaces in the computer name. I once
lost several hours trying to install a card until I figured out that it was
a bad idea to use spaces! It confuses Windows badly.*

Big networks can have more than one Workgroup. But since you're setting up a
little network, you want to make sure everybody on the network has precisely
the same Workgroup name in this box. You can put anything you want in the
Description box.

Finally, the Access Control tab (Figure 8-111) lets you choose between allowing everybody equal access to your disks and printer or setting up specific
access rules for each individual.

Note that "equal access" doesn't mean "free access." Once the network is
going and you've chosen File and Print Sharing under the Configuration tab,
you can specify passwords, read/write restrictions, and all sorts of things, down
to the folder level, in Explorer: simply right click on the folder or printer and
pick Sharing.

**Figure 8-111.
You can control
access by assign-
ing passwords or
allowing certain
users in**

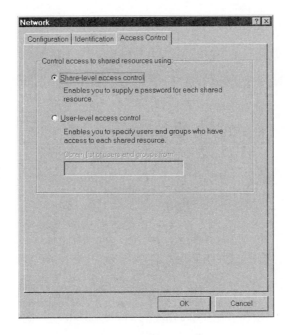

The "Obtain list of users and groups from" box is gray unless you're connected to a network server.

If you're thinking of setting up a client/server network, I strongly recommend that you get a copy of Microsoft's BackOffice Small Business Server. It combines NT Server with many of the BackOffice products and makes installation and maintenance a breeze. Well, maybe not a breeze, but a mild gale. Compared to any other client/server networking product I've ever seen, BackOffice Small Business Server hides you from most of the (very) dirty work.

If you're installing a new peer-to-peer network from scratch, it's probably a good idea to reboot the machine once all the settings are in place. After you've set up everything through the Network applet on all your computers and rebooted all the machines, try clicking on Network Neighborhood to get a list of the other computers on your network.

If you have problems finding other computers, the first thing to blame is the wires: go back and double-check all the connections. The second thing to blame is the Workgroup name: go back to each machine, look in the Network applet, and make sure the name is spelled precisely the same way on every one (and while you're at it, make sure the computer names are all different). If those all look good, pick one machine as a guinea pig and go through the network troubleshooter on that machine.

Once all the machines are visible in Network Neighborhood, there's one *crucial* last step. You have to explicitly enable sharing for each drive (or folder) and each printer you want accessible over the network. Go into Explorer, right

**Figure 8-112.
This level of sharing gives full access to the drive to anyone on the network**

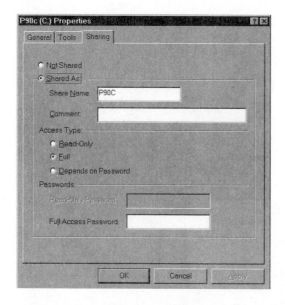

click on the disk or folder or printer you want to share, pick Sharing, and select the level of sharing you feel comfortable with, as in Figure 8-112. Once sharing is enabled, other PCs on the network can get to the shared drivers (or folders) by simply clicking on them in Explorer's Network Neighborhood folder. They can also install your printer to work on their machine by double clicking on the printer in Explorer's Network Neighborhood.

Explorer tries to give you visual clues as to which drives and folders have sharing turned on—it adds a hand ( ) to the objects icon in the tree pane, so, for example, changes to .

 There's a bit of a security issue here. If you let just anyone on the network into your data, well, you let *just anyone* on the network into your data. Once you've opened the gate, a nosey coworker or somebody walking by an unattended PC connected to your network would be able to look at the files you've released. So think a bit about security before you open up your whole machine, and consider whether free access to your data is an altogether good thing.

The rest of the things on the Configuration tab look mighty intimidating. Dial-Up Adapters. IPX/SPX protocols. TCP/IP. Lots of alphabet soup.

 Yeah, it's too bad nobody translates this stuff into plain English. A dial-up adapter is a modem, or maybe a direct cable connection (see Chapter 3)—in other words, a way to attach to other computers that isn't "on" all the time. The adapter entry in the Configuration tab is created automatically when you install Dial-Up Networking from the Add/Remove Programs applet.

IPX/SPX is the language ("protocol") Novell Netware uses for Netware computers to converse. TCP/IP is the language of the Internet and most UNIX machines. NetBEUI is Microsoft's "little" network protocol, which is appropriate for very light loads on small networks. In general, it doesn't hurt to install all three protocols; having them all available may come in handy some day.

 This really is amazing stuff. When it works, it's magic. You'll never need to put up with sneakernet again: printing on the group's laser printer, say, is just a point and a click away—as easy as printing on the printer right next to your computer.

■ Passwords

Chapter 3 discusses Passwords, including the way to set up multiple users for a single machine and the place in the Registry that's modified to adapt to more than one user.

 There's one very important subtlety you need to know about before you even think about looking at the User Profiles tab (Figure 8-113).

Changing your PC from a multiple-user machine to a single-user machine (which you do by clicking the button marked "All users of this computer use the same preferences and desktop settings" button) may be fraught with danger.

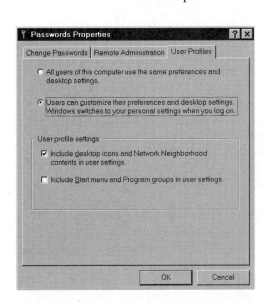

Figure 8-113. The (extremely dangerous!) User Profiles tab

One time when I changed from multiple users to a single user, Win98 deleted all the folders underneath `C:\windows\profiles`. And it did so without warning, without telling me if any important files lurked under that folder. I couldn't repeat it but I'd suggest caution.

So before you change to single user, examine closely everything under `C:\windows\profiles`. If you find anything there, back it up! And if you find a file called `outlook.pst` there—the primary data file for Microsoft Outlook (this is the default location for an Internet Only installation)—don't even bother trying to convert to single user. You'll lose more time futzing with Outlook than you'll ever regain by having a single-user machine.

If you're here because you want to get rid of that stupid logon screen—the one that asks you for a password every time you start Windows—the topic is covered in detail at the beginning of the preceding section on the Network applet.

■ Power Management

Figure 8-114. Default "Always On" power settings

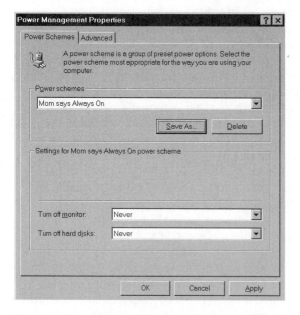

Figure 8-115. Genuine "Always On" power settings

Windows 95 used a power management technology called APM, for Advanced Power Management. Win98 can handle both APM and the newer Advanced Configuration and Power Interface (ACPI) specification. Unfortunately, as we went to press, Win98's ACPI capabilities seemed to be, uh, substandard. Undoubtedly new hardware will be set up specifically to conform to Win98's interpretation of the ACPI specs, but if you bought an ACPI machine in early to mid-1998 (particularly portables), you may be better off disabling Win98 power management and relying on the routines built into the BIOS of your PC.

How to disable Win98 power management? It's easy. Bring up the Power Management applet (Figure 8-114). Change the "Turn off monitor" box to read Never and the "Turn off hard disks" box also to read Never. Click Save As, and give your honest-to-goodness-always-on power scheme a name. In Figure 8-115, I've chosen the name "MOM says Always On." At least you can trust MOM to keep your machine "always on," even when Microsoft plays loose and fast with the terminology.

That's the first strike against Win98's power management. The second strike we discussed back in Chapter 6: when you install Win98, the default power-down settings turn off your monitor after 15 minutes of no use and turn off your hard drives if they haven't been used for an hour (Figure 8-114). That's ludicrous for all but the most power-miserly portable systems, and we strongly recommended, back in Chapter 6, that all Win98 users change the default settings the minute they install Win98.

And the third strike? Sometimes Win98's power management puts hard drives and monitors to sleep—permanently. Many Win98 users report that, no matter what they do, they

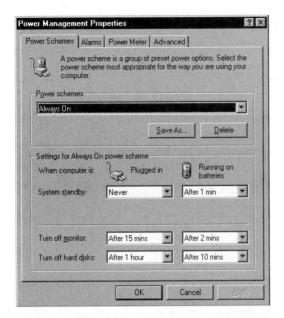

Figure 8-116. Power Management for portables

can't "wake up" older machines that have been rendered somnambulant by the Power Management settings.

There's a separate Power Management dialog for portable computers. It looks like the screen in Figure 8-116. The Alarms and Power Meter tabs let you specify how and when Win98 should notify you of impending doom. Unfortunately, like all the other power management routines, these don't always work as advertised, and in many cases, the power management routines provided by Win98 are actually in conflict with the power management routines built inside your portable's BIOS.

There's a full description of ACPI and APM in the Windows 98 Resource Kit. As always, it presents a good theoretical case, which may or may not work on your particular hardware. Just scan the online version for ACPI.

If you don't want your system to sleep with the fishes, here's what you can do.

- Test your system to see if it will "wake up." Go into the Power Management applet (Figure 8-114) and set it to turn off the monitor after 1 minute and turn off the hard disks after 3 minutes. Then wait about 4 minutes. If you can't get the system to come back to life (wiggle the mouse, and when you get the screen back, try to navigate around in Windows Explorer), completely disable Win98 Power Management.

- If your machine has built-in power management and you trust it more than you trust Win98's, completely disable Win98 Power Management using the steps outlined earlier in this section, and use the built-in power management in your PC's BIOS.

- If you want to use Win98 for power management, your PC's BIOS may include routines that will thwart your efforts—for example, if you tell Win98 to power down your monitor after 1 hour but the monitor goes blank after 30 minutes, chances are good that the BIOS power management schemes have taken over. In such cases, try to disable your PC's BIOS power management routines and see if Win98 will take over. If that doesn't work, you may want to get a new BIOS. Contact your PC manufacturer to ask about the availability of new BIOSes. Make sure the BIOS has been tested for Win98 power management compatibility.

- Even if you decide to use the Win98 routines, don't be intimidated by Win98's default settings. They stink. Change them.

Figure 8-117.
Power
Management in
the Registry

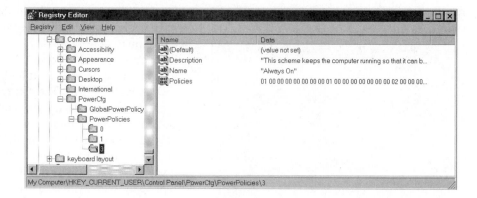

Power Management settings are stored in the Registry key **HKCU\Control Panel\PowerCfg** (Figure 8-117).

 I think there's a bug in the Always On scheme. While the name would have you believe that this scheme would keep your PC always on, in fact it keeps the monitor on for only 15 minutes and the disks spinning for only an hour. Take a look at the **PowerPolicies/3** key in Figure 8-117, particularly the Description value. It says, **"This scheme keeps the computer running so that it can be accessed from the network. Use this if you do not have network wakeup hardware."** That's exactly what I would expect from the third PowerPolicy—the Always On power scheme. But the settings generated by the scheme don't follow the description. Not even close. It's gotta be a bug.

 ## ■ Printers

I discuss the Printer applet in Chapter 3. The Control Panel's Printers icon just sweeps you off to the Printers folder; there is no separate Printer applet.

In the Registry, if you want a list of all valid printers, take a look at the key **HKLM\System\ CurrentControlSet\control\Print\Printers**. If you want the currently active printer, try **HKLM\Config\0001\System\ CurrentControlSet\Control\Print\Printers**.

 ## ■ Regional Settings

This rather innocuous Control Panel applet serves up a gold mine of Registry entries. Although you'll find that Win98 uses the entries pretty consistently—change the format of the time in the Registry, say, and the clock in the Notification Area stands up and salutes—Windows applications in general are notorious for ignoring these settings. Some software developers who write the major

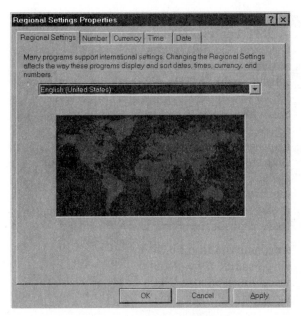

Figure 8-118. Regional Settings applet

applications don't even know they *exist,* the worst ignorance of all. So, while you might hope that changes made in this applet will ripple to all your applications, don't be surprised if you find out differently.

The first tab that appears in the Regional Settings applet is the, uh, Regional Settings tab (Figure 8-118). The dropdown list offers you a wide variety of choices (Bokmål Norwegian, anybody?). Think of these list entries as schemes—their primary purpose in life is to establish a whole bunch of settings, which you can later modify by clicking other tabs. Should you change the scheme in the list, be sure to click "Apply" before proceeding to another tab.

There's an amazing amount of intelligence built into the Number tab (Figure 8-119). If you choose a Country/Language combination in the Regional Settings list where number representations vary, the dropdown boxes reflect the locally recognized alternatives. For example, choosing English (United States) forces the Number tab to show . as the decimal symbol and , as the digit grouping symbol. Yet the German choices allow either . or , as the decimal separator and , or . as the digit grouping symbol—precisely the options widely used in German-speaking locales. Bravo!

Figure 8-119. Number formatting options on the Number tab

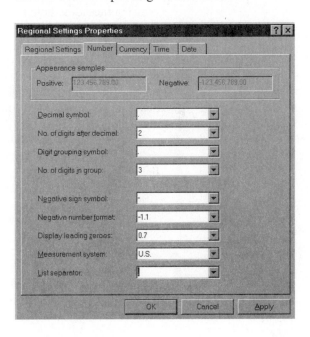

**Figure 8-120.
Regional Settings'
Currency tab**

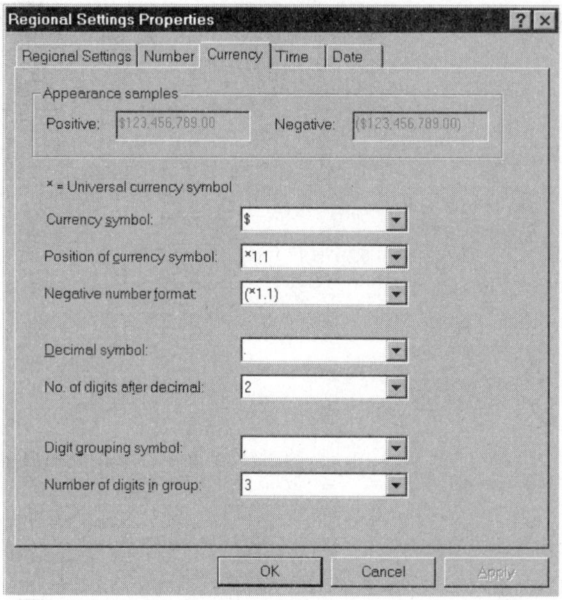

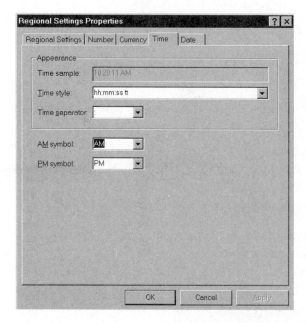

The Currency tab (Figure 8-120) is every bit as intelligent as the Number tab. For example, if you choose Sweden under the Regional Settings tab, the Currency tab will not only display the correct unit of currency (kr) but also as a default, Windows positions the symbol correctly—*after* the value (3.50 kr).

Undocumented fact: You can even type in a character number for the currency symbol by pressing **NumLock**, holding down **Alt**, and typing the four-digit character. This is important in places where fonts have single nonstandard characters for the currency (for example, some Spanish fonts have Pst as a single character for pesetas; Portuguese fonts have a single Esc character for escudos; Thai fonts have Bt in one character). Excellent work, Redmond!

Alas, after two panels of glory, Microsoft really fell down on the Time tab; it's full of bugs. The Time sample box (Figure 8-121) gives a pretty good indication of how the time will appear in, say, the Date/Time applet. The Time separator and the AM and PM symbols all seem to work as you would expect.

Figure 8-121. Time format in Regional Settings

But the Time style box is all bollixed up. In general, you're supposed to construct a template of the time in this box: **hh** stands for hour, **mm** for minute, **ss** for second, **tt** for the time symbol (AM/PM), **HH** for hour on a 24-hour clock. (The doubled **hh** and **HH** ensure that a zero appears at the beginning of single-digit times; **hh** at nine o'clock shows 09.) You're also supposed to be able to put in text, using ' (single quotes) to set it off. Try typing **'MOM time' hh:mm:ss tt** in that box and hit **Apply**. See?

To clear out the mess, pick **H:mm:ss**, hit **Apply**, and then go back to **hh:mm:ss tt** or whatever you like. Bummer.

Windows 98 can claim "year 2000 compliance" largely because of the two-digit year interpretation setting at the top of the Date tab (Figure 8-122). It's a very solid implementation, as far as I can tell, for programs in the Win98 suite. The real problem, of course, is that not all applications use this setting. As of this writing anyway, Microsoft Office applications ignore it.

The terminology for year 2000 calculations may be a bit confusing at first, but you'll get used to it. The settings shown in Figure 8-122, for example, say that the two-digit date 00 should be interpreted as 2000; 29 should be interpreted as 2029, but 30 should be interpreted as 1930.

The final tab in the Regional Settings applet, the Date tab, lets you pick Windows' default formatting for dates. The Short date format is used in Explorer and other WinApps.

Figure 8-122. Short and Long dates

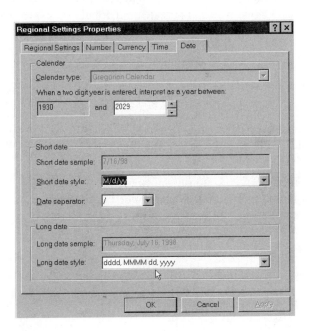

Undocumented fact: In Word 97, if you click on Insert, then Date, the first two options offered are the date in Short date and Long date formats, respectively. WordPad, on the other hand is too lazy to bother checking for your settings.

 While you're here, change the long date to get rid of one of the **d**'s in **dd**. It should read **dddd, MMMM d, yyyy**. Not many people want to see leading zeros on their dates!

The Registry abounds with Regional settings. The full list of available Country/Language schemes is located in **HKLM\System\CurrentControlSet\ Control\NIs\Locale**. The Country/Language is identified in that key with a number: **English (United States)**, for example, is **00000409**. The number of the currently selected Country/Language appears in **HKCU\Control Panel\International** as the value **Locale**.

There are also keyboard layout settings linked to the Country/Language number, located in the key **HKLM\System\CurrentControlSet\Control\ keyboard layouts** (which just happens to be one of the few keys in Win98 that isn't capitalized very well!).

Though the Number, Currency, Time, and Date settings associated with Country/Language schemes aren't stored anywhere in the Registry, they appear to be built in to Windows itself, with parts stored in the file **\windows\inf\locale.inf**. That's really a shame, for at least two reasons. First, you can't assign unique settings to a Country/Language scheme: if you change the currency symbol for Spanish (Modern) from Pst to $, the change "sticks" across languages—if you then switch to Portuguese (Standard), you probably want the currency symbol to switch over to Esc, but it stays at $. Bummer. Second, you can't create or distribute your own set of Country/Language schemes: Win98 wouldn't even know how to handle them.

 Sounds to me like Microsoft needs to rethink how it handles schemes in general. There are so many places where Win98 uses schemes, or something like schemes, but each one is handled in a different way, and switching among them can be very confusing. Uniform schemes, I say!

The Regional settings all appear in **HKCU\Control Panel\International**. If you have nothing in that key except **Locale**, it's because you haven't made any changes.

Taking the entries from the top of the Number tab dialog (see Figure 8-120):

- The Decimal symbol is value **sDecimal** (default value for English (United States) is the period).
- No. of digits after decimal is **iDigits** (default is 2).
- Digit grouping symbol is **sThousand** (default is a comma).
- No. of digits in group is in **sGrouping** but stored in a weird way (for example, a value of 5 is stored as 5;0—and we can't figure out what the semicolon signifies) (default is 3).

- Negative sign symbol is **sNegativeSign** (default is the (-) minus sign).
- Negative number format is stored as a code in **iNegNumber**—**0** is for the (1.1) format, **1** is for -1.1, **2** is for - 1.1 (with intervening space), **3** is for 1.1-, and **4** is for 1.1 - (with intervening space) (default is 1).
- Display leading zeros is a code in **iLZero**—**0** for no leading zero, **1** for a single leading zero (default is 1).
- Measurement system is a code in **iMeasure**—**0** for metric, **1** for U.S. (default is 1).
- List separator is in **sList** (default is a comma).

The list separator is used internally in Win95 and rarely appears to the user. The Currency tab settings:

- Currency symbol ($) in **sCurrency**.
- Position of currency symbol is a code in **iCurrency**—**0** for $1.00, **1** for 1.00$, **2** for $ 1.00 (with intervening space), and **3** for 1.00 $ (with intervening space) (default is 0).
- Negative number format is a code in **iNegCurr**—**0** for ($1.00), **1** for -$1.00, **2** for $-1.00, **3** for $1.00-, **4** for (1.00$), **5** for -1.00$, **6** for 1.00-$, **7** for 1.00$- (just in case you have to keep track, the preceding have no embedded spaces, and the following have one embedded space), **8** for -1.00 $, **9** for -$ 1.00, **10** for 1.00 $-, **11** for $ 1.00-, **12** for $ -1.00, **13** for 1.00- $, **14** for ($ 1.00), and **15** for (1.00 $) (default is 0).
- Decimal symbol is **sMonDecimalSep** (default is a period).
- No. of digits after decimal is **iCurrDigits** (default is 2).
- Digit grouping symbol is **sMonThousandSep** (default is a comma).
- Number of digits in group is **sMonGrouping**, with the same strange format used in **sGrouping** (default is 3).

Over on the Time tab, things are stranger. The Time style (h:mm:ss tt) setting translates into three Registry entries. One of them, **sTimeFormat**, contains the time format string, just as you see it. But a second entry, **iTLZero** appears with a value of 1 if the time format dictates that the time appear with a leading zero. And a third entry, **iTime**, appears with a value of 1 if the time format is for a 24-hour clock. The Time separator (:) is **sTime**. The AM symbol (AM) shows up as **s1159**, and the PM symbol (PM) is **s2359**.

> What are you kvetching about? We had to put those entries in the Registry for compatibility purposes. Windows 3.1 set similar flags. Youse guys had the gall to document them in the original *Mother of All Windows Books*. Now everybody and his bro' uses the Win3.1 settings, and we had no choice but to maintain them.

<Gulp> The truth at all costs, says I. Rounding out the Regional Settings in the Registry, the Date Tab has some more strange settings. **sShortDate** has the Short date formatting string (M/d/yy), just as it appears on the Date tab. In addition, though, **iDate** shows up with a 1 if the day is put ahead of the month, 2 if the year appears before the month. The Date separator (/) is **sDate**. Finally, **sLongDate** has the Long date formatting string (dddd, MMMM dd, yyyy).

■ Zounds! . . . er, Sounds

Lap me in soft Lydian airs.

—John Milton, *L'Allegro,* 1632

The Control Panel's Sounds applet (Figure 8-123) is quite straightforward. In a nutshell, Windows and Windows applications make certain "events" available to the system—"Starting Windows" being the classic example, plus application-specific events, such as receiving an e-mail message. By using this applet, you can tell Win98 to play a particular **.wav** file whenever the event occurs. There are buttons to let you choose new sounds and test them before they're assigned to events.

Sound schemes are handled very well in this applet. I talked about that extensively in the discussion of the Mouse applet, as the methods are quite similar. In Win95 it was easy to obliterate a Sound scheme—in Win98 it's almost impossible.

Registry entries for sounds are stored in a rather bizarre hierarchy, even by Windows 98 standards. Default sounds (those that will play for any application) are in **HKCU\AppEvents\ Schemes\Apps\.Default**. Sounds that play for Explorer events are in **\Schemes\Apps\ Explorer**, sounds that play for Media Player are in **\Schemes\Apps\MPlayer**, and so on. Within each key is a list of events that are sound-enabled: **\Explorer**, for example, has the **\Explorer\ EmptyRecycleBin** event; **\.Default** has **\.Default\SystemStart**, and many more.

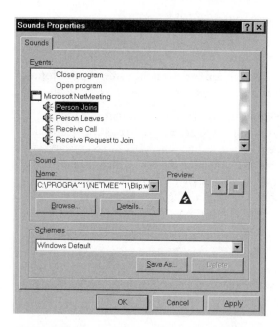

Figure 8-123. Assign sounds to events in the Sounds applet

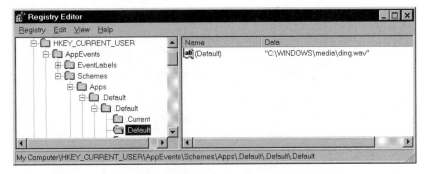

Figure 8-124. `\.Default\.Default\.Default (Default)` is a, uh, humdinger

Underneath each of *those* keys is yet another group of keys, including at a minimum the Current sound and the Default sound. So, for example, the Empty Recycle Bin event has two keys, `\Explorer\EmptyRecycleBin\.Current` and `\Explorer\EmptyRecycleBin\.Default`. Each event key thus constructed has one value, the `(Default)` value, which is a pointer to the applicable `.wav` file.

 Given that explanation and the fact that the default sound for any recognized Windows event is the `ding.wav` file, would you care to guess the value of the key (hold your breath): `HKCU\AppEvents\Schemes\Apps\.Default\.Default\.Default (Default)`?

 ■ System

Ah, Tam! Ah, Tam! Thou'll get thy fairin';
In Hell they'll roast thee like a herrin'.

—ROBERT BURNS, "Tam O'Shanter," 1790

The Control Panel's System applet (Figure 8-125) must be considered the Mother of All Applets. Think of system as being a collection of advanced, detailed utilities for Windows—or, if you prefer, as a set of velvet steps to the innermost circles of Windows hell—in many cases eclipsed by individual utilities in Windows 98. You can get to the applet either by double clicking on the System icon in the Control Panel or by right clicking on My Computer and choosing Properties.

**Figure 8-125.
Control Panel's
System applet**

The Device Manager tab lets you track down your PC's resources. The Hardware Profiles tab sets up alternative "profiles," theoretically for PCs that change hardware frequently. Theoretically. The Performance tab lets you juggle with Win98's innards. Let's take each tab in turn.

Device Manager Tab

The Device Manager, which lurks under the Device Manager tab (Figure 8-126), is a marvelous "sniffer" application that gives you a highly accurate view of what hardware sits inside or is attached to your PC. In Device Manager you can also do the following.

- Look at and manually adjust IRQ, DMA, and I/O address assignments for every piece of hardware (except Plug 'n' Play hardware, which theoretically never needs adjustment).
- Tell Windows 98 to keep its hands off IRQ, DMA, and I/O addresses that you want to reserve for hardware that hasn't yet been installed.
- See how devices are physically connected to the PC.
- See what drivers are loaded for a particular piece of hardware.
- Find out if devices aren't working properly or if they've been disabled by Windows or the hardware itself.
- Configure some of your ports and set other hardware options.
- Change drivers for any hardware device.
- "Hunt" for unused IRQs, DMAs, and I/O addresses.

**Figure 8-126.
Initial face of the
Device Manager**

 Some of these functions are duplicated with the new Win98 System Information system. I show you which ones appear in SysInfo as we take the Device Manager through its paces.

 Are you confused by all these TLAs (three-letter acronyms)? Not to worry. While we look at many of the details shortly, the basic idea is pretty simple: there are a limited number of IRQs, DMAs, and I/O addresses available inside a PC, and no two hardware devices running at the same time can use the same IRQ, the same DMA, or the same I/O address. So, for example, if your modem uses IRQ 3 and you install a sound card that also uses IRQ 3, all hell will break loose. For a much more definitive explanation, see *The Mother of All PC Books*.

As Plug 'n' Play hardware becomes more prevalent, the importance of Device Manager will diminish: when devices can change their IRQ, DMA, and I/O addresses under control of the PC, the need to futz with this stuff by hand will disappear. But as long as there are older devices that have to be configured by hand (typically with a pair of pliers and a Lilliputian jumper, but occasionally with software) and as long as some Plug 'n' Play devices don't play as well as they should with their siblings, the Device Manager will remain one of the truly pivotal Windows utilities.

When you bring up the Device Manager tab (Figure 8-126), you'll find a complete list of the hardware within and attached to your PC, listed in alphabetical order by what Microsoft calls "type." We'll dive into all the options available for examining the types in a moment, but for now, let's look at what you can do with Computer, highlighted at the top of the list. The Computer type should probably be called Summary: information you gather with Computer highlighted applies to the PC as a whole.

With Computer highlighted, push Properties. You'll be treated to a complete list of assigned IRQs, or Interrupt Request Numbers (Figure 8-127), and the hardware device using each IRQ. (IRQs are numbered from 0 to 15, corresponding to the 16 wires inside your computer that can force the central processor to interrupt its calculations and tend to outside business.) You can get the same kind of list by using the System Information manager (Figure 8-128): click Start, Programs, Accessories, System Tools, System Information, double click on Hardware Resources, click IRQs.

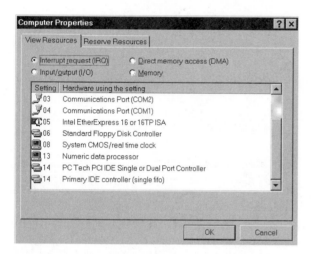

Figure 8-127. IRQs listed through the Device Manager

Watch out for duplicated IRQ numbers. Sometimes a device is listed twice with the same IRQ (for example, the IDE Controller in Figure 8-128 is listed twice with both at IRQ 14). But worse, if you have two different devices using the same IRQ, disaster may result—sometimes. The details are a bit confusing, and you might want to refer to *The Mother of All PC Books* for edification.

Click the View Resources' Input/output radio button and you see a complete list of all the I/O addresses used by your system and peripherals (Figure 8-129). I/O addresses are locations of external ports that devices use to communicate with the PC itself. If two different devices use the same I/O address, they can write all over each others' data.

Figure 8-128. Same PC's IRQs using the System Information utility

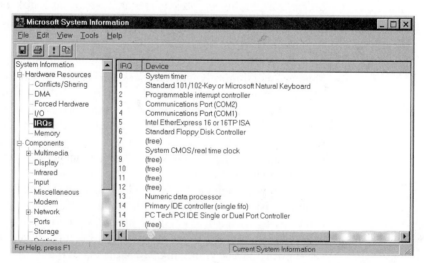

Figure 8-129.
I/O addresses us-
ing Device Man-
ager

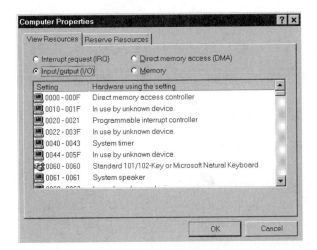

Similarly, SysInfo shows the addresses by clicking on the I/O item (Figure 8-130).

The addresses are listed in hexadecimal. Regardless of which utility you use—Device Manager or SysInfo—this list isn't as useful as the list of IRQs, simply because there are so many of the suckers, but the information contained here is vital to the hassle-free operation of any PC.

 If you compare Figure 8-129 and Figure 8-130, you notice that Device Manager claims several addresses are "In use by unknown device." It's been my experience that, in all such cases, Device Manager is wrong and System Information is correct. (Or, more accurately, System Information agrees with third-party system sniffers.)

**Figure 8-130.
The same I/O ad-
dresses using
SysInfo**

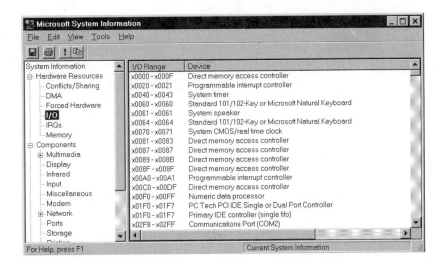

You might think discrepancies like this don't speak well of Microsoft's programmers' abilities. Ah, but I would disagree! The fact that the two reports don't match means that they're using two different programs—two different detection techniques—and, while that may lead to discrepancies, it also gives you a "second opinion." In the best of all possible worlds, both utilities would use different code to report their results, both reports would match, and both would be correct. Until we get to that point, I'd much rather have a 50/50 chance of one report being wrong than an absolute certainty that the only offered report is wrong some of the time.

Gee, you sound as if you like your watches not to run on the principle that that way they are right twice a day.

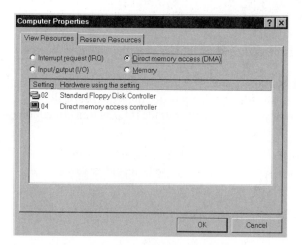

Figure 8-131. Device Manager's DMA list

Click the Direct memory access (DMA) radio button in Device Manager and you'll see a complete list of used DMA channels, as in Figure 8-131. In the SysInfo utility, the same list appears when you click DMA (Figure 8-132).

DMA channels, numbered from 0 to 7, correspond to the eight different locations on the DMA Controller chip inside your PC that allow peripherals to send data quickly and directly to the processor's main memory. It's important that no two devices share the same DMA channel so that they don't end up clobbering each other when transferring data into memory.

Figure 8-132. Analogous DMA listing in SysInfo

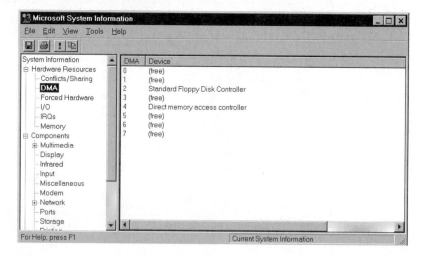

Figure 8-133. Device Manager's list of reserved upper memory locations

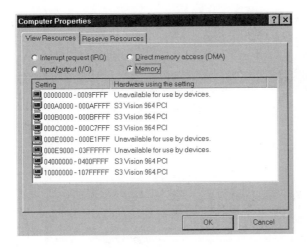

Some specific locations in memory are set aside (or remapped) for video cards and occasionally for other high-speed devices in the region above 640 K and below 1 MB—the so-called upper memory area. (And here you thought Win98 had got rid of that old-fashioned concept!) Click on the Device Manager's Memory radio button and you'll see which parts of upper memory have been set aside for those devices (Figure 8-133).

 SysInfo has a similar report, but it seems to overlook areas in upper memory that have been blocked off by the Plug 'n' Play handler (Figure 8-134). When push comes to shove, I would trust the Device Manager's report over SysInfo's.

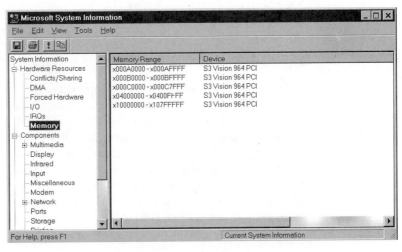

Figure 8-134. SysInfo's upper memory report on the same machine

Figure 8-135. Reserve IRQs, DMAs, I/O locations, or upper memory blocks here

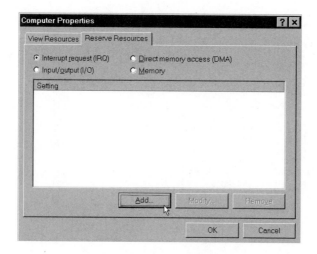

Bring up the Device Manager's Reserve Resources tab (Figure 8-135) and you'll have an opportunity to set aside IRQs, DMAs, or I/O addresses—reserve them—so that Win98 won't use them when it assigns resources in the Add New Hardware Wizard. To add new reservations, click the Add button. If you try to reserve an IRQ, DMA, or I/O address that's already in use, Win98 will warn you. There's no comparable capability in the SysInfo utility.

 Device Manager will print a system report. With Computer highlighted in Figure 8-126, hit the Print button—but I don't recommend you use it for two reasons. First, this report isn't nearly as detailed as the one given by SysInfo (click File, then Print). Second, we had very obscure sporadic problems with the accuracy of the printed report in Windows 95, and I'm not completely sure the problem has been fixed in Windows 98. Far better to run with the full report from SysInfo.

 Those are the options available when Computer is highlighted in Figure 8-126. Let's backtrack now and see what else awaits in under the Device Manager tab when we look at individual devices.

With the "View devices by type" radio button checked, you can look at the various logical groupings of hardware devices and the actual devices installed on your machine. For example, under CDROM, you'll find the name of your CD-ROM drive (Figure 8-136); under Hard disk controllers, you'll see the various kinds of hard disk controllers installed on your machine.

A similar report in SysInfo, though, goes several steps further (Figure 8-137). It not only lists the CD-ROM; for example, it also goes out to the CD-ROM, reads a file, verifies that the device is working, and gives you statistics about transfer rate, CPU utilization, and the like.

Figure 8-136.
Device Manager's
report on CD-
ROM drives

Figure 8-137.
The SysInfo re-
port is much more
complete

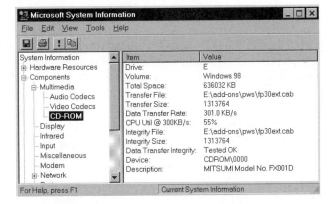

Click the "View devices by connection" button in Figure 8-136 and Win98 will show you how it all hooks together, per Figure 8-138. The internal logical connections show up on the screen: which devices are connected to what controllers and how they all fit onto the PCI bus. It's a very impressive view of the inside of your machine. This screen is particularly valuable for verifying that the hardware you thought you bought is what you actually got. If you've ever wondered whether your IDE hard drive controller really does go through the PCI bus, this display will show you in a snap. While SysInfo has much more detailed information about the individual pieces in your machine, there's no comparable report in that utility to show you how the parts hang together.

Figure 8-138. Graphic representation of how it all fits together

Figure 8-139. Problems with the SCSI controller reported by Device Manager

Sometimes when Windows 98 detects that something is wrong, it will draw your attention to the potential problem by putting a yellow exclamation point on top of the device's icon, as in Figure 8-139. In this case, the SCSI controller didn't have the correct driver, and Win98 alerted us by putting a yellow exclamation point on the BusLogic MultiMaster icon. Win98 is also supposed to raise the yellow exclamation point flag if the resource settings you have listed for the device don't match the physical settings on the device itself.

 If you have a yellow exclamation point and suspect there's a resource conflict—either the jumpers on the board don't match the settings Win98 has stored away or two different devices are trying to get at the same IRQ, DMA, or I/O address—Windows has a troubleshooter that may help. Click Start, then Help. Under the Find tab, type **conflict**, then click List Topics. Choose Troubleshooting Hardware Conflicts, and follow the instructions.

The Refresh button on the Device Manager tab tells Win98 to go back to the Registry and rebuild its list of all the devices and the resources they use. It does *not* force Win98 to scan for new hardware.

It's not all that difficult to install two copies of the same "device"—effectively telling Win98 that you have two keyboards, or two mice, when in fact, you have only one. That's why the Remove button is on the Device Manager tab. Should you ever accidentally install the same device twice, there will be a repeated entry on the Device Manager tab. The challenge is to find out which, if either, of the two devices is installed properly (usually by clicking on the device, then clicking Properties, as we see in a moment). If you have a repeated entry here and can figure out which one is the correct one, select the wrong one and hit the Delete button. If both of them appear to be the same, flip a coin and delete one or the other.

If you accidentally remove a valid device, DON'T PANIC! Pick Cancel on the Device Manager tab, if you can. If not, just reboot. Windows 98 often detects the hardware automatically the next time you reboot and may restore the old device without even telling you, much less asking your opinion. If the device appears to be well and truly gone, though, you'll have to go through the Add New Hardware Wizard to re-install it (see Chapter 6).

If you remove what you think is a critical device, like your display, don't think that Windows will refuse to run. It'll just shift to a generic driver. On one system we saw, the display somehow got terribly confused and complained that it was not correctly installed when we looked at the Display applet. The only way we found to fix matters was to remove the display in Device Manager, reboot, and use Add New Hardware to have Windows re-install the proper driver.

And don't forget Safe mode, which will boot with generic drivers for the basic hardware.

You can get a wealth of information about individual devices by double clicking on the device in the Device Manager tab (or clicking the device once and clicking Properties). While SysInfo gives you most of this information (and a lot more detail), it won't let you play with the settings—and sometimes you need to take Windows 98 into your own hands and change things.

I'm going to step you through the details of setting up an AWE-32 sound board. I chose the AWE-32 sound board because it uses quite a few resources, and sound boards are notorious for conflicts. This is the same sound board we installed with the Add New Hardware Wizard earlier in this chapter. When you double click on the sound board on the Device Manager tab, the General tab of the Properties dialog for the board appears (Figure 8-140).

The "Device status" box says that the device is working properly. Of course, Win98 isn't smart enough to know if it really *is* working properly. But if you see the "working properly" message, it means that there are no obvious resource conflicts and that the device seems to be responding properly to inquiries from the PC (although for some devices, a "proper" response is no response at all!).

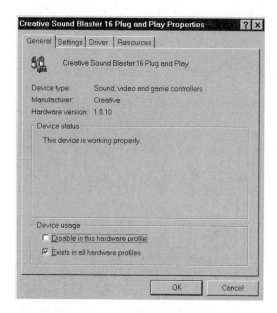

Figure 8-140. Sound Blaster properties

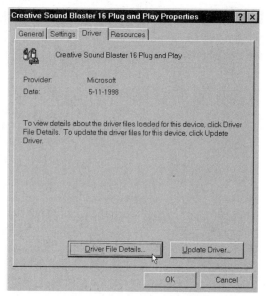

Figure 8-141. The Driver tab tells you who provided the driver—but not who wrote it!

Figure 8-142. The hand that rocks the driver cradle

Down at the bottom of the General tab you can choose whether to enable the card in all hardware profiles or if you want to disable it in the current hardware profile. We talk more about hardware profiles—the easy way to set up portable PC docking stations—later in this chapter.

The AWE-32's Driver tab (Figure 8-141) shows you who provided the driver files that make the board work. That's only a very small part of the story. To see who really did the hard work—and who to blame if something goes wrong—click the Driver File Details button (Figure 8-142). This list is less important for the rote recital of 13 driver names than for the help it lets you provide to tech support people. (Yes, it takes 13 driver files to make your Sound Blaster work!) You can tell the techdroid on the phone which drivers are installed, with version number, in a matter of seconds.

If you have a new driver, Figure 8-141 is as good a place as any to install it. Click Update Driver and follow the bouncing ball. You'll be transported to the Add New Hardware Wizard's Select a Driver box.

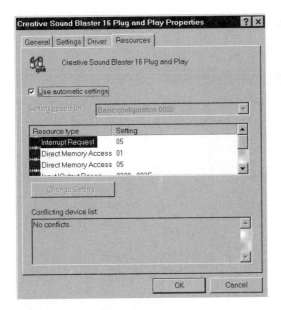

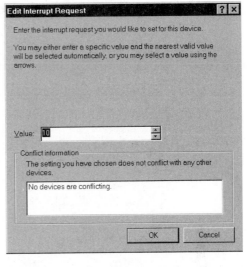

Figure 8-144. Manually changing an IRQ, DMA, or I/O address can be . . . challenging

Figure 8-143. IRQs, DMAs, and I/O addresses are all listed here

The cantankerous part of the AWE-32's properties sits beneath the Resources tab (Figure 8-143). As long as there are no conflicts, it's much, much easier to leave the "Use automatic settings" box checked. That gives Win98 maximum flexibility in assigning resources not only to this board but to all the other devices in your system. If there's a conflict, though, you have to uncheck the "Use automatic settings" box and try to find a compromise. Click the resource that you want to change (say, the IRQ), then click Change Setting, and you'll get an Edit dialog like that in Figure 8-144.

Flip through the choices and see if any shows up with "No conflicts" in the "Conflicting device list." If that works, as it did for IRQ 10 in Figure 8-144, hit OK and you're done. If it doesn't work, your only resource is the Troubleshooting Hardware Conflicts, described earlier in this section.

 Once you find a group of settings that leaves all your devices conflict-free, your travails aren't yet over. In many cases you have to physically yank the board(s) out of your PC and change jumper settings or DIP switches. And the only guide you have is the hardware's manual or tech support line. If you should find yourself in that position, keep two things in mind: (1) doing the same thing was a *hell* of a lot harder before Windows 95; (2) when Plug 'n' Play really starts working, this will all be a not-so-fond memory.

Figure 8-145.
CD-ROM Settings
tab for auto insert
notification

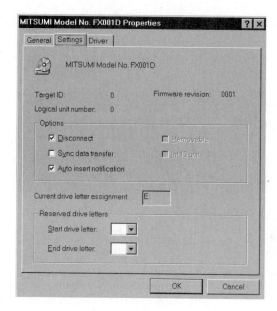

A few additional settings and oddities accessible from the Device Manager tab are worth mentioning.

- CD-ROM drive entries (as in Figure 8-145) let you choose whether to disable Auto insert notification, which in turn can kill off Autoplay and Autorun; they also allow you to assign a permanent drive letter to your CD-ROM drive.

- The Dial-Up Adapter device, under the Network Adapter device, includes not only modems (as you would probably expect) but just about any networking connection that isn't permanent—it's a virtual device to provide networking capabilities in situations where you don't have a network card, for example, where networking is accomplished, via a modem.

- If you have an "IO read data port for ISA Plug 'n' Play enumerator" <*whew!*> device listed, take a look at its Resources tab to make sure I/O space has been assigned to it.

 Not all devices appear on the Device Manager tab. For example, my Colorado Memory Systems Jumbo 250 doesn't show up anywhere—even though it works just fine with Windows 98's back-up routines. I have no idea why Win98 summarily skips some types of hardware.

Registry entries for these devices are located in various keys under **HKLM**, with **\Enum** being a favorite. I would strongly recommend against changing them manually inside the Registry. If you use the Device Manager to change an IRQ or other resource for some device, look for the changes to be reflected in a value called **ForcedConfig**.

Hardware Profiles Tab

 Here's the concept. You have a portable PC with a docking station. You need to keep two completely different hardware profiles: one for the portable on the road, the other for the portable tethered to the station. The Road profile includes a small, 256-color monitor, a small keyboard with no number pad, and a single hard drive. The Dock profile includes a 21-inch monitor, a full-scale keyboard, and a 20-GB RAID-5 bank of hard drives. Every time you boot your PC, it asks if you want the Road or the Dock profile, and Win98 configures itself accordingly.

 Here's the reality. Win98 needed this "profiling" capability to support Plug 'n' Play. Since it was there anyway, Microsoft put a rather hokey people interface on the front of it and turned it into a feature that many people might think they want but that few people could actually use (Figure 8-146). There aren't too many situations where you would want to manually create multiple hardware profiles and choose from them when Win98 boots. Why?

- *The fancy new hardware doesn't need it.* If you have Plug 'n' Play hardware, Win98 figures out what's working on the fly; there's no need to create a second hardware profile because the hardware is detected as soon as it's available.

- *Sometimes even old hardware doesn't need it.* If you have older hardware, Win98 still goes through a detection phase when it boots, and it's often smart enough to pull in the drivers and settings it needs for the hardware at hand.

Figure 8-146. Road, Dock, and Original spicy configurations

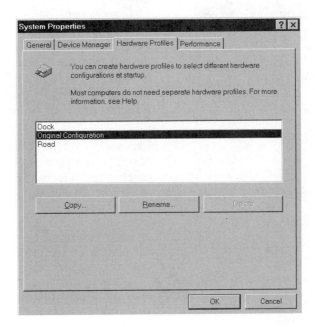

In our experience it's unusual to have two real-world profiles so similar that manual intervention is necessary, yet so different that Win98 couldn't compensate on its own. Yes, you can create one profile for, oh, 640 × 480 resolution and a second for 800 × 600 and have Win98 prompt you for your preferred profile every time you boot. Or you can install Tweak UI (discussed later in this chapter) and not worry about it. Given that caveat, creating multiple hardware profiles for very different hardware setups—say, a docked and an undocked portable—is easy. Here's how.

- Start by installing drivers for all the hardware that you'll use for *all* your various profiles. Typically, that will involve using the Add Hardware Wizard to install every piece of hardware both on your portable and on your docking station.

- Then, in Control Panel, double click on System and bring up the Hardware Profiles tab. You'll see the profile that includes all the hardware in both configurations listed as Original Configuration.

- Click the button marked Copy. You'll be asked to provide a name for your new profile. You can use just about anything. We made two new ones— one called Dock, the other called Road. Click on the profile you want to change—say, Dock (eh, what's up Dock?).

- In the Registry, this second profile is identified by the key **\0002**. For example, where the original configuration information is stored in **HKLM\Config\0001**, the second hardware profile's config info is in **HKLM\Config\0002**, and so on. The third profile is **\0003**.

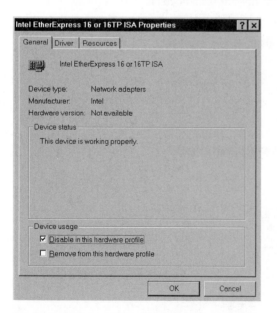

- Finally, you need to go back to the Device Manager tab and, one at a time, double click on each piece of hardware that you want to exclude from the selected hardware profiles. At the bottom of the General tab on each applicable device, you'll find two check boxes. Check the top box to remove the piece of hardware from that particular profile.

- In the example in Figure 8-147, the EtherExpress 16 card has been excluded from the "Dock" hardware profile. The box has been checked accordingly.

Figure 8-147. Removing the EtherExpress 16 from the currently active profile

The procedure for creating multiple hardware profiles for minor differences—say, one for 640×480 resolution, and another for 800×600 resolution—is similar. Just set up all your preferences for the one setting, go into the Hardware Profiles tab, and hit Copy. Highlight the new profile, and go back and make the changes you want for the second profile. There's no Save button: Win98 remembers the last settings you establish for each chosen profile.

 In theory, that's how you're supposed to set up hardware profiles. In practice, I haven't seen it do much more than behave as an admirable Win98 parlor trick. Chances are pretty good you won't want to go through the hassle.

Performance Tab

Back in the days of the original Windows 95 *oh!* so long ago, some performance tuning could be expected on just about any new installation. Over time, though, Microsoft discovered that the old Win95 settings didn't work as well as they should, so they goosed them all a bit—using many of MOM's old tricks from *The Mother of All Windows 95 Books*, we might add.

With Windows 98, the System applet's Performance tab (Figure 8-148), like so many other Performance tabs we've seen in this book, is primarily a troubleshooting tab: it's the place you can go when Win98's fancy acceleration routines outrun your hardware. This is where you look, when Win98 is screwing up, to see if you can throttle back some of that wonderful performance and get the bloody thing to simply *work*.

If you're not using any real mode drivers—that is, old-fashioned drivers designed to work in DOS—your Performance tab should look as clean as a hound's tooth. This particular machine (Figure 8-148) is running 32-bit file and disk access (that's what File System: 32-bit means—it has nothing to do with FAT32). It's also using the optimized Win98 routines for virtual memory and disk compression.

The phrase "Your system is configured for optimum performance" really means "You don't have any real mode drivers installed that are gumming up the works." There are still several points you should check before you're satisfied that your system is, indeed, configured for optimum performance.

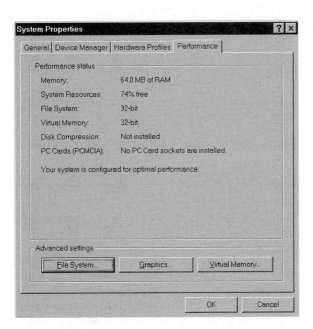

Figure 8-148. No real mode drivers, ergo "optimal performance"

**Figure 8-149.
Real mode drivers
do exist—they're
just getting
harder to find**

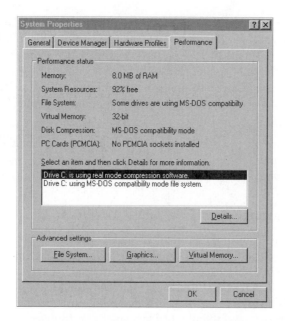

The machine that posed for the screen shot in Figure 8-149, on the other hand, is using one real mode driver for disk access and one for disk compression—most likely old Stacker routines that weren't vetted by the Win98 installer. The solution in this case is to contact the manufacturer for replacement 32-bit drivers or to convert to FAT32.

If you have any real mode drivers, don't even bother with the rest of the Performance tab—the big performance boost you'll get is in zapping out those drivers. Fix the big problems before you tackle the little ones. Check Chapter 6 for several hints on how you might go about exorcising the 16-bit beasts.

If you push the Performance tab's Advanced settings/File System button, you'll find the Hard Disk tab (Figure 8-150). For "Typical role of this machine," you get three choices:

- "Network server" allocates extra disk buffer space at the possible expense of application work area.

- "Desktop computer" tries to strike a balance between applications and disk access.

- "Mobile or docking system" minimizes memory usage while increasing the frequency of buffer flushes (in case the battery gives out).

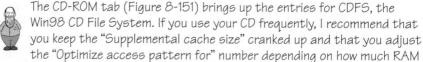 *The CD-ROM tab (Figure 8-151) brings up the entries for CDFS, the Win98 CD File System. If you use your CD frequently, I recommend that you keep the "Supplemental cache size" cranked up and that you adjust the "Optimize access pattern for" number depending on how much RAM is in your PC: if you have less than 8 MB, single-speed (which creates a 64-K cache); if you have 8 MB or more, quad-speed (which creates a 1,238-K cache). Extra CD cache space for multimedia applications makes a big difference.*

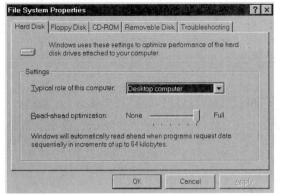

Figure 8-150. The hard drive almost always comes optimized for top performance

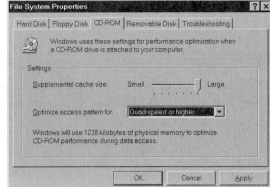

Figure 8-151. Go for the biggest buffers if you have more than 8 MB of memory

The Removable Disk tab (Figure 8-152) has an interesting setting. This is where you can enable "write-behind caching" on your removable disks—a technique that can speed up hard disk access but at the same time make your system much more vulnerable to destructive behavior if the power suddenly goes out. With write-behind caching enabled, your system can save up multiple writes to the hard drive, sort them out so that they're in some sort of optimal sequence, and perform all of them in an ordered batch.

 I'm too chicken to enable write-behind caching. I'd rather wait an extra few seconds, instead of being worried about pulling out a ZIP cartridge too soon.

In spite of the dire warning on the Troubleshooting tab (Figure 8-153), checking any one of those boxes doesn't make your PC disappear in a billowing cloud of

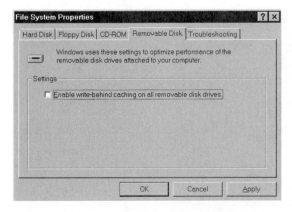

Figure 8-152. Write-behind caching can be harmful

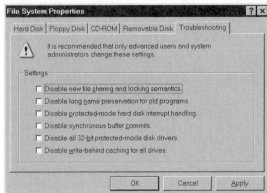

Figure 8-153. For throttling back Win98's power

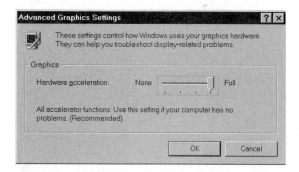

Figure 8-154. Make the video slow down in this dialog

smoke, although they will bog your machine down. Mostly, they're increasingly unnecessary last-ditch ways of turning off advanced Windows features, primarily to accommodate old hardware and software that doesn't behave itself. For a full description of the various options, consult the Windows Resource Kit.

Back on the Performance tab (Figure 8-148), if you click the Graphics button, you'll have an opportunity (Figure 8-154) to decrease your video system's performance in pursuit of greater compatibility. Set the slider back one notch if you're having trouble with the video card's hardware cursor. Back two notches and you also move processing of bit block transfers from the video card to the PC. If you set it on None, you move all video acceleration functions from the video card back to the PC.

 If you find that setting this slider back makes your machine more stable, get on the phone and scream at your video card manufacturer. Tell 'em MOM told you it was OK.

Finally, if you click the Virtual Memory button on the Performance tab, you'll be offered a chance to manually change the location and size of **win386.swp**, the Win98 swap file (Figure 8-155). In spite of the warning, there's absolutely nothing wrong with pointing Win98 to a drive that's faster or has more room than the drive Win98 automatically assigns to itself. Just be sure the drive has enough room; running out of swap file space can be a deadly experience. If you leave the Maximum file size set at "No maximum," Win98 will know that it can grow as needs dictate; if you change it, Win98 will assume that you're specifying an absolute ceiling—which is not a good idea.

Figure 8-155. Adjust the swap file at your own risk!

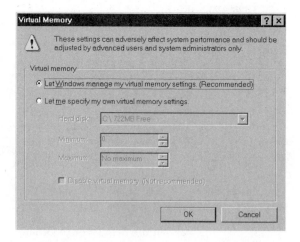

Registry settings for the Hard Disk tab are in **HKLM\Software\ Microsoft\Windows\CurrentVersion\FS Templates**, with values for **PathCache**, **NameCache**, **BufferIdleTimeout**, **BufferAgeTimeout**, and **VolumeIdleTimeout**—all of which are described at length in the Windows Resource Kit—plus the undocumented **ReadAheadThreshold** value, which tracks the size of the read-ahead buffer reported in the dialog.

The CD-ROM tab affects Registry settings in **HKLM\System\ CurrentControlSet\Control\FileSystem\CDFS**, with the undocumented values **CacheSize** (set by the "Optimize access patterns for" selection) and **Prefetch** and **PrefetchTail** (both of which are set by the Supplemental cache size slider).

The Troubleshooting tab puts new values in the Registry's **HKLM\System\ CurrentControlSet\Control\FileSystem** key. Full details are in the Windows Resource Kit. Those of you who remember struggling with the Windows 3.1 **.ini** file value called **VirtualHDIRQ** might want to look it up in the WRK. You'll get a kick out of reading about the old Emperor in his new Win98 clothes.

The WRK explains how settings in the Graphics dialog are reflected in the **[Windows]** section of **win.ini** and the **[Display]** section of **system.ini**. From there, they migrate to the Registry key **HKLM\Config\0001\Display\ Settings** in values **SwCursor**, **Mmio**, and **SafeMode**.

Virtual Memory settings are kept in **system.ini**! They're in the **[386Enh]** section, with entries such as these:

```
PagingDrive=D:
MinPagingFileSize=5120
MaxPagingFileSize=102400
```

Both of those the numbers are bytes. If **MinPagingFileSize** is missing, Win98 assumes that the paging file can shrink as small as it likes. If there is no **MaxPagingFileSize**, it can grow to fill the entire disk.

■ Telephony

Windows 98 includes complete support for TAPI 2.1—the Telephone API that allows programs to access voice/telephone features on a suitably enabled modem. While TAPI offers a wide range of capabilities, the support you find in the Control Panel is limited to adding and removing drivers.

The primary dialog you see when you bring up the Telephony applet is the Dialing Properties dialog—precisely the same dialog you saw back in the Modems applet, as Figure 8-85. It allows you to specify the local area code, set up ten-digit dialing, and the like.

Click the Telephony Drivers tab (Figure 8-156) and you can add or remove TAPI drivers. Beats me why they aren't treated like all the other Win98 drivers, but they're not.

Figure 8-156.
Add and remove
Telephony drivers
here

The NDISWAN TAPI Service Provider you see in Figure 8-156 provides TAPI support for ISDN connections. Unimodem is the TAPI support in Win95, with a few enhancements.

■ Tweak UI

Tweak UI is the only Control Panel applet that isn't officially a Control Panel applet; we talk about installing it in Chapter 6. If you haven't yet installed it, break out your Win98 installation CD, navigate to the folder `\Tools\Reskit\Powertoy`, right click on `tweakui.inf`, and pick Install.

Microsoft says it doesn't support Tweak UI—and they don't, probably to keep their phone lines from overheating. But every system we've seen running Win98 runs Tweak UI just fine. There's no reason we can imagine for bypassing this impressive system tool.

Almost all of the Tweak UI utilities (and there are dozens of them!) directly manipulate one or two settings in the Registry. If you've been reading this book sequentially, that's wonderful, because Tweak UI will have you plumbing the depths of the Registry in no time.

Let's take the Tweak UI tabs one at a time.

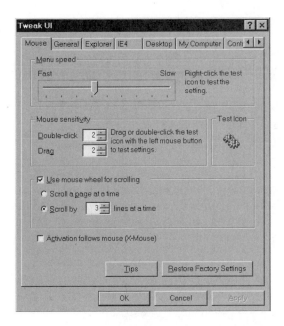

Figure 8-157. Tweak UI Mouse settings

Mouse There's absolutely no question in our minds that all of the Tweak UI mouse settings (Figure 8-157) should be in the Mouse applet. Unfortunately, that isn't going to happen any time soon.

The "Menu speed" box controls how quickly submenus (or cascading menus) appear when you pass the mouse pointer over them. You might think Fast would be good—and based on the test suggested in Figure 8-157, it certainly seems snappy—but you should try this setting on the Start Menu. If you set it too fast, Win98 goes into the herky-jerkies when you scroll your mouse along items in the Start Menu: it's too busy trying to open the submenus to keep up with your mouse. Very disconcerting.

The "Menu speed" box control's Registry key **HKCU\Control Panel\Desktop MenuShowDelay** value. Fast is zero; Slow is a number so large it appears in **Regedit** as **-2**.

We've already played with the Double-click sensitivity value, back in the Mouse applet earlier in this chapter. (Sensitivity in this case refers to how close together two clicks must be in order for Win98 to recognize it as a double click.) The number that appears in the Double-click spinner is actually half the amount stored in the **DoubleClickHeight** and **DoubleClickWidth** keys in **HKCU\Control Panel\Desktop**: if you run the spinner up to 4, for example, both of those keys will get the value 8. The 8 just means that you have a box 8 pixels wide by 8 pixels tall, centered around the first click, in which you must click again for Win98 to recognize the two clicks as a double click.

The Drag spinner in Figure 8-157 tells Win98 how far you have to move the mouse (in pixels), with the left mouse button held down, before Win98 recognizes the action as a drag. The number you pick in the spinner is transferred to two Registry entries, **HKCU\Control Panel\Desktop** values **DragHeight** and **DragWidth**.

If you have an Intellimouse (or a mouse with a recognized spinning wheel), the "Use mouse wheel for scrolling" box becomes available. All the settings in this box change the Registry key **HKCU\Control Panel\Desktop**'s **WheelScrollLines** value. If you uncheck the box, **WheelScrollLines** is set to zero. If you click the "Scroll a page at a time" button, **WheelScrollLines** is set to **-1**. Otherwise, the number that appears in the spinner is used for **WheelScrollLines**.

Get a load of the final box in Figure 8-157. Microsoft doesn't even bother to tell you what X-Mouse is! Basically, if you check this box, Windows 98's "focus" travels with the mouse: move the mouse over a Word window and Word gets "focus"; move the mouse over a Control Panel window and the Control Panel gets focus, and so on.

This X-Mouse check box controls the Registry key **HKCU\Control Panel\ Desktop**'s **UserPreferencemask** value. With X-Mouse off, the value of **UserPreferencemask** is **ae 00 00 00**. With X-Mouse on, the value changes to **af 00 00 00**.

General Here's a nice hodgepodge of settings that really should be in all sorts of different locations—none of them in an officially unsupported Windows add-on, of course (Figure 8-158). The effects you can change are these:

- *Window animation* controls the way Win98 shows "trails" when you minimize or maximize a window. This setting ties in with the Effects tab in the Display applet (Figure 8-53): checking the "Animate windows, menus and lists" box there also checks this one; unchecking this box grays out the "Animate windows, menus and lists" box.

- *Smooth scrolling* controls the "trails" in Explorer when you scroll.

- *Beep on errors* is a strange setting that took forever for us to track down. As best we can tell, unchecking this box keeps Explorer from playing the "Default sound" in the Sounds applet (Figure 8-123). The reason this is so odd is that it accomplishes the feat not by changing the **\.Default** key in **HKCU\AppEvents\Schemes\Apps** (which would also change the sound in Figure 8-123), but by placing a value in the key **HKCU\Control Panel\Sound** called **Beep**, set to **"No"**!

- *Menu animation* controls the "sliding" you see when you click on a menu item. It behaves much as *Window animation*, above.

- *Comb box animation* affects the "sliding" you experience when you click the down arrow on the right side of a Windows combo box. It behaves the same as *Window animation*.

- *List box animation* sets up "sliding" in list box controls when you scroll through the list box contents. It behaves the same as *Window animation*.

- *Menu underlines* is another setting that seems to change behavior only in Explorer. It controls whether Explorer underlines the hotkeys on menus (for example, the "F" in "File"). We couldn't find any other application that uses the setting—not even the ones in Microsoft's own Office 2000.

- *X-Mouse AutoRaise* (as the Tweak UI Help file mentions) doesn't belong here at all. It should be on Tweak UI's Mouse tab. If you have X-Mouse enabled, at the bottom of Figure 8-157, Win98's "focus" travels with the mouse—when the mouse pointer goes over a window, that window gets fo-

Figure 8-158.
It says General,
but it really
means "all other"

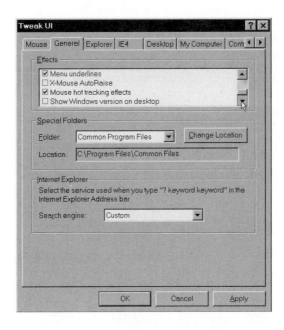

cus. If you also check this "X-Mouse autoraise" box, Win98 also moves the window in focus to the front, so you can see it. So much trouble for such a little thing! This setting changes the first byte of the **HKCU\Control Panel\Desktop** key's **UserPreferencemask** value. It changes the initial **a** to an **e**, for example, **ef 00 00 00**.

- *Mouse hot tracking effects* controls whether Win98 shows a ToolTip on the Minimize, Restore, and Close buttons in the upper right corner of windows. It, too, plays with **UserPreferencemask**, changing the initial **a** to **2**, for example, **2e 00 00 00**.

- *Show Windows version on desktop* puts the Windows' version number ("Windows 98 4.10.1998," for example) in the lower right corner of the Desktop. You have to reboot to make it happen, and it's not necessary to have "View Active Desktop as wallpaper" enabled.

 An important note. If you ever need to know precisely which version of Windows you're running, click Start, Programs, MS-DOS Prompt, and type **ver /r**. The **/r** switch ensures that you see all the details.

The Special Folders box in Figure 8-158 lets you change the location of certain system folders. Tweak UI claims it can change all these system folders: Common Program Files; Desktop; Document Templates (for Office); Favorites; My Documents (also primarily for Office); Program Files; Programs (that is, the programs that appear on the Start Menu's Programs entry); Recent Documents; Send To; Start Menu; and Startup.

I won't swear that all of these work, but I was astounded—dumbfounded—to see that changing My Documents here actually worked, rippling all the way through the appropriate nooks and crannies of Office 2000. Absolutely amazing.

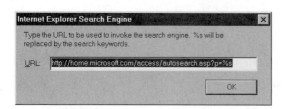

Figure 8-159. Specify the URL and parameters for your custom search engine here

The final box on the General tab in Figure 8-158 lets you pick which Web search engine you want Internet Explorer to use when you type **? something** in the URL space of the browser. You can choose from predefined hooks into Alta Vista, Excite, HotBot, InfoSeek, InfoSeek Ultra, Lycos, Magellan, MetaCrawler, Open Text, WebCrawler, or Yahoo!. Or, if you like, you can pick Custom, and Win98 will let you type the URL of your favorite search engine in a box like that shown in Figure 8-159.

This box changes the value in the Registry key **HKCU\Software\ Microsoft\Internet Explorer\SearchUrl**.

Explorer You thought the preceding General tab entries specific to Explorer (Smooth scrolling, Beep on errors, Menu underlines, and SearchUrl) meant that we were done with Explorer settings in Tweak UI? Ha! In fact, there's a whole separate crop of them on the Explorer tab (Figure 8-160).

The "Shortcut overlay" box controls which graphic is "pasted over" icons associated with shortcuts. While Win98 usually puts a hooked arrow in the lower left corner of shortcut icons, you can actually pick any valid icon to paste over shortcuts. You can see the effect in the Before and After pictures.

This setting changes one of the values in **HKLM\Software\Microsoft\Windows\ CurrentVersion\Explorer\ShellIcons**, specifically one with the weird name of **29**! We talk about good ol' **29** in Chapter 9 in the section on Registry hacks.

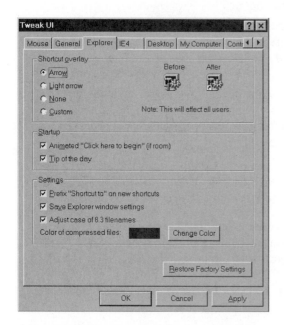

With two exceptions, the rest of the settings in Figure 8-160 are pretty straightforward. "Click here to begin" is the bouncy graphic you probably saw in the Taskbar on startup, way back when you first installed Windows. The tip of the day appears on startup, too, until you clobber it. Win98 puts "Shortcut to" at the beginning of the filename on new shortcuts unless you uncheck this box. (Yes, this one works in Win98—it was spotty in early versions of Win95.)

Figure 8-160. Explorer settings in Tweak UI

I tried and tried and couldn't get "Adjust case of 8.3 filenames" to do anything. Try it yourself. With this box checked, create a new text file on the Desktop called, oh, **TEST.TXT**. Win98 will take it upon itself to change the name to **Test.txt**. Fair enough. Now uncheck the box (you'll have to restart Windows). Create another new text file called **TESTA.TXT**. Win98 magically changes it to **Testa.txt**. The box doesn't seem to do anything.

 The final button—the one that lets you change the color of compressed files—definitely doesn't do anything unless you install the compressed file support available in the Win98 Plus! Pack. It's hardly worth the effort.

IE 4 Though the tab says IE 4, much of this part of Tweak UI also deals with Windows Explorer, the Start Menu, and related utilities.

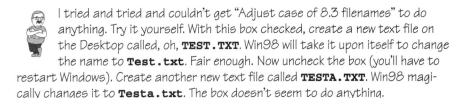 This Tweak UI tab really gives me the willies. I don't know what it's doing, most of the time—except that some parts of it are so obviously screwed up and other parts so poorly worded, I'd be very wary about trusting any of it.

For example, Figure 8-161 shows that the Active Desktop is enabled—but on this particular machine, at the time the screen shot was taken, Active Desktop most definitely was *not* enabled. If you right click on "Active Desktop enabled" and pick "What's This?" the ToolTip you see (Figure 8-162) is the one associated with "Show Documents on Start Menu"! Try it.

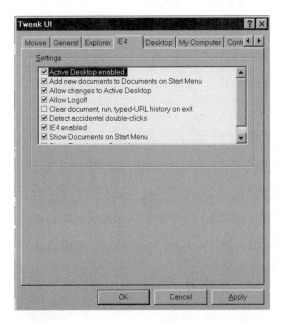

Figure 8-161. IE 4 settings—but are they, really?

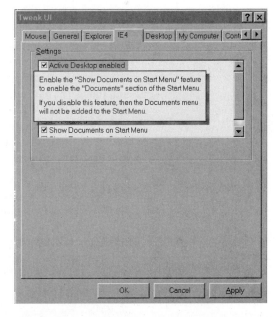

Figure 8-162. ToolTip for "Active Desktop enabled"

As best we can tell, here's what these options will do (ignore Tweak UI's built-in documentation, which is wrong over and over again).

- *Active Desktop enabled* does *not* mean "View my Active Desktop as Web page"—what most Win98 fans would call "Active Desktop enabled." But if you uncheck this box, you won't be able to right click on the Desktop and pick *any* of the Active Desktop options. More than that, the Display applet won't even show a Web tab (Figure 8-55)! If you want to be very, very sure you won't accidentally turn on anything associated with Win98's Active Desktop, uncheck this box.

- *Add new documents to Documents in Start Menu* has absolutely nothing to do with adding new documents to the Documents list on the Start Menu. If you check this box, every time IE opens a file, that file is added to the Documents list on the Start Menu. If you uncheck the box, IE won't bother putting the file on the Documents list. Gad. Sometimes I wonder if Microsoft has a compulsory course in obfuscation.

- If you uncheck the box marked *Allow changes to Active Desktop*, Win98 won't show the Web tab on the Display applet. That effectively keeps you from modifying the `.htm` file wallpaper, ActiveX controls, and pictures shown on the Active Desktop. But you'll still be able to turn Active Desktop's "View as Web page" on and off.

- *Allow Logoff* shows/removes the Logoff line immediately above the Shut Down line on the Start Menu. That's the one that lets you quickly log off and log on as a different user. One little problem. If you uncheck this box and click Apply, the change *isn't applied*. It won't "take" until you restart Win98 (or log off and log on again).

- If the *Clear document, run, typed-URL history on exit* is checked and you restart Win98, the Start Menu's Documents list gets cleared out, the list of commands you've previously typed into the Start/Run box is eliminated, and the list of old typed-in URLs (available from the dropdown button to the right of the URL Address box in Internet Explorer) likewise is nixed. Amazingly, though, the History of accessed URLs (which you see when you click the History icon on IE's Toolbar) remains intact. If you have any interest in these capabilities, use the Paranoia tab, documented later in this section.

- According to the Tweak UI documentation, if you uncheck the box marked *Detect accidental double-clicks*, a double click will be treated as two single clicks when you have Explorer or the Active Desktop set up to respond to single clicks. (That's the setting you'll find in Windows Explorer's View/ Folder Options/General/Settings dialog.) We tried and tried and couldn't get it to do anything. Your mileage may vary, but don't rely on this Tweak UI "feature."

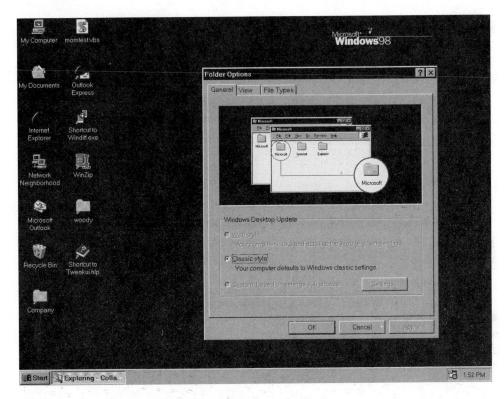

Figure 8-163. Desktop with "IE 4 enabled" turned off

- If you uncheck the box marked *IE 4 enabled*, you might expect IE 4 to be disabled—as in turned off. Not even close, although I suspect if this setting *did* work it would make Janet Reno and her crew happy. As you can see in Figure 8-163, unchecking the box still allows you to view the Active Desktop as a Web page (and thus use your own **.htm** file as wallpaper). It doesn't interfere with the operation of IE 4—just click File, click Run, type **iexplore**, and hit **Enter** and you'll see. But it does disable two of the buttons on the Windows Explorer's View/Folder Options dialog, and it gets rid of the Quick Launch Toolbar, next to the Start button. Far as we could tell, that's the whole story.

- The *Show Documents on Start Menu* and *Show Favorites on Start Menu* items work pretty much as advertised: uncheck the box and the Documents and/or Favorites lines on the Start Menu disappear. One little problem: the Apply button doesn't work. As was the case with Allow Logoff, you have to restart Win98 for the new settings to kick in.

All I know is that when I started playing with the Show Documents and Show Favorites check boxes, Win98 started going weird on me—I got an item at the bottom of the Start Menu that said "Eject PC"; I couldn't get Favorites to show up on the Start Menu, even with the appropriate box checked. Problems came and went; I couldn't duplicate it long enough to run a screen shot to show you here, but based on that experience, I have to believe these settings are all bad mojo.

 Now you know why Microsoft won't support Tweak UI. If any other part of Win98 had been this screwed up, there would've been hell to pay.

Desktop Long the favorite hunting ground of Registry gurus and newbies alike, Tweak UI's Desktop tab (Figure 8-164) deals with most of the built-in system icons.

A couple of icons—My Computer and My Documents—are conspicuous by their absence on this list. And Internet Explorer (which also appears in the list as The Internet) shows up several times, even though none of the instances in the list seems to have any control over the icon that appears on the standard Win98 screen.

 Two of the actions you can specify for most icons—Show on Desktop and Rename—are pretty straightforward. That Create As File option, though, is very poorly described. Microsoft should've called Create As File something like "Create shortcut to system icon." Here's what's really happening.

**Figure 8-164.
The Desktop tab lets you show (or hide) system icons on the Desktop, create a shortcut, or rename the system icons**

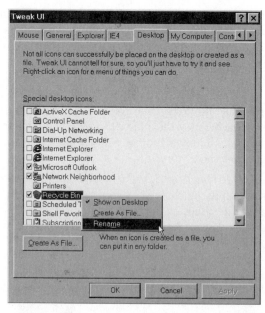

Most system icons can't be moved inside folders. If they appear anywhere as icons, they have to be on the Desktop. Recycle Bin is a good example: if you try to drag the Recycle Bin icon into another folder, Win98 won't let you. On the other hand, you can create a shortcut to a system icon and move it anyplace you like. A shortcut to the Recycle Bin, for example, can go in any folder.

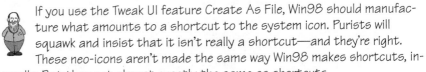 If you use the Tweak UI feature Create As File, Win98 should manufacture what amounts to a shortcut to the system icon. Purists will squawk and insist that it isn't really a shortcut—and they're right. These neo-icons aren't made the same way Win98 makes shortcuts, internally. But they act almost exactly the same as shortcuts.

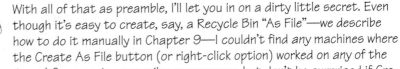 With all of that as preamble, I'll let you in on a dirty little secret. Even though it's easy to create, say, a Recycle Bin "As File"—we describe how to do it manually in Chapter 9—I couldn't find any machines where the Create As File button (or right-click option) worked on any of the system icons! Once again, your mileage may vary, but don't be surprised if Create As File turns out to be a complete dud on your PC.

My Computer You might expect a tab marked My Computer to be concerned with the My Computer icon, but it isn't. Instead, this ho-hum tab lets you hide drives. If you uncheck the box next to a drive—say, C: as in Figure 8-165—the drive no longer appears in Windows Explorer. It also refuses to appear when you double click on the My Computer icon and doesn't show up in Windows File Find.

Figure 8-165. Hide a drive with a click

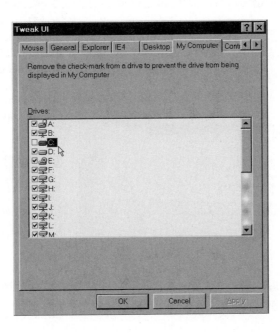

Of course, the drive doesn't really disappear. You can still see it from the DOS box or run programs on the "missing" drive from the Start/Run dialog. Although you won't see the drive listed in the dropdown "Look in" box in most applications' Open dialogs, you can get to it by typing the drive name on the File name line, as in Figure 8-166. Other machines networked to your PC can still see the drive. You're the only one who can't see it. Files on that drive are still accessible through the Documents list on the Start Menu, via Favorites in any of a dozen different applications, or from the Most Recently Used list in practically every commercial application.

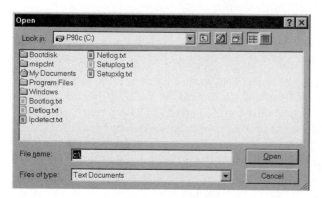

Figure 8-166. Finding the "missing" drive

Once again, the Apply button seems to work, but it doesn't most of the time: you have to restart Windows to have the "missing" drive disappear.

All in all, this tab could provide the setting for a fairly elaborate practical joke ("Good grief! I can't find my C: drive!"), but it doesn't seem to have much real-world application.

Control Panel Tweak UI's Control Panel tab (Figure 8-167) gives you the opportunity to remove specific applets from the Control Panel: uncheck the box by an applet and the next time you bring up Control Panel, that applet won't appear. The magic? The Control Panel tab just makes changes to **control.ini**, the file that drives Control Panel, adding unchecked applets to the **[don't**

Figure 8-167. Various Control Panel applets

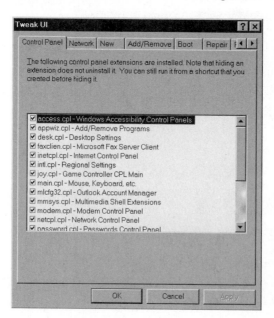

load] list (Figure 8-168). Since **.cpl** files that appear in **control.ini**'s **[don't load]** section aren't loaded, Control Panel won't pick up the specified applet. Short, simple—and it works!

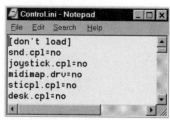

Figure 8-168. Uncheck the Display applet and desk.cpl gets the deep six

Network The Network tab holds a rather nifty utility built into Tweak UI. It automatically logs you on every time you start Win98. Some people like it, some people hate it—if you have a tendency to start typing as soon as you see the logon screen, Windows can get sorely confused and have a hard time completing the logon. But if you can be patient and wait for Tweak UI to run its logon program, you'll never have to type your logon ID or password again.

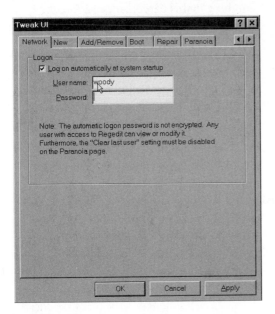

To get automatic logon rolling, just check the "Log on automatically at system startup" box at the top of the screen (Figure 8-169). Note that you must provide your logon ID and password. Also note that, as the screen warns, your password will be stored in the clear—anybody with access to Regedit will be able to read it.

If you enable auto logon, TweakUI turns the Registry **HKLM\Software\Microsoft\ CurrentVersion\Winlogon** key's **AutoAdminLogon** value to **1**. It also sets up **HKLM\Software\Microsoft\Windows\ CurrentVersion\RunServices** to run **TweakUI.cpl**'s program **TweakLogon**. Clever and effective.

Figure 8-169. Automatic logon, compliments of Tweak UI

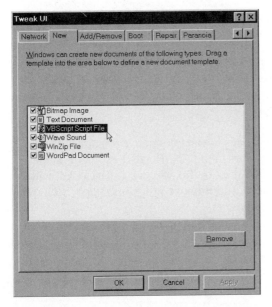

New This tab lets you make changes to the list of files that appears when you right click on the Desktop (or in a blank area of Windows Explorer) and pick New. In Figure 8-170, I've clicked and dragged a **.vbs** file—a VBScript script file—onto the window.

If you'd like to make VBScript files available in the New lineup (Figure 8-171), here's how to do it.

- Create a new, empty text file.
- Rename it with a filename with extension **.vbs**.
- Click and drag it onto the window on the New tab of Tweak UI.

Figure 8-170. Click and drag almost any kind of file and it will appear in New

Figure 8-171. VBScript files are now in New

Win98 takes the file you drag onto the window and uses it as a template. Since there's nothing in this particular **.vbs** file, the "template" is just an empty text file with the filename extension **.vbs**. As you know from Chapter 7, Win98 is already set up to recognize text files with the extension **.vbs** as VBScript script files. So it's quite simple, really, in this case.

If you have a more complicated situation—say, you want to create a totally new file type with a new filename extension or you want the template to contain some "boilerplate" text—bring up the Tweak UI Help file, **tweakui.hlp**, and look in the Index for "template troubleshooter."

The situation with templates is actually a bit more complicated than it would appear here. For full details, look at Chapter 9, in the section "**\ShellNew**."

 To me, the nicest thing about this tab is that I can remove items from the New menu. After all, how often do I make a new Wave Sound? It just clutters the New menu and this lets me remove it. And, since its only a check box, I can use Tweak UI to restore any item I've previously removed. Elegant.

 Tweak UI does its magic when you uncheck an item by renaming the **ShellNew** key to **ShellNew-** with a minus at the end. If you recheck the box, it removes the minus.

 The idea of renaming a Registry key with a minus at the end when you uncheck a "please use" box should ring a bell. It's exactly what System Configuration utility uses for its Startup tab (see "System Configuration Utility" in Chapter 6).

Add/Remove This Tweak UI tab does not add or remove programs. Instead, it controls the list of names that appears in the Add/Remove Programs applet. Compare Figure 8-172, which shows the Add/Remove tab of Tweak UI, with Figure 8-173, which is the associated Add/Remove Programs applet. See how both figures refer to the same programs?

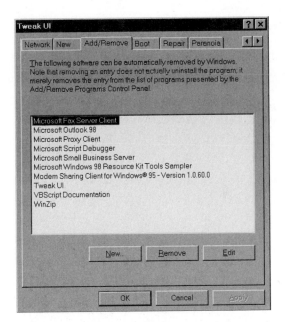

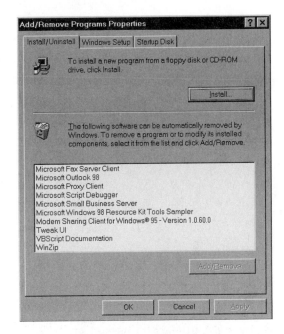

Figure 8-172. Programs on the Tweak UI Add/Remove tab

Figure 8-173. Programs in the Add/Remove Programs applet

 Using the Add/Remove tab in Tweak UI, you can modify the list of programs that appears in the Add/Remove Programs applet. So, for example, you can remove a program name from the list so you won't accidentally remove the program itself. If I wanted to make sure I couldn't remove, oh, the Win98 Resource Kit Tools Sampler, I'd use the Add/Remove tab in the Tweak UI applet to remove the line "Microsoft Windows 98 Resource Kit Tools Sampler" from the Add/Remove Programs applet.

This tab can come in handy if you remove a program and it manages to uninstall everything except its own name on the Add/Remove Programs list. Strange, but it does happen.

Boot This Tweak UI tab (Figure 8-174) controls the contents of **MSDOS.SYS**, in accordance with the myriad details discussed in Chapter 7.

 The only setting I can't get to work is the Autorun ScanDisk "After prompting." As you may recall, Win98 runs Scandisk every time you reboot, if it detects that Win98 wasn't shut down properly (through the Start/Shutdown Menu). An "After prompting" setting here is supposed to force Win98 to prompt you before running ScanDisk on an improper shutdown. As we mentioned in Chapter 7, we never could get it to work that way.

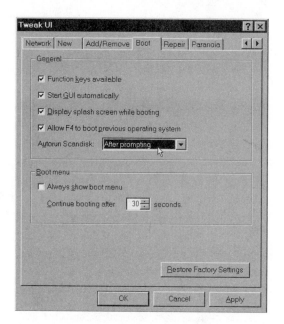

Figure 8-174. GUI face for `MSDOS.SYS`

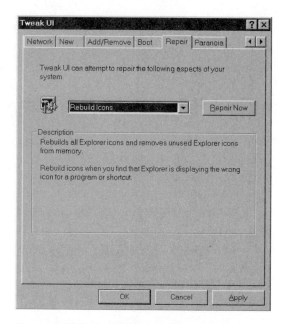

Figure 8-175. Tweak UI can fix an amazing array of fairly common Win98 problems

Repair Stuff happens—but sometimes Win98 can recover. That's where Tweak UI's Repair tab comes in. The options on the Repair tab (Figure 8-175) can

- Rebuild system icons by completely redrawing the system icon pictures, both on your Desktop and in Explorer. Note that if you've changed one of the system icons—made My Computer a whirling dervish, say, using the Display applet's Effects tab—the Repair feature here will rebuild the icon you've chosen, not revert to the "standard" icon.

- Fix the Fonts, Temporary Internet Files, or URL History folders. Each of these folders is supposed to behave a little differently from everyday folders. If they no longer function the way they're supposed to, Tweak UI can bring them back to life.

- Restore filename extension associations. If double clicking on your **.bmp** files no longer brings up Microsoft Paint with the file loaded, this will fix the problem.

- Make Regedit show all its columns. If Regedit no longer shows you Name and Data columns, this is supposed to fix it.

- Restore all overwritten system files from back-up copies stored in **C:\windows\SysBckup**. It's a drastic step, but one you can take with a simple click.

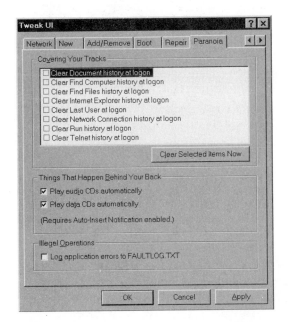

Figure 8-176. Use the Paranoia tab to cover your tracks

Figure 8-177. Map Network Drive holds the Network Connection history

Paranoia Finally, Tweak UI's infamous Paranoia tab (Figure 8-176) lets you wipe out various stored histories. It also has a couple of additional purely miscellaneous settings. The history files are these:

- Document history appears on the Start/Documents menu.

- Find Computer history is on the Start/Find/Computer menu.

- Find Files history is on the Start/Find files or Folders menu.

- Internet Explorer history is the list of typed URLs in the pulldown Address list. It's important to note that this does not include the history of which URLs you've visited, which you can see by clicking IE's History button on the toolbar.

- Last User is the logon ID of the last user to log on to this machine.

- Network Connection history is actually the Map Network Drive dropdown list (Figure 8-177) that you can access from Map Network Connection in My Computer or from various other applications.

- Run history is the list in the Start/Run Menu.

- Most obscure of all, Telnet history is the list of computers you see if you run Telnet (Start/Run and type `telnet`), then click on Connect and Remote System.

"Things That Happen Behind Your Back" are just the two different kinds of autoplay Win98 supports. Auto insert notification is established in the Device

Manager; see Figure 8-145. You must have auto insert notification enabled for either autoplay setting to take effect.

Finally, "Log application errors to FAULTLOG.TXT" is supposed to make Win98 append the contents of the Details screen to **C:\windows\ faultlog.txt** whenever a general protection fault (GPF) occurs.

 I was surprised at how well this option works. Every GPF I could trigger caused Win98 to append the Details information to **faultlog.txt**. While purists will probably want to run Dr. Watson in Win 98 (Start, Run, **drwatson**), this option is a good fallback.

 ## ■ Users

The Users applet is covered extensively in the Chapter 3 "User Profiles" section. Each user has a unique Registry key, **HKEY_USERS\logonid**. So, for example, a particular PC might have **HKEY_USERS\barry** and **HKEY_USERS\woody**. Those, combined with the **C:\Windows\Profiles\logonid** folders, do all the heavy lifting.

Chapter 9

Oh Registry, My Registry

We must make allowances for whoever does a thing first.

—*Greek proverb*

Welcome to the graduate course on Windows 98. Your assignment for the next two hours is to learn enough about the structure and contents of the human brain to self-administer a prefrontal lobotomy. I'm afraid the campus bookstore hasn't yet received copies of *The Mother of All Anatomy Books*, so you'll have to make due with the Bodily Resource Kit. You'll note that the BRK spends twenty-five pages on "brain," six pages on "structure," one page on "lobes," and a paragraph on "prefrontal" but sadly neglects to say anything about "lobotomy." That's OK. I'm sure you'll be able to pick it up once you get into the thick of things. Scalpels are available for your experimentation in the box marked Regedit.

OK, OK. The Registry ain't *that* bad. Yeah, it's true that the Registry is Win98's brain. And yeah, I have to admit that the Windows Resource Kit for Win98 covers the Registry a whole lot better than the Win95 WRK. Still, the official documentation doesn't say much about where to poke and prod to get the Registry to do what you—or I—want it to do.

Microsoft would have you believe that the Registry can be manipulated only by very sophisticated users. But all too often when you ask Microsoft for tech support, the first question you hear is "Do you know how to use Regedit?" The simple fact is that there are hundreds, if not thousands, of reasons why you might need to edit your Registry and precious little documentation on how or why or what.

You might think this chapter is the place to start when pursuing Registry things. It isn't. A very large part of Chapter 8 is on the Registry—Barry and Woody just disguised it as a discussion of the Control Panel so you wouldn't freak out. If you're beginning with the Registry and want to learn more, or if you want to tweak anything contained in the Control Panel, start with Chapter 8.

■ Regedit

The best partner for dice playing is not a just man, but a good dice player.

—P<small>LATO</small>, The Republic, ca. 370 B.C.

 Ready to roll the dice? Excellent. We have some really good dice players on MOM's crew, and we'll show you the ins and outs. Let's start by assuming that you've already seen the Registry and used Regedit at least once. If you're completely green at editing the Registry, go back to Chapter 8 and start at the beginning. This is the Advanced Registry course, not Registry for Dummies, OK?

 Hey! Even Dummies need to learn how to use Regedit. You act as if it's some big deal, but you and I both know that—as long as you're careful and make good backups—there's no reason why you shouldn't take your Registry into your own hands.

Keys, Values, Names, and Data

Let's start by taking a detailed look at Regedit itself and getting some of the (confusing!) terminology down. Click Start, then Run, type **regedit**, and hit **Enter**. You'll see something like Figure 9-1. Click a **+** sign and the entry expands. Double click on a name in the right-hand panel, and the Regedit Edit box pops up, so

**Figure 9-1.
Regedit under the
magnifying glass**

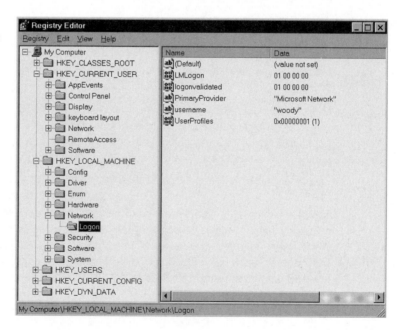

Figure 9-2.
Regedit edit box

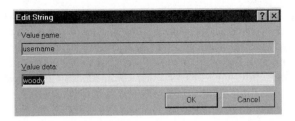

you can change the value (Figure 9-2). Click once on almost anything and hit the **Del** key to delete it. Click on Edit, then Find, and you can search for particular values or strings. You already know all that.

 Now, to get the terminology straight, start by forgetting everything you've ever read about the Registry. (The Windows Resource Kit is confusing as hell.) Let's start with a clean slate. In Figure 9-1, every line in the left-hand box is called a **key**. Every line in the right-hand box is called a **value**. So, for example, the left-hand thing that appears as **HKEY_LOCAL_MACHINE\Network\Logon** is a key, and it has five values. The right-hand thing that appears as **username** "woody" is one of the values.

Admittedly the terminology is a bit weird. (I, for one, tend to think of **username** as a part of the key, with "**woody**" as the value—and I'll bet you do, too.) But we're talking about Official Microsoft Definitions here: any semblance to rationality is entirely coincidental. As you can see in Figure 9-2, the first part of the value (**username** in this example) is called the *value name* and the second part of the value ("**woody**" in this example) is called the *value data*. This terminology is an extreme example of techie obfuscation, but we'll stick with it to stay compatible with the official documentation.

Look at the key side of Figure 9-1. See the six high-level keys? They're called **HKEY_CLASSES_ROOT**, **HKEY_CURRENT_USER**, **HKEY_LOCAL_MACHINE**, **HKEY_USERS**, **HKEY_CURRENT_CONFIG**, and **HKEY_DYN_DATA**. For reasons I discuss in the next section, we generally deal with just three of those keys: **HKEY_CLASSES_ROOT** (which I will abbreviate **HKCR**), **HKEY_CURRENT_USER** (abbreviated **HKCU**), and **HKEY_LOCAL_MACHINE** (abbreviated **HKLM**).

Now look on the right side of Figure 9-1. See how the first Registry value name is listed as **(Default)**? That's a special value name: while you can change the **(Default)** value data—the part marked **(value not set)**—by double clicking on **(Default)**, you cannot delete **(Default)** and you cannot create a second **(Default)** value name. Every key (that is, every line on the left side of Regedit) has exactly one **(Default)** value (that is, one and only one **(Default)** value name on the right side).

Every value has three parts: the value name, the type of data contained in the value (indicated by the icon to the left of the name), and the value data itself.

The other value names in Figure 9-1, **LMLogon**, **logonvalidated**, **PrimaryProvider**, **username**, and **UserProfiles**, show how value names can be just about any combination of letters or numbers, including spaces.

Spaces are significant (**Primary Provider** is different from **PrimaryProvider**), but capitalization is not (**PrimaryProvider** is the same as **primaryprovider**). In Windows 95, Registry key name capitalization flip-flopped all over the place. In Win98, it looks as if a copy editor took a red pen to Windows' internals (heaven knows it needed the makeover!) and in most places you'll find more or less reasonable capitalization.

There are three different flavors of value data.

- *String* value data are normal characters, numbers and the like, including just about any oddball character you can imagine, including quotation marks. (For you programmers, it's a variable-length, null-terminated string.) The little ⓐⓑ icon in Regedit signifies that this value's data is string.

- *Binary* value data is just a variable-length hexadecimal entry. Double click on a value name and Regedit shows you the value data both in hex and in ASCII translation (Figure 9-3). Cool. The 🔢 icon in Regedit signifies that this value's data type is either binary or dword (see the next list item). When you overwrite binary data, be careful to make sure that you overwrite only the bytes you want to overwrite—because of the way the editor works, it's very easy to alter the size of a binary entry accidentally. Practice with it a couple of times and you'll see how it works.

- *Dword* value data is the standard PC hex double-word. Programmers call a double-word (four bytes of data, each byte containing two hex digits) a *dword*. It's usually interpreted as a number that can range from zero to FFFFFFFF hex—commonly written 0 × FFFFFFFF. In decimal notation, that's zero to 4,294,967,295. Note how, in the UserProfiles value of Figure 9-1, Regedit shows both the hex (in 0 × . . . format) and decimal representations (in parentheses) of every dword value. The only difference between a dword and a binary value is that the former has a fixed length of four bytes.

**Figure 9-3.
Editing a binary
value**

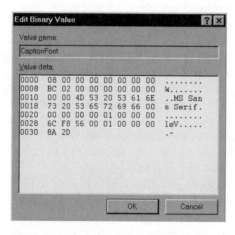

(value not set) is a special null value (er, value data) that appears to be valid only in **(Default)** entries; at least, I couldn't find it used with anything but **(Default)** entries. Although Regedit puts the 🔤 icon in front of null values, **(value not set)** is *not* a character string. You can't search for it. If you use Regedit's editor and type in the data **(value not set)**, you get a string with that value, not a null! The only way I've found to reset a value to **(value not set)** is to click on **(Default)** and hit **Del**.

Zero-length strings (often called "empty strings") show up in the Regedit right panel as a pair of quotation marks with nothing in between. Although there is a technical difference between a zero-length string and a null **(value not set)** value data, in practice I haven't seen any difference in the way the two are treated in the Registry or in Windows as a whole.

(zero-length binary value) is another special null value, this time for binary value data. Again, it is *not* a character string. You can assign the null **(zero-length binary value)** value to a binary entry by double clicking on the value name and deleting everything in the Regedit edit box.

You're bound to ask, sooner or later, "What's the real meaning of those different types of value data?" Well, I hate to disillusion you, but there isn't any. Choice of a particular data type seems to be a reflection of what the programmer was feeling like on the day she decided to add the entry. One of the best examples of how the types become jumbled sits in the Registry key that deals with window sizes and fonts, **HKCU\Control Panel\Desktop\WindowMetrics**. If you look in there, you'll find lots of numbers (e.g., the height of the title bar) stored as string data and lots of strings (for example, the names of fonts) stored as binary.

 And why are the **EditFlags** values—which are always four bytes long—stored in the Registry as binary data instead of dword? Got me. Anybody who tells you that string data are for characters and binary and dword data are for numbers obviously hasn't spent much time in the Registry!

New Keys and Values

Adding new keys and values to the Registry is as simple as clicking Edit, then New, or equivalently, right clicking inside the Regedit dialog. Following Explorer's folder metaphor, clicking Edit, New, then Key adds a new key (that is, a left entry in Regedit) below the currently highlighted key, as in Figure 9-4. As soon as the new key is added, you'll notice that it has one automatically generated value attached to it with a value name of **(Default)** and value data of **(value not set)**.

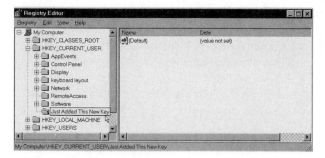

Figure 9-4. A new key gets a **(Default)** value of **(value not set)**

While creating a new key is pretty easy and more or less intuitive, there's a trick to making the Regedit approach to creating a new value rather easy. Start by clicking the key you want to receive the new value, then click Edit and New and choose string, binary, or dword. (Equivalently, you can right click on the key and pick New, then string, binary, or dword; or you can simply right click in the right side of Regedit and pick New, then string, binary, or dword.) The new value will have a name of **New Value #1** (or **#2**, **#3**, etc.), and if you type immediately, you overwrite the name.

 Here's the trick: once you've typed in the new value name, hit **Enter** twice. That immediately brings up the Regedit edit box (Figure 9-2), and typing in data at that point is easy. Every other method for typing in new data is a PITA.

When you create a new value, the default value data varies, depending on what kind of value you've created.

- *String* value data starts out with a zero-length string.
- *Binary* value data starts out as **(zero-length binary data)**.
- *Dword* data starts out **00 00 00 00**, four bytes of zeros.

In general, Windows ignores new keys and values that you've typed in manually. There are lots of exceptions, though: for example, some schemes (see Chapter 8) are established by sticking keys in the right place, in a process analogous to sticking folders in Win98's **\Windows\Start Menu** folder to add new items to the Start Menu.

 It's always safer to change keys associated with the Control Panel by playing with the Control Panel's applets themselves instead of Regedit. Unfortunately, as discussed many times in Chapter 8, the Control Panel's applets often fail to give you access to all the Registry settings. As the saying goes, necessity is a mother.

Don't delete keys willy-nilly, even if they have no values other than **(Default)**. In many cases, the mere existence of a key (even a value!) is important information for some part of Windows or an application.

Figure 9-5.
Creating a text
file with the se-
lected key and all
the keys below it

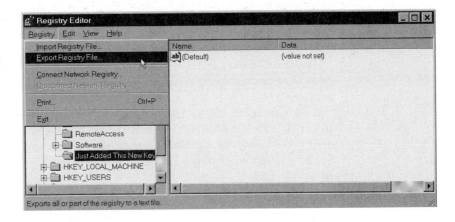

Import/Export

Regedit allows you to export all the values for a single key, or all the values for all the keys underneath a specific key, to a simple text file (except for the data in and under the key **HKEY_DYN_DATA**, which can't be exported under any circumstances). To use the export capability, click the key you want to export, then click Registry and Export Registry File, per Figure 9-5. Type in a filename for the exported file; Win98 will suggest you save it as a **.reg** file. The resulting file has entries for every value in the chosen key, plus the values of every key underneath the chosen key. To export the entire Registry, click on My Computer, then Registry and Export Registry File. It's a real disk hog: a typical exported Registry will take 1 MB of space or more.

 I recommend that you ignore Windows' suggestion and save exported Registry files with any extension *other* than **.reg**. **.txt** seems like a good choice, as you'll often want to look at and/or edit the resulting file. If you save the exported file as a **.reg**, accidentally double clicking it will immediately merge the file with the current Registry—a potentially hazardous happenstance.

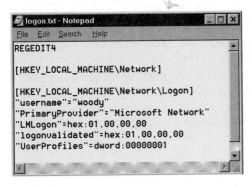

Figure 9-6. HKLM\Network saved as a
text file

If you export starting at the **HKLM\Network** key shown in Figure 9-1, you get a text file that looks like Figure 9-6. The key **HKLM\Network** has just one value, **(Default) (value not set)**, which doesn't appear in the exported text file.

There are several points worth noting. See how the file starts with a line that says **REGEDIT4**? I talk about that line—hallmark of a **.reg** file—in the section "Merging **.reg** Files." Next, look at how the keys are handled. Each key appears on one line in **[brackets]**. While the Registry itself is hierarchical, a **.reg** file is just a straight, flat text file. The Registry's hierarchy is reflected in the key names. Also note that the **(Default) (value not set)** value doesn't create any entry at all in the **.reg** file. Finally, take a close look at how value names and string, binary, and dword values appear in the **.reg** file. Looking at a raw **.reg** file can be a bit jarring at first, but give yourself some time and you'll come to appreciate the symmetry in the beast.

There are four odd values that appear in **.reg** files from time to time.

- While a **(Default) (value not set)** value doesn't appear in the **.reg** file at all, a **(Default)** **"some value"** entry generates a line that looks like this:

    @="some value"

    The **@** sign apparently is used to take the place of a **(Default)** value name.

- Empty binary values look a bit odd, too. If your Registry has a **ValueName (zero-length binary data)** value, it shows up in the **.reg** file as

    "ValueName"=hex:

- Double quotes in string value data are preceded by a backslash. For example, a value name of **Test** and value data of **An "award winning" book** appears in the **.reg** file as

    "Test"="An \"award winning\" book"

- Apparently because of the way double quotes are treated, backslashes appear in the **.reg** file doubled. For example, a value name of **Another Test** and value data of **C:\windows** appears in the file as:

    "Another Test"="C:\\windows"

While exporting with Regedit covers a multitude of sins, importing with Regedit is not very sophisticated. You tell Regedit to import a file by clicking Registry, then Import Registry File, and picking a file to import. Regedit doesn't really import anything. It simply merges the selected **.reg** file with your Registry, just as if you had double clicked on the **.reg** file while in Explorer. I talk more about merging **.reg** files in the section "Merging **.reg** Files."

■ Care and Feeding of the Registry

Life is warfare, and the sojourn of a stranger in a strange land.

—Marcus Aurelius, *Meditations,* ca. 170

 Enough on Regedit for the moment. No doubt you're wondering by now what exactly the Registry is. The answer, it turns out, has an easy part and a hard part. Now that you've seen what the Registry looks like, you're ready to understand both parts.

The Registry is a centrally maintained warehouse of information that programs—including Windows itself—use to store and retrieve information. Microsoft feels that allowing (even requiring!) programs to use a central warehouse is better than letting them store data ad hoc: a central store is easier to manage and can be much more efficient than the ad hoc approach. On the flip side, though, storing all your eggs in one basket means that if the warehouse goes up in flames, all of Windows can, too. That's the easy part, the conceptual part, the part you already know.

 Microsoft, though, seems to want you to do what they say, not what they do. Not only are **win.ini** and **system.ini** still used for some data (see, for example, the section "Media Control Interface—Do You Mean Mike McCurry?" in Chapter 2) but a number of Windows 98 applets continue to use private **.ini** files instead of the Registry, for example, **exchng.ini**, **control.ini**, **wavemix.ini**, **mspclnt.ini**, and **telephon.ini**.

Physically, the Registry is an amalgam of data from two or three files,[†] plus a bunch of things that are created on the fly whenever Win98 gets going. And that's where things start getting complicated. Let me first explain which files are involved and how they get mashed together to make the thing we call the Registry. Then I'll go into some detail about six methods you can use to change those files when things go bump in the night. All six of these methods are in addition to Regedit, of course, which can change Registry values (and the underlying files).

Registry Genesis

The designers of the Registry had to take into account three conflicting sources of information when creating Registry entries.

1. The information about a specific PC—what hardware exists, which ports are being used, what kind of printer is attached, and on and on. In a very

---

† If a network administrator has established network policies, there may be more than three files involved. These **.pol** files can get pretty hairy; since they're advanced networking files, they're mercifully beyond the scope of this book.

broad sense, this information is stored in a file called **system.dat** and becomes the Registry key **HKEY_LOCAL_MACHINE**.

2. The information about the currently logged on user—how the Desktop is laid out, which files were most recently used, how fast the mouse moves, and much more. Again in a very broad sense, this is stored in a file called **user.dat** and becomes the Registry key **HKEY_CURRENT_USER**.

3. The collective restrictions embodied in the **.pol** files—what kind of access is permitted on the machine and under what circumstances it is permitted. Settings in **policy.pol** find their way into many parts of the Registry.

 I waffled a bit in those descriptions because they aren't at all cut and dried. For example, I would've thought the system font—which can be changed with the Control Panel's Desktop applet, Appearance tab—should be a **user.dat** setting, like, oh, the Active Title Bar's color. It isn't. For good technical reasons, the system font is a **system.dat** setting.

In the simplest of all possible worlds—a PC with one hardware profile (see Chapter 8, System applet, Hardware Profiles tab), a single user profile (see Chapter 3, Password applet, User Profiles tab), and no restrictive **policy.pol** file—the Registry is constructed from the files **system.dat** and **user.dat**, both in the Win98 **\windows** folder.

If the PC has more than one hardware profile, all the information about the different profiles is stored in the file **\windows\system.dat** and the information is accessible, regardless of which hardware profile is in effect, with Regedit. I talk more about hardware profiles and how their settings end up in **HKEY_DYN_DATA** in the section "Dynamic Data." For now, suffice it to say that all the Registry's hardware information—regardless of which hardware profile may be in effect—resides in **system.dat**, and Win98 is smart enough to pick and choose the information it needs to build a Registry that accurately reflects the current hardware configuration.

Constructing the Registry is considerably more complicated if there is more than one user profile defined on a PC. Chapter 3 goes into considerable detail about how Win98 stores multiple profiles, and you should refer to the discussion there if you're in the dark. As a quick refresher, if there are two user profiles defined on a PC—say, one for logon ID *barry,* and another for logon ID *woody*—there will be three **user.dat** files on the machine: a default one in the Windows folder **\windows\user.dat**; one for *barry,* stored in his own Windows profile folder, **\windows\profiles\barry\user.dat**, and one more for the user *woody,* **\windows\profiles\woody\user.dat**.

If a user bypasses the normal logon sequence on a multiple user profile PC (by, say, hitting **Esc** when presented with the logon screen), the Registry is constructed as it would be if there were only a single user profile, that is, by combining **\windows\system.dat** with the file **\windows\user.dat**. In essence, **\windows\user.dat** is the "default" user data file, pressed into service when Win98 can't identify which user profile it should use.

On the other hand, if a user logs on normally to a multiple user profile PC—say, *woody* logs on—the Registry is constructed by combining three files, not the normal two: **\windows\system.dat**, which provides the information for the Registry's **HKLM** key; **\windows\profiles\woody\user.dat**, which provides the information for the Registry's **HKCU** key; and **\windows\user.dat**, which provides the information for a little-used key called **HKEY_USERS\.Default**.

Try finding *that* information in the Windows Resource Kit!

It all sounds a little convoluted, but it isn't, really. When a new user logs on, a personal copy of **\windows\user.dat** is placed in the user's **\windows\profiles\username** folder. (Or, equivalently, the user gets her own copy of **HKEY_USERS\.Default**, which becomes **HKCU**.) If the correct box is checked in the Passwords applet User Profiles tab, the user also gets her own customizable **\Start Menu** and **\Desktop**, both located in the **\windows\profiles\username** folder, along with as many as seven other folders, as described in the "User Profiles" section of Chapter 3.

The Registry is modified to point to the new **\Start Menu** and **\Desktop** folders, so any changes made to the Desktop and Start Menu affect only the new user. Network administrators can set things up so that the **user.dat** travels with the user on a network: if you log on from machine A, you get the same **user.dat** you get if you log on from machine B, so all your settings travel along with you. It works pretty well.

It doesn't work all that well. Among many other things, if MOM installs, oh, Office 97, the installer is smart enough to change MOM's **\profiles\mom\Start Menu** so that her Start Menu is updated to include all the new Office applications. That's fine. But the Office installer isn't smart enough to look for, much less change, Billy's **\profiles\billy\Start Menu**, so the next time Billy logs on, he won't have the applications on his menus, even though Office 97 is available on the machine. That isn't, strictly speaking, a Registry problem. But it's a big problem, nonetheless. The ability to customize menus and Desktops cuts both ways, and many users (including this one!) find it very confusing.

Registry Checker (aka ScanReg) in Windows

The first and best way to take care of your Registry is via the new Win98 utility known as the Registry Checker (ScanReg to its friends). To get it going, click (get this) Start, Programs, Accessories, System Tools, System Information. Then in the SysInfo utility, click Tools, Registry Checker. This may be the best-hidden system tool in Win98.

It's a whole lot easier to click Start and Run, type **scanreg**, and hit **Enter**. That's why the Registry Checker is probably best known to Win98 cognoscenti as ScanReg.

 To be accurate, there are two programs: ScanReg, which runs under DOS, and ScanRegw, which runs under Windows. If you invoke ScanReg from the Run line, the Registry Checker is smart enough to realize that it's running under Windows and automatically brings up ScanRegw. The distinction is not entirely academic: ScanRegw, since it's running under Windows, won't try to fix the Registry on the fly; instead, it'll tell you to pop out to DOS and use ScanReg.

No matter how you kick start it, the Registry Checker takes a look at your Registry for very obvious (and usually deadly) Registry screwups. The Registry Checker isn't smart enough to check for the most common Registry problems—filename extensions associated with nonexistent programs, say, or flotsam left over from lousy uninstallers—but it can detect a few problems. Ninety-nine times out of a hundred, you come up with a clean bill of health.

Win98 runs ScanRegw every time it boots. ScanRegw "prunes" away dead Registry branches if they exceed half a megabyte in size. (When you delete a key in the Registry, it remains inside the file, marked "not used" and hidden from Regedit.) ScanRegw also maintains a series of Registry backups in compressed files named **rb###.cab**, where **###** is a number, starting at 000. The exact method for constructing those **.cab** files is a bit complex, so hang in there while we go through the details.

If you do nothing to change the Registry Checker's default settings, ScanRegw maintains a five-deep set of backups, named **rb000.cab** through **rb004.cab**. Those files are stored in the hidden folder **C:\windows\sysbckup**. Each **.cab** file contains copies of the Registry files **system.dat** and **user.dat**, as well as the ancient files **win.ini** and **system.ini**. The five-deep history is maintained by date: every time it runs, ScanRegw looks to see if there's been an **rb###.cab** file created already on that date. If not, it creates a new one, cycling through the **rb000.cab**, **001**, **002**, **003**, and **004** filenames.

 It may surprise you to know that the **user.dat** file stored away in the **rb###.cab** files is always the "system" **user.dat**—the one stored in **C:\windows**, not the **user.dat** for the user who's logging on, stored in **C:\windows\profiles\username**. That's a controversial choice, because it means that no customizations for any user are ever backed up by the system.

 Yes, but on the other hand, it means that the system will probably boot using the backed-up **user.dat**. At most, full system restoration may require re-installing some programs and changing a handful of settings.

Figure 9-7.
`Scanreg.ini`
controls the
Registry Checker's
activities

```
Scanreg.ini - Notepad
File  Edit  Search  Help
;
; Scanreg.ini for making system backups.
;

;Registry backup is skipped altogether if this is set to 0
Backup=1

;Registry automatic optimization is skipped if this is set to 0
Optimize=1

ScanregVersion=0.0001
MaxBackupCopies=5

;Backup directory where the cabs are stored is
; <windir>\sysbckup by default. Value below overrides it.
; It must be a full path. ex. c:\tmp\backup
;
BackupDirectory=

; Additional system files to backup into cab as follows:
; Filenames are separated by ','
; dir code can be:
;       10       : windir (ex. c:\windows)
;       11       : system dir (ex. c:\windows\system)
;       30       : boot dir (ex. c:\)
;       31       : boot host dir (ex. c:\)
;
;Files=[dir code,]file1,file2,file3
;Files=[dir code,]file1,file2,file3
```

A very large handful, if you ask me.

Anyway, that's the simplified version of how ScanRegw works. In fact, the actions of ScanReg and ScanRegw are controlled by a file called **scanreg.ini**. See Figure 9-7 for an example.

As far as we could tell, **Backup** and **Optimize** (the "pruning" action for removing dead Registry entries) work as described in Figure 9-7. **MaxBackupCopies** controls how many **rb###.cab** files are maintained, as expected.

We had some trouble with **BackupDirectory**, though. It's a very picky setting. You cannot place a backslash at the end of the directory name. For example, **BackupDirectory=C:\temp** doesn't work. Also, we couldn't get this setting to put the **.cab** files in the root of any hard drive; **BackupDirectory=C:** doesn't work. That's the bad news. The good news is that if ScanRegw can't figure out where to put the **rb###.cab** file, it's stuck in **C:\windows**.

Independent numbering schemes are maintained in each folder. So, for example, if you have an **rb000.cab** and **rb001.cab** file in **C:\temp** and you change **scanreg.ini** to point **BackupDirectory** to **C:\temp**, the next back-up file will be called **rb002.cab**.

Finally, you can tell ScanRegw to back up more than the standard **system.dat**, **user.dat**, **win.ini**, and **system.ini** files by completing the **Files=** entries in **scanreg.ini**, per the instructions shown in Figure 9-7. For example, if you want ScanRegw to back up your **C:\autoexec.bat** and **C:\config.sys** files every time it does a backup, you would include the line

> **Files=30,autoexec.bat,config.sys**

at the end of **scanreg.ini**. And, no, we tried but couldn't get files in other folders (for example, **C:\windows\profiles\woody\user.dat**) to work.

ScanReg in DOS

Running **scanreg.exe** in DOS presents several interesting possibilities. If you just restart in DOS mode, navigate to **C:\windows\command**, and simply run ScanReg, the Registry Checker takes a look at your **system.dat** and **user.dat** files and confirms that they're valid. You're given a choice to restore individual **rb###.cab** files, if you so wish.

ScanReg in DOS has three important command line switches.

- **Scanreg /backup** creates a new **.cab** back-up file, according to the settings in **scanreg.ini**. Unfortunately, the DOS version of ScanReg can't compress files so, even though the file has a **.cab** filename extension, the files inside an **rb###.cab** file generated by a forced **/backup** are not compressed.

- **Scanreg /fix** forces the Registry Checker to examine **system.dat** and **user.dat** and reconstruct the Registry, from scratch, using those files. When it's done, it rewrites **system.dat** and **user.dat**, presumably "fixed" and absent of whatever demons may have dogged them before you ran the Registry Checker.

- **Scanreg /restore** presents a list of **.cab** files and lets the user choose among them, restoring one of the backups. You can get the same effect by simply running ScanReg and choosing View Backups.

 There are some **rb###.cab** file numbering subtleties when using ScanReg in DOS. I couldn't nail down the details, but using the DOS version of the Registry Checker creates files with **###** numbers greater than the maximum indicated by **scanreg.ini**. In addition, I've seen files called **rbbad.cab** generated using the DOS version. Strange.

Copying .dat Files

By far the easiest and safest way to back up and restore the Registry is through the Registry Checker, in both its Windows and DOS incarnations. That said, though, there's nothing to prevent you from keeping track of your own **system.dat** and **user.dat** files and replacing them manually, should the situation arise.

 You might want to consider direct manipulation of **user.dat**, if only to preserve copies of the file that applies to your particular logon ID.

 It's also theoretically possible to extract one backed-up system file from your favorite **rb###.cab** file and only restore that one file by simply copying over the existing copy in **C:\windows**. Extracting a single file from a **.cab** is trivial in Win98—just click and drag. But if you're stuck at the DOS command prompt and want to extract a file, you're in for some interesting times, compliments of the DOS command **extract**.

When you run the **extract** command, you have several options, which are generally indicated thus:

```
extract [/A][/E][/Y][/L Target_Directory] Cabinet_Name
    Files_To_Extract
```

Target_Directory is the place you want the extracted file(s) to go. If you don't specify one, Win98 sticks the extracted file in the current directory. Put quotes around **Target_Directory** if it includes embedded spaces.

Cabinet_Name is the name of the **.cab** file **extract** is supposed to look in.

Files_To_Extract is a list of files to extract, separated by blanks. You can use ***** and **?**, the usual wild cards.

/A tells **extract** to look at all **.cab** files beginning with the one called **Cabinet_Name**. You shouldn't need it when extracting **rb###.cab** files.

/E is the same thing as using ***.*** for **Files_To_Extract**. For example, if you have the command line

```
extract /E /L C:\temp C:\windows\sysbckup\rb003.cab
```

extract extracts all the files in the **rb003.cab** cabinet and places them in **C:\temp**.

/Y means "answer yes." Usually **extract** prompts the user before overwriting a file. If the **/Y** switch is used, it's as if the user answered Yes to all those prompts.

Finally,

```
extract /D Cabinet_Name [Files_To_List]
```

lists all the files in **Cabinet_Name** matching **Files_To_List.** If there is no **Files_To_List**, **extract** lists all the files in the cabinet.

Merging `.reg` Files

You now know that you can change Registry entries one at a time using Regedit or wholesale by using the Registry Checker or by copying over the **system.dat** or **user.dat** files. There's a fourth way to change the Registry that I want to cover before we get into the structure of Registry keys. You can change the Registry by using a **.reg** Registry merge file. I showed you a small but typical **.reg** file in Figure 9-6. Basically, a **.reg** file is just a simple text file that begins with the line **REGEDIT4** and contains Registry keys in [brackets], with values following the keys. Running the **.reg** file (by double clicking on it; right clicking on it and choosing Merge; or, from inside Regedit, by clicking Registry then Import Registry File) merges data from the **.reg** file into the Registry. You can also merge **.reg** files with the DOS version of Regedit.

It isn't quite that simple, of course. We're talking Registry, here. If you expect simple, you're definitely in the wrong place. When Win98 merges a **.reg** file, it processes entries under each [key] as follows.

Step 1 Windows looks at the [key]. If it starts with **HKEY_DYN_DATA**, Windows spits out an error message and stops processing the **.reg** file. Ma Windows won't let you touch any Dynamic Data keys or values.

Step 2 If the key exists, Windows skips to Step 4. If it does not exist, Windows tries to create a new key with that name.

Step 3 If the key starts with **HKEY_CLASSES_ROOT**, **HKEY_CURRENT_USER**, **HKEY_LOCAL_MACHINE**, **HKEY_USERS**, or **HKEY_CURRENT_CONFIG**, a new key with the indicated name is created, and a value of **(Default) (value not set)** is entered for the key. If the key starts with anything other than one of the five established root names, you do *not* get an error message—in fact, you aren't notified of any problem at all—and the new key will *not* be created. Windows skips down the **.reg** file to the next key and starts again at Step 1.

Step 4 If there are any values listed in the **.reg** file under the key, they're processed one by one. If a value name exists, the value data in the Registry is overwritten with whatever data appears in the **.reg** file. (Note that if the type of value data in the **.reg** file is different from the type of value data in the Registry, the Registry entry takes on the **.reg** file's data type—so if the Registry entry has, say, a binary zero and the **.reg** file has a character string ABCD, the Registry entry is changed to be a character value, with data ABCD.) If the value name does not exist, a new Registry value is created, based on the entry in the **.reg** file. Processing continues with the next key at Step 1.

Wait a minute! If I read that right, you're saying that there's no way to construct a **.reg** file that deletes a key, deletes a value, or even renames a key or value. All you can do is add new keys under one of the politically correct five root keys, add values, or change value data. That's it. Ouch.

Figure 9-8.
The `.reg` merge lie

 Actually, Barry, it's worse than that. When merging `.reg` files, if Windows doesn't understand a particular line in the `.reg` file, it just ignores the problem and goes to the next line, ultimately giving you the happy news that everything is well (Figure 9-8). Error messages are rare. Meaningful error messages are nonexistent.

Which leads me to one of my favorite bugs in all of Win. . .dumb. When Windows merges a `.reg` file, it looks at the first line of the file to make sure it says **REGEDIT4**. If you screw up that line just slightly—say, type **REGEDIT 4**, with a space—Win98 skips merging the whole file but still gives you the Figure 9-8 message saying that everything has been merged successfully!

If you find that merging a `.reg` file doesn't do what you think it should, take a look at the file. Chances are good there's a quote missing or a period in the wrong place or a slightly misspelled name. Remember, when you're working with `.reg` files, you're working without a net.

`.inf` and the Registry

Those funny installation files I talk about in Chapter 7, the `.inf` files, can also manipulate Registry entries. They are set up that way to allow hardware manufacturers to put things in your Registry when you set up their hardware. Of course, you can take advantage of them, too, if you don't mind playing around with `.inf` files.

Let's shed a little light in this bastion of darkness. For our purposes, an `.inf` file can tell Win98 to add or delete keys and/or values to the Registry. An `.inf` file is a simple text file that looks a lot like an old-fashioned Windows 3.1 `.ini` file, with sections, keys, and the like. You "run" an `.inf` file by right clicking on it and choosing Install. (Networked users who have their installation "pushed" using **msbatch.exe** may also have `.inf` files installed via a program called **infinst.exe**—but that's a rather complex topic, well beyond the scope of this book.)

 In our case, Install updates Registry entries. There's no error checking, no testing mode, no chance to see if the update proceeded without problem—indeed, there's no way to find out if the update even ran, except by examining the contents of the Registry to see if they were changed. The syntax—at least the part of the syntax that I understand—is a bit strange, but that's par for the course.

Every `.inf` file (at least, every `.inf` file that works) starts with two lines:

```
[Version]
signature="$CHICAGO$"
```

where **Chicago** can be uppercase or lowercase.

 Chicago was the code name for the early betas of Windows 95. It's immortalized in this strange place.

Every `.inf` file (at least, every `.inf` file that works by right clicking and choosing Install) has a section that looks more or less like this:

```
[DefaultInstall]
AddReg = Some_Section
DelReg = Some_Other_Section
```

 Note that this is different from what the Windows Resource Kit says in Appendix C. From what we've seen, for the `.inf` file to be installable with a right click, you *must* use **[DefaultInstall]** as the name of the one and only Install section. (You 'Softies can see why if you look at the Registry key **HKCR\inffile\shell\install** command, where **DefaultInstall** is clearly demanded.)

The **AddReg =** line points to another section in the `.inf` file that contains a list of all keys and/or values that are to be added to the Registry. The **DelReg =** line points to another section in the `.inf` file that contains a list of all keys and/or values that are to be deleted from the Registry. An Add section might look something like this:

```
[Some_Section]
HKCR,txtfile\shell\SomeNewCommand\Command,,,"ZapIt.exe %1"
HKCU,AppEvents\Schemes\Apps\MyNewApp\Open\.Current,,,"tada.wav"
```

The general pattern for these entries is **MajorKey**, **Key**, **Value Name**, **Flags**, **Value Data**. The **MajorKey** is one of the abbreviations

- **HKCR**, which is an abbreviation for **HKEY_CLASSES_ROOT**
- **HKCU**, which is an abbreviation for **HKEY_CURRENT_USER**
- **HKLM**, which is an abbreviation for **HKEY_LOCAL_MACHINE**

and we talk about it later in this chapter. I have absolutely no idea what **Flags** means; I could find no details in any of the documentation, nor could I find any working examples.

The first line adds a new key to the Registry called **HKEY_CLASSES_ROOT\ txtfile\shell\SomeNewCommand** (assuming one does not already exist, of course). That key has a **(Default)** value—all new keys get at least one value with that name—with **(value not set)** for data. In addition, there is a second key that is set up called **HKEY_CLASSES_ROOT\txtfile\shell\ SomeNewCommand\Command**, and it has a **(Default)** value data of **ZapIt.exe %1**. You'll see in the section on **HKCR** how that might be a valid entry, adding a new command to the right-click context menu for text files.

The second line adds the key **HKEY_CURRENT_USER\AppEvents\ Schemes\Apps\ MyNewApp\Open\.Current** to the Registry, with a **(Default)** value data of **tada.wav**.

As you'll see in the section on **HKCU**, this is a legitimate Registry entry that tells Windows to play the **tada.wav** sound every time an application called **MyNewApp** starts.

A Delete section might look like this:

```
[Some_Other_Section]
HKCR,txtfile\shell\SomeNewCommand\Command
HKCU,AppEvents\Schemes\Apps\MyNewApp\Open\.Current,,,"tada.wav"
```

The first line deletes the key **HKEY_CLASSES_ROOT\txtfile\shell\ SomeNewCommand\Command**, but it leaves the key **HKEY_CLASSES_ROOT\ txtfile\shell\SomeNewCommand** intact.

The second line deletes the key **HKEY_CURRENT_USER\AppEvents\ Schemes\Apps\MyNewApp\Open\.Current**, but it leaves all keys above it intact. This line also shows you that you can leave the extraneous garbage **(,,,"tada.wav")** at the end of the line and the key will still be deleted.

As best I can tell, you can have any number of Add and Delete sections in the same **.inf** file, but if a single key or value appears in both an Add and a Delete section, heaven only knows whether the key or value will show up in the Registry after the **.inf** file is through running. Following is a perfectly legitimate Registry-manipulating **.inf** file, which will run on your machine. To run it, simply create a New text document, type this in, rename the file with an **.inf** extension, right click on the file, and pick Install.

```
[Version]
signature="$Chicago$"

[DefaultInstall]
AddReg = MomLikesThis
DelReg = MomSaysGiveItTheHeaveHo

[MomLikesThis]
HKCR,txtfile\shell\SomeNewCommand\Command,,,"ZapIt.exe %1"

[MomSaysGiveItTheHeaveHo]
HKCU,AppEvents\Schemes\Apps\MyNewApp\Open\.Current
HKCR,txtfile\shell\SomeOtherCommand\Command,,,"ZapIt.exe %1"
```

I believe all of this is previously undocumented.

The Mysterious Sixth

That makes five ways to change Registry keys—Regedit, Registry Checker, manually changing `.dat` files, using `.reg` merge files, and "Install"ing `.inf` files.

Think we've hit all the ways of changing the Registry? Well, there's one more way. Sometimes you go in with Regedit and delete a key or a value. Then you come back a day later and the key or value has mysteriously reappeared. Change it or delete it, and a day or two later it comes back again. What could be happening?

There seems to be a small set of settings in `win.ini` that Win98 takes on itself to post to the Registry every time Windows restarts. If you repeatedly delete or change an entry and can't figure out why it's changing back, look first in your `win.ini`.

Note that these settings are *different* from the ones that are migrated from Win3.1 or Win95 to Win98 during installation. They're also different from the settings that are intentionally maintained in `win.ini` for compatibility purposes. These settings are actually copied, wholesale, from `win.ini` to the Registry every time you start Windows.

Final Word on `.reg`

 If you ever need to compare two different `.reg` files to see how they differ, you have to try WinDiff. Install the Windows Resource Kit sampler on the Win98 CD, and it will suddenly appear as file `windiff.exe` in the folder `C:\Program Files\Win98RK`. There isn't much documentation, but there doesn't need to be, eh? Click File, then Compare two files, and WinDiff steps you through opening the files (see Figure 9-9). Click View, then

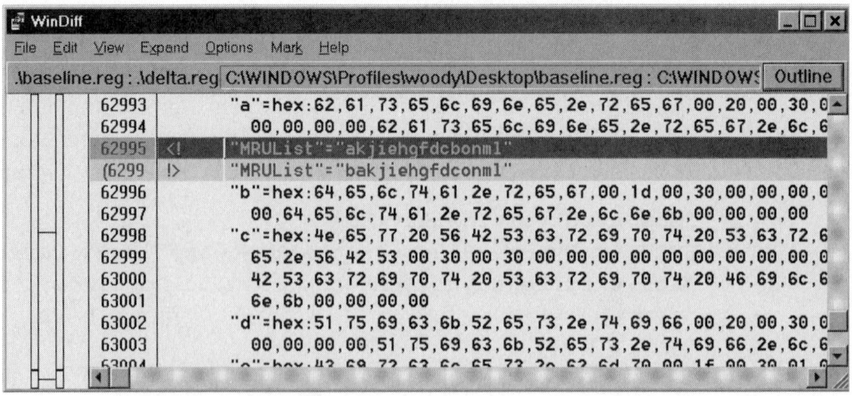

Figure 9-9. WinDiff—the ultimate way to compare files, especially Registry back-up files

Expand, for WinDiff to find all the differences between the two files. Hit **F8** to hop from delta to delta. Very cool.

 One last crucial point before you start poking around with your Registry. The Windows Resource Kit and every book I've seen that discusses **.reg** files would have you believe that you can save a complete backup of the current status of a key or group of keys by exporting a **.reg** file from Regedit. Then, presumably, you can muck around with the key all you want, and if you get into trouble, merging the **.reg** file back into the Registry sets everything right. Well, you now know that that isn't entirely true. If you manually add a value to a key, for example, merging the old **.reg** file won't get rid of the value. If you rename a key, merging the **.reg** file won't remove the renamed key, it'll just restore the old key. In some cases—particularly when Win98 is looking for the presence of a key or a value—that can make a big difference. Using **.reg** files will *not* restore your Registry: to make a full and complete backup, you have to make a copy of the **system.dat**, **user.dat**, and **\profiles\ username\user.dat** files and use them appropriately.

Alternatively, you can save a key to a **.reg** file, do whatever you like to that key in the Registry, then when you're ready to restore the key to its original status, manually delete the key before importing the **.reg** file back into the Registry. This approach leaves you hanging without a key for a while, so use it with extreme caution.

 Some books strongly suggest that you *not* use Regedit directly to change a value or key in the Registry. They insist that it's better to export a Registry key, make changes to the resulting **.reg** file, and then merge the changed key. I say balderdash. While it's certainly important to make a backup of any key before changing it—and an overall backup of the entire Registry from time to time, too—this slavish insistence on only editing a **.reg** text file is a crock.

Just for starters, you can't delete or rename keys or values using a **.reg** file: if you want to delete anything, you have to go in with Regedit and do it manually. More than that, though, mucking around with the **"oops"="C:\\weird\\\".reg\\file\\\"format"** is a pain in the neck. Miss one of those dumb doubled-up backslashes, or type in a quote without a requisite backslash, and you not only screw up the Registry setting, the merge is so dumb you'll never even know something went wrong!

Besides, manually editing **.reg** files adds several extra steps to the process of editing the Registry—you have to export the key, use a text editor, then re-merge the key—without giving you any benefit.

 Working with **.reg** files often leads to errors. It's slow. It's cumbersome. And it doesn't add any safety to the process. So why bother? Keep good backups, and use Regedit directly.

■ Gettin' Around

Whatever deceives seems to exercise a kind of magical enchantment.

—PLATO, *The Republic,* ca. 350 B.C.

 It's taken me this long to poke around the periphery of the Registry, and for that I apologize, but it's important that you know whence the Registry originates and how you can safely change it. Now it's time to jump in with both feet.

You may find some of what follows rather rocky going. As is so often the case in Win98, there are dozens of new concepts you need to "get"—and for everything to make sense, you have to "get" them all at the same time. The Registry is a very complicated place. So take your time, and bite off small chunks. Make sure you have your computer handy, and follow along in Regedit as we take a look.

The Registry, as mentioned earlier, consists of six major keys (I call them "root keys," but you can call 'em chicken soup, if you like). Figure 9-10 shows you what the root keys look like from Regedit's point of view.

If you've read this far in Chapter 9, it probably won't surprise you one bit to discover that there's some real sleight of hand going on here. For openers, there are really just three root keys, and one of those three can't be changed at all by you. And therein lies a story . . .

Aliases

The root key **HKEY_CURRENT_CONFIG** is a sham. It's just an alias, a handy bit of shorthand that points to the current configuration information in **HKEY_LOCAL_MACHINE**. If you have just one hardware profile, or if you have multiple hardware profiles but Win98 is currently using the first profile, the current configuration information is in **HKLM\Config\0001**; **HKEY_CURRENT_CONFIG** is the same thing as **HKLM\Config\0001**. What do I mean by "the same thing"? Pop into Regedit and scroll down to **HKLM\ Confg\0001\Display**. Double click on **(Default)** and give it a value of **Mom says HI**. Scroll down to **HKEY_CURRENT_CONFIG\Display**. See how

Figure 9-10.
Root keys

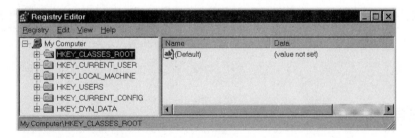

Figure 9-11.
Mom says HI in
a replicated key

the value has changed, as in Figure 9-11? Now single click on **(Default)**
and hit **Del**. The value data turns into **(value not set)**, right? Scroll back
to **HKLM\Config\0001\Display**. It's reverted to **(value not set)**, yes?

Three of the root keys are really aliases for other keys. Microsoft set them
up that way to make it easier for programmers to get in and out of frequently
used parts of the Registry. For example, a program that makes changes to entries
for the current hardware configuration could monkey around with **HKLM**, query
the Registry to see which hardware profile is in use (it's almost always **\0001**),
and then work directly with **HKLM\Config\0001** (or whichever hardware profile happens to be in effect). Instead of requiring programmers to go through
all that garbage, it's far, far simpler for the Registry to set up this pseudokey
called **HKEY_CURRENT_CONFIG** and just point it to **HKLM\Config\0001** (or
whichever hardware profile happens to be in effect). That way, programmers
need only monkey around with the aliased key **HKEY_CURRENT_CONFIG**, and
the system will take care of the rest.

Let's take an eagle's-eye view of the Registry's root keys and how they are
interrelated.

Classes

 The root key **HKEY_CLASSES_ROOT** (**HKCR**) is an alias for **HKLM**
Software\CLASSES. It's a huge key; on my test machine—the one
with very little application software—there are more than 800 subkeys
for this key alone. This is where Windows goes when it wants to associate a filename extension with a particular program or a group of Windows objects with actions on the objects. When you double click on a filename, run
something with the Start/Run command, or right click on just about anything,
Windows checks this key to see what to do. I talk about **HKCR** extensively, as it
harbors a very large percentage of Win98's cool power-user tricks.

 We actually put **HKCR** at the top of Regedit to make it easier for users
to find the settings they want to look at most often. Not that I'm encouraging people to change their Registry settings manually, of course.

Current User

The **HKEY_CURRENT_USER (HKCU)** root key is also an alias. If there is only one user profile, it's an alias for **HKEY_USERS\.Default**. If the machine is set up for multiple user profiles, it's an alias for the **HKEY_USERS\username** associated with the currently logged-on user, or, if the user bypassed the logon screen, **HKEY_USERS\.Default**.

HKCU was set up as an alias to keep programmers from having to constantly figure out which user is currently logged on to the machine.

Much information about Windows itself sits in the key **HKCU\Software\Microsoft\Windows\CurrentVersion** and the keys directly underneath it. I talk about **HKCU** extensively in the rest of this chapter: it's a whole lot easier than constantly referring to "the **HKEY_USERS** key for the currently logged-on user."

Speaking of convenience, why in hell do I have to click down seven levels in the Registry to get to the Windows settings? If Microsoft is going to insist that it takes seven-level and eight-level keys to organize its own information (like, say, **HKCU\Software\Microsoft\Windows\CurrentVersion\Explorer\Streams\12**), the least they could do is provide easy ways to get to the common fifth-level keys like **HKCU\Software\Microsoft\Windows\CurrentVersion**. There should be some sort of bookmark capability or at least a handful of common keys with icons on a toolbar, for heaven's sake.

Local Machine

HKEY_LOCAL_MACHINE (HKLM) contains information about the PC, the information stored in **system.dat**. I talk about **HKLM** extensively later in this chapter, too.

The big key in **HKLM** is **HKLM\Software\Microsoft\Windows\CurrentVersion**, which is roughly analogous to the **HKCU** key with a similar name but generally includes machine-dependent (instead of user-dependent) data.

That reminds me of one of Microsoft's best manglings of the English language. Everywhere you look in Windows 98—even in Tweak UI, for heaven's sake—you find reference to "per-user" and "per-machine" settings. As far as I can tell, a "per-user" setting is one that changes when the logged-on user changes. As such, it usually refers to a setting stored away either in HKCU or in one of the **\windows\profiles** folders. A "per-machine" setting is one that doesn't change when the logged-on user changes. As such, it's likely to be stored in HKLM or some folder other than **\profiles**.

Users

The root key **HKEY_USERS** has either two or three subkeys. On a single user profile machine, there's one subkey called **HKEY_USERS\.Default** (note the period) and another called **HKEY_USERS\Software**. Same on a multiple user profile machine where the currently active user bypassed the network logon: there are only **\.Default** and **\Software** subkeys. On a multiple user profile machine with a logged-on user, there's a **\.Default** subkey, a **\Software** subkey, plus one more subkey for the active user. The name of the subkey is the same as the logon user name of the user, which in turn is the same as the name of the **\windows\profiles\username** folder (Figure 9-12).

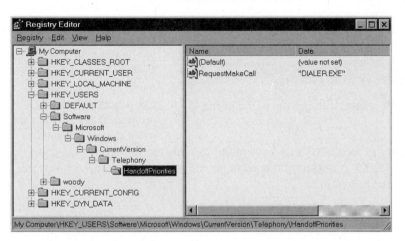

Figure 9-12. HKEY_USERS with user Woody logged on

Lots of sources, including the WRK, tell you that there are **HKEY_USERS** subkeys for all valid users: "This key contains information about all the users who log on to the computer." That isn't true, as a quick glance at any multiple user profile machine's Regedit confirms. If it were true, you could go in and monkey around with other users' settings—a definite no-no. Amazing how many books and articles just parrot the official documentation, without even looking at the real world, eh?

 That **\Software** subkey no doubt started as a wonderful attempt to collect all the settings that should be valid for most users, much as the new **C:\Windows\Application Data** folder picks up settings that don't necessarily apply to the **\profiles**. Pity Microsoft didn't implement it. I looked high and low and couldn't find any settings other than the really absurd one you see in Figure 9-12, which must have something to do with Telephony.

I don't refer to **HKEY_USERS** very often simply because the data you're most likely interested in changing sits inside the alias **HKCU**.

Current Configuration

Root key **HKEY_CURRENT_CONFIG** is another alias, as explained in the preceding section, "Aliases." This one points to the currently active hardware profile, most commonly **HKLM\Config\0001**.

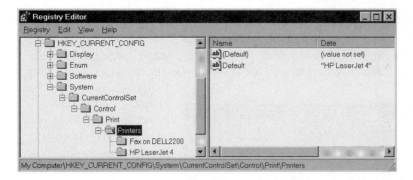

Figure 9-13. Use `HKEY_CURRENT_CONFIG` to get the name of the active printer

We don't talk about `HKEY_CURRENT_CONFIG` in the rest of this chapter because none of the `HKLM\Config\0001` information is particularly interesting, with one exception. If you're browsing quickly through the Registry to retrieve the name of the currently active printer (or writing a program that needs to find it, for that matter) and there's any chance the PC may have multiple hardware configurations, you should use `HKEY_CURRENT_CONFIG` to get the name, per Figure 9-13, instead of `HKLM\Config\0001`.

Dynamic Data

Quite probably the least understood key of all, the third real root key `HKEY_DYN_DATA` contains information about the current hardware configuration (in the `\Config Manager\Enum` subkey), in addition to a whole slew of performance data (in `\PerfStats`).

It's important to realize that the `\Enum` subkey here really does describe the machine in its current state—Plug and Play devices and all. `\Enum` is maintained dynamically. On startup, once the profile has been established, Win98 uses `HKLM` hardware information (generally stored in keys identified by `\0000`, for hardware that isn't dependent on the profile, or the profile number, such as `\0001`) to configure the machine, and all the information on the current configuration is transferred to `HKEY_DYN_DATA`.

As an example, Figure 9-14 shows the kind of information that's stored for your PC's programmable interrupt controller. The `HardWareKey` value here points to detailed information stored in `HKLM`, per Figure 9-15.

Figure 9-14. `HKEY_DYN_DATA` information on the programmable interrupt controller

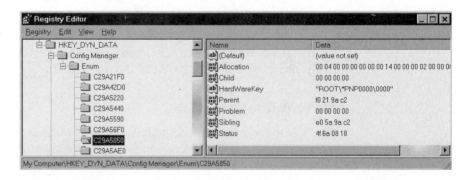

Figure 9-15.
Detailed PIC data referred to by HKEY_DYN_DATA

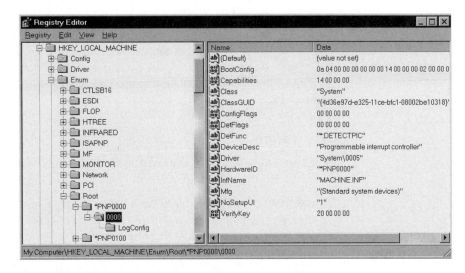

Since the PIC is always the same, regardless of hardware profile, its information is stored in a key named **\0000**. Similar information for, say, a monitor—which can be changed, based on hardware profile—is stored in keys named **HKLM\Enum\MONITOR\DEFAULT_MONITOR\0001, \0002, . . .** where the number of keys depends on the number of hardware profiles defined on the machine.

 Although you can't change any of the values in **HKEY_DYN_DATA**, the **\Enum** subkey is the ultimate place to go if you need the absolute truth on what Windows thinks is attached to your PC. By following the pointers there back to **HKLM\Enum**, where human-readable hardware descriptions await, you can tell precisely what hardware is active.

Now let's go through each of the big three root keys one at a time and see what kind of mischief we can get into.

■ HKCR

Half the world knows not how the other half lives.

—George Herbert, *Outlandish Proverbs,* 1640

The **HKEY_CLASSES_ROOT** key (or **HKCR**) is an alias for **HKLM\Software\ Classes**. It's a machine-related key, stored in **system.dat**, that doesn't vary depending on which user has logged on. It's used to store information about file types, entries on right-click context menus, and some property sheets.

Wait a minute. You think I'm going to buy the Microsoft Party Line about **system.dat** containing all the data in **HKLM** and **user.dat** storing all the data in **HKCU**? I don't believe it for a second. It's too clean, and Win98 is anything but clean. I bet if you looked hard enough, you'd find some of the **HKCU** data in **system.dat** and some of the **HKLM** data in **user.dat**.

Orientation

HKCR contains hundreds of entries. The sheer volume can be overwhelming until you discover that there are really only six different kinds of entries.

- **HKCR*** key, which contains links to commands that will (1) appear whenever you right click on any file or (2) create new property sheet tabs when you bring up the property sheet for any file

- **HKCR\CLSID** key, which lists "class IDs"—those mysterious 32-character identification numbers (commonly called CLSIDs)—and the icons, programs, and various settings associated with each CLSID

- Hundreds of **HKCR\.extension** keys, identifiable by the period at the beginning of the subkey name, each of which associates that particular filename extension with a program ID (which I'll call a ProgID)

- Hundreds of **HKCR\ProgID** keys, which contain commands appropriate for the ProgID—such as Open or Print—plus icons and occasional miscellaneous information pertaining to the ProgID

- **HKCR\Unknown** key, which behaves much like a **HKCR\ProgID** subkey but applies to files with extensions that don't appear in **HKCR** (Figure 9-16)

- If you have QuickView installed (it isn't part of the default installation; see Chapter 3), the **HKCR\QuickView** key lists all the filename extensions for files that have supported QuickView viewers.

 I get into details momentarily, but I want you to pause and consider one thing. Perhaps the single most brilliant part of the design of Win98 is its ability—even its *willingness*—to have programmers and users go in and change these settings. When you hear that Win98 has an "extensible shell" or when you read that a package has "Windows shell extensions" or when you install a new software package and suddenly find that it has put its tentacles into all sorts of fancy places (right-click context menus, say, or property sheets), this is where the magic originates.

Figure 9-16.
HKCR\Unknown key

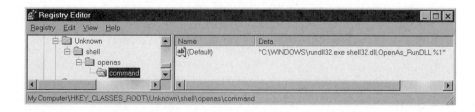

Thank you, thank you. Actually, it took quite a leap of faith on the part of our developers to put these extensibility hooks into Windows so that developers can weave their new programs into the fabric of Windows itself instead of patching onto the periphery with jackhammers and earthmovers. In the past we tended to build monolithic, insular systems, thinking that we were giving our users the best possible technology and discouraging developers and advanced users from piddling around in places they didn't belong. What we found, though, was that developers and advanced users would hack into the bloody thing anyway. Taking a cue from our applications people (where Word was, arguably, the first significantly user-extensible Windows application), we decided that, this time around, we'd build Windows so that it could be customized reliably by thousands of developers—thus, shell extensions like these.

That's a nice sales pitch, Billy, but I think what you really found was that you couldn't keep up with all the other developers. Microsoft doesn't have a monopoly on smarts, you know, and these other developers brought important new ideas to the party that Microsoft either didn't think about or decided not to implement. By giving them solid hooks into Win98 itself, Windows could start looking more like an easily extensible, customizable system, instead of an unstable deck of cards that threatened to collapse each time an outside developer had a great new idea.

Whatever your religious inclinations, the simple fact is that these **HKCR** keys give users and developers alike an unparalleled opportunity to customize the way Win98 works. We show you in Chapter 3 how a few changes to **HKCR** can turn the dumb way Win98 handles Explorer windows into a much smarter configuration. Now we're going to show you the rest of the story.

\.extension to \ProgID and Back

By far the majority of entries in **HKCR** are **HKCR\.extension** subkeys that point to **HKCR\ProgID**s and the **HKCR\ProgID** subkeys. The method Win98 uses to link extensions to ProgIDs is simplicity itself. Take simple text files, the ones with a **.txt** extension. Figure 9-17 shows you how Win98 has associated the **.txt** extension with the ProgID called **txtfile**, using the **(Default)** value for the **HKCR\.txt** key. If you look in your Registry, you find the same association.

When Win98 needs to know what to do with a **.txt** file, it looks in **HKCR** for a key called **HKCR\.txt**. It then takes the **(Default)** value of that key and uses the

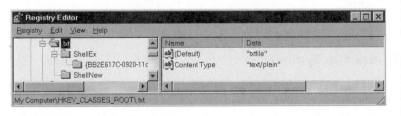

Figure 9-17. .txt in the Registry

Figure 9-18.
Associated
`txtfile` entry

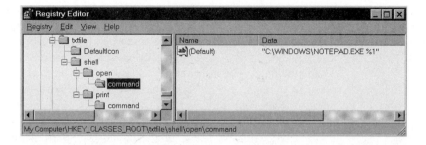

Figure 9-19.
Icon specified by
an icon number
of 1

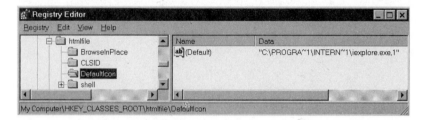

value data to search for a ProgID—in this case, **`HKCR\txtfile`**. Figure 9-18 shows you what the **`txtfile`** ProgID entry in the Registry looks like.

Multiple **`HKCR\.extension`** keys may point to the same ProgID. For example, unless you've done something to change it, if you look in your Registry you find that both **`HKCR\.htm`** and **`HKCR\.html`** point to the ProgID **`htmlfile`**, which is the ProgID for HTML files. Also note that the extensions need not be three characters long: they go from one character on up.

 If you look at Figure 9-19, you see how the **`HKCR\htmlfile\`** **`DefaultIcon`** key contains information Win98 uses to produce an icon (on the Desktop or in Explorer) for each file with the **`.htm`** or **`.html`** extension. The **`(Default)`** value of this key follows the usual Win98 icon-naming conventions, that is, it contains the name of a file containing an icon (generally, a **`.dll`**, **`.exe`**, or **`.ico`** file) and if the file has more than one icon in it, a number that points to which icon you've chosen. Icon numbers start at zero, so the value data **`C:\PROGRA~1\INTERN~1\iexplore.exe,1`** in this entry would signify the second icon in the file **`iexplore.exe`**.

 This is a great example because it also shows how Windows 98 hard-codes the "~1"-style shortened filenames into some Registry entries.

ProgIDs and File Types

The **`HKCR\txtfile\shell`** key (Figure 9-18) holds all the details Windows itself needs to handle **`txtfiles`**, and that gets a little complicated.

If you open up Explorer, click View, then Folder Options, bring up the File Types tab, and scroll down to the Text Document line, you see something like

---

Figure 9-20.
txtfile entry in
Explorer's
View/Options
dialog

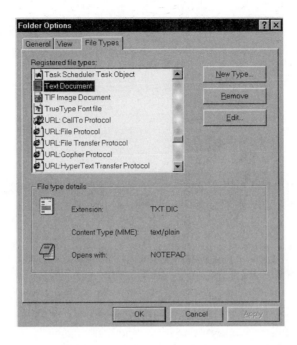

Figure 9-20. Every time you open the File Types dialog, it looks at all the entries in **HKCR** and builds a big table, listing all **HKCR\.extension** keys, their associated **HKCR\ProgID** keys, and a whole bunch of ancillary stuff. The Registered File Types list in Figure 9-20 is constructed in a rather complex way.

- Windows scans all the **HKCR\.extension** keys and keeps track of all the referenced ProgIDs. These are potential candidates for inclusion in the Registered File Types list box in Figure 9-20.

- Windows then looks at all the **HKCR\ProgID** keys that were referenced by **HKCR\.extension** keys. It collects the **(Default)** values associated with those keys. If the **(Default)** value data is **(value not set)**, that **HKCR\ProgID** is ignored. Otherwise, the **(Default)** value data is used as a potential entry in the Registered File Types list box.

- Finally, Windows looks for values called **EditFlags** under each of the **HKCR\ProgID** keys. If it finds an **EditFlags** value name, the value data may force Windows to either include or exclude this key from the Registered File Types list box. For example, in this way, a ProgID like Drive appears on the list even though it has no associated extension. I discuss all the **EditFlags** in the section, uh, "Edit Flags," coming up in a bit.

Figure 9-21.
Where the "Text
Document" de-
scription comes
from

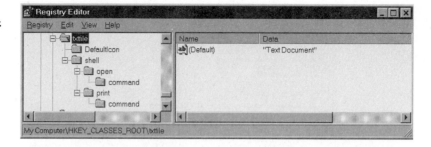

Figure 9-22.
HKCR\.DIC also
points to
txtfile

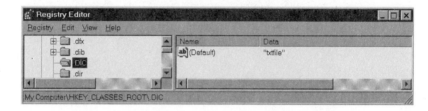

As you can see from Figure 9-21, the **HKCR\txtfile** key's **(Default)** value data is **"Text Document"**, and that's the entry that gets put in Figure 9-20's Registered File Types list box. If you look at the File Type Details box in Figure 9-20, you see that the File Types tab can tell you a few more things about the **txtfile** ProgID (although, surprisingly, the ProgID itself never appears).

- The Extension line tells you which **HKCR\.extension** keys point to **HKCR\txtfile**. In this case, **HKCR\.txt** and **HKCR\.DIC** (**.DIC** being the extension for Microsoft Office dictionary files; see Figure 9-22) both point to **HKCR\txtfile**.

- The Content Type (MIME) line just displays the data of the **Content Type** value in the **HKCR\.txt** key, as in Figure 9-17, which is supposed to tell you something about the kind of Internet Multimedia Extensions data that would be included in a Net file with this extension.

- The Opens With line actually traces all the way down the **HKCR\txtfile\ shell\open\command** key (see Figure 9-18) and extracts the name of the program stored as that key's **(Default)** value. It also retrieves the icon associated with that program and displays it here. Pretty impressive, no?

 If you click once on Text Document in Figure 9-20 and then click Edit, you get something that looks like the Edit File Type box shown in Figure 9-23. I go into some detail on the Actions box momentarily, but first let's look at the less interesting features of the Edit File Type box.

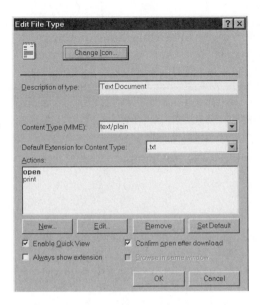

Figure 9-23. Edit `txtfile`

- If you click Change Icon, you have an opportunity to change the contents of the **HKCR\txtfile\DefaultIcon** key, which in turn affects the icon displayed in front of all **txtfile** files in Explorer or on the Desktop. Note in particular how you can change only the icon for the entire ProgID, not the icons for individual extensions.

- If you change Description of Type, you modify the **(Default)** value data for **HKCR\txtfile**, just as you would expect.

- The Content Type and Default Extension boxes merely let you choose from all the **HKCR\.extension** values that go into this ProgID. (Recall that **Content Type** is a value of the extension, not the ProgID, so there may be several of them.) Since **txtfile** has two associated extensions, **HKCR\.txt** and **HKCR\.DIC**, there are two choices in the Default Extension box.

- Down at the bottom, unchecking the "Enable QuickView" box removes the entry in the **HKCR\QuickView** subkey for the filename extension listed in the Default Extension box—in this case, **.txt**. Curiously, checking the "Enable QuickView" box doesn't restore the **.txt** entry in **HKCR\QuickView** but instead puts a **\QuickView** subkey underneath the ProgID (in this case **txtfile**), with a **(Default)** value of *. The presence of the **HKCR\txtfile\QuickView** key adds QuickView to the right-click context menu for all **txtfiles**, as we see in a moment in the section "Keys and Context Menus."

- The "Always show extension" box creates a value in the **HKCR\txtfile** key called **AlwaysShowExt**. The data for that value doesn't matter—all that's important is the presence of the value. When Explorer finds a ProgID with an **AlwaysShowExt** value, it always shows the filename extension for that ProgID, even when the View/Options box marked "Hide MS-DOS file extensions for file types that are registered" box is checked. If you've ever wondered why **.dll** (ProgID = **dllfile**) and **.sys** files (ProgID = **sysfile**) always appear in Explorer with their filename extensions, look at their ProgID keys and you'll see that they have an **AlwaysShowExt** value. Note that **AlwaysShowExt** is a valid value for **HKCR\ProgID** keys only: if you put an **AlwaysShowExt** value in an **HKCR\.extension** key, it will have no effect. There's also a value called **NeverShowExt** that does precisely the opposite. (Look at **HKCR\DocShortcut**, **HKCR\lnkfile**, **HKCR\piffile**, and **HKCR\ShellScrap** for samples.) It has to be set manually.

For what it's worth, there's a value called **NoExtension** that is used for Briefcase files. If you look at **HKCR\.bfc\ShellNew\Config** you probably see a **NoExtension** value. Briefcases never have extensions. The **.bfc** entry here is a complete phantom. The only reason for its existence, as far as I can tell, is to provide a place for the **HKCR\.bfc\ShellNew** key so that New Briefcase will show up in the Desktop's right-click New menu. Apparently **NoExtension** was invented to keep this little kludge from confusing users. Oh, how I love a nice kludge in the mornin'!

So much for the easy parts of the Edit File Type dialog. Let's look at the tough one.

\shell

The Actions box in the Edit File Type dialog (Figure 9-23) puts a pretty, relatively easy-to-use face on one of the most powerful features of Win98. It lets you define new entries for the right-click context menus and, in some cases, lets you choose the "default" action—the one that Win98 takes when you double click on a filename. To really understand what's going on, though—and to see how Win98 occasionally screws things up royally—you really have to see how changes here are reflected in the Registry.

Pick the first action in the alphabetical list, the one marked **open**, and click Edit. You should get a dialog similar to that in Figure 9-24. See how the command **C:\windows\notepad.exe** in Figure 9-24 is translated into the similar (but different) command **C:\windows\notepad.exe %1** in the Registry, Figure 9-18? **%1** says to Windows, "Put the name of the current file right here before you run the command."

It's all automatic. Any command entered into the Editing action for type: dialog for a particular action name gets a **%1** stuck on the end, and the resulting command goes into the Registry's **\shell\actionname\command** key's **(Default)** value.

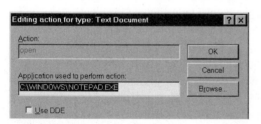

Figure 9-24. open File Type

If you go back to the Edit File Type dialog, click on the **print** action, and click Edit, you see how the print action actually happens—with a **/p** command line switch fed to Notepad, as in Figure 9-25. The resulting Registry entry (Figure 9-26) once again gets a **%1** appended to it. That **%1** is all well and good for some programs, but for others it can be the kiss of death. See the section "%1 Bugs" later in this chapter.

The "Use DDE" box at the bottom of the dialogs in Figures 9-24 and 9-25 opens up an extended box that lets you enter Dynamic Data Exchange commands (Figure 9-27), which are placed in the **\shell\actionname\ddeexec** key and keys underneath it (Figure 9-28).

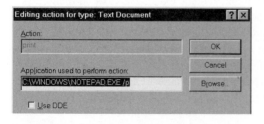

Figure 9-25. print in File Type

**Figure 9-26.
print in the
Registry**

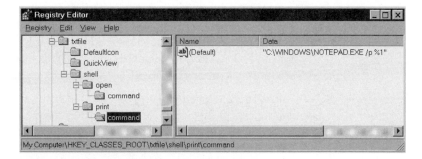

**Figure 9-27.
DDE for Word
2000 in File Type**

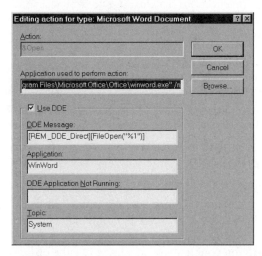

**Figure 9-28.
DDE instructions
located in the
Registry**

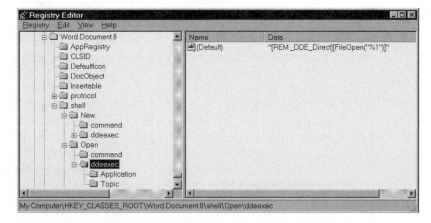

The standard Word 2000 **.doc** file open command **(ProgID =
Word.Document.8)** is implemented as a DDE command. If you have Word
2000 installed on your machine, look at the Explorer File Type called Microsoft
Word Document and the key **HKCR\Word.Document.8**. Oh—in case you
wondered, the **/n** switch on the Word command line starts Word without a
default document, the **Document1** you probably know and love.

A thorough discussion of DDE is beyond the scope of this book, but suffice it to say that you can use DDE in many situations where a command line doesn't give you all the options you need to implement a particular action. Many more details are in *Windows 3.1 Programming for Mere Mortals*, by, uh, Woody Leonhard.

 Far as I'm concerned, it's very odd that Explorer and the Registry only implement old-fashioned Dynamic Data Exchange, and not OLE Automation—er, ActiveX technology—which is infinitely more flexible and more stable, especially under Win98. Microsoft probably figured it would have to create an entire macro language to drive OLE Auto—or force people to buy Visual Basic 6, which would be a very popular decision, all the way from the front page of *InfoWorld* to the most obscure offices at the Justice Department. Oh, well. Gotta leave something for Win00, I guess.

 Before I leave the **\shell** discussion, I should mention that a very few **HKCR\.extension** keys have **\shell** subkeys under them. (The **\shell** subkeys almost always go underneath **HKCR\ProgID** keys.) I've been told that these **\shell** subkeys exist for backward compatibility.

Default Action

Let me cap the discussion of the things you can do with Explorer to change **HKCR** by looking at the so-called "default action" for ProgIDs. Move back to the Edit File Type box (Figure 9-23) for a moment. See how the **open** action name is highlighted? That's because **open** is the default action for **txtfiles**—if you double click on a **txtfile** the **open** action is invoked; if you right click on a **txtfile**, **open** is highlighted.

Most of the time, the default action for a ProgID key is **open**. Notable exceptions include audio files, where the default action is **play**. In general, you can change the default action for a ProgID by clicking the action you want to become the default in the Edit File Type dialog, then clicking Set Default. (Sometimes Edit Flags prevent you from doing so; see "Edit Flags" later in this chapter.)

The new default action is stored in the **HKCR\ProgID\shell** key as the **(Default)** value. If the **(Default)** value data is **(value not set)** or an empty string, a default action of **open** is always assumed, if that action exists. If it does not exist, the default action is chosen from the other so-called canonical verbs (**print**, **explorer**, **find**, **openas**, and **properties**), if any of those exist. And if none of those exist, the first action, listed alphabetically, becomes the default action—although it isn't advertised as such on the Edit File Type dialog.

HKCR* and \unknown

Now that you know how the **HKCR\.extension** keys are related to **HKCR\ProgID** keys, **HKCR*** and **\unknown** should be pretty obvious. The **HKCR*** key contains entries that apply to all files, regardless of their filename extension.

The **HKCR\Unknown** key contains entries that apply to files with extensions that do not have an **HKCR\.extension** key. Not surprisingly, the **HKCR\Unknown** key contains an **AlwaysShowExt** value so that Explorer will always show the unregistered filename extension. Its default action (and only action, for that matter) is **openas**. This is the only **openas** action that appears in the default Windows SetUp. When Windows encounters an **openas** command, it is translated to Open With on the context menu.

 Many files without recognized extensions are ASCII text files. You might want to add an action for **HKCR\Unknown** called **notepad**.

Directory, Drive, Folder

Files, files, files. All we've been talking about so far is files. Well, Windows does a lot more than files, and **HKCR** covers many nonfile bases. Just for starters, **HKCR** has four **ProgID** keys that have nothing to do with files.

- **HKCR\Folder** contains information used whenever you right click on a "virtual" folder, like My Computer, Network Neighborhood, Printers, or Dial-Up Networking, or bring up a property sheet for a folder. (By "virtual" folder, I mean one that isn't physically a folder on a disk drive.) Actions are **explore**, which just cranks up Explorer, and **open**.

- **HKCR\Drive** holds information used when you right click on a drive or bring up a property sheet for a drive. (More accurately, **\Drive** refers to root directories, including those on mapped drives.) The only action in a fresh Windows installation is **find**. (If you took our advice in Chapter 3 to make Explorer smart, **open** is also an action, as are several others if you followed all our advice.) Windows has some built-in code that makes **HKCR\Drive** a daughter of **HKCR\Folder**, in the sense that whenever you do something that would use the contents of **HKCR\Drive** Registry keys, Windows behaves as if all the entries under the **HKCR\Folder** key were stuck under **HKCR\Drive**, too. So, for example, the **explore** action from **HKCR\Folder** shows up on the context menu when you right click on a drive.

- **HKCR\Directory** has the settings for physical folders—those things that used to be known, in pre-Win95 days, as directories. The only action is **find**—again, unless you followed along in Chapter 3, in which case you have **find**, **open**, and several others. Windows also treats **HKCR\Directory** as a daughter of **HKCR\Folder**.

- **HKCR\AudioCD**, similarly, has nothing to do with files. It has one action, **play**. Amazingly, though, in the Win98 hierarchy, **HKCR\AudioCD** is considered to be a daughter of **HKCR\Drive** (which, in turn, is a daughter of **HKCR\Folder**).

All this daughter key cum object-oriented inheritance would be very touching if it were implemented worth a damn. As it stands, the only Registry inheritance is this obscure four-way interaction with **Folder** as the, uh, mother, **Drive** and **Directory** as the two daughters, and **AudioCD** hanging off **Drive** like a neglected stepsister. It's hardcoded into Windows; there's no way to set up your own inheritance schemes and it isn't documented anywhere. Worst of all, the "inheritance" doesn't obey any traditional inheritance rules: stick an **open** command in **Folder** and another one in **Drive**, and they *both* show up on the context menu! Sheesh.

HKCR\CLSID

Perhaps the most important nonfile part of **HKCR** revolves around treatment of class IDs, numbers that uniquely identify programs, commonly called **CLSID**s. No doubt you've seen class IDs. They're written down as 32-hex characters in an 8-4-4-4-12 pattern, like this: {21ec2020-3aea-1069-a2dd-08002b30309d}. Pretty hard to miss. Lots of Win98 tricks in books and magazines use **CLSID**s, but the articles always seem to start mumbling when trying to explain *why* the tricks work. That's too bad, really, because the concept is pretty simple, and the implementation in Win98 isn't that much more complicated.

Microsoft has set up a simple way for programmers to come up with a unique number, a unique **CLSID**, for each program they create. The procedure for getting the number isn't really important; the important point is that each **CLSID** is unique, so Program A from Adams Amalgamated in Atlanta has a different number from Program D from Dubious Distribution in Dubuque, and both of those numbers are different from the hundreds of numbers Microsoft has assigned to its hundreds of programs in Win98.

All right, you want the details, don't you? Inquisitive bugger. There's a program called **guidgen.exe** in the Win98 Software Development Kit. For some reason a different program called **uuidgen.exe** is included with the Win98 Driver Development Kit. When you run either program, it looks at the current machine's network card for the unique number assigned by the board manufacturers, combines that information with the current day and time, and pops out a unique 32-hex-character number. The chances of any two different copies of **guidgen.exe** or **uuidgen.exe** running on two different machines coming up with the same **CLSID** are roughly equivalent to the chances of the Beatles getting back together and giving a free concert on top of the Apple building in January 2099, or the chances that Bill really knew all the lyrics of the Stones' tune "Start Me Up" before he bought the rights.

You already know that when Win98 wants to figure out how to handle, oh, **.txt** files, it looks in the Registry for **HKCR\.txt** and proceeds from that point. In a very similar manner, every time Win98 encounters a `CLSID`, it looks up the `CLSID` in `HKCR\CLSID` and runs the indicated program, which is usually a standard Windows `.dll` file.

What's a little bit different is the myriad ways Win98 can bump into a `CLSID`. Let me try to list all the ways I know about (this is probably far from exhaustive).

- A `CLSID` can appear as a filename extension. Just as the `.txt` extension triggers a lookup in the Registry for `HKCR\.txt`, a `CLSID` extension also triggers a lookup in `HKCR\CLSID`. I haven't been able to get this to do anything interesting, but if you put the `CLSID` for a particular application (for example, Excel) at the end of a filename, Explorer will show the file to be of that type (Excel Spreadsheet).

- A `CLSID` can appear as the filename extension for an entry on the Start Menu. This is the mechanism behind the trick for putting the Control Panel, Printers, or Dial-Up Networking flyouts on the Start Menu, as described in Chapter 3. When your mouse goes over the Control Panel entry on the Start Menu, Win98 looks at the filename of the entry, strips off the `CLSID` filename extension, looks in `HKCR\CLSID\{21ec2020-3aea-1069-a2dd-08002b30309d}`, and brings up the indicated program (from the `InProcServer` key), which is smart enough to say, "Oh! I'm on the Start Menu! I better show the Control Panel flyout."

- A `CLSID` can appear as a value or even a key in the Registry. Take a look at Figure 9-29, a shot of `HKCR\*\shellex\PropertySheetHandlers`, for examples of both. When Win98 is looking for a program in the Registry and hits a `CLSID`, it just jumps down to `HKCR\CLSID` and runs the indicated program. Programmers call this sort of setup a level of indirection.

- A `CLSID` can appear as the "extension" name of a folder. You didn't know folders could have extensions? Try this: right click on the Desktop, pick New, Folder. Type in a name like this: `mom.{21ec2020-3aea-1069-a2dd-08002b30309d}`. Hit `Enter`. See how the `CLSID` for the Control Panel (the monstrosity that starts out `{21...}`) turned this plain-Jane folder into a copy of your Control Panel folder? (Go ahead and hit `Del` to get rid of the folder: don't worry, you won't delete any of the Control Panel applets.)

Figure 9-29.
Dueling CLSIDs

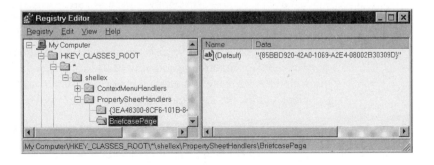

Figure 9-30.
Common CLSID
entry

If you look at your **HKCR\CLSID** entries, by far the most common situation is for the **CLSID** itself to be assigned a name in the **(Default)** value and for the key to have one or two subkeys, called **\InprocServer** and/or **\InprocServer32** (see Figure 9-30). Those subkeys, more often than not, contain the names of programs called by Win98 to handle OLE with the named application.

Why does this have to be so complicated? I mean, why use **CLSID**s at all? Why not just put program names in there and have Win98 use standard program names?

 I can see three good reasons to use **CLSID**s.

- They're a uniform way of approaching a potentially weird syntax. (Can you imagine having a folder called **folderoll.C:\windows\ program files\myapp.dll**?)

- They alleviate the problems with duplicate program names. (What if two different companies come up with very different programs called **foobar.dll**?)

- There's some potential for simplifying updates—to specify a new handler for a given **CLSID**, an installation program need only change the **HKCR\CLSID** entry, instead of trying to hopscotch throughout the entire Registry.

Besides, OLE needs **CLSID**s, so why not?

Keys and Context Menus

You've seen how the **HKCR\.extension** and **HKCR\ProgID** keys are constructed and how parts of the keys can be maintained by Explorer's View/ Options File Types tab. You've also seen how the **HKCR\Folder**, **\Drive**, and **\Directory** keys interrelate and how **CLSID**s set up a single-level indirection, both within the Registry and out in the world of Win98 as a whole. Now, let's take a look at how the keys and values change the way Win98 works.

Figure 9-31. Right click on a .txt file

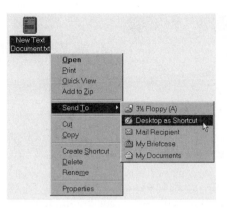

Tweak UI Alert! *Everything discussed in this section can be changed by using Tweak UI. If you want to make the change—and couldn't care less about learning how or why it works—use Tweak UI. It's discussed at length in Chapter 8.*

When you right click on a file, either in Explorer or on the Desktop, Win98 creates a context menu like the one shown in Figure 9-31. In Chapter 3 I talk about the items on the context menu below the first horizontal line— how Send To connects to the **\windows\SendTo** folder, and so on. Now you're in a position to see how the top items come into being.

When you right click on a **.txt** file, Win98 looks in the Registry for **HKCR\.txt**. The **(Default)** value of the **\.txt** key is **txtfile**, so Win98 looks at **HKCR\txtfile**. In this example, the key **HKCR\txtfile** has three subkeys.

- **HKCR\txtfile\DefaultIcon**, which specifies the icon you see above the **.txt** filename in Figure 9-31. (This key also controls which icon you see in Explorer.) I talk more about **DefaultIcon** shortly.

- **HKCR\txtfile\QuickView**, with a single value of **(Default)**. Apparently this key works with QuickView, though I'm not sure why or how.

- **HKCR\txtfile\shell**, which has two subkeys, **HKCR\txtfile\ shell\open** and **HKCR\txtfile\shell\print**. Since the single value in the **\open** key is **(Default) (value not set)**, per Figure 9-32, Win98 uses the name of the key—**Open**—as the first context menu choice. If **(Default)** had a value other than **(value not set)**, it would have been used in place of Open on the context menu. Similarly, the single value in the **\print** key is **(Default) (value not set)** (Figure 9-33), so Print becomes the second entry on the menu.

Figure 9-32. The \open key has no (Default) value

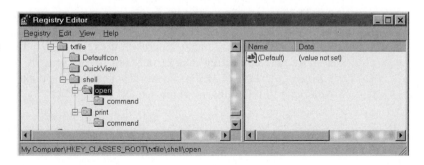

Figure 9-33.
Similarly, the
\print key has
no (Default)
value

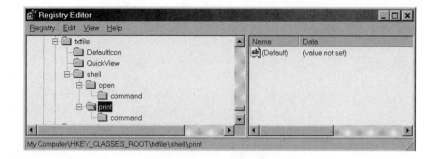

In this example, **HKCR\txtfile\shell** has a value of **(Default) (value not set)**, so the default action—the one highlighted in the context menu and the action that will be taken if the file is double clicked—is set to Open, as described earlier in this chapter in the section "Default Action."

This multiple use of **(Default)** can be confusing, so let me emphasize that there are two different ways **(Default)** is used to construct the context menu. The **(Default)** value for the **\shell** key determines what the default (highlighted) menu choice will be. The **(Default)** values for actions—which are always subkeys of **\shell**—determine the names of the actions on the context menu.

 That's a big part of the story about the way Registry keys turn into context menu choices, but there are several more details. In the earlier section "Directory, Drive, Folder," I told you about the fledgling "inheritance" scheme Win98 establishes among the Registry's **HKCR\Folder**, **\Directory**, **\Drive**, and **\AudioCD** keys. Because of this inheritance, the context menu for **\Directory** includes all the menu items from **\Folder**, the **\AudioCD** context menu includes all the menu items from **\Drive**, and the **\Drive** context menu, in turn, includes all the menu items from **\Folder**.

Also, the name that appears on the right-click context menu comes from the **(Default)** value for the action's key. For example, the Sarah's Smart Setup version of Explorer described in Chapter 3 assigns to the key **HKCR\Folder\ shell\open** the **(Default)** value data **FolderView**. So, while Windows may think this is an **open** command, the user who right clicks on a folder actually sees a FolderView entry on the menu.

That's generally true: if the **HKCR\ProgID\shell** key has a **(Default)** value (at least, one that isn't a blank string), the **(Default)** value is used as the text on the context menu. Microsoft uses this feature for internationalization: **HKCR\Directory\shell** in Spanish Windows 98, for example, has a **(Default)** value of **Abrir**, so Abrir appears on the context menu, where American Windows users would see Open.

Wait a minute, wait a minute. Something's fishy here. You're telling me that when Win98 encounters a key with a name like **\open**, it's smart enough to capitalize the name so that the entry Open appears on the context menu? I can buy that. But how does Win98 know to turn **\find** to Find? And how does it figure which characters on the menus should be underlined, making them accelerator keys? Where's all that stuff stored?

I haven't the slightest idea. Some of the accelerator keys are specified by ampersands (**&**) in the **(Default)** values of the **\shell\command** keys—where the ampersand precedes the key that is to be underlined and become an accelerator, as is the general convention in Windows programming—but much of the accelerator key recognition must be built into Win98's core code, somehow.

It may have something to do with what the Windows Software Development Kit calls "canonical verbs," **open**, **print**, **explorer**, **find**, **openas**, and **properties**. (The SDK also lists **printto** as a canonical verb, but it never appears in context menus. **printto** is the default action taken when an object is dragged onto a printer icon. Thus, Windows can keep track of two different print actions for a given ProgID: the **print** action appears on the context menu; the **printto** action is for drag and drop.) I believe Windows uses the list of canonical verbs in order, if no default action has been selected for a given ProgID. Several canonical verbs are "translated" before they appear on the context menu, with the strangest translation being **openas** to open with.

\shellex

Time to let the other shoe drop. Many **HKCR\ProgID** keys—in addition to the **HKCR*** key and more than a few **HKCR\CLSID** keys—have subkeys called **\shellex**, a key name reserved by Windows 98 for so-called "shell extensions." That's a strange name for such a ubiquitous tool, really, because (as we'll see) bone-stock Win98 ships with hundreds of **\shellex** "extension" programs. Win98 shell extensions are not just for add-on software; Win98 itself uses them relentlessly.

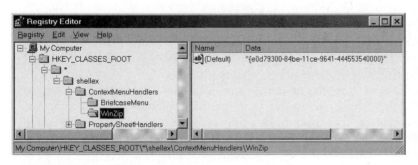

Figure 9-34. shellex for WinZip

\shellex programs are always referred to by their **CLSID**s. If you look at Figure 9-34, you see just how. The **\shellex** subkey hangs off an **HKCR\ProgID** key, **HKCR\CLSID\{...}**, or **HKCR***. Then there's a subkey that describes the kind of shell extension. Finally, there's an application name set as a subkey with a **(Default)** value that points to the **CLSID** of the associated program.

Following are the subkeys under **\shellex** that control when Win98 runs the listed programs.

- **\shellex\ContextMenuHandlers** programs are run whenever the user right clicks on a file, folder, drive, or directory with the given ProgID, an icon with the given **CLSID**, or—in the case of **HKCR*\shellex\ContextMenuHandlers**—any file at all. Win98 ships with many **\ContextMenuHandlers**. For example, **HKCR\CLSID\{00028b00-0000-0000-c000-000000000046}\shellex\ContextMenuHandlers** controls the contents of the context menu for the Microsoft Network icon. The sharing option on drive context menus comes from the **(Default)** value data in **HKCR\drive\shellex\ContextMenuHandlers**.

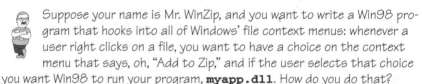

Suppose your name is Mr. WinZip, and you want to write a Win98 program that hooks into all of Windows' file context menus: whenever a user right clicks on a file, you want to have a choice on the context menu that says, oh, "Add to Zip," and if the user selects that choice you want Win98 to run your program, **myapp.dll**. How do you do that?

Well, if you're Mr. WinZip, you start by writing a special kind of program called a context menu handler. The context menu handler puts "Add to Zip" on the context menu, and it runs a program called **myapp.dll** if "Add to Zip" is chosen. Once you've created the context menu handler, you run **guidgen.exe** to get a unique **CLSID**. Then you write an installer that puts your program's **CLSID**, along with a pointer to **myapp.dll**, into **HKCR\CLSID**. Finally, the installer puts the **CLSID** in the **(Default)** value of the key **HKCR*\shellex\ContextMenuHandlers**, just as you see in Figure 9-34.

- **\shellex\PropertySheetHandlers** programs are run whenever the user picks the associated property sheet, typically (but not always) from the bottom of the context menu. Win98 also ships with many **\PropertySheetHandlers.** Try a little experiment. Right click on an AVI file and pick Properties (Figure 9-35). In Regedit, click **HKCR\avifile\PropertySheetHandlers** and export the key (Figure 9-36). Then delete the **\PropertySheetHandlers** key. Bring up the property sheet for the same file (Figure 9-37). See how the Details and Preview tabs are missing? That's what a property sheet handler does—manipulates the appearance of the property sheet. (Be sure to restore the Registry by importing back the key!)

- **\shellex\CopyHookHandlers** programs are just like context menu handlers, except they're fired up by a right click before Windows lets the user copy, move, delete, or rename a folder. The resulting context menu is manipulated by the copy hook handlers programs, and Windows essentially asks the handler if it's OK to perform the requested action. You can see copy hook handlers in the **HKCR\Directory** and **HKCR\Printers** keys.

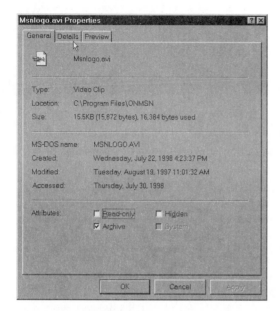

Figure 9-35. AVI file with
\PropertySheetHandlers intact

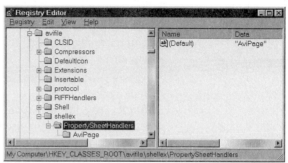

Figure 9-36. Registry key that controls the AVI property sheet

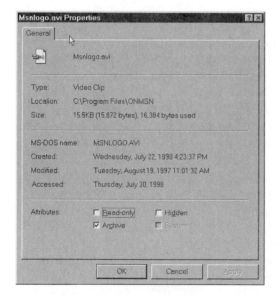

Figure 9-37. Same file's property sheet with
\PropertySheetHandlers removed

- **\shellex\DragDropHandlers** programs are added to the context menu that pops up when you right drag and drop a file onto the object with the drag and drop handler. You can see drag and drop handlers in the **HKCR\ Directory** and **HKCR\Printers** keys, too.

- **\shellex\DropHandlers** programs are called when something is dragged onto an object. For example, **HKCR\lnkfile** has a **\shellex\DropHandlers** program to let Win98 redirect files dropped onto a shortcut so that Win98 can act as if the file were dropped onto the program itself. You'll usually see **\DropHandlers** attached to data files—program files usually take care of their own drag and drop activities. The difference between a drag and drop handler and a drop handler is that the former defines items that appear on the context menu that pops up when you right drag and drop, while the latter defines actions that are taken when a drop is made without any menu involved.

- **\shellex\IconHandlers** programs are run whenever Win98 needs to redraw an icon, either on the Desktop or in Explorer. **HKCR\lnkfile\shellex\IconHandlers**, for example, stores the **CLSID** of the program used by Win98 to help draw icons for shortcuts. Amazingly, the program does not draw the bent arrow on shortcuts—it draws the icon underneath!

- **\shellex\DataHandler** programs are run when Win98 transfers data between programs: the key's **CLSID** routine includes translators to handle unusual clipboard data formats.

 Some books tell you that you can remove the shortcut arrow by removing the **IsShortcut** values from **HKCR\lnkfile** and **HKCR\piffile**. Although that certainly does get rid of the arrows, it might also have side effects (although, admittedly, I haven't hit any yet). You're far better off using Tweak UI to do the job neatly and easily—or, if you must fuss with your Registry, by adjusting the **shell32.dll,29** value in **HKLM\S\M\W\CV\ explorer\ShellIcons**, as I discuss later in this chapter in the section "More Iconoclasms."

\ShellNew: Keys and the "New" Context Menu

 Tweak UI Alert! *Everything discussed in this section can be changed by using Tweak UI. If you want to make changes to the New context menu— and couldn't care less about learning how or why it works— use the utility. Tweak UI won't tell you anything about how templates behave, but if you don't want to get your hands dirty hacking the Registry, you probably won't be too intrigued by templates anyway. Fair enough. Tweak UI is discussed at length in Chapter 8.*

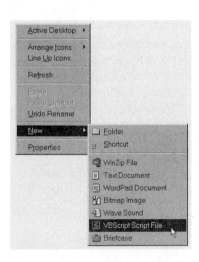

Figure 9-38. The Right-click New context menu

When you right click on the Desktop (or on an empty part of Explorer or a folder window) and pick New, Win98 gives you an opportunity to create new files in a vast array of formats (Figure 9-38). All of the choices you see on the New context menu come from **HKCR\.extension** subkeys called **\ShellNew**. For example, if you right click on the Desktop and pick New, one of the file type choices you see is Text Document, or **.txt** file. That menu item appears because of the **HKCR\.txt\ShellNew** key. If you choose Text Document from the menu, Win98 will create a new **.txt** file and place it on the Desktop. The initial contents of that file are controlled by values under **\ShellNew**.

Figure 9-39. Registry entry that controls the contents of New .txt files

The names on the New context menu come from the **(Default)** value data of the **HKCR\ProgID** key associated with the specific **HKCR\.extension** containing the **\ShellNew** key. (Whew!) For example, **HKCR\.txt** has a **\ShellNew** key (see Figure 9-39). When Win98 constructs the New context menu, it looks at the **HKCR\.txt (Default)** value data and finds the associated ProgID **txtfile**. Looking at **HKCR\txtfile**, Win98 finds that its **(Default)** value data is **Text Document**, and sure enough, that's what's on the New context menu for a new **.txt** file.

When Win98 creates the new file, it looks for values in the **\ShellNew** key in this order.

- If there is a value named **NullFile**, Win98 creates an empty file. Otherwise,
- If there is a value named **FileName**, Win98 creates a copy of the file listed in the value data and places that copy on the Desktop (or within the folder, if the user right clicked on a blank part of an open folder). The **FileName** data need not include the full path of the "copy from" file if the file is located in the Win98 **\windows\ShellNew** directory. Otherwise,
- If there is a value named **Data**, Win98 takes the binary value data and creates a new file containing the binary data. Otherwise,
- If there is a value named **command**, Win98 runs the command but only under certain circumstances. For details, see the section at the end of this chapter about Word and the New context menu.

The new file is given a name of **New**, followed by the entry in the New context menu. For example, a new **Text Document** is called **New Text Document.txt**. Finally, once the new file with its new name sits on the Desktop, Win98 looks in the **\ShellNew** key for a value called **command**. If such a value exists, Win98 scans the command string data entry, replacing all **%1** occurrences with the name of the new file, and then runs the command.

 I was looking for Registry origins of the two menu entries at the top of the New context menu. I finally found the shortcut information stuffed under **HKCR\.lnk\ShellNew**—the Command value there is a bit unusual because it brings up the Shortcut Wizard. I never did find the key for a new folder.

One of the nice implications of the **\ShellNew** key is that you can cut down the number of programs listed when you right click the Desktop (Figure 9-38). Say you don't ever create new Wave Sounds and you'd like to delete that entry from the New context menu. It's easy to do it manually—so easy you might prefer it to cranking up Tweak UI.

Get into Regedit. Click on **HKCR**, scroll to **.wav**, right click once on the **\HKCR\.wav\ShellNew** key. Pick Rename, and give it any name you like. Hit **Enter**. Now try the New context menu. See how the Wave Sound entry disappears? (You could delete the key, but by renaming it, you still have it around if you ever want to restore it. Tweak UI just puts a minus sign—actually a hyphen—at the end of the key name, resulting in **\ShellNew-**.)

Edit Flags

You're probably wondering about those mysterious Edit Flags I mentioned earlier, the ones that can force a particular ProgID to appear on—or disappear from—the Explorer File Types tab and can keep you from changing the Default Action on a particular ProgID. Well, there are actually two different kinds of Edit Flags, those that are values of **HKCR\ProgID** keys and those that are values of an action, two levels lower in the tree (for example, **HKCR\batfile\shell\open** on your system probably has an **EditFlags** value). Let's take a look at the higher-level **HKCR\ProgID** keys' Edit Flags first.

Warning! ¡Cuidado! Achtung! These flags are internal to the operating system. They may change in future versions of Windows. They are officially undocumented. Use them at your own risk, and don't be surprised if you have to change them again when you change versions of Windows.

As you can see in Figures 9-40 through 9-43, **EditFlags** is a value in **HKCR\ProgID** keys that consists of four bytes. The last two bytes are not used by the Explorer File Types tab; the third byte is associated with multimedia, but I'm not sure exactly how.

Figure 9-40.
HKCR\AudioCD
Edit Flags

Figure 9-41.
HKCR\batfile
Edit Flags

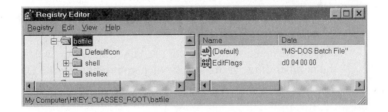

**Figure 9-42.
HKCR\drvfile
Edit Flags**

**Figure 9-43.
HKCR\exefile
Edit Flags**

**Figure 9-44.
Remove button
grayed out in the
File Types dialog**

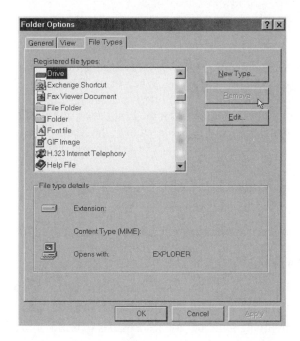

Many of the Edit Flags involve graying out buttons in two dialogs. The first dialog (Figure 9-44) is the one that appears when you pick the File Types tab in Explorer's View/ Options. When I say, "Such and such Edit Flag grays out the Remove button on the File Types dialog," I mean that if you click on a ProgID on this dialog and the Edit Flag in the Registry for that ProgID is set to **1**, the Remove button on this dialog goes gray—you won't be able to use it.

Figure 9-45.
Remove button
grayed out in the
Edit File Type dia-
log

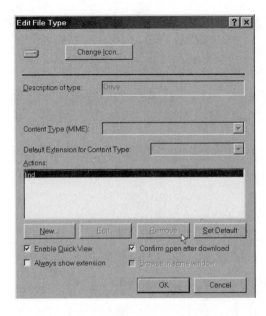

The second dialog (Figure 9-45) is the one that appears when you pick the Edit button from the first dialog. When I say, "This other Edit Flag grays out the Remove button for the Edit File Type dialog," I mean that if you click on a ProgID in the first dialog and hit the Edit button and the Edit Flag in the Registry for that particular ProgID is set to **1**, the Remove button on the second dialog goes gray *no matter which of the Actions you pick.*

 I know that sounds complicated, but if you fiddle with the Edit Flags a couple of times, you'll see how it works.

To understand the meaning of the first two bytes in Edit Flags, first expand them from hex to binary notation. (For example, a hex **d** is 13 in decimal, or 8+4+1, which translates to **1101** in binary. Remember that?)

In Figure 9-40, **02 00** hex expands to **0000 0010 0000 0000**.

In Figure 9-41, **d0 04** hex expands to **1101 0000 0000 0100**.

In Figure 9-42, **01 00** hex expands to **0000 0001 0000 0000**.

In Figure 9-43, **d8 07** hex expands to **1101 1000 0000 0111**.

Reading from left to right (which is *not* what programmers usually do, but if you aren't a programmer, you'll find it a whole lot easier to follow), here is what a **1** in each of the 16-bit positions means.

Position 1 *The Remove button for the Edit File Type dialog* (Figure 9-45) *is grayed out, no matter which of the Actions you choose.* Looking at the expanded Edit Flags just shown, you see that the Remove buttons in both

batfile—which appears on the File Types tab as MS-DOS Batch File—and **exefile**—which appears as Application—are grayed out. Go into Explorer and look at MS-DOS Batch File. That's precisely what happens. There is one exception to this rule, explained shortly.

Position 2 *The Edit button for the Edit File Type dialog is grayed out, no matter which of the Actions you choose.* Again, if you look at Explorer, you find that the Edit buttons in **batfile** are grayed out, which agrees with the binary Edit Flags. There is one exception to this rule, explained shortly.

Position 3 *The New button for the Edit File Type dialog is grayed out.* I couldn't find this flag used anywhere in the Registry.

Position 4 *The Remove button on the File Types dialog (that's the first dialog, Figure 9-44) for this ProgID is grayed out.* This keeps the user from removing the entire ProgID. In Explorer, the Remove button in both Application and MS-DOS Batch File is grayed out, per the Edit Flags.

Position 5 *The Edit button on the File Types dialog for this ProgID is grayed out.* This prevents the user from adding to or changing any of the actions or the icon for this ProgID. In Explorer, the Edit button for Application is grayed out, but MS-DOS Application's Edit button is not.

Position 6 *The ProgID has an associated extension.* I couldn't find this flag used anywhere in the Registry.

Position 7 *Include in the File Types tab Registered File Types list.* Normally, a ProgID has to have an associated **HKCR\.extension** key to be eligible for listing. When this bit is **1**, as it is with **HKCR\drive**, for example, the ProgID is listed with the registered file types whether it has an **HKCR\.extension** key or not.

Position 8 *Do not put on the Explorer File Types tab Registered File Types list.* **drvfile**, the ProgID for **.drv** driver files, shown in Figure 9-42, is one of those excluded from the list. If you look at the File Types tab, you won't see Device Driver listed, even though there is an associated extension.

Positions 9, 10 *Not used.*

Position 11 *In the "Editing action for type" dialog box (see Figure 9-25), the Use DDE box is grayed out.*

Position 12 *In the "Editing action for type" dialog box (see Figure 9-25), the name of the .exe file in the "Application used to perform action box" cannot be changed.*

Position 13 *In the "Editing action for type" dialog box* (see Figure 9-25), *the "Application used to perform action" box is grayed out.*

Position 14 *The Set Default button in the Edit File Type box is grayed out, no matter which of the actions is chosen.* This is the case with **batfile**, where you're not allowed to change the default action from run (open) to print, unless you hack the Edit Flags—essentially, set this bit to 0. See Chapter 3 for details.

Position 15 *The Change Icon button in the Edit File Type dialog is grayed out.* I have no idea why Microsoft, in creating **exefile**, decided to turn on this bit *and* the one in position 5, which effectively prevents you from even getting to the Edit File Type dialog.

Position 16 *The "Description of type" box in the Edit File Type dialog is grayed out.*

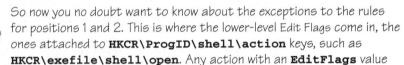 So now you no doubt want to know about the exceptions to the rules for positions 1 and 2. This is where the lower-level Edit Flags come in, the ones attached to **HKCR\ProgID\shell\action** keys, such as **HKCR\exefile\shell\open**. Any action with an **EditFlags** value can override the rules for positions 1 and 2, providing the data for the action's **EditFlags** value starts with **01**. For example, if you create a new action for **exefiles** called **george**, and the key **HKCR\exefile\shell\george** contains a value called **EditFlags** with data **01 00 00 00**, you discover that the **george** action in the Edit File Type Actions dialog box has both the Remove and Edit buttons available, even though the two buttons are grayed out in the rest of the actions in that box.

In Figure 9-46, you can see the Edit Flags associated with the action **george**. In Figure 9-47, note how the Edit and Remove buttons are active for **george**, even though they're grayed out for all the other actions. When you create a new action by pushing the New button here, a lower-level **EditFlags** value is automatically created for the new action, with the data **01 00 00 00**. That means you will be able to edit your manually created action even if all the other actions are grayed.

Figure 9-46. New action george with Edit Flags set to override the Edit and Remove buttons

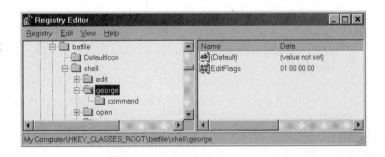

**Figure 9-47.
Action george
overrides the
settings for the
rest of batfile**

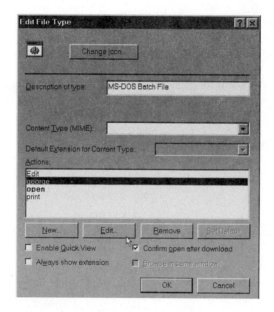

The ability to change your Edit Flags (and remove Win98's training wheels) is an important one. I've seen people—including some people who should know better—recommend that you change certain entries in the Registry manually because Explorer's View/ Options File Types tab's Edit capability for that particular ProgID is grayed out. **WRONG!**

If any File Types key is grayed out and that's preventing you from changing Win98 to work the way you want, your best solution is *never* to hack the Registry **\shell** keys directly. Your best solution is *always* to change the Edit Flags for the ProgID that's causing you problems and then use the File Types tab to make the changes you want. Why? Because once you've changed the Edit Flags to let you in, making changes from the File Types dialog box is very easy—and (with the exception of the %1 Bug, coming up next) almost always consistent with what Windows 98 expects. The chances of making a bad mistake are greatly enhanced when you're tackling entries manually. Minimize your exposure by using the simplest possible and most robust tools—in this case the File Types dialog box—after you open up the forbidden parts of the Registry.

Don't screw around with the Edit Flags without understanding what you're up to! While you might want to zero out the bit in position 2, which keeps you from changing the default action associated with some ProgIDs, you don't want to mess up, say, position 7 for Drive, as that would take it off the File Types list. A bit of caution is called for.

Oh, Woody! You don't have to be so conservative. I plunked around the Registry for a bit and came up with the following list of minimalist **EditFlags**, which you can use as long as you're cautious about how you change the **open** action.

Table 9-1.	
HKCR *Key*	*Minimalist* **EditFlags**
\AudioCD	02 00 00 00
\AVIFile	00 00 00 00
\batfile	00 00 00 00
\comfile	00 00 00 00
\Directory	02 00 00 00
\dllfile	00 00 00 00
\Drive	02 00 00 00
\drvfile	00 00 00 00
\exefile	00 00 00 00
\file	02 00 00 00
\Folder	02 00 00 00
\lnkfile	00 00 00 00
\piffile	00 00 00 00
\sysfile	00 00 00 00
\vxdfile	00 00 00 00

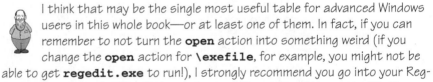 I think that may be the single most useful table for advanced Windows users in this whole book—or at least one of them. In fact, if you can remember to not turn the **open** action into something weird (if you change the **open** action for **\exefile**, for example, you might not be able to get **regedit.exe** to run!), I strongly recommend you go into your Registry right now and make all those changes. The power of the entire File Types shtick will be available to you, unfettered.

The basic rule is simple. To remove Windows' training wheels, use an **EditFlags** value of **02 00 00 00** for those few cases where you have a type that has no extension but you want to appear in the File Types list (that probably means exactly the four special built-in types and the type called **\file** added by Internet Explorer) and otherwise use **00 00 00 00**.

%1 Bugs

Some incredibly advanced Windows applications—say, Notepad—are smart enough to take a command line like

Notepad C:\windows my test file.txt

and figure out that it should load the single file called **my test file.txt**. Other Windows applications (I won't mention Word 2000 by name) are too dumb to understand a command line that looks like

winword My Document.doc

and figure out that it's supposed to open up a single document called **My Document.doc**. Instead, when Word is confronted with that command line, it tries to open a file called **My.doc**, and then it really gets confused, gobbling up the rest of the command line. Really smart for the flagship application of the world's largest software company, eh?

It's even worse than that, Woody. If you feed Word 2000 the command line

winword C:\My Documents\New Work\abc.doc

it will start Word, then look for three documents: **C:\My.doc**, **Documents\New** (with no filename extension), and **Work\abc.doc**. I kid you not!

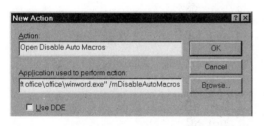

Figure 9-48. **Open Disable Auto Macros** for Word documents

Nowhere is this bug more infuriating than in the creation of your own commands, using the File Types New Action box Action command. Win98 insists on sticking a **%1** on the end of any command you create, and that can drive programs like Word batty. In Figure 9-48 you can see how I created a new command for Word documents called **Open Disable Auto Macros**. (If you have Word 2000, you can do the same: in Windows Explorer, click View, Folder Options, File Types, click Microsoft Word Document, click Edit, then New.) The "Application used to perform action" box looks like this:

"C:\program files\microsoft office\office\winword.exe" /mDisableAutoMacros

It starts Word by running the old WordBasic command **DisableAutoMacros** (that's what the **/m** command line switch means—it runs old WordBasic commands). That WordBasic command has Word start without running any auto macros—a technique that can be helpful if there are problems getting Word going.

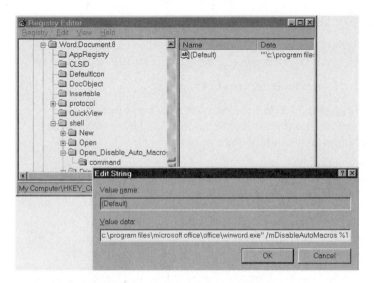

In Figure 9-49, you can see how Win98 added a gratuitous **%1** to the end of the command line.

If you right click on a **.doc** file and pick **Open Disable Auto Macros**, it works just great as long as there are no spaces in the filename or in any of the folder names leading up to the file. Right click on **C:\AnyOldDocument.doc**, say, pick Open, and Disable Auto Macros, and Word starts with the command

/mDisableAutoMacros
C:\AnyOldDocument.doc

Figure 9-49. HKCR\Word.Document.8\shell\ Open_Disable_Auto_Macros command (Default) key, generated with a gratuitous appended %1

that disables auto macros and loads **AnyOldDocument.doc**. Wunnerful, wunnerful. But what happens when you right click on

C:\My Documents\abc.doc and pick Open and Disable Auto Macros? Word is fed this command line:

/mDisableAutoMacros C:\My Documents\abc.doc

Word, in its infinite wisdom, tries to open **C:\My.doc** (giving you an error message) and then **Documents\abc.doc** (giving you another error message). Bummer.

Fortunately, the solution is quite simple. If you go into the Registry's **HKCR\Word.Document.8\shell\Open,_Disable_Auto_Macros\ command** key and change the value of **(Default)** to

"C:\program files\microsoft office\office\winword.exe"
/mDisableAutoMacros "%1"

(note the quotation marks!), Word works just fine. If you make that change, Word is fed the command line

/mDisableAutoMacros "C:\My Documents\abc.doc"

and all is right with the world. Amazing, no? Windows should automatically include the **"%1"**, of course, rather than just **%1**. Yet another bug.

Where the Icons Come From

You can assign an icon to any ProgID most easily by using the File Types tab, choosing the ProgID in question, hitting Edit, and then Change Icon. (You can do the same thing manually by altering the **(Default)** value for the **HKCR\ProgID\DefaultIcon** key.) In the case of **.exe**, **.scr**, **.ico**, and **.ani** files and the like, Win98 extracts the icon from the file itself, of course.

Figure 9-50. Explorer punts when trying to create an icon for .foo files

Figure 9-51. WordPad icon

Figure 9-52. Redrawn .foo icon, now associated with Word-Pad

But what does Windows 98 do for a picture—either on the Desktop or in Explorer—when no icon has been provided? Windows is pretty tricky on that score. In Figure 9-50, I created a new icon on the Desktop and gave it an extension of **.foo**. Windows didn't know what to make of this new extension, so it punted for an icon. The icon you see there is the generic "I don't know what the hell to put on the screen" icon that Win98 uses when it's clueless in Seattle.

In Figure 9-51, you can see the icon for WordPad. You've seen it a million times. Now, if I right click on **MyStuff.foo** and tell Win98 to Open it with WordPad, making sure that the box marked "Always use this program to open this type of file" is checked, Win98 automatically constructs an icon for **.foo** files that superimposes a scaled-down version of the WordPad icon on a blank sheet of paper, per Figure 9-52.

Pretty cool, eh? Many icons work this way: If you associate an open action with the extension, a new icon is constructed superimposing a scaled-down version of the Open program's icon on a blank sheet of paper. Windows does this only if an explicit icon hasn't been assigned to the ProgID in the **DefaultIcon** value.

■ HKCU

Mystery is the wisdom of blockheads.

—Horace Walpole, *Letter to Horace Mann,* 1761

The Registry key **HKEY_CURRENT_USER (HKCU)** contains user-specific information stored in a **user.dat** file. It's actually an alias for **HKEY_USERS\ username**, where **username** is the logon name of the currently logged-on user. In a single user profile system or when the user has bypassed logon by hitting the **escape** key, it's an alias for **HKEY_USERS\.Default**.

**Figure 9-53.
The eight high-
level HKCU sub-
keys**

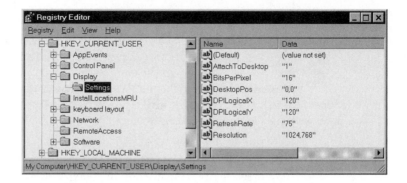

Orientation

HKCU has eight high-level subkeys (Figure 9-53).

 Although I don't claim to understand the details of many of them, here is an approximation of what those keys control.

- **HKCU\AppEvents** revolves around Application Events—the things that can trigger beeps, whoops, giggles, and fizzes. I talk about these oddly convoluted keys extensively in the Chapter 8 section on the Control Panel's Sound applet, but I go into a little more detail momentarily, particularly for Windows applications.

- **HKCU\Control Panel**, as you might imagine, primarily deals with settings established and manipulated by the Control Panel. A big part of Chapter 8 discusses these keys. There are separate keys for **\Accessibility** (for details, look in Chapter 8 for the Control Panel's Accessibility applet), **\Appearance** (the Display applet), **\Colors** (also the Display applet), **\Cursors** (the Mouse applet), **\International** (mostly the Regional Settings applet), **\Keyboard** (the Keyboard applet), and **\Mouse** (the Mouse applet).

- **HKCU\Display**, an oddball key, has only a handful of entries (as you can see in Figure 9-53), and they're all repeats of information found elsewhere. For example, Figure 9-54 shows how several of the settings are repeated in **HKLM\Config\0001\Display\Settings**—which is where you would expect to find data on refresh rate, resolution, and the like. I have no idea why Win98 puts the same information in two different places.

- **HKCU\InstallLocationsMRU** points to the places last used for installing Win98 components. I talk about it more in a moment.

**Figure 9-54.
Redundant infor-
mation from
HKCU\Display—
but this is where
it belongs!**

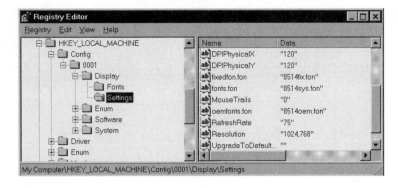

- **HKCU\keyboard layout** has very little information in it; most of the keyboard settings are in **HKCU\Control Panel\keyboard**. Beats me why Microsoft constructed this separate key. **HKCU\keyboard layout\ preload\1** contains just the country code (see Chapter 8, Regional Settings applet). If multiple keyboard languages are chosen in the Keyboard applet's Language tab, they're listed as **\1**, **\2**, **\3**, and so on. The **\toggle** key apparently represents the key combination that switches among the languages.

- **HKCU\Network** contains some data on recently connected network drives. It's a jungle in there—but thankfully a *small* jungle, if your network is simple.

- **HKCU\RemoteAccess** covers your Dial-Up Networking connectoids and all the details necessary to dial and connect to your dial-up services.

- **HKCU\Software** is a huge key that would take years to explore completely. In a nutshell, any software package that has user-specific settings (and most do) is supposed to put a subkey in here for the manufacturer, then subkeys off that subkey for its major products, and subkeys off those for major revisions of the software, and more subkeys off those for components. That's why you see entries like **HKCU\Software\Pinecliffe\WOPR\97\Enveloper**. If you're trying to solve an application-specific problem, this is where you should start looking.

 In the rest of this chapter, I look at only the one **HKCU\Software** key called **HKCU\Software\Microsoft\Windows\CurrentVersion** (give it the abbreviation **HKCU\S\M\W\CV**), and I only briefly touch on some of the hundreds of keys that live there. There's a similar key called **HKLM\Software\Microsoft\Windows\CurrentVersion** (**HKLM\S\M\W\CV**) that controls Win98 settings that aren't specific to a single user. I talk about them in the section on **HKLM.**

Now let's take a look at some of the more interesting facets of **HKCU.**

**Figure 9-55.
Events that can
trigger sounds**

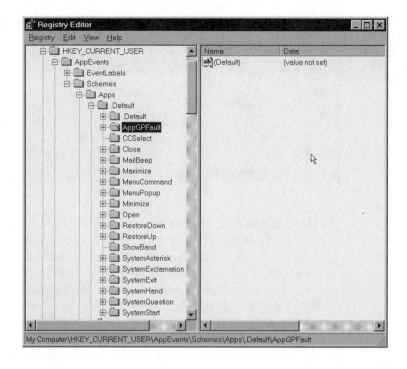

Sounds

 Any Windows program can immortalize the events listed as keys in Figure 9-55 with song (or at least a **.wav** file).

In case the abbreviations aren't too obvious, here's a translation of the tough ones. **AppGPFault** (the person who thought of that one must've been in a bizarre mood) happens when an application generates a general protection fault (GPF). **CCSelect** in the Registry corresponds to Select sound in the Sounds applet. **SystemAsterisk** sounds whenever a dialog box with an Information symbol (I) appears. Similarly, **SystemExclamation** is for dialog boxes with exclamation points, **SystemHand** is for dialog boxes with stop signs, and **SystemQuestion** is for dialog boxes with question marks.

Say you want the sound **C:\windows\tada.wav** to blast over your speakers every time you start the calculator. No problemo. In Regedit, bring up **HKCU\AppEvents\Schemes\Apps**. Then add a key with a name that precisely matches your application's program name, in this case **\calc**. For a sound that corresponds to starting a program, use the **\Open** key and its subkey **\.Current** (for the currently active sound, of course). Finally, set the **HKCU\AppEvents\Schemes\Apps\calc\Open\.Current** key's **(Default)** value to **C:\windows\media\tada.wav** (Figure 9-56). That's all it takes.

**Figure 9-56.
Starting the
calculator with
"tada"!**

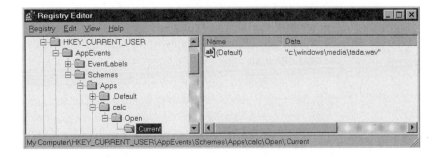

You can do the same thing for other actions by replacing **\Open** in the key name by **\SystemAsterisk** or any of the other events just mentioned. It's pretty impressive that you can customize things so thoroughly (only a very small percentage of all the available events can be controlled through the Control Panel's Sounds applet).

MRUs

Windows maintains several most recently used (MRU) lists. One of the lists you've no doubt encountered is the list of file specifications used in the

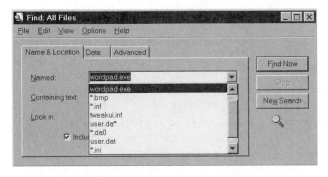

Figure 9-57. The Start/Find file MRU list

Start/Find dialog: Win98 keeps track of which file spec strings you've looked for and lists them in the Find dropdown box (Figure 9-57).

The key **HKCU\S\M\W\CV\ Explorer\Doc Find Spec MRU** contains the Find MRU list. As you can see in Figure 9-58, the key contains a whole bunch of values with value names that are letters of the alphabet, plus one value called **MRUList**. That's a general pattern in every Win98 MRU list.

**Figure 9-58.
Where the
Start/Find file
MRU list lives**

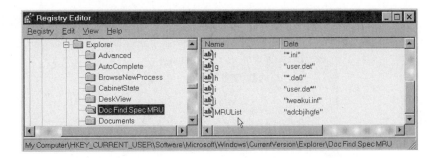

Win98 maintains the MRU list by changing the value data of **MRUList**. In Figure 9-58, the data reads **abcdjihgfe**, which is just shorthand for "the last-used document is stored in value **a**; the next most recently used is in value **b**; the next one is in **c**; and so on, down to **e**."

 If you think about it for a minute, you can see why Microsoft uses this simple method for keeping track of MRU lists. It's quite efficient. If you use the find criterion mentioned in value **c**, for example—the third most recently used file specification in this example—Win98 doesn't have to update the value data for **c**; it just has to move **c** to the front of **MRUList**. The time savings for any one MRU list isn't much, but if you multiply dozens of MRU lists by hundreds of uses a day, it becomes significant. Well, maybe not that significant, but it's still a cool way of handling MRUs.

The important thing to know about MRU lists is that you can get rid of them by deleting the single value called **MRUList**. In some cases (but not in this one), you also have to restart Windows—the Shutdown option "Log on as a different user" is sufficient. In this case, deleting the **MRUList** value in Figure 9-58 will completely wipe out your Start/Find file spec list.

It's also important to know that even when Win98 alphabetizes a list for you—as it does with the Start/Documents list—you can still retrieve all the information about most recently used items on the list, should you need it, by examining the appropriate **MRUList** value (Figure 9-59).

 Speaking of the Start/Documents MRU list, it follows the general pattern of Win98 MRU lists you've been talking about, but it has an interesting twist: the entries in the MRU list don't point to the files themselves but in fact point to shortcuts to those files maintained by Windows in the hidden folder called **C:\windows\recent**. If you want to wipe out the Start/Documents MRU list, you can either delete the **HCKU\S\M\W\CV\Explorer\RecentDocs** key's **MRUList** value and restart Windows, just as you would with any other Win98 MRU list, or—much faster—simply delete all the files in **C:\windows\recent**. Without the shortcuts in the folder, Win98 doesn't know which files were most recently used.

Figure 9-59. Start/Documents MRU list

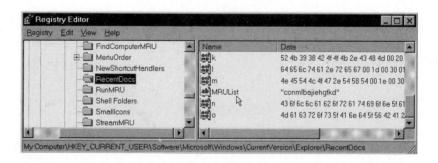

Woody, your memory must be the first or second thing to go! If you want to wipe out the whole list, you right click on a blank part of the Taskbar, pick Properties, go to the Start Menu Program tab (where else would it be? <grin>), then hit the Clear button near the bottom!

In addition to the Start/Find file spec and Start/Documents lists, I've found the following MRU lists in the Registry.

- The locations used to install Win98 components are in **HKCU\ InstallLocations MRU**. You might want to go in and adjust this Registry key, but before you do, check out the key **HKLM\S\M\W\CV\Setup\ SourcePath**, covered later in this chapter. It's much more likely to be the key you want.

- The MRU list for the computers you've searched for, using the Start/Find/Computer feature, are stored in **HKCU\S\M\W\CV\Explorer\ FindComputerMRU**.

- The command lines used in the Start/Run box are in **HKCU\S\M\W\CV\ Explorer\RunMRU**.

- The data structures Explorer calls streams (discussed in the next section) have an MRU list maintained in **HKCU\S\M\W\CV\Explorer\ StreamMRU**. Win95 handles up to 29 streams by including values of **a** through **z**, **{**, **}**, and **|**. Win98 has 100 streams labeled 0 to 99 (plus Desktop) and StreamMRU is a binary key.

No doubt there are others.

Streams and Restoring the Desktop

This is one of the great unsolved mysteries of Windows 98, as far as I'm concerned. Read on, read on.

*Explorer uses temporary storage areas in the Registry that it calls streams. They're located in **HKCU\S\M\W\CV\Explorer\Streams\0** on up. One of the streams holds all the information about the location of icons on your Desktop: it's called, not surprisingly, **HKCU\S\M\W\ CV\Explorer\Streams\Desktop**. (The actual objects on the Desktop are read from the folder **C:\Windows\Desktop** and the **HKLM\S\M\W\CV\ explorer\Desktop\NameSpace** key that I discuss later in this chapter.)*

Don't know about you, but I spend quite a bit of time and care arranging my Desktop, and I *hate* it when stuff is moved around. I click on the wrong button, or Win98 suddenly decides to rearrange my icons, and it really drives me nuts. Unfortunately, Windows doesn't have an automatic method for taking a snapshot of the Desktop and letting me restore the Desktop to my preferred arrangement: one accidental right click and there's no way I can say, "Undo, damned Spot!"

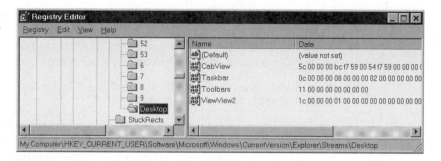

 There is a method for storing and restoring the Desktop, but I could only get it to work on single user machines. So if you're on a multiple user machine, take a quick gander here, but don't bother trying to go through the paces—unless you'd like to tackle a very intriguing problem.

Here's my procedure for storing and restoring the Desktop.

1. Arrange the Desktop however you like it, then (this is vital!) save it by either restarting Windows or clicking Start/Shutdown and clicking No.

2. Crank up Regedit and look for **HKCU\S\M\W\CV\Explorer\ Streams\Desktop** (see Figure 9-60). Export the key to a file, say, **C:\savedesk.reg**.

3. If your Desktop ever gets screwed up, change your **autoexec.bat** file to include a line that says **regedit C:\savedesk.reg**. Then restart Windows. *Boom!* Your old Desktop is restored.

 That's a very cool trick, but it works only on single user machines, most likely because the **regedit C:\savedesk.reg** line changes only the primary **user.dat** file—the one in **C:\windows**. I tried and tried to put together a line for **autoexec.bat** that would change the correct **user.dat** in a multiple user machine. The one that looked most promising went like this:

```
regedit /L:C:\windows\system.dat
    /R:C:\windows\profiles\woody\user.dat C:\savedesk.reg
```

but it didn't work! I've finally given up on this one. There has to be something strange going on—but I'm darned if I can figure out what it is . . .

Run **and** RunOnce

I talk about the **HKCU\S\M\W\CV\Run** and **\RunOnce** keys in Chapter 6 in the section "How Windows Starts." The important thing to realize: the programs stored in these keys are run *after* the user logs on (assuming the machine is set up for logon) and *only* for the current user (if somebody else logs on to the same machine, the programs are not run). There's a definitive list of all the **\Run**s in the discussion of **HKLM**.

**Figure 9-61.
Cross-reference of
key system folders**

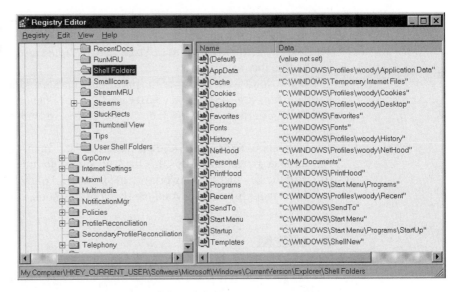

\Shell Folders

The key **HKCU\S\M\W\CV\Explorer\Shell Folders** contains a cross-reference between folders with special meaning to Windows and the physical location of these shell folders on disk. For example, as you can see in Figure 9-61, the value name **Desktop** has the data **C:\WINDOWS\Desktop**, telling Win98 that information about the Desktop can be found in the folder **C:\WINDOWS\Desktop**. Pretty simple. The key also has values for every system folder you can imagine.

 Although you can change any of the locations by futzing around with this key—and several magazine articles recommend that you do so—you're much better off simply changing the name of the folder in Tweak UI, if Tweak UI will handle it. Look at the Special Folder box on the General tab in Tweak UI, described in Chapter 8.

 Explorer is pretty clever about maintaining this key for you. If you rename or move a shell folder in Explorer, it automatically adjusts this key.

Other HKCUs

I talk about the multimedia settings in **HKCU\Software\Microsoft\Multimedia** in Chapter 8, in the section on the Control Panel's Multimedia applet.

HKCU\S\M\W\CV settings span a huge range. Settings for many Win98 applets—Backup, Media Player, Paint, Resource Meter, Sound Recorder, Volume Control, WordPad, even Regedit—as well as games sit in the key

HKCU\S\M\W\CV\Applets. Settings for the entire Windows Desktop, in addition to the Explorer application, reside in **HKCU\S\M\W\CV\Explorer**. Internet Explorer settings live in **HKCU\S\M\W\CV\Internet Settings**, as you would probably expect.

If you don't want Favorites to appear on your Start Menu, go to **HKCU\S\M\S\CV\Policies\Explorer**. Create a new dword value called **NoFavoritesMenu**, and give it a value of **1**. Restart Win98 and Favorites will disappear.

I talk about **HKCU\S\M\W\CV\Policies** later in this chapter, when I get into ultimate power users' tips. It's the key you use to hide some Desktop icons. (It's also the key that the network-oriented System Policy Editor works with, and that—thankfully—is beyond the scope of this book.)

■ HKLM

The key **HKEY_LOCAL_MACHINE** (**HKLM**) contains information that pertains to the PC as a whole, from **system.dat**.

Orientation

The **HKLM** key has eight subkeys (Figure 9-62).

- **HKLM\Config** has entries for each hardware profile. On a single hardware profile machine (see the discussion of the System applet in Chapter 8), there's only one subkey, called **HKLM\Config\0001**. On a multiple hardware profile PC, you'll also see **HKLM\Config\0002**, and so on. Each profile has up to four subkeys. One, called **\Display** holds information about the system fonts and metrics (see the discussion of the Display applet in Chapter 8). Then there's an **\Enum** key with some leftover PNP settings. The **\Software** key rattles down to an area with **ProxyServer** settings (Figure 9-63). The fourth, called **\System**, finally tells you—about ten levels down—which printers are installed and which printer is active. That's the whole ball of wax.

Figure 9-62.
HKLM's eight keys

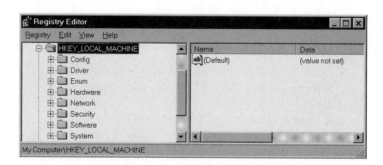

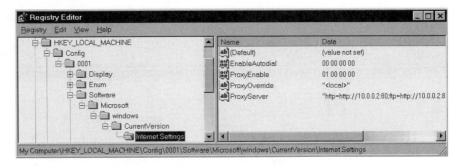

Figure 9-63. The `HKLM\Config\0001\Software` key leads only to `ProxyServer` settings

- On every machine we've seen, **HKLM\Driver** has a single subkey, called **4**, with no values. I think that's somebody's idea of a Halloween joke.

- **HKLM\Enum** contains "bus enumerator" information—basically, a list of all the hardware that's installed on the machine (regardless of hardware profiles), descriptions, and resources such as IRQ numbers, DMA channels, and drive letters.

- Another very strange subkey, **HKLM\Hardware**, has information about the machine's floating point processor and the assignment of COM ports. An earlier version of the Windows Resource Kit said it was used by Hyperterminal. I can't find any reference to it now.

- **HKLM\Network** contains the current user's user name—that is, the user name that will appear as the default the next time Windows restarts and puts the logon dialog on the screen—as well as the **PrimaryProvider** entry.

- **HKLM\Security** concerns network security and contains information about the domain and its administrator.

- **HKLM\Software**, by contrast, is a gold mine of settings. I describe the **HKEY_CLASSES_ROOT**, alias **HKLM\Software\Classes**, earlier. Application software packages that have user-independent settings are supposed to put all those settings here, listed by company name. A complete description of the hundreds of entries in **HKLM\Software\Microsoft\Windows\CurrentVersion** alone could probably fill another book this size. This is the mother lode for user-independent Registry entries.

- **HKLM\System** has only one subkey, **\CurrentControlSet**, but the subkey contains an impressive array of scary-looking entries. The WRK says that this key is used during startup, but that's only part of the story: at the very least, some boilerplate text stored in **HKLM\System\CurrentControlSet\control\PerfStats** is used by the System Monitor. Stuff in this key finds its way into all sorts of nooks and crannies.

**Figure 9-64.
Number of the
current hardware
profile**

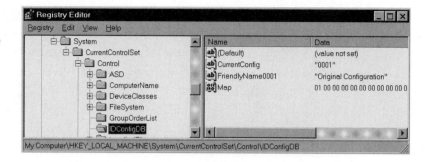

For example, when Win98 determines which hardware profile is the active
profile (usually on startup, but it can be changed manually with the Hardware Profiles tab), it sets the value **CurrentConfig** in the key **HKLM\
System\CurrentControlSet\control\IDConfigDB** to the number of
the currently active profile (see Figure 9-64). Although the **HKLM\System**
key is fun to browse through, I haven't found any need to edit it directly
and thus don't talk about it.

 There doesn't seem to be a whole lot of thought given to the structure of **HKLM**. Sometimes I think these keys were put together with
chewing gum and bailing wire, designed by committee, and reviewed by
a random number generator. I mean, the name of the current printer
for a single hardware profile machine is in the key **HKLM\Config\0001\
System\CurrentControlSet\Control\Print\Printers**, in a value
named **Default**—no, not **(Default)**, the key's default value, but in a real-
live value with a real-live value name of **Default**.

 And, as you can see in Figure 9-65, there's absolutely nothing else from
\System on down the many-deep chain of keys. C'mon, Redmond!

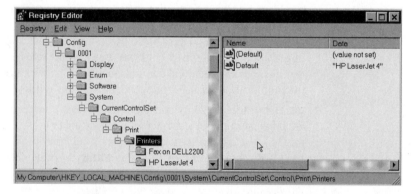

**Figure 9-65. The active printer sits eight levels deep, in a value named
Default!**

App Paths

Most of the interesting keys in **HKLM** live in **HKLM\Software\Microsoft\ Windows\CurrentVersion** (**HKLM\S\M\W\CV**). It's a huge key, with hundreds of subkeys.

 So how does Win98 find programs? Good question. As best I can tell, the Start/Run box looks for programs with names typed into the box in the following order:

1. In **C:\windows\system**
2. In **C:\windows**
3. In **C:\windows\command**
4. If it still doesn't find the program, it looks along the DOS path, which was probably established in **autoexec.bat**.
5. If it doesn't find the program after all that, it looks in the Registry for a key called **HKLM\S\M\W\CV\App Paths** followed by the name of the program. For example, if the user types **test.bat** into the Start/Run box and **test.bat** isn't found in Steps 1 through 4, Win98 looks for the key **HKLM\S\M\W\CV\App Paths\test.bat**. If it finds the key, Win98 *runs the program* listed in the **(Default)** value of the key.

 *Yes, you read that correctly. You might think Windows would use the path information in the **(Default)** key to find the program, but you'd be wrong. In this example, if the key **HKLM\S\M\W\CV\App Paths\ test.bat** had a **(Default)** value with the data **C:\windows\ calc.exe** and there was no **test.bat** in **\windows\system**, **\windows**, **\windows\command** or along the DOS **path=**, Win98 would run the calculator, **calc.exe**. Go figger.*

 *This is so that if you don't have an **autoexec.bat**, and hence, no MS-DOS **path=** set, you could still type **Excel** and the system would go out and find the correct version of Excel to execute (assuming, of course, that Excel properly registered itself when it was installed). Also, the **\App Paths** stuff works from the MS-DOS **start** command too. So **C:> start excel** would work just fine. We were very serious about making sure your system would work just fine if you had a zero-length **autoexec.bat** and **config.sys**.*

 I talk about a supremely cool way to use this key for shortcuts in the Start/Run box at the end of this chapter.

The **\App Paths\progname** key can have one more value, called **Path**, which sets the search path used by the program in the **(Default)** value when it is run. All good Windows programs callable from the Start/Run box are supposed to register themselves in this set of keys.

This feature is available only for 32-bit Windows applications. Since all the old 16-bit applications (primarily those designed for Windows 3.1) share a common address space, there are no provisions to have a per-process environment like the one for 32-bit applications. In fact, the whole feature of per-application paths is implemented entirely in the shell with no changes to the underlying kernel!

In case you programmers out there are curious about how it's actually implemented, when you run an application from the shell or the MS-DOS prompt, the shell simply reads the contents of this key, shoves it into the lpvEnvironment argument of the **Create Process()** *API, and feeds it to the kernel. The kernel itself has no specific knowledge of per-application paths: it just gets this per-address space environment string from the shell.*

Run, RunOnce, RunServices, RunServicesOnce

Here's the definitive list I promised of all six **\Run** *keys and when, precisely, the programs mentioned in the keys' values actually run. This list is a little more detailed than the one on startup in Chapter 6 because you now know where all the bodies are buried.*

1. The logo appears on the screen.

2. If there's a **winstart.bat** in the **\windows** directory, it runs and must complete before anything else happens.

3. **HKLM\S\M\W\CV\RunServices** and **HKLM\S\M\W\CV\ RunServicesOnce** run after Windows is initialized but before the logon screen appears. (All of the **Once** keys contain the names of programs that are run just once, then are deleted from the key. The plain **Run** keys, by contrast, contain the names of programs that are run every time Windows restarts.) Two oddities. First, users may log on before the **\RunServices** and **\RunServicesOnce** programs complete, and if they do, the next programs in the list start. In other words, **\RunServices** and **\RunServicesOnce** are not showstopper programs; they aren't required to complete before Windows continues. Second, if you shut down with the choice "Close all programs" and log on as a different user, all of the programs that were started with these two keys are shut down and then are *not* restarted as Windows comes back up again.

That's not the whole story. It's a security issue. Programmers need to be aware of the fact that if the application calls the **SetServiceProcess()** API, then it will not be terminated when one user logs off. It also won't show up in the C-A-D dialog after that API is called. However, applications like that *must* be aware that there is only one security context systemwide in Windows 98. As a result, if User A logs on, whatever applications were started from that **\RunServices** key inherit whatever network security privileges User A is allowed. When User B logs on, those network permissions are then changed out from under the service process to those of User B.

4. The **HKLM\S\M\W\CV\RunOnce** programs start *and finish*. These are showstopper programs: Windows will not proceed until all of the programs in this key have completed.

5. The **win.ini load=** and **run=** programs are started.

6. Then the **HKLM\S\M\W\CV\Run** programs are started.

7. Finally, the **HKCU\S\M\W\CV\Run** and **HKCU\S\M\W\CV\RunOnce** programs are started. The programs in Steps 5, 6, and 7 may finish asynchronously, at any time.

You now know nine different ways to run programs when Win98 starts. One of them is bound to do whatever you want.

And don't forget that in addition to these nine ways, there are the two StartUp groups and the possibility of setting Task Scheduler to run programs on startup.

Other HKLMs

You can control the default behavior of the MS-DOS configuration options described in the section of Chapter 3 called "The Penalty Box." Check out the keys stored under **HKLM\S\M\W\CV\MS-DOSOptions** (Figure 9-66), including **\CD-ROM**, **\Doskey**, **\DOSSettings** (for **DOS=HIGH,UMB** and variants), **\EMS**, **\Himem**, **\Lock** (for direct disk access), **\Mouse**, **\Net**, **\Smartdrv**, and **\Vesa** (for VLB support). These keys exist primarily to make it easier for

Figure 9-66. MS-DOSOptions for the penalty box

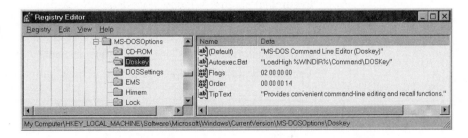

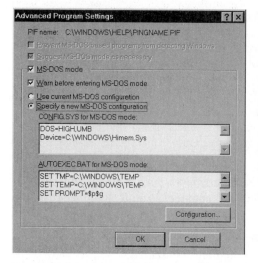

Figure 9-67. Advanced properties for DOS programs

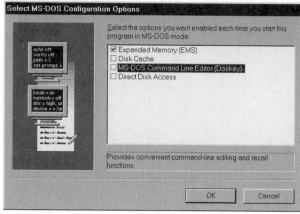

Figure 9-68. Associated Configuration Options box

hardware manufacturers to customize default penalty box settings on their systems, but you can use them, too.

Autoexec.Bat and **Config.Sys** values are strings that appear in the penalty box's **autoexec** and **config**, respectively (Figure 9-67), if the key's box is checked in Configuration Options. The **(Default)** value for each key becomes the description in the Configuration Options box (Figure 9-68). The Order value controls the order of lines in the resulting **autoexec** and **config**—larger numbers are attached to keys with lines that appear toward the end of **autoexec** or **config**. The **TipText** value appears at the bottom of the Configuration Options box.

 The **Flags** values underneath these keys appear to control their appearance in the Advanced Settings dialog. As best I can tell, here are the valid value data for the first byte of the **Flags** value and what they imply in the Configuration Options box.

- **00** means that the key does not appear in the Configuration Options box.

- **02** means that the key appears unchecked in the Configuration Options box.

- **07** means that the **Autoexec.Bat** or **Config.Sys** value appears in the default **autoexec** and/or **config**, in the Advanced Settings dialog, and there is no option for this key in the Configuration Options box.

- **1b** means that the key appears checked in the Configuration Options box.

Figure 9-69.
The `SourcePath`
value points to
the installation
CD

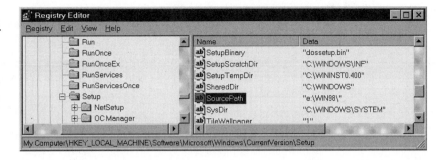

 HKLM has a handful of additional keys that may prove useful to you. But whatever you do, don't take some books' advice and change **HKLM** to start truncating long filenames. As it comes straight out of the box, Win98 changes long filenames into short filenames by cutting down the filename to six characters, then appending a tilde and a number to the name: **MyLongName.doc** becomes **mylong~1.doc**. The crew talk about that extensively in Chapter 2.

If you go to the key **HKLM\System\CurrentControlSet\Control\ FileSystem** and add the value **NameNumericTail** with data **0**, Windows suddenly starts truncating filenames: **MyLongName.doc** now becomes **mylongna.doc**.

What's wrong with that? Well, some programmers—including, as Billy explained earlier, the programmers who put together Windows 98—assumed that shortened names have tildes and wrote that assumption into their code. Don't ask me why, but they did. Anyway, **NameNumericTail** will break enough software that it just isn't worth the hassle.

There's a very useful key called **HKLM\S\M\W\CV\Setup\SourcePath** that I've modified on several machines (see Figure 9-69). When Windows 98 needs an installation disk (either a floppy or the CD), it first looks at this key to see which drive letter it should first query. If Win98 finds the disk it wants in the path mentioned by this key, it just goes over there and snags what it needs, without even asking the user. For example, if you have your installation files copied to **C:\winstall** and **\SourcePath** points there, you'll never hear a thing as Windows whooshes straight to the installation files. If it doesn't find the data it needs here, it pops up a dialog that lets the user browse and takes the information for the browse dropdown list from the key **HKCU\InstallLocationsMRU**.

The funny thing is that the **HKLM\S\M\W\CV\Setup\SourcePath** key is never updated. Even if you install Win98 components from a new location a hundred times, Win98 isn't smart enough to automatically look in the new location; it always hits you with the stupid browse dialog box. If you go in and manually change this key to point to the disk drive you use to install new Win98 components, Windows will never hit you with the browse dialog box again.

And that concludes the tutorial part of the chapter. Time to have some fun!

■ Registry Hacks, Ultimate Power Users' Tricks

 Talk, talk, talk. It took us more than 70 pages to cover the basics. What I want to know is how I use this stuff to make Win98 cooler. You know, the best of the hacks.

 It's important that you understand the basics and get the lay of the land before trying advanced tricks. And oy! what tricks they are! Most books and mags extol the virtues of Send To. Well, sonny, this stuff is so advanced it puts Send To to shame.

The first big hack, of course, is my method for making Explorer "smart," as explained in Sarah's Smart Setup toward the end of Chapter 3. The second big hack is to go into **HKCU** and make MOM's modifications to take the training wheels off of the File Types tab, as shown in Table 9-1. Now let's see what other mischief we can get into.

Renaming, Moving Desktop Icons

I'll bet the question I hear most often from advanced Win98 users is "How do I get rid of the ^&%$#@! icons Win98 put on my Desktop?" Sometimes their language can be a little shocking, but it's hard not to sympathize with them. After all, My Computer is the kind of thing you'd expect to find on an 8-year-old's Desktop, but hardly the sort of power icon you'd want in the upper left corner of, oh, the National Security Advisor's main screen, eh? Well, here's everything we've found about changing My Computer, Network Neighborhood, Recycle Bin, My Documents, and Internet Explorer. The first two are a bit of a disappointment, but the rest succumb sooner or later to a coherent Registry attack.

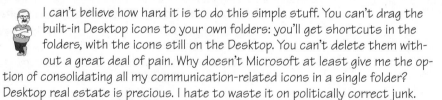 **Tweak UI Alert!** *Many of the hacks discussed in this section (but not the extremely cool ones for Internet Explorer) can be changed by using Tweak UI. If you want to make the change—and couldn't care less about learning how or why it works—use Tweak UI. It's discussed at length in Chapter 8.*

I can't believe how hard it is to do this simple stuff. You can't drag the built-in Desktop icons to your own folders: you'll get shortcuts in the folders, with the icons still on the Desktop. You can't delete them without out a great deal of pain. Why doesn't Microsoft at least give me the option of consolidating all my communication-related icons in a single folder? Desktop real estate is precious. I hate to waste it on politically correct junk.

First the easy part. You know how to change the names of the Desktop icons, right? For any icon except the Recycle Bin, it's easy: just right click on the offending icon and pick Rename. While it's true that some of the names are hardwired (for example, My Computer will show up in a few places, including the root of every key in Regedit, even after you change the name on the Desktop icon), it's a good start for getting rid of the most embarrassing aspect of the icons, their touchy-feely names. You can even "delete" the name on an icon entirely by simply renaming the icon with a single space.

If you want to change just the icon pictures for the Desktop icons, look for the following keys.

To Change This Icon	Change `HKCR\CLSID\{This}\DefaultIcon`'s (Default) Value
My Computer	`{20d04fe0-3aea-1069-a2d8-08002b30309d}`
Network Neighborhood	`{208d2c60-3aea-1069-a2d7-08002b30309d}`
Recycle Bin	`{645ff040-5081-101b-9f08-00aa002f954e}`
Internet Explorer	`{871c5380-42a0-1069-a2ea-08002b30309d}`
My Documents	`{450d8fba-ad25-11d0-98a8-0800361b1103}`

 By the way, as far as I know the information for Internet Explorer and My Documents is previously undocumented. You can change the icon for My Documents in Tweak UI—but Microsoft apparently wanted to keep the icon on Internet Explorer immutable! Heh heh heh. As MOM likes to say, "You can run in Regedit, but you can't hide."

To change the name of the Recycle Bin, go into `HKCR\CLSID\{645ff040-5081-101b-9f08-00aa002f954e}` and change the `(Default)` value data to whatever name you like. It's kinda funny because the right-click Rename option for all the other Desktop icons simply changes the appropriate `CLSID`'s `(Default)` value. Hard to imagine what possessed Microsoft to not permit the same sort of right-click name change on the Recycle Bin, thus forcing you to use Tweak UI or (better!) manually hack the Registry.

If you want to move icons around, the procedure is a bit tougher.

My Computer Several books recommend that you get rid of your My Computer icon by going into `HKCU\S\M\W\CV\Policies\Explorer` and adding a dword value called `NoDesktop`, setting it to **1**. You can try that if you want to—on rebooting you won't see the My Computer icon—but I'd suggest you first consider poking out your eyes with a sharp stick.

 When I was writing about My Computer for the Windows 95 version of this book, I started fooling around with the **NoDesktop** value. Most of the time, when I set it to **1** and rebooted, I got either a completely blank screen (**Ctrl+Alt+Del** time) or just the Taskbar. Once, though, I crashed my whole system. Hosed it royally. When I re-installed, every time Win95 started, it immediately crashed with a GPF in Explorer. It took me two full days, with our editor breathing down my neck for MOM's overdue book, to get back up and limping. Restoring my carefully made backup of the Registry (with **NoDesktop** set to **0**) didn't help. I had to completely erase Win95 from my hard drive and re-install from DOS 6.2. Fact. While I can't swear it was all the fault of **NoDesktop**, I'm convinced the setting had something to do with my problems. And if it crashed that badly in Win95—well, I'll be hanged if I'm going to try it again in Win98.

Which leads me to several important points. First, remember that merging an old copy of the Registry does *not* overwrite new values, like this **NoDesktop** value. You have to go into the **.reg** file and manually add a **"NoDesktop"=dword:0** line in the right place to remove the effects of a **NoDesktop 1** setting. Failing that, you have to copy over old copies of **system.dat** and **user.dat**, making sure you put the old **user.dat** in the right place, if you have a multiple user profile system.

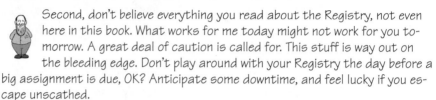

Second, don't believe everything you read about the Registry, not even here in this book. What works for me today might not work for you tomorrow. A great deal of caution is called for. This stuff is way out on the bleeding edge. Don't play around with your Registry the day before a big assignment is due, OK? Anticipate some downtime, and feel lucky if you escape unscathed.

Finally, a bit of advice from my friend, Dr. Ruthless: Don't play around with the Registry too much. Sex may be for Dummies—at least that's what the good doctor tells me—but playing with the Registry requires a keen mind and a deft hand. Play with it too much and you may go blind.

I'm too chicken to get rid of My Computer completely: it seems to be too tightly tied into Windows itself. But I *do* know how to make it invisible so that you can't see it on the Desktop! The icon shown for My Computer on the Desktop is stored in the key **HKCR\CLSID\ {20d04fe0-3aea-1069-a2d8-08002b30309d}\DefaultIcon**, in the **(Default)** value. You can put the name of any icon in there you like, or use the **filename,iconnumber** convention (where **filename** contains more than one icon, and **iconnumber** is the number of the icon, the first icon being icon 0). For example, to use the sixth icon of **C:\windows\ moricons.dll**, which is icon number 5 in the Windows counting method, set the value data for **(Default)** to **C:\windows\moricons.dll,5**.

The coolest part of this is your ability to use "transparent" icons—ones that take on the underlying color of the Desktop itself. There's a completely transparent icon floating around, which is distributed with Visual Basic, in the file **screen.ico**. See if you can run down a copy. If you assign the **(Default)** value of the **HKCR\CLSID\{20d04fe0-3aea-1069-a2d8-08002b30309d}** key to **screen.ico** (copy it to your hard disk first, of course), the My Computer icon will disappear entirely! If you then rename My Computer to a single space, you'll never see it again. Out of sight, out of mind. Outta sight!

Network Neighborhood

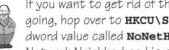

If you want to get rid of the Network Neighborhood icon, get Regedit going, hop over to **HKCU\S\M\W\CV\Policies\Explorer**, and add a dword value called **NoNetHood**, with data of **1**. Reboot Windows, and Network Neighborhood is gone. As best I can tell, this **NoNetHood** setting prevents you from browsing the network to see what's on it—the Network Neighborhood icon on the Desktop disappears, of course, but so does the Network Neighborhood entry in Explorer and the Network Browse capability in File Open boxes and several wizards. Yet **NoNetHood** does not prevent you from attaching to drives on the network, using UNCs. In addition, if you've told Win98 to automatically attach to the given resource on startup, the connection will be made. Thus, the major effect of **NoNetHood** is to curtail your searching ability—while your ability to attach to network resources stays intact. You can always retrieve Network Neighborhood, if you miss it, by simply removing the **NoNetHood** value or setting it to **0**.

Recycle Bin Unlike Network Neighborhood, the Recycle Bin is docile as can be. While you can't drag the Recycle Bin into a folder, you *can* create a fully functional clone of the Recycle Bin—and it's a real clone, identical to the original, including full drop functionality in drag and drop deleting—which can be moved anyplace you like. If you then delete the original Recycle Bin, the clone can take its place.

Right click on the Desktop, pick New Folder. Type in the name **Zap.{645ff040-5081-101b-9f08-00aa002f954e}**. (The **Zap** part can be anything you like: whatever you type to the left of the period becomes the name of your new Recycle Bin.) Hit **Enter**. Test this new Zap can out—move it into a folder, double click on it to see the items in the can, drop an unneeded file on top of it, and verify that the file was removed from its previous location and moved to the can.

If the Zap can works for you, delete the old Recycle Bin by going into Regedit, looking for the key **HKLM\S\M\W\CV\explorer\Desktop\NameSpace\{645ff040-5081-101b-9f08-00aa002f954e}**, and deleting it. Restart Windows, and the old, rigid Recycle Bin is history.

If you just want to change the Recycle Bin icon, be aware of the fact that the Recycle Bin actually has two different icons in three keys, all stored in **HKCR\CLSID\{645ff040-5081-101b-9f08-00aa002f954e}**. The icon in the **(Default)** value's data is the icon that's currently shown on the screen. If you empty the Recycle Bin, the **empty** value is moved into **(Default)**. If you then add anything at all to the Recycle Bin, the **full** value is moved into **(Default)**. Remember: two icons, three keys, and **full** doesn't mean "full," it means "not empty."

**Figure 9-70.
Tweak UI Internet
Explorer Create
As File**

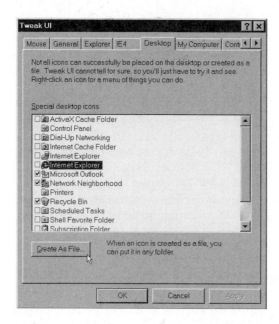

Internet Explorer Once you know the right CLSID, moving the Internet Explorer icon is easy, too. Create a clone by right clicking on the Desktop, choosing New and Folder, and naming the folder **Internet Explorer.{871c5380-42a0-1069-a2ea-08002b30309d}**. When you're satisfied that it works correctly, right click on the original Internet Explorer icon and pick Delete. Piece of cake.

 Wait a minute! Tweak UI has a Create As File option for the Internet Explorer icon. Why don't you just use that?

 Most systems, in fact, have *two* Internet Explorer listings on the Desktop tab of Tweak UI (Figure 9-70) and a third listing called The Internet, and as far as I can tell, the Create As File option doesn't work very often—if at all—on any of them. Microsoft was pretty much forced to have a Delete option when you right click on the Desktop's Internet Explorer icon, just to placate the conspiracy theorists. But they sure went to great lengths to make it difficult to move the icon off the Desktop or to use a different picture. MOM's crew found ways to do both, and they both hinge on the new-to-Win98 CLSID **{871c5380-42a0-1069-a2ea-08002b30309d}**.

More Iconoclasms

Tweak UI Alert! *All the settings discussed in this section can be changed by using Tweak UI. If you want to make the change—and couldn't care less about learning how or why it works—use Tweak UI. It's discussed at length in Chapter 8.*

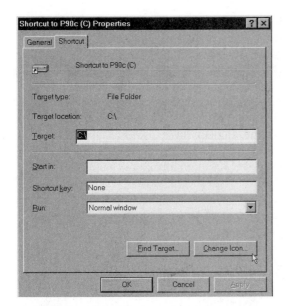

Figure 9-72. List of all the icons in `shell32.dll`

Figure 9-71. Shortcut's Change Icon button—gateway to the icon lister

Icon Numbers By far the vast majority of icons used on the Desktop and in Explorer come from a file called `C:\windows\system\shell32.dll`. Any time you want to see which icons sit in that file (or any other file for that matter), right click on any shortcut on the Desktop and pick Properties. On the Shortcut tab, click Change Icon, as in Figure 9-71. When you get to the Change Icon dialog (Figure 9-72), click Browse, and browse over to `C:\Windows\System\Shell32.dll`.

 Each icon in a file has an icon number. Here's how to "count" icons, Win98 style. Start with the icon in the upper left corner of the Change Icon dialog. On the screen in Figure 9-72, you would start with the icon that looks like a sheet of paper with the Windows logo on it. That's icon 0. Now move down one picture. That's icon 1. Move down again, and you're at icon 2. Down one more time (to the closed file folder) and you have icon 3. Next, hop over to the top icon in the next column—in Figure 9-72 that's the picture of the open file folder. That's icon 4. And so on.

 If you look at the highlighted icon in Figure 9-72—the one that looks like a disk drive—that's icon 8.

Icons abound in almost every file you can imagine. The easiest way to see what's available is to simply click on the Browse button in the Change Icon dialog, then pick files that appear with tiny icons in front of the file names. There's a list of the files stuffed with the most icons in Chapter 8 in the discussion on the Display applet's Effects tab.

Changing System Icons There's a way to change the basic icons Win98 uses by hacking yet another Registry entry. This one is in **HKLM\S\M\W\CV\ explorer\ShellIcons**. If you do not yet have a key with that name, create it; it will be worth the effort. By changing values within this key, you can change the basic icons used by Windows itself. For example, if you don't particularly like the standard short-cut arrow in Figure 9-73 and prefer the alternative shortcut arrow in Figure 9-74, one simple value in this key will change all the lower left arrows to upper left arrows throughout Windows.

Figure 9-73. Standard shortcut overlay arrow

Figure 9-74. More distinctive— and arguably more visible— shortcut overlay arrow

Windows numbers its icons internally. For example, it knows that the standard shortcut arrow is icon 29. But before it actually paints an icon on the screen, it looks in this key to see if there's an override. Thus, using this key, you can tell Windows, "Whenever you need to draw icon 29, use my preferred icon instead of the one you usually use" (Figure 9-75).

 Wondering where the "29" comes from? Easy. That's the icon number in **shell32.dll** that Win98 normally uses. If you look at the arrow icon in Figure 9-73 and carefully count the icons shown in Figure 9-72, you'll find that the standard arrow icon is icon **shell32.dll,29**.

An important little note here: when you specify an icon's filename and icon number, use a comma to separate the two but no space. Thus, **shell32.dll,29** specifies icon 29 (the thirtieth icon) in **shell32.dll**.

Values within the **HKLM\S\M\W\CV\explorer\ShellIcons** key have the **shell32.dll** icon number as the value name and the new file and icon number as the value data. For example, if you want to change the shortcut arrow from the standard arrow (**shell32.dll,29**) to the alternative arrow (which we found in **C:\windows\system\wmsui32.dll,36**), you would set up a value in this key with the name **29** and the data **C:\windows\system\ wmsui32.dll,36** (see Figure 9-75). That tells Windows, "Whenever you need to draw icon 29, use the icon **wmsui32.dll,36** instead of the one you usually use." If there is no value named **29**, Windows uses its default icon for the short arrow, **shell32.dll,29**. See how that works?

Most of the **shell32.dll** icons appear in Figure 9-72, but in the interest of maintaining your eyesight and sanity, here's a short list of the icons Windows uses most commonly.

Figure 9-75. The Registry setting that controls the arrow in Figure 9-74

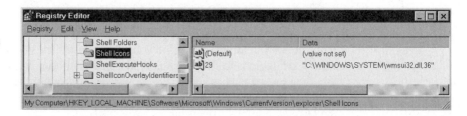

What the Icon Is Used For	Icon Number
Default document icon	0
5.25" floppy	5
3.5" floppy	6
Tape drives	7
Local hard drives	8
Network hard drives	9
Disconnected network drive	10
CD-ROM drive	11
Computer in Network Neighborhood	15
Printers in Printer folder	16
Entire network in Network Neighborhood	17
Workgroups in Network Neighborhood	18
Superimposed for shared drives or directories	28
Superimposed for shortcuts	29

Thus, if you want to change the icon used for Printers in the Printer folder, you need to create a value in the **HKLM\S\M\W\CV\explorer\ShellIcons** key with the name **16** and data that points to the new icon.

You have to force Win98 to reconstruct the entire Desktop before changes in the **\ShellIcons** Registry key take effect. The simplest way we've found to do that without restarting Windows is to right click on the Desktop, choose Properties, pick the Appearance tab, choose Icon from the Item dropdown list, crank the Size up by 1, hit Apply, and then move the Size back down by 1, hitting OK all the way back out. Or you can use Tweak UI's Repair tab.

Thumbnails

 In the section "The Fifth View: Thumbnails" in Chapter 3, I show you how to turn on thumbnail previews for graphics files on a folder-by-folder basis. Win98 does that by modifying the **desktop.ini** file in each folder so changed. This Thumbnail shows thumbnails—previews—of graphics in Windows Explorer.

There's another way to see previews. And, as you might imagine, it involves the Registry. Usually a **.bmp** file either on the Desktop or in Explorer will show a generic icon, one that signifies that the file is a **.bmp** (see Figure 9-76). While Windows is smart enough to show you thumbnail sketches of the icons in **.exe**, **.ico**, **.cur**, and **.ani** files, it reverts to a generic icon for **.bmp**s. You can change that by (what else?) hacking the Registry. If you go into the key **HKCR\Paint.Picture\DefaultIcon** and change the **(Default)** value to have the data **%1**, your **.bmp** files will suddenly appear with thumbnails (Figure 9-77).

Figure 9-76.
Typical Large Icon
view in Explorer
(or, in this case,
the Start/Find
dialog)

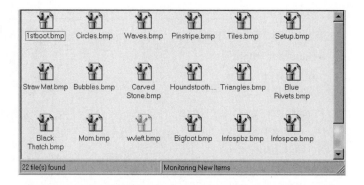

Figure 9-77
Large Icon view
with the %1 .bmp
hack

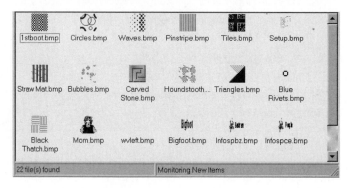

 You better warn them about the side effects of this change, Woody. There's a reason Microsoft didn't do this as the default in Windows 98 and left it to supersleuths to discover: showing **.bmp** thumbnails takes a significant performance hit. It's especially heinous when you open a floppy drive and Win98 has to scan all the **.bmp** files to extract thumbnails. Personally, I like the pretty pictures, but I didn't think our users would want to put up with the delays.

 Yep, and there's another hitch. No matter how hard I tried, I couldn't get thumbnails for **.jpg** files (CLSID jpegfile) to appear using this kind of Registry hack. Somehow the hooks just don't appear to be there. Of course, if you're serious about seeing thumbnails of your JPEGs, you'll want to use Thumbnail View, via the trick in Chapter 3.

Run Accelerators on the App Path

Here's my favorite Registry hack. I have a handful of programs that I'd like to "accelerate" in the Start/Run box. For example, instead of typing **regedit** in the Run box to run Regedit, I'd like to set things up so that simply typing **r** and hitting **Enter** gets Regedit going (and maybe typing **w** to start Word). Turns out it ain't the least bit difficult.

Figure 9-78.
Type **r** in the Run
box and Regedit
will run

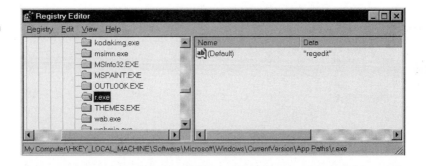

Figure 9-79.
A w.exe entry for
Word 2000

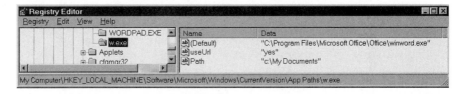

If you go into **HKLM\S\M\W\CV\App Paths** and add a key called **r.exe** with
a **(Default)** value that points to **regedit** (see Figure 9-78), Win98 will be
smart enough to translate an **r** typed in the Start/Run box into the **regedit**
command: when it doesn't find a file or program called **r** along its usual path, it
looks in **HKLM\S\M\W\CV\App Paths** for the program and finds it there.

Similarly, an **HKLM\S\M\W\CV\App Paths\w.exe** key with a **(Default)**
value pointing to Word will force Win98 to run Word whenever you type **w** in the
Start/Run box. As you can see in Figure 9-79, which is specifically for Word
2000, you can even establish a starting path for an application in **\App Paths**
by adding a value called **Path** to the appropriate key.

Watch out! Windows ignores **\App Paths** entries with **.bat** or **.com** extensions. It's pretty weird: in the old DOS world, **.exe**, **.bat**, and **.com** extensions were all considered when matching commands with filenames. Not so in
Win98: you must use an **.exe** extension in **\App Paths**.

Good luck with the Registry! May it bring you as many hours of fun as it
has to MOM's crew. And keep your powder dry.

> *O Captain! my Captain! our fearful trip is done!*
> *The ship has weather'd every rack, the prize we sought is won.*
> *The port is near, the bells I hear, the people all exulting.*
>
> —WALT WHITMAN, *Leaves of Grass,* 1855

NetMeeting *(continued)*
  video calling with, 384
  voice calling with, 383
NetMeeting Resource Kit, 423
Netmonitor, 475
Netscape Communicator, 152, 429
Netscape Navigator, 152, 429
NetShow, 385
NetShow Resource Kit, 423
NetWatcher, 403
Network, 662–669
  Access Control tab, 666–667
  accessing, 662
  components, 665
  Configuration tab, 665–666
  Identification tab, 666
  selecting share level for, 667–668
  setting up peer-to-peer network with, 664–668
  turning off logon screen, 662–663
Network briefcase, 357–358
Network devices, 515–516
Network Interface Card (NIC), 664
Network Neighborhood, 280–281
  folder structure of, 68
  removing icon from Desktop, 793
Network, Tweak UI, 711
Networking, 148–150, 342–362
  adapters for, 149
  briefcases and, 355–358
  Client for Microsoft Networks and, 149
  Dial-Up Networking and, 343–347
  Dialer and, 359–360
  Direct Cable Connection (DCC) and, 350–354
  Hyperterminal and, 358–359
  installing printer for, 249–252
  logon scripts and, 347–350
  MCA and, 12
  Microsoft Network (MSN) and, 361–362
  overview of, 342
  protocols for, 149
  sharing resources and, 149, 487
  TCP/IP stack and, 149–150
  UNC filenames and, 150
  WinChat and WinPopup, 360–361

New menu, 182
New, Tweak UI, 711–712
Newsgroups, 154, 295–296
NIC (Network Interface Card), 664
Notepad, 390–391
Notepad+, 431
Notification Area
  context menu for, 165
  ToolTip and, 165
  using icons of, 165–166
  volume control and, 166
NT File System (NTFS), 10
Null value, 721
Number tab, 673

O

Object graphics. *See* Graphics, vector
Object Packager, 402–403
Objects, 50–51
OLE, 63–66
  client and server for, 65
  extensions for object sharing, 65
  file extensions, 66
  file types for Win98, 66
  history of, 63
  linking and embedding with, 64–65
  OLE automation and, 65
  videos and, 405
OLE/Com Object Viewer, 423
OLE DB (database), 65
OLE/Dependency Walker, 423
Online Services folder, 363–364
  America Online (AOL), 363–364
  CompuServe, 363–364
  Microsoft Network (MSN), 363–364
  Prodigy, 363–364
Open, common dialog, 55–57, 224–227
Open With
  common dialog, 224–227
  File Manager and, 226–227
  limitations of, 225–226
  using with ASCII text files, 225
Option buttons. *See* Radio buttons
Options, Backup, 331
Organic Art Screen Saver, 421

Addison-Wesley Computer and Engineering Publishing Group

How to Interact with Us

1. Visit our Web site

http://www.awl.com/cseng

When you think you've read enough, there's always more content for you at Addison-Wesley's web site. Our web site contains a directory of complete product information including:

- Chapters
- Exclusive author interviews
- Links to authors' pages
- Tables of contents
- Source code

You can also discover what tradeshows and conferences Addison-Wesley will be attending, read what others are saying about our titles, and find out where and when you can meet our authors and have them sign your book.

2. Subscribe to Our Email Mailing Lists

Subscribe to our electronic mailing lists and be the first to know when new books are publishing. Here's how it works: Sign up for our electronic mailing at http://www.awl.com/cseng/mailinglists.html. Just select the subject areas that interest you and you will receive notification via email when we publish a book in that area.

3. Contact with Us via Email

cepubprof@awl.com
Ask general questions about our books.
Sign up for our electronic mailing lists.
Submit corrections for our web site.

bexpress@awl.com
Request an Addison-Wesley catalog.
Get answers to questions regarding
your order or our products.

innovations@awl.com
Request a current Innovations Newsletter.

webmaster@awl.com
Send comments about our web site.

cepubeditors@awl.com
Submit a book proposal.
Send errata for an Addison-Wesley book.

cepubpublicity@awl.com
Request a review copy for a member of the media
interested in reviewing new Addison-Wesley titles.

We encourage you to patronize the many fine retailers who stock Addison-Wesley titles. Visit our online directory to find stores near you or visit our online store: http://store.awl.com/ or call 800-824-7799.

Addison Wesley Longman
Computer and Engineering Publishing Group
One Jacob Way, Reading, Massachusetts 01867 USA
TEL 781-944-3700 • FAX 781-942-3076